JESSE

By the same author:

CASSIUS MARCELLUS CLAY
HOW TO THINK AND WRITE
MUSE OF FIRE: APPROACHES TO POETRY
WILLIAM FAULKNER: THE JOURNEY TO SELF-DISCOVERY

BEST-LOVED SHORT STORIES OF JESSE STUART

JESSE

◇

The Biography of
an American Writer

JESSE HILTON STUART

◇

H. Edward Richardson

McGRAW-HILL BOOK COMPANY
New York St. Louis San Francisco
Toronto Hamburg Mexico

1 2 3 4 5 6 7 8 9 D O C   D O C 8 7 6 5 4

ISBN 0-07-062307-4

LIBRARY OF CONGRESS CATALOGING IN PUBLICATION DATA

Richardson, H. Edward (Harold Edward), 1929–
  Jesse: the biography of an American writer, Jesse Hilton Stuart.
  Includes bibliographical references and index.
  1. Stuart, Jesse, 1907–   . 2. Authors, American—20th century—Biography. I. Title.
PS3537.T92516Z84   1984   818'.5209 [B]   84-924
ISBN 0-07-062307-4

Book design by Marea Epes.

DEDICATION

To all who, loving life, have the courage to live their talents and beliefs with exuberance and determination, who strive lifelong to give the best of themselves, knowing their lives will make a difference, who dare out of defeat to create triumph, and so live committed to the uplifting hope that the world will be better.

I walked in the wind today . . .
though I die tomorrow.

—Jesse Stuart, letter from
Edinburgh to Oscar Sammons, Mar. 21, 1938

Contents

THE W-HOLLOW WORLD
OF JESSE STUART

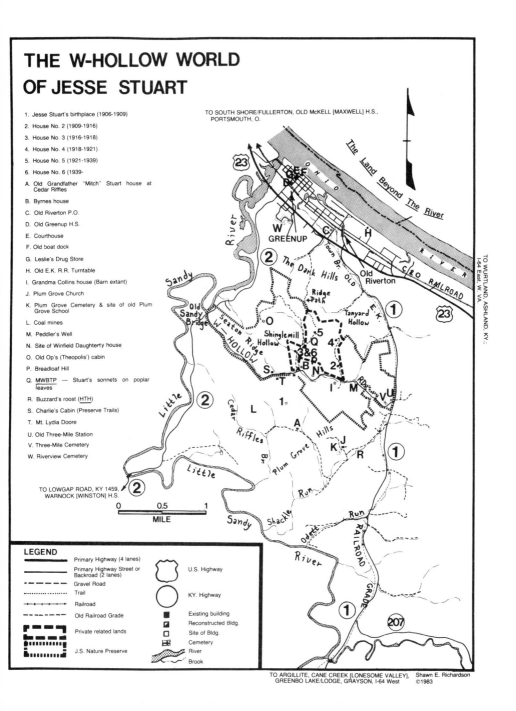

1. Jesse Stuart's birthplace (1906-1909)
2. House No. 2 (1909-1916)
3. House No. 3 (1916-1918)
4. House No. 4 (1918-1921)
5. House No. 5 (1921-1939)
6. House No. 6 (1939-

A. Old Grandfather "Mitch" Stuart house at Cedar Riffles
B. Byrnes house
C. Old Riverton P.O.
D. Old Greenup H.S.
E. Courthouse
F. Old boat dock
G. Leslie's Drug Store
H. Old E.K. R.R. Turntable
I. Grandma Collins house (Barn extant)
J. Plum Grove Church
K. Plum Grove Cemetery & site of old Plum Grove School
L. Coal mines
M. Peddler's Well
N. Site of Winfield Daughterty house
O. Old Op's (Theopolis') cabin
P. Breadloaf Hill
Q. MWBTP — Stuart's sonnets on poplar leaves
R. Buzzard's roost (HTH)
S. Charlie's Cabin (Preserve Trails)
T. Mt. Lydia Doore
U. Old Three-Mile Station
V. Three-Mile Cemetery
W. Riverview Cemetery

TO SOUTH SHORE/FULLERTON, OLD McKELL [MAXWELL] H.S., PORTSMOUTH, O.

TO WURTLAND, ASHLAND, KY.; I-64 East, W. VA.

TO LOWGAP ROAD, KY 1459, WARNOCK [WINSTON] H.S.

0   0.5   1
MILE

LEGEND

Primary Highway (4 lanes)	
Primary Highway Street or Backroad (2 lanes)	U.S. Highway
Gravel Road	
Trail	KY. Highway
Railroad	
Old Railroad Grade	Existing building
Private related lands	Reconstructed Bldg.
	Site of Bldg.
J.S. Nature Preserve	Cemetery
	River
	Brook

TO ARGILLITE, CANE CREEK [LONESOME VALLEY], GREENBO LAKE/LODGE, GRAYSON, I-64 West

Shawn E. Richardson ©1983

Acknowledgments

This book would not have been possible without the cooperation and encouragement of both Jesse and Naomi Deane Stuart, so my greatest debt is to them. The forty-two interviews I had with Jesse and numerous conversations with Naomi are merely indicative of the many hours we spent together, most of them since June 1978, when the research was commenced in earnest. From the outset I was given access to all necessary papers, records, and manuscripts, even personal correspondence, and a totally free hand in shaping these resources into the life. For admitting me "behind the scenes," as Alexander Smith wrote of that essentiality for a satisfactory portrait, I remain especially grateful. Although upon occasion I showed portions of the typescript to Jesse and Naomi or read from it to them, and from time to time requested their assistance to ensure accuracy, I was never once asked to have my writing reviewed. As the Stuarts have been so supportive, the work has been as much a joy as a labor. Because I have received such creative latitude and full trust, my gratitude is truly heartfelt.

Jesse Stuart's life has been enormously full and rich. Although the available resources could easily have justified a three-volume *omnium gatherum*, my guiding purpose has been rather to concentrate upon the most significant events of the life, balancing them with those aspects of background and local color that lend life to significance. I have aimed to keep myself out of the way as much as possible, allowing the subject to speak for himself, revealing his life the way it was—indeed, to permit Jesse, through his own words whenever possible, to tell his own life story. I hope the result has been, to adapt Thomas Carlyle's definition of biography, a reasonably accurate likeness of the earthly pilgrimage of Jesse Stuart. Certainly I have tried to produce a true portrait.

My special thanks are due Jesse Stuart's family—Sophia Stuart Keeney, Mary Stuart Nelson, James Mitchell Stuart, and Glennis Stuart Liles—all of whom are numbered among the interviewees listed in the back of this book. Throughout the five years and more that have gone into the research and writing, James Stuart has lent many kinds of personal assistance, guiding me through the physical places so familiar to Jesse as he grew up in W-Hollow and later wrote of them, the farms he plowed, the ridges and hollows he walked every foot of, and Riverton, Greenup, and other parts of Greenup County now transmuted into the enduring literature of his lifework.

Similarly, Jesse Stuart's many neighbors, friends, classmates, and teachers have helped me immeasurably in detailing Jesse's life with their impressions and anecdotal insights as his world memorably engaged theirs. Most but by no means all these names are listed in the interviews in the section "Abbreviations, Works, and Interviews" at the back of this book, to which I refer readers. All these are deserving of further acknowledgment here, but the limitations of space dictate that I mention only a representative few: Thurman Darby, Eunice Mitchell Harper and the members of the Greenup High School Class of 1926, William and Irma Warnock Collins, Grace Hilton Carter, Essie Hilton Roland, E. P. Hilton, Elta Cooper Kotcamp and her son, Dr. Wayne Kotcamp, Robert E. Hatton, Lena Wells Lykins Voiers, Virginia Monroe Tippett, Virgil Sturgill, Roland Carter, Lucille Jordan Palmer, Winnie Palmer McDonald, Barnie Greene Hutchens, Lawrence Edwards, Alfred Leland Crabb, J. E. Windrow, Paul J. Davis, Maud King, Lena Nevison, Opal Rice McKee, Dr. H. B. McWhorter, Horace "Choppy" Thomas, Elizabeth Hale, Kathryn Geny, DeRoy Givens, and Richard Prince.

To the many who shared with me the warm hospitality of their homes as well as reflections on their friendships with Jesse Stuart, I am particularly obligated, especially Greenup Countians James and Betty Stuart, Oscar and Ann Sammons, Ethel Bush, Elmer and Scottie Heaberlin, G. Sam Piatt, and Ethel McBrayer, and Ashlander Paul G. Blazer, Jr. I wish to thank Robert Penn Warren for taking a morning and afternoon of a late winter day on the Yale campus to talk with me about Jesse Stuart, for the resources of his reminiscent Foreword in Jesse Stuart's *Head o' W-Hollow* (1979) and Introduction to *The Best-Loved Short Stories of Jesse Stuart* (1982), and for his gracious hospitality. I am also grateful to Rick Meng, April Derleth, and Kay Mulcahy for discussing their memories of Jesse Stuart and August Derleth with me, then pointing me to the large collection of Stuart letters to Derleth on file in Madison, Wisconsin.

My obligation to Kentucky author James Still for allowing me to review Jesse Stuart's letters to him, commencing in 1929 and continuing into the 1970s, is large, indeed. For sharing other such letters with me I am similarly indebted to Charles E. Bess of Flat River, Missouri; Clem Carson of Tifton, Georgia; Carleton F. Wells of Ann Arbor, Michigan; and John Bird of Wallingford, Pennsylvania. Earl Hobson Smith granted me two interviews and gave me a personally conducted tour of the campus of Lincoln Memorial University at Harrogate, Tennessee, pointing out places associated with Jesse Stuart's years there as a student.

Jesse Stuart's good friend Richard M. "Pek" Gunn was kind enough to guide me over Nashville and its environs in search of old friends of Jesse's Nashville days, and I am deeply indebted to him and to other Nashvillians who know Jesse Stuart: Elizabeth Hale; Edward K. Hardy, Elizabeth Hale's brother-in-law, who granted me two most helpful interviews; Philip Davidson, who directed me to several resource persons in Nashville, as did Edgar H. and Ivar Lou Duncan, and T. D. Young of Vanderbilt University; Catherine and Ella Puryear Mims, Professor Edwin Mims' daughters; and Kathryn Geny, Jesse Stuart's classmate in Robert Penn Warren's 1931/1932 class in contemporary literature.

It would be difficult to overstate my indebtedness to Jesse Stuart's bibliographer, Hensley C. Woodbridge (also editor of the *Jack London Newsletter*), on whose *Jesse and Jane Stuart: A Bibliography* I have heavily relied. Others whom I wish to thank and without whose help this book would be thinner and less substantive are listed under "Abbreviations of Works by Others about Jesse Stuart" at the back of the book. Two biocritical studies I wish to acknowledge here as well are Ruel E. Foster's *Jesse Stuart* and Everetta L. Blair's *Jesse Stuart: His Life and Works*, especially for such penetrating insights as that on Stuart's literary achievement in the short-story genre treated in the former, and the useful assemblage of general information on Stuart's literary career contained in the latter. Of practical use to any Stuart scholar are Lee Oly Ramey's pioneering thesis, "An Inquiry into the Life of Jesse Stuart as Related to His Literary Development and a Critical Study of His Works," and Frank H. Leavell's solid dissertation, "The Literary Career of Jesse Stuart," both of which contain otherwise unobtainable material. Especially significant are Mary Washington Clarke's folkloric study *Jesse Stuart's Kentucky* and J. R. LeMaster's continuing works of thorough scholarship, including *Jesse Stuart: Selected Criticism* and, more recently, *Jesse Stuart: Kentucky's Chronicler-Poet*. As editors, the two last-mentioned scholars have probed the significance of Stuart's literary achievement in *Jesse Stuart: Essays on His Work,* which stands as the best collection of scholarly commentaries on his work to date. Special approaches to Stuart's work can be seen in Lee Pennington's *The Dark Hills of Jesse Stuart,* which examines Stuart's prose and poetry through a symbolical lens; in John Howard Spurlock's *He Sings for Us,* a sociolinguistic study of the Appalachian subculture as Jesse Stuart's works interpenetrate and reflect it; in Dick Perry's *Reflections of Jesse Stuart on a Land of Many Moods,* a provocative collection of Stuart's thoughts on his life, land, and art; and in Wade Hall's apt critical reviews and piquant monograph, *"The Truth Is Funny": A Study of Jesse Stuart's Humor,* which rewards readers with uncommon stimulation. I thank them all.

I am in debt to William Boozer, Charlotte Salmon, Kenneth Clarke, Julian Lee Rayford, John R. Gilpin, Jr., Lawrence Edwards, and Earl Hobson Smith for their contributions to Stuartiana. More indirectly, I wish to acknowledge several scholars and their works for providing useful information on those Fugitives and Agrarians at Vanderbilt University whose paths crossed Jesse Stuart's at a time when, despite many personal difficulties, the convergence was propitious for his literary development: Louise Cowan's *The Fugitive Group: A Literary History,* Donald Davidson's *Southern Writers in the Modern World,* John Tyree Fain's *The Spyglass: Views and Reviews, 1924–1930, by Donald Davidson,* M. Thomas Inge and T. D. Young's *Donald Davidson,* Fain and Young's *The Literary Correspondence of Donald Davidson and Allen Tate,* Robert A. McGaw's *The Vanderbilt Campus: A Pictorial History,* and Donald Davidson's *The Tall Men.* Other bibliographical details pertaining to these works can be found in the Notes.

I am especially grateful to Elizabeth J. Graves, Librarian, and Geneva Viers, Assistant Librarian at the Carnegie Library, Lincoln Memorial University, for their help with the Jesse Stuart materials available there. To Keith M. Heim, Head of Special Collections, and Jerry A. Herndon, Curator of the Jesse Stuart Collection at the Pogue Library, Murray State University, Murray, Kentucky, I wish to express my thanks for their cooperation in making available the resources of the Jesse Stuart Collection housed there, and especially for providing photocopies of the Stuart Scrapbooks. Other librarians and libraries to be thanked and commended include Frank P. Grisham, Director of the Joint University Libraries, and Assistant Directors of Special Collections Frances Hardie and Mildred S. Rawlings for their assistance in arranging access to Stuart's letters to Donald Davidson, and for providing photocopies of this correspondence; Linda Bauch, Senior Archivist at the Tennessee State Library and Archives in Nashville, for making available their materials; Ernest E. Weyhrauch, Director of Libraries, Sharon McConnell, Curator of the John Wilson Townsend Collection of the John Grant Crabbe Library, for the use of their library materials, and Charles Hay, Archivist, Eastern Kentucky University, Richmond, Kentucky, for the use and copying of the tape recordings of Jesse Stuart's lectures as writer-in-residence there during the mid-1960s. For making available Jesse Stuart's letters to James Still and for providing me photocopies of them, I wish to thank Jack D. Ellis, Director of Libraries, and John Forbes, Coordinator of the Appalachian Collection, Morehead State University, Morehead, Kentucky. I am grateful to Evelyn Stevenson and J. E. Windrow of George Peabody College of Teachers for allowing me to review a large file of Stuart materials; to Gerald Ham, Head of Archives and Manuscripts of the State Historical Society of Wisconsin at Madison, for arranging my study and photocopying of Stuart's letters to August Derleth; to John Bird, for providing me access to his file of letters from Jesse Stuart, dating from World War II; to John T. Demos, Dean of Libraries, University of Louisville, George McWhorter, Curator of the Patterson Rare Book Room of the Ekstrom Library, and Delinda Stephens Buie, Assistant Curator, for their consistent cooperation and assistance in making available to me, often on a moment's notice, essential materials in the Jesse Stuart Collection housed there. I also wish to thank Ruth Culpepper of the Interlibrary Loan Department of the Ekstrom Library for her help and that of her staff in procuring, somehow, even the most difficult-to-find items for my research.

Among those whose reviews, articles, or letters are alluded to or quoted and to whom I wish to pay proper credit—other details of publication being in the Notes—are Malcolm Cowley, *New Republic;* John Gould Fletcher, *Poetry: A Magazine of Verse;* David McCord, *Yale Review* and *New Yorker;* Horace Gregory, *New York Herald Tribune Books;* Roy Helton, *Philadelphia Inquirer;* Paul Jordan-Smith, *Los Angeles Times;* Merrill Moore; Walter Paschall, *Atlanta Journal;* Henry E. Christman, *Knickerbocker Press;* Isabel Ackerman, *Lexington Herald;* John Chamberlain, *New York Times;* W. B. Ward, *New Day;* Eda Lou Walton, *Nation;* Franklin P. Adams, *New York Herald Tribune;* Lois Colley, *Eastern* (KY) *Progress;* Mark Van Doren, *New York Herald Tribune;* William Rose Benét, *Saturday Review of Literature;* Ralph Thompson, *New York Times;* Elizabeth Hardwick, *Lexington Herald;* Margaret Trotter; William Lyon Phelps; Charlotte Salmon, *Southwest Review;* Amy Vanderbilt; Morton Clark; Pinkney R. Allen, *Louisville Times;* George Scarbrough, *Chattanooga Times;* Nancy Grimes, *Portsmouth Times;* Raymond Brewster, *Huntington Herald-Advertiser;* J. Donald Adams, *New York Times Book Review;* Burton Rascoe, *Esquire;* George Buchanan, *News Chronicle* (London); Clip Boutell, *New*

York Post "Daily Magazine"; Lewis Gannett, *Boston Transcript;* May Cameron and Henry Beckett, *New York Post;* Chet Anderson, *Huntington Herald-Advertiser;* Earl Mittendorf, editor, *Greenup County Citizen* ed. of the *Russell* (KY) *Times;* Rena Niles, *Louisville Courier-Journal:* T. M. Longstreth, *Christian Science Monitor;* I. L. Salomon; Russell MacFall, *Chicago Sunday Tribune;* Elinor Richey, *Tracks: Chesapeake and Ohio Railway;* Malcolm Conley, *Ashland Daily Independent;* Robert A. Thornbury, *Louisville Courier-Journal* magazine; Helga Sandburg, *New York Herald Tribune Book Review;* Bordon Deal, *Saturday Review of Literature;* V. P. Haas, *Chicago Sunday Tribune;* Annie Laurie Williams; Bruno R. Neumann; Carl Leiden; Fanny Butcher, *Chicago Sunday Tribune;* William Plumley, ed., *Poems from the Hills;* Robert Hillyer; Hal Marc Arden; George Wolfford; William Boozer, *Nashville Banner;* Don Edwards and Andy Mead, *Lexington Herald-Leader;* G. Sam Piatt, *Ashland Daily Independent;* John Patterson, *Pittsburgh Press;* Beaufort Cranford, *Detroit News;* Norbert Blei, *Milwaukee Journal;* Morton S. Corwin, *Miami Herald,* and for his letter to Naomi Deane Stuart; and Katherine Paterson, *Washington Post Book World.* These and many others are credited in the Notes.

The completion of this work would have been considerably delayed had not timely if modest grants augmented my own funds in meeting research and writing expenses. In this connection, and for other good reasons as well, I wish to express my gratitude to several colleagues at the University of Louisville: X. J. Musacchia, Dean of the Graduate School; Lois S. Cronholm, Dean of the College of Arts and Sciences; Arthur J. Slavin, former Dean of the College of Arts and Sciences and now Justus Bier Distinguished Professor of Humanities; John A. Dillon, Jr., former Dean of the Graduate School and now Director of the Systems Science Institute; William F. Ekstrom, former Acting President and now Professor Emeritus of English; and Thomas A. Van, Chairman of the Department of English.

Others who have in various ways added to the reservoir of information out of which this book was written deserve acknowledgment here, among them Paula Wells, Fred A. Engle and Allen Engle, Frances Street, Zetta Sturgill Stephenson, and painter-writer Charley Robertson. I am indebted to Teva Meadows, managing editor of the *Russell Times-Trader,* who spent several hours assisting me in finding and photographing old editions of the *Greenup County Citizen* at Russell, Kentucky, containing many of Jesse Stuart's travel columns. I also wish to acknowledge Hargis Westerfield for his Introduction to the 1964 reprint of Stuart's *Harvest of Youth,* and Charles K. Wolfe for providing information on Theron Hale & His Daughters in his *The Grand Ole Opry: The Early Years, 1925–*

35 and for his helpful letters concerning the old-time fiddlers Jesse Stuart may have heard in Greenup. I thank Sally Fitzgerald, editor of *The Habit of Being: Letters of Flannery O'Connor* (New York: Farrar, Straus and Giroux) for bringing to light O'Connor's letters to Cecil Dawkins and T. R. Spivey relating to Jesse Stuart's participation in the 1959 Vanderbilt Symposium with her and Robert Penn Warren. I also wish to credit J. R. LeMaster for making available his interview with Jesse Stuart, published in the *Indiana English Journal,* vol. 8, no. 4 (Summer 1974). Although space forbids my mentioning all those who made memorable contributions to the literary gathering *Jesse Stuart and the Greenbo Sessions,* May 1980, for a weekend in "Stuart Country," the courtesy book of scholarship demands that I acknowledge and express my thanks to Delinda Stephens Buie for her statistical report on the sessions; to John T. Flanagan and Maude Adelaide Hochstrasser for their letters to Jesse and Naomi Stuart following the sessions, from which excerpts appear in this book; to William Boozer for references I have made to his "Jesse Stuart: An Appreciation," published in the *Kentucky Review* (1981); and to Wade Hall for my allusions to his "Foreword" in the 1980 reprint of Jesse Stuart's novel *Trees of Heaven.*

A sense of duty and of gratitude prompts me to mention the Reverend C. I. Scofield and the Reverend John W. Howell, for my references to their interpretations of Luke 17:21 as they bring light to Jesse Stuart's concept and use of the verse. No acknowledgment would be complete without mention of my editor, Lou Ashworth of McGraw-Hill, who has also been Jesse Stuart's editor. Throughout our work together, she has somehow managed to combine incisiveness with tolerance, patience with tight deadlines, and apt critical suggestions with constant encouragement, for which I am deeply grateful. Finally, I wish to thank my family, whose assistance to me has been no less than substantial: my son, Shawn, who prepared the map of "The W-Hollow World of Jesse Stuart"; my daughter, Jill, who accompanied me to W-Hollow and took useful notes; and my wife, Antonia, who made several trips to W-Hollow and elsewhere with me, took notes, did much of the typing, and once again provided helpful critical insights.

—H. EDWARD RICHARDSON

Louisville, Kentucky
March 15, 1984

JESSE

1

Daybreak: W-Hollow
1906–1918

◇

The log cabin stood on a high hilltop overlooking W-Hollow on one side and Shacklerun Valley on the other. A photograph taken in the late 1930s records a young man standing, arms akimbo, in front of the abandoned house, blocking the camera's eye from the narrow doorway. A panel of lumber leans against the front window, nearly obscuring it from view. Mountain pines stipple the distant horizon. Sawbriers, iron weeds, ragweeds, milkweeds, and tree sprouts impinge upon the place, while in the foreground a circle of barren yet pathless earth surrounds a patch of weeds and an old washtub, its bottom tilted up to the camera's view. It is difficult to discern whether the man looks at the camera or the washtub, or somewhere between. The roofline of the cabin poorly disguises a sagging ridgepole. The dilapidated roof appears to be made of hand-riven oak shingles. The camera's eye detects no chimney. The watercourse below on the southern side of the hill away from W-Hollow is recalled as "a lonely spot"—a place where one could listen to the sounds of Cedar Riffles Branch traversing "the stony riffles on silent nights" on the way down to the Little Sandy River, but if "the wind is blowing through the pine trees the water cannot be heard." In this house four miles by road from the nearest post office at Riverton, Kentucky, on the Ohio, Jesse Hilton Stuart, the oldest son of seven children of Mitchell and Martha Hilton Stuart, was born August 8—the child of the cabin in 1906, the persona to be created by the man-artist in 1907.[1]

It is strange how far back memory will reach and what it chooses to hold, montages of life-infused detail: wind howling around the hilltop shack and through the cedars, the barking of the foxes and squirrels and hound dogs across the night, flocks of honk-honking wild geese wheeling through the skies in Ls, Ws and Vs, brown autumn fields, winter snow fields when sundown "left a red radiance in the sky," and crows marauding gleefully through the farmers' cornfields, exchanging guard duty to eat the corn, then rising; those "black birds shining in the icy air and their caw-caws against the wind were things to be remembered."[2] The boy remembered, too, visiting the coal bank with his father, riding in the coal buggies on iron tracks, and learning that rats in the coal shaft were his father's friends. What the boy's mind absorbed provided the source for "Vacation in Hell," a short story published more than a generation later, in which a father of seven children says to his less fortunate mining partner, "I never liked a rat until I come here. . . . I didn't know there's one good thing to be said fer a rat. But here is one thing. He warns us when there's danger in th' coal banks. We can see 'im runnin' out."[3] By heeding these grisly little friends, "Mick" Stuart, as Jesse's father was known, had barely escaped death.

The infant Jesse had his first narrow breather with death while living at his birthplace, although he could not remember the incident. He was sick with "summer complaint," as his mother called it. Martha Stuart's youngest brother, Jiles Hilton, was home on furlough from the Marines at the time and was at the little hilltop shack. Martha picked Jesse up from the bed and, thinking he was not breathing, panicked and started for the coal mine to get Mick. Her brother, patient and unexcitable by nature, stopped her. He laid the boy on a table and worked with him until he was visibly breathing. The family credited Jiles Hilton with saving little Jesse's life.[4]

By November of 1909, Mitchell Stuart had left the mine and become a tenant farmer, most likely the winter before. Jesse remembered being with his sister, Sophia, then six, huddled under a laprobe close to Martha Stuart, their feet in the straw as she drove their sled. He and Sophia (called "Sophie") got up so close to their mother that her elbows bumped their shoulders as she reined in the horse. A larger sled pulled by a yoke of oxen carried their household goods. Heavy flakes of snow struck their faces, and the hilltop wind penetrated their clothes, but they were used to the cold. Their destination was a three-room log cabin in W-Hollow, named for the W-shaped creek itself. "And our place," Jesse Stuart later wrote, "was to be on the [center] of the middle prong of the W [i.e., of the creek in W-Hollow]."[5]

Bright spots in the boy's memory were associated with the family hearth—the evenings after his father had got in the firewood, when the family gathered in front of the fireplace to roast potatoes and chestnuts, pop popcorn and make "lassie balls," and crack hickory nuts and walnuts on the stone hearth. He remembered his mother sewing and knitting socks and sweaters, sometimes piecing quilts, and the cat playing with the yarn. His earliest clear memory was setting the house on fire. Speaking in his typical conversational manner, he elaborated, "That little house in the hollow. I was only about two years old, used a broom. I got a little toy broom and this fire ate the broom, so I took it over and stuck it to the window curtain. Mom was a strong woman and put it out." Before he knew his alphabet, his mother, who had gone to grade school, taught him a few childhood rhymes on winter nights:

> Mother's knitting stockings
> Pussy's got the ball;
> Oh, don't you think that winter
> Is pleasanter than all?[6]

In his own words, his first memories of the land were "the hills. It has always been the land—wild plums, poplar trees, redbirds, mules, geese. I hunted eggs down the [W-Hollow] creek; our chickens laid eggs away from the chicken house—they laid them under the ferns and rock-cliffs, in hollow logs and stumps and the pawpaw groves. And the beauty of the land, the four seasons—autumn first, the brown hills of autumn."[7]

Of his birth his oldest sister, Sophia Stuart Keeney, born September 3, 1903, recalled, "I barely do remember his birth. I was standing at the door, and someone was with me, this lady. I was kicking the door and crying. My father mined coal then, and this lady took me down to the place where he worked, and we looked around there, and then she brought me back." She went on, "The lady let me go in then, when we got back, to see my new little brother." Years later Jesse Stuart said, "I believe Dr. Morris delivered me," though he was not sure. In *Beyond Dark Hills* he and a man named Dr. Torrey had words when the doctor attempted to give him unsought advice. "The one disgrace I've had in life," Jesse told him, "was when you came to deliver me on a stormy August night and got there too late. You are still too late to know what's going on!"[8]

Jesse Stuart's memories of his early years in the second little log house (still standing and occupied in W-Hollow at this writing) were as impromptu and natural as snapshots in a family album. He early learned that the woodland pewees were reliable weather prophets. Each spring a dusky-topped, whitish bellied couple came at garden plowing time, more dependable even than the bluebirds, singing their wistful song that had named them, their *pee-a-wees* with the rising lilt at the end. Living there close to the middle fork of W-Hollow, not two-tenths of a mile from Peddler's Well, he and Sophia had the run of the long green valley pastures. Brave in daylight they ventured to the place where long ago a peddler had been murdered, all his earthly goods stolen, and his body and broken, bloody buggy thrown down the well. Here people saw strange lights at night, but Sophia and Jesse never went by there after dark.[9]

One day in early June of 1911, the brother and sister walked down the path to W-Hollow Road. Looking across the widest green sweep of the hollow, they saw a hearse drawn by a span of big horses drive out from the home of Nathaniel and Lydia Collins. Mr. Collins had been ill for a long time, and although Jesse was too young to understand, Sophia told him, "Mr. Collins is dead." Behind the hearse followed a line of buggies, people on horses, others riding in surreys, and many walking on the way to nearby Three Mile Cemetery, located on a hilltop just outside the entrance to W-Hollow. "They are hauling him in the front wagon. He is taking his last ride."

"What is 'dead'?" Jesse wanted to know.

"He can't breathe, and he can't move," Sophia said, but her four-year-old brother still did not understand. To explain she tried to catch a butterfly but had to settle for an ant. She laid it on a rock in the road and then crushed it with another rock. The ant did not move anymore. Sophia said that Mr. Collins would be buried and go back to the earth, the ground, just like the ant that would soon go back to the dirt. "This was when I was first told about death," Jesse later wrote. "I didn't like it."[10]

The boy remembered going to the fields with his father when he was six years old. In time he would associate his father with the permanence of a mountain, although Mitchell Stuart, thin and wiry, was only five feet eight and averaged a slight 134 pounds. "I had chores to do to help him and I was proud of them. I carried drinking water for him, and I walked along behind him when he was plowing to uncover the corn that had been buried by dirt from the plow. When I got tired, I'd go to sleep under a shade tree."

Jesse was hoeing tobacco by the age of six. The heat of the sun-drenched field burned into his memory as well as the sight of long rows contouring the hillside, the smells of "hot parched soil worming up between his toes," and the familiar smells of "burdock, pursley, smart-weed and cockleburrs." He remembered the "peck-peck of bright-handled goose-neck hoes all day long." Much later, in the story "Whose Land Is This?" the author, through his fictional alter-ego Shan, recalled a nearby tobacco field his father had rented close to his Grandfather Hilton's house, where Jesse/Shan first wormed tobacco: "I remember it was the first place I ever pulled a tobacco worm from the stalk—I pulled it in two and buried it in the soft black smelly dirt of the tobacco balk." The boy worked barefooted, memorably in the chill of autumn dawns:

> In paradise I found life first a battle.
> When I was six I worked at thinning corn,
> I went to work before day in the morn.
> At four each morn I rose to feed the cattle
> Before the chickens flew down off the trees.
> And when I found the cow on autumn morn
> I drove her up and stood on the warm leaves
> Where she had lain, to get my cold feet warm.[11]

Sometime during Jesse's third year his father carried him on his back to the schoolhouse at Plum Grove, which then stood across the hilltop from the site of the present church, on what is now the front portion of the main graveyard. A rural Republican of some grassroots influence, "Mick" Stuart had got himself elected school trustee for his district. He was interested in hiring competent teachers, but he put most of his physical energies into clearing the grounds and building a cistern and toilets for the boys and girls. "Since I didn't get any education, I don't want my youngins to grow up in this world without it," he told Jesse. "They'll never know what they're missin' until they don't have it. If I could only read and write!" From the time the boy was five, Mick Stuart talked to his son about school soon to begin at Plum Grove, and so filled him with the idea that he could hardly wait.[12]

Jesse had good reason to remember his parents as being different from each other. He observed the differences before he understood them, and stored them in his mind—undemonstrative love and conflicting voices and actions, differences in appearance, politics, religion, and individual natures. His mother had the prominent Hilton features suggestive of an Indian: as a young woman she was dark-complexioned, with high cheekbones accenting her attractive face and crow-black hair, though her hair quickly grayed in later years. A descendant of a stubborn English family that had made its way into Kentucky from North Carolina, she was a slender five feet eleven inches tall. She preferred the open fields to housework; yet by the time Jesse was ten years old he realized that neighborhood women "came to Mom for things." She showed them how to darn, to cut out dresses, to pattern and to piece quilts. "She would wait on their sick." The Hiltons were a people slow to anger, but "persistent against force when angered." They loved their homes in the hills, had a penchant for bright colors and books, and were distinguished in the mountains as Baptist preachers and "good larners." The patriarch of the Hiltons as Jesse grew up was Grandpa Nathan, at fifteen a Confederate in John Hunt Morgan's camp, later a timber cutter, and a lifelong Democrat. He was the model for Grandpa in "Another April," a story in which the mother of a boy full of questions remembers Grandpa's prime of life when "he'd walk out on the snow and ice barefooted and carry wood in the house and put it on the fire." Dramatically the boy's eye follows his grandfather as the old man totters through scenes of the new spring earth and dialogues with his ancient friend, a terrapin with "1847" cut on its shell. Both the Grandpa of the story and Grandpa Nathan Hilton lived into their nineties.[13]

Jesse Stuart wrote that his father's family descends from Raphy Stuart, his great-grandfather, one of six brothers who emigrated from Scotland's Firth of Forth and eventually came to Wythville, Virginia. One of the brothers died, one remained in Wythville, but the others scattered. Raphy Stuart settled on the Big Sandy River in eastern Kentucky. According to family lore the brothers were, without exception, at least six feet two, and Raphy Stuart was six and one-half feet tall—thus the author's autobiographical chapter heading "Tall Figures of the Earth" in *Beyond Dark Hills*.

Mitchell "Mick" Stuart, the author's father, bore the name of his father. The first Mitchell Stuart, Jesse's grandfather, was a knock-down-drag-out fighter. A woodsman and colorful log-rafter on the Big Sandy, he married twice and fathered nineteen children. He was a hard-working, hard-drinking, land-clearing timber cutter and Republican of violent propensities. Jesse's father took him by train to visit Grandpa Stuart at his home in the Big Sandy country, near Buchanan in Lawrence County by the railroad, in sight of the river. The old man grabbed the boy by the neck with the crook of his cane and gave him the "dutch-rub," that awful knuckle-on-scalp torture other small boys had occasion to know. "I cried and tried to get away," the author recalled. "I was afraid of him. He was twice as large as my father and had a great long beard. . . . If I had met Grandpa at night I would have thought he was The Devil." Although the family could never learn the details, the circumstances surrounding the old man's death offered the likelihood of murder.[14]

In 1901, when Grandpa Hilton got wind of his girl's impending marriage his response was frantic: "My heavens, my daughter is marrying an outlaw when she marries Mitchell Stuart!" Young Mick Stuart was only twenty-one at the time, but Nathan Hilton, having heard of the older Stuarts, was mistakenly judging his future son-in-law by them. Still, his outburst sheds a bright, quick light on those opposing mindsets of the Stuarts and Hiltons that the boy kenned before he was old enough to understand.[15]

Small wonder that as a child Jesse began to store in his mind the details, the events, the very atmosphere of familial conflict that in time brimmed over into such autobiographical pieces as "The Storm." In this story the boy tells what he sees and hears from the inside out as "Mom lifts the washrag from the washpan of soapy water" and "washes my neck and ears." The sound of verbal conflict clashes above his innocence. Her "I can't stand it any longer, Mick," and his "We're different people . . . Sal. If I say things that hurt you, I can't help it" are set off against the child's preoccupation with a toy his mother has given his baby brother, "a threadspool that Pa whittled in two and put a stick through for me to spin like a top," in local idiom "a pretty." The child-narrator persistently draws the parental argument into a broader familial arena, in which the innocence of the child powerfully, if unconsciously, contends with the tensions and subdued passions of the parents:

> I look at the pretty Herbert holds in his hands. Herbert looks at it with bright little eyes and laughs.
>
> "Mom, he has the pretty Pa made for me," I say. "I don't want him to have it."
>
> "Quit fussing with your baby brother," Mom says as she puts my hand into the washpan and begins to scrub it.

Perhaps the mother and father had better part since they cannot get along together. Will she take the children?

> "They are mine. . . . I gave them birth—and I remember—and—I'm going to hold them." Mom looks hard at Pa as she speaks these words.

She objects to his changeable nature: "laughing one minute and the next . . . raising the roof with your vile oaths." But Mick pushes his case, she her threatened leave-taking:

> "We just aren't the same people," Pa says. "That's why I love you, Sal. You're not like I am. You are solid as a mountain. I need you, Sal. I need you more than anyone I know in this world."
>
> "I'm leaving," Mom says. "I'm tired of this. I've been ready to go twice before. I felt sorry for you and my little children that would be raised without a father. This is the third time I've planned to go. Third time is the charm. I'm going this time."

. . . "Listen," says Pa, "I heard something like April thunder!"

Pa holds his pipe in his hand. He sits silently. He does not speak. Mom squeezes the washrag in the water again. Now she listens.

"I don't hear anything," says Mom. "You just imagined you heard something."

But Pa has heard distant thunder, and he knows the signs, "A mare-tail in the sky," then "the martins hurrying to their boxes," and then the real thunder. The boy sees his mother look at the martin boxes and thinks, "She remembers the day when Pa made the boxes at the barn. . . . Mom helped him lift the poles into the deep post holes. . . . I'd just got rid of my dresses then and started wearing rompers." She hurries to finish packing, but the rain comes. The boy thinks, "It sounds like you'd thump with your knuckles on the bottom of a washtub." His mother looks at the flowers of April, "snow-white patches of bloodroot blooming around the cliffs . . . the pink sweet Williams growing by the old logs," the flowerbox "Pa made for her," and she hears the questions of her children. "If we go, Mom, who'll cook for Pa?" She sees "through the rain-washed windowpane the bench Pa made," where they would sit "at the end of the grape-arbor and string beans." She knows that had they gone they would have been caught in the heavy rainstorm on the dirt road. The boy reads it in her face. She hardly notices the rain stopping, the sun coming out, or what the boy sees in his father: "A shadow falls over Pa's brown, weather-beaten face." For she has already made her decision:

"The third time," says Mom, "that I've got ready to go. Something happened every time. I'm not going."

. . . Pa puts his pipe back in his pocket. His face doesn't have a shadow over it now. Pa looks happy. There is a smile on his September pawpaw-leaf-colored face.

In a scene of tender reconciliation, the parents walk out together. Only then does the boy's attention revert to his play pretty. "I go into the front room to see if Herbert has my top in his hand. It is my top, for Pa made it for me."

Jesse Stuart later said, "That's the way I remember it."[16]

While living at the house on the center of the middle fork of W-Hollow Creek, the boy learned a hundred chores: feeding the chickens shelled corn, gathering eggs, bringing in kindling and wood, pitching down hay for the livestock, helping his mother bring in cows for milking, getting a bucket of nubbins, feeding the hogs, drawing water. His father led him by the hand over the farm and sometimes carried him on his back. "I learned to love the things he loved," among them his first memory of a cornfield, the rows "curved like dark-green rainbows around a high slope," the blades of corn rustling in the wind. Mick Stuart claimed that he could understand their whispers, but Jesse

> . . . reasoned that before anything could speak or make a sound it had to have a mouth. When my father said the corn could talk, I got down on my knees and I looked a stalk over.
>
> "This corn hasn't got a mouth," I told my father. "How can anything talk when it doesn't have a mouth?"
>
> He laughed like the wind in the corn and hugged me to his knees, and we went on.

Following his father's lead, the boy explored the woods, climbed trees, and stared at three large blue eggs of a fussing crow. He learned about snakes and their ways, the differences that counted between the blunt-tailed copperhead and the man-befriending blacksnake, the poisonous water moccasin and the playful green garden snake. On walks with his father and mother he mastered lessons in nature lore he would later teach to other children. There was a kind of clock in nature. One of the early signs of spring was hazelnut blooms, "soft yellow-green tassels like spears on corn tassels, clinging to lifeless little branches" of these clustering bushes. Spring often arrived with the first wild flowers of late March or April, the low, leather-leafed trailing arbutus with its spicy pink and white flowers. Then the white-petaled percoon, or bloodroot, stippled the slopes. The serviceberry trees blossomed before the dogwood, wild crab apple, and redbud trees, and before one could chew the ripe mountain-tea leaves. The high purple-crowned Queen-of-the-meadow came along in August and September, as well as the somewhat shorter ironweeds with dusky-rosy pink and purple heads. Later on into October, especially in the dew-laden flats, the low blue-violet clusters of hardy ageratum appeared. He learned to read the finer bark of the black locust tree well enough to distinguish it from the heavier bark of the yellow locust. He could tell the smooth-barked white oak from the thicker, tough-barked chestnut oak, and the light gray bark of the sugar maple from the ridged gray bark of the tulip poplar. One late September his father introduced him to the fruit of the pawpaw tree. "Did you ever taste a banana in your life that was as good as a pawpaw? Did you ever see anything prettier than the clean sweet golden fruit of a pawpaw?" After the first frosts in October, he ate ripe persimmons, too, sweet as dates. "The persimmon is a candy tree," Mick Stuart told him. "It really should have been called the gumdrop tree." Ever after the boy saw the ripe fruit as browning gumdrops on the frosty ground.[17]

It was a time before the sawmills came into W-Hollow. After the corn was "laid by" one July, Sophia and Jesse left Herbert and their infant sister, Mary, at home and set out to Plum Grove School early in the morning over a two-mile country path. Herbert Lee was a handsome little child with brown eyes and "black curly hair . . . real wavy," but he was only three years old and had to stay with his mother. He was Jesse's main playmate, for Jesse did not really count the girls—Sophia and their cousins, Grace and Essie Hilton, who lived nearby and often walked to school with them. Heading southward down the middle fork of W-Hollow branch, "We met foxes in our path many a morning." Squirrels barked and scampered over the children's heads in the tall timber up the hills and on the bluffs, and rabbits hopped across their path. They crossed W-Hollow Road and went on southward where, at this writing, a barn stands, marking the Collins homesite, and then over Collins Hill by "Grandma" Collins' apple orchard, through the Wheeler woods and across the pasture where a bull roamed and produced no little apprehension in the children: "We dared not wear red."[18]

If, as Plato said, the direction in which education starts a man determines his future life, then Calvin Clarke shares with Mitchell and Martha Stuart an important early formative influence upon the boy. Just eighteen when they met, Clarke, the "Iron Hand" of the later stories, first taught Jesse his multiplication tables and "words—to read, spell and write." Words and people fascinated the boy, for "thirty-five people were a multitude for me to see together," and "words are marvelous things." Words "are something which you can do anything with but take hold of with your hands." Learning them, excited beyond caution, he put words on paper—a note to Mabel Jones—and threw it to her across the aisle that separated boys from girls. His exhilaration was short-lived. Iron Hand Clarke promptly whipped him. His enthusiasm unsubdued, Jesse learned his primer "forward and backward" that first year, and was never to forget the first poem he memorized from an old primer:

Oh Mother look at the moon,
She's riding so high,
For tonight she looks
Like a lamp in the sky.
Last night she was smaller
And shaped like a bow,

But now she is larger
And round like an O.[19]

Competitive and hyperactive, he determined to work "to get ahead of everybody in my class." He especially wished to overtake his sister Sophia, who tattled on him. "Sis" told on him daily when he fought at school or "tried to do some miraculous thing before the other students . . . such as jumping off the highest fence post." Worse, she was "the direct cause of my mother examining my neck and ears every morning before I went to school." In the game of fox and hounds at Plum Grove, in which the biggest and fastest boy was the fox, Jesse was as yet only an ambitious hound.[20]

Sometimes during the fifteen-minute recesses, the boys and girls gathered in a circle to play "the needle's eye" and sing a song the boy never forgot:

The needle's eye that does supply
The thread that runs so true,
Many a beau have I let go,
Because I wanted you.

Many a dark and stormy night,
When I went home with you,
I stumped my toe and down I go,
Because I wanted you.

Although he no longer threw messages across the schoolroom to Mabel Jones, he loved to write little prose sketches and to rhyme words. It simply gave him pleasure to write what he saw—trees budding in the spring, percoon blooming in the yet bare March woods, white clouds rolling "above the daisy-covered pasture hills, . . . and it was poetry." He wrote his first theme when he was eight. It was, by his own account, "about the Easter rabbit laying eggs in the garden and covering them with straw," and when he read it before his Plum Grove classmates they responded by jumping up and down, clapping their hands, and laughing. "Well," Jesse said, "I guess the rabbit did lay eggs in our garden. Mom said it did anyhow." The teacher smiled and once again the students burst into laughter. Jesse "was sore at the whole class."[21]

He had just completed his second year at Plum Grove when his only brother, four-year-old Herbert, "took down" with what was then considered "some kind of fever"—probably bronchial pneumonia. Herbert died on Monday, January 12, 1914. Jesse remembered his father sitting on a box beneath an apple tree without leaves, just a little sun on the January day, his father wringing his hands and saying: "It is too unbearable to stand. If we could have only had a doctor here in time to have saved him." The funeral procession, led by a spring wagon with a pine box roped to it, wound five miles through the Plum Grove Hills; from Plum Grove Church itself it went two hills and two valleys beyond and directly south, and then east of the road leading on to Argillite. This was a hillside of Grandfather Nathan Hilton's farm then, the only land Martha Stuart's family owned. Born in 1851, Nathan Hilton was in his early sixties, still a strong and active farmer. Jesse's mind forever held the image of his grandfather standing in the blowing January wind, "his white hair tousled," pointing the way for the driver. "Right this way," he said, and cut the wire fence of his pasture. There were pine trees, newly dug earth thrown up nearby, Baptist hymns, a mountain preacher who would not take pay. Years later the author would write, "I remember how cold my feet got standing in the mud, and how the people cried. All of the others in the family cried but I did not. I cried when I went back home and he was gone." Angrily the boy vowed never to go back to that pine grove again.

In the autobiographical story "Brothers," Herbert becomes "John." Back from the funeral, the boy-narrator notices "how the tears would drop from Mom's eyes" as she sat before the fire, silent, darning a sock. The boy expresses his resentment, a sense of injustice rather than grief:

> God is not a fair man, Mom, or he would have let John play in the sand with me. John sleeps under the ground, Mom. You know how hard that is. I don't want ever to sleep under the ground. I want John back to play with me. I don't like to play doll with Sophia and Mary over there under the grapevines where that old goose has her nest.[22]

He found little consolation playing with the girls—his sisters Sophia and Mary, and his cousins Grace and Essie Hilton—although they remember the fun they had swimming together. Grace later said, "You know, we didn't know anything about sex, so we had this old frog pond down there in the hollow where we all played together." Essie added, "We didn't know anything about anything, because we hardly went anywhere. We went swimming in the nude, all of us, and it was so much fun because there was a lot of green scum on the water that made it good and slick for sliding." They both laughed gloriously. The man-artist remembered, too, both in biography and fiction, "how I went in swimming with the girls—how I hated to go in swimming with them. How I laughed when they slid over the slate rocks where the frogs had been, into the knee-deep water. I remember the minnows that took to the willow roots and hid when we jumped naked into the water." His cousins were not specific about how the fun ended, but Jesse Stuart later wrote that his mother one day came across the potato vines and told him, "Jesse, you must find you another swimming hole and quit swimming with the girls."[23]

The mix of feelings that made him both enjoy and hate swimming with the girls, aside from being a natural reaction of a pre-puberty male, appears to have stemmed from a hardly surprising conflict between a fun-loving nature and an unconscious guilt: "I didn't think it fair that [Herbert] should sleep in the ground and I could go on playing in the sand forever—see the spring come with birds, green leaves on the willows, Sweet Williams on the cliffs. Hens cackling. Geese chasing the butterflies. And [Herbert] not there."[24]

He played and tumbled and was as familiar with the woods as any Indian could have been. One day he ventured away from the little three-room log house at the center of the middle fork of W-Creek. He was thirsty and lay on his stomach, feeling the roots of an old tree under him as he drank from a stream of cool, blue, inviting water. He was sick for six months with typhoid fever, at one point so weak he had to be "lifted on a sheet." Neither could he feed himself, his arms and hands had been so weakened. His hair fell out. His limbs were flaccid and useless. In time his hair grew back, but he had to learn to do everything all over again—to feed himself, to stand up again, and then to walk. Later, before the Stuarts moved from the little house, he was exploring the woods when again thirst struck him. This time he found enticing water bubbling "from the rocks" not far away. He came down once more with typhoid fever, "but it didn't hurt as much as the first time."[25]

He was the only boy his age in W-Hollow and had been swimming and playing by himself for over a year after Herbert's death when a man carrying a small leather bag rode up to the house on a large sorrel horse, dismounted, and went inside. In a little while Jesse's curiosity got the better of him and he decided to find out about the man. At the door the man told Jesse, "You will hug my neck when you see what I brought you," and then the man went on out toward his horse. Jesse went inside and saw his mother smiling. She pulled back the sheet, and he saw the baby. She said, "Here is your brother that the Doctor fetched you."

"Where did he get him?" Jesse asked.

"From behind a stump over there on the hill," his mother said.

Jesse Stuart later wrote, "I took back to the hill where the Sweet Williams grew. I looked behind every stump on the hill. I was hunting for babies. Funny, as many hens' nests as I have found behind those stumps and had never found a baby. I ran to the house and told Mom I'd hunted for babies and couldn't find any. Then said Mom: 'Only doctors can find babies.' "[26]

This was the birth of James Mitchell Stuart, to be the most sustaining friendship of his life, the brother he had lost and found again.

The year that followed was one of the happiest times of the boy's life. At least two of the most joyful of childhood memories center about the bushy-topped white oak tree, which still stands in the backyard of the little log house. This was the tree upon whose then low branches the famed fighting rooster "Nest Egg," also the name of one of Jesse Stuart's most widely read stories, last roosted. The rooster had been hatched by a fierce old Sebright hen. Following his mother's advice, Jesse/Shan had moved a nest egg away from the nest, but had left the egg close enough that the hen could roll it back with her bill; however, he had been technically honest with his mother in taking the egg out of the nest, and he showed her three places on his arm where the hen had pecked him and brought blood. A strong young rooster who survived scratching for a living in the woods, Nest Egg grows straight and tall, and steps out proudly on his tiptoes and whips all the old roosters. Neighbors who enjoy cockfights are disappointed and sore when Nest Egg kills their best. After Pa refuses a hundred-dollar offer for the rooster, the Stuarts/Powderjays begin to notice that their chicken flock is growing—while the neighbors' flocks diminish. The neighbors think they are the victims of a chicken thief, but are not so sure when they see their chickens with the colorful Powderjay rooster. They wonder about Pa. He is indicted for stealing chickens, but the case is thrown out of court. The wondrous rooster "tolls the hens" to the farm until the Powderjay flock has doubled; the chickens flourish. Pa, threatened by a barn-burner, is uneasy at night; but by day the Powderjays gather eggs in bushel baskets and sell them in town. One day the rooster does not awaken the family with its lusty crows, and the boy and his father find him beneath the white-oak-tree roost where a screech owl had pecked a hole in his head while he was asleep. "That damned owl fouled 'im," Pa says, and the two cry over the death of Nest Egg.[27]

Near the white oak, too, is the well-remembered pasture where the daisies were white and the wild roses pink. Once he hunted there for the milkcow, Gypsy, through sawbrier clusters and small pines, whose needles were weighted with "dew drops . . . like little lumps of polished silver until the sun lifted them skyward in ribbons of mist." That day he found the smart old cow in the alder bushes, shunned by the biting flies, and he drove her to "the big bushy-topped white oak that didn't shade anybody but Gypsy, my mother, and me." While Martha Stuart milked the cow, the boy lay on his back and looked through half-shut eyes at the blue sky and "changing leaf pictures." It was a happy time, this world of pastoral contentment. "I was nine in this year of 1916, and I loved everything about it." It was, despite the dark moments, a world the man-artist would cherish and record in 1955 as a life-giving vision in the "Prologue" of *The Year of My Rebirth,* and later as the short story "An Angel in the Pasture."[28]

Each school year or term was composed of about six months, usually from late July into winter as weather allowed up to February. Calvin Clarke taught the schoolboy his first two years, and a part of a third. Twenty-one-year-old Nora Riggs, who taught him for the rest of his third term, was the first of his teachers who had been to college; after that term, she returned to Eastern Kentucky Teachers College at Richmond to complete her senior year. Although Jesse usually walked to school with his sisters and cousins, that year he walked from Mrs. Collins' farm on to Plum Grove with his teacher, who roomed at the Collins house. He had read an article about Harvard in the newspaper and hoped to study there someday. Sharing a dream—and wanting to impress a teacher he thought "so pretty and so nicely dressed"—he told her of his ambition to attend what he believed to be "the greatest and oldest" college in the United States.[29]

In their spare time and often before school he and Sophia practiced their lessons at home. Jesse burned up so much energy he was nearly always hungry. His lunchbox consisted of a five-pint bucket, the contents four ears of boiled corn (from August to frost), eight biscuits spread with cooked apples, buttered cornbread, a bottle of milk, and pie or cake. He ate at morning recess, lunch, and afternoon recess. Yet by four o'clock, as he later wrote, "I was always hungry."[30]

Each day going to and from school, he saw "Grandma" Collins' bright red apples on the orchard trees. The old lady had offered the Stuart and Hilton children all the windfall apples they could eat, but the boy disdained these lowly fruit as "soft, mellow apples that tasted like meal." When he saw the juicier red globes shining fresh on the trees, his eyes got big and his mouth watered. For several days he hung back from the girls and stealthily partook of the forbidden fruit, until Sophia got wise to him. Although she promised not to tell on him, the next day when he got home Martha Stuart was waiting in the yard with her well-used willow switch. When questioned he produced the apples and held them out in his hand.

"You've been raised not to steal," she said, and hit the boy's legs with the switch. Jesse began to cry as she ordered him to return the apples to Grandma Collins.

"I can't!" Jesse balked.

"But you will!"

Consistently she met reluctance with force, and switched the boy all the way down to the main hollow. They crossed the footlog over W-Creek, where she "let up," to Jesse's relief, but she again "lit in" on him and whipped him steadily until they reached the white fence in front of the Collins house. His legs "were streaked with red whelps." The weeping boy stood in front of the house and cried all the harder. Mrs. Collins heard him and rushed to the door before he could knock. "What's wrong?" she asked. "Is someone dead?"

He confessed his sin, then handed her the apples. He never forgot the old woman's faded blue eyes, her slat bonnet pulled low over her forehead. She used her apron to "wipe a tear from the corner of her eye," and said, "You are an honest boy." Blinded by his tears, Jesse stumbled at the gate. "It was the hardest thing I have ever had to do in my life."[31]

Jesse accepted the punishment from his mother without question, but he swore revenge, first hoping to "whip" the tattler, then to entice the notoriously feared Wheeler bull into attacking the culprit; but he could never place the blame with certainty. His sister had promised she would not tell on him, and he believed her. Honesty was a sacred matter in the Stuart family. Although Sophia might tattle, she would not lie. Grace or Essie might have told his mother, but he could not be sure as to the guilt of either. These girls had learned of their Aunt Martha's intolerance of dishonesty firsthand, but had once escaped retribution through a clever technicality of their own invention. Jesse's mother had a "prize apple tree" filled with green apples that hung over a flat roof. "She had seen us taking apples and warned us not to pull the apples off her tree. Well, we climbed up on the roof and ate the apples but left the cores hanging on their stems." Apparently the ruse worked, "and Aunt Martha didn't get mad because she was afraid we would get sick."[32]

Sometime in 1915 or 1916 Jesse and his family moved for the third time. This move took the Stuarts to the head of W-Hollow, then the "last log house" up the last prong of W-Creek, now the remodeled and many-times-enlarged home of the Jesse Stuarts. Jesse led the cows to the third log house, not more than a mile away, and made a return round trip for the chickens. Their new home consisted of two log rooms, separated by a dog trot, standing at the juncture of Shinglemill Branch and the final prong of W-Creek. It was "the most desolate place I have ever seen." He recalled the time as World War I, and remembered that his new brother, James, still wore dresses. There was a patch of blackberry briars by the house, outside the window near which, many years later, he would place his desk and write. "I cut a patch of blackberry briars out of there I wish you had seen. It was as big as a small stack of hay. My mother wanted 'em cut, and I got out there and cut them. Every room of this house leaked through the roof. Behind the old front log room then was a log kitchen, and the present dining room was a dog trot," or what the Stuarts called an "entry." The author recalled that "the garden was right in front of the house, and the road was closer to the house then. The barn was across the road. Right where the driveway is we used to raise onions. That is fertile ground. It is excellent ground." Even now the home seems comfortably remote, up at the head of W-Hollow and tucked back into the outlet of the smaller hollow known as Shinglemill; but then it seemed so far back from civilization that Jesse Stuart was inspired to write of the place, in what may have been more truth than hyperbole, "Owls hooted from the dark timber at midday."[33]

The move to the head of W-Hollow made the trip to Plum Grove School something like a mile longer. Sometimes Sophia carried her shoes, putting them on when she reached the foot of the hill, for the family could afford only one pair a year for each child. Jesse, like other boys, walked barefoot. His appetite to outlearn all others was as keen as ever, and he fought with the other boys for physical supremacy as he competed academically with everyone. His fourth-term teacher, Elta Cooper, was a small, bright woman who had graduated from high school and received teacher preparatory training in normal school. She remembered Jesse as a child who played harder than anybody in school, "running and jumping over them—just *wild!*" A good disciplinarian, "Miss Elta" instructed her students in manners as well as in academics. Under her alert eye and motivating praise, Jesse continued his rapid progress—two grades each term. Before he was ten, he was placed in the seventh grade.

Although she afterward followed Jesse Stuart's career closely, she recalls him best when he was ten years old, "the few months I had him in the 7th grade in 1917." It was such a severe winter that the term was only six months long. She remembers "snow and sometimes ice on the ground from December 8th, 1917." Fortunately for the Stuart children,

"Martha Hilton Stuart . . . was a remarkable person. . . . She kept her family well clothed and fed with her hard work and talents." Concerning an incident the author relates in *To Teach, To Love*—her forthcoming marriage to returning soldier Earl Kotcamp, and her students' becoming so enthusiastic they had to be kept in after school and talked to about their manners—Mrs. Kotcamp took gentle exception. "It was at election time in 1917 so the boys used 'Earl Kotcamp' instead of a candidate to yell for! as they were going across a pasture field on their way home." This is not Jesse's explanation for his, Aaron and Ed Howard's, and Glen Hilton's shouting "Hurrah for Earl Kotcamp and Miss Elta." Another detail "a little different" is that "I never kept anyone after school. They had so far to walk home and some of it through woods I wanted all of them to go together. Then at recess the next morning I said, 'Now all of you who were yelling on the way home yesterday please remain in your seats.' I only talked to them."

Of Jesse's competitiveness she writes, "Jesse always wanted to win every ball game or at marbles, even if it was playing London Bridge. He looked forward to the arithmetic matches we had on Friday afternoon [and] always had his slate up first and the correct answer. In spelling matches he always finished at the head—these matches I gave to 5-6-7-8th grades together. Another thing I remember well was his love for grammar, as we called it then, [and] that was unusual for a boy. We thought of grammar as a girls' favorite and arithmetic as a boys' favorite. Not so with Jesse. He liked to work with the language, liked to diagram sentences on the blackboard so all the class could see them—nouns, verbs, adjectives, adverbs, etc., were fascinating to him."

A 1917 photograph of Elta Cooper's Plum Grove School shows Jesse on the right end of the front row, squatting down barefoot but up on his toes, as if in arrested motion, holding Morris Sinnett's shoulder with his right hand to balance himself. "The picture," Mrs. Kotcamp said, "was taken in front of the school house in September, 1917. . . . He was a worker even at that early age, wanting to excel in everything at play and in class . . . could compete with any eighth grade student." In a game of fox and hounds, Jesse was now the fox and, admittedly, felt the full glory of the honor.[34]

As the boy had been introduced to the axe and sprouting hoe at six, he learned to cut corn with his father in his ninth year. Mick Stuart taught him to see corn as "a beautiful flower when one of the stalks silked and tasseled," and henceforth corn became a subject of poetry. He surprised his mother and father when he told them that "someday I'm going to own all the land you've ever rented in W-Hollow!" The parents laughed at the boy's dream that escaped in words before he could hold it in his thoughts, but they remembered it. Apparently he was in dead earnest, for his cousin Grace recalled substantially the same statement from the same period: "When Jesse was a little boy and we were walking down W-Hollow Road, he picked up a handful of fresh dirt and said, 'Here, Grace, smell this dirt. It's the best smelling thing on earth. Someday I'm going to have me a lot of land and own all the farms in W-Hollow.' " The furrows his father had plowed into the rented hillsides and level bottoms along W-Creek had been permanently carved into Jesse's mind; he would later write, "Our hearts were in our land. Parts of our hearts were buried in the land that we had rented."[35]

As the seasons passed, the Stuarts continued to clear new ground from long-grown-over, fertile hillsides, slopes, and valleys, but the growing season of 1918 was so rainy that much of the corn "rotted in the sour earth." What did grow was ruined by crayfish. Fruit was bad. "The cattle took murrain," the author later recalled. His father was bedfast with severe influenza, and James was too young to do much work.

The circumstances of the family's survival during this tragic winter in the nation's history are narrated in "Dark Winter" and "Spring Victory," as well as in his personal story, *Beyond Dark Hills*. In that winter of 1917/1918, his mother tells the older son, now ten, "Your Pop is dyin'," and sends him on the family horse to get the doctor. After the doctor's first visit, the boy meets him once a week at the entrance to W-Hollow and brings him to the house. He and his mother cut a black oak tree, hook it to the horse with a drag chain, and take it to the wood yard where they cut it into logs. The mother sends her son to cut white oaks with his pole ax and bring them to her. She then cuts them into splints and weaves peck, half-bushel, and bushel feed baskets. He sells them and brings home staples—salt, sugar, coffee, meal, and lard—and any remaining money. He hunts their food, too, and hangs as many as forty skinned rabbits on the joist of the smokehouse; he traps skunks and mink, and skins them for money. The chickens and guineas that survive the dark winter have to be destroyed because of "limber neck" or "maggots in their craws." In March the boy is sent hurriedly for the doctor again, and a new baby is born. "Spring Victory" concludes as "Mom stood in the late March wind with our tiny brother wrapped in a blanket in her arms. She kicks the dead leaves away with the toe of her shoe from a clump of blooming violets," a symbol of hope, as "Pa rest[s] between the handles of the plow." It was, in spite of all, a "Spring Victory."[36]

But "Dark Winter" does not end with the new life. The action continues into April. Mr. Woodrow, based on the real Winfield Daugherty for whom Jesse worked from the ages of nine to twelve, hires the boy at twenty-five cents a day, for Jesse/Shan is now "big enough to plow." The boy works from "sunrise in the mornin to sunset" and gives his money to his parents. When father and son are planting corn, Shan sees "Mom comin down the path to the clearin. She is wringin her hands and cryin." The new baby has died. The child is buried on the mother's father's farm. The boy remembers the spring wagon leading the way "through the April mud" and the "drizzling April rain." His youngest little brother, the boy thinks,

> rests in the dirt of the world. We leave him on the hill, a part of us, my father, mother, my brother and my sisters. We leave him a part of the Kentucky earth. It is strange to leave on a hill to sleep so long, one that you have seen breathe and move tiny fingers and blink an eye and cry like a little squeakin mouse.

The story ends as the family tries to beat the rain by racing the horses back home, and they see the sun—"first time today," the mother says, "that I have seen the sun."[37]

Jesse Stuart says that both stories are facts as he remembers them, with some changes of names and dates because, as he has often said, "I do not want to hurt anyone." In the autobiographical *Beyond Dark Hills*, the author says that as the winter of 1917/1918 broke, "My youngest brother [Martin Vernon Stuart] was the victim of pneumonia fever [bronchial pneumonia] and lasted only a few days. He had died the same way that Herbert Lee had died." Although Jesse had vowed four years before that he would never return to the pine grove marking Herbert's grave, he did return. Smoldering under that act of custom and familial loyalty, however, was a growing ambivalent attitude toward himself and his world as the tragic circumstances of hill life once more rushed in upon him. Conflict arose between the boy's emerging tendencies of self-assertion and submission; these powerful archetypal themes were soon to find expression, shape and form in his work as he developed the conscious techniques of literary artistry to handle them. Though the motif would appear in such early works as the developmental *Harvest of Youth* (1930) and the successful "poetry with muscles" in *Man with a Bull-Tongue Plow* (1934), it would thoroughly penetrate a term paper written in white heat during early spring, 1932, and later published as *Beyond Dark Hills* (1938)—rebellion versus submission to poverty, love of home and father juxtaposed with the desire to escape mountain doom. This raw scene of self-assertion, building after the death of Herbert Lee on January 12, 1914, and breaking through the mask of submission after the death of Martin Vernon on April 7, 1918, fairly leaps out of the page:

> My father and I were walking to the barn. *I refused to* step in his tracks anymore, as I had done before when there came deep snows. *I made a path of my own.* I said to myself: "You were born among them—you'll die among them. You'll go to that pine grove where we went. . . . You will lie there forever in that soil. Your night will then have come when man's work is over. Since you have brought us into the world, isn't there some escape from fevers? Can't we move to a place where we can get a doctor easier? There two of my brothers are dead and sleeping over there by that pine grove. Don't they have the same right as I have to be here? Now they are gone, I repeat. Life for them was a tragedy. They had better not have cost my mother the pain of birth—dying young when it can be prevented. . . . *Now these hills will not always hold me. I shall go beyond them some day.*" [italics added]

But as yet he was a child, fresh out of Miss Elta Cooper's Plum Grove School class, and could not see beyond his dark hills, except through the angry heart of youthful rebellion or the eye of imagination, or in the visions of books, or from the mountain summit of his daydreams.[38]

2

Out of Mountain Shadows
1918–1925

———◇———

Sometimes Jesse missed school and worked all week for Winfield Daugherty, the model for Fielding Flaughtery in *Beyond Dark Hills*. He remembered the man as "a big Irishman, about six feet four inches tall. He used to ride a horse and shoot quail with a Winchester." The boy sacked sweet potatoes in sawdust for seed. Using a mattock with a short handle, he dug strawberry plants for resetting until the stooping "kept my head dizzy." Daugherty was a severe taskmaster, remembered ever after as "the most selfish man I ever knew on the face of this earth," but whiskey eventually got the better of him. Each Saturday at noon he paid Jesse $3.15 for the week's work, then proceeded to get "dead drunk." Jesse was warned by the old men, "Son, don't let him get you to drinking licker." On Saturdays when his boss's legs were getting limber, Jesse maneuvered Daugherty onto the bed of an express wagon among the sacked sweet potatoes, where he passed out. Then Jesse drove him over the rough furrows and laughed to see the sacks of potatoes bump against him.

It was a kind of poetic justice, for Daugherty had reported Jesse to Martha Stuart for stealing his melons. "Did you see him?" she asked.

"No, but he left footprints."

"Did the thief have a high arch?"

"He sure did," Daugherty said, and took Martha Stuart to see the evidence. There were the footprints in the sand.

"Yeah," she acknowledged, "he's my boy all right." The high-arched tracks were in the big bottom over to the south of Dead Man's Curve in the W-Hollow Road, no more than a half mile from the Stuart cabin. Yet Martha Stuart did not punish Jesse that time. Perhaps she reasoned that if Daugherty were not bent upon firing the culprit, why should she punish him? and more, the boy was working hard enough and regularly enough for the big self-centered farmer that a few melons, the value of which would have otherwise gone to whiskey, could be overlooked.[1]

Meanwhile, things had changed at Plum Grove School. Miss Elta had left after the 1917/1918 year. Mitchell Stuart had been narrowly defeated as trustee, and a new teacher, Claris Brown, had been employed. She was a young, inexperienced woman, who had only a grade-school education and maintained but little discipline. Alf Sinnett, the father of Jesse's schoolmates Morris, Everett, and an older girl, declared, "We've got no school. My boys . . . ain't larning nothing but meanness. My girl . . . was about to fergit all she larned and would have if she hadn't walked out and come home."

On one particular hot summer day that Jesse happened to attend, two students were sent for a bucket of well water. They returned, and "Miss Claris" had emptied her drinking cup and the bucket was dry by the time one of the boys whispered something in the teacher's ear. Out loud she cried, "Don't drink that water!" but it was too late. On the way back from the well, it was revealed, the boys had stopped in the shade of willow trees by Shacklerun Creek, and at least one of them "urinated in the bucket." As the teacher gagged, the alarmed children, realizing what had happened to their drinking water, vowed revenge. Eventually, the delinquent boys were expelled, but it was clear that Claris Brown was no disciplinarian. In such an atmosphere Jesse worked more school-days than he attended Plum Grove School.[2]

By the time he was twelve, he quit working for Winfield Daugherty. Jesse and his father took advantage of the wartime prices by cutting corn in the Riverton bottoms for twenty-five cents a shock. The old EK (Eastern Kentucky) Railroad crossed the C&O tracks at the junction of Riverton and Greenup and ran down to the river then. The turntable was located on the present site of the town's swimming pool; today's spacious level lawns of river-view homes were rich cornfields then. At that time the big white house of the president of the EKRR, "Sturge" Bates, was there for Jesse and his father to look up at as they cut corn. Any two-story house then "was a mansion to me," Jesse later said.[3]

In the winter of 1918/1919 he cut wood with a hard-working neighbor who became the model for his short story "Wilburn." The boy in the story, of a younger age than the actual Jesse, idolizes this Paul Bunyan of a man, whose face literally shines in the sunlight. The boy comes to recognize Wilburn as a dynamic force in their agrarian world. If Wilburn takes a turn of corn to the mill, the boy wants to do the same. Wilburn plows with oxen, and the boy happily follows, hearing the rooty earth popping and seeing the sprouts and stumps roll out. He, too, wants to plow like that. Wilburn helps with house raisings, and the boy works with him in the log woods. He goes fox hunting with Wilburn, too, and remembers "the nights of the hound-dog music and the stars and the wind." He admires the way Wilburn "laughed in the moonlight under the fluffy green of April." Then in that terrible winter of 1917/1918, the year when the real Mitchell Stuart was bedfast with influenza and most of the family were ill, Wilburn proves himself to be as tender and efficient a nurse as he had been a powerful plowman. The boy never forgets the big man's ministrations, his bringing him his medicine and buttermilk, and his father's compliment, "Wilburn is the finest man that ever put his foot on shoe-leather." Thus was to emerge another story as the man-artist would remember it. He depicted Wilburn true-to-life, using the real first name of Wilburn Crump, and as the black he was. However, the story was rejected by publisher after publisher, until he took out the part about Crump's being black. Later, Jesse worked with Wilburn Crump in making cross-ties for the C&O Railroad. The two averaged thirty ties a day at ten cents a tie, and worked six days a week. In the brisk late autumn mornings of 1918 on his way to cut timber, and during the following years of 1919 and 1920 in the tobacco and cornfields, the boy would sometimes hear the sound of the Plum Grove school bell, and listen, and yearn to be back in school. "If I could have, I would have returned to school when I heard the Plum Grove bell."[4]

The happy sound of armistice bells and train whistles in Greenup, only a mile away as the crow flies across the bony chine of hills, was never to be forgotten by James Stuart, Jesse's younger brother. The family had moved or were moving to the fourth childhood home Jesse was to know. This time it was his Uncle Martin Hilton's farm, located north of the house at the center of the middle prong of W-Creek, above where James had been born a little more than three years before. Now the Stuarts were living at the tipmost end of the middle prong upon a steep bank. In the front yard a sulphur spring ran out under beech trees, and hollyhocks grew around the house with its rock chimney. It turned out to be a good year, with large corn and potato crops that meant "life in the hills."[5]

During the war, Mitchell Stuart had worked as a section hand with the C&O Railroad at four dollars a day, "big money" to the Stuarts, and by 1920 he had managed to put himself in debt for a three-hundred-dollar, fifty-acre farm, making his down payment with two cows. The old Jack Sinnett farm, as it was known, was potentially good land with much rich new ground, but disadvantaged by three glaring faults: no house, no barn, and no easily accessible road. However, the new Stuart land bordered the Martin Hilton farm, where the Stuarts were living. This gave them ample opportunity, after their regular work hours as tenants and at other possible times, to clear away the sassafras, pine, and sawbrier sprouts. They also moved an old house Jesse's Uncle Martin let them have onto their new farm and had a barn-raising.[6]

With his father working each day on the railroad to make payments on the land, more farm work than ever was required of fifteen-year-old Jesse. Even the chickens had "to scratch for a livin' " that spring. The family put into practice the father's homely maxim to "make every edge of the ax cut that would." Martha Stuart and her daughters, Sophia and Mary, hoed corn and cut weeds, while Jesse and Grandfather Nathan Hilton began construction of the first house to be owned by the Stuarts in W-Hollow. During the spring of 1921 they cut oaks for house logs and roof shingles. Twenty-nine people, the author later wrote, came to the house-raising in September. Jesse and his grandfather had built the foundation and, with the help of a professional carpenter, put in windows and hung doors; most of the work they did themselves, right down to building the rock chimney in the center of the six-room, two-story house.[7] As much as Jesse admired Grandfather Hilton, the old gentleman was not always pleasant to work with. When a rock slivered under his hammer, Grandpa said, "Dam that Grant-wroughted thing!" and threw his sledge over the hill. The hill the author wrote of is a good twenty-five feet high, and he fetched his grandfather's sledge back each time.

During these months, the boy learned a valuable lesson in diplomacy as his grandfather in the daytime, and his father in the evening, attempted to persuade him to become a citizen in one of their two worlds— Grandfather Hilton's Democratic, Confederate, and Baptist (like his mother's); and his father's Republican, Yankee, and Methodist, the heritage of the Stuarts before him. These two worlds had since his earliest memories spun off a seemingly eternal quarrel that sometimes alienated his mother and father for a week at a time. Jesse was to explore his predicament in the short story "Two Worlds." High on Seaton Ridge overlooking the Ohio River—the boundary of North and South so close to where he had been born and grew up—the boy and his grandfather, an experienced stonemason, split a huge rock for the chimney they were building for the family home:

> I realized more than ever how I lived in a divided world. Here I
> had been born to divided parents. I had grown up with two good

parents whom I loved. But I had heard them quarrel over the North and South, over Lee and Grant, over the Democrats and Republicans, over the Methodists and Baptists until I thought the roof of our house would be lifted up and float away. I sometimes wished it had gone off to scare them. I wished it would rise and float away everytime they quarreled, which was so often we would have lived in a house without a roof.

In the midst of this sectional contention, a solution gradually evolved. Jesse decided that he could not go against any of those he loved, at least not openly. Rather, he "became a diplomat" and "played neutral" for the time being, for "this was the only way out."[8]

On August 30, 1921, the seventh child and third daughter, Glennis Juanita, was born. The Stuarts moved into the unfinished house about November. Reflecting the family's collective relief and natural joy, Stuart wrote, "Home at last. And it was good to have a home . . . a place where wind blew off the pine tree tops and passed over our house. We smelled pine fragrance in the winter wind there. It was a lonely place. It was desolate. But it was home."[9]

The circumstances surrounding this first move of the Stuarts into a home of their own are explored in the heavily autobiographical story "The Builders and the Dream." Pa (Mick) and Mom (Sal, sometimes Sall) are troubled over her brother's last visit. Uncle Mel Shelton has the habit of dropping in on his sister and comparing their respective families in such a way that Mom's feelings are hurt and the Powderjays are insulted. Shan relates the story of how Pa had left Warfield Flaughtery's farm and agreed to farm Uncle Mel's, for Pa's crops had failed. However, Uncle Mel's land has proved poorer even than Flaughtery's. The Powderjays, meanwhile, have bought a farm of their own, but there is no house on it. Motivated by Uncle Mel's overbearing attitude, Mom declares, "The best way to whip him is to build a house on our own land." At suppertime the Powderjays talk about their dreams for the new house on their new farm. First, however, they must raise three acres of tobacco and ten acres of corn as agreed on Uncle Mel's steep slopes. Pa works for the railroad to make payments on the family's farm. Mom and the girls will do the farm work while Shan, whose age is stated as fourteen, and Grandpa Shelton, an old man, build the house. Even Shan's five-year-old brother, Finn [James became six on August 11, 1921], worked at "taking care of the new baby, Glenna [Glennis]."

Family jealousies and accompanying incidents of pettiness follow, along with Uncle Mel's frequent abuses, Mom noting that he is "coming up here once a week and bawling me out." Shan wants the use of enough land for popcorn and melon patches, but Uncle Mel refuses. The Powderjays learn that Mel Shelton's reputation for bullying tenants is truly earned. In a rash of spite, he makes the Powderjays move their chickens off his land for "tramping the ground." He threatens to sue his sister's family for a delayed planting schedule. He raises "another racket" with his sister because Shan has allowed a cow to step a few inches out of the grass path. Mel Shelton's outbursts and his trembling lips reveal what really disturbs him most: the fear of losing a long-existing family competition between brother and sister. Through Shan's thoughts the author reveals,

> I knew how jealous he had been of us when we had made better grades than his children, our first cousins, in school. We had led our classes and Uncle Mel couldn't stand it. And Mom could beat Aunt Effie making clothes. When Mom made dresses for my sisters, they were the prettiest dresses at school. And Uncle Mel's girls went home and told their parents and that hurt them. And I knew we could build a better house than Uncle Mel had.

At one point in the story, when Mel Shelton sees his sister plowing, "he started cussing Pa," but Sal Powderjay stands up to him: "You've made me plow, Mel Shelton. . . . You, with your overbearing temper and your mean ways. But we will beat you yet." And the Powderjays do just that. The conflict so steeped in extended sibling rivalry is given added zest and the victory is made sweeter when noble old Grandpa Shelton decides he will make his home at the new house with the Powderjays and help them clear more new ground for crops that would never grow with quite the same flavor on Mel Shelton's land—land that Shan's Pa describes as just "a white sand under a little loam."[10]

In leaving the third farm in late 1918 the Stuarts had in fact moved from Winfield Daugherty's land to that of Jesse's Uncle Martin Hilton. The results in a general way followed the outline of the story and are closely consistent in a surprising number of details. Martha Hilton Stuart's older brother had indeed developed the unfortunate habit of dropping in on his sister every week or so to give her what he called a "round" or "going over," and the habit continued even after the Stuarts had moved into their own new house. At a later date, young James appeared in the midst of one of the "rounds." When his mother began to shed tears under the verbal barrage of her older brother, James walked in and, being a Stuart with no hesitation about imminent violence, ran his Uncle Martin off. Under difficulties similar to those imposed by the Powderjays' relative-landlord, the Stuarts did manage to bring in good crops from two farms and complete their first home sufficiently to move into it by early November. Even the suppertime talk is authentic. Whereas in the past Mick Stuart had told his family about the old days when he cleared land and fenced it with split chestnut rails and plowed it with oxen and sowed it with wheat and corn, he now talked of plans with more immediate, exciting prospects. Some differences between the story and the facts exist. For example, the fictional baby is taken care of while the logging for the house is done, although the real baby was not to make her appearance until late August, a few months after the logs actually had been cut. The mother's plowing follows her baby's birth in the story, while in reality, had Martha Stuart plowed tobacco, she would probably have done so in late spring while still pregnant. But these are differences of detail rather than of substance, simply to fit the author's aesthetic purposes. Similarly, he compresses time and the educational theme, one suspects to better fit his dramatic intent, for the real Jesse was not to enter school and take competitive tests until the following year, 1922. But even the final detail of the story coincides with the facts. The hero of Martha Stuart's stories, her powerful timber-cutting father who had once picked up a rock so heavy that when he put it into a wagon bed "it went through the floor," did choose to live with Martha and her family rather than Martin and his family.

The differences between the Stuarts and the Hiltons may have acted as a stimulus to achievement, but years later the writer would question the benefit of such competitions. "Don't tell me rivalry is good for children. It's the worst thing in the world. In our family we had rivalry with the Hiltons. Mom said, 'Get them, children, get them!' " That part of the memory was not pleasant. As Jesse fictionalized the conflict, however, the joy of the Powderjays' triumph over the Sheltons—in effect a family feud fought with work, self-sacrifice, and pride instead of bullets—dominates bitterness.[11]

Whatever the differences between the Stuarts and the Hiltons, they were not serious enough to interfere with the children's education. The outrageous water-bucket incident resulted in changes for the better at Plum Grove. Everett Hilton, a first cousin five years older than Jesse, got the teacher's job at Plum Grove. He was a high school graduate and had finished first in the Greenup County teachers' examination. At Plum Grove he organized a baseball team. In one memorable sixteen-inning game, his boys defeated the larger Greenup High School team. Within a few months of the beginning of his five-year tenure, the school underwent an academic reawakening. "E.P.," as he was known, not only attracted the students to the school, but also went out and brought them in from fields and woods. "I got Jesse out of the cornfields," he said, "where he had been working. I took eight of the students at Plum Grove my first year and pointed them to high school. I kept the eight, including Jesse, one hour late each day for the added training." Everett Hilton remembers Jesse as "an average student excepting the field of literature and writing. In those areas he excelled." Distinctively, he recalled, "Jesse and my sister Essie used to play with words and make little rhymes. They had fun doing this, but Jesse was different. He had a knack of remembering the unusual. He remembered every little anecdote and detail, and of course he lived in the woods, and knew everything about this [W-]hollow."[12]

The year 1921/1922 was a busy one for Mitch and Martha Stuart's older boy. He had new ground to clear even before the house was begun, crops to tend, the house to help build and finish after the family had moved in, scarce work to find and do for meager wages, and school to attend, however sporadically. Even so, Jesse still found time for games and mischief. As early as 1915 he and his cousin Glen Hilton and Aaron and Ed Howard climbed trees in the valley of the last prong of W-Hollow. They used to "stick sticks back in hollow places and chase flying squirrels out . . . and make them fly." They also had a kind of wild peach tree racing game. The idea was to find wild peach trees in bloom—worth ten points. It was a running game, and Jesse wrote, "I liked to think I ran faster than the wind blew." In late March and early April Jesse would run ahead to espy the "pink blossoms blooming in the cool winds." The stark nudity of leafless trees intensified their beauty for the mountain boy. He liked to hear the others behind him, "breathing hard with their tongues out," and gloried in shouting, "I've found another one . . . in a cove near a white oak . . . my tree." Then he would go on, never stopping for a second look.[13]

"Big Aaron" Howard, the largest and oldest of the boys, was the leader of the W-Hollow gang. It was he who had pitched all sixteen innings of the Plum Grove upset over Greenup High, and his fictional counterpart emerges as a prominent character in three stories Stuart wrote reflecting the boys' teen-age prankishness. In "Saving the Bees," Big Aaron is described as a sixteen-year-old with "big arms and a big bull-neck." His hands are "hard as rocks," and "he has a heavy beard on his face." By far "the stoutest boy" in the Plum Grove hills, he intends "to free . . . the honeybees in this country," reasoning they "don't have liberty anymore." The boys, including Jesse/Shan, agree with their leader's sense of injustice at the slavery of the bees. Wild bee trees are rare "in these parts," and it is not fair to make the honeybees "work their lives away for a lazy bunch of people." Paradoxically, this includes the boys' own parents, among the gang's planned victims. After first agreeing to an oath of absolute silence never to be broken, the boys stealthily take the "bee gums" and, heavy as they are, manage to secrete them in a locust grove of the wild woods so remote that "the hoot owls holler in the daytime." In a series of Twainian adventures, the boys spirit away hive after hive—fifty in all—and carefully place them on rocks in the locust grove. At one time the boys are sprinkled with buckshot, and the shots "fall like rain," but they escape. Their last theft is characterized by a wild night ride on a stolen Old Line Special handcar, adding zest to their thievery with painful bee-stingings and nearly disastrous gun-shootings. Baffled outrage grips the Plum Grove citizens, causing more than one to make such remarks as "I'll tell you the world is going to hell." The boys divert guilt from themselves by lying beautifully, and are never really suspected.

"Tradelast" is another of the Shan-Big Aaron stories. In this adventure the boys' shenanigans ironically culminate in true happiness and benefits for all; for Big Aaron and Shan's tradelasts, related to Cief Meadowbranch and Miss Dovie Maynard respectively, bring dramatic changes to the two lonely people's lives and result in a delightful marriage. Years later the author acknowledged the reason he had not earlier written the events into story: "Big Aaron and Little Edd and Cousin Penny and I were afraid to tell about giving them tradelasts that were false. We were always ashamed of this after we grew up." But after the principals' deaths, the author reasoned, "they would never know," and so wrote the story. The earliest of the three stories, "Coming Down the Mountain," centers on Aaron and Little Edd's discovery of their "Pappie," passed out, his neck "limber as a wilted milkweed," his head "drooped like a big sunflower on a hot September day." Testing Pappie's besottedness, Little Edd snaps his ears, first stretching them "until they looked thin enough to see through," then letting them snap back to his head "like old rubber." The boys take Pappie home on a borrowed mule, having first secured him to the saddle with a rope. Immediately the mule begins to buck and kick, then paw and bray, reducing a soon-conscious Pappie to pain, prayer, and a vow never to fox hunt and drink again. The drunk has been cured by a handful of cockleburrs put under the saddle by Pappie's enemy, who had loaned the boys the mule to take their father home.

Big Aaron and Little Edd are fictional extensions of the Howard boys. The family actually lived up a smaller hollow branching off of the middle prong of W-Creek, not far from the log house the Stuarts had lived in until 1915. As the story reveals, the elder Howard loved moonshine, and it was common knowledge that the family made some of the best. Many of the incidents of such stories paralleled those in the adolescence of Jesse Stuart.[14]

Such prankishness was to extend well into his high school years. One evening Zetta and Wade Sturgill went by the Stuarts' for a visit. Returning after dark by the empty log house at the foot of the hill, abandoned since 1918, they heard strange noises and an eerie groaning, as though it were haunted. They ran home as fast as they could and arrived "out of breath [and] almost hysterical." Another time, too, someone played ghost with similar results, and when the Sturgills related their adventure to their mother, she said, "You know that's Jesse Stuart. Don't you remember when he sent your Dad a valentine in March?" It was a valentine with "a big heart with a woman on it," and it read, "I'd pull down the stars and the moon if you would let me ride with you and your little mule team." Jesse's youthful frivolity was doubtless triggered by Dave Sturgill's purchase of a new mule team. The Sturgills' reaction is revealing. "We kept it from my dad," Zetta Sturgill explained, for "he didn't like jokes and we knew he would mention it to Jesse."[15]

During the summer of 1921, Jesse went over Seaton Ridge and down Academy Hollow looking for work. He found a job helping to lay new streets for Greenup; it paid thirty cents an hour. He worked a tenhour day and until noon on Saturdays. The townspeople objected to paying for the new streets that went by their houses, but they had to pay. Jesse's job was digging out old cobblestones and bricks. On a dare he threw a piece of watermelon into a boy's face and was promptly fired. Instead of walking off the job, he went to another work crew, watched what they were doing, and got busy putting sacks of concrete into a mixer. It was hot work in July, but he continued for a time without further incident. He was hired back the next summer of 1922. His boss had the "oddest name I'd ever heard"—John Pancake. The man's clothing struck the boy as odd, too. "He used to come out there in a dark suit and white shoes." Jesse worked through his sixteenth birthday and until school began in September. Main Street was a white strip of new concrete, and "the yellow leaves were skipping along on it." At the corner of Harrison and Perry Streets, Greenup High School struck the concrete-spattered boy as "a beautiful place, a bluish gray brick building with a spire shooting above the tops of the elm tree."[16]

What had motivated his decision to get a high school education? He had no end of work to do at home, but three months earlier he had made the decision by taking the high school entrance examination. He realized that the two months spent studying with Everett Hilton at Plum Grove had been essential, for altogether he had received only twenty-two solid months of formal education. In spite of the fact that he had not noticeably impressed his cousin, Jesse seemed "to float" right through the exam, and the questions of each section seemed easy for him. Yet he failed composition, the subject he thought he knew best, by one point—just under the minimal 60. However, because his subject sections taken together were well above average, the school officials allowed him the extra point in composition and let him enter high school. Later, he would refer to this decision as the "turning point of my life." The day of the exams he ate his first oyster stew at Callihan's Restaurant across from the courthouse on Harrison Street, close to Front Street on the Ohio River. He had never tasted anything better. When he reported his test results to Everett Hilton, his cousin said, "Jesse, I don't see how you pass. You're a good guesser."[17]

There can be no doubt that the family rivalry was as strong as ever. Sometimes Jesse's mother was very direct about it. "Get them, children," she would say, and at other times, "Love the Lord and beat the Hiltons." But a deeper motivation for Jesse was her often expressed desire to be proud of her children. To Jesse she had said, "I want you to grow up and be such a man that when you walk down the street in Greenup, someone will look at you and say, 'There goes Martha Hilton's son.' " The boy never forgot her words. Nearly as powerful an incentive were Mitchell Stuart's expressions of pride in Everett Hilton's academic accomplishments; these repeated tributes set Jesse's ambition afire to emulate and, if possible someday, to surpass his cousin. Less clear but perhaps even deeper than these motivations were those of personal pride and self-respect, and something else, insistent though inchoate, to be articulated within months, when he would acknowledge his ambition to write a book.[18]

Now he was in Greenup High School. The schoolwork and the six-mile walk over Seaton Ridge and down along Academy Branch to Greenup High and back to W-Hollow each day were not nearly as hard as the farmwork that he, Sophia, and the other Stuart children were used to. The path led northward from the Stuart house past the rock jutting from the hillside, where he and Grandfather Hilton had cut several layers and shaped the stone to build the chimney, down into the valley of the recently planted apple and peach orchard, up along the woods bordering the pasture until the woods crossed the meadows and grew thicker. On for perhaps a half mile to the high peak by the stile, where the path led over into the steep declivity of ashes, oaks, poplars, dogwoods, and beeches. Back to his left behind oak sprouts, a sycamore tree, and a hickory, Wilburn Crump lived with his family; and here a wagon and sled road began. Farther down the hill, up on a high flat bank to his right, lived one of Uncle Frank Sparks' daughters, and Uncle Frank and his family lived just down the hill in a little white bungalow along the narrow hollow road. At another lived Uglybird (Alf) Sinnett, close to a big black oak tree. Farther down was the fork of the road where it met Academy Branch. Here Brady Callihan lived, an enterprising handyman and carpenter if there ever was one, who could also do blacksmithing; he had devised his own system of running water, piping the water from a spring he had boxed in with concrete nearly sixty yards to the rear of the house.

On out toward what is now Route 23 was the "Bricktop" Crawford property, the home of the man who operated the Riverton depot at the junction point between the C&O and the old EKRR, back of the present location of the Kenner Lumber Company. Today, the Academy Hollow Road leads directly to a Gulf station at the new four-lane Route 23; but in the 1920s Jesse and Sophia would cross the tracks and turn northwest, parallel to the Ohio River, close to Dilley's General Store, and walk the final mile downriver to Greenup High School, although if Jesse were in a hurry he would sometimes follow the C&O tracks along the same direction until he reached the livery stable just south of the school, and take Harrison Street to the side entrance.[19]

His first semester went well enough in English, Latin, and history, but algebra caused him trouble from the beginning, and came near to being his downfall. When he became discouraged because of low grades in the course, he stayed home from school; but he found little sympathy there. Sophia remembers that their mother "almost worked him to death." Then his teacher, Miss Lena Wells Lykins, a Transylvania graduate and principal of the Greenup High School from 1921 to 1923, went over the ridge path to his home and chided him. She smiled, too. "Quit Greenup High School because you can't get a subject, huh?" It was a big, friendly smile, as the author would later describe it, "a big 'howdy' smile that lights up her whole face, her eyes twinkling with good humor and curiosity." Then she said, "Jesse, are you going to be a quitter? Are you going to let one subject keep you from finishing high school? You're not going through life like this!" She met his family. Later she told him, "If I fail you in algebra, you won't be the first one I have failed." She asked Jesse to light her way back over the mountain to Academy Branch, for she had to go to a dance. The twenty-six-year-old woman told him that he would write a book someday if he worked hard enough. It was then that his "first stirrings of ambition," as he later wrote, rose within him, "simply because she had so much confidence in me." As he carried the lantern on the way over the ridge path, he decided to take her advice and stick it out. Perhaps next year algebra would be "as easy for you as walking over this mountain." His eagerness to learn and his natural verbal ability evoked a guess-who compliment from Jesse's history teacher Miss N. E. Hamilton, whom Miss Lykins later remembered as an older "brilliant woman." To the boy's delight, Miss Hamilton pointed him out in front of his classmates as a future "Patrick Henry in this room," a bit of praise causing the other students to tease him, but nevertheless motivating a sensitive youth hungry for recognition.[20]

"Do you remember, Oscar, in 1922, when a handful of rural students attended Greenup High?" Jesse Stuart wrote years later to a close friend. Oscar Sammons had grown up on his father's farm. His father was not a wealthy farmer, but he was a wise one; other farmers in the region often came to him to get advice and to borrow money. Although Oscar had seen Jesse with Grandfather Hilton at church, the two had gone to different country schools, Oscar attending the rural school at Whetstone, on the west side of the Little Sandy River about six miles by highway from Plum Grove, no more than four as the crow flies. Whereas Jesse walked the Seaton Ridge path in all weathers, Oscar rode a horse to Greenup High during his freshman year; he was "saving up" for a bicycle. During his freshman year, Jesse was nearly six feet tall and weighed a scant 110 pounds. He remembered Oscar as a boy thinner than he, riding up to the school from the four-mile trip out Whetstone Road, so stiff with cold in the saddle that the teachers sometimes had to help him off the horse. "He was almost frozen." But the two boys from the country had something in common. Some were there because they had to be, but these two boys wanted to get an education.[21]

Another student destined to be a lifelong friend, Elmer Heaberlin, remembered the first day he met Jesse Stuart in high school, on the second floor of the old building on the corner of Harrison and Perry Streets. "Jesse was just an overgrown country boy like I was, and we talked about the grades we made on the county exam." Elmer's father, Charles Heaberlin, was an accountant; Elmer had practically grown up with an adding machine, so he knew math. "We also discussed our ages. I was . . . almost thirteen. Jesse was about two years older than I was . . . fifteen or so." Jesse was "tall, gaunt, wore knickerbockers. Most did. Long stockings. And he had a dark complexion. . . . spelled his name *Stewart* then." Jesse admired Elmer's math ability. "What impressed him to start with," Elmer Heaberlin said, "was that I completed the first year of algebra myself, just picked it up, took the book, and when I went into high school algebra there wasn't anything I didn't know. I did the work and took the exams because I liked to, but I was excused from them. The teacher [Miss Lykins] would take my paper and look at it and smile, and write a hundred on it. And of course, Jesse, who was having problems with the course, saw this." As Jesse would return to W-Hollow each day, and Oscar rode out Whetstone Road, Elmer walked upriver along the railroad tracks, a distance of about four miles to Wurtland, although sometimes he was lucky enough to catch a slow-moving C&O freight.[22]

By spring of his freshman year, Jesse was in charge of the farm, for his father was working daily on the railroad section. Jesse plowed the oats early that year. When the cows were turned out to pasture, the timothy and orchard grass were flourishing. He plowed the land, harrowed it, and planted the corn and potatoes. With the help of his mother, sisters, and James, the tobacco was finally set and the first hoeing finished. He did all the plowing that spring. By summer, an unusually hot and rainy one, pumpkins lay over the fields and beans wrapped around the cornstalks. Mitchell Stuart bragged on his son, declaring that his boy "worked the mules down lean." Yet the farm was not, by the boy's own admission, "the same place" for him. His mind was on the newly discovered world of Greenup High School—and those smiling girls in new dresses "going along talking about nothing in particular." He could not forget "that flashy red sweater Burl Mavis wore," as well as "Fred Mansfield's pretty necktie. . . . Lord, that was lots to live for, and the world was big."[23]

His imagination caught hold of old things, and he remembered his long-cherished but rarely admitted ambition to go to Harvard. He associated evidences of antiquity with education, noticing that the steps of the schoolhouse "were wearing thin." He asked local citizens about the age of the building and discovered it was among the most venerable on the Ohio River. Restlessly, the youth now dreamed of a someday when he would receive an appointment to West Point. By July he had applied for and was accepted for a month's training at the Citizens Military Training Camp at Fort Knox, close to Louisville, Kentucky. Seizing upon the opportunity for travel, he took the longest possible route there, by way of North Vernon, Indiana. He felt the inevitable urge of maturity; his seventeenth birthday was rapidly approaching. At Camp Knox the farm boy, now nearly six feet tall and weighing perhaps 130 pounds, was quickly dubbed "Gawky" and put on the Awkward Squad for speaking while standing at attention. He cried tears, as boys will, but "it did no good," for as he soon learned, "the army is no place for tears."[24]

His name is listed in the Camp Knox annual, *The Mess Kit,* as "Stewart, Jesse," of Riverton, Kentucky. As he stands in the group picture of the CMTC roster for Company I, First Regiment, Infantry, one receives the impression of a serious adolescent with a head of thick, dark hair. In the upper margin is an inked notation, apparently in his hand, "J. Stuart / cross on body." Camp began with the arrival of the youths at the Louisville depot on Friday, July 27, 1923. They had scarcely been introduced to reveille and drill when on the next Friday, August 3, an "Extra" declaimed the death of President Harding, to whom the annual would be dedicated. On the next page is a pleasant portrait of Calvin Coolidge, inscribed "To the Success of the C.M.T.C.," with the date "1923" and his signature affixed. In writing of this experience later in *Beyond Dark Hills* and *To Teach, To Love,* the author would not mention the passing of his seventeenth birthday, the minimum age requirement for trainees.

The August days passed quickly with hikes, the routine of mess, laundry, and practice on the rifle range; but there was some pure fun too—intramural baseball and track, a tug-of-war, and a dance at the Hawaiian Gardens down at Fourth and Broadway in Louisville. There were picture days, and, finally, the last review. On August 24, the boys drew their civies and checked in all military equipment; they went home Saturday, August 25.[25]

Jesse enjoyed exercise and marching at review and excelled with the rifle, but the discipline and routine were torture for him. He hated bayonet practice, and never could get "mad" enough for it to make much sense to him. When he threw a bucket of water on a corporal, he was given a cold mud bath for punishment. He was put on KP for leaving his leggings in the barracks and having unlaced shoes at reveille. He was tossed up in a blanket, fell to the ground, and was sore for weeks. His impulsive ambition to go to West Point, if not to Harvard, began to fade. Yet the trip had been a memorable adventure for him; he had never before been more than fifty miles from home, and the fact that he had achieved it all on his own and paid his own way strengthened his confidence. He came home as the leaves began to turn and fall. The hungry crows commenced their raids on the field corn that would soon be cut and shocked. Wild geese honked in their old formations. Around the supper table, his family welcomed him back again, and he held them spellbound with his stories of faraway Camp Knox and Louisville, though he left out more than he told. That autumn promised a rich harvest, and the Stuarts saw the reward of their hard work. His mother had pickled beans, canned berries and peaches, and just finished canning apple butter and wild grape jelly. To the youth home was beautiful and, as he later wrote of that return, "the best place in the world after all."[26]

Two of the Greenup High School city boys in particular, Jesse thought, wore good sweaters and clothes. Earl Woodman and Estille Howland were the most likely models for Burl Mavis and Fred Mansfield in *Beyond Dark Hills*. Now that Jesse had turned seventeen and was a sophomore in high school, he was getting too big for knickers. He was determined to have at least some clothes as nice as those of classmates. During the late summer and fall of 1923, he earned fifty dollars for new clothes and books for himself and Sophia by making cross-ties from his father's black oak timber and by hunting and trapping rabbits, opossums, raccoons, and skunks in the woods and selling the hides at Banner Produce, located one block downriver from Greenup High at the corner of Washington and Perry Streets. Now a parking lot marks the spot of the business, founded in 1912. This was the store of David Darby, father of Jesse's classmate Thurman. Oscar Sammons remembers it as a store with a few groceries, a lot of poultry bought "on foot," and a good assortment of such herbs as ginseng and yellowroot. When the weather got cold, Mr. Darby bought rabbits and hung them out on a wire. People came along, took a rabbit off, and paid for it. Sometimes Jesse sold the meat of his hunt and then got the hides back for sale at Banner Produce. In the autumn wagons loaded with cans of sorghum molasses lined up out front waiting to sell their produce.[27]

That fall of 1923, Jesse "railroaded" the corn in order to save it as feed for the stock from an early frost. As his father had taught him, he tied each shock with one middle band and two outward bands so that it would withstand strong winter gales. One autumn Saturday, to his father's disbelief, he cut fifty-four shocks, and then he went out and cut twenty-four more by moonlight. Mr. Stuart "opened his eyes wider," Jesse later wrote of his father's astonishment. The youth bought a new suit of clothes across the Ohio River at Ironton; it was a gray tweed with long pants, and at eighteen dollars it was expensive. Consistent with the youth's clothes-consciousness, his future wife remembered that

> in his sophomore year he started wearing long pants, and every morning he walked in . . . from W-Hollow across a high hill to the street across from my house, where he waited to carry my books. I don't know whether I loved him then, or just admired him, but I never forgot the day in April when he told me I was beautiful.

He had come a long way since she had first seen him the year before in 1922, when he had stood beneath an elm by the walk leading to Greenup High. She remembered exactly what he wore: "corduroy knee pants, black stockings and brogan shoes. The elbows of his black pullover were reinforced with leather patches. He had been trapping, and the teachers complained about the scent of skunk on him. I looked at him and he looked at me, but neither of us spoke."[28]

Miss Lena Wells Lykins had left after the spring semester of 1923, settling in nearby Vanceburg, and her temporary successor was a Mr. Robinson. During Jesse's sophomore year of 1923/1924, he took his English classes with Miss Virginia Monroe, newly graduated from Georgetown College near Lexington, Kentucky. Years later he wrote the teacher, "I never knew you'd finished college then and [were] only twenty until much later. I was a boy too. . . . I remember I made A's for you. And I thought you were very pretty." Mrs. Virginia Monroe Tippett remembers Jesse Stuart as a keenly attentive, eager student. "His eyes were . . . pretty. He looked straight at you. You can tell when a student is paying attention and learning." His themes, as she recalls, were written about the things he was familiar with—his home, the woods and nature. Once when a student named Thelma asked why Jesse had received a better grade on his theme than she had received on hers, Miss Monroe very directly told her, "Jesse deserves a better grade, Thelma, because he wrote a better theme than you did." Though his teacher did not remember the incident, the author never forgot it, and years later reminded her of it. During the remainder of his sophomore year, Jesse finished with three A's—in English, history, and general science—but a C+ under Miss Katherine Bailey was the best he could do in algebra. The strange subject was to remain something of a puzzle for him.[29]

As Mrs. Tippett remembered, the principal, Mr. Robinson, was not a well-organized school official. His discipline was so poor and the students so unimpressed that they were soon calling him "Barney Google" behind his back, after the comic-strip character. At mid-year he was replaced by Dr. Robert E. Hatton, a native of Columbia, who had received his B.A. from the University of Missouri, where he did further graduate work. His wife, née Harriett Lewis McFarland, was born at Lexington, Missouri, in an area known as "Little Dixie." Her mother, Elvira Evelyn Early, was the sister of General Jubal Anderson Early. Her father was the Reverend William B. McFarland, President of Marshall College in the 1850s. The two were married by the time they taught together at Roanoke Female College in Danville, Virginia. The 1905 yearbook, *Echoes from R. C.,* lists "Robert Edwin Hatton, A.M., Ph.D." as president and his area of instruction as philosophy and natural sciences; Mrs. R. E. Hatton is "lady principal." The handsome young couple are depicted side-by-side, he in a high white collar and pince-nez, she dark-eyed and pensive. It was a small but distinguished institution. The Director of Music was Professor Felix Heink, brother-in-law of famed opera and concert singer Madame Schumann-Heink, perhaps the most celebrated contralto of her time.[30]

In the summer of 1921 the Hattons settled in Catlettsburg, Boyd County, Kentucky. They moved the Union Stock Food and Manufacturing Company, in which they held stock, to Catlettsburg, but continued to teach school as they conducted the business. Dr. Hatton became both superintendent and principal of Greenup High School, perhaps as early as the late fall of 1923, and probably began his duties at the end of the first semester when Mr. Robinson left, in January of 1924. Robert Hatton, Jr., who was then in college at Marshall University, recalls that his mother was teaching at Greenup by 1924, the beginning of Jesse Stuart's junior year. Since Catlettsburg is approximately twenty-two miles from Greenup, no small distance for daily travel at the time, the Hattons took rooms in Greenup at Mrs. Webb's on Front Street, although the couple retained their home in Catlettsburg. Certainly by the fall semester of 1924, Mrs. Hatton commenced teaching English. During the first semester of his junior year, Jesse Stuart made an A with Mrs. Hatton, and followed with another A in the spring 1925 semester. Sometime during Jesse's junior year, Robert Hatton, Jr., substituted for his father, who took a short leave to go to Florida. Evidence in the school records shows "Stewart" as the family spelling of Jesse's surname; but as Robert Hatton, Jr., recollects, Jesse "always resented the 'ew' [and] wanted the 'ua.' " Mrs. Hatton soon whetted Jesse's interest in the literature and traditions of Scotland and England. His friend Elmer Heaberlin recalls that he was "infatuated with the Stuarts of Scotland and England. Jess *loved* the Scottish. He just spelled [his] name the way he wanted to. He just changed it and nobody seems to know the difference." Concerning the youth's difficulties with algebra, bookkeeping, and plane geometry, the younger Hatton remarked, "Jesse's love was always English, not math." Of 1924/ 1925 he remembers that he and his mother would walk over from the Webb house to the old Columbia Hotel on Main Street, just across from Lawson's Hardware, and take their meals. Jesse would come by sometimes before and sometimes after school to talk with Mrs. Hatton about his work. A graduate of Missouri Central College in Lexington, she was well prepared to teach English, journalism, and music. In appearance she was tall, five feet eleven inches, the exact height of Martha Stuart, the writer later recalled; she was slow-moving and soft of voice, the opposite of her husband, a big man well over six feet tall, quick and energetic, who called the boys at Greenup "Buster" and the girls "Tootsie." By his wife he was called "Mr. Hatton"; he called her "Hattie." Knowledgeable in the ways of human nature, he preferred "Mister" to "Doctor," and endeared himself to those around him by once remarking, at least so his son recalled, that " 'Ph.D.' stood for Piled higher and deeper."[31]

Mrs. Hatton, then in her late fifties, saw something in the boy. She asked the students to write about the things they knew and to read their themes weekly in class. This was exactly what Jesse liked, for he had already learned at Plum Grove that he could get satisfying attention and recognition by reading his themes aloud, and hadn't Miss Monroe begun to praise his themes at Greenup the year before? At Plum Grove, the writer would later say in *To Teach, To Love,* "every pupil listened when I read a theme." Many times they had laughed, too. These social stirrings added to his natural pleasure in using words, building them into sentences, sentences into paragraphs, and paragraphs into a theme or a story. In Mrs. Hatton's class, though, he had a "different kind of audience, a more critical and a more appreciative one." He took several pieces of writing to class each "Theme Day" and was disappointed if he did not get to read more than once. Sometimes he read for students who had not written their assignments. In allowing this arrangement, Mrs. Hatton doubtless enjoyed hearing Jesse read, too. Even so, he did not get to read as much as he wanted. He would later write of these days, "I have taken as many as twenty-four pieces of creative writing, theses, articles, and poems at one time [to class]. I wasn't exactly bashful."[32]

Jesse wrote of his boyhood experiences and natural surroundings, the flora and fauna of his hills and woods, his pets and a few of the people he knew. Later he would write of their lives and deaths and of lessons learned in the school of hard knocks, and of stories that his mother, father, Grandpa Hilton, and Uncle Jesse Hilton had told, for if a story was unusual enough the boy would remember every detail. Some he reported from life on the farms where the Stuarts had lived, among them the story of the remarkable rooster "Nest Egg," and at least the germs of several of the stories eventually to be published in *Head o' W-Hollow* and some of the poems to appear in *Harvest of Youth.* Mrs. Hatton gave Jesse a volume of Robert Burns' poetry. He read and understood the Scottish ploughboy and his work. "Highland Mary," "John

Anderson My Jo," and "The Cotter's Saturday Night" were among his favorites. Mrs. Hatton also taught music, and when the boy heard "Flow Gently, Sweet Afton," he choked with emotion. "I had never heard words more beautiful than those," he thought. He carried the Burns volume with him like a talisman, and read it avidly whenever he could, even at the plow when he rested the mules. "I feasted on the poetry of Robert Burns," he wrote of this time. "It seemed as if something big in life had taken hold of me." Gradually, his urge to emulate the well-dressed town boys in high school did not seem as important as his desire to write. Sometimes the Hattons gave him a sweater or coat or some article of clothing young Robert had abandoned, and he took whatever they gave gladly, for he had identified fully with their love for other, higher things, in contrast to which clothes were merely means or necessities. "And my prayer," he recorded, "if I ever prayed one then, was to write poetry that would endure like the poetry of Robert Burns."[33]

Sometime as early as his freshman year, he had purchased an orange fountain pen, and now he used it to good purpose. It had long been his habit in the early winter mornings before daylight to go to the kitchen and build a fire in the wood range. As the kitchen warmed, he sat on the woodbox close to the stove and read and studied and wrote. He had done this at the old house down the hill, the third farm at the head of W-Hollow where he had lived in 1916, 1917, and 1918—then later at the Martin Hilton house the Stuarts had rented—and now at their house on the hill where the wind sang through the pine groves and across the peaking roof above the story and a half he and Grandfather Hilton had built four years ago.[34]

Writing haunted him. In the spring he heard whippoorwills calling across the newly plowed fields, and he sought the silence of the woods in evening. "I would steal quietly," he later wrote, watching the young rabbits at play in the pasture, hearing the caw-caw of the crows, having pencil and paper (not risking the loss of his pen), and go into the pine grove at twilight to write his themes for Mrs. Hatton. He would take his time and try to write well. "I would sit there and write and rewrite a theme . . . about pine trees then, the stars, the sound of the wind and the evening sky." Sometimes he would carry a lantern with him and hang it on a broken branch of a dogwood tree, and work on his themes. He took them to her. They talked of his themes and Burns and, capitalizing on the boy's enthusiasm, she loaned him several books on Scottish history to read. She praised him: "There is a flavor of the soil and a picture of the sky and the trees in your themes."[35]

By this time Jesse's friend Oscar Sammons had saved enough money to buy a bicycle, which he rode to school. He and Jesse saved their good clothes for special occasions and asserted their social identity by organizing the Overall Club, to which more than half the rural students of Greenup High eventually belonged. Jesse is remembered by Oscar Sammons and other friends as never having been in a bad humor. However, "he was more sober-minded in high school than later," Judge Sammons recalls. "He looks serious in his pictures, and that grinning personality one often associates with Jesse . . . came later. He always liked talking and joking, though, and even in those days he was ahead of the others in joking and in being good-humored."[36]

Jesse's football prowess their sophomore years, Judge Sammons contends, is somewhat exaggerated in Stuart's work. "There were only about thirteen boys on the team when we went out, and Jesse and I were both pretty skinny little fellows, but he was bigger than I was." Judge Sammons tells of their being taken on the traveling squad to Louisa, Kentucky. "We had got into trouble with the coach for going out and eating before the game, so it looked like we weren't going to play, but when two of the boys got hurt, Jess and I got into the game. The coach *had* to put us in. And well"—Sammons laughs at the recollection—"Louisa just ran *all over* us." High school football was fairly primitive then, and when the Greenup Tigers voted on their new school colors, "we chose green because we could get the old pool table covers from Louie Hoffman's Pool Room to make our letters."[37]

Judge Sammons' memory of Mrs. Hatton's influence on Jesse is vivid. "I have known Jess to bring in big tulip poplar leaves to Mrs. Hatton. They had poems on them, where he had taken a stick and scratched them, probably on the way to school. She had given him a copy of Burns' poetry. She was very influential . . . , and she encouraged him more than anyone during [that time]." Robert Hatton remembers, too, how "Jesse used to take Mother out to pick wild flowers together— in April and May Solomon's-seal, trillium, and wild Sweet Williams, the last a blue phlox variety with pale blue petals spoking out from their centers like fuzzy windmills—and in the fall misty blue ageratum, snowy snakeroot, and asters of many varieties." And, he remembers, these simple pleasures were "real to Mother and to Jesse." He uses the word "earthen" to describe their commonality of quiet joy. "There was nothing phony in this"; "He brought flowers to her—the wild flowers out of W-Hollow, time and again." Together the teacher and student talked about Scotland, literature, and writing. "My mother really was an artistic person. While she was very Scottish, my father was more British. I remember the Burns book she gave Jesse. That was very precious to Mother, who was entranced with her Scottish ancestry. . . . She would share that with Jesse, and that may have been the reason he became so fascinated with the Scottish." On his visits home, the younger Hatton distinctly remembers, "Jesse was my mother's favorite. She saw in Jesse everything that she wanted to do. She saw *her* creativeness *in him.*"[38]

If Mrs. Hatton was Jesse Stuart's literary mother, Dr. Robert Edwin Hatton was a surrogate educational and spiritual father; indeed, he was a vigorous paternal symbol to many Greenup High students. Opal Rice McKee remembers that "everybody loved him. He would call the boys 'Buster,' and when he pointed his finger, they'd better move, too. He was a big man. Quick. He was just super." Jesse made an A in general science and received the superintendent's compliment of having "horse sense." In his bookkeeping class with Mr. Hatton, however, he encountered more difficulty. His course grade is listed as a C. Plane geometry nearly proved his downfall, though he resisted the subject until his senior year. The first semester, so he writes, he received a D−, but he determined to take the subject over, declaring, "I'm going to learn it," and he did eventually achieve a B standing both semesters. He also took Bible from Mr. Hatton his senior year. "He was a devout old Baptist," Stuart later recalled. "He'd been president of two small Baptist colleges." In that course they read and discussed the Bible "from cover to cover." Sometime during the course, Luke 17:21 made an enormous impression upon the boy, as if it defined some special need, or became the very cornerstone of his developing personhood. The context is that of the Pharisees' questioning of Christ on the subject of the coming of the kingdom of God. It will not come with "observation" or outward show, Christ said, then,

> Neither shall they say, Lo here! or,
> lo there! for behold, the kingdom of
> God is within you.

Years later, the writer would declare, "It stuck with me all my life and it's the forerunner of *The Kingdom Within*—my novel. Because it stuck with me through all my life."[39]

The combined influence of the Hattons on Jesse Stuart appears to have come along at just the proper time to fire the boy's struggling ambitions and to expand his visionary hopes. As early as 1922, he later wrote, he had conceived of a seven-year plan "to finish high school and write a book." He had discussed his ambition to write a book two years before with Miss Lykins, and under Miss Monroe's and Mrs. Hatton's tutelage he was already writing some of the poems that would appear in his first volume of poetry and some stories, such as "Nest Egg," that would later be published. Indeed, his inscription penned on the flyleaf of *Harvest of Youth* reads in part, "To Virginia Monroe Tippett / my former teacher / and a good one / . . . Some of these might have been written in your class." Whether the youth heard Mr. Hatton explain the Kingdom-within verse in the Bible class his senior year, or had occasion at an earlier time—in the spring semester of his sophomore year or during either semester of his junior year—for it to register upon his consciousness with such force is not clear. The possibility exists that he heard Mr. Hatton speak of it in assembly, or at the Hatton home ("I was very fond of the Hatton family," he later wrote), or in any number of conversations, of which the young Stuart was notably fond, or even in a Sunday School class Mr. Hatton may have taught. Certainly the boy's love of literature and newfound joy in composing poems and themes were manifest by his sophomore and junior years. Yet, as significant as his early efforts to write were, or as important as Mrs. Hatton's influence upon him and those ingrained motivations stemming directly from the familial pride of the Stuarts might have been, it was Mr. Hatton whom he credited with catalyzing a kind of transcendental spiritual realization, an experience that, from the retrospect of years, crystallized the youth's determination to find purpose in life and achieve fulfillment. "I hope young people can find somebody," the poet laureate later said of this event, "who can point out to them some little piece of scripture that can hold them like that quotation from the Bible held me, 'The kingdom . . . is within you.' That *expanded* me. I knew that I could do anything."[40]

No creative writer, of course, is tied to fact, but rather uses fact for creative and dramatic purposes. In both *Beyond Dark Hills* and *To Teach, To Love* the author at times tends to bring together and blend events of his high school years. For example, although he links Mrs. Hatton's teaching with his sophomore year, the best evidence indicates that Mr. Hatton did not begin his duties at Greenup High School until January 1924, and Mrs. Hatton did not commence teaching until even later, most likely at the outset of Jesse's junior year in the fall of 1924. In April of 1924, he would later write, he reached a turning point in his life, applying a newly realized philosophy of accomplishment to plowing, harrowing, and planting eight acres of new ground in corn. In the story, "Victory and the Dream," Jesse Stuart's persona Shan says, "I had the greatest sense of accomplishment I ever had in my life. . . . I had realized a dream. . . . I felt there wasn't anything I couldn't do. . . . There wasn't a subject in Greenwood High School I couldn't pass . . . [not] a baseball game on our schedule we couldn't win. . . . I knew now that I could go to college, even if my father didn't have any money to give me and I had none of my own. I knew that I could and I would find a way. . . . I had found that sense of accomplishment. I had needed it as much as any young man alive. Now I knew that I would never be whipped or defeated again." With substantively the same thematic emphasis the author pointed out the very ground where, he told Dick Perry over thirty-five years later, Mick Stuart did not believe him when he told him that "I could do it with a young pair of mules . . . but I did it all right." Further, "I plowed, harrowed, and laid it off and planted it. I felt if I didn't do it I would never be more defeated in my life. I went after things that way." In the short story, not unexpectedly, some autobiographical differences exist. Although Jesse, like Shan at sixteen, was about six feet tall, Jesse did not weigh 180 pounds, seventy pounds more than he described himself as weighing less than a year before. In the short story the new ground plowed in the week of his spring vacation contains about eight acres, whereas the author later described a twenty-acre field to Dick Perry and expanded the time of plowing to two weeks; and in the story Shan's friend Poss Sparks handled the corn planter while Shan laid off the corn ground. Finally, Jesse was seventeen his sophomore year rather than sixteen, but, as before, these are differences of detail rather than of substance.[41]

The student's desire "to do something in life," so strongly encouraged and defined at Greenup High School, tended to reinforce Martha and Mitchell Stuart's hopes for their son. Shan's father, described in "Victory and the Dream" as "a wiry, slender, red-faced man with big blue eyes and a long big nose," who "never weighed more than 140 pounds and not less than 126 after he grew to manhood," and who has a job "on the railroad section," is unquestionably and clearly Mitchell Stuart transmuted into fiction. The father looks with pride upon his son's efforts to be "a young Sampson," and when he sees the boy's determination to accomplish a demanding task, he declares, "I'm proud of you. . . . You're going to high school. And I didn't have a school in my day to attend. And you will work, Shan! I've got confidence in you, my son!"—to which Shan directly responds, "This made me feel very good." Similarly, the high school junior also talked with his mother. He spoke with her in the milk-gap, when they milked the cows together, but only after he took his mother's apron and put it on, for, as Martha Stuart said, "My cows are not used to men folks." His mother's ear was a sympathetic ear. "You know," she told him, "sometimes I have felt like I would just like to get out and go and go and go. I have felt that these hills could not hold me. And if I had been a man I would have gone."

They would talk on in the milk-gap while Jesse zigzagged two streams of milk into a two-gallon zinc water bucket.[42]

So he was writing. He had read in Burns' lyric poem "My Heart's in the Highlands" a line about "the straths in the green valley below," and identified the phrase with green strips of land down in the valley of the Ohio River, seen from his own path over Seaton Ridge. Certainly, he thought, "my heart wasn't in the lowlands." Clearly he was under the spell of Burns, and felt Mrs. Hatton's influence—and that of others as well. In the Greenup High School library he had read Emerson—his essay "Nature," especially the lines

> . . . if a man would be alone, let him look at the stars. . . . In the woods, we return to reason and to faith. . . . Nothing can befall me in life—no disgrace, no calamity . . . which nature cannot repair. . . . In the wilderness, I find something more dear . . . than in streets or villages. . . . Standing on the bare ground,—my head bathed by the blithe air, and uplifted into infinite space,—all mean egotism vanishes. I become a transparent eyeball; I am nothing; I see all. . . . I am part or parcel of God.

He thought of Emerson as he walked over the ridge path to and from high school, and later he would declare the Concordian's shaping power upon his youth; "Emerson lived with me. He walked up that ridge with me." Yet Burns and Emerson and the Hattons and his own family's hopes for him did not explain why he burned to write. Seven springs later he would reach for a deeper, more authentic cause rooted in the land he intimately knew. "It was because of the wind I heard in the dead leaves and the loneliness of sounds at night."[43]

In the spring, fragrant white blossoms of the apple trees attracted the boy. When wind blew through the spreading, round-topped trees in the old orchards along the woodland edges, floating the white flowers to the earth, he thought about man and the seasons. These trees would bloom again next April, and the blossoms would be young again. Emerson's idea of harmony between man and nature, sympathetic correspondence, did not seem to hold here. No, the way of nature was not the way of people. "I would bloom but once and then I would go back to the earth and be silent and cold forever." Whereas springtime trees spoke life and beauty, the carrion-seeking buzzards spoke death. Shoemakes [sumacs] put forth their sticky red leaves "with a sour smell on damp spring days," and then the blackberry briars bloomed under the apple trees. The windy fragrance from them, he thought, "is enough to make man jealous of bees."

Such intimately sensuous woodland experiences welled up in the youth's heart—inspired him to write, surely—but also inspired him to shout to the wind, the sky and the stars:

Won't you listen to me for a moment? My voice is not strong, but won't you listen? I tell you again and again I have something to say. I have walked in the silence of the night. I have talked to the stars. I have tried to be strong as the oak trees I have leaned against and on whose bark I have put my hands. I have clenched my teeth to keep from crying when the wild geese flew over the brown autumn fields with their honk-honking cries. I wanted to follow them. I have lived among the things I loved. I have put my hands on them. I have talked to them but they could not understand. Now I have something to say to you. I want to say it in words beautiful as the stars. Can't you listen to my voice while I am still beneath these blooming apple trees?[44]

3

Schooldays and Steel Mills
1925–1926
———◇———

One day Jesse Stuart came out of W-Hollow on his way to Greenup High School. Near the railroad tracks at the first crossing, where little Riverton then merged with larger Greenup, he saw two black boys who were, as he later put it, "just beating the hell out of" a smaller boy. It was little Bill Collins, son of a local man who worked in Lawson's Hardware Store. "They had him penned up, and they were working him over."

Young Jesse Stuart ran up and said, "What's goin' on here?"

The Collins boy said, weakly, "They're about to kill me."

"You!" Jesse said, and grabbed the larger of the two boys. He knocked him down, then picked him up and, holding him by the top of his head and the seat of the pants, "kicked him clear back into black town." The W-Hollow youth then worked the other one over right in front of little Bill Collins until, so Jesse Stuart recalled, "He said he'd had enough."

From that time on Bill Collins, as boys will do, worshipped the older youth.

Sometimes Jesse would go home with Bill after ballgames and stay the night. Mr. and Mrs. Will Collins were happy to have their son's friends by anytime. Jesse and his parents knew the family through Grandma Collins, and through her Bill Collins' parents had learned to respect the Stuarts as poor but honest people. Mrs. Collins always prepared a large breakfast for the boys, and although Bill sometimes objected to eating a large bowl of steaming oatmeal covered in cream, Jesse led the way with genuine gusto, and Bill more often than not followed suit. "Bill thought I was a Jack Dempsey," and, said Stuart, "I was a husky among those boys."

Bill used to visit his grandmother's farm in the summertime, where he noticed Jesse and Sophia, along with the Hiltons and sometimes the

Howards, on their way to Plum Grove School right up through his grandmother's homeplace. "Their school was different from ours; they started in the summer." Jesse was living up at the tip of the middle prong of W-Creek when Bill first got to know him. Bill Collins remembers talk of the Stuarts having "a log raising" for the house that Jesse built with his grandfather and in which he lived during high school. Bill liked hunting and camping and always had a cabin in the woods, even if only one built of sassafras poles upon a hill. "He had a bed and a supply of canned foods laid in," Jesse recalled. The boys hunted all over the area of the Collins and Mitchell Stuart farms and camped out sometimes even in the winter. "Bill Collins and I slept together many a night and nearly froze to death."

To young Bill Collins Jesse was "tall and brawny for his age, a stout kid, and he had worked out on the farm. Jesse didn't have in his mind any mean stinkin' things to do and was as honest as anybody I can remember. My folks had no objections about us getting together for that reason. My mother liked him particularly. He often came to our house in Greenup, after a fair at the school or something, maybe as late as eleven o'clock in the evening, sometimes without invitation, and stayed with us. Mother invited him anytime he wanted to stay all night, and Jesse was welcome."

In the summer of 1923, after the crops were in the ground, the two close friends went on a camping trip to the Carter Cave country close to Grayson where they could hunt, fish, swim, and "just lie back." Bill Collins remembers that they hitchhiked part of the way, for it was a long walk. Out in the cave country they met a friendly farmer by the name of Baker, who had a pretty little daughter about seven years old. His six to eight acres of land composed a natural canyon, entirely fenced by nature, except for some stones and an iron gate. He said, "You boys can go on down by the river bank and camp there."

That night he invited the boys to go to church with him and his family. "Well, we went," Collins recalls. "We waded the Tygart River with him. He carried his wife across and then his little girl. And then we went up a solid rock cliff of about twenty-five feet on a ladder he had built so he could go to church, and on through the woods to an opening in a pine forest." There they found benches of split logs in the middle of the pine grove and two or three preachers of the Pentecostal Church. "Before the meeting," Collins said, "four or five people began talking in tongues." Jesse and Bill were open-mouthed. "We'd never seen anything like that before!" Since it was dark by the time church was over and the farmer did not want to chance the river, they all had to walk around three miles to the bridge. It was a cool wet night, and the farmer would not let them stay in the pup tent. "He put us up in the spare bedroom nice as you ever saw," Collins recollects. "We had a good breakfast the next mornin' and that was our first night out to camp."

The next night they did stay in the tent but moved upriver about one mile closer to the caves, away from Grayson and the Bakers' house. Before the day was over, though, Mr. Baker showed them a cave of his own. "It's not as big as Carter Caves but it's a dandy," he said. Collins is excited yet at the memory: "Well . . . there was a hole through the ceiling of the cave just about like a manhole. He said, 'I'll show you another up there.' And sure enough, there was another one, really strange, unique." The boys stayed on in the cave country several days and nights. Collins remembers their fishing on the creek bank, although most of the time he put out the fishing pole while Jesse sat up on the bank and read. One night they got "soakin' wet," and had to return to Grayson to dry out.

Jesse remembered the Walden-like existence of those drowsy days, and his reading the poetry of Tennyson and Burns. When their food ran out, the boys hiked twenty miles to the EK Railroad and caught the train back to Riverton. He would recall details of the trip that Bill Collins did not: the lowland where they camped was called Horseshoe Bottom; they fished all day long and once made a raft to sit on; the turtles kept them from swimming in the Tygart River; expert with a .22, Jesse demonstrated his shooting prowess—learned not from Camp Knox as Bill thought, but from "shooting squirrels out of the tall walnut trees near home"; they ate their kills of bullfrog-legs, squirrels, and several ground-hogs, although Bill "wouldn't touch a piece of groundhog," even though "they were fat on earing corn" and just "a great dish." Jesse recollected the bees feeding on buckwheat blossoms, the long hours of reading, then leaving his books on a shelf of rocks in the cave for Farmer Rankins, as he apparently later named the character suggested by Farmer Baker, the friendly man who had treated them to his hospitality.

Thurman Darby, whose father ran the produce business, was another of Jesse's close friends. The family got to know Jesse well because the youth often made extra money by bringing animal hides in for sale. During World War I there was an increased demand for ginseng, yellowroot, and May apple, and from time to time the woods-wise boy sold them at the store. Later, after he had begun attending high school, Jesse was so successful in bringing in lucrative skunk pelts that the unmistakable odor hung on, earning him the nickname "Polecat." It was apparently at about this time that Naomi Deane Norris received her first impression of the mountain boy in the Greenup High School yard; but though inwardly sensitive, Jesse's pride was so strong that he generally gave no inkling that he felt insulted. In face of the seeming unawareness and general good nature that met such gibes, the nickname proved only temporary. Indeed, Elmer Heaberlin and Judge Sammons do not remember the nickname at all, but Stuart himself recalls that it lasted a short time. In the generally pervasive aura of adolescent ridicule the boys, aware of how quickly Academy Hollow wound up into a woods thick with wildlife, began to refer to it as "Cattymount Hollow." By the time he was a senior Jesse's compact, muscular build, strength, personable manner, and comparative maturity earned him another cognomen—"Poppie," which he carried into later life.

One day at Greenup High Jesse ran physically into someone on the playground and split his pants. Thurman took him across the tracks to his home where Mrs. David Darby mended the trousers so he could return to school right away. The brick front porch on Chesapeake Street next to the C&O tracks became familiar to Jesse Stuart by his senior year. Sometimes he stayed there as often as every other week—as Thurman Darby recollected, "when something was going on at school or when the weather was bad." As her son remembers, the author accurately quoted Mrs. Darby in *Beyond Dark Hills:* "Now come any time and make yourself at home. . . . The key will always be above the door. Remember you are welcome here."[1]

In the summer of his junior year, 1925, when he was farming a heavy crop, he accidentally went into a schoolroom where a teacher's examination was about to get under way. He sat for the test and passed it, earning a second-class certificate, although up to that time he had completed only twelve high school units. By late summer he completed two successful months of teaching at Cane Creek Elementary School in the southern end of Greenup County a few miles from Hunnewell, a station of the old EKRR line. Many of the biographical events of this summer are treated in *The Thread That Runs So True,* in which Cane Creek becomes Lonesome Valley.

Jesse first roomed and boarded with a family much like the Conways. The father was a trustee, and although Jesse did not argue with him, after his first month of teaching, "I got out of that place." Guy Hawkins' real surname was Felty, and as in the book, the boy had blacked Sophia Stuart's eyes before Jesse fought him, again much as in the book. "I weighed about 150 then," he recalled, setting the context of the fight. "I hit him hard enough that I split my shirt from the neck clear down my back." Jesse said that the big boy got into line "after he got the message," then, reflecting further, added, "I don't know how I kept from breaking his jaw. Boy, I hit him."

Most of the characters in *The Thread That Runs So True*, of course, parallel real people. There truly was a neighboring girl who played her guitar and sang songs while he tried to teach; according to the author, her fictional name and actual name were the same—Cochran—although she did not later marry a character such as Ova Salyers. Similarly, a talkative man like Burt Eastham worked in those hills, digging out and hauling coal, an echo in type of Uncle Frank Sparks of W-Hollow. Interestingly, the author's brother, James Stuart, related a story of his helping Uncle Frank Sparks measure his haulage accurately and thus avoid being swindled by hauling more coal than he was being paid for. The story is nearly identical to that of Jesse Stuart's story of Burt Eastham, who learns a similar lesson in the practical value of an education.

Jesse Stuart did wear a white suit one moonlit evening up toward Carter County, hoping to keep a date with an attractive teacher named Woods, although May was not her first name; she had been going with a steelworker from the American Rolling Mills at Ashland (Aukland Steel in the book). Jesse was egged and tomatoed and shot at precisely as in the book. After watching the two contending religious groups at Cane Creek, much as those in *Thread*, Jesse moved down into "the Valley," actually Hunnewell, to stay with a kind old couple named Batson in the book, Wilson in reality. "They lived in the finest house there, a big frame house," the author said, "originally built for an EK Railroad family." Much to the surprise of the Wilsons, who had previously believed teachers could not do much farm work, Jesse milked their cows for them, and they learned to respect and trust him enough to loan him the use of their pony, although Jesse invented the name "Sundance." After two months of teaching at Cane Creek, Jesse returned in September to high school at Greenup. The transition is handled smoothly in *Thread*, covering the balance of the six-month rural school year in less than four pages and completing Part I. "I invented those other months," the author said, "to give a whole year's picture."[2]

After paying his room and board, he had nearly a hundred dollars with which he purchased new clothes to augment the Robert Hatton hand-me-downs that Dr. and Mrs. Hatton had given him. More than the money, however, he had gained new confidence in himself. At Greenup High School he did substitute teaching in math and history, and sometimes met classes for absent teachers in the grade school. In the fall he was regular left guard on the football team and did some punting, but he encountered severe competition from Malcolm Norris, a strong hand-some boy of "high-cut" build, who more than once kicked the pigskin the length of the football field. Jesse was also president of the YMCA and the Hi-Y Club, Christian organizations high on Dr. and Mrs. Hat-ton's approved list of student clubs. During his senior year he was so busy with school activities that he stayed about one-third of his nights in Greenup, usually with such families as the Collinses or Darbys, al-though many families welcomed him. During his junior year he had made A's in English and history, but received a C − in Latin. The summer of hard work farming and teaching, followed by increased substitute teaching and a rash of club, athletic, and some social activities, apparently cut into his grades his senior year, when the record reveals a drop well below the 3.27 overall average attained during his first three academic years. Even in English, a subject in which he had a record of three A's and three B + 's up to his final semester, his grade fell to an atypical C, a decline that must have puzzled Mrs. Hatton as much as it may have pained Jesse.

From his boyhood days at Plum Grove he had now and again spent a few idyllic hours with a neighborhood girl who lived over by the Little Sandy River at Put-Off Ford. Edith was the daughter of Charlie Greene, a farmer who sometimes crossed paths with Jesse's father. Later, about the time Jesse discovered Robert Burns, he envisioned Edith as his own imaginary Highland Mary. Her surname became a kind of assonant verbal image of his Romantic dreams, the Maria Sheen of his poetry and *Beyond Dark Hills*. Even at Plum Grove he had competed with Big Aaron Howard for the privilege of going swimming in the waterhole nearest her house. He had gone through the meadows to get the cows with her. Down at Put-Off Ford, when dew shone on the cane tops, they had stolen off together to play in the john-boat and row it up to Shackle Run, not far from the farm where Jesse's Grandfather Mitch Stuart had lived at the time of the boy's birth. Under the shade of birches—at least in the boy's mind if not in fact—they had put their hands together and then put them under water while holding Bibles in their other hands and so pledged their troths in true Burnsian fashion. The Little Sandy became the River Ayr. He later described her as "tall, strong, slender and beautiful" and wrote of her "dark skin and the curved lips and the white teeth." Years later, Jesse Stuart did not remember her as good looking, but James Stuart's memory differs. She was "a small girl—beautiful, with dark hair and striking blue, dark blue eyes." During Jesse's senior year, as he wrote in *Beyond Dark Hills*, he urged Maria to stay with her aunt in Greenup so they could go together to the *Cotton*

Blossom Show Boat. Strains of "Dixie" from the calliope excited them. She called him "Stuart," and some nights Jesse did not get home until three in the morning. In *Beyond Dark Hills* the author enlarges upon their dates, speaking to Maria Sheen, "Let us take in all the coming attractions on this river—the *French Sensational,* the *Water Queen* and the *American.*" But the tone is that of an expansive youth exaggerating a pocketful of money during a new and rebellious phase of life when he had little money indeed. Then he tells her, "Let's go in big fashion," belying the modest circumstances of his real situation. "That was symbolical," the author explained in a clear effort to diminish any literal interpretation that readers might tend to place upon the part of his personal story treating his friendship with Edith Greene, although he admitted knowing and seeing her on through his youth and young manhood.

Indeed, most of Jesse Stuart's friends of this period recall little more of Edith Greene than her family name and the general impression that she was attractive and went out with a variety of young fellows. At the time Jesse was often carrying Naomi Norris' books to school, although she was two grades behind him, and he thought she was socially above him. However, Jesse's close friends to a person recollect Rose Bergmeier as his high school sweetheart. Her father, Joe Bergmeier, was a barber who had his shop next door to the old Columbia Hotel on Main Street. Jesse Stuart recalls him as "a real German. He had a pear-shaped head [that] sat on broad shoulders," and the man simply "loved beer." He would have a "big glass . . . right there while he was cuttin' hair. He'd blow the foam back a little and say, 'If the Lord ever made anything better than beer he kept it to himself.' " Reflecting, the poet summed up his view of Rose: "I wish I'd held on to Rose . . . from the time I went to high school until the time I left. Oh boy, she wasn't good-looking at all, but there was no better girl than she was. An ardent Catholic . . . She was a dandy! I frequently visited her over there on Laurel Street."

Judge Sammons remembers Jesse's bringing his lantern over the ridge path from W-Hollow after dark, extinguishing it and leaving it on a nearby tree before going on to the Bergmeier house at 507 Laurel Street, across the street from St. Lawrence Catholic Church, a quaint little cathedral reminiscent of a Currier and Ives print. "They might have gone to a showboat, where they tied up at the bottom of Harrison and Front Streets—maybe the *Majestic,*" Thurman Darby offered; but more likely they went to Charles Taylor's movie house a few blocks up East Main Street from the courthouse. Both classmates recollect well enough that neither they nor Jesse Stuart had much time for "playing around" while they attended Greenup High. "Jesse and I had to haul it home to get work done," Thurman Darby said. "Elmer [Heaberlin] had to go all the way to Wurtland." Sometimes if they had a little spare change they would stop off at Bruno Cardi's restaurant, next door to the present site of Clovis Hurt's Chevrolet Garage close to the movie house, and get a sandwich or Coke. The boys especially liked Hoot Gibson and Tom Mix movies, though "picture shows" were a rare treat for them.

Jesse could be mischievous and was something of a practical joker. Eunice Mitchell Harper won't ever forget the time she sat by Jesse in Mr. Hatton's study hall. "If students talked he would make them get down on the floor. Jesse would talk, but I wouldn't say anything because I knew if I did Mr. Hatton would make us both get down on the floor." Mrs. Harper's eyes twinkled. "And *I* didn't want to get down on that floor." Elmer Heaberlin recalled that Jesse went through a period of writing anonymous letters in a backhanded scrawl, "sometimes for revenge and sometimes for entertainment—or both—just practical jokes." The anecdote of the "love pills" is one of his vivid memories. The senior class sold candy, and the extra boxes of candy were kept in Mr. Hatton's office. " 'C'mon, Heab, let's get us some love pills,' Jesse would say, and we would slip into the office and help ourselves. If the door was locked, we would go in over the transom. One day we caught Oscar Sammons sneaking in there—" and Heaberlin reflected, "—I'm not sure whether we caught the Judge going in over the transom, or he caught us, but we were all in it together then. I remember after school Jesse and I would go up the railroad track eating the love pills." The boys also liked to drop into Hoffman's Pool Room, operated by the father of their classmate Katherine Hoffman, just across Harrison Street from the courthouse, where "we ate the best hot dogs." Still and all, the very best food was served in the Callihan Brothers Restaurant on the site where the Van Hoose Apartments now stand. Their "luscious hamburgers" sold for only ten cents apiece.

Jesse Stuart is depicted among nineteen other students of his Greenup High School graduating class as they faced north in front of the double-door entrance on Harrison Street. They stood in four rows, using the steps as platforms to allow the maximum exposure of each senior's shoulders and face; it seems obvious that Jesse Stuart stepped down from the fourth row, leaving a vacant spot by Estille Howland and taking up a space on the end of the third row next to Kyon Murray, who stood between Jesse and Oscar Sammons, and cocked her head a little to one side in order to look around Irene Barney (Griffith) and smile at the camera. Another photograph taken that day was one of Jesse Stuart,

Oscar Sammons, Thurman Darby, and Jimmie McCoy, the class president. Stuart is almost at attention; all have their hands behind their backs. Oscar Sammons appears more relaxed than the others, and only he wears a suit.

However formative or deep the schoolboy Jesse's relationships were with Edith Greene and Rose Bergmeier, they were significant enough that he kept their photographs, along with his class pictures, in the section of his albums allotted to his Greenup High School days. Two informal poses of Edith Greene with a friend, Nellie Griffith, in front of a house in Catlettsburg, Kentucky, provide little detail, but they reveal her to be the taller of the two women. The photos show a dark-complexioned, slender young woman of seemingly happy disposition, smiling as she stands in pumps, wearing an informal dress with a large collar and bow, and sporting a watch or bracelet on her wrist closest to the camera. Jesse Stuart's friendship with Edith Greene lasted until after she moved to Catlettsburg. "I knew her a long time up there," he said. Rose Bergmeier's photograph is a studio pose. Signed "Lovingly /Rose," a large-ed young woman with clear-cut nose, mouth, and chin looks from under low bangs of her short coiffure directly at the lens. Irma Warnock Collins, a junior that year, recalls distinctly that she was "a compassionate, understanding person." Jesse Stuart acknowledged her as a possible model for the fickle Jo Ann Burton in his short story "Slipover Sweater," but "without the shallowness," he emphasized. "She used to be kind of crazy about me," he mused.[3]

In May 1926, at the age of nineteen, Jesse Stuart graduated into a world of ambivalence toward himself. His father asked him to stay on the farm, for he was in debt, and even though he still worked for the C&O he was unable to hire hands to do the work. James was not quite eleven years old—too young to plow. The older brother gave the matter considerable thought. Doubtless, the memory of the winter of 1918 still burned in Jesse's mind; nor could he forget the talks with his mother in the milk-gap, the vow to "go and go and go," to make something of himself. Recognizing the harsh, elemental life of his father, the youth challenged himself: "Now must I follow the footprints of my father?" Self-assertion warred with submission.

For a few weeks he seems to have submitted, but despite the rigor of farm work, he reacted physically to the tension. At first he taught Mary and James to ride the gentler of the two horses the family owned; but in leading the way on Fred, the faster of the horses, he rode bareback—Indian fashion—"as fast as the wind." Indeed, he wrote, "I tried to outrun the wind" as the horses traversed the ridge roads. He rode to his hilltop birthplace and witnessed its decay under the elements. To neighbors' astonishment he jumped Fred over gates. The children followed, screaming their fright and delight. "Them Stuart youngins is plum fools," a neighbor complained, "just a raising hell with them horses." Jesse grew increasingly restive under the restraint of his dark hills. "I dreamed of something beyond the hills," he wrote, echoing his mother's words, "I wanted to go and go and go. I wanted to do something." One night in the chip yard, before he left W-Hollow, he told his father, "Fifty acres of land is not a big enough place for me."

In *Beyond Dark Hills,* Stuart amplifies the conflict that resulted in his first inward and private, if not outward and open, breakaway from home; it is tied in with Maria Sheen and a carnival at Cole's Field just west of Greenup. First his eye had been taken by the colorful life of the showboat, again when he had been with her. "I wanted flashy colors, gay clothes, parties, romance . . . more than all the dark woods and the white clouds floating over. There was beauty in dancing women on a show boat, their bodies swaying to lively music." Then the carnival fascinated him: "the painted showmen, the dancing girls, the vagabond life and the plaintive thrumming music of the merry-go-round. . . . I made up my mind to get a job and follow it." The bright lights catalyzed his resolve to escape.

That night after he took Maria home and went himself, it was four o'clock in the morning before he sneaked into the house. It had been a hot walk over the ridge path, and he described the quietness with which "I slipped to the water bucket and gorged on water." Almost viciously he realized it was his last night home "for a long time," he wrote. He lit the oil lamp, looked over his three small rows of books, and was suddenly "tired of everything." What began with a slipping of his grades his senior year, culminated in his throwing the books "one by one" out the window. The books were suddenly "all deceitful things." He had "acted crazy over them for a little while." The tone of the disillusionment mixes interesting images: abstract books against the desire for a life one must "put his hands on"; Scotland's River Ayr against Kentucky's Little Sandy; his Maria Sheen against Burns' Highland Mary. The disparities confused him into tears, or as Stuart wrote, "A brown-skinned farm boy put his face against the quilts his mother had made for his bed and cried."

He did not really go to bed that night. The next day he avoided his father. Jesse wrote that the next morning he burned the books he had thrown out of his window, close to the twin hickories where his mother washed clothes near the chip yard. After plowing a few hours, he went back to the house and told his mother he was leaving home. She was not surprised at his decision, and told him to "be a good boy," and to return whenever he wanted. "Take care of yourself," she advised, and "remember, chickens come home to roost." As he left the hollow by the ridge road, each stone of the chimney he and Grandfather Hilton had built, the logs, the roof, the fruit trees he had set out, the reaches of land he and his father had cleared, and the fences were suddenly intimate as old friends. Yet the old life seemed empty, and he was impelled by the thought that he would be free from the farm and hard toil forever.

He got a job with the carnival taking tickets for the merry mix-up, and wrote that he stayed with it when it moved from town to town along the Ohio River toward Cincinnati. However, before the entourage reached the Queen City, he was fired for giving away free rides and taking a turn with the girls while their boyfriends took tickets in his place. But as he put miles between himself and home, he could not shake loose from the memory of Maria Sheen—whether an inspirational symbol or a warm-blooded lover does not seem so important—and identified her beauty with his feeling for the cornfields. He penned two sonnets to her in his tent one night, recounting their childhood days together, their adolescent dream of marriage, her description:

> Her skin is milk-weed dark, her eyes sky-blue,
> Her teeth are blood-root white, her hair is black
> As thick rain-clouds . . . her lips are soft as new
> Bark peeled from a slippery-elm and her back
> Is straight as a horse-weed upon the shore.
> Her legs are brown as the buff-colored corn. . . .

In poetry he declared an intention he would not declare so exclusively in reality:

> I think of her that I shall see once more,
> The sweetest mountain girl I've ever known.

Coming home, so he wrote, he pondered his childhood ambition to go to Harvard; off and on he had been aware of it since his Plum Grove days when he had talked with Nora Riggs about it, but now he was mature enough that "I laughed when I thought of the jump from a street carnival in the hill towns of Kentucky to Harvard." Deriding his own despondency, a bit like Melville's sea-bound Ishmael, and having nothing else to do, he wrote a poem "Harvard or the Sea," penning these lines of bleak resolution, "Then Great Seducer Sea, / Be last to pant and lick your wet lips over me."

But we have James Stuart's word that, although Jesse worked for a carnival that came to Greenup that summer, he never left Greenup with it. He doubtless did talk with the carnies during the summer days and nights, alcoholic fire-eaters and roustabouts alike; he could have been fired for giving free rides, and may have been promised a job if he would follow the carnival along the Ohio River towns; but in reality he submitted to the old routine of farm work and the duties of home. It was only in his creative imagination that he built upon the local color of the carnival, asserting himself and projecting his rebellion from home. In reality there had been no answer to his eleven-year-old brother's question, "What will we do here without you? No one is left to plow." Though he yearned to leave he innately realized, "I was rotten for doing it." Yet the conflict between self-assertion and submission had given rise to the rebellion of which he wrote, the exaggerated dramatizing of the runaway carnival episode, the sullen return to Greenup from remote Ohio River towns, and the shunning of his home at the head of W-Hollow.

Only later in the summer, when the crops were laid by and his sense of responsibility and conscience unburdened to that extent, could his growing self-assertion dominate familial submission. The juncture of imagination and reality, the mid-point of rebellion and submission, of thought and action occurred when he joined a group of young Greenup men and went to Camp Knox, for him his second and last encampment. Assertively, he relates stories of a Greenup tough called Mack, "the gun man and the razor man from Plum Grove." The author later acknowledged that the character was based on Jack Dysard, the model for Sparkie at a younger age in *Hie to the Hunters*. "He wasn't all that bad. He wasn't a knife man—far from it. I exaggerated that, but he'd fight and he'd shoot." The photographs of this period, however, only hint at Jesse Stuart's inner stirrings, revealing a spick-and-span soldier from his glistening and neatly parted hair down to the tightly wound puttees, or "leggins" as Jesse referred to them. In one photograph he poses seated, his arms folded and legs crossed, with another soldier, Wren Menifee. Also in the group of Greenup soldiers was Elmer Heaberlin. The government paid transportation, meals, and board for a thirty-day period. "Jess was in the horse-drawn artillery, and I was in a different unit and a different company," Heaberlin recalled. "Jesse told them about me and I played baseball with my unit because they thought I was a terrific player. [He] always liked to build things up. We were in separate units, but just occasionally I'd see Jess around there." In another snapshot Stuart stands at ease in wide-brimmed hat with leather chinstrap along with soldiers Newall from Indiana; Staggers from West Virginia, who later became Congressman from that state; and Artner from Ohio. Two other snapshots reveal soldiers Staggers, Heishman, and Stuart as comrades-in-arms, nearly aggressive in their militant seriousness as their attention is riveted to the lens.

Once again Stuart did not "take well" to military training. He questioned the whole idea of "practice on how to kill men," which "seemed queer to me." On Sundays he visited the artillery ranges and witnessed how the 75-mm guns tore the earth and everything around them to pieces. When he failed to salute officers, he was put to cutting wood, pulling weeds, hauling garbage, and cleaning latrines, or so he wrote. Despite having burned his books just weeks before, he suddenly hungered for reading matter again. He read Edgar Allan Poe, Burns, and later *Carlyle's Essay on Burns,* edited by Edwin Mims; but when he left books out on his bunk he and the whole floor of his barracks were graded down. "This seemed as crazy as hell to me," Jesse recorded his thoughts, and "I rebelled against the whole works."

Sometimes at night he went to the nearby Haymarket Theatre and saw such films as *God's Country and the Woman, The Vanishing American,* and *North of '36,* and then slipped back into his barracks after taps, outrunning the Officer of the Day when necessary. Finally he was caught with his clothes on in his bunk. The sentence was light—seventeen laps around the barracks. He redeemed himself on the rifle range though and excelled in foot drills. He was six feet tall and weighed, perhaps, 150 pounds. Whereas he had been humble and compliant in 1923, he was now recalcitrant and questioning. Yet his pride was sufficiently strong that he achieved the distinction of being selected among four men as one of the best soldiers in camp. Maneuvers became a vivid memory as planes drummed overhead and artillery battalions and infantry echoed cannon and machine-gun fire across the thirty-four-thousand-acre camp reservation. Despite his venting rebellion, he folded back into submission long enough to step up to get his medals "like a little hungry boy takes candy . . . one medal for track, the other for shooting." Years later, he looked at a photograph of the rifle pit area in his album, remarking, "We were down in those pits. We gave 'em their scores as they shot over us. . . . The bullets that went over that, you'd just ear 'em plunk right above your head into the target. I worked those pits, put the scores up on a long wooden handle."

Under live fire of a rifle grenade citizen Stuart, not unlike Stephen

Crane's Henry Fleming in *The Red Badge of Courage,* "wanted to run," for "I could not help it." The flattery of medals notwithstanding, submission and fear finally gave way to anger. "You know what I got mad about in the army? They put up horses in artillery. Those beautiful white horses with flaxen manes." The impressionable young man's thoughts foresaw the inevitable mutilation, and he wrote of "their guts ripped out and hanging down from their sides." The idea of horses in war haunted him. "I thought of the horses all the time." He reasoned that "man could find places to hide in. . . . But a horse just had to stand and take war as it comes. He is slaughtered and, like the men in most wars, for no reason." But what had horses to do with the troubles of human beings? Why should horses be dragged into war? "There ought to be a universal law against it." Because he was a Republican in Kentucky, he wrote years later, he did not receive a West Point appointment, adding parenthetically, "Now I'm thankful because I didn't belong there."[4] He was thinking of the horses.

When Jesse Stuart and Elmer Heaberlin returned to Greenup from Camp Knox in early August, Jesse went to work at American Rolling Mills (ARMCO) in Ashland. The chronology of the thirty-six-page chapter "Cool Memories of Steel" in *Beyond Dark Hills* is elusive. Jesse wrote that he left steel-mill work to "go to college on September the twelfth, 1926." However, his record at ARMCO shows that he was employed on August 9, and worked his last day in 1926 on September 17. His second stint at the steel mills did not occur until the following summer vacation from college, when he commenced working June 2, 1927, and worked through September 10. Of the 1927 period Jesse declared, "I hugged every bit of time I could get." These were his only periods of work at ARMCO, altogether totaling almost five months.

The habit of honesty learned from Martha and Mitchell Stuart is humorously evident in the author's description of his hiring at the ARMCO employment office, where he put a piece of paper with "21" written on it in his shoe, so "if John Findlay asks me if I'm over twenty-one I'll tell him the truth." Actually, he had celebrated his twentieth birthday the day before he was hired. Of the man who hired him, John Findlay, as he calls him in *Beyond Dark Hills,* Stuart said that "Floyd Berry was the man. He had big gold teeth and was something else." The author also linked the character of Ruddy Flannery with Floyd Berry, who ran a huge blacksmith shop known as the Grey Iron Foundry for the mills. There Jesse worked his way up to the furnace, heating heavy pieces of steel to be shaped by "ten-ton thugs" from a giant air hammer. He also learned striking with a sledgehammer, but as his way with words and numbers became obvious he frequently found himself doing office work for Ruddy Flannery's Second Division shop.

Flannery's men claimed to be "the meanest bunch in these mills." They were practical jokers with no subtlety, as Jesse soon learned. Overtime work had cut into his weight, and he had dark circles under his eyes. Ruddy Flannery kidded him about being a boy instead of a man and asked him to step into his shovel. "Steady now as I bring you up. Hold onto my shoulder." In an eyeblink Jesse flew ten feet through the air and lit in the slack tub of water. The men hooted and Flannery "showed his yellow teeth." Jesse also learned to rip off the hippockets of his pants so the men wouldn't slip cigarette butts into them. "Say, Perry," Jesse records one of the men's wisecracks, "how is your wife and my child?"

One of the most blatant of practical jokes was played on Jesse Stuart's roommate, an adulterous piano player who explained to Jesse that he was "just aching for a woman," and proceeded to show the young man anatomically "what women's done for me. . . . Ain't this a hell of a shape for the 'siff' to leave a man in—though I'm well of it." Jesse's response was "He made me fear women," and he wondered if the piano player's wife noticed. "I wonder if she has ever known another man so that she could make the comparison." Determined to "put the skates" under the piano player quickly, Boss Flannery had young Jesse buy "one of the largest loaded cigars you can get" and several more. Stuart returned and passed out the smokes, holding the last for his roommate. It exploded. The piano player screamed to the accompaniment of flying cigar pieces and Flannery's men threw the startled fellow into the slack tub. He left the shop, never to return. "He went out cursing and wet as a drowned chicken." Of this anecdote Jesse later said, "[Floyd Berry]'s the one who sent me to get explosive cigars . . . for the men. He gave me the money. . . . I went and bought them. I brought them back and one whole day . . . they was going off in the shop."

Stuart's view of sexuality in this work is brashly if ingenuously frank. He meets Mattie, "the friendliest person there," who loans him two dollars. The dollars felt "quite warm where they had been against her leg." She tells him what she does to live and to support her children in Cincinnati. "I want to raise 'em right," she explains, "and never let them know I've throwed myself away." She tells Stuart that she is called "Red Hot Mattie." Three passions of the men at the steel mills, he soon learns, are drinking, womanizing, and gambling. He learns how such men as Charlie Wampie and Foreman Sheff "got to 'Weedmonkeyin' together," taking Charlie's "Chivy roadster, a couple of blankets, and a little licker and how we did get them. But we got a whole lot of them rotten stinking kind. And God, when one of them 'Weedmonkeys' smells she's enough to vomit a buzzard. But hell, me and old Sheff took 'em on together." Fighting is a fourth passion and in this personal story Jesse Stuart relates his fight with Spike McCartie, who has insulted his grandfather, Mitch Stuart. During these months of exhausting work at the steel mills Jesse's own pastimes appear to have been writing, sleeping, reading, and dreaming of going to college. If his poetry of the period, such as "Batter Me Down, Life," bespeaks a determined faith in himself and an ability to recover from defeats in life, then the sonnet "Sleep" suggests a desire to escape from pain and disappointment into "Where we give up the body and the brain / And lie in peace in our long night of sleep."

The young Jesse Stuart, though frank and open with his close friends, nevertheless kept many things to himself. As late as the Camp Knox experience of 1926, Elmer Heaberlin doubted that Jesse's ambition to go to college had crystallized. However, Jesse wrote that while at ARMCO he got a catalog from Vanderbilt and investigated expenses there as well as at Harvard and the University of Virginia. Although these schools were his first choices, circumstances inclined him more practically toward a self-help college such as Berea. His brother James remembers Jesse's returning to W-Hollow before he left for college, but the dramatic personal story of *Beyond Dark Hills* continues to emphasize his alienation from home. Though close to home, he didn't return, but did wonder "what my folks were doing at home" and "how my father felt towards me now"; yet he is more determined than ever to follow his mother's unfulfilled desire "to get out and go and go and go." He recalls their talks in the milk-gap his sophomore year when he had discovered the new world of Greenup High, a time that now seemed so long ago.[5]

After paying all his debts, Jesse bought a pasteboard suitcase in Ashland for a dollar, but he had a lot to learn about the role of a college man. The job in steel, standing six feet from the intense heat of the pieces, had reddened his face to a brick color and singed his eyebrows and hair above his forehead so that he looked more like a fierce Indian than a Kentucky mountain boy hitchhiking down to where the Bluegrass meets the Cumberlands. Neither had he learned to wear a sweater with a letter or to put college decals on his suitcase, so he had some difficulty catching rides. He was two days in covering the 135 miles to the Berea campus. Fortunately, Mattie had made him some sandwiches. Being a woods-wise youth, he camped along the way, sleeping in a haystack his first night. He washed and brushed his teeth in creek water.

He was not to be disheartened, for he felt the freedom in the very air of a dream being lived. After five weeks of labor, often working overtime, the young steelworker took such hardships as joys. The outdoors lent gusto to his journey. The scenery of the eastern Kentucky hills was fresh to him, the clean air he breathed in marked contrast to the polluted air of the Grey Iron Foundry; the atmosphere was already "slightly tinged with the smell of autumn leaves." Although Jesse declared in *Beyond Dark Hills* that he had shipped his trunk to Berea ahead of him and, apparently, went straight to his destination, in actuality he looked into several colleges along his way—first Morehead Normal School on Highway 60, and then Kentucky Wesleyan, located in Winchester in 1926. He veered south from Winchester, taking either Kentucky Highway 388 or U.S. 227 to old Dixie U.S. Highway 25 leading through Richmond to Berea. He knew that Eastern Kentucky State Normal School and Teachers College was in Richmond, but he did not believe he could go there and work his way through.

When he reached Berea, he was interviewed by Dean Hendrix and told there was no room for him. The dean recommended another college to Stuart—Lincoln Memorial University, just across the Kentucky border at Harrogate, Tennessee. Jesse caught an L&N train and arrived at the institution on September 20, 1926. At registration, he sought out the end of the line so that the other students would not hear him tell Dean Charles D. Lewis that he had only $29.30 with which to register. It was a long line. The girl in front of him noticed him. He had no way of knowing that she was worried about the same thing, although she had $150.00 with her. She saw him as "a tall slender lad, about 150–160 pounds." He was tieless, his shirt open at the collar, and he wore a short-waisted blue wool mackinaw jacket. He "looked as if he were growing too fast for his clothes." There was something unusual about him. His hair "seemed to part itself on one side and fall to the other in a dark mass," but that was not it. His forehead was burnt and face deeply bronzed. He looked "rather like an Indian lad" to her. As time went on, she spoke to him. What he answered "was less than 'No,' " and he did not smile once. The boy "was not very cordial to anybody; he just looked as if he wanted to be alone." The line inched on through the September day.

It was late morning by the time he reached the dean. The girl in front of him registered and went on. Then he handed his registration card over, and explained his circumstances. His funds were very little, even for a man who wanted to "work a half-day and go to school the other half." They talked it over.

"Where are you from, Stuart?"

"Northeast Kentucky."

"I'm from Kentucky, too," Dean Lewis said. "I grew up in the mountains of Kentucky—back where the hoot owls holler in the day-time," and he laughed.

"I'm from that land too," Stuart bandied, "where the hoot owls holler in the daytime." The dean laughed again and, although Stuart embellished the facts, learned of his Berea colleague's recommendation of LMU. He looked closely at the youth with the singed hair and strange fire tan.

"Please try me on a full schedule and let me work all the spare time I have," Stuart said. "See if I can't pass my school work. I would like to try to work my way here and do a few other things!"

"I'll take you on your face!" The dean decided to enroll him and help him get a job on the college farm. "You've got an honest face!"[6]

Jesse Stuart was a college freshman at last.

4

Torchlight in the
Valley Mists
1926–1929

—————◇—————

People used to ask Jesse Stuart what college he went to, and he would reply, "I went to the college that'd take me. I did. I had a time finding a school that'd take me. Nobody wanted me. Do you know that? No one wanted me."

At Harrogate, Tennessee, Lincoln Memorial University put the youth to work. As a freshman he worked in the hayfields, dug potatoes, filled silos, cut corn, and raked leaves. Working half a winter with a gang of boys to lay the water line from Cudjo's Cave to the campus, he dug ditches, sometimes through frozen earth. He dynamited rocks in the quarry, swung a sledgehammer and beat the rocks into smaller rocks so he could feed them into a pulverizer, and wheeled the stones in Irish-buggies. Later he helped spread granulated limestone along white walkways over the LMU campus. He got odd jobs, too, washing Professor Kroll's car in front of his cottage, on a level place just across the uphill road from his house, back of the present parking lot between the Farr Building and the library. He did masonry work for faculty members, including the librarian, Mrs. Iris Grannis, and gardening for Mrs. Trosper. Although he was very fond of the Trospers, he never forgot the disgust with which he walked off the job when Mrs. Grannis' German shepherd bit him. "Oh, it didn't hurt much," she said, as he left. By autumn of 1927 he had a job drying pots and pans in the kitchen and working in the dining room of stately Norton Hall. In 1928 and 1929 he was editor of the campus newspaper and literary magazine, *The Blue and Gray,* and also delivered the college mail.

Of these days, one of Stuart's two favorite teachers at LMU, Earl Hobson Smith, wrote that he was "a progressive student" who made "fine grades" in his courses. The text in public speaking was *Aristotle's*

Rhetoric, to Smith the very " 'New Testament' of Thought." In the fall of 1926, Professor Smith critiqued the freshman's first college speech, "How I Became a Blacksmith in the Steel Mills," and found it "concrete." When Stuart expressed hopelessness about his own promise as a speaker, Smith quickly told him, "Everybody is always a public speaker." As Smith remembered, these were happy days for the youth. "He was so full of life, vitality, and the love of living and doing for others that his hardships merely gave zest to Jesse's living."[1]

The girl in the registration line in front of Stuart turned out to be Lucille Jordan of Greenville County, South Carolina. He saw her again the morning after registration in the dining room and "warmed up" considerably. Students could choose to sit wherever they wished, so he chose her table. They introduced themselves to each other. She was nineteen and had bobbed hair, a cultured southern voice, and thoughtful demeanor. There was something about her that he liked, as one likes a friend, a sister. He sat at her left that day and kept the same seat during the years they remained at LMU. She was sure he was younger than she.

As he had become an above-average worker at ARMCO, he was clearly an above-average, if inconsistent, student at LMU. The second-quarter College Honor Roll of March 16, 1928, lists Jesse Stuart with a 2.35 standing (A = 3 points, B = 2 points), twelfth in rank of the twenty-five students so honored. The next quarter, spring of 1928, he improved his standing to 2.41. These were his two best academic quarters at the college; although the forty-eight hours he took in English and creative writing earned him a total of 119 honor points, a standing in these subjects of approximately 2.48, he was busier writing and publishing poetry, prose sketches, editorials and articles for *The Blue and Gray* and other small periodicals than studying for honors.[2]

In his sophomore year, admittedly Jesse's "golden year" at LMU, nearly everything seemed to go his way. True, his first-year English teacher, bespectacled Miss Kathryn Howard, had denigrated his sonnet "Muddy waters, how I have loved your crying," advising him to "get away from sedge and muddy waters and the night wind. Write high, beautiful things like Shakespeare, Keats, Browning, and Longfellow. Don't waste your time on such low, vile things."

Now his teacher was Harry Harrison Kroll, who advised the students,

> Get that story on paper. . . . Write the wildest stories that ever happened in your community. You can't get them wild enough. Get all the old scandals. Let them kiss and love but no four-letter words.

Be more skilled at writing than to use these. Do them by implication. Write between the lines. Get them down so they won't die! Write like you talk! Just tell the story! Get it on paper!

During 1927 and 1928, when Kroll was teaching at LMU, Jesse stated that he wrote, excluding poems, stories "that later made forty-three publications, including *Esquire, Harpers* [sic], and *Colliers* [sic]. The majority of my short stories in *Head o' W-Hollow* . . . were written in [his] class." Moreover, the trunk he had sent to Harrogate from Berea contained "approximately five-hundred poems and numerous articles and stories," as well as a wire hanger "filled with rejection slips," for "not one magazine or newspaper editor would have anything I had written." When the first twenty poems he submitted were also rejected, he determined to become editor of *The Blue and the Gray.* His roommate, Mason Dorsey Gardner of Duck River, Tennessee, nominated Jesse with "a flowery speech," but he was soundly defeated by "a very pretty girl." Stuart later said that shortly after her election "she became extremely nervous—I believe she had to leave school for a semester." Again Stuart was nominated at his own request by Gardner. This time his opposition was "a beautiful girl," who later became Miss Lincoln Memorial University. She trounced him, too, but "strangely enough, something happened to her," Jesse related. She too "became extremely nervous" and "had to resign her editorship." At this point the English faculty stepped into the situation and appointed Jesse editor in 1928. In a burst of jubilation, "the first thing I did was to publish my first poem, 'The Cumberland Call.' "

However, the earliest published poems of Jesse Stuart to come to light as of this writing are not that one but three that appeared in the October 15, 1927, issue of *The Blue and Gray*, "Dead Farm," "The Ohio River: Evening," and "Sleep Spell." Unsurprisingly, they are schoolboy-ish pieces, requiring a close reading to perceive hints of the musical lines and vigorous images of the poet to come. In "Dead Farm," for example, "Slow shadows move across the place, / The clouds are drifting out of space," and "When darkness settles, the lone winds howl, / And about the ruins gaunt foxes prowl." In "Ohio River," the persona's isolation is dramatized and even the river is "desolate . . . / Where the dark waters moan,"

And the reeds bleed and quiver;
Just when the day was dying
And the white caps going down;

When the killdees were flying
Over the gray walls of town.

"Sleep Spell" is the most musical of the pieces, and anticipates the poet's rich combination of earth and sky images, as the first stanza shows:

The autumn wind is wailing
Where the leaves are dying.
The copper moon is failing,
And the white clouds flying.
And the darkness deep
Makes me want to sleep,
Want to sleep.

He was not writing poetry only. By 1927 he was typing prose at the rate of at least thirty thousand words a quarter for Professor Kroll, who advised, "Crank 'em out, boys. Get your ideas and crank 'em out! The words will come." It was in this class that Jesse wrote a twenty-page manuscript later published under the title *Tim*, now a collector's item for Stuart buffs, as well as the first drafts of most of the stories to appear in *Head o' W-Hollow* in 1936.

But poetry was his most compelling literary love. By 1928 a little booklet, *Lyrics from Lincoln Memorial University,* carried his photograph and four of his poems. "Directed" by Professor Kroll, *Lyrics* also featured the works and likenesses of Winnie Palmer, Louise McCamy, Iva Daugherty, and Roland Carter. In a group photo of Kroll's class, Jesse Stuart sits between Iva Daugherty and Winnie Palmer on the second row, cradling his knees with his hands and smiling at the lens. Three of Stuart's poems in the collection are reprints of December 1927 publications, but "Things I Have Loved," an echo of Rupert Brooke's "The Great Lover," makes its first appearance; it would be reprinted in the Bristol *Herald-Courier* the following year. The "Foreword" of *Lyrics* states that it contains the work of "mountain boys and girls," most of whom "are very young." It notes that "they typify the mountain spirit—a freedom of spirit that knows no superior save God" and acknowledges "the soil from which they sprang" as the source of their "true feeling for beauty." The last paragraph concludes with more than a hint of prescience, "We leave it to the reader to recognize the value of investment in such potential genius."

Of this group several stood out in Harry Kroll's mind. "As a student," Kroll wrote of Stuart, "he was absorbed in creative writing and literature. . . . I don't remember that he ever talked of anything but writing and reading poetry. Our little group of so-called creative writers met two nights a week down at Avery Hall, presumably for an hour a session. Actually we knew no hours. We'd read and talk and mutter and argue for two hours, or into half the night. Just talking, sitting in the classroom awhile and then going out and lying on the campus grass under the elms and hackberries and stars, murmuring this and that, Stuart in his jerky Kentucky eloquence, Roland Carter in his measured ecclesiastical manner, Louise McCamy in her cultured voice. . . . Stuart might bring up a word. 'Isn't that a beautiful word?' He might remember a name from a lichened tombstone back in his Plum Grove. 'Isn't that a good name?' He might stare through the branches of the trees at Thunder Mountain. 'It would make a poem.' He would talk perhaps of his toil in the steel mills, and what a laboring steam locomotive looked like on a zero morning, pouring smoke and steam against an icy sky. 'It had drama. There's a poem there.' He wrote it, I remember, and it was published in a railroad magazine."[3]

In 1928, Jesse Stuart published at least one poem in *Palo Verde* and another in *The Kentucky Folk-Lore and Poetry Magazine*. During the period until September of 1929 he was frequently published: seven poems in *The Blue and the Gray*, one partial reprint in *The Railsplitter*, two poems in *American Poet*, one in *American Poet, 2*, two in the Bristol *Herald-Courier* (one a reprint), and one in *Sonnet Sequences*. In addition, by the summer of 1929 he signed a contract with a Howe, Oklahoma, publisher to print his first book of poems, *Harvest of Youth;* to be published in August 1930, it would carry a number of reprints and revisions of the LMU years. "This was," Stuart later recollected, "an exciting time in my life."[4]

At Harrogate the author was known both as "Stuart" and as "Jesse." Inez Williams, "Most Attractive Girl" in the 1929 yearbook *Railsplitter*, inscribed her photograph in the poet's copy,

> Jesse,
>> Please don't drop by the side of
>> the road any memories that you may
>> have of me. I shall always remember
>> you.
>>> Just,
>>> Inez

Fred Fennell, a fellow member of Gamma Lambda Sigma and circulation manager of *The Blue and Gray* under Stuart's editorship, wrote in his editor's yearbook, "I shall always remember you for your literary achievements. Also you always had one of the opposite sex near you."

If the LMU years were times of hard work and hard study seared with creative energy, they were also charged with extracurricular activities, friendships and courtships, and good old-fashioned fun. He wrote of the feats of the Debate Club, composed of such talented students as Elmer Heaberlin, Ernest W. Fields, John A. Ivey, Paris Houston, Fred Fennell, Theodore Elmer Cox, and Edgar Beverly. In literary fields he competed with James Still, Roland Carter, Lawrence Edwards, Worley M. Hughes, Don West, Winnie Palmer, Iva Daugherty, Louise McCamy, Ida Mink, Katherine Harris, and the eldest member of Professor Kroll's journalism class, Mrs. Bessie Anderson. He went on hiking parties and climbed the Pinnacle with such students as Edith "Bill" Jones, no mean poet and writer herself, and Mabel Adams, a talented painter, during the fall semester of 1926. In Jesse Stuart's photograph albums are the likenesses of such close LMU friends as Ernest Fields, Mason Dorsey Gardner, and Elmer Heaberlin who put in their stints as his roommates. He somehow found time to belong to the Student Volunteer Band, dedicated to Christian service, with Rand Boring, Edith Rogers, Calberta Baird, Hattie Atkinson, Pace Davis, and Ida Maudlin. At the edges of the wooded mountain slopes north of the water tank, he and Elsie West either photographed each other or had their youthful poses snapped into immortality in a field of pasture daisies. Of these daisies the author wrote, "They looked like blooming fields of white cotton."

Lawrence Edwards met Jesse Stuart in the fall of 1927 and remembers seeing him on campus "conversing with verve and gusto." He would be "probably on his way to the library . . . or to the toolshed." Edwards recalled Stuart's "yellow-paper littered room." Elmer "Heab" Heaberlin, one of those who, along with Mason Dorsey Gardner, helped the poet with his math, saved some of the comic epitaphic verse his roommate left on the floor or bed, or gave him to read and "just forgot about." One could have been written about a tall fellow student who gorged on condiments in the dining hall:

Within this mound lies Judas Rickles.
White-robed, gloved hands, he sleeps securely.
He left this world by overeating pickles,
Six-two, thumbs down, black-haired and curly.

Another could have been directed toward his biology professor, Frank C. Grannis.

Here lies in a pine box Petroleum Flanagan
Beneath these cockleburrs and thin crabgrass.

He proved apes were descendants of the man
And that he was brother to the ass.

In Professor Grannis' class, dissection was for him a dreaded chore, and he was always grateful to Lucille Jordan, who "cut up frogs for me."[5] In truth, she did more than that. On some mornings at their table in the dining room, she noticed that "he would look as if he hadn't had enough sleep, and he wouldn't be talkative." More than once he "might, before the meal was over, slip into my lap some manuscripts and say in a low voice, 'I want you to read these when you get upstairs. Tell me what you think about them.'" She liked his work and recalled many years later having read "Nest Egg." Lucille Jordan was a science major with a combined assistantship in biology and home economics. Jesse often came by the science building, even on winter evenings, on his way to the dining room. If Lucille had not finished the slides and preparation for the next day's laboratory, her upstairs light would be on. He would come in and wait for her to walk over to the dining room with him. She always believed that he did not want her to walk alone across the campus. "He never said it, but his actions proved it." She was like a sister to him and he was comfortable with her. One such night he came in and sat backward in a straight chair, with his hand on the top rail and his chin on his hand. On the shelf in front of him and behind her was a jar containing a human fetus. "He sat there in a deep study of the figure in the jar, and finally said, 'We certainly ought to love our mothers.'" She made no comment, and in a little while they went on to the dining room.

He began working in the campus kitchen during his sophomore year and fell out with the head waiter, one "Spence Fillis" in *Beyond Dark Hills*, and the two fought it out in the presence of the matron of the dining room. The man picked up a chair and drew it back, but Jesse hit him first just below the ear with his fist. A vicious fight ensued. Fillis was a short, tough man, and the muscular Kentucky sophomore had his hands full. Jesse's reach proved decisive after Fillis hit him with the broad side of a bread knife across the heart. With a blow reminiscent of the one with which he had floored the Felty boy at Cane Creek over two years before, Jesse stood on his toes and "threw" a punch so hard, he later wrote, that he ripped his shirt "across the shoulder." The matron, wielding a poker, tried to stop the fight. "A man fighting a boy! You ought to be ashamed." The knock-down-drag-out ended when Fillis could not get up. His eyes were blacked, but Jesse's hands were "bursted open" and his "wrists strained."

Of that night, Lucille Jordan recalls that she and Jesse had planned to go with other students for a mountain outing; she went with a group of them down to the dining room where they were to meet Jesse when he got off work. He was late and finally the others went on, leaving Lucille to wait. In a little while he came out the side entrance. "He was quite frustrated, I could tell." Although he had tried to straighten his clothes, they were messed up, "and he had been roughed up . . . though I later found that Henry Willis was in worse shape." On the way back down the mountain that night he told her about the fight: "An insult to a girl had triggered his reaction. It was a fight in her defense, because the girl didn't have a brother there to defend her. He tried to defend the girl's honor."

Although other girls' reputations may have been impugned by Fillis, the one that apparently precipitated the battle was, ironically, the hostess of Jesse's own dining table, Lucille Jordan herself. Jesse's quiet response to the events of the evening apparently succeeded in keeping the offending information from her, just as he would have protected his own sisters.

Questioned years later about whether the fight was real, Stuart replied with surprise, "Did it take place? It sure as hell did."

"Just the way you describe it?"

"I whipped him over that kitchen finally."

The "block of a man," Henry Willis, apparently liked to bully the girls at the Norton Hall dining room. When word of Stuart's feat in whipping him got around, as Stuart later remembered, "All these girls tried to buy me ice cream or Cokes or something, because he had been so mean to the girls."

The feverish writing, publishing, and conflict were much in mind when Kroll wrote of Stuart years later, "I recollect him as a powerful, muscular lad, quick on the draw with a double fist, and glib with the most amazing flow of poetry I ever listened to from a human mouth." Kroll recalled, too, that the youth had done much reading. "He knew them all, had read them all, and his memory had blotted up ten thousand poetic words and phrases. Keats, Shelley, Byron, Robert Burns—his favorite poet . . . for certain obvious reasons; Whittier, Robert Frost— they were all in his blood and bone. In addition, he had an unerring eye for form and color in field and hill; and a flavorsome appreciation of people as he met and loved or hated them—and he did both with a right good will."

After the fight, Jesse thought surely he would be expelled, and "I had my trunk packed." But Kroll intervened. During some kind of official conference, Kroll "came down there all flustered. You know, that big man, wearing a big overcoat. And he said, 'I'll get the best lawyer out of Knoxville.' He said, 'Hell, he's not leaving here. You bring any of these damned boneheads here, like Henry Willis, and you put them up against somebody that's got some sense like Stuart!' " At one point, Jesse recalled, "Kroll's language got even more colorful. He got so angry he said, 'I'll see that that s.o.b. gets off this campus,' and 'I'll tear this school apart.' Apparently, the administration got afraid of Kroll"; but both Willis and Stuart were allowed to stay on, although the school officials apparently left the decision of whether or not the "dining room boss" would be allowed to remain at LMU up to Jesse. "Let him stay," Jesse decided. "He won't bother me."[6]

Lawrence Edwards wrote for the student paper while Jesse Stuart was editor. He recalled that Stuart's "pals" included Don West, John Ivey, and Professor Elliot Van N. Diller, a young instructor from Harvard who had come to LMU "to practice teaching psychology and philosophy." He was, Stuart said, one of the "dollar a day" men from the East who sought genuine teaching experience. Granting that "Diller was as bright as he could be," Stuart observed that he was unsuccessful in implementing his knowledge in the violent freshman–upperclassman confrontations that took place. Jesse and his cohorts, outnumbered by a large class of rebellious mountain freshmen, first lost a tug-of-war competition arranged by Diller "to keep the hostilities from getting serious." The instructor purchased a new hatchet and arranged a ceremony at night in Democrat Hollow "that would rival the Magna Carta in England—and each side agreed and we buried that new hatchet," but Diller did not truly know the mountain boys. "The very next day fighting between us broke out again and we . . . were soundly defeated." Diller was not easily discouraged. Some variations exist among Stuart's descriptive manuscript, the more embellished short story, and the account in *To Teach, To Love,* but the author wrote in the first of these, "The professor suggested putting [a] white flag in the top of a sturdy tree— that our upper classmen use twenty-five men to take it from the tree— which they did, not leaving a branch on the tree—a battle that almost destroyed LMU's basketball team and sent several of our men to the hospital in Middlesboro, Kentucky."

When asked about where in fact he was during this battle, in the tree, watching, engaged, or where, Jesse Stuart replied, "I was *in* it! My Lord, I was in it!"

"Were you up the tree?"

"No, I was down on the ground with people sitting on me. . . . Elmer

Heaberlin came up there . . . he was in it and he started to pull the men off me, and they got him down there and they really worked him over."

The campus hostilities became the source for Stuart's "How Sportsmanship Came to Carver College," with Elliot Van N. Diller becoming the model for the foppish Professor Dixon. "What I liked about this young tall, well-dressed teacher with the hairbrush mustache was he applied his Psychology. He was a peacemaker." Even though Diller "never understood us," he concluded, the man "was on the right track."[7]

In *To Teach, To Love* the author mentions other teachers who remained vivid in his memory. Frank C. Grannis, the protozoology professor who lacked "feeling for life"; the feuding of Mme. Frances Eppinger and Dr. Lucia Danforth, who deployed their respective German and French armies of loyal students outdoors under two famous campus trees on the greensward just northwest of Duke Hall; the lovable and kind campus nurse, Ida Shifley; the handsome but bribeable education professor, W. S. Woodward, who thought two good twenty-five-cent cigars worth "a standing-up A"; and the unfortunate successor of the unforgettable Kroll, the pseudonymous Dewitt Davis, possibly suggested by English teacher G. R. Floyd.

In publishing a seven-page character sketch of Harry Harrison Kroll in *To Teach, To Love*, Jesse acknowledged the teacher's inspirational and formative influence. Certainly with more generosity and imagination than either Hemingway or Faulkner expressed toward their common mentor and friend Sherwood Anderson, Jesse Stuart caricatured his benefactor in his *Esquire* short story "The Crazy Professor." Jesse described Kroll as "a big ruddy-complexioned man," who "looked to me like some of the men I had known at the steel mills," but the "color in his face made him look more like a farmer." A native of Indiana, born of Dunkard parents, he was a graduate of Peabody College, who had originally entered as a special student, which probably meant that he had no high school diploma. He made his way through the South by working in cotton fields and by taking pictures of children on a pony. Though married with three sons and an annual salary of only twelve hundred dollars, he managed to help Jesse Stuart along with loans and odd jobs. He was "the first flesh-and-blood writer I had ever seen," Stuart wrote; and he showed Jesse the first check the youth had ever seen for short stories. Elmer Heaberlin recalled that Kroll "had Jesse writing about his life at the steel mills. . . . That was the sort of thing he wanted." As early as Jesse's sophomore year, Kroll told him to return to his country after he finished college and to write of his own people. "These are things in your own backyard that need to be written," Kroll advised.

LMU students often saw Kroll's lights burning after midnight, and they knew the reason when in 1928 he published his first novel, *The Mountainy Singer,* much to the delight of his students. The 310-page book is more a story of the Tennessee mountain country, where the Cumberlands go into Virginia, of the folkways of speech and song, of daily snatches of life in family and hill country, in schoolhouse and church than of firmly etched characters. Danny Hubbard and Shoon Westbrook are not so much fully developed characters as participants in a local-color panorama. When Kroll concentrated upon the vivid mountain scenery and the mores of his people, however, the stiffness and artificialities of his style fell aside and his characters became more believable. A hundred pages into the novel, for example, the subdued passions of the adolescent boy and womanly girl are effectively counterpointed by post-storm scenes that vividly portray nature and, in the process, passionately reveal the undercurrent of the characters' elemental stirrings. Danny sees not Shoon, but "her form pushing through the tall iron weeds in the pasture." Doubtless such authentic descriptions appealed to Jesse Stuart as he read of "the mountains darkish green-brown . . . cut out against the distance like cameos," or of descriptions of cornfields and the "drying of the dew, and blue-and-white marked with morning-glories." Perhaps he identified with the "hero's feel of the mule's ridgebone under him" as "the touch of a renewed friendship," or warmed to the easy cadences of "country store, grist-mill gossip." It was a modest creative work that struck home; according to Jesse, it was the first ever written by a teacher in the English Department while teaching at Lincoln Memorial.

When the book became the center of a local storm of controversy, most of the faculty condemning it, he was surprised. One elderly Ph.D. declared that it was "just plain sexy." Stuart reported that "men on the campus said it made them love their wives more when they read it," and "one male faculty member tore his copy of the book in two and laid both ends in the fire." Whether true or not, Jesse always believed that there was another, more destructive critic of Kroll on the faculty, "an attractive woman . . . a New Englander," he thought. "She was the type they all fell for; she could have knocked any man's eyes out. I think she was the one who got Kroll fired—so he said. She backed him up in the library and tried to possess him." However, Kroll wouldn't be possessed, "and she took it out on him. She was after him." Kroll certainly wrote Stuart as much years later, refusing to sympathize with "your sense of tragedy" at the woman's demise:

There was something ironic that she would die with a beauty device caressing her dome. For if there ever was a woman eaten out with vanity and self importance it was [she]. . . . I remember I could have had her. She practically gave me to know this one day in the library in the stacks when we were secret and alone. Mrs. Kroll says she hated me because I "spurned" her. I didn't exactly spurn her, I simply didn't accept the invitation.

"The only teacher at Lincoln Memorial in my time there with a Ph.D." was Dr. Lucia E. Danforth, Jesse wrote. She was not Jesse Stuart's teacher, but he remembered her social and academic feud with his German teacher, Mme. Frances Eppinger, whom he recalls as "a delightful, friendly teacher," a native of Dresden, Germany, who had studied at the University of Berlin. She preferred good German beer to "the sweet wine" of France, which "makes the head woozy!" The two teachers stood like Germany and France before World War II, worlds apart, and "There was no Alsace Lorraine." Whether Dr. Lucia Danforth was the faculty member who found *The Mountainy Singer* "just plain sexy," or she or some other faculty member was the chief gossipmonger in the Kroll affair is not clear, but Kroll was, according to Stuart, "eventually dismissed from his position because of his lascivious writing." The students at LMU quickly learned "that creative writing is as explosive as a stick of dynamite . . . It's dangerous!"[8]

Jesse Stuart and Barnie Greene first dated during Christmas vacation when he stayed on campus to work, and she returned early from her home at Sneedville, Tennessee, to bring him some fudge, mystifying her parents by going back so soon. She and Jesse ate at the same table in the dining room of Norton Hall, although she liked to take frequent breaks at the "Hunkstand," where Jesse joined her when he could. Social life buzzed around the sweet shop.

During spring of 1928, Barnie Greene's brother Kyle and his girl-friend picked her and Jesse up at the LMU campus for an Easter weekend visit to the Greenes' home at Sneedville, in Hancock County, Tennessee, a break from the college routine which Jesse had especially welcomed. Barnie Greene Hutchens recalls an open car, a Durant, she thinks. On the way to her home over the sixty miles of gravel road southeast of Harrogate they caught sight of "a great crowd" gathered around "a large log house," and quickly surmised that it was a funeral. "Let's stop," Jesse said, and out of politeness or curiosity, perhaps a combination of both, his hosts obliged him. Of this experience Jesse later wrote an "Autobiographical Reminiscence," which sets the scene of tragic reality out of which "Mountain Funeral," one of his finest lyrics was created:

> We could not stay about the house
>   Where so many were crying;
> We pushed on through the sobbing crowd
>   From where the corpse was lying.
>
> We walked the path behind the house
>   Among his blooming trees
> And wondered if he dreamed again
>   Of gathering fruit from these.
>
> His lank bay mules he used in plowing
>   The sandy upland loam
> Played in the barnlot willow-shaded
>   Behind his mountain home.
>
> His rusty ax stuck in the block.
>   In the furrow set his plow;
> The calloused hands that used them
>   Were cold and lifeless now.
>
> The bees he loved were working on
>   The tall wind-waves of clover;
> The evening winds he loved to hear
>   Were softly blowing over.

Barnie Greene remembers some of the same details—the yard, the willow trees and mules—but whereas Stuart writes of "a large log house," she calls "a little white weatherboard house." Of the dead man she said, "He was just a poor farmer," and added, "but Stuart probably saw a whole lot more than I did." She does not remember his writing on an envelope in the car with his pen as he relates, only the image of creative urgency. "It came to him and he just put it down. It was just born in him." Of this and other poems flowing out of his pen she remembers, "And he would read them to me. He didn't care, if you knew him that well. He is very open. Stuart is just what he is."9

In many ways, if not academically, LMU was a struggle for Jesse Stuart. His natural metabolism and the demands he placed upon his energy made him nearly always hungry. He had been pleased all along with his place in the dining room, not only because it was by Lucille Jordan, but also because more girls sat at the table, and that gave him more to eat. His job in the kitchen and dining room provided access to more food, too. Once after drying pots and pans he helped himself to a can of pork and beans, sopped the can dry with a piece of bread, and later became gravely ill. The voice of the school nurse, "pretty, thirtyish, unmarried Ida Shipley [sic]," etched the words onto his mind: "Jesse, if something happens to you, tell us who to notify." Similar to the average person's concern about wearing good, freshly laundered underwear to thwart the shame of being in an accident and revealing holey and dirty underwear on one's stunned body or corpse, he remembered thinking vaguely, "How could my poor parents get my dead body from LMU? And what would they think of their son, of whom they were so proud because he was in college, getting poisoned on a can of pork-and-beans he had stolen?" After a week he recovered. Later, he posed with Nurse Shifley in a winter snow, both smiling brightly. He cherished the photograph. "Every boy in that school was in love with her," he said. "She saved my life once."

The preceptress of Norton Hall, Mrs. B. B. Huntzinger, had trained the dining-room table hostesses to improve the boys' behavior, as Lucille Jordan subtly attempted to do at Jesse's table. At one evening meal a girl cried out loud, "Let loose of my leg, you damned old fool, Paul Sykes." The culprit suggested is Paul B. Dykes of Limestone, Tennessee, who used to date Jesse's associate editor for the *Blue and Gray*, Winnie Palmer (McDonald). The incident very likely appealed to Jesse not only because of its actual occurrence and innate humor, but also because it was an irresistible opportunity to play a joke on the LMU yearbook editor. Yet according to his closest friend and roommate, Elmer Heaberlin, "Jesse was innocent [then], and he just wasn't knowledgeable about a lot of things that maybe other college kids would know . . . until after he got through college." To illustrate, Heaberlin said, "Ten of us ate at [the] table. . . . One day I was sitting at the upper end, and Jesse was at the very lower end. A whole line of girls was in between us, and Jesse hollered up, 'Heab, what does pregnant mean?' I just laughed and said, 'Wait till we get to the room!' And he was a sophomore in college!"

Heaberlin enjoyed kidding his hometown buddy. "When Jesse was out for track—he ran cross-country—he got quite concerned about a breaking out on his legs, spots on his legs, and I rubbed it in. . . . I told him, 'Jess, you've got the plain old zip.' I coined that for VD. His eyes get wide open when he really takes something in. He got very serious and very concerned if he thought you were telling him the truth. It was probably just an allergy or diet or something, but he was sensitive about anything like that—spots on his legs—still is!" Heaberlin laughed. "He always ran to Miss Shifley. She took care of him, yes, from the time he got sick."

Yet Jesse was so fascinated with words that he was not always sensitive to the context of his language. "We'd kind of kid each other," Heaberlin recounted, "and use off-color terms, as college boys do. When we'd get ready to go someplace, I'd say, 'Jess, let's urinate first' and we'd go. Well, one time we were at the nurse's office, and after he saw Miss Shifley and we got ready to leave, he says to me—She was standing right there!—'Come on, Heab, let's urinate,' and started for the john. Miss Shifley just smiled when we left. We were still dumb kids."

Having confidence in Lucille Jordan, Jesse often came to her with his problems. Sometimes it was a simple thing, the loan of a quarter; but he also sought her advice in more sensitive matters, such as his table manners, "what fork to use, some little thing" that might have worried him. When all was said and done, the upshot of her advice to him was "just be yourself and be natural." She perceived something in his behavior that declared itself, "and that was really *real* and anything else would be superficial and insincere. And there wasn't anything insincere in Jesse, and I think that was what I recognized." Later he told her that the advice "had helped him somewhat."

She remembered that he was "perfectly free in whatever he did," and what he did often carried with it a kind of "natural" appropriateness, if not always a conventional dignity. "Kroll was his ideal," of course. Jesse used to go to his little white clapboard house before he knew much about Strauss and Beethoven, and sit on Kroll's doorstep and listen to his record player. She recalls "Black Is the Color of My True Love's Hair," "Barbara Allen," and the Scottish ballads, such as "Flow Gently, Sweet Afton." That was "the real stuff," he thought then. She remembered reading somewhere that Jesse Stuart would later regret not having written music. "I thought that odd because *all* of his writings are musical; I mean rhythmic. I remember when I first noticed his walking or when he was just walking by himself, his motions were musical, rhythmic. He had music in his soul and it expressed itself in his physical moves. It was a half-dancing-like step—just energetic, expressive."

Lucille Jordan's advice was as applicable to his writing as to his table manners. A *Blue and Gray* editorial entitled "Forever Free," though unsigned, is one of several on the page in the prolific senior's editorial style. It amplifies not only Lucille Jordan's observation that he was "perfectly free" in what he did, but also Barnie Greene's comment that writing "was just born in him":

> Writing is one form of vocation, or play that will allow any person to be free as the wind. You once get started to writing and the urge will carry you onward, capturing most of your time, but leaves you with the satisfaction of having accomplished something. It helps you in school work, knowing how to take the thought from a book and rearrange it into your own style of words which will make a new idea of it. So, why not write? It will make you free.

Free to live and to write, Jesse perceived humor naturally even in ordinarily somber situations. The Student Volunteer Band took on the mission of helping an old lady at Cumberland Gap, as Lucille Jordan remembers. The woman in need was a miner's widow. Her son and husband had gone to work in the Kentucky mines and they never came home again:

> She lived right there in a little shack on the railroad in Cumberland Gap. She had no stove and no window, and [our] group that found such needs collected money and bought her a stove and put in one little window so she could have daylight, especially on the winter days. [We] went over there on a Sunday to give her a Bible, too. She put the Bible in a pillowcase in a box and pushed it under her bed. So when we were there, we said, as customary, "Aunt Mary, we would like to read from the Bible." She could neither read nor write. "Oh, yes," she said, and pulled that Bible out, and we read to her and were about ready to start back to the campus and were outside her door. She had young chickens that were feathered out, and they were roosting in the corner of the chimney. She told us they were disappearing, but she finally found the problem. It was, she explained, this big rat that was catching them. And she said, very definitely with her finger pointing at us, "I'm going to kill that son-of-a-bitch!"

"And with that Jesse fell down on the ground and rolled and laughed. When he laughed, he laughed *all over*. It was the only language she knew, of course. That was her vocabulary, and she found it strange that a college boy would get that kind of reaction."

Barnie Greene Hutchens remembers Jesse Stuart as "a real jolly, happy person. He was clean-cut, hard-working." She thought a moment and remarked that he could be serious, too. "His eyes," she said, "were a kind of bluish gray." She laughed, recalling "how he peered at you when he looked at you—real serious, you know, and he would squint his eyes." She laughed again. Winnie Palmer McDonald recalled that "Jesse had a twinkle in his eye. He always looked like he was thinking of something pleasant and funny . . . or up to something."

Considering the flurry of Jesse's college activities, it may be difficult to remember that most of his time in fact was taken up with working his way through school, going to classes, and writing. "Now he was popular," Winnie Palmer McDonald pointed out. "Everybody liked him, but he wasn't somebody who partied a lot or would have won a popularity contest. I don't think he ever had an enemy. He was very outgoing, an extrovert, never saw a stranger, never ill at ease . . . no matter who it was. Nobody ever intimidated Jesse in any way. He was a person who said what he thought. . . . An extreme individualist."

After Jesse Stuart and Barnie Greene went their separate ways, Joe Atkins in his column "Joker Joe's Jabbers" wanted to know "if Jesse Stuart is fickle, or just likes variety?" Under "Things That Never Happen" he considered such impossibilities as "Prof Diller without his mustache," "all the boys being permitted to spend Wednesday at Norton Hall," and "Jesse Stewart [sic] neglecting his work." The work, his studies, his social life were all somehow tied in with his absorbing creative interests. According to Earl Hobson Smith, "He fell in love with the prettiest girls; but, true to a campus poet's nature, the love affair ended in new sheaves of poems."

As Edith Greene had become the Maria Sheen of his high school inspiration, Barnie Greene would become the Wilma O'Shean of *Man with a Bull-Tongue Plow*. So she filtered through his romantic imagination, though not, perhaps, without a few scars to try his memory in years to come. Before he left LMU in 1929 he wrote "this sonnet for Bonnie," redolent of the valley mists at Harrogate in which their youthful love had bloomed:

Do you remember April evenings when we
Tripped side by side on tender orchard grasses
Beneath the spreading cloud-white apple tree?
Do you remember night birds' fluttering passes
Into the shower-drenched wind-quivering leaves?
And the cloud-patched sky, the wry-faced moon,
And sleeping valley mists, do you remember? It grieves
Me to forget—Our lives broke then—broke soon,
Too soon we drifted down corridors of time
With new lovers following after. And now,

The grass is dead, the winter's rainy slime
Marks jet-black each leafless apple bough.
Can you remember a dread that banished?
A love that faded? A joy that vanished?

The last issue of *The Blue and Gray* Jesse edited lists him as a guest of honor at the Beta Kappa Annual Banquet, along with Margaret Brooks, a slender girl from Alabama he dated his senior year, Chester Hobbs, and Gertrude Bales. He must have gained some consolation from the outcome of the faculty vote honoring the senior class members in several categories. The faculty members selected Jesse Stuart as the "most original" student; he also shared honors with Ralph Shanks, Helen Hatfield, and White Orr as "most rebellious student." Although he was initially distressed from his near shutout from class-elected honors, the record does not reveal that he let his feelings openly show. The tone of his editorial farewell is undiscouraged, even gracious. He was complimentary toward his staff for their cooperation. Aware of the paper's audience, he wrote, "We get more enjoyment when we know that you enjoy reading it." His poetic conclusion is a blend of traditional hope and resignation: "So we as old staff members pass the torch on to the new student writers of this college. Keep it burning. So now, the year is at an end. Let the fire darken. Let the book close."

"From the first," Winnie Palmer McDonald recalls, "Jesse Stuart knew exactly where he was going." Was she surprised that he became a successful writer? "Not at all surprised," she replied, recalling his ambition. In everything he did, he seemed to be reaching above himself, trying to be better than he was. In so doing he had established something of his own identity as a writer and a poet, and he did not hesitate to let his fellow students know it. Even at this early time of his development, he had evinced an uncanny ability to perceive detail straight from life with a deep-down, close-to-the-soil validity, as he demonstrated in "Mountain Funeral" then, or later in Battle Keaton's beard. Such responses to reality did not simply emerge from his consciousness; rather, they were compelled forth. As Walt Whitman did not allow any artificial barriers or false modesty to stand between him and what he said and wanted to say, Jesse's awareness sometimes came through so strongly that, as he strove to express it, it appeared to some who did not know him well enough as conceit. "He was open," Barnie Greene explained. Apparently he felt good about himself "as a writer," she emphasized. "He wouldn't have made it if he hadn't." Mrs. McDonald agreed that

Jesse Stuart's youthful self-awareness sometimes came on so strongly that some resented it or misconstrued it as conceit. "He would say just what he meant." Earl Hobson Smith, however, saw no exaggerated estimate of his own abilities or self-importance in young Stuart, and maintained that "Jesse's special, straightforward way of expressing himself is one of his most attractive personal traits. . . . Those who mistake his directness for conceit often miss his true humility."

Before he graduated he had ample opportunity to exercise his humility, too. Although he received a few of his classmates' votes as "Man Done Most for LMU," Jesse Stuart was shut out of all other honorific categories by the votes of his own 1929 class. Mrs. McDonald attributed this situation to a little period of youthful jealousy. "You see, when we were having all these poems published in the writing classes, there were some of the boys who resented it, and they resented Jesse, and they resented our poems." Three or four of the boys, she thought, cut one of his poems out and pinned it on the outside of his door one night, and some fights nearly broke out. "That's why, the last year I was there, I quit writing." She laughed, musing. "But that didn't affect Jesse. He could have cared less. They just resented his ability."

If talent was doing what it could that spring, genius had been doing what it must. Within two weeks the school paper carried the caption JESSE STUART WINS HONORS over the byline of Don E. Thomas. The piece details Stuart's winning two of three first places and one of three second places in a creative writing contest. His story "Red Whiskers" and poem "My Loves Will Remain When I Have Passed" were the firsts, and his short story "Kindness" was awarded second place. He had all through the year been active in other areas, too, including athletics and dramatics. The 1929 *Railsplitter* depicts him in uniform with the winged "L" on his jersey. The legend reads, "Jesse is a man who believes in hitting everything hard. In track he trains hard. While the other boys are running on the cinders, he is trotting on the Ridgeroad [sic] where the going is hard. Jesse is an endurance man who can be banked on." But Hoyt Morton of LaFollette, Tennessee, veteran "hurdler and . . . hard runner," was more impressed with Stuart's courage and creative flair than his athletic prowess, writing across his own photograph next to the editor's, "Jessie [sic] remember the day we met in the hayfield. I shall always remember you as the poet. Keep it up Jessie I am for you." Hoyt "Hog" Morton had good reason to remember the hayfield. During Stuart's initiation to farm labor just after his arrival on campus, "Hog" had contrived a joke with other boys, mimed a violent "fit," and attacked the Kentucky

"Yankee," hoping to send him scurrying. But Stuart sidestepped the charge, hit "Hog" with a pitchfork, and left him stunned on the ground. Hoyt Morton later became the Claymore Jones of *Beyond Dark Hills.*

The prior winter athletic events and farmwork had given way to cultural activities. The *Mountain Herald* carried an article from the *Middlesboro Daily News* noting that members of the Woman's Club, agog over the forthcoming concert of Madame Schumann-Heink, were recipients of a "delightful entertainment" from LMU students, among whom was Jesse Stuart. He read "a group of original poems" for the ladies and then acted in a one-act play, "The Dust of the Road," along with fellow students Louise McCamy, John Ivey, and Hubert Kirby.

Jesse received an invitation to the Commencement Exercises in the Duke Hall of Citizenship scheduled for June 4, but his Bachelor of Arts degree was not officially conferred until completion of the summer session, August 22, 1929. The *Railsplitter* featured his poem "L.M.U. Walkways" below a photograph of two young women standing on a road in a patch of tree-filtered sunlight. The oval senior picture of Jesse Stuart of Riverton, Kentucky, shows him in a dark striped suit with a bowtie, his hair neatly combed, his face young and purposeful, the eyes fixed as though on a distant, half-dreamed goal. For a working student his campus achievements seem surprisingly numerous and varied: member of Gamma Lambda Sigma 1926–1929, Vice-President in 1926, Secretary in 1927, Treasurer in 1928, and Art Critic in 1929; and member of the Glee Club in 1927. In addition to achieving publication honors and a letter in track, he was a member of the Kentucky Club, 1927–1929 (Vice President in 1928), and a member of the Student Volunteer Band for two years (Treasurer in 1927 and Secretary in 1928). In 1927/1928 he had been a member of the YMCA, and he joined the Dramatic Club in 1929. A member of the Writer's Club the same year, he had also written for *The Blue and Gray* throughout the three years of his college career, and is listed as Editor-in-Chief for the years 1928 and 1929. Below his list of student achievements is this observation:

> He does not need the spectacles of books to read nature. He does not need the precedent of others['] intellect to be intellectual. He conquers adversity with the same zeal that he enjoys prosperity. In this aspiring, determined man genius does not lie dormant. In the future Stuart must inevitably occupy the Pinnacle with America's greatest poets.

The quotation under Jesse's biographical note: "What Price Glory?" One nice irony of American literary history is that on the same page with

Stuart's senior picture and biographical note are those of the Senior Editor of the *Railsplitter* of 1929, James A. Still of Fairfax, Alabama.[10]

From the time Jesse had come to Harrogate, he had found it necessary to assert a self-protective aggressiveness—in the hayfield from the first day, at the rock quarry when he had hit the overbearing student foreman "flat-wise against the ribs" before walking off the job, and in the dining room with Henry Willis. Jesse was ready "to take on" another student, this time one who had criticized and mocked his poems, but the boy backed down when Jesse invited him outside behind Duke Hall of Citizenship. He had always had to defend himself, and though he had not expected so much of it at college, it had come as no real surprise. Still, he had mixed feelings about college.

There were other ambivalences more difficult to resolve. As editor of the campus paper, he had sometimes helped write the captions for photographs that found their way into yearbooks and albums, like "Grant-Lee in Blossom Time" and "Grant-Lee Hall Where College Men Live." Handsome old building though it was, it was the same hall, as Elmer Heaberlin related, in which the two had been sleeping in an iron bed when they got "an awful dose of bedbugs." They attached a hose to the hot water faucet of the shower room and jetted hot water into every crack and crevice. "We scalded everything . . . the bedsprings!" One time canned beef had been served and not only he, but virtually the whole school body had been stricken so severely with stomach cramps and diarrhea that the sewage system was flooded and the toilets failed to flush in both the boys' and girls' dormitories. Bedbugs, bad canned food, and ptomaine poisoning were not exclusive to Lincoln Memorial, he knew, but he had not expected these things.

Another surprise was the quality of teaching at college. Although many small colleges had faculties not necessarily superior to that of LMU in the 1920s, perhaps few had professors like W. S. Woodward, "tall and straight as a ramrod with a Gary Cooper face," who, so Jesse wrote, had raised his grade in an education course from that dubious range between a B + and A − to "a standing-up A without any trimmings" for the bribe of two twenty-five-cent cigars. Whereas most of his teachers at Greenup High School had been "outstanding," he had experienced only two who were "great" and "inspirational" at LMU—Harry Kroll and Earl Hobson Smith. He believed he had received better training in the four years at Greenup than in the three years and two summers at Harrogate.

It was the dismissal of Kroll, however, that had crystallized his deepest dissatisfaction, although Kroll was only the tip of the iceberg.

Others were swept out or had to resign. Outspoken Don West, away on a visit in Georgia to see his sick mother, was sent a telegram saying he was not to return to campus; but West did return, at first hiding out in a cabin where Stuart took him stolen food daily and delivered letters from West's girlfriend and future wife, Mabel Adams. West was eventually reinstated. "It hurt me to see these teachers go," Stuart wrote in *Beyond Dark Hills*. Yet he learned that even academic wars ended in some peace and, if not necessarily in forgiveness, at least with hopeful stoicism. Kroll had almost taken Chancellor John Wesley Hill out with him, but after he had lost and Jesse came by to tell him goodbye, Kroll told him, "Some day this school will bloom like a flower." In the months to follow, though, "the place seemed empty after they had gone."

Thus the feeding of the young poet's idealism was sporadic at best, and all the high moments that could be salvaged seemed to be offset with so much cry and so little wool. In the bitterly fought Herbert Hoover–Al Smith campaign in the fall of 1928 the new LMU labor boss, J. D. Walker, deputy sheriff of Claiborne County, Tennessee, a Democrat, had promised the large young work force of the college relief from their chores on election day. In *To Teach, To Love*, the author recounts how he and the others were crowded against the railings of a truckbed and taken to vote for Hoover, first to Cumberland Gap, then to Arthur, another voting place in the county. Hustled back to campus, the students were fed a hasty lunch over the objections of the argumentative Henry Willis, then transported to Sewanee to vote for the third time that day. Election day had been "harder than campus labor," but Hoover carried Claiborne County by a huge plurality. "There was never a protest or a word said about it," Stuart wrote. "It passed over like a bright autumn wind blowing over the multicolored hills in Claiborne County, Tennessee."

Pride had struggled, too, in the depths of his poverty. When he and Elmer Heaberlin returned to Harrogate in 1927 from a summer of hard work in the steel mills at Ashland where they had just earned funds sufficient to pay their college expenses, they both swallowed their pride and went out to "the barrels"—clothes sent for LMU students from all over the nation. "We went out and went through everything in the barrel," Stuart recalled, "and we decided if we had to wear clothes like what was in those barrels, we'd go back to the steel mills." Some of Stuart's dissatisfaction, doubtless, was the result of his own recognition of the wide contrasts between the faculty and students at Harrogate and those he imagined to be at the universities of his adolescent dreams—Harvard, Virginia, and Vanderbilt.

Stuart's answer to the world he encountered was not so much an aesthetic analysis through writing; rather, he possessed even then an ability to keep one foot planted in earthy substance, the other in the more ephemeral territory of an ever-conscious, seemingly childlike innocence. Somewhat as Mark Twain with Huck Finn, Jesse Stuart guided his Shan Powderjay and other personae, including himself as narrator, into the core of life, playing, learning, adventuring, living whatever human experience lay to hand, no matter how outrageous. As bruising to burgeoning idealism as the election experience may have been—in his private feelings he admitted to being "scared" afterward—he had other crises in his life and used them as a basis for a short story eventually published in *Esquire.*

Jesse could undergo such experiences and remain seemingly involved, yet stand aside when involvement may have been personally destructive, and do so with a kind of wide-eyed innocence, inwardly registering every detail so that he could ultimately channel his outrage into literary art. This suggests not only a remarkable artistic intuition to deal with the material of life at hand, a kind of instinctive negative capability, but also underlines one of Stuart's singular traits: When he chose to focus the frame of his creativity upon a subject, he possessed the ability to survive life's bitterest, most disillusioning experiences and, more to the point, to make of even the gall of reality one artistic triumph after another.

With a nature so constituted, it should not be a total surprise that, when Jesse added up the balance sheet, he discovered through the cloud of ambivalence a positive image of himself, of what he sought to be: "I wanted to make LMU proud of me—this small school, without money or prestige, that had taken me in off the road where I was a hitch-hiker. . . . I had tried other, better-known colleges that had refused me entrance. It was Lincoln Memorial that had given me a chance. I would be eternally grateful." The college at Harrogate had been "a second home to me. It had been my second mother." He had found in those ambivalent years, after all, a safe if ungentle refuge for his youth; a torchlight in the valley mists to light a consuming creative urge that already had him in its grasp and would not let him go.[11]

5

"Harvest of Youth"
1929–1930

————◇————

Jesse finished his undergraduate work during the summer quarter of 1929, and his B.A. degree was conferred Thursday, August 22. He seems to have remained on campus to receive his degree, but was home again by Sunday, August 25, one among less than a half-dozen native college graduates of Greenup County, which then had a population of approximately twenty-three thousand. That year his poems continued to appear almost monthly in small literaries. "Sin" came out in *Anthology of Magazine Verse for 1929*, edited by W. S. Braithwaite and published in New York. "Desire" and "Hurt Not the Proud" were in the April issue of *American Poet*, and "Like a Strong Tree" appeared in the June issue of *American Poet, 2*. "Mountain Farmer" was printed in the *Bristol Herald-Courier* on July 14; and, appropriately for his homecoming, "My Mountain Home" was published in the September issue of *Sonnet Sequences*.

That his literary activities on campus were well known is evident in several autographed inscriptions in his 1929 *Railsplitter,* such as these: from Grace Bolton, "I shall always remember you as 'the poet' "; from Ralph B. Stout, "You are to be complimented in that you are a genious [sic] in poetical ways"; and from Merlin Gillfillin, "I shall always remember you for your literary achievements." His roommate Elmer Heaberlin, having acquired no mean reputation as a debater, declaimed in the back of Jesse's annual, "I believe our Alma Mater is sending forth into the world a poet, a man, a person of whom she will someday be proud and when that day comes . . . I shall arise and rejoice with you in your great hour." Jesse was more than pleased to have his poems "collected" in Braithwaite's *Anthology,* writing to James Still, it "doesn't take money to get them there either and it's a real collection." Jesse was walking in the wind.

Yet he was under no illusions about what he needed to do to make a living. He left Harrogate with only ten dollars in his pocket, owing the college one hundred dollars (and fifty cents). This time he had put decals on his suitcase before he hitchhiked, but a thunderstorm caught him in the mountain darkness of eastern Kentucky. As young Ben Franklin had once sought a Philadelphia meetinghouse in which to spend a night, the mountain youth turned to shelter in a country church. He ran along the highway as the rain poured and lightning flashed, illuminating "a thousand white tombstones" in the churchyard. The door was locked so he entered the ivy-covered building through a window and found an organ cover to lie under as "the hailstones tattooed on the windowpanes and water streamed down them and shut my visage from these ghosts." There he reminisced about such college friends as Don West, Jimmie Still, Barnie Greene, Margaret Brooks, and Louise McCamy. He wondered about Harry Kroll, and about what would happen to Dean Charles D. Lewis, who had admitted him to the college that "Abraham Lincoln had asked General Howard to establish for 'his people.' "

Nostalgic reflections led to contemplation of his future. The lightning flashes around the church seemed to emphasize his awareness that "America was on the boom." Like no few other teachers before and since, upon graduation he was certain of one thing: "I wouldn't teach school." Seemingly "opportunities for a young ambitious man willing to work and to strive were unlimited." Two of the last three summers he had worked at the American Rolling Mills in Ashland, and he believed he should return to where a job in steel awaited him.

There he had found a lot of good material for writing, too, and not only about the steel mills. One short weekend he had left Ashland on a Saturday to visit his Uncle Marion on Twelve Pole Road near Ceredo-Kenova, West Virginia. A longtime U.S. marshal, his uncle "was about six feet four, had a steady cold blue eye, walrus mustache and was a man without humor." In the Sunday morning paper, Jesse read a news article about a religious sect that planned to meet that very night. Those people would "take up a 'dead sister and she would live again. She would walk and breathe.' "

"Uncle Marion, I want to stay another night," he said. "I like it so well here. And I want to go and see them dig this woman up, to see her 'live again.' "

His uncle put on his "specs" and read the article. "They're crazy people," he said. "If I had a warrant to arrest them I'd like to put all in the cooler. That's where they should be."

Jesse remembered how his uncle looked straight at him with his cold blue gaze. "I wondered if he might not think his nephew, who was a college student, wasn't a little crazy too." His uncle relented, finally saying, "If you want to see this crazy tomfoolery of ignorant crazy people . . . all right."

It was the kind of local color Jesse was after. He journeyed to the rural graveyard on foot. "And here I found drama of its kind. I saw people the likes of whom I never knew existed. . . . an unusual story enacted before my eyes." But Kroll did not think the story had a strong ending, and Jesse was discouraged from sending it in to a magazine for several more years.

His first Christmas at LMU, in December 1926, he had become homesick and, with a dollar borrowed from Don West, thumbed his way back to Greenup for a reunion with his family. Images of "winter oak trees" and "gray December skies" ran through his mind, the delighted surprise of his mother who was saving him the chicken backs he liked so well, that last Christmastime gathering with his family—James with a new .22 rifle, Mary and her new dress, Glennis and her doll, his father's new leather coat. He had talked with his father as they walked over the farm hunting rabbits one day, and he had known again "the real sweetness of living down against the soil." That following spring of 1927 he and Elmer Heaberlin had come home together, taking the train to Ashland, then catching a Blue Ribbon Line bus down to Wurtland. Elmer would always go home by way of his mother's Nazarene Church on old Highway 23 and Virginia Street. Up in front of the church was an exhibit Jesse photographed in his mind—"things a-hanging up there where they'd taken them off sinners . . . [brass] knucks and pistols, and down below a bottle of gin or liquor. And we'd go in that church, and Elmer would go up into the pulpit and say a silent prayer." Then they would walk on to the house on Heaberlin Road, where Elmer's mother would take them into the center of the living room and there, by a little table, get down on her knees and "start prayin' that her son and his classmate had returned from school . . . two boys who had gone out to try to improve themselves, and the Lord had been good to them and brought 'em back, and she prayed the awfulest prayer you ever heard there." It was the first time, Jesse later acknowledged, "I was remembered in a prayer because I had gone to college," and he was impressed. After the prayer, "We'd get up and go to the table, and we'd have minced pie and coffee. For our return, every time, that's what we got."

For Jesse to get home, he had to hike on down to Riverton and take the familiar old path up Academy Branch and over the high hills to his father's farm. That spring his mother took him out for a walk, as his father had the Christmas before; as they went through her garden they talked. She told him about Brother Tobbie's preaching against education: "He got up and preached . . . on mothers sending their children away to college where they would be educated right for hell. He looked right at me when he said it. He knowed you was away, you know. Oh, he just made me so mad!" Jesse listened closely, and asked if Brother Tobbie had repeated his outrageous pulpit story about receiving "the call" while he was mowing hay. "Yes," his mother continued, "he did go over that old story again about the Lord calling him to preach. . . . I got tickled when he said he just fell off the mowing machine like he was shot when the Lord called him." If he had told that story at Lincoln Memorial, Jesse thought, the boys would have hooted at him; they would have thrown rotten eggs and said he was crazy.

Out on the farm in the evening, he and his mother had listened to the insects of the night chirring their oratorio, the aria of the whippoorwill. "Mom, you know I think the whippoorwill is the lonesomest bird I ever heard. It makes me want to cry to come back among these hills and hear a whippoorwill."

"They're not half as lonesome as a night hawk when it screams," she said.

They had walked on into the evening, talking.

Now the last long summer at LMU was over and he was spending his final night out on the road. He knew his family was proud of him, for he had "got to be something." But now he had to use his college education. Perhaps he could move up fast in steel. He had done well in college, "something like a B average," although he had "never stopped to count it up." He had learned a lot about writing, too, and now he wondered if he would ever become the writer that Harry Kroll was. There in the church his thoughts raced "until sleep came and all was nothingness."[1]

Bill Collins remembers well working in Lawson's Hardware Store in Greenup and often seeing and talking with Jesse during the years after he graduated. That summer he particularly recalls picking Jesse up and giving him a ride out toward W-Hollow. "He told me the story of sleeping out in a church, in a piano robe." Whether his friend dropped him off where Highway 1 enters W-Hollow or at the foot of the hill near Academy Branch is not clear, nor is it important; the drama of Jesse's personal story required that he focus his return on the familiar ridge path. In *Beyond Dark Hills* the first person he sees is coffin-maker and hollow-dweller "Uncle Rank Larks," neighbor Frank Sparks in fact. The old prophet of the hills greets Jesse with "I knowed you'd come back to drink of lonesome water. . . . I seen you over there one day when you was a little shaver down on your knees and bending over drinking water out'n th' crick. I said to Sam: 'Sam, that boy's not goin' to leave these hills. Look at him there with the ferns around his eyes. He's drinking lonesome waters.' " In a kind of one-man choral outpouring, Uncle Rank recounts the deaths and changes that have taken place during the graduate's absence, and the young chronicler's brain records dialect and all: "The old people just keep a-drappin' off." Among them are the efficient old German farmer, Henry Wheeler, whom Jesse calls "Annis Bealer," and the fundamentalist preacher, Brother Tobbie. According to Uncle Frank, he "wasn't nigh right with the Lord," for "he put a double-barrel shotgun to his temple and pulled both barrels . . . blowed the whole top of his head off." A virtual catalogue of the dead continues to emanate from Larks' mouth until Jesse leaves him standing by the barn.

He goes on over the ridge path, thinking, "I am going home. I shall soon be home. The trees I love are all around me now," and he feels once more his brotherhood with the beeches, dogwoods, maples, oaks, pines, and poplars. "The desolate sweep of land lies on every side. . . . I am coming back for all the good I can do in the hills." Home again—it was so good to see it—and "my folks were glad to see me there." It was the life he liked and he reflected upon it. Yet in doing so he kept his inmost feelings to himself, for "I didn't want people to know how much I loved the hills and how much I had hated them." Rebellion having run its course, submission was on the ascendant:

> It took life beyond these hills to make one love life among the hills. I had gone beyond the dark hills to taste of life. I found it sour when I went beyond where the blue rim of the hills touches the sky. I had wanted to go beyond and find out all that was there. I wanted to taste of life. I tasted of it from books and steel and the merry-go-round. It was not sweet like the life in the hills.

Doubtless his rebellion against his father, against the fifty acres that could not hold him, against the dark hills and what they represented of ignorance, poverty, body-staggering work, and primitive health facilities, against the narrow confines of Brother Tobbie's fanatical religion were all of a unit now—a darkness upon which light from the transforming experience of education could be shed, illuminating heartbreaking beauty in the shadows. After knowledge gained, the independence of making his own way, and the change that other places and people can bring to a young man, there remained the still-acknowledged devotion to father and mother and family, to the land that drew his deepest emotions, to the people who could intuit religion if not explain it, and to a God of a perception higher than he could put into words. Years later, Stuart spoke of his religious conflicts at Lincoln Memorial and of doubts among the students: "And you know I—I got afraid—if I denied there was a God that God would strike me down. I'm a hill man, and you can't find hardly a person in these hills that doesn't believe in God."

Further articulating his thoughts out of the context of Romantic literature, he was convinced that "God manifests himself in nature and in man. I know He does." In *Beyond Dark Hills,* he declared his spiritual joy in the land. "The sod puts one close to nature. Call it God, if you will." Recounting that beauty—"old orchards white in apple-blossom time, ridges of green Irish potato vines, the blue streams running between the dark hills, the lonely sounds at night. . . . Rabbits in the dead weeds and foxes barking from the ridge tops at night"—his Romantic attitude toward God was bespoken. "And I can't bear to let God pass. The worship of God is something too beautiful to pass." Once, he felt, "I wanted to make myself believe that there was no God," only to see "as my people had seen . . . the great consolation of God in the beauty of the hills." It was not the first time he had sought God in nature and found an explanation that met his needs:

> Say that God is in the wind, that God is in the dead leaves flying over the September hills in Kentucky, but don't leave God out. I once heard something about the ancient song passing deathward mournfully. It seemed to me that God was an ancient song among the minds of many people, and that he was passing deathward mournfully. But the hill people still saw God. He was the great force that drew them together. He called the inner something of their bodies, greater than flesh and bone, to walk out under the trees and pray.

The mystic and affirmative tone of this passage is juxtaposed not with his mother's greeting, but with her announcement that there is a teaching job awaiting him at Warnock, Kentucky. In *The Thread That Runs So True,* his family is "proud" and "rejoicing" upon his return, for he is a college graduate. His father is not at all receptive to Jesse's ambition to work in steel. Rather, Mick Stuart informs him of the school superintendent's holding a teaching job for him. His mother is more imperative. "Yes, go see him at once, Jesse. . . . You know I don't want you to go back to the steel mills." Resorting to pride and family tradition, both parents exhort their son to teach, his mother reminding him of her grandfather Preston Hilton, who was both preacher and schoolteacher. "I want you to teach school," she repeats. "I'm proud of you, Jesse. You're goin' to amount to something." In *Beyond Dark Hills*, however, the conversation over the teaching job is characterized by more conflict. When Jesse declares that the monthly wage of one hundred dollars "isn't any money at all," his mother responds, "It's more than any of us has ever made in this family," and she strongly advises him to take it. Further, she assumes that he *will* take it. In *To Teach, To Love* his mother asks him what he is going to do. When he answers, "I don't know," she says, "I know what you're going to do. You're going to teach school. . . . There's a place waiting for you." And he wrote, "I always listened to my mother." In retrospect, then, as August turned into September in 1929, the pendulum of rebellion had begun its swing back toward submission. He would not, after all, strike hot steel again as a blacksmith in the American Rolling Mills at seven dollars a day. He would instead be a schoolteacher at one-room Warnock High School for a hundred dollars a month.[2]

Jesse Stuart tells the story of his year of teaching at Warnock High School in Part II of *Thread*. It was Robert J. Nickel, Superintendent of Greenup County Schools, whose policies Jesse was later to oppose so vigorously, who offered him the hundred dollars a month (an unusually low salary for a teacher with a bachelor's degree) to teach at "Red Hot High School," so nicknamed "because a steam engine blew up there." Though hesitant to teach algebra, he promised himself then and there to learn the subject; and in *To Teach, To Love* he takes the job, saying, "Mr. Norton, I'll be your faculty." The longer version in *Thread* is substantially the same, although the latter work employs "Winston" for "Warnock" and "Larry Anderson" for "Robert J. Nickel." In his conference with the superintendent in both works, his grades in algebra are represented as being higher than the B and D he had actually made in two quarter classes, although Jesse is careful to declare his own doubts concerning his ability to teach the subject. There is no superintendent's conference in *Dark Hills*. His mother mentions the superintendent's name as "Mr. Blair," and the time between Jesse's late-August return and the commencement of his teaching at Warnock is taken up with a series of striking local-color descriptions of the places associated with his childhood and youthful writings.

Warnock High School was a dilapidated converted stable. It had also been used as a lodge hall and was inhabited with mud daubers' and wasps' nests and the nest of a mavis before Jesse and his students cleaned the building from top to bottom. In the months to come he would take the county roads on weekends back and forth between Warnock and W-Hollow—out the W-Hollow Road to Highway 1, then south about four miles through Argillite to the Low Gap Road (now Highway 1459), northwest about two miles to the juncture of Highway 2, then west about three miles over Raccoon Hill and across Tygerts Creek to the large valley opening up around Warnock—even by present-day roads a journey of perhaps twelve or thirteen miles. He took this first journey to Warnock, so he wrote in *Thread*, in "the Reo Speed Wagon that carried mail and passengers," a roofed but sideless vehicle that rode over the dusty road like earlier stagecoaches, but more rapidly, "the only communication line between Landsburgh [Greenup] and Winston [Warnock]."

In this work the author introduces the reader to several of the fourteen students he taught that year. The first ones he met were "Snookie" and "Robin Baylor," based on the real "Snook" and Robert Taylor, sons of "Ottis and Lucretia Baylor," in fact Ott and Lucy Taylor, with whom he roomed and boarded in a two-story white frame house that still stands at Warnock. One of the memorable students was "Budge Waters," about whose awkward appearance Jesse wrote, "I'd never seen a youth in my life that looked anything like him. I'd never seen one with his peculiar actions when he walked. He used his hands to pull against the wind." He "swaggered" when he walked, too. This special child with the gifted mind and memory was based on the real Charles Rice. Others remember him well, too, how he "walked all over" and "kind of jerked his head when he walked . . . but a brilliant fellow." There was "Rena Warnock," a descendant of the pioneer family that had given the area around the Tiber River [Tygarts Creek] its name. Another was Betty (then called "Bessie") Stephens, who ten years later would wed the author's brother. These and others of the fourteen were to hold a special place in Stuart's heart because they were "good timber to work with"; they were "ambitious descendants of a landlocked people" who gave him "their best," so he gave them his best in return.

Betty Stephens Stuart recalls vividly her early impression of her young teacher. He was six feet tall and weighed about 160 pounds. "They called him Mr. Stuart. He was slender, straight as an arrow, dark complexioned with dark eyes—no," she corrected herself—"*blue* eyes. He had dark hair, parted on the side. He wore a V-neck sweater or a sweater that was buttoned, and he always had a necktie on. His expressions were serious, unless something funny would happen. Then he laughed. He sure . . . had fun with us."

That September he wrote James Still that he was teaching a branch of Greenup High School "established out in the County, eleven miles from a railroad station. I have fourteen students—intelligent youngsters and willing to work." By late October he was describing Warnock as "a paradise," writing, "My work is so easy and the children are so worthwhile that I give them all I have and love them so. They are the selected few and come for many miles to school. Some of them come eight and ten miles. One day one will ride a horse, and next day drive a Ford." He attended dances and socials in the Warnock area—"cornhuskings, apple-peelings, bean-stringings, square dances." In addition to teaching regular school subjects, he also instructed from nature's hornbook. He went rabbit and quail hunting with his students, and he taught the boys to hunt 'possums and 'coons "where the persimmons and pawpaws grew," taking special care to show them how to care for and to barter their animal pelts for money, clothes, and books.

He often went home on weekends and brought books to those students hungriest for knowledge. Leaving the Ott Taylor house one cold snowy December afternoon, when there were six inches of snow on the ground, he became lost in a snowstorm after nightfall. Hard flakes that "felt like grains of corn" blinded him in an "incessant sweep of wind." He survived the bitter night by carrying eight fodder shocks to one place, improvising from them a snug dwelling, and sharing it with the field mice and the ticking of his watch. This incident actually took place close to the present area of Greenbo Lake, about six miles by road from W-Hollow. As the author recounts in *Thread*, the next morning he stopped at Ephraim Gullet's gristmill to brush the fodder out of his hair, warm himself at a potbellied stove, and drink hot coffee before going on his way to W-Hollow. Eunice Mitchell Harper, a Greenup High School classmate, recalls that after he slept out on the hill "that night in the snowstorm in the corn shocks," he stopped by the Mitchells' home on the Low Gap Road and had coffee and breakfast.

Concerning this incident as well as others, Betty Stephens Stuart recollects that Jesse often brought books to the students at Warnock; the spot where he spent the night out in the snowstorm is on Raccoon Hill, about four miles by car from where she and James Stuart live on Raccoon Road. She also remembers that the students rode with their teacher into Greenup High School on horses, some students on mules, and took examinations at the old school building on the corner of Harrison and Perry Streets. "We hitched up our horses at the big long fence back of the old high school building." She clearly recalls the Warnock students' taking tests and Charlie Rice's winning "all kinds of contests and prizes." A local news story reported the Warnock youth's first prize in history and civics with a 94, while Greenup's Woodridge Spears took the first in literature.

Jesse was still writing every chance he got. He had made a "contract" with James Still: "I cannot write to you [except] when I place some thing in a reputable magazine," and of course, the contract worked both ways. By October 7 he had written with some pride of an acceptance—"a nice little English sonnet to come out in *Sonnet Sequences,* published by the Dreamland Press at Landover, Maryland." He had sent the poem away five months before and would not have known it had been published had he not gone home to W-Hollow and found it in some "scrap papers the kids ditched in the trash can." They had thrown the magazine away, thinking it was a circular. When he opened it to page 74, he saw in print for the first time "My Mountain Home," later to reappear in *Harvest of Youth* and *Man with a Bull-Tongue Plow.* After he drew his first check for teaching he purchased a pica typewriter and proudly typed a letter to Still: "I'm due to write you a letter." For autumn he had already placed two sonnets with *Sonnet Sequences,* other pieces in *International Poetry Magazine,* the *Kentucky Folk-Lore and Poetry Magazine, The Poet's Scroll,* and Braithwaite's *Anthology.* Not having heard from his LMU classmate in more than three weeks, he generously added in consideration of their agreement, "Still, I'm . . . going to . . . grant you permission to send me a one-cent card if you have never placed anything. I'm going to get something ahead and stay that way so when I wish I can send you a letter." About the house that served as the Warnock post office and grocery, Jesse wrote, "I sent and received more letters from the post office than anybody."

By spring he was keeping the mailman Ron Bradford and his pack horses busy on the wet roads. In April he received his first money for a published work, two dollars for a one-page article entitled "The Value of Well Kept Yards," published in *Home Circle.* He published six more poems by the summer of 1930. "Heaven Enough," a vigorously paced sonnet variation anticipating the Stuart to come, made its appearance in London in *The Spring Anthology:*

> Heaven for me will be an April field
> With an orchard wind striding gallantly.
> Heaven will be new Nature's rarest yield.
> Each tree will be a gusty rain beat tree.
> Heaven, I know, will have the wooded hills,
> White cherry sprays, one long shrill note of sun,

> The cloudless blue, the silver singing rills,
> The laughing crow . . . but not oblivion. . . .

He wrote James Still that he had been dating two girls with cars who "fell and fell hard for me here." Of the two, "one drinks and swears and yet is straight . . . the rough youthful type, carefree and happy. The other is too angelic for me. I like the rough one best for we enjoy life. Boy, I'm telling you I'm living my youth . . . proud of it too." Having broken up with Barnie Greene and Margaret Brooks, he continued, "I said I would not look at another girl but they are looking me up." He confided in Still, "I love a girl free with a kiss, not only to me but others, a lover of the wind at night, and the glare of city lights and passing crowds. . . . I rather doubt if some have loved theirs as I have mine." Whether arising out of mere confessional commentary or out of a sudden whim of epistolary imagination, the vaunting remark, when coupled with such flaring poetic flippancy as "Foreknown," leads one to speculate that his courtships in the spring of 1930 were continuing to culminate in new poems if not in durable premarital relationships:

> What is last year's rain to you
> And what is last year's snow
> Same as any tender flame
> That flares before you go?
>
> What are yesterdays to you?
> What are the songs you sing?
> A smile, a tear, maybe a sigh,
> Perhaps not anything.

Whatever the true nature of his social life that spring, he seems to have remained largely immersed in his teaching and creative work. Reacting to "the jazz phantasy that has swept our country the last decade," he published an essay, "The Higher Type of Mountain Ballad," which reveals genuine knowledge of and firsthand insights into the genre in general and four ballads in particular. Remarking on the ballad "I Am Free Again," he points to "the essence of freedom in the very first line, which is the typical mountain spirit, 'Oh, I am free, I'm free again,' " and observes, "It is a ballad of freedom and has a tragic ending but still keeps, beyond reach, that poignancy of lilt which some of the really great songs fail to maintain." Further, "pride is the characteristic element regardless of the inner sorrows that sometimes depress that noble mountain spirit, that irresoluteness and independence" in "I'll Be All Smiles

Tonight." He is impressed with "the beautiful play of words and the rhythmical swing that seems to roll and flow like one of the highland rivers. There is a sincerity in this song which is direct from the heart. . . . [It is] a typical mountain ballad of the higher type." Such songs, Jesse concluded, "have been sung two centuries by people who are as stern and beautiful as the rugged hills they love." He addressed the reader: "Then why break away from a worthy tradition that has been handed down through countless generations and especially when it is the very soul of noble people bursting into song and highly emotional music?" His affirmation and joy of mountain life sing through this introductory piece of simple eloquence.

Having developed an excellent reputation as a teacher at Warnock and having strong credentials, Jesse Stuart was offered the principalship of Greenup High School for the 1930/1931 school year. "I won't be called 'polecat' now!" he responded. Although he did not mention his old nickname in *Beyond Dark Hills*, probably because of youthful sensitivity, by the time he was in his forties he recalled hunting skunks back in the autumn of 1922 and the fact that he "was scarcely ever without a little of the scent" at Greenup High School. Now, "I go back to take over!"[3]

Both pride and practical need urged him back to college to prepare himself for the new task ahead. During the year at Warnock, he had earned enough to repay LMU his remaining college expenses and to save enough, along with a loan from the Greenup bank, to allow him to attend Peabody College in Nashville, Tennessee, for the late summer session. A year before he had noticed in small poetry magazines advertisements of publishing houses offering to print books for pay. One of the poets whose work Jesse had seen, Ernest Hartsock of Atlanta, Georgia, had published such a book and had sent it to the young Kentuckian with enthusiastic comments. "It was a real nice little book," Jesse recalled, admitting that the idea fell on rich new ground ready for seed. Why not get his own book of poems published? He had been working since summer, off and on, to put the little book together from approximately five hundred early pieces, including those he had recently published. In a happy mood he wrote James Still early in 1930,

> I would love to have you to go with me on a few of my solitary night rambles through the woods. I have gone alone all this past autumn. I am going in about two hours from now. This is a fine night, thousands of stars and a little old sickle moon.

He concluded,

> James, before I say "Guten Nicht" I want to tell you . . . about "HAR-
> VEST OF YOUTH": I did not include many of my old poems in this
> collection. I have a fear that it is only a youthful adventure. Some
> of my verse is rather filled with pathos and humor is lacking. This
> is about all I have to say, altho I am a mite enthused over the
> adventure. I have not signed the contract yet but I am going to sign
> it. . . . He wants to bring out two-hundred and sixty copies in the
> first edition and I want three hundred. That is the difference.

He borrowed the money from a Greenup County farmer, Andy Johnson,
and made a hundred-dollar down payment on his first fifty copies; after
that exchange, both parties had agreed that 250 more copies would be
forthcoming for an additional fifty dollars. However, when Jesse received
the first copies in the mail at Peabody in mid-August 1930, he knew he
would not be paying any more money to Scroll Press. "I knew that I had
been swindled."

Harry Harrison Kroll remained his ideal as a writer; sometime
during the previous summer of 1929 he had visited Kroll, and written
to James Still shortly afterward, "He's absolutely the most interesting
man in Tennessee." His former teacher had made him feel welcome.
Jesse found him still at work on his *Cabin in the Cotton* and "taking his
time." He was "working hard and living fine," saving money, wearing
"the same old clothes," driving "the same old Dodge," and was "the same
old man." He had "a fine house and plenty of new furniture and it's
pretty well kept too." Stuart had been impressed with Kroll's advice to
young writers. "He knows what he's talking about," especially "in the
novel and short story." Almost wistfully he noted, "I wish I could have
stayed with him awhile." Small wonder that Jesse Stuart, the student to
whom Kroll had given nine quarter hours of A's in creative writing,
dedicated his first book

TO
HARRY HARRISON KROLL
Genius, Novelist and Southern Realist
These Artless Poems of My Youth
Are Dedicated
With All Good Reasons

Commenting on this dedication years later, Jesse said, "I overdid it, but
'with all good reasons.' You know, Kroll was good to me." He never

forgot the seventy-five cents for washing his teacher's car, and the money
he earned from other odd jobs like putting a backwall in Kroll's fireplace,
which "wasn't drawing worth a darn." And there was the Henry Willis
fight, when Kroll was prepared to get a lawyer to keep the volatile
Kentuckian in school at Harrogate.

One need read only the thirty-four poems of the final section of
Harvest of Youth to understand why Jesse in time considered his first
publication the offspring of a literary sin requiring confession. To say
the pieces are derivative and immature is nearly enough; indeed, one
suspects they were strategically placed in the last section, but despite the
editorial ploy to diminish their visibility, even the most tolerant of readers
may have difficulty forgiving "Tennessee Farmer," which shows the poet
at his earliest and worst:

> Ott Davis spent his life on his farm:
> In Tennessee he died
> . . . .
> The weird bells of his upland sheep
> Ring not to do him harm.
>
> His children, Mary, Rube, and Glennis
> Rotate wheat, rye and cane;
> While tall pine trees grow with the weeds—
> Despite the wind and rain.
> He sleeps in shadows of the pines—
> With epitaphs on his tomb;
> His children follow in his steps—
> Are going to their doom.

Biographically, "Mary" and "Glennis" are, of course, names of the poet's
sisters, and "Ott" the nickname of the farmer with whom he had been
rooming and boarding at Warnock. "Rube" is not merely a form of
"Reuben," but also slang for an unsophisticated countryman, the "hick"
that he did not want his brother James to become. Thus, as poor as it
may be, the piece reveals a fatalistic tracing of the destiny of an upland
farmer and his family toward mountain doom. He seems to have been
striving to attach something of the universal theme and power of "Mountain Funeral" to his effort, but failed in nearly every respect, leaving
only the gleaning of his mindset for biographical purposes. Although
"Fug[i]tive" is a happier failure, it seems to have been written in response

to a reading of Stephen Vincent Benét's "Ballad of William Sycamore (1790–1871)." Jesse depicts his pioneer subject "Decaying strangely into earth and stone / . . . in the black sod where they left him lie. / . . . His powder horn rusts on the puncheon floor." Aware of "his rude sires who have gone on before," the poet prays, "God, let him still keep his pride 'round him / . . . In a world where his deers and elks have found him." The section further confirms the biographical consistency with Edith Greene as "My First True Love," and introduces the local color of Plum Grove Church into Jesse's published work for the first time in "My Peoples' [sic] Prayers." Most of the remaining poems consist of epigraphic quatrains, short pieces, and college reflections, the best of the latter being the musical and amusing "Carver Life":

> I made my vows like a fool for love
> I kept vows under cover;
> If Love was late, I would not wait,
> I found another Lover.

> With Love for this, with Love for that,
> With Love for everything,
> Free as the wind, why should I mind
> What future years would bring?

"Carver Life" recalls the title poem, "Harvest of Youth," in which he refers to his persona as "this young braggart sowing grain."

Despite the poet's often declared shame about his first "brain child," in its other three sections the book, though expectedly schoolboyish and imitative, nevertheless contains some good and some excellent pieces, promising better things to come. Eighty poems are contained in the four sections, several of which are of biographical significance.

He chose to call the first section of sixteen poems, half of them quatrains, "Out of the Night." While the source and influence of William Ernest Henley's "Invictus" seem obvious enough, some critics have pointed to the general direction of the author's early obscurity and the dominant elegiac tone of the pieces in the section. Upon his return from LMU, his mother had urged him to "get out . . . and look around over the old places where we used to live." He had visited "the house where I was born" at Cedar Riffles and other places as well. Echoes of the poet's past—the abandoned homes of his infancy and youth and those of former neighbors—impinge upon "What There Is to an Old House." The boy's Christian experience is recounted in "Free God." Once compliant and "Attentive as an old man / After he has run wild," the youth has since met "Sin":

> He bade me walk freely in
> And love him to the core.

"Sin" has become the youth's "bed fellow," until on his own he read his "dusty Bible / From cover to cover," rediscovering "one God . . . a jealous Lover" in March trees and winter wind "Blowing wildly and free." The unorthodox youth found God "in Sinful flesh," too. Indeed, "I found him everywhere": for the poet's God, not unlike Emerson's or Whitman's, was large and contained multitudes:

> He had a tremendous soul
> Of all under the sun.
> And the bloods of his people
> Were to him as one.

One of the poet's "Epitaphs" was "For Elmer Heaberlin":

> If Heaberlin's Loves come to him here,
> Forget the words: "I love you so."
> Flesh bearing rank, scholastic grain
> Within some weeds will surely grow.

What did the poet mean exactly? For answer Mr. Heaberlin, having discussed the quatrain with the poet, said, "Jesse thought I was about as smart a kid as he knew, I think . . . he was saying I was so brilliant that after death, if nothing [else] were produced in this life, at least [some] scholastic grain would have to come forth from around the grave." Similarly, Jesse wrote "Consider the Poet" for another LMU classmate, Roland Carter, a young man of both literary and ecclesiastical leanings whom he deeply respected. With both these men he had formed what were to be lifelong, sustaining friendships.

That Jesse's early work could be derivative is evident throughout *Harvest*, but especially in the epitaphic quatrain "Poet":

> If there is life beyond the grave
> He lives in future bliss.
> If there is not another world.
> He made the most of this.

Before composing these lines in college, he had probably read Robert Burns' "Epitaph on William Muir":

If there's another world, he lives in bliss;
If there is none, he made the best of this.

And he might well have read John Masefield's lines from "August, 1914":

If there be any life beyond the grave
(It must be near the men and things we love.)

He may have read either or both poets' lines as early as high school, but at any rate they dropped back into his mind somehow, to emerge as a full-flowing quatrain he genuinely believed he wrote freshly out of his own thoughts. He did write some of it, and although the result may be an improvement over both originals, the total effect is, nevertheless, that of a rearrangement or readaptation of these older lines.

Clearly the best poem in the section is "Mountain Funeral," in which Jesse attached the ballad measure to that poignant human experience on the trip home with Barnie Greene and her brother, discussed in the previous chapter. "I Know the Gypsy Wind Too Well" is an epigrammatic swipe at the fickleness of life. "Last Lover" juxtaposes images of passion and death, presaging both the method and theme of some of the *Bull-Tongue Plow* poems. Stuart's persona recognizes Earth as his "last lover" in the poem of that title. He is calm in kissing her earthen lips; the paradox is that other lovers of Earth "lie with her under cover, / Lie with her forever curiously still." Stuart's persona in "The Winner" runs a most ironic race, against his will, with Death. The descriptive naturalness of the runner's muscles set to run and running tends nearly to balance his opponent's grim eminence. Then as the persona falters, loses his breath, and "Death romped by him," the persona's teammates *cheer*—a stunning paradox leaving the reader to cogitate upon the strange human perversity that turns upon its own kind.[4]

"Slabs from a Sun-Down World," the second part of the slim volume, contains ten poems generally of more ambitious length than those in the other three sections. Jesse Stuart frankly admitted that the "Language" of this section was from Carl Sandburg, whom he later acknowledged not as the greatest poet or even a major influence on his work, but as "My Hero" among a 1920s group of poets that included Edgar Lee Masters and Robert Frost, and then "my first choice of the modern American poets" of the decade. While the small library of Greenup High School held mainly more conventional American and English poets, he may have read there and in textbooks such poems as "Chicago," "Fog,"

"The Grass," and "Cool Tombs." He remembered that he "dearly loved" the last of these, recalling one phrase he easily identified with—"lovely as a pawpaw." In 1922, the year he entered Greenup High, Sandburg's *Collected Poems* was published, and in the summer months of 1926 and 1927, while working as a blacksmith in the steel mills at Ashland, he regularly bought books of poetry, including those of Sandburg, Frost, Masters, and John Gould Fletcher. "I became a robust Artist with a sledge-hammer that Mr. Sandburg immortalized in poetry," for "he spoke a poetic language I understood. And when he sang of railroads and passenger trains, my father knew these and had talked about them at our supper table." There were other kinships, too. Sandburg's father had worked on the railroads, and Sandburg "had to work his way" at Lombard College in Galesburg, Illinois; by 1930 an even stronger point of identity was the fact that the Illinois poet's first work "had been privately published."

As Sandburg's burial references in "Cool Tombs" and "The Grass" are rendered concretely in workmen's terms, the verb naming the noun or the tool (Lincoln in the former was "shoveled into the tombs," and the grass urges, "Shovel them under. And let me work"), the young Stuart echoes the image and phrase in "River Railroad Man," commencing "Shovel under this old river railroad man." Clearly this poem springs from firsthand recollections of his father on those chill dawn walks over the ridge path and down the C&O railroad tracks, when Mick Stuart "heard mean winds strike the cold wiring on / zero mornings. / And whistle through the lonesome treetops." The poet's synesthesia in such images as the winter wind-whipped frozen wiring establishes a further kinship in "Railroad Sounds," although the comparatively larger scope of images in this poem seems well within the free-verse tradition and influence of such works as Walt Whitman's "To a Locomotive in Winter." As Sandburg's protagonist in "Chicago" asserts himself as "builder" of a nation, Stuart's persona in "Fantasy in Black" declares, "I am an atom and a builder." The 1928 publication of "Six Hickories" at Lincoln Memorial establishes both the temporal and substantive contexts of "Steel Gang" in *Harvest of Youth*, clearly revealing the Sandburg influence as mountain steel workers (no longer sawyers) imperatively demand the reader's attention:

Listen: we were dogging steel, somewhere
Between Six Hickories and Muldraugh Hill . . .
Daring, stormy . . . we chewed tobacco and flapped
Broad-rimmed and dusky felt hats . . .

"My City" is an autobiographical depiction of the young man's view of Riverton and Greenup, complete with such details as a "dirty wharf boat landing," a schoolhouse, and Riverton's old "octagon sided post office." Many of the Stuart classmates are suggested by their first names, as one may see by the addition of surnames in brackets throughout this excerpt:

> We went to the dirty wharf boat landing
> So tired of being tired
> And bought tickets for Pittsburg in the east
> St. Louis in the west . . .
>> Elmer [Heaberlin], Bert [Bertice Smith], Estille
>> [Howland], James [Jimmie McCoy], Oscar [Sammons],
>> Thurman [Darby], Edith [Craft West or, perhaps,
>> Edith Greene], Grace [Hilton], Irene [Barney
>> Griffith], Elizabeth [Forbes Smith], Kyon [Murray] . . .
> Proud, bent, daring to go . . .

Eventually, they all return home, at peace with the past and their niche in life, to a city "the dead remember, / In a city where the wind loves the dead."

Jesse's imagist phase is best illustrated with "Silhouettes," stylistically reflective of such pieces as Ezra Pound's "In a Station at the Metro," but with an unsuppressed kinesthetic flair:

> Hard, clear
> Chiseled profiles
> Of black bodies trees
> Swerving in the wind
> At sundown

He could only have brushed the surface of Pound by then; his deeper reading of the expatriate poet would come later. He did have ample opportunity to read such poets as Hilda Doolittle and Amy Lowell as well as Pound. Of this period, Jesse later wrote, "I imitated the Imagists— Glad I got in on the tail end of this miscarriage of poetry." Eliotic images prevail in "Undulated Season," which recounts in cyclical imagery a young man's view of the seasons or stages of promiscuous love, bearing some kinship to the Maria Sheen/Quadroon Mott symbolism of his own creative youth. She is "a tiny flame / in a tiny town that hath not understanding / when March tree sap / was turbulent young blood," and when the "March wood veins / drink the sweet from her body." The images of "copper August" and "t[aw]ny arms clutching / dry concrete breasts for nourishment" lead to "dark alley ways / called time," where she, the "tiny flame in a tiny town / lies limb to limb with any lover." Birds mate in their season, and old men talk, though "gone is she / who was so beautiful." While the style repeatedly echoes Eliot, the substance remains Sandburgian; Stuart's symbolical Maria Sheen has become, at least in the poet's imagination, like Sandburg's Chick Lorimer, the "wild girl" whom "everybody loved," and who is literally "gone." His lyrical description of autumn, with its repeated images of yellow, anticipates another to follow within two years in *Beyond Dark Hills*:

"Undulated Season"	*Beyond Dark Hills*
. . . yellow the winds drift . . .	Mellow is the wind and yellow are the leaves and yellow is the mist about the pools. . . . Almost yellow is the tobacco and yellow is the corn. . . . Yellow the noonday September sun.
. . . the winds drift yellow . . .	
. . . time is yellow with plum leaves . . .	

Winter brings the cycle full circle. The persona is in her grave symbolically if not physically, wrecked by "storms turbulent," and she is inhumed with her sins in communion with hosts of those gone before, "so the old men say who remember / sins of the world buried," with winter— the winter of time and repeated snows—covering them. Though she may be the subject of gossip, the ultimate lover, Death, will surely question only the productivity of that life or any life compared to "sterility"; for the ultimate measure of life, the poet seems to say, is what was done with life.

"Vagabond Houses" is also related in imagistic method and theme, while the dramatic narrative "Black April" is a synthesis of influences: it evokes the epitaphic style of Edgar Lee Masters' *Spoon River Anthology*, contains naturalistic verbal echoes of Stephen Crane's "God Is Kind," and blends something of the substance of Stephen Vincent Benét's ballad celebrations of American pioneers. Further, it is thoroughly infused with autobiographical elements such as those in personal stories like "Dark Winter." Flint Sycamore "moved to W-Hollow" with "his wife, Lucy, by his side," and "sifted pine tree loam / Through his scrawny fingers" until he found "a place to build." They eat a ham supper, daub a "pine pole house," and plant corn only to have April rains rot it in the ground, sour the potatoes, and drown the cane. The crows laugh and the winds sing their mockery. In response to Flint Sycamore's defiant refrain "God, I'll beat you yet," his first-born dies, the horses "took the murrain," and "marshland fever / Cut Flint down / Like a weed in autumn," leaving only "two dim lettered / Lichen sandstones" upon which, much later, marveling travelers speculate. Ironically, the scene shifts to twelve men in white clothes picnicking on "rarest food," for "God is kind." They see the two "lichen stones"

> Shaded by a tall grass of undying beauty:
> Shaded with a wild cherry
> With a thousand white sprays
> Daring the wind . . .
> Life from the richest earth;
> Life from a daring dust;
> April life from the bosom
> Of Flint Sycamore.

The biographical elements demonstrate that the poet was working out of his own material: the memory of that 1917 rainy growing season of rotted corn in the sour earth, when the cattle took the murrain; the move of the Stuarts to the third farm at the end of the last prong of W-Hollow Creek; and the following winter of his father's near death, the birth of Martin Vernon Stuart February 12, and the infant's death April 17, 1918. At least one student of Stuart has noted the parallel, writing "during a lengthy illness in the winter of 1918 Mitch Stuart almost followed Flint Sycamore."

One perceives the poet's cyclical vision at work in "Black April" as well as in other poems in *Harvest of Youth;* for although the April of Flint Sycamore is indeed black, those who follow the pioneer's effort literally enjoy April life blooming from the tragic pioneer's "daring dust." Clearly Jesse identified his father, his mother, and his parents' people with all the Flint Sycamores gone before them. Of these forebears he would later write, "They were not prisoners, debtors, ne'er-do-wells, or cast-offs from the seaboard settlements, as some rumors have reported them to be. They were the most aggressive pioneers, brave with dreams and visions, who had come from the Old World of the British Isles to establish new homes and a new country in a wilderness."[5]

"Sonnets: Juvenilia" is the third section of *Harvest of Youth.* It contains twenty-four poems in experimental sonnet forms, six of which compose a preview to *Man with a Bull-Tongue Plow,* where they were to reappear in 1934 as numbered sonnets:

HOY	*MWBTP*
"To Muddy Waters"	Sonnet # 223
"Batter Me Down, Life"	Sonnet # 224
"My Loves Will Remain when	
I Have Passed"	Sonnet # 225
"My Mountain Home"	Sonnet # 232
"To Edith"	Sonnet # 236 ("To B. G.")
"Silent Earth"	Sonnet # 240

Although several of these, as well as others in the section, have been previously discussed, they deserve further comment. "Harvard or the Sea," for example, arising out of his desire to attend an "old college," a dream he had laughed at more than three summers before when he imagined "the jump from a street carnival in the hill towns of Kentucky to Harvard," was by no means a dead dream. In September of 1929 he wrote James Still, "I'm just waiting like a strong man does to win a race—a bit shaky—for the time to come when I can pack my trunk and go to Harvard. I'm going Still—watch me."

He had been reaching back into the past in more ways than one. The past-haunted sonnet "Loneliness" had appeared originally in the *The Blue and Gray* that May:

I still remember when you went away
On that red morning in the summer drouth;
When dry winds blew out of the warm south,
I still remember all you had to say.
Vines then that draped the stucco wall
Have turned buff-colored in the sun.
Beech leaves are slowly dropping one by one,
And south going birds only stop and call.
The loneliness and life's little things back
You to me again. The desolate autumn rains
Tapping the roof, streaking the window panes
And gambling with night's deserted waste of black
I cannot forget. My soul is lost in you
As deep as space, and wide as space is blue.

Between the initial publication of "Loneliness" and late August of 1929 he had visited Barnie Greene again. "Barney and I had a quarrel before

I left there and then confessed how much we really loved each other and both said we were sorry we had ever seen each other. . . . I doubt seriously whether I'll ever love another girl like I once did her. Look how happy I was last summer when she was away. . . . I am [happy] when I can't see her."

She had, indeed, gone away—she went home that summer of 1929 and taught school the same academic year that Stuart taught at Warnock. During this time she met an engineer with the Tennessee Highway Department, Ernest Hutchens, and the two started dating. Although she and Jesse had begun to drift apart, he did go to see her in the summer of 1929. "Stuart and I were dating others at LMU," she said. She had begun to date Ernest and "we just kinda left it that way." When Stuart returned the next summer, he found that Barnie Greene had changed her name to Mrs. Ernest Hutchens. "Stuart stayed at Dora Testerman's place," she recalled, "but he came [to Sneedville] to talk to me. He told my friend that he couldn't believe that I was married to anybody but him." His bold move had surprised her, for she just could not "figure someone doin' a thing like that." Her husband did not like it very much, but she talked with Jesse anyway. "He just wanted to know if I was happy. I told him I was. We parted as friends, and that's the way I always wanted it to be, because he was a *dear* person, I thought."

The sonnet "Margaret" was inspired by Margaret Brooks, "a very high-level girl, very decent and very fine, out of Birmingham, Alabama." She was a tall, slender, black-haired girl whom he had dated his senior year. Sometime in the summer of 1929 he made his way to Birmingham and caught a street car out to her home—"fine folks," he wrote James Still, who hailed from Fairfax, Alabama, himself. "I believe that's the best home I ever visited." Stuart remembered that she talked much about her ancestry and the old Confederacy. "I had a great time with Margaret, but we are more divided now than ever." His poetry sings of her in the context of "summer stars' meteoric flashes" and concludes with these six lines:

> She would saunter off when the full moon rays
> Shone on Spring's snowy rows of apple trees
> And listen to the night wind harmonies,
> Knowing beauty is all that really pays.
> When my soul is empty and hope withdrawn,
> She beams a jewel on the breast of dawn.

Of the remaining sonnets in the book's third section, "My Loves Will Remain When I Have Passed" intensifies memories of "sleepy mountain towns" while "the cold / Nosing winds" play "in November corn stubbles." Vanished is the "swimming time of night." As the title indicates, "August Night" conforms to a seasonal schema as "quiet stirs of August wind / Blows [sic] through the trees. . . ." Anticipating the John and Kathaleen of *Album of Destiny,* not published until 1944, "Clean Fingers Sloped in Farewell" finds a seasonal patterning in the image of "Autumn rain / On his shoulders" as two lovers part. The recollection of Elsie West, with whom he posed in a field of daisies above the LMU campus, may have been the incentive for composing "to a Georgian Lass," a sonnet celebrating "our merry youth in Nature's garden." Finally, "Returned" is an imaginative fulfillment of "one swift-breathed yesterday." The scene is "springtime in sunny Tennessee" where "eerie birds sing in the boughs to solace me / And clouds blow westward over Lincoln Memorial." The poet desires to walk along "old roads curved into tree-lined places, / To visit favorite haunts" in this piece written in praise of friendship. Perhaps he had in mind the rare and careless hours laughed away at the Hunkstand. He wanted to see again "familiar faces," to "live now as I did then," and to "feel at least as free" as in his college years.

Although he had liked Warnock, he was glad to get away from the place and back on a college campus, as he wrote Naomi Deane Norris. He was looking ahead to the upcoming year as principal of Greenup High School. He had gained some financial independence, paid off his college debts, and even purchased a radio powered by a Delco battery system kept at his father's house in W-Hollow. Sometimes on Saturday evenings, the Grand Ole Opry came in loud and clear from Station WSM in Nashville, Tennessee. Everyone liked the old folk music and the country fiddle, Uncle Dave Macon, the Fruit Jar Drinkers, Deford Bailey and his harmonica; but among his favorites was a different kind of hoedown band known as "Theron Hale and His Daughters," Mamie Ruth and Elizabeth. No one could play "Listen to the Mockingbird" the way the Hales could. Further, he had published his first book, such as it was. How he wished now that Kroll had taught him how to prepare a manuscript! How he wished he had had a good editor, that the book had been accepted on a royalty basis! As August ebbed he knew he was going home by way of eastern Tennessee and Harrogate, so his thoughts turned eastward toward old friendships there. He decided, with some mixed feelings, to inscribe a copy of his new book to Lucille Jordan, and wrote,

> Dear Lucille: Tho this book is somewhat wrecklessly shattered
> by the handling of hands and shipment, it is the first autographed

copy of my first book. Since we are intimate friends, you will know that part of this verse is stormy and morose as my career of 23 yrs. has been. I trust that you will not be wholly deceived in the lad you ate by for 2½ longer years and had you as hostess and friend, and you, too, were a noble friend indeed. I remember you as a very proud character living your own life—what more may be said is buried in my mind.

Jesse Stuart   Aug. 20, 1930[6]

6

Nashville
1930–1931

———◇———

. . . One night in the late fall of 1931, the Vanderbilt graduate student stood on a corner of Church Street in downtown Nashville and wrote a poem on an envelope, while all around him the crowds were moving along in the pre-Christmas rush that begins in late November. His attention was compelled to the paper, to the pen in his hand which seemed to hold him in its control, and he kept on writing on the envelope. . . .[1]

Nearly a year and a half before, in the summer of 1930, Jesse Stuart had taken five hours of graduate work at George Peabody College for Teachers in Nashville, making A's for three hours and C's for the other two. His English 471 course in Modern Poetry was taught by Randall Stewart, "a good teacher and one of the fairest," the Kentuckian remembered of the man who later joined the Vanderbilt faculty just across Broadway from Peabody. Those late summer weeks at Peabody were as tinder to the still-hot embers of ambition that had first begun to smoke at Harrogate, where the student-poet had discovered the books of the Fugitives and Agrarians. "I had read poems in magazines and books written by members of this group. I wanted to take graduate courses under these men, whose poems, stories, articles, and nonfiction books I had read." Back in 1926 he had read Professor Mims' book on *Carlyle's Essay on Burns,* a copy of which he put under his shirt and took from the Army Library at Stithton near Fort Knox. He knew that Mims, "The White Knight of Arkansas" as people called him, was the powerful chairman of the English Department at Vanderbilt. That much-admired paternal figure was an important part of the tradition of a university where, as Jesse believed, "teachers wrote books and farmed."

He had believed, too, that he could identify with such people. After

117

all, had he not farmed and published poetry much as they? Since the summer before he had worked on the poems clustering under four seasonal divisions. He was not sure how good they were. So far they had not seemed to "sing with life," but he would finish them and then maybe they would. The north temperate zone of Greenup County had four of "the most beautiful, distinct seasons of any segment of earth," he believed, and the land possessed "a beauty *so* conducive to poetry." Perhaps the help he needed with them would eventually come from Vanderbilt.[2]

And he had a book, too, of sorts, even if it was published without a dust jacket and without critical praise, except for two local write-ups. One of these was a review by Vergil Leon Sturgill, an Ashland, Kentucky, high school teacher who years earlier had moved the young Burns thrall with his readings at the Greenup High School assembly. Shortly after the book was published, the poet inscribed a copy,

> To Leon Sturgill   a brother poet

When the best that is in us fades away
And goes somewhere into the world's far ends
We'll sit before the fire with old time friends—
And smoke our pipes and drink and sometimes pray
And talk about the cool swift hours of yesterday
When we were free as dust, and winds that blow
Before the fire we sit—our dreams burn low;
The fading woodfire turns the room to gray—
Drink Comrades! Drink! Come closer to the fire!
And smoke and pray unto your heart's content—
I love you all—from that same element
We came. Back we shall go. And my desire
Will be, turn pages of a book before the fire
And laugh, and say: "Good night", and then retire.

There had been a few notices and comments in such small poetry magazines as those in which his poems had appeared, but he knew from the time he saw the first copy the book was not quite right. He had expected a better book with better print on better paper. The threads were loose throughout the back of the book and he handled the first copy tenderly:

> I held the book in my arms as a mother holds her firstborn baby. I ran around showing it to three or four grey-headed professors not interested in poetry at all, and as they didn't want to embarrass me, they didn't comment. So I ran to a few women to show it, and they were more sympathetic.

Years later he would strip away all youthful vanity from the moment he extracted the first copy of *Harvest of Youth* from the mail. "You know when I got that book out of the box I almost vomited. They had paper backs—thin paper. And it was just terrible. I got sick to my stomach. Just real sick."

When Superintendent Robert J. Nickel told the new principal of Greenup High School that his salary was a third less than the expected $1500 for nine months—only $111 per month—Jesse set his jaw and decided to save expenses by living at home. He took the ridge path down to Academy Branch and into Greenup each morning, often leaving early with his father, who proudly walked before him and knocked part of the dew off the ragweeds. Still the plants showered their clouds of golden pollen upon his trouser legs and cuffs. He saw Sam Leslie at the corner drugstore, where he left several copies of *Harvest of Youth* to be sold. He sent a few copies to the small magazines, ostensibly to thank them for publishing his poetry in the past but actually to solicit reviews of his book. One way to forget *Harvest of Youth* was to work hard at his new job. He taught English, which he enjoyed, and kept his young faculty busy. Later in the fall, a board member took him aside and told him something that was the talk of Greenup: "You have dyed your pant legs where they have lost their original color, and . . . you have dyed them a color that doesn't match the rest of your suit."

In order to comply with the rule that teachers live in Greenup while they teach and to avoid the dew-drenched ragweed and tongue-wagging about his sulphur-colored trouser cuffs, he had moved to the Columbia Hotel where his room and board totaled $40 a month—more than a third of his monthly paycheck. There, from his high room overlooking Main Street to the east and west and the intersecting streets to the south, he learned about the town's night activities—"loud voices and hilarious laughter"—voices familiar to him, for nearly thirty percent of his high school students were among those up past midnight. From his room Stuart could watch the town bootlegger sell his wares out of his topcoat, worn even in mild weather. Through cooperation of the women of the PTA, a curfew was passed; by nine o'clock students had to clear the streets, gambling fathers to cease gambling at sports events, and students to cease gambling at school. With better habits at home the students learned more and their grades improved. In short, the women cleaned up the town, and Jesse Stuart, who had wisely given them their rein, was credited with a new era of discipline.[3]

One of the interesting people whom he had come to know in the year past was Hulda Cooper, an English and creative writing teacher from New York whose natural love for language was infectious enough to impress even young James Stuart, then in his senior year. She saw in the dialect of the students a natural poetry and discussed her ideas with the principal—the prefix *a* and the dropping of the *g* of *-ing* endings, as in "a-goin," "a-playin," and "a-singin." Hulda Cooper visited the students' homes and soaked up the local color firsthand—sorghum making, the smokehouses stocked with cured meats, and cellars filled with home-canned goods. She heard the old-time music at country dances. James Stuart recalled that Miss Cooper's hair "kind of strung down and she combed it over on one side." A "very thorough teacher" who used "plus and minus letter grades," she was also one of his two favorite teachers; the other was Margaret Waggoner, who was also a friend of Jesse's. These two teachers suggest respectively the characters of Helen Kirsten and Martha Welch in *The Thread That Runs So True*.

That year Charles Rice had roomed and boarded with the Stuarts in W-Hollow so he could more easily attend Greenup High. Betty Stephens was completing her senior year at the school, staying at the Greenup home of pretty, blue-eyed Ethel Brown, a friend and fellow senior. Betty thought that Jesse, in future years her brother-in-law, "always had something new and interesting to teach in class every day," whereas she "despised" tall, skinny James Stuart then, advanced in school for his years. The year before he had been expelled for "either fighting or skipping school," but when James and several others sought entrance in good faith, Jesse reinstated them. With James in particular there were conditions. "Boy, I worked," he remembered, "because he wanted me to go to college."

At the May Day Fair in 1931 Jesse Stuart had run into a young woman from Cane Creek, who, in the six years that had passed since he had taught at his first school, had married another of the Cane Creek students and given birth to five children. She was the Cochran girl remembered for playing her guitar and singing while he taught school. She told him enough that he realized nearly everything at Cane Creek had changed in those intervening years, the saddest being Mr. Wilson's passing at Hunnewell. The sudden recollection set him to musing on the transience of life, a theme increasingly to pervade his work.

He had come to know his young faculty well and developed a lasting friendship with Lewis "Mack" McCubbin, a "Smith-Hughes man" who taught agriculture and science and as such was paid more than any other teacher, part of his salary coming from the Commonwealth of Kentucky for visiting and instructing farmers. He became the "Lonnie Maxwell" of *Thread*. During the school year Jesse Stuart went on his friend's note three times to help him pay for his car and other expenses necessary to his work. William "Bill" Harrell struck Jesse Stuart as "one of the best teachers Greenup ever had"; he was to emerge as "Bill Hadden" in *Thread*, and Charlie Wilson, the high school teaching coach, the oldest and only married member of the faculty, appeared in that work as "Coach Watson."

At the end of the school year Jesse reapplied for the principalship with the condition that his pay be raised to $1500 annually, the salary he had originally expected. Superintendent Nickel kept him impatiently waiting only to inform him finally, "We didn't hire you. . . . You asked too much." The familiar pattern of change had set in. That year he had had dates with several different girls, among them Margaret Waggoner and Naomi Deane Norris. (Naomi had been attending Morehead College and was teaching school to pay her way.) Now Hulda Cooper and Margaret Waggoner had returned to their homes. One rumor he never knew the truth of was that Miss Cooper hitchhiked her way back to New York, either for lack of funds or for the experience. Charles Rice, who had memorized "Thanatopsis" in its entirety, later migrated north to Wyandotte, Ohio, where he had a family and for many years kept the records of his real estate business filed away in his remarkable brain.[4]

In the spring and early summer of 1931 Jesse and James Stuart worked on a tobacco crop in W-Hollow, hoping to earn their college expenses together. James wanted to go to Berea and Jesse to Nashville again—if possible to Vanderbilt, for the dream of studying under and being part of the Fugitive-Agrarians remained strong. Before July the tobacco leaves were literally suffocated from heavy rains, and they whitened, died, and rotted. Jesse Stuart borrowed $250 from the Greenup National Bank and divided $100 of it between his mother for household needs and James, who successfully matriculated at Berea College in September. That summer Sam Leslie sold four copies of *Harvest of Youth*. "The books absolutely would not sell, regardless of the fine write-ups I got in two local papers." Meanwhile, he had given away a few copies, and he took some along with him to Nashville.

In Nashville again, he stayed in Room 109 of Kissam Hall on the Vanderbilt campus, his transcript having been sent to Dr. Edwin Mims, Chairman of the Department of English at Vanderbilt, for evaluation. Whatever the problems necessitated by farmwork at W-Hollow, gone for naught because of the May and June rains, by mid-July he had scheduled a heavy load of 14 hours at Peabody College, most of them in English, and posted a letter to Naomi Deane Norris in answer to her own, complimenting her letter as an "impressive one." He sympathized with her not going to college that summer. "We can get to the place where we want to break loose and go places and see things. A teacher should be ready for work when school begins. This is good advice but I know that you don't need it. You have taught as much as I have but I've had an adult group. There is a lot of difference." His plans for attending Vanderbilt were much on his mind, his excitement at the new world and slower old culture obvious:

> If I stay here next year, I shall, perhaps, shift to Vanderbilt altogether because it is a more classical type—on the order of Harvard, Yale and Oxford. Deane, Vanderbilt is an immense place—eighty acres in building[s]. From 30 to 40 men are constantly employed to look after the buildings and grounds. They are "niggers" for the white man here as a usual thing is a man of leisure and certainly never bends to ditch digging and the like. The South is a grand old place. You would like the slow South. It just seems like everybody is slow here.

In response to her apparent inquiry, he wrote, "No, no one waits for me at a brick house on the hill," not identifying the reference. From "up there" he hears only from "very intimate friends like Elmer von Heaberlin Esq." Of the teachers only Lewis "Mack" McCubbin writes, and he is surprised that "not even Miss [Margaret] Waggoner" writes. "She knows where I am. I sent her my address. That's all I can do. I've made an effort. . . . Next time you see her ask when she has heard from me. If she says not any you tell her you have gotten all the letters you can carry from me. She used to kindly [sic] ask me about you. I never could understand." He mused, "Those good old days are gone." But he was "having a glorious time and a hustling one too," for "life is far greater as a student than a teacher." With newsy levity and ingenuous frankness he finished:

> I tell you there are more girls here than anyplace I've ever been. Put a boy where there are plenty of girls and few boys he doesn't notice the girls like he does if they were scarce. I haven't had a date on this campus since I've been here except with an old gray haired lady and we get "Chaucer" together. Everybody in that class is a college teacher. See where I am don't you. Competition is too keen. Golly I started to write you a personal letter—is this one? I've just rambled along like an old T model Ford. So here I close with [. . .] and good night and ——

Jesse Stuart

It was his first letter, so far as the record shows, to the woman who was to become his wife more than eight years later.

Marriage had been far from his mind. Apparently having raised the question—as epistolary banter or out of curiosity is not clear, since her letter does not survive—Naomi Norris told Jesse about Lewis McCubbin's having given Dorothy Vernon a diamond. Expressing surprise over "Mack's" engagement, he responded, "But long association has a tendency to malgamate [sic] couples," and then, somewhat skittishly, he returned to his own case:

> The girl I go with here, has a date tonight with another boy from Kentucky. I have a date with Harriette Brendle from Greensboro, North Carolina. Does that sound like matrimony? I don't know how that could have started. It would be impossible for me to marry even if I wished. Besides, besides—and beware! beware!

In addition to Naomi Norris, Jesse Stuart was writing other young women during 1930/1931. He had sent Margaret Waggoner his address. Betty Stephens and Lucy May Scott were among those he corresponded with from Morehead. Betty Stephens remembered, "He used to write letters from Kissam Hall. I admired him as a teacher, and the other girls would get so jealous every time I got a letter." During the summers of the early 1930s, Naomi Norris also noticed this reaction among other coeds who knew Jesse Stuart but were not so fortunate as she in receiving so many letters from him. In partial explanation for his brother's propensity to write often and at length, James Stuart observed, "Jesse lived by the pen. He'd communicate two doors down, why he write a letter!"

"The girl I go with here" was Elizabeth Hale, one of the two talented daughters of Theron Hale of "Theron Hale and His Daughters" of WSM Grand Ole Opry fame. Jesse had met her in July 1930 by passing chance through a young theologian, Edward K. Hardy, studying in the Vanderbilt School of Religion (later Divinity). He was the son of Dr. Chester Hardy, an M.D. and President of Trevecca Nazarene College in Nashville. The two young men shared an interest in the Grand Ole Opry. "Where do they broadcast it, Ed?" Jesse inquired.

"Down at the National Life Building. In fact, my girl friend and her sister and her father are really stars on the program, 'Theron Hale and His Daughters.' "

"Why, I've heard them over the radio in Kentucky." Jesse grew suddenly excited. "You know them!"

"I certainly do. . . . Mamie Ruth and I are engaged. I go down to the program every Saturday night. Meet me at the steps of the First National Bank. I'll wait for you at the door."

From an upper floor of the old National Life Building, located on the southeastern corner of the intersection of Union Street and Seventh Avenue, diagonally across the street from the present site of the Hyatt Regency, the Grand Ole Opry held forth to half a nation over radio station WSM. Jesse saw banjo-picking Uncle Dave Macon with his plug hat, gold teeth, and goatee—"The Dixie Dewdrop." The Fruit Jar Drinkers were lean, gangly Tennessee hill men, who lived up to their name by sneaking drinks whenever they could, despite the presence of watchful prohibition-era policemen. Then Theron Hale and his daughters appeared. He was an old-time fiddler and Mamie Ruth Hale was a talented violinist. According to Hardy, Elizabeth Hale chorded along on the piano and sometimes played the mandolin. Jesse also saw Deford Bailey, a hunchbacked black man, who made his harmonica talk. The entertainers performed during two sessions, usually until midnight, and then signed off when "the roosters crowed and the pawpaws pawed and all good things come to an end."

Before the evening came to an end, he noticed a coolness between the Hales and the Fruit Jar Drinkers. Theron Hale and his daughters shunned the wild mountaineers. In all the Saturday evenings Jesse attended the Grand Ole Opry, he never saw Theron Hale and his daughters speak to the Fruit Jar Drinkers. In getting to know the Hales in the weeks to follow, and in talking with Ed Hardy, he would learn why. He was invited out to the home of the Hales at 306 Scott Avenue. Coming out of an eastern Tennessee Baptist background, the family had become affiliated with the Nazarene Church at 510 Woodland Street in East Nashville. Theron Hale, a handsome man with a showman's personality, was a teetotaler. His daughters had been Nazarenes from their teens, and they were devout practitioners of their faith.

Ed Hardy and Mamie Ruth Hale had been courting for several years and were about to be married. Jesse was attracted to Elizabeth and, despite religious differences, he found the naturally gifted musical family attractive. Mamie Ruth was something of a concert violinist. She attended the Nashville Conservatory of Music and had studied for more than a year under respected violinist Eric Sorentine. She played with attractive authority, her eyes flashing to the music. Whereas Mamie Ruth was outgoing and often scintillating, Elizabeth was quiet, and while not exactly shy, more introverted than her sister. Elizabeth was about five feet four inches tall and weighed about a hundred pounds then. She was

pale, blonde, petite, wasp-small of waist, and shapely. "Mama Hale," as
Ed called the girls' mother, was a marvelous cook, and after her sub-
stantial Sunday meals, they would sit around the living room. Sometimes
Theron Hale would pick up a fiddle and play for anyone who might
listen. Mamie Ruth might play the violin, or Elizabeth the piano, and
Ed would sing. Jesse would join in. In the evening they would go to
"First Church" on Woodland Street, where Ed often led the music. These
were pleasant, restful Sundays. There were two swings on the porch
then, and sometimes Jesse and Elizabeth would sit outside on one and
Ed and Mamie Ruth on the other. In weeks to come Jesse talked with
Elizabeth about his studies and his dreams, as he had with Barnie Greene
three years before; he sometimes read her his poems. More than anything else he wanted to be a poet and a writer. She admired the young
Kentuckian, especially his "forthright character, honesty and integrity,"
as she later wrote.

During the Peabody summer session of 1931, Jesse Stuart was in
Nashville in time to attend the spirited, happy wedding between the
young minister and the vivacious violinist on June 25. Together Jesse
and Elizabeth threw rice and saw the couple off at Union Station at the
corner of 10th Avenue and Broadway, where the green and gray structure of stone and Tennessee marble still stands in its Romanesque splendor. Antic songsters filched a wheelchair and insisted on pushing the
bride and groom around the huge concrete boarding deck, singing, "Ten
little baby fingers, ten little baby toes . . ." The couple rode off to Birmingham to Ed's ministry. The Hardys often returned to Nashville to
visit and for Ed to take additional course work; within a few years they
would move back to Nashville for good. During their visits, as Ed Hardy
recalled, he and Jesse would talk, as like as not on the Vanderbilt campus.
Both studied under Mims at different times. "Sometimes Jesse would
ask me to look over something he had written, a poem or paper or
article. 'Here, Ed, won't you take this and just look it over?' and I would
take it." And they talked about more serious things. One day Ed saw
him in his janitor's work clothes and just asked, "Are you doing cleaning
in Science Hall, Jesse?"

Jesse told him intently, " 'Yes, Ed. I'm working in Science Hall
cleaning. Ed, anything I can do, whatever sacrifices I have to make, I'm
going to finish school and prepare myself to give what I have to give in
the field of writing.' Or words to that effect," he qualified. Hardy admired
the Kentuckian's genuineness and sincerity. "I liked him from the very
first, and I have every reason to believe it was reciprocal." They talked
at other times, too, about their ambitions. "Jesse's ambition was always

to write. That's what he was going to do. I was much impressed from the first that of the young men our age, he was one who was going to make it in the future. There was no question in my mind at all. Jesse Stuart was going to write."[5]

The summer session at Peabody was far from an easy one. Jesse met formidable professor-author Alfred Leland Crabb for the first time. In contrast to the quiet demeanor of the slender six-foot educator, the highland poet saw himself as a "semi-raw youth, energetic, blustery, over-talkative—full of notions and dreams—a 225 pounder, who never grew physically or mentally tired and never had enough money to buy himself enough to eat." His clothes were, confessedly, "never as neat as the professor's." One day Crabb called Jesse into his office and began asking questions—historical questions. "What do you think of Andrew Jackson?"

"Andrew Jackson was great because he acted first and discussed it afterwards. He was a fighter and doer, and he fought only when he thought he had to fight." He told Crabb he was impressed with Jackson because he "didn't mind a fight he believed was right and just, before he was President and after he was President." Before the summer was over, Crabb invited Stuart into his office again and repeated the questions. "You asked me these questions before, but I don't mind answering them again." However, he did wonder why the Peabody professor was "trying to probe me." The well-groomed man did not "speak with precision, but he did speak with caution"—so different from himself, Jesse thought. "I suppose we were opposites." He was sure Professor Crabb did not like him.

In his letter of July 25 to Deane Norris, he inquired about friends and teachers. The time of year triggered fond images that poured out in romantic retrospect:

School beginning—the bell ringing for recess and the careless kids at play. Nothing looks better to me than to see a young girl, neatly dressed, and intelligent looking, standing out amid her group of youngsters. (The Shepherdess and her flock). Deane you should fill my description of a teacher and do. I know how those days are in Greenup County when teachers assemble from all parts. . . . I like to be in Greenup on those days. . . .

Things can pass at home that people don't notice there—but being away with strangers they turn their selves to home sometimes. You know how that is—for me it has been strangers and always

"Hello, I'm glad to meet you"—and always "Good-by—be good if I never see you again."

Always always, Stuart

By August 19 his decision to attempt the year of work at Vanderbilt had firmed up. "In September I start class work over here in Vanderbilt in a big way," he wrote. "I'm looking around now and grabbing all the work I can for next year. You know I have to hustle." He was not worried about what the year held for himself, "but I do worry about my little skinny brother. He's entering Berea in September."

By late August Jesse Stuart was already "grabbing" such jobs as laundry collector and encountering the raw humor of a few anatomy and medical students:

I have a roommate now. Guess! It is a cat. How he got in here, I don't know. He's a pretty big fluffy fellow. I think people carry them off and throw them out here. I saw a little skinny hound pup over at Wesley Hall today. The medical students nab all of them they can get to work on. I hear dogs howling every time I pass the hospital. The other night when I was collecting laundry, a boy asked me to run through his pockets and get the stuff out. I found a negro's ear in one pocket. I felt kindly funny when I pulled it out.

He would be staying on at Vanderbilt "until next May"—that is, "I hope to be." He would have his master's degree then and some work on the Ph.D. "I'm quite too young for a Ph.d. [sic] I'm not craving one anyway." Even in the heady Vanderbilt atmosphere, he remembered himself, his origins, and assured Deane Norris he would not forget them:

No Deane I don't care if I would get a Phd [sic] from Vanderbilt, Harvard or Yale or have half the money Henry Ford has. I'd never be sophisticated. I'd always have to be just what I am and who I am with nothing to be proud of or be proud for. I'm just Jesse Stuart—no more—no less and no one else.

Near the end of the summer session he sent his fourth letter of the summer to Naomi Deane Norris, postmarked Wednesday, August 19. "Tonight is a big hard night for me. This week end [sic] I have three examinations. One in Chaucer, one in Greek Literature and one in Children's Literature." The next week he left Kissam Hall and traveled to northeastern Tennessee, taking a long way home through places he wanted to see again, especially Lincoln Memorial University and Harrogate, Tennessee. He was in Greenup in time to have a few more dates with Naomi Norris and to see his brother, James, off to Berea College. For dates they went to ball games, school activities, and dances. Sometimes they went to movies in her car, and sometimes they double-dated with friends who had a car, such as the Fred Maynards.

By early September he had returned to Nashville. The sobering thought of the upcoming year at Vanderbilt faced him. Energetic Dr. Randall Stewart, then in his twenties, had taught his Chaucer class. Although Jesse had made a B with him before, the competition had proved keener in the Chaucer class, and the little old gray-headed lady he had studied with had not been much help. His final course grade was C. The consolation was that Stewart "was a good teacher . . . and I got to know him very well."[6]

To add to the question of his unspectacular summer grades, Jesse Stuart had deeper problems. He felt himself "a stranger" and "afraid." Holding nothing back, he told Professor Mims of his circumstances, his hopes and doubts, his financial limitations and plans to work for his expenses. When he officially registered for the fall semester, Mims said, "It looks as if you've got something big before you, Stuart. I don't see how in the world you can do it and do yourself justice." He listened carefully to the distinguished man with the mustache and goatee, looked at the piercing dark eyes under dark arching brows, the rondure of high forehead blending into a nearly bald pate. As he talked, Jesse could see a gold tooth glittering in the back of the left side of his mouth. Of that moment he wrote,

> He was right. But I was not turning back. I was going through with the ordeal. Hell, stand up and face the thing like a student should. Why show clay feet on the spur of the moment when the whole tryout was coming off? Well, I was going to stay.

That September he went up Wesley Hall stairway toward his room on the third floor, and there in the murky light he saw "the familiar outline of a tall rugged man sitting at the window," looking out over smoke-clouded Nashville. The figure turned around and spoke: "Stuart, what in the world has brought you here!" It was Don West.

"More education . . . my M.A."

"I'm getting my D.D. this year, preaching and working in the slums."

"Same old Don West!"

"In flesh and blood but not in spirit. I've been kicked out of three churches since I preached in the mountains. I've seen so much human suffering, Stuart, that I've grown bitter. I've been trying to save human beings on earth instead of preaching to them of a reward in heaven."

The two stood and talked, and Jesse Stuart mused on his old LMU friend's "heart big as all-out-of-doors," remembered their track days together, felt a sudden surge of good feeling. "I always felt as strong as a mountain alone, and as strong as two mountains when with Don West." Learning of Stuart's meager funds West said, "Why don't you register in the School of Religion, Stuart? You can get by there on the money you have."

"Hell, I can't preach. I don't ever intend to. If I were called on to lead in prayer I'd sink through the floor."

"That's not the thing, damn it! Others are doing it and they're not ministerial students. You could too."

"Yes, but do you know what they are when they use religion for a blind like that? They are a bunch of cheats. That's exactly what they are. I don't intend to do it unless I have to leave Vanderbilt University. Then I'd have to drop two of the courses that I'm taking in the English Department for a couple of courses in the School of Religion. Well, I don't intend to do it."

There was much Jesse had admired in Don West—his rough good looks, his energy, the freedom of his hitchhiking and globe-trotting. West had thumbed his way over the country and taken a bicycle and walking tour of England, Belgium, France, Germany, Denmark, Norway, and Sweden; he had run two miles in 9:26 and cleared the high jump at six-three.

On the third floor of Wesley Hall, Jesse had also met sculptor-poet Julian Lee Rayford. Rayford was living in a back room on the same floor when, as he later wrote, "one afternoon, in pops this big country boy from Kentucky."

Immediately Jesse said, "You're a sculptor?"

Rayford admitted it.

"And you're a writer?" Rayford had published in the *American Mercury* and *New York Herald Tribune,* and he was cocky about it. Immediately Jesse began talking about his own work. He had published "Desolation," in the Fall 1930 issue of *Prairie Schooner,* as well as a dozen other pieces since; and "Brother to the Dust" would appear in *Schooner* the next summer. Though young, Rayford was a serious artist who would in time sculpt models of American folk heroes for the Public Works of Art Project in Washington, D.C. Rayford struck Stuart as comical, perhaps because he insisted on reciting his poetry in a high-pitched voice. Rayford was original in other ways, too. Though not a matriculated student, he had on his own initiative studied anatomy and dissected cadavers, making sketches of bones, ears, muscles, and skulls. The two laughed and suddenly became friends, as Rayford remembered. He was amused at Jesse's good-natured garrulousness and liked him immediately. Before their first meeting was over, the Kentuckian was telling Rayford "he could run the mile faster than a hound—'and look at this leg, boy I can run!' "[7]

During the fall, Jesse and Don West had occasion to see their LMU mentor, Harry Harrison Kroll. In mid-November the *New York Times* carried a review of his new novel, *Cabin in the Cotton,* sympathizing with its social message but condemning it as a novel. On the same day *Books* complimented it as "A worthy effort, the sincerity of which one must respect," but backhanded its artistry as "unimpressive." About two weeks later Allen Tate, referring to Kroll as "A Mississippi Dreiser," gave the book a surprisingly tolerant reading. In this work Kroll's hero, Danny Morgan, succumbs to the wiles of the planter's daughter, Nordie Lord, and to the riches of fine clothes and motor cars. Tate discerned an arresting parallel between Kroll's "fuddled" hero and Dreiser's Clyde Griffiths. Remembering well that Kroll had worked hard on "his Cotton novel" at Harrogate, then into the summer of 1929, Jesse could not resist traveling more than a hundred miles out into northwestern Tennessee to see him again. There he found Kroll "had a house he'd rented up on the hill and he was driving a Hudson car. And boy! he was living it up. . . . I think he got $50,000 for the rights." Bette Davis and Richard Barthelmess would play the lead roles in the film.

Don West had been working on a little collection of dialect poems and was arranging for the Art Print Shop of Trevecca College to publish it. Julian Rayford did a portrait for the frontispiece and West wanted Harry Kroll to write the Foreword and Jesse the Introduction. Both obliged him. Jesse finished his Introduction on November 21, writing that West's poems were "nearer the soil" than James Whitcomb Riley's, though admitting that the Hoosier poet's were "more universal." West "has confined himself to a region where the dark austere summit lines of the sky limit the horizon"—his "barrier"—and "he seldom goes beyond." Folksy and unpretentious, the poems of *Crab-Grass* struck young Stuart as "terse and original," yet, perhaps out of his strong friendship for West, he contented himself with an introduction more biographical than critical. According to Rayford, however, the fifty-page black book with a brass-colored imprint of a log cabin on its cover "seemed to put a little more fire under Jesse and he began writing more intensely. . . . Gradually . . . surely, I came to know an artist was living there on the third floor with me."

Early in the fall Jesse had met William R. Moses. The two shared an interest in literature and nature, and walked and talked on the Vanderbilt campus. Sometimes on Sundays they went to Centennial Park to see the Parthenon or took a streetcar to the end of the line and walked the country roads. In time, "Will" Moses became Jesse's closest friend at Vanderbilt. However, when they first met, Jesse looked strange to the Minnesota native. Moses was familiar with country people, since most of his mother's family were from farms or small towns, but most of the rural background he was familiar with was that of central Minnesota, not of northeastern Kentucky. "And Jesse, always a man with the courage of his convictions, came on strong." In contrast to his sudden rapport with Julian Rayford, his friendship with Will Moses, then in his senior year at Vanderbilt, developed more slowly. On at least one occasion, probably on one of the rambles around Centennial Park and the Parthenon, Jesse and Will were accompanied by Elizabeth Hale, and on another by Don West.

Though memorable, such moments of delight were not frequent. That fall he had "grabbed" four jobs. When football season came, he caught the fever, writing home as early as August 19, 1931, "Vanderbilt has already begun to crowd. Foot ball [sic] is in the air. Coaches smoke their fat cigars and long stem pipes and laugh and talk football." He wanted to sell programs at football games but was told all the jobs were taken. Remembering the time he was fired on the Greenup Street job, and while unnoticed began working with another gang and continued to get paid, he just got himself some programs and began selling. "It worked beautifully. I made a little money and saw all the games free." He sold coupons for car-repair "bargains," too, and worked in the Wesley Hall cafeteria an average of two hours each day, receiving in return eleven meals a week. On these, largely, he survived—"one on Sunday, two on Monday, one on Tuesday, two on Wednesday and Thursday, one on Friday and two on Saturday. The week-ends were hardest." He worked for nearly three months sweeping the lofty-ceilinged rooms of Science Hall, polishing its high windows, waxing the oak floors and high baseboards, and cleaning toilets. He worked from six to seven in the morning and from two until five in the afternoon. "I had one distinction," he later wrote. "I was the only white janitor at the University." Will Moses never forgot his first impression of Jesse Stuart: "His trousers, or one pair of his trousers, were so worn at heel that an arc, almost a half circle, of the cloth was gone." Moses had been accustomed to seeing poverty, "but I had never seen the like of that."

It would be a mistake to think Jesse Stuart had been unconscious of his clothes. Indeed, he believed it was such clothes that helped him get the janitorial job, for the personnel manager who hired him, one who had also worked his way through college, "saw my worn shirt with split places around the shoulder." As early as his LMU days, Elmer Heaberlin remembered Jesse's sensitivity about his appearance—even "little things"—and his extreme sensitivity about customs and common decencies.

One morning the custodial foreman at Vanderbilt, a man the author later called "Rister," watched him run a wire through several rolls of toilet paper and put a brown wrapper on them. "What are you wrapping that toilet paper up for?"

"I don't want those girls standing up there on the walk to see me carrying it across the campus."

"Oh, you don't? Well, all the other janitors do it."

"Well, here's one sure as hell not doing it, Rister. I am a janitor but I'm not going up across the campus with an armload of toilet paper."

"Well, ain't girls seen it before?"

"That may be true, but don't we have a certain amount of decency between us and self-respect? If we didn't we'd all use the same toilets." The foreman did not like Jesse Stuart's attitude. He wanted to say something to the big student but hesitated. "By the way he approached me," Jesse wrote, "I knew he was afraid."

One afternoon shortly after lunch at the Wesley Hall cafeteria, Jesse had heard someone call his name. He looked up from the steam and heat of dishwashing to see Lena Wells Lykins Voiers and her new husband, Gus, who ran a clothing store in Vanceburg, Kentucky. She was right there looking at him with her "big 'howdy' smile that lights up her whole face." Through the steam she spoke, "Well, well, look where I find you. Up among the clouds as always." What a genius the woman had for keeping up with students and making timely appearances! She had been his first principal, had come into W-Hollow and goaded him back to Greenup High School to struggle with algebra because he had believed he would write a book someday; later, she had come by the boardinghouse in Ashland when he was striking steel and encouraged him to go on to college in September; he had seen her later still, after his graduation from LMU and at Warnock when his students began to win academic honors—and now here! After he got off work, they had time to talk. Her visits always put "new life, hope, and ambition" in him and "to listen to her gave him renewed faith in his future." Such faith and fervor, though invisible, moved him. After they visited he wanted to do something for her. Swallowing all mixed feelings and hesitation, he threw caution to the wind and inscribed for her a copy of *Harvest of Youth.*[8]

As the leaves had turned and thinned on the southern campus in the big bowl that was Nashville, he was not so sure about what he was learning, only that his urge to write was increasing. He had to make a note to the Business Office for eight dollars before completing registration and had no money left with which to buy books. Fortunately, he ran upon an agreeable Georgian who loaned him his books. Clem Carson vividly recalled their first encounter:

> I had just bought my books for my first classes and stopped in a diner for a bite to eat, when a dark-haired fellow . . . came up to me and introduced himself as Jesse Stuart. He was a sizeable fellow and looked like a fine physical specimen. He asked questions about the books, how much they cost. . . . After looking at one in particular, which we were to use in our lyric class under Donald Davidson, he asked permission to use it for an hour or two. I went on to my dormitory room, thinking maybe I had been rooked out of a new book.

But Carson did not have to wait very long until he heard a knocking at his door. It was Jesse, who returned the book. The two sat and talked and "he and I became good friends" from that time on; "on other occasions he borrowed books from me as well." That first quarter Jesse either borrowed or read what he could in the library and, unfortunately, at other times, did without. When he was not studying he was writing, and he was writing more than he was studying. He called a growing sheaf of seasonal sonnets "Songs of a Mountain Plowman," but he was far from satisfied with them. They evoked the beauty of the four north temperate zone seasons he knew so well, but he "was disappointed that they didn't come alive . . . that they didn't sing!" One day in the library stacks he pulled out a translation of the *Eclogues* and read those "idyllic pastoral poems." Then he read Vergil's *Georgics,* too, and was upset. Jesse's own "Songs of a Mountain Plowman" was organized in four books— four seasons—much like the Mantuan poet's. There in the shelves for all the world to see was Vergil's *Georgics,* "praising the farm people and the rustic life of the Roman Republic . . . a beautiful book," and consequently, even though there had been little if any Vergilian influence on his own work, he was "disheartened" about sending his book to a publisher. Why not take the time he was using on sonnets, poems, and stories—for he was writing sketches of prose, too—and spend it on more study and class preparation? The growing book of sonnets was doing him little good, especially since he kept the pieces hidden away, but "it was just in me to write poetry and I did not suppress the desire." When the conflict between intellectual desire and creative compulsion built to a climax a few months later, the explanation spilled out:

> Poetry took me along. It made me its servant. I couldn't handle poetry. That is funny to say but I heard Lum Dryasdust say something funnier at Vanderbilt: "I'm reading the sonnets of Shakespeare now. I'm getting inspiration from them to write. I'm reading Edgar Allan Poe's 'Poetic Principles,' about how to construct verse. I'm going to sit down and write poetry when I get my term papers off and have a little time. I want to be a poet. I want to write novels too."
> Oh, dear Lum Dryasdust! You are taking poetry along with you. It doesn't have you by the heels and drag you everywhere you go, through the steel mills, and the leaves, through the pasture fields and the cornfields, through the tie-timber woods, at the plow and everywhere you go. No, you are going to sit down and write poetry, when you get ready. . . . Poetry puts you down and makes you write. . . . Poetry will tell you to let the term papers go to hell. It will make you lie to your teachers.

Jesse had never known a stranger. One day he stepped up to a student, the "Oscar Boswell" of *Beyond Dark Hills*, and complimented his poem in the university magazine—possibly the *Vanderbilt Observer*. It was a poem "about the ghosts of dead leaves following you on the street."

"I'm glad you think it was poetry. I do not."

But Stuart knew better, and interpreted the remark as "false modesty." He said, "Well, I try scribbling verse too. I've placed a few poems in one-horse magazines."

The student only smiled. Stuart's sensitivity rose up. "I believed that he didn't believe me. I think that he thought I was a faker." Neither did Jesse Stuart think the teachers at Vanderbilt would believe he had written over five hundred poems in three years of college while he paid his expenses by working. "They would think I was a newspaper crooner, —a poem-a-day keeps the doctor away." Years later he denied that Oscar Boswell referred to his classmate Randall Jarrell, or to any other specific student. "It had nothing to do with Randall Jarrell. I didn't like him. He was an ass. Donald Davidson couldn't stand him. Jarrell tried to take [Davidson's] classes over. He did not understand anybody, [for he was] too wrapped up in himself. Walter Sharpe was another one in that class, too," Jesse said. Boswell was "a personalized idea, and so was Lum Dryasdust—a personalized idea. I got the idea of 'Dryasdust' from Carlyle's

Sartor Resartus in Mims' class. I was good in that course; and I underlined my copy of that book."

For all these reasons he was unsure about college—a stranger afraid. He realized he had left "flat impressions" on Mims, Davidson, Warren, and Wade, his professors. Vanderbilt was so different from LMU, where he had been able to learn and work and write and, most important, still succeed. The fear of failure, and worse, of misrepresenting himself to others was frustrating. His logic told him that his plight was his own fault. He had begun to think about a thesis on John Fox, Jr., and had pored through the stacks of theses at both Vanderbilt and Peabody to find them "dryasdust" too. In their metal shelves, "they were all covered with dust. The only time they were ever used was when a student wanted to see what one was like before he wrote his." His thesis director at Peabody was "dryasdust," too. "Oh Lord, he couldn't talk without fixing his words artificially. A big professor, dull as a frow."[9]

. . . Now, the crowds were busy in downtown Nashville. Despite the Depression, the stores were already lit up for the Christmas season and blinked in festive decoration. He yearned to go home for a few days at least, but the poem had been blowing him along as a northeast Kentucky wind blows a yellow autumn leaf. He screwed the tip back on his pen, put it in his pocket, and looked at the envelope in his hand. A wind colder than autumn's tousled his dark hair over the right side of his forehead. He stood on the corner of Church Street and read,

> Be with me courage, for I walk alone,
> Although I have no fear of night and gloom.
> The earth is wide and there is spacious room
> For human creatures on her streets of stone.
> Be with me, courage, in this trying hour
> When stars are hard to barter for thin bread,
> (Be with us all in this dark hour of need)
> The lonely poor with dreams, the rich with power.

> The leafless tree in winter stands alone
> Dreaming of leafy days and sunny Spring
> When birds alighted in her boughs to sing.
> Now somewhere out by changing winds I'm blown,
> A yellow leaf to drift with time away
> The silver moments of my swift brief day.

By the arrival of the Christmas holidays he had little money left. His janitorial job at Science Hall was over and he had no job to give him hope of getting more money. He had tried the newspaper offices for reporting jobs with no luck. Now that Christmas had come, the Wesley Hall cafeteria trade had slowed to a trickle; the cafeteria closed entirely for three days of the Christmas vacation.

On January 4, 1932, Jesse caught a ride through from Nashville to Ashland, Kentucky, and was back in Greenup. He had to pay interest on a note at the bank or disappoint Forrest and Lillie King, his co-signers. It was the first Monday of the month, sales day in Greenup, and the courthouse square was thronged with county farmers, townspeople, merchants, and all kinds of goods for selling and trading, from old plug horses to cheap clothes being auctioned from the back of a truck. It was a warm day for January in Kentucky, but the wind was rising. An old blind couple named Haley played fiddle and guitar and wailed in "long-drawn-out sentimental voices" such old-time favorites as "In London Far City," "Sourwood Mountain," "The Hangman's Song," "The Little Mohee," and "Loving Nancy." Jesse had forgotten about stars being "hard to barter for thin bread." He went to the bank to have his note renewed. Several people kidded him about his education. A few wanted him to run for Superintendent of Greenup County Schools against Robert J. Nickel. It was sunset by the time he took the familiar ridge path home up past Uncle Frank Sparks' place, on up the trail through a hundred trees he knew intimately—patches of dogwoods and black oaks. It was the path he had walked to school. Impulsively, he went over to the black oaks and put his hands on their rough black bark. It was getting dark and the winter wind rustled dried leaves on the branches. He looked up and saw the stars coming out. The hill leveled out by a cornfield where he stood just a moment to hear the wind rattle the blades of fodder in the upright shocks along the edge of the trees; it "sang lonesome-like in the bleak treetops." The familiar joy of home suddenly flooded through him—"Oh, but it was great to be back again! I could forget school life. I could be free. I could run with the wind. I could act crazy out there on the ridge." He thought of his poem "The Trail," written right there on a white oak stump by the side of the road in December of 1926, when he had returned after his first quarter at Harrogate. He went down the long, sloping pasture along the hilly woods to his left until he reached the orchard of peach and apple trees he had set out in 1926. He stood in the moonlight and turned right to descend through the orchard and small pasture and up a slight incline to the chipyard. Through it and he was home again, his feet under the table. He was eating chicken and pickles and cornbread and butter and sausage with sage and drinking sour buttermilk just the way he liked it.

James was seventeen and home from Berea College. The two stayed up most of the night talking. Mitchell Stuart was working hard on the railroad section but still did not have the farm paid for. Martha Stuart had sold eggs and cream to help pay James' college expenses at Berea. Sophia and Mary were married now and only Glennis was living at home. Just as some of the people in the town had suggested, Jesse's father urged him to run for superintendent of county schools. James left for Berea early Tuesday morning and Jesse followed at noon, up the same ridge path. At the orchard fence he sat down on his suitcase and thought of his boyhood dreams of Robert Burns and his Kentucky Highlands— these hills. This was the land he had once hated and wanted to leave. He had even cursed it, but now it occurred to him that, like his father who had often declared his wish, he wanted to be hauled to one of these hills for his "last long sleep." Sitting there at noon on January 5, he wrote the sonnet "Return":

> Kentucky, I shall return to you some day
> To live out in your wind and rain and sun
> And watch your trees and fields together run
> And orchards whiten with the blooms of May.
> I shall go back and sit before the fires
> At home and tell tales with a fellow rover,
> Before I'm cold and the best of life is over;
> We'll tell of drinking days and fighting sires.
> I shall go back to tramp the crimson leaves
> That spread like quilts upon the frosty ground.
> I'll take my gun and faithful hunting hound
> And be alone where wind in treetops grieves.
> Kentucky, your dwindling autumn streams
> Flow out across old meadows of my dreams.

That night his Greyhound bus took him across the Bluegrass. By morning he was back in Nashville on the Vanderbilt campus.[10]

7

"Beyond Dark Hills": Vanderbilt 1931–1932

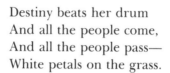

Destiny beats her drum
And all the people come,
And all the people pass—
White petals on the grass.

(Lines written at Vanderbilt,
April, 1932, *Beyond Dark Hills)*

He castigated himself for writing poetry when he should have been studying for his English classes and working on his thesis. Too much of his time had gone into sweeping Science Hall, selling garage coupons and football programs, taking trays off the conveyor belt and cleaning pots and pans at Wesley Hall cafeteria. He resolved to discipline himself to study. Then, in spite of his resolve, he let poetry grab him to write the sonnet "To Three Low Grades" anyway. It was a way of dealing with his problems—one C in Mims' Victorian Prose and Poetry, one C in Davidson's English Lyric Poetry, and one C in Wade's American Literature. Only in Robert Penn Warren's class had he made a B—and an overall B standing was necessary for a graduate student to attain an M.A. "Red" Warren was the youngest of his teachers, not much older, Jesse believed, than he himself. Warren was friendly enough to share his tobacco pouch with his students, though Jesse himself did not smoke at that time. Warren was tall and thin and retained something of those shy, self-effacing qualities Allen Tate was to remember from their first meeting in Walter Clyde Curry's office eight years before, when Warren was just as tall and even thinner. "He had a long quivering nose, large brown eyes, and a long chin—all topped by curly red hair."[1]

Actually "Mr. Warren," as Jesse addressed his teacher on campus, was in his twenty-sixth year during most of the three academic quarters of their association in 1931/1932. The Guthrie, Kentucky, native had been one of the Fugitives even before he received his degree at Vanderbilt and studied for his M.A. at Berkeley. Only the year before he had been a Rhodes Scholar at Oxford. Warren had published a book on John Brown, *The Making of a Martyr* (1929), and was one of the twelve Southerners who had essays published in *I'll Take My Stand,* the widely known testament of the Agrarians published in 1930. Though Warren was a western Kentuckian and Jesse Stuart an eastern Kentuckian, both had served at Camp Knox near Louisville in the Citizens Military Training Camp and had their names printed in the summer yearbook, *The Mess Kit,* Warren in the 1922 edition and Stuart in the 1923 and 1926 editions.[2]

Other members of Jesse Stuart's class with Robert Penn Warren included Lacey Reynolds, Logan Tuthill, and Viston Smith, as classmate Kathryn Geny recalls. She was a junior then, taking the course for undergraduate credit, and remembers how the class used to love to listen to "Robert Penn," as she and other students spoke of him. To her mind Warren was "poetic, intellectual," and Jesse Stuart was "earth earthy." One day the class discussed the popular novel *Elmer Gantry.* Jesse was impressed with the realism of the work and gave as an example of his opinion, so she seemed to recollect, Sinclair Lewis' description of the hair on Elmer Gantry's arms. "I can see Robert Penn cringing right now. For Jesse to mention the hair on Elmer Gantry's arms—the thought that Jesse Stuart would pick out that for discussion!" However, Mr. Warren thinks that Ms. Geny may have *Elmer Gantry* "mixed up" with Eliot's "The Love Song of J. Alfred Prufrock," in which Prufrock expresses "a hint of revulsion . . . of neurotic repudiation" at the image of hair on the arms, and confused Prufrock's unrealistic response with his own because he may have read the poem in character. Ms. Geny also observed that Jesse was quick to engage in class discussions and seemed to know what he was talking about. "Jesse sat right on the end of the row, and he picked up on everything he could. Jesse was always interesting to us in the class." Sometimes Jesse and Warren "argued," she remembers, but in a spirited classroom atmosphere that allowed for discussion. Warren recalls that discussions with Jesse and others were "not uncommon" in the class. Jesse was "very frank. He would speak his mind; he was thinking out loud. He didn't speak to please. I remember that distinctly."[3]

But Jesse Stuart's newfound excitement at having discovered an English heaven with his Vanderbilt teachers, who were authors, too, "was constantly marred by my always wanting food." Soon after his formal resolution "to conform and study all required subjects," he sat in Warren's Contemporary Literature class just before noon:

> About twenty of us are listening to Robert Warren talk about Elizabeth Madox Roberts. He goes on lecturing. I don't get it all. My stomach keeps on bothering me. It is empty. I forgot to drink water before I came to the class. Drink plenty of water for water is good to drink. The head is dizzy and the whole body feels sick. Drink good cool clear water and drink plenty of it, for it makes the sickness leave the body. Drink water when you are hungry so that your guts won't growl and the girls next to you won't hear and laugh. I don't mind a boy hearing but I hate like hell for one of the girls to hear. But their guts would growl too if their stomachs were empty. I only forgot to drink water. My stomach has ripped out a long growl. I bend over and press my hand on my stomach. It ceases slightly. My arm grows tired pressing down on my stomach. I remove it for a rest. My guts let out another long growl. Damn guts, I'd like to put my hands on them and squeeze them in their emptiness and confusion. I'd stop them from embarrassing me. I didn't quite get all that Warren said. It is only five minutes until the bell. I can see the clock in the tower from my window. I'll be glad when the five minutes are gone.

The eleven meals a week had been enough to sustain his weight at about 192 pounds and to fuel his enormous energy, but not enough to assuage the distraction of nearly constant hunger, especially now that the late Nashville winter was upon him. He had learned in the steel mills to drink water and lick salt to increase the turgidity of his body cells. The water was filling—"good fodder," as he put it—but, of course, no substitute for food. Hunger etched itself deeply in his waking hours at Vanderbilt. Yet "the hunger of the mind, as strong and constant as the beating of my heart, overcame the hunger for food." Stirred by these elemental needs, he soliloquized, "Cramp your guts when they growl. Push them against your backbone with your hand flat against your stomach. But don't cramp your dreams."[4]

One evening Julian Lee Rayford took Jesse Stuart out to 3802 Whitland Avenue, perhaps three miles west of the Vanderbilt campus, to meet Sidney Mttron (pronounced Me-TAT-tron) Hirsch, one of the early Fugitive poets with interests in Oriental civilization, linguistics, and journalism. The gifted son of a cultured Jewish family, at the time he was living with his sister, Rose, and brother-in-law, James Frank, a scholarly merchant and, like Hirsch, an early Fugitive. Both were given to the role of Maecenas, and the Fugitives had met from time to time at one of their homes from 1913 to 1928 to discuss their work. Allen Tate wrote Donald Davidson that he thought of Davidson, Ransom, and himself as the "Final Causes" of the Fugitive movement, Hirsch as merely the "Efficient Cause." Invited by Donald Davidson to a Fugitive meeting in 1921, Tate perceived Hirsch as a person of "vast if somewhat perverse erudition . . . a mystic and I think a Rosicrucian, a great deal of whose doctrine skittered elusively among imaginary etymologies. . . . Shining pince-nez stood up on his handsome nose, and curled Assyrian hair topped a massive brow." Others were more respectful. Davidson remembered that the Fugitives grew silent when

> Sidney Hirsch picked out some word—most likely a proper name like Odysseus or Hamlet or Parsifal, or some common word like fool or fugitive—and then, turning from dictionary to dictionary in various languages, proceeded to unroll a chain of veiled meanings that could be understood only through the system of etymologies to which he had the key. This, he assured us, was the wisdom of the ages—a palimpsest underlying all great poetry, all great art, all religion, in all eras, in all lands. All true poets possessed this wisdom intuitively, he told us, solemnly, repeatedly.

Julian Rayford thought of Hirsch as the founder of the Fugitives, Olympian in his learning, a true exemplar of "everything ideal a man should be." He told the Kentucky poet something of Hirsch, "the intimate friend of painters, poets, novelists, sculptors, philosophers." Hirsch had associated with Rodin, Isadora Duncan, Percy Mackaye, Paris Singer, James Earle Fraser, and Edward MacCartan, and all kinds of people called on him in Nashville. Stuart should not be uneasy, Rayford remembered advising him; but "Jesse was nervous about going out there to Whitland Avenue that night."[5]

The man with the reputation of a Nashville Buddha, however, received Jesse Stuart with generosity and food. He fed the young poet that night and many nights afterward. In time, Jesse took whole sheaves of poems to Hirsch, who must have divined something of that "palimpsest underlying all great poetry" in the Kentuckian's work. "Sidney liked Jesse," Rayford recalled, and "it always cheered him when Jesse came around." That first night their vibrations must have been strong indeed, for "pretty soon," Rayford reminisced, "old Jess was telling him how fast he could run and showing him his leg." Within a few weeks Jesse Stuart would write,

I was a welcome visitor at any time. [Sidney] never censored my work. It was always praise and encouragement. His home was filled with good books. His place was home to me. In addition to the bread of dreams he gave me along with the other youth of the land who'd come and stay a week or longer with him . . . big plates of potatoes, big slices of cheese, green onions, milk, bread. . . . Ah, those feasts there when I ate food until I was ashamed, and then he stacked more on my plate![6]

Hirsch spoke pleasantly, "Your teachers used to come here. Donald Davidson came to me when he was just a boy in Vanderbilt University. I have many of his youthful poems now. He was the handsomest youth I've ever seen. When the war came on he enlisted and became an officer. Once he captured five Germans single-handed. The war didn't do him any good." Stuart was impressed and found his horizons widening. Before another season was over he would write, "Religious leaders of India came there, Robert Frost had been there, and G. K. Chesterton, Clarence Darrow, Edwin Markham, George Russell, Vachel Lindsay, and T. S. Eliot! It was great to hear about these people."[7]

When Jesse Stuart saw his grades for the first quarter at Vanderbilt, "my legs weakened," he later acknowledged. Almost intuitively he sought out Donald Davidson, who lived in an apartment in Wesley Hall with his wife, Theresa, and their daughter, Mary. The couple were in their thirties and, with their twelve-year-old, Jesse thought they composed "a good family scene." As early as the spring of 1928 at Harrogate, Jesse had read Davidson's weekly literary page in the Knoxville *Journal,* and his column "The Critic's Almanac" had thoroughly engaged his attention. Many of the Agrarians and Fugitives had reviewed and commented on literary topics in "The Weekly Review: A Page about Books," and it was one of the lures that had drawn him to Vanderbilt. Economic pressures of the Great Depression, however, had brought Davidson's ambitious enterprise to a close the year before Jesse enrolled at Vanderbilt. Davidson had published two books of poetry, *An Outland Piper* in 1924 and *The Tall Men* in 1927. It was generally known that he was the driving force behind the Agrarians and was editor of *I'll Take My Stand,* as well as author of one of the twelve essays. Davidson had published articles in *Creative Reading, Forum, Saturday Review of Literature, Sewanee Review,* and other literaries. Distinguished and friendly, there was something very human about Davidson that gave the student confidence.

"There is something very fine about his face," Jesse later wrote of his teacher. "He had black keen eyes. They were so alive. He talked with his eyes; he showed friendliness with his eyes." So, though the telling shamed him, Jesse confessed to Davidson his problems and dreams. "What was I down there for, anyway, bothering Davidson?" he wondered, but went on talking, and Davidson said, "Oh yes, I understand." Did Davidson truly understand "what amounted to trivial dreams?" Even though he might not finish his coursework that year, his teacher told him, "You don't have to get an M.A. before the sun goes down. Take your time about it. Don't worry. I understand." Jesse had got something off his chest, and he felt relieved.[8]

He was "always the first student to enter Davidson's class and the last to leave." Although he had continued to borrow textbooks from classmate Clem Carson, he eventually acquired a copy of the English lyric poems for Davidson's class. Those Elizabethan lyrics the class studied echoed the ballads of his eastern Kentucky hills. Davidson loved the old songs and ballads as did Jesse, so the student felt a cultural kinship with his teacher. "I was brave enough to show him poems" in two sheaves, one of derivative poems of such earlier influences as Sandburg, Rupert Brooke, and lesser-known poets such as one about whom Stuart had written an elegiac sonnet published the previous September in *Sonnet Sequences*:

To Ernest Hartsock, 1903–1930

This day the amber clouds go drifting
    south
Across the Georgian threshold where
    you lie;
I wonder why the glorious young
    must die
And why at you Death spread his
    cruel mouth—
Clean, happy lad with laughter on
    your lips;
Love of life, free as the winds that blow;
Your brain the living fires of sunset glow;
Young with proud music on your finger tips.

If there is life beyond your Georgian grave,
Shelly [sic], and England's own dear Rupert Brooke,
And Keats have met you there, I know. They took
You by the hand and led you where they have

Strange splendors found—where beams the shining
    sun
You are with them, a young immortal one.

It was Hartsock who had encouraged Jesse to publish his *Harvest of Youth*. The young Georgian had not only known of Davidson and the Fugitives, but had praised Davidson as a Southern critic of significance, one who "had become an active force in our literary life."[9]

Davidson lost no time in turning Jesse away from such conventional, post-Romantic figures, as well as from the obviously imitative poems of *Harvest of Youth*. Certainly no stranger to Hartsock's work, Davidson took *Narcissus and Iscariot* from him, so Jesse recalls, leafed through it, and told him, "Stuart, don't be a pretty boy." Davidson put down the thin volume. "These are pretty-boy poems." Again, the graduate student noticed Davidson's eyes. His professor certainly did a lot of things with his eyes. Davidson said that Rupert Brooke was a pretty boy, too.[10]

It was Jesse Stuart's second sheaf of poems that caught Davidson's attention. There was something in them. "Your natural poems are the ones," he told Stuart. "This is your trend to follow." It was a moment that would endure, perhaps be glorified in the Agrarian's memory. Nearly a quarter of a century later he would recall the Kentucky youth standing in his office in Calhoun, just off the northeast corner of the site of old Wesley Hall (what is now the greensward behind the Joint University Libraries):

> The bundle in his hands contains some pretty but rather worthless poems of his that had appeared in certain even more worthless poetry magazines. They were what he thought he was supposed to write in the way of poetry. But the bundle also contained a rough draft of what later became his "[Elegy] for Mitch Stuart," which was something Jesse Stuart really meant when he was thinking of Kentucky and the world.[11]

In the weeks that followed, Jesse got down to work on his thesis on John Fox, Jr., but his heart was not in it. Donald Davidson thought Jesse had difficulty with term papers because of his long work hours and his compulsive creative absorption. The truth was that Jesse had not learned to write a genuine research paper at Lincoln Memorial. Not having been trained in formal research technique, he was frustrated in competing with formally trained students. Still he continued to drive himself to the library and immerse himself in reading master's theses and learning by example. Painfully, he began to force out the writing; but a few weeks later, in a burst of creative energy that would find expression in *Beyond Dark Hills,* he rebelled: "God help me! God help us all! God help this dry educational system! God give it a backbone to hold to and not dry theses. . . . Don't strike matches around theses or wear tacks in your shoes."[12]

He thought of himself as a writer and a poet. One day he was walking across the campus with one of the students with whom he took all four of his graduate classes. Just who the student was is not clear, but the two were discussing such writers as Davidson, Warren, Tate, and Ransom when Jesse said, "I'm a writer, too! I've written a book."

"What's the title?"

"*Harvest of Youth.* It's poetry."

"Who published it?"

"Scroll Press."

"I never heard of Scroll Press."

"It's at Howe, Oklahoma."

"Isn't that a vanity house?"

Jesse did not answer.

Later, he was sure the student had gone to the library vainly to seek his book. "After this experience, which embarrassed me and really cooled me, I knew I'd never tell another person I'd written a book until I had written one published by a good house on a royalty basis. Then, I'd shout it to the world: I've written a book. I also knew and I knew only too well, I'd kill *Harvest of Youth.* I'd murder my own book."[13]

Other discomfiting incidents occurred, of which he sometimes seemed hardly conscious. Sometime after Kroll's success with *Cabin in the Cotton,* Jesse, Don West, and Julian Lee Rayford took Harry Kroll out to Whitland Avenue. They rode out in style in Kroll's new "Hudson Super Six," and introduced the author to Sidney Hirsch. That evening, Rayford remembered, Jesse sat in an antique chair with thin legs and leaned back against the wall while the chair strained with his weight. It "cracked and creaked," and they were uneasy, even as Hirsch began to fall into his pattern of attentive listening and comment; but even Hirsch may have noticed, for as Rayford remembered, "I think we all sweated over that chair." It apparently "never bothered old Jess a bit!"[14]

Meanwhile, despite confusion with his term papers, the demands of physical work, and omnipresent hunger, his newfound relationship with Donald Davidson brought him renewed determination to succeed in academic work and genuine encouragement, even excitement about his future prospects as a writer. He dug back into "Songs of a Mountain Plowman." Although as a seasonal unit—a book as he had originally planned it—it still did not satisfy him, groups of the poems certainly told something of himself he desired to express. Moreover, he very much wanted Davidson's reaction to them. In the batch he also included two longer pieces, the substance of the nineteen-stanza "Elegy for Mitch Stuart" in six parts, and another poem of thirty-three decasyllabic couplets with one three-line stanza sandwiched in the middle, which he called "House in the Wind." As the second quarter continued, he visited the professor's office in Calhoun Hall with increased frequency. "I'd walk up to ease his door open to see if he were in." Although the graduate student had misgivings about taking his teacher's time, increasing confidence overcame hesitancy. Jesse remembered that Davidson "had the good manners never to tell me he was too busy to see me."[15]

Davidson was more than a teacher to Jesse; he was a counselor, patient listener, and friend, yet not so formal a friend that the student could not talk over his "ideas and dreams" with him. In advising him "to write naturally" in his own way and of the things he knew best, Davidson clarified the most immediate vision and love of creativity the young man had developed in W-Hollow. People may have joked about Davidson's conservatism, not only because he was a leading Agrarian, but every fiber of his personality exuded a profound commitment to a literary, philosophic, and moral tradition often identified with the Old South. Jesse Stuart knew the student-wise anecdote well: If a horse and buggy ever pulled up on the Vandy campus and stopped, Donald Grady Davidson would get out. Yet beneath the surface was the man, behind the lecturer the humanist, under the teacher the poet; and poet to poet their minds found rapport. Warren observed that Davidson was "a magnificent teacher," on the one hand "a hard-boiled intellectual," on the other "a poet"; and "he possessed a deep sense of folk culture." This became "a bond between him and Jesse." Davidson "had a natural sympathy for Jesse's poetry and liked it very much, and he was terribly fond of Jesse." For Jesse Stuart, Davidson's classroom and office were "my little bit of Heaven on the Vanderbilt University campus."[16]

In the months to come the Kentucky poet began to receive increased attention among both faculty members and at least some of the Agrarian circle. About the middle of January Allen Tate wrote Donald Davidson from Clarksville, Tennessee, that he had accepted Harriet Monroe's invitation to edit a Southern number of *Poetry* magazine. He asked Davidson for his own contribution and other specific recommendations. By February Davidson sent along his own poem, "Aunt Maria and the Gourds," to be published in the May 1932 issue. During this period he also saw that Tate received some of Jesse Stuart's long and short poems. About this time, Julian Rayford completed a relief portrait of Allen Tate, and sometime in late January or early February Tate was up in Wesley Hall visiting Rayford in his room. He asked Rayford if he knew Jesse Stuart.

"Sure!"

"What do you think of him?"

"I don't know. He's a big country boy." In explanation of his comment years later, Rayford wrote, "Hell! I didn't see much in Jesse. I was twenty-two then, and I didn't see much in anybody but myself. I was out to encompass my own world and I was full of my own conceit."[17]

In early February Rayford got into trouble, as a result of which he was to credit Jesse Stuart with the unwitting favor of perhaps saving his life. A theology student disliked Rayford and so stated to Jesse Stuart, who unwisely told Rayford about the matter. One night with Jesse present, Rayford and the other student got into an argument. Rayford could not control his temper and struck "the preacher" so hard that four stitches were needed to repair his face. "I'm right proud of you for walking over to the hospital when he had his eye patched up," Jesse later told Rayford. Though Rayford was evicted from Wesley Hall, he was nevertheless grateful to Jesse Stuart, for within two weeks Wesley Hall was destroyed by fire.[18]

On February 19, Jesse heard the fire siren, and from his third floor room looked down on the firemen throwing water up. "Oh, it won't amount to much," he thought. "It can't. Now I'll take out a little stuff and put it under that green tree in the yard." He took three shirts and a picture, possibly one Elizabeth Hale had given him, and put them in a suitcase. Outside he stood and watched his room devoured by the flames reaching down from the roof where the fire had begun. He ran back upstairs but was blinded by the smoke. While trying to rescue some books from the fire he split the crotch of the trousers to his one good suit. By 5:15 P.M. Wesley Hall was engulfed in flames. When the fire was out, only a few walls and most of the cafeteria were left standing in the smoking pile of ruins. He had lost what clothes he had, about fifty sonnets, other poems, and a novel fragment. His thesis on John Fox, Jr., and a term paper he had revised five times were gone, along with his old Oliver typewriter. His cafeteria job was put into abeyance, and his eleven meals a week also vanished in the flames of Wesley Hall.[19]

Jesse Stuart and Bill Chandler were able to get "a free room" at Kissam Hall. A little more than a year later he would write Donald Davidson, "You know what a hard year 1931–32 was—the fire at Wesley Hall and how hard the year was on people in general." The frequent caricature of the Great Depression, a carefree tramp going along the road with a bindle over his shoulder, must have appealed to the two roommates, for within weeks Stuart wrote, "I marched away from those ashes on February 19th and each of us promised the other that we would hang together." And each carried his remaining personal belongings "in 'turkey' fashion, as if he was going to a lumber camp." To the main question—Would he stay at Vanderbilt?—Jesse's response was "Hell yes," even if nearly all his personal belongings were gone. "Let them be in ashes. I would arise from the ashes and be stronger than when I fell among them."[20]

The maid at Kissam Hall patched up the split crotch of his pants, and Bill Chandler got eggs from his folks on the farm. Together they bought old bread—two loaves for a nickel then—cut the mold off and cooked in their room. Sometimes they had cheese. "Often Sidney Hirsch supplied me with food." His friend Lewis "Mack" McCubbin, the car-owning "Ag" teacher at Greenup, loaned him a suit of clothes so that he would have a change; it was "a little tight but I managed to wear that suit." His former roommate at LMU, Elmer Heaberlin, who had married Maurine ("Scotty") Scott, an LMU girl and was then striving to make ends meet while teaching at Wurtland High School in Greenup County, complied with his request for assistance by sending a box of clothing, some food, and a little money. In gratitude, Jesse soon responded to the Heaberlins with a snapshot of himself and Elizabeth Hale. She is standing on a yard wall of Tennessee rocks about two feet high; though Jesse stands on the ground level, she appears hardly half a head taller than he. Both smiled at the camera. On the back of the photograph is inked

Jesse and
Elizabeth Hale
(Grand ole Opr
Star)
Nashville, Tenn
Jesse a student
at Vanderbilt

Throughout Nashville, clothes were collected. Stuart let one hand-some brown suit, "too big for anybody else but it just fitted me," hang for a long time, for his home-instilled pride rebelled at taking "anything given to me second-hand or first-hand." However, when his pants could be patched no more, his determination to stay in Vanderbilt no matter what the cost overcame his pride. "I went over and got the big suit," he recorded. "It was a fit. It looked very good on me but I always felt guilty in wearing that suit of clothes." So deep was the conflict over that suit that he never cared for the color brown in a suit of his own again.[21]

In this time of what Elizabeth Hale would later refer to as "our financially lean years," she was there to care and help. Jesse managed to see her about once a week. Many times he walked the four miles to 306 Scott Avenue to save the streetcar fare of ten cents. In addition to Saturday nights at the Grand Ole Opry, Jesse and Elizabeth saw each other at church. In the long autumn, and even more frequently as winter waned, the two went for drives in her family car with friends, or for "rambles," at least on one occasion with Bill Moses and his girlfriend around Centennial Park. While in no way feeling inferior, Jesse was sensitive to their differences right down to their clothes. "I hardly had clothes to wear when I saw her—she dressed well—she stood by me like I was a millionaire." When he went to the Hales' home, Elizabeth asked, "Have you been to supper?"

"Yes," Jesse always answered.

But she would put the food out on the table and say, "I expect you're hungry. You can eat a bit, can't you?"

Even though she disguised her perceptivity, Jesse knew she knew, and "very well she understood I was hungry after I'd clean up the table. I'd actually clean the table and sop the dishes. That home cooked food was so good after getting out and scrambling for what I could get." He confided to his friend Carson, "Many a time at Vanderbilt, I went away from the local students there—bought some little thing at a restaurant . . . then I picked up the left-over pieces of light-bread and ate them. And Carson, I was glad to get them." The next year he would write Davidson, "I've been so damned hungry that I've eaten scraps from restaurant tables. . . . And this has not been long ago." Years later he would declare, "Every time I stand on the Vanderbilt campus, I get hungry." He would develop the habit of leaving nothing on his plate. "My going hungry so often in the past has put a stricture in me against wasting food. I know somebody somewhere is hungry."[22]

About this time he received a donation of five dollars to help replace textbooks destroyed in the Wesley Hall fire, and he also received a sonnet prize of five dollars from *Muse and Mirror,* where two vigorous fourteen-line poems had appeared. In "Autumn Potency" Jesse's persona watches black oak leaves blown to the ground by winds with voices "like wounded quails"; autumnal meadows are mown, wildlife retreats, and geese migrate. The persona desires to fly with the "gray restless birds," communicative as "words from this brown autumn's mouth," but he can only "bite my lips . . . to keep from crying." The second sonnet, "Four Sweethearts Go to Bed with Death," is seasonally progressive and continues the wind imagery into winter. The avian image becomes a "keen-eyed crow" flopping his frosty wings against the frozen timber," querying, "Who sleeps beneath this January cover?" Perhaps of biographical significance, the names of "sleepers" Elizabeth Hale and Marvin Smith appear in the poem. Ed Hardy recalls that Elizabeth Hale's close friend, Carrie Louise Benz, later married Marvin Smith and that the four friends shared many happy moments together, including a visit to Jesse Stuart's home in W-Hollow the next summer. In "Four Sweethearts," however, the themes of the transience of life and the inevitability of death dominate the poem with heavy, prophetic certitude. Implicit in both poems, too, is the threat or fear of something indefinable, more amorphous than winter and death, to which the persona can only react—perhaps the desire to be free as migratory birds that "in streams go south," escaping the very coldness the persona must endure. Despite the overwhelming pitch of love's emotional intensity, the realization that snow will indeed cover "many a forgotten lover's lover"—Elizabeth Hale and her "John," and "Sly Marvin Smith" and his "Joan," too—stands as a calming paradox of life-affirming passions. Of the largess of the five-dollar donation, the need for textbooks notwithstanding, and the five-dollar prize from *Muse and Mirror*, the poet-student later wrote, "I saved this ten dollars for food."[23]

From Clarksville, Allen Tate wrote Donald Davidson on March 10 of his rejection of Jesse Stuart's poems for the May 1932 Southern number of *Poetry*:

Stuart shows some good qualities, but I don't see how I can use any of this stuff in this number. In the longer pieces there are flashes, but the short ones lack the headlong freshness of some lines in the long, and are merely clumsy. (It is a minor point: but the boy should learn that *lie* is not a transitive verb.) But he does have a genuine flair, and being near him you have a good chance to give him pointers. It seems to me that he doesn't know what emotions and images belong together, and he has no sense of the leading image of the poem. His composition, to put it another way, is bad. Yet it is obvious that this fellow has some experience that he is trying to understand—a genuine problem; don't you think that this kind of integrity is a fine basis to work from?

One can hardly imagine lines more in opposition to each other than Tate's "You have no more chance than an infusorian / Lodged in a hollow molar of an eohippus / Come, now, no prattle of remergence with the ὄντως ὄν" (translated as "in actuality"), and Stuart's

> O clansmen, weep!
> Mitch Stuart's dead!
> Old age took him
> At home in bed.
> No Van Horn put
> A bullet through
> Mitch Stuart's head.

Assuming that the early drafts of "Elegy for Mitch Stuart" and "House in the Wind" were in the batch Tate read, as Jesse later believed and so declared, it is strange that the graphic elegy to be published less than a year later in *American Mercury* and the hauntingly piquant couplets of "The House in the Wind," soon to appear in *The Yale Review*, were not dignified with at least a titular reference by editor Tate. Donald Davidson's choice of editor, then, his recommendation notwithstanding, was hardly fortuitous for the struggling Kentucky poet. Davidson did not try to "criticize" Stuart's poems as the Fugitives had so directly done each other's work. He seemed to have realized intuitively that such an approach would not work. Remembering the "hungry, burning, fighting, zealous boy who wrote the *Bull-Tongue Plow* poems," he observed, "*How do you criticize or teach a flowing river?*" For "it was perfectly clear that Jesse Stuart was a river of poetry—and heaven knew what more."[24]

Actually, the teacher had helped the student "to smooth out some wrinkles and to put . . . into rhyme" the "Elegy for Mitch Stuart," although part of Jesse's basic developmental problem had been the need to move away from the free verse he had been imitating. Other than such obvious exceptions and his guidance in the courses on the English lyric, Davidson contended that he had not instructed Jesse as to technique or form. Clearly Stuart was the kind of student who did not study to create, but rather, "the poems burst out of him." Consequently as a young poet he had a "habit of overdoing things," but he would outgrow that. Davidson perceived something rare in his student's plaintive images and commonplace words, as in the poet-student himself, that went straight and purely to the heart of things. He would eventually acknowledge in Jesse an ability even rarer for any literary artist to achieve, a kind of convincing magic:

> I think he is on "my" side in what he writes; and that's what his readers think, I do believe—"He is on *my* side," they must be saying. "Here is *one* writer who is not on that 'other' side—who is not away from us." Isn't that enough? The larger part of it, though, the gift of art, is there, too, in potent quantity.

He recognized his pupil's genius, as he told Frank H. Leavell, "from the first poems that Stuart shared with him," though he was cognizant, too, of the hard times against which he struggled. He knew that Jesse "did not have time to do his school work and that he often did not have enough to eat." Perhaps Davidson discerned in the poems of the raw youth before him something of the "*bardic* tradition," which he would later acknowledge as the poet's restoration of something that had been thought "entirely obsolete and lost." Years later, Davidson rhetorically questioned the weight of his shaping hand in Stuart's early big-name publications: "Did Jesse Stuart, true Kentuckian, true poet, need more than a prod, or a gentle poke, to discover for himself that what he really meant was what he ought to write?"[25]

Whatever else may be said of his role in catalyzing the creative career of Jesse Stuart, Davidson knew originality and quality when he saw it. Sometime after Allen Tate's rejection of the first Stuart poems, Davidson reemphasized for Jesse that the natural pieces were his "trend to follow," especially with "Elegy for Mitch Stuart":

"Send it to H. L. Mencken, editor of the *American Mercury*."

"But I can't even make the little magazines. I send to them, and all I send is returned."

"That is just it. You're cut out for the big magazines. Send it."

Even then Jesse was not convinced. He told Davidson what he had heard of Mencken's derision of American poetry, the waspish editor's opinion that there was no poetry then "fit to publish" in the country.

Davidson nodded and smiled encouragement. "His bark is bigger than his bite." Later that spring Jesse managed to get the poem off to the *American Mercury* and then promptly forgot about it. By the end of the second quarter, he had pulled his grades up to a B level in both Davidson's and Wade's classes and maintained his B standing in Warren's course. Mims' class was still a problem but he seemed to be turning the wintry corner of his graduate career. Spring lay ahead.[26]

Jesse Stuart first saw Allen Tate by the spirea bushes along the little street in front of the Vanderbilt bookstore. Tate had come down to the university from Clarksville on one of his frequent trips. That Jesse had mixed feelings about the well-known Fugitive-Agrarian critic seems hardly surprising. Tate's rejection of his poetry must have smarted, yet the younger man was by no means squelched by Tate or by what he represented. Indeed, Jesse tended to be in sympathy with the Agrarians and most of the essays he had read in *I'll Take My Stand,* which no graduate student in English at Vanderbilt at that time could miss. He knew Davidson and Warren were good friends of Tate's; Tate had published many Fugitive poems and a good book on Jefferson Davis, and he was an active editor and poet. The January *American Mercury* "Check List of New Books" carried a brief review of Caroline Gordon's new novel, *Penhally*, depicting the changing South. Jesse thought it "wonderful" that a man and his wife both could publish books, and he respected the quality of their writing.[27]

Tate was slender and short of stature. He was about thirty-two then, but despite the receding hairline that emphasized his prominent forehead, he looked no older to Jesse than a college graduate student. His egg-shaped head seemed too large for his small body, yet somehow fitting for a literary polemicist of such dry wit. At the time Tate was absorbed in literary activity. Having lived in New York and free-lanced for the *Nation*, the *New Republic*, and the *Herald-Tribune*, he had recently moved to a farm given him by his brother in 1930, near Clarksville. The year before he had published *Poems: 1928–31*. He was the Southern editor of *Hound and Horn* and would join his wife on her Guggenheim Fellowship in France in June. His mustache shifted above an ever-present cigarette as he conversed with Jesse about creativity in general, and in particular about "two very important poets, so he thought, looming high upon the literary horizon, Ezra Pound and T. S. Eliot." Jesse had already used some Eliotic imagery in "House in the Wind," and would very soon experiment further with "Waste Land" images in *Beyond Dark Hills*. Impressed by Tate's inspired mood he "read and reread" Eliot's major poem and dug into Pound. "I read all I did or didn't understand and pretended I understood what I didn't understand." By the end of the academic year, however, Jesse would discard Ezra Pound: "I couldn't make myself believe something I didn't believe"; and though later he would travel to and write in considerable detail about Greece and Rome, stippling his work with proper nouns steeped in classical significance, he never dropped a Greek phrase into a poem in his native language with the assumption that those few to whom the meaning was significant would get it.[28]

One day when Jesse went into Davidson's office, Allen Tate was there. The three talked briefly. Jesse commented on Tate's "Ode to the Confederate Dead." Later he praised some of Tate's work as "grand poetry" and wrote Davidson that "Ode" was "not surpassed in our language the way I see it." That day, though, he was impressed with Davidson's "Litany," a poem that had appeared nine years earlier in the *Fugitive*. An eighteen-line poem in three stanzas, it dealt with weather beating wildly at a farmer's door while inside a child, oblivious to Nature's tumult, slept. Jesse identified his own life with the child's and thought it a fine idea. "Too soon, too soon," sang the incremental repetition, the child must bow his head to the sun and even to the moon to plow and run furrows and bind sheaves for the family's bread. The idea struck Jesse's own creative chords even though he had read the poem only once. The idea bubbled in the very core of his own creative energy, something as yet undefined yet very near his own thoughts.[29]

In Professor Mims' class in Victorian Literature, Jesse had an "incomplete" the second quarter. Mims was then nearly sixty and still vigorous. With his trim inverted-V mustache and pointed goatee, his image was formal and grandfatherly; Jesse and other students thought of him as "a very old man," although most realized that he did not carry a cane because he really needed it. Often Jesse Stuart saw him walking along the campus, smoking his pipe and tapping his cane at "every alternate step." His students were required to memorize many lines of poetry, so many the Kentuckian forgot the number, although it has been estimated at five hundred or more. Mims' poetic ideal was Tennyson, but because Jesse Stuart did not care much for Tennyson, he failed to memorize the minimum requirements; nor was he successful in writing formal papers for Mims. To awed students Mims was "thunder and lightning" in his classroom. Once when students failed to get the text of an assigned poem, he remarked with Mimsian disdain, "I am more and more amazed at the unlimited ability of the human mind to resist the entrance of knowledge." Jesse's reaction to Mims was not unlike that of Donald Davidson seventeen years earlier, when he took Mims' survey course and felt as though he had been "hit by a cyclone." English literature, he discovered, "had a history. . . . Mims' broad acquaintance with different periods was . . . tremendously exciting."[30]

On his first paper Mims did not give Jesse a grade, for his work was "too poor to grade"; however, Mims did single out one of his paragraphs on his experience in the steel mills as "interesting and fairly well written." This notation, along with a B− on a term paper he had written for Davidson, provided some encouragement. He took a week to write another paper for Mims on Carlyle. "This will be an A paper," Jesse thought. But when Mims looked the paper over he failed to find "a single thing about Carlyle," and again would not accept the paper. Later, Jesse went over the paper, and "I couldn't find anything about Carlyle in the paper; only in three places I had imitated his prose."[31]

Knowing what was expected, Jesse worked harder in Mims' Victorian Lit. than he had ever worked in any other class. Now in his last quarter and having been stung by rejected papers, he determined "to write one that would stick." Mims' assignment was for an original autobiographical paper of about eighteen pages. Jesse's response was immediate: "That pleased me very much—the idea of writing an original term paper—something that concerned our own lives." He would tell his professor about himself, how it was to live in the hills of Kentucky, how he had dreamed of going to Harvard and Virginia but had gone to the college that would take him—LMU—and then to Vanderbilt. He wanted to write about how disappointed he was in "finding colleges were not what I thought they were." He wanted Dr. Mims to know about how hungry he had once been for knowledge. He started the paper in late March and finished it in early April, a creative outpouring of eleven days.

One day Jesse wrote thirty-seven pages. He wrote at night, sometimes through the night, but he attended his classes in the morning. He became more excited with the idea, then absorbed in it. Each morning he took what he had written to "Mr. Warren," who told him "it was good," and advised him "to keep it up if I had to throw everything else aside." About the first of April 1932, he wrote,

> Blindly I've beaten these words out. They feel like drops of blood on the eardrum. I beat them with a hammer and forged them with heat cleavers to make them undouble the small pictures I have gathered in the album of my brain. Some of the words got cold too soon and I could not twist them into the shape I wanted them. And you will not care for many of the pictures I have saved. I hope you like what I have had to say about the trees and the horses and skies full of stars. It won't matter much about the bread and onions and my grandfather hanged in the old house. It does not matter about a family moving from place to place and clearing the land and moving on. And the snakes, and the buzzards, blackberries, and copperheads and dead horses by the blue stream and bones in the sunlight don't matter very much. But since I have gone beyond the dark hills I think of a pasture field and pines, and a strong woman with hair turning white now, who goes there with a hoe and a basket of flowers on Decoration Day . . .[32]

Such were the borrowings of his restless memory of life in the hills—those countless pictures of W-Hollow walled off from the meandering Ohio by Seaton Ridge. Now he remembered one time especially when he had returned from Portsmouth, Ohio, going upriver toward his home. "At the bend of the river just before you get to Greenup you can see all of Seaton Ridge . . . spread out before you. I looked up and saw the hills against the sky and they looked dark. I thought, 'Beyond those dark

hills is my home.' *Beyond—Dark—Hills*." And so he titled his paper for
Dr. Mims. He had beaten out the words on a borrowed typewriter. Now
if he thought about it even his dorm room in a way was borrowed, too,
an institutional largess bestowed after his own had burned in the Wesley
Hall fire. The stack of paper had not been borrowed; it was given to
him by his friend Katherine Atherton Grimes, a poet and writer whose
office in the old *Southern Agriculturalist* building was a favorite stopping-
place on his walks downtown. And he had borrowed the money to come
to Vanderbilt, his books from Clem Carson, and a suit for a change from
Mack McCubbin. The funds with which he had registered for the third
quarter of graduate work were also borrowed; his security had been Don
West, although West did not know of his obligation until he came to
Jesse's room one day to say he had arranged a meal a day for his friend
at a boardinghouse on nearby Highland Avenue. "Don, if you ever get
a note with your name signed to it and I'm dead, you pay that note. If
I'm living, remember I'll pay it if I have to crawl and work to do it."
When Jesse was on the last chapter of his paper for Dr. Mims, West
came to the door again and remarked, "I hear the poems you slipped
under Davidson's door are going well here. I heard he read them to the
class."

"It's been a new Vanderbilt to me since Donald Davidson got those
poems," said Jesse. He told West about Boswell's turning friendly—
Boswell, who had once ridiculed him for saying he wrote poetry.[33]

Now he stacked the manuscript on a piece of stiff cardboard and
put three heavy rubber bands around it to make it look thinner. Waiting
until he was the last student, fearful Mims would not accept it, he handed
in the paper. The professor hefted it and spoke abruptly, "You write all
of this for me to read. Stuart, you aggravate me—you are not passing
my work and then you go and write all of this." He strode away, grum-
bling, sucking on his pipe, tapping his cane, and holding the big paper
under his arm. Jesse stood there, ashamed for imposing on Mims at
such a busy time in the spring.

A week later Jesse was on his way to see Robert Penn Warren when
Professor Mims semaphored with his cane and invited Jesse into his
office. The two looked at each other. Mims' eyes were piercing. Jesse let
his own gaze pierce back. "If he was going to start a row with me," Stuart
thought, "I would not stand it any longer." Then Mims said, "I have
been teaching school for forty years and I have never read anything so
crudely written and yet beautiful, tremendous, and powerful as that
term paper you have written."

Mims was smiling at him—a hard smile, it was true, but a smile.

Jesse was floored, as if he "had been hit between the eyes with a bullet."
Was he sincere? Jesse wondered. "Do you really like it?" he asked.

"I took it home and let the family read it. It is a great piece of work."

Even Dr. Mims' daughters had seen his paper, then? He had met Ella Puryear Mims on the Vanderbilt campus, had seen her often, but Catherine was teaching in New Jersey. He thought Ella Puryear, only a sophomore then, was very nice, and he had heard both girls wore culture on their sleeves. Years later Ella Puryear could not recall seeing the manuscript, but said, "I remember a good deal of talk about it, though. It was quite a thing to turn in a three-hundred-page paper for a fifteen- or eighteen-page assignment, and it made quite an impression."

"I can't go out with you to lunch today," Mims was saying, "but I am paying for your lunch—here, take this dollar and eat on me today." He held out the dollar.

Jesse did not want to take it, but he believed he could not very well refuse. Overjoyed, he grabbed it and broke for the Pie Wagon, the diner down the hill from Calhoun Hall on Broadway at 21st Street, across from the old Phi Delta Theta House. Very soon poetry grabbed him to write again in what surely is an object illustration of his declaration, "Writing for me is an escape for overenjoyment":

> There is a pie wagon down on Broad Street
> That keeps good pies and coffee black as ink,
> The place where intellectuals used to meet,
> Survey their scanty food and eat and think.
> I was no intellectual, but I went
> And listened to the silly things they said.
> I got more for the money that I spent
> Is why I went—I drank instead
> Of listenin' to Will Shakespeare's "Tragedies."
> And now I think I shall go back and meet
> The intellectuals there and discuss fleas,
> Order my lunch with five baked pies and eat
> And drink black coffee with white rings of cream,
> Discuss Shakespeare and fleas and eat and dream.[34]

At the time Jesse wrote "Beyond Dark Hills" as a term paper, he had not, of course, composed those portions about Mims' reception of it, his breaking for the Pie Wagon with the dollar, nor the book's tenth and final chapter, to be entitled, "Man with a Bull-Tongue Plow." That chapter would follow five years later while he was in Scotland on his Guggenheim Fellowship. The book had not been written to be published, he later wrote Davidson. "It was written for a term paper. To tell you the truth I've never wanted it published. But the [E. P. Dutton] Company wanted it and asked and asked." His misgivings were both professional and personal. "If it wrecks me I'm just gone." He wanted to give "honest impressions" in the paper, but in so doing he feared his own relatives would be upset. "My brother is bound to raise hell when he sees himself in the book." Jesse was especially apprehensive about his depiction of Lincoln Memorial University, but he thought it was a fair treatment. To Davidson he admitted, "Poor students didn't get good training!" To have moved from LMU to Vanderbilt "was like changing worlds." The shock of the Vanderbilt experience was as quick and definitive as a chemical reaction, crystallizing his deepest interest: "It made me write!" In the weeks that followed, Mims passed Jesse's work among the faculty. Warren recalled Mims' excitement and consternation: " 'My God, this boy turns in a thing like this. *What* am I to do with it?' It was a remarkable thing. Mims and I were not 'pally,' so his mentioning it to me—he must have been hit hard." When Julian Lee Rayford encountered Donald Davidson, Davidson told him that "Jesse had written a work of great significance." He said that "only a genius could have done it." Davidson was further convinced that the book should be published.[35]

The faculty climate at Vanderbilt was culturally as well as creatively and academically invigorating for Jesse. John Donald Wade had come there in 1928 with a particular interest in advanced research in American literature. A pro-Southern gentleman from Marshallville, Georgia, he had a well-known biography on Augustus Baldwin Longstreet to his credit. He had also published a learned history on John Wesley in 1930 and was fond of discussing both Methodism and the Civil War—topics of some interest to the Kentuckian. An established Agrarian, he had written a long, impressive piece, "The Life and Death of Cousin Lucius," for *I'll Take My Stand*, more of a short story than an essay or a polemic. Wade was "the personality" among Stuart's professors, and his American Literature class was Jesse's largest. "We were not only taught but entertained in his class." Younger in spirit than his forty years, Wade was rumored by the girls to be a "good catch," and he was in demand at parties. "No one I knew on the . . . faculty had the sense of humor and laughed as much as John Donald Wade," Jesse later wrote. He was invited to take rides around Nashville with Wade and his best friend, bachelor Edd Winfield Parks, an owlish teacher, a writer and a Georgian. As Jesse recalled, their talk was mainly of writing and literature. A pleasant man with considerable wisdom, Wade had a knowledge of people and manners. He was by turns eloquent and salty, lighthearted and profound. From him Jesse learned something of the true distinctions between regions of the country. Wade's Georgia was as different from Stuart's Kentucky, so he later thought, as England from Scotland. To Jesse, Wade was an object lesson on why Donald Davidson wrote of sectionalism. When the final quarter's grades were posted in Calhoun Hall, Jesse had scored by two points the highest grade in Wade's American Literature course. It was more than an A to him. "It was a victory, a victory!"[36]

John Crowe Ransom was away that year at Oxford University, where he had been a Rhodes Scholar nearly twenty years earlier. Before his departure, however, Jesse got to know him "fairly well." He wanted very much to know Ransom, for Ransom was one of the reasons he had come to Vanderbilt. Jesse had read his four books and admired his poetry before he had enrolled at Vanderbilt, but coming to Vanderbilt out of the LMU experience and being confronted with Ransom, he was initially "frightened out of his skin." It was Ransom's aloof and distant manner that Jesse did not at first understand, the professor's own concept of manners and gentility that gave rise to an exterior difficult for anyone to penetrate, though Ransom was known informally by the faculty as "J. C.," "Johnny," or "John." Jesse eventually came to know the "very, very kind gentleman" underneath the social carapace, and Ransom would, upon his return from England, read Jesse's poetry and advise him about its publication. Yet he did not know the side of Ransom that such colleagues as Warren knew, a man who loved games, could play with children and stand on his head—a witty, "rollicking companion," who could, even in concluding a formal letter, give in to a mood of sudden whimsy and by way of a P.S. declare that he had been moved to "drop a furtive tear." Short and stockily built, Ransom reminded Jesse of Emerson's description of Thoreau, though only in physical sense for their literary styles widely diverged. One of Jesse's classmates was Ellene Ransom, the professor-poet's sister. At least twice she invited him out to her home on 16th Avenue to meet her parents.[37]

Nashville and Vanderbilt were not all work for Jesse Stuart. One Sunday morning on the narrow street between Wesley Hall and Calhoun, Dr. Mims walked and smoked, his cane "tattooing at alternate steps" and his pipe leaving a plume of smoke in the warm spring air. "Stuart," he asked, "what are you doing this Sunday morning?"

"Nothing," he answered, suddenly finding his arm hooked with Mims' cane and himself spinning around to face the Arkansas bard.

"You're a wild man," Mims remarked. "Get a coat on and go to Sunday School and church with me. I'll wait on you."

If he had any plans of going to church with Elizabeth Hale and their friends in East Nashville, he ignored them and went that Sunday with the department head to stately West End Methodist Church. Mims even taught the Sunday School class. Increasingly Jesse became aware of how widely Mims was known. He was, without exception, the finest lecturer the Kentuckian had ever heard, and apparently many others agreed. One story Jesse and other graduate students heard more than once was that of a woman sitting on the front row in his class. Mims was really getting carried away as he did sometimes with his own eloquence. Suddenly he interrupted his own lecture and looked at her. "Young lady, why aren't you taking notes?"

"Dr. Mims, I don't have to. My mother gave me hers."

It was part of the living legend that was Mims.

Although memorizing hundreds of lines of poetry was not Jesse's idea of learning, he accepted Mims' standards and blamed only himself for not meeting them. He admired his teacher and perceived strengths other than his inspired ability to bring Carlyle's *Sartor Resartus* to life or to quote Whitman endlessly. "And what a sensible liberal he was!" Mims spoke all over the South and elsewhere, sometimes espousing views of the Anti-Lynching League, saying things, so Jesse recalled, "only Dr. Mims could say." At that time Mims believed in civil rights for blacks but, according to his daughters, not in social equality. He stood alone between contending groups, not liberal enough for the liberals of his time, but too liberal for the conservatives.[38]

"Red" Warren wore baggy tweeds in those days. He was very interested in the poems Jesse brought him, including some later lost in the Wesley Hall fire. Years afterward, Warren would recall the Kentuckian as "an impressive youth, tall, powerfully built, dark-haired, keen of eye, full of all sorts of curiosity, intellectual and otherwise." Their youth, perhaps, drew them more closely together, for both were aware of the not always subtle paternal stance of the department head. Mims once a week would rap on the English faculty's office doors with his cane and "lead them all on a march to town for lunch." Walking east on Broadway, they passed Union Station, and usually stopped at Mrs. Fitzhugh's Dining Room, where they talked over hot coffee and fried chicken; sometimes they talked heatedly, Fugitive versus the Victorian tradition of Mims. Mims knew his faculty would thrive on the dialogue and conflict of ideas. Jesse Stuart always believed Mims to be a kind of academic father to the Fugitives, especially in the sense that he taught many of them; and Jesse believed, rightly or wrongly, that Warren was, in this sense, still Mims' student. He had heard Mims at quarter's end admonish him, "Red, you get those grades in on time." It seemed to Jesse that if the English faculty were the most gifted of families, then Mims was its father.[39]

A sophomore that year, Ella Puryear Mims remembers Jesse walking across the campus, and on a few occasions she stopped and talked with him. "He was a big, handsome fellow, down from the mountains . . . and very different. Not very meticulous in his dress. I remember a bright blue shirt for some reason." Her friend Fannie Cheney told her Jesse Stuart always looked as if he were "bustin' out of his clothes." Smiling, she recalled, "Jesse was colorful, you couldn't miss him." The general impression was that Jesse's lack of polish could be put down to the Depression. The students knew that he was poor, worked hard at jobs most white students did not work at, and had lost nearly everything he owned in the Wesley Hall fire. Another observation was to them baffling at the time: The mountain boy spent more time with his professors than with the students. And there was something even more distinctive about his personality. "Robert Penn Warren saw it," Kathryn Geny remembers, "and you could tell it in class definitely. It was his own self-confidence. Jesse knew about writing, and he was determined to write. He knew the people he wanted to write about, and he knew who could help him to learn to write. He seemed more mature to us." Kathryn Geny could see what Ella Mims glimpsed, too, that "strong quality, that masculinity, something you have to admire in Jesse Stuart." The students would have liked to have had more contact with him, "but he didn't seem to have time for us. He was too busy for us."

Warren remembers, "I liked him, and I hope he liked me." The young assistant professor found the mountaineer "a good narrator." Jesse was "full of tales and small events and anecdotes . . . really carrying his world with him all the time, and that was my immediate interest. His conversation was totally natural." There was a maturity there, too. "He had early a grip on the kind of world that meant most for him. . . . I think the most impressive thing about him was a kind of self-certainty he had, a kind of self-respect. It could never cross his mind or feelings to be different from what he was."[40]

The very day Mims had called him into his office to compliment his term paper, Jesse had finished a 479-line poem, "Whispering Grass," and was on his way to show it to Warren. Already he had begun to write more of his different kinds of sonnets, for an idea was stirring within him. As the poems grew into a sheaf, he felt the familiar pull. Years later he would speak of the time as a "writing spree." During his remaining days at Vanderbilt he would continue writing as many as thirty or more of these pieces, but he was not sure what he would do with them. He would just keep on writing. Having seen the daily accumulations of Jesse's prose resulting in a remarkable paper and seeing the prolific poetry build, Warren realized that Jesse Stuart was a driven artist—"already a compulsive writer, as though all the life he had absorbed was struggling to find a way out, and perhaps to achieve its own meaning."[41]

Although Jesse continued to call his young teacher "Mr. Warren" in class, outside he was "Red," and the two became friendly enough that Warren invited his fellow Kentuckian to his home. Jesse had heard much about the Agrarian movement with its emphasis on " 'pro' back to the farm and 'anti-'industrialization of the South." Warren and the Agrarians were articulating to some extent what Jesse Stuart believed he had been living. The relevance of Agrarian theory aside, he desired to see just how his professors were not only literary agrarians but also practicing, down-to-earth men of the soil. He knew Warren was an Agrarian, of course, and when Warren mentioned he "lived in the country" and invited the "curious-to-talk" graduate student out for a walk in the woods, Jesse could hardly wait to see his farm. Already a keen observer, he had noticed his young professor "walked fast and took long strides." He "leaned forward when he walked as if facing a strong wind. His red hair was often tousled in the wind." But as Warren remembers, he and Jesse did most of their walking once they got into the country, for his white-washed shack, where he lived with his wife, was located beyond a convenient walking distance five or six miles east of Nashville on the beautiful Burch estate bordering the Cumberland River. They drove out, Warren recalls, in his baby Austin. When they arrived, the scene was not at all what Jesse had expected; and he laughed when he saw "not rolling fields of corn and tobacco," but the Warrens' little white cottage at the foot of a formal vegetable and flower garden. But Warren's hospitality warmed him, and he was delighted to see his teacher in a domestic atmosphere with his wife—"Cinina," as she was known to friends—a woman "of Italian descent, soft-spoken, and very pretty." Her resemblance to Naomi Deane Norris of Greenup, he thought, was striking. At the time, Jesse recalled, Warren was working on a manuscript of *Night Riders*, and from some of the manuscript beside the typewriter Jesse kenned the author's writing habits. Warren "would write a word, halt, type-in another word and another until he got the right one. He was careful with word choosing in his time of creativity." He could even interrupt his composition with errands, then return to the typewriter and pick up "the thread of thought and go on."

As amusing as Warren's life "in the country" struck him, Jesse was interested in his contemporary literature teacher's life outside the classroom. On another occasion the two went swimming in the Cumberland River, and Warren, a distance swimmer, performed the Australian crawl "about as fast as a man could trot alongside the river bank to keep pace with him." At the pool in the Peabody gymnasium one day Warren was lying on the diving board when Jesse came by and grabbed him by the calf of the leg and said, "You've got an awfully good leg for a little man."

One evening Jesse went out to the Warrens' with others and the group got into a political discussion. The philosophy of strong Jeffersonian Democrats vied with eastern Kentucky Republicanism as Jesse entered into the fray. It all seemed healthy enough until they sat down at the table. As Jesse later recalled, his exasperated teacher said, "You vote for Hoover and eat my food!"

Perhaps the accusatory revenants of his youth, isolation and ridicule, those two real horrors that stimulated the autobiographical story "One of the Lost Tribe," suddenly rose up where he least expected them, stirring his discomfort and menacing him once again. He struggled to control himself but was on his feet immediately. "I don't have to eat your food." He started toward the door, but Warren caught him and smoothed over the situation as best he could. "I stayed and ate dinner," Jesse recalled, "but I never felt welcome at Warren's after that. I didn't feel comfortable there."[42]

As the Tennessee spring warmed into late April and May, the flood of creative energy swept with it memorable nostalgic colorings of indelible hues. For Jesse it would become a "flowering literary springtime . . . when all the teachers were young and very gay." His professors and others had recognized the strictures he had encountered; now they perceived, at first bit by bit and then with an insistent plastic breadth, something of his remarkable talent. Intuitively, perhaps, they made way for his growth, reflected in the burgeoning season.

Sometimes he hiked through Centennial Park over to Whitland Avenue to see the friendly Fugitive, Sidney Hirsch, and hear him descant upon Oriental philosophy and religion, to pursue with him "the secret meaning within hidden things," and always to read a few poems. Hirsch never censored his work and always praised it. On occasion his old friend Don West would be with him. Hirsch would graciously feed them, and sometimes it was three in the morning before they returned to the campus. The late hour was a lonely hour, and they heard

> ducks quacking in Centennial Park. We would hear the soft Tennessee winds of spring combing the white hair of the spirea and the sweet-scented blossoms of the magnolia trees. A moon would be leaving the sky and the hoofs of the heavy horses drawing milk wagons would be pounding emptily on the stone streets breaking the silence of the morning.[43]

At least once a week Jesse and Elizabeth Hale enjoyed their dates and, weather allowing, they walked together along the quiet streets, through the park, across the campuses of Nashville, along roadsides, and into the woods and hills. These moments were idyllic, except for one unfortunate incident. Sometime before he left that spring, they walked together in the evening until they found themselves out on a hill. Jesse had taken out his handkerchief, perhaps to wipe his brow, but he left it on the ground. "I've always been a bad one for leaving my handkerchief lying around," Jesse said, reflecting on the incident. In a little while the couple's privacy was interrupted by a large man who approached them as they stood on the hill not far from the side of the road. An older man followed the large man. Other Vanderbilt students, Jesse heard, had been arrested by roving constables who seemed to get a special pleasure out of preying on privacy-seeking couples. Their exact words are not recorded, but the injustice of the incident burned into his mind. "She was scared to death," he remembered. When the constable came up with the old man and accosted them in words Stuart would later recall only as "awful," he stood up for his rights and his lady.

"Young man, you get smart with me, and I'll show you what I can do with you."

"I'm not gettin' smart with you," Jesse replied. "I am smart, but I'm not gettin' smart with you."

Jesse and Elizabeth were arrested.

Of the details of the event he said years later, "We were just there together. We had been walking beside the road." Then noticing his handkerchief on the grass, he stooped to pick it up. The constable lifted a restraining hand and spoke: "Don't you touch that handkerchief. That's evidence." The insinuation infuriated Jesse, but he retained control of his emotions. Several influential Nashvillians took part in the affair, vouching for the high character of the two young people. Vanderbilt officials were especially critical of the overzealous local authorities. Donald Davidson was familiar with the case, as well as Jesse's friend Ed Hardy. "It did cause a furor," Ed Hardy remembered, and recalled that Jesse and Elizabeth were totally exonerated and the case expunged from the record. "I remember that well." But for the Kentucky youth, the ordeal was a humiliating experience, the injustice and irritation of which chafed at his sense of fair play and belittled his cherished integrity. When remembered, the outrage was to anger him the rest of his life.[44]

Jesse waited in Calhoun Hall for the last quarter's grades, knowing he had already brought his three-quarter average up to the standard requirement of a B level in Davidson's and Wade's classes. He had every confidence he would sustain his B performance in Warren's Contemporary Literature, perhaps even raise it to an A, especially since Warren had so consistently encouraged him in his creative progress. So in effect, he believed, he had only Professor Mims' class to hear from. Still elated over Mims' praise of his paper, Jesse nevertheless played his own devil's advocate, thinking that if Mims passed him, Mims "would not be the teacher I thought he was." But "if he flunked me or held my work up he was a teacher." Even though Jesse had worked hard to make up some of his assignments, he had not completed all of them, nor had he done the required memorization. Mims had praised the paper, but how would the paper stack up against his deficiencies?

Mims was, indeed, the teacher Stuart thought he was: "Work unfinished. No grade." There was no grade on the term paper either, only the characteristic, barely legible scrawl, "I've told you before what I think of this." Jesse Stuart's official graduate record shows blank columns for his third quarter of work in both Mims' and Warren's classes; a subsequent analysis by Vanderbilt officials indicates, at least officially, that Jesse "did not enroll in 3rd quarter," nor does the record show that he ever removed a second-quarter I in Mims' class. All other evidence, however, shows that he was in attendance in both Mims' and Warren's courses as well as in Davidson's and Wade's throughout the third quarter; and Jesse himself believes he attended all his classes through the third quarter. At that time a graduate student in English needed thirty-six quarter hours and a thesis for the M.A. degree. He did not have the thesis, of course, and he was shy an additional six quarter hours at Vanderbilt; perhaps some portion of his nineteen hours of graduate work at Peabody, most of them in English, could have been used to resolve the question of the six additional hours. Then, had he received full credit for Mims' and Warren's classes and attained the required B average, he could have chosen to rewrite his thesis, off campus if necessary, and upon its acceptance receive his degree.

The real mystery here lies in whether or not Jesse was, in fact, enrolled in Mims' and Warren's classes for the third quarter. The official record says he was *not* enrolled, despite his well-established presence in those courses. Is it possible he simply did not pay his tuition for these courses because of severe financial limitations, and thus no credit or enrollment was officially recorded, not even "Incompletes"? Why did Mims have an I grade entered for Stuart the second quarter, and nothing for the third quarter? The evidence of Jesse's attendance throughout the third quarter in both these courses is amply satisfying. One obvious chronological detail is that he did not even submit the 322-page term paper for Mims until the third quarter was under way. He was taking his work on that same paper to Warren "nearly every morning" during its writing. And as he wrote Davidson years later from Scotland, he not only did the paper in eleven days, but also "attended classes too!" Could he have literally followed Warren's advice "to throw everything else aside" in order to give his creative "spree" full sway? Given Jesse's traditional view of academic responsibilities and nearly religious attendance at class, such an explanation hardly seems likely. Furthermore, at the end of the third quarter, so he wrote in *Beyond Dark Hills,* he was waiting in no little anticipation to receive his grades, having already known of his A in Wade's American Lit. and his B in Davidson's English Lyric Poetry classes. Yet, he embellishes reality when he translates the latter into an A. In fact, the B Davidson assigned Jesse for his third-quarter grade functioned as an A, raising Jesse's total class average in Lyric Poetry, including his first-quarter C, to a B. A note on his transcript, keyed with an asterisk by the third-quarter B, reads "B average for year." To simplify and to dramatize the scene, certainly more effectively than an explanation such as this, Jesse chose to call it an A, more of a symbolical than substantive change.

All well and good for Davidson's class, but what of Jesse's rendering of an A in Warren's third-quarter class, when the official transcript shows a blank column (perhaps with an erasure) and the notation "did not enroll in 3d quarter"? If their brief clash over politics affected Warren's judgment of Jesse during the third quarter, neither ever indicated it. Before Jesse left Vanderbilt, "long before . . . we became friends," Warren later wrote. Jesse Stuart carried no bitterness toward either Mims or Warren, and while recognizing their differences, seems rather to have respected them and cherished their friendship in the years to follow, as they did his in both letter and deed. Warren later used Jesse's short stories in his capacity as editor of *The Southern Review,* in his own widely used text *Understanding Fiction,* and in other publications. Despite Warren's penchant for the New Criticism, not the most suitable critical lens through which to view either Stuart's poetry or his fiction, he praised Jesse's fictional strengths and wrote of his "real talent," evident as early as his Vanderbilt days. Jesse resigned himself to Mims' evaluation of his classwork declaring, "Hell, I deserved it. I didn't do all that memory work he asked." Warren's class, though, would appear to have been a different kettle of fish. Already having achieved two Bs in two quarters, what happened the third quarter? And what of the A in Warren's course Jesse reports in *Beyond Dark Hills*? Is it possible Jesse made it up out of whole cloth? Unlikely, for he later wrote that Mims' class was "my only course at Vanderbilt in which I didn't receive a grade." And what of the possible erasure in that third-quarter column for Warren's class, a photocopy of which Warren looked over forty-nine years later, commenting, "Might be a B under there . . ."? No one now can remember the details to unravel the mystery of Jesse Stuart's grades at Vanderbilt.

Hardly the absent-minded professor, even Mims could not remember such details though they were comparatively fresher when he tried. From Nashville, in 1943, Mims wrote Jesse, "There is one thing I have wanted to correct in your account of our relations. I am asked in all your lectures, did you give me full credit for 'discovering' you, or— blame me for not letting you get your degree. Well, I'd rather you [had] written *that paper* than have secured all the degrees that ever were. . . . I've said that in many lectures all over the country for I always play you up when I am talking. . . . I don't remember all the facts, but I have the impression that you didn't stand a final examination, or didn't finish your thesis." That Jesse considered completing a graduate degree by taking coursework beyond the end of his third quarter seems evident in his question put to Mims, could he get an M.A. without writing a thesis? In answer, so Jesse wrote, Mims referred him "to the dry pages of the catalogue" and asked him "to read for myself, and that was that." Yet Mims had taken him more than once for lunch to his charming old Victorian home, just a short walk from Science Hall. There they had talked and Mims had moved and inspired him when at one point he said, "If you were a son of mine, I don't know what in the world I would do with you. You're unusual, just some kind of special genius." Is it any wonder that, to the young man from W-Hollow, Vanderbilt was "a bunch of paradoxes"?[45]

In his most private thoughts Jesse had mixed feelings about his Vanderbilt experience. Some seeming inconsistencies he amusingly reported—teachers writing books until no one was excited over the appearance of a new one; the smoking of pipes, cigars, and cigarettes in class; the fiercely private attitudes about one's getting "stewed"; the university police's patronizing of academic scions "meandering lifelessly" through the groves until they were tucked into bed; ministerial students playing poker and not always with unmarked decks; professors keeping jugs of illegal Tennessee corn-licker and Warren's saying, "I've got a real moonshiner now . . . and I hope he doesn't get too much trade so he'll continue to make good corn"; the quaint idea of a university as a place upon a hill, "unmolested throughout the years, going on quietly and watching the students come and go." Other doubts and misgivings he put down to his own shortcomings, noting as late as 1970, "Vanderbilt was a great school, but I didn't understand it until years later. I wasn't ready for it." Such thoughts would be subject to visions and revisions in the retrospective years to come.[46]

In the remaining weeks of his last quarter, remembering the missed tackles of the fall, he impulsively went out for spring football practice. For three days he battled other bodies on the gridiron, "a little weak on a meal a day," yet he was impressive enough to be offered an athletic scholarship. Irony of ironies, on the condition that he would return, he was also offered a scholarship in English. Yet these successes could neither hold nor turn him long from a deeper yearning, a distant voice heeded and growing stronger. Through the early spring and into late May he had dreamed of home—of the dogwood trees in W-Hollow that "stand out among the thin-leafed oaks like white spreading sails," and he thought of "crabapples in bloom, and crows flying into the pine woods." He had naturally put them into prose and song, and now was writing increasingly of them. His thoughts turned insistently north-by-mountain-east.

He put what he had into a borrowed suitcase, and went over to say goodbye to Donald Davidson. The professor earnestly advised him, "Jesse, go back to your country. Go back there and write of your people. Don't change and follow the moods of these times. Be your honest self. Go back to your country, as William Butler Yeats is writing of his native Ireland. Your country has your material." At another time Jesse recalled Davidson's mentioning Robert Burns, who wrote of Scotland, and Sir Walter Scott, too. Davidson did not stop with advice; he had words of encouragement, too. "I wish you success," he said, and "I hope you have a million readers someday."[47]

Jesse Stuart had come to Vanderbilt because he heard of the Fugitives and Agrarians, and he had read their work. He had studied under some of them and spent hours with others. He had learned something of the way they looked and thought and spoke, and he had seen them in the context of their place and in some cases even of their homes and families. But he was already changing his mind about wanting to join the Fugitives or Agrarians:

> I didn't want to join anything literary. I had my reasons. I came to the conclusion that a writer should be an individualist, that each tub had to set on its own bottom my mother used to tell me. I thought the writer had to grow up like an uncultivated giant tree in the forest and not be one in a row of cultivated trees. He had to be, as each great writer is or has been, a word-mountain personality. Each had to build his mountain of thought and storyline, turning phrases into word-fabric, individually in his own choosing as Shakespeare, Chaucer, Dickens, Hardy, Yeats, Burns, T. S. Eliot, Twain, Emerson, Thoreau, Whitman, Hemingway, Faulkner, and others had done. In group agreement (and why would they be joined?) there would be danger of amalgamation to make a composite word-mountain. This idea formulated in my mind at Vanderbilt, and for thirty-six years I have not deviated.

But although it fairly accurately expresses his feeling at the time, this declaration was made formally and long after his departure from Vanderbilt. In 1932 he was too young to declare his independence completely, to break so totally in fact and in spirit from the Vanderbilt group. Indeed he would seek their guidance, nourishment, advice, and influence for some time to come. From the lonesome waters of W-Hollow, he would turn back and refresh himself at the Pierian spring of Vanderbilt; for if Vanderbilt had hurt him, it had changed him, too—a normal, painful growth.

Frustrated the year long by an academic preparation all too thin, his study diluted by menial labor, embarrassed by his poverty and hand-me-down clothes, distracted by continuous hunger, he strove through his dubious battle until his creative energy carried him onward to an individual victory of which he and his professors were only dimly aware. His lifelong difficulties had become and were becoming the growing substance of what he wrote. Something in him insisted on shaping life—his life and the lives about him—into prose and song. Unlike others, he required no induced mood, incentive, or inspiration; something as natural as breathing took hold of him and he wrote, as he had from the time he was eight years old. That something carried him along and would not let him go. His writing was as natural, as compulsive as ever, yet he knew what he had written in his year at Vanderbilt was very different from his earlier pieces. The sonnet forms he was composing now, for example: between them and the *Harvest of Youth* poems were a depth and distance that aroused his curiosity. The before-and-after contrast was dramatically pleasing to him. He would keep writing the sonnets for he could not do otherwise. It was as if they, or writing, chose him to write them. But more than that, he was aware that the year at Vanderbilt had stirred him deeply and he was a better writer. This was what he most desired. He would never be a scholar and do research papers in Victorian prose and poetry, or a thesis on John Fox, Jr.; he did not even want to—but he would be a poet and a writer. Other things to be written were more important than graduate work. Now he *knew* it more than ever, with sudden confidence and an overwhelming sense of purpose taking him away from graduate school rather than back to it.[48]

When he thought of Warren's Agrarian ideas beside his formal garden Jesse had to smile. Yet real writing and real farming could go together, he believed. Even Chancellor Kirkland, he had observed, used his hoe with skill among his beds of iris, and Warren and Kirkland symbolized the possibilities. He, Jesse Stuart, could fulfill them. He would go home and farm *and* write, and practice what the Agrarians preached. He saw Clem Carson on the steps of Kissam Hall and asked, "Can I borrow five dollars to get home on?"

"I'll go to the cafeteria, Jesse, and see." That was the place at which Carson had been cashing his checks, but this time the cafeteria was closing for the summer and could not accommodate him. "I have two dollars that you can have," Carson offered.

"I think I can get by on that."

Carson readily handed the money to Jesse, for he had already learned that Jesse was good for his word. "If he told you something," Carson would write years later, "you could bank on it being the way he said it was."

Jesse said goodbye to Will Moses, too. The friends promised to visit each other at their homes in W-Hollow and Springfield, Ohio, where Will's father edited a newspaper. Of his farewell to Elizabeth Hale in the last days of May and early June little is known, but they may have discussed plans for her to come to Kentucky, for soon afterward she would make the trip to W-Hollow with friends, and he would write of her visit in letter and song. Prior to leaving he stood with Don West as "the long line of students passed us in caps and gowns." Surprised to see him, West wondered why his old LMU chum was not in the procession. Jesse explained to West that both his "unfinished assignments" in Dr. Mims' class and his thesis, burned in the Wesley Hall fire, would have to wait, for he was going home.

On West End Street close to Vanderbilt, he carried his suitcase into the best ice cream parlor in the city, Candy Land, to see his friends Julian Lee Rayford, Sidney Hirsch, and Sidney's sister, Goldie Frank. Jesse just wanted to say another goodbye. He said it and walked to the door, opened it, and stepped out into the hot late May day. The volatile sculptor was moved by the parting. There was something about Jesse Stuart that got hold of people. "I felt pretty sad over seeing him go, for a part of me went out with him."

Jesse had "Whispering Grass" with him, the sheaf of poems he had taken to Warren. Rides were scarce for hitchhikers. He had to pay for a tourist cabin when rain and nightfall caught him, but the next day he drank a cup of coffee and rode a truckload of dynamite through Kentucky northeast to Olive Hill. Behind him, somewhere along the miles of hot, oozy asphalt highway, he had lost the whole sheaf of poems.[49]

8

"Man with
a Bull-Tongue Plow"
1932–1933

————◇————

"When I knock the door will be opened," he wrote dramatically of his homecoming, but his return was at first unnoticed by his family. By moonlight he walked up Academy Branch and over the familiar ridge path, down the pasture and through the orchard, and stepped quietly onto the back porch. He went into the kitchen. He put a stick of kindling into the cookstove and with it lit the wick of a kerosene lamp, adjusted the flame, put down the chimney, and adjusted it again to a smokeless light. It was as if he had just come in late at night once more, ready to eat from the pie safe. Things were just the same as his mother had always kept them. He helped himself to a plate of cold biscuit bread, ham, and milk. Then he climbed the stairs to his old room.

His brother James was "a long object lying in my bed." He had returned early from Berea College on May 27. Jesse looked from his window down toward the lower valley of W-Hollow. The scene was different from the great old elm trees outside Kissam and Wesley Halls. Here the poplars below the hogpen were covered with dew and in the rustling wind looked like "a silver cloud in the moonlight." He heard whippoorwills calling from the hilltops, beetles in the wet grass, and, presently, hound dogs chasing a fox out on town ridge. He saw the "light of fireflies on the meadow." The taste of home-cooked food was in his mouth, and it was good past telling. He would not be hungry here, he thought, and lay down, still looking out the window. Each day would have three meals instead of one. And so he thought and heard and saw until "the nothingness of sleep" overcame him.

His father's loud voice awoke him. "Roll out'n there, James. You can't get anything done and sleep all morning. Get out'n there, I say, before I come up there with a bucket of water!"

"Just in the minute," James mumbled. "Just in the minute," and lay there.

Jesse used to hate hearing his father's voice rolling him out of bed, but now he was glad to hear it again. "James," he said, "let's get up!"

"You here! Well, fine! We've got plenty of work to do. You've just come in time. Got more work here than five men can do. It's about to work me to death. Pa sold the horses. Got a span of mules, Jack and Barnie. Horses couldn't stand the new-ground plowing."

It was not yet four in the morning when the boys got to the dabbling-pan and wiped the wrinkles out of their faces. They drank hot black coffee as their parents welcomed Jesse home. His father was glad to get another work-hand: "Never needed you so, Jesse, in my life!" His mother said, "You're looking good. Looks like you've had plenty to eat."

Through winter and spring he had drunk water and licked salt to assuage his hunger. He said, "Oh, yes, you know me. I'll always manage to get plenty to eat." James quickly noticed his brother did not look like himself, "His flesh . . . too full in the neck and jaws sort of—bloated."

Outside the moon drooped over the town ridge, and a "swarm of stars" was blinking "at a dew-covered world." Before leaving for work on the railroad section, Mick Stuart told the boys to get the weeds out of the corn. He took the lantern and started over the ridge toward Greenup—still the family's main route to the outer world, for there was as yet no road. In a little while, all Jesse could see of his father was the lantern he carried, a light under the starlight; and he watched until the moving spot of yellow was lost behind the trees and brush far out the ridge.[1]

Once more Jesse found himself clearing new ground, and he and James chopped the weeds and hoed around the corn. They had to chop black oak sprouts from stumps, ragweeds, sourwood sprouts, and the worst—sawbriers. At first Jesse could not keep up with his brother. James, who would be seventeen in August, was thin and strong. Wearing only pants shorn off above the knees, he was at home in the hot sun. As Jesse himself had done in the past, James now took the bottom row and told his older brother to come on.

"I'm weak or something, James. I just can't take it. I'll get back on my feet after a while."

Within a week the corn was "clean as a hound's tooth."

Martha Stuart plied Jesse with such familiar fare as cornbread and buttermilk—such foods as would "stick to your ribs"—and the physical labor was invigorating. "I could feel the strength come back to my body," he wrote. "The flesh that I gained at Vanderbilt University that made me look well-kept was not good flesh. It was bloated on my stomach. My soft flesh started going down as wind leaves a balloon." He began to hold his own in each row of corn, and gradually he caught up with James "until he stepped up and let me have the bottom row of corn again." As he had five years earlier devoured his fingerprints in the white bread during his lunch break at the steel mills ("when we touched food, we got black on it"), he now ate the product of his work again—this time "roastenears" from the early corn. For the noon meal his mother had cooled buckets of milk in the well. He and James had "seven big roastenears apiece," and they drank "five pints of cool sweet milk at noon with the cream on it." He later wrote, "We were brown as autumn black-oak leaves. I was the strongest that I'd ever been in my life." He wrote his friend from Vanderbilt, Clem Carson of Tifton, Georgia, that he was down to a trim 170 pounds.[2]

Sometimes he would begin in the early morning and plow until ten o'clock, finding an old satisfaction in the fresh smell of the brown earth turning out from his plowshare. Then he would let the mule into the pasture and help James cut sprouts the rest of the day.

"Boy, come right out'n college after you got your Master's degree and get back in the old saw-briars and sassafras sprouts with a big one-eyed grubbing hoe!" James spoke with young brash irony. "Getting somewhere, aren't we, boy!" Jesse listened as James continued, and then the teenager made a sudden confession: "I've never told you but I didn't make it at Berea College the last semester."

"You mean to say you didn't pass?"

"I mean to say a lot of things." He showed his brother a letter that said he would not be admitted to Berea College next year. Jesse looked the letter over as James, leaning on his hoe handle, complained of one particular sentence, "We don't think you are the type of boy to finish college." The youth continued, "That makes my blood boil, too," he said, then confessed again, "I smoked down there." Although he was told at Berea that he could not write a passing theme, in time he would write his own story of the Berea experience with such effectiveness that it would be published in the February 1933 issue of *The American Mercury* under the title "A Freshman at Fishbone."[3]

The older brother took all of this in and returned, "What are you going to say when I tell you I didn't get my Master's degree? It doesn't make my blood boil."

"You didn't!" What Jesse said shocked him and stirred his pride, too. "That's fine! Both in the same boat and I'm not so bad after all."

Sometimes in the early afternoon when the noon meal was over, Martha Stuart would join them in the field. "You can't do anything with her," James told his brother. She was like all the Hiltons—"has to have her way." Their mother handled a gooseneck hoe expertly. Wearing her slat-bonnet, she usually worked about two hours, smoking her pipe, and then went back to the house to prepare supper.

Though James had tried to keep his poor grades from his mother, she had found him out. In her way Martha Stuart was still trying to teach her children, especially James, to apply themselves. It was moral, she believed, to do so; for "idleness was the devil's workshop." Each day she said, "I want you boys to amount to something. You have one life to give. You must make your life count." That summer crystallized the experience out of which Jesse Stuart, years later, would publish the story "A Mother's Place Is with Her Son." In the story two brothers learn a lesson in sweat and honesty from an iron-willed mother. That the story dates from late spring of 1932 is clear from the younger brother's (Finn's) being sent home from college and the mother's age, "fifty years old now." Martha Hilton Stuart was actually fifty the summer of 1932.[4]

One day when Jesse was plowing the bluff corn, below the house and above the spring just under two small poplar trees where Martha Stuart used to wash clothes, he put into action what he had already told James. "I'm in a different University," he had said. He did not need teachers to tell him "this is good or that is good." He would write to suit himself, "the way I damn well please." Thus academically disaffiliated and joyously free, at home in his hills, blessed with rest from hard labor in the boiling sun, he sat upon his bull-tongue plow beam and wrote:

Sir,
    I am a farmer singing at the plow
And as I take my time to plow along
A steep Kentucky hill, I sing my song—
A one-horse farmer singing at the plow!
I do not sing the songs you love to hear;
My basket songs are woven from the words
Of corn and crickets, trees and men and birds.
I sing the strains I know and love to sing.
And I can sing my lays like singing corn
And flute them like a fluting gray corn-bird;
And I can pipe them like a hunter's horn—
All of my life these are the songs I've heard.

And these crude strains no critic can call art,
Yours very respectively, Jesse Stuart.

He wrote six sonnets that day, resting his mule while he wrote.[5]
When a day's labor was finished, the two brothers took their dogs with them on a two-mile romp to Riverton, where they swam in the Ohio, the dogs swimming right along with them. Jesse had already begun writing sonnets and sonnet-like poems at Vanderbilt, an average of one every few days all through April and May after he had completed the "Beyond Dark Hills" manuscript for Mims' class. Now it was as if he were living out the imagery of such lines as

The long bright isle of crystal channel water
. . . broken by my body plunging down
And little swirl holes in the water after
I have gone down to touch the muddy bottom . . .

Taking his mother's advice to heart, he would, indeed, make his life count, and in more ways than one; for had he not turned away from the lure of nearly all Vanderbilt represented in higher education—the scholarship offers, the challenge of the "dry as dust" research paper so foreign to his creative urgings, the temptations of a pleasant campus life, and conversational respites with other graduate students and with tobacco-smoking faculty members—in order to return to W-Hollow and to write of it? Had he not written of that longed-for return to where, even now, in the waters of the ancient river, as it laved his flesh and muscle and bone, he was being born again into the heart of the land he loved above all others? So he wrote:

When I go to the land where I was born,
When I go there to give this flesh rebirth,
There I shall dive into a deeper stream
And I shall drown or come up with a dream.[6]

In June the late summer daylight wanes slowly in Kentucky, and after work in the fields Jesse and James often went to square dances, sometimes at the home of the neighboring hill family of Fred and Maude Moore. Their daughter Virginia Moore provided an incentive for the poetry written to the "mountain Lydia Doore" of *Man with a Bull-Tongue Plow,* which would break upon the literary scene in 1934:

Yes, I shall come tonight, the moon is full;
A block of white-ash wood caught in the leaves . . .
I shall be there and we must dance together;

And we shall dance until the early morn—
Oh, we shall dance and put our lips together
When we go home through dewy fields of corn.
And Lydia, if we see a shooting star
You make your wish before it fades away—
Then we can hold our hands in running water
And make one wish of all the things there are—
Choose that one wish that's been a cherished dream;
Old women say it will come true hereafter.

Years later the poet would qualify any possible misunderstanding of the literal facts of inspiration provided by the girl. "The family lived up the hollow here," but "oh my heavens! . . . It was imagination! I used that material, and just let my poems go."

"Will" Moses made good his promise to visit Jesse at W-Hollow that summer. He took a bus down from Springfield, Ohio, to Portsmouth, then got another bus going upriver that dropped him off on the Ohio side across from Greenup. There he caught the ferry over to the village at dusk. Moses had been reading "My Kinsman, Major Molineux" and, being imaginatively inclined, he felt rather like Robin ferrying across the river to the town at the beginning of Hawthorne's short story. Other parallels between the experience and the story seemed to follow as the young man walked around Greenup asking people there and in Riverton if they knew or had seen Jesse Stuart. Everyone knew Jesse, but no one had seen him recently. As to the way to W-Hollow, he was told it was "about three miles away, across the hills," but Moses questioned his ability to find his way there on his own in the dark. He spent the night at "a kind of lodging house run by one Aunt Molly," Aunt Mollie Womack, whom Jesse Stuart would fictionalize as Aunt Effie Winston in *Foretaste of Glory* (1946). At breakfast the next morning, as Will Moses remembered, "Jesse burst in. He had come to town coincidentally, to be greeted on all sides by the news that a mysterious stranger was looking for him."

Moses had "a little mustache" then, James Stuart recalled, and his brother and Moses, being good friends, were "talking all the time."

One night the two friends attended a square dance at the Moore cabin, where they stood shoulder-to-shoulder with the other guests against the wall and watched the dancers. A barn-raising had taken place that day, and although Jesse had not worked with the others and had spent the day out in the woods, they went anyway. It was a memorable evening for the Ohio youth. The local people "seemed to feel that it was proper to be polite to me without quite looking at me." One young man walked up close to them, eyed Jesse and jerked his thumb at Moses, asking, "Would your friend like to come out and have a drink?"

Despite the fact that Jesse's reputation was that of "a very abstemious man, then and later," the two joined the young fellow in a drink of friendly sociability. Moses' impression was to linger for decades: "That was the first time I had tasted sorghum whiskey from a glass fruit jar, and I found it very impressive."

Later that evening, Moses recalled, a fight broke out on the dance floor. It stopped abruptly. The defeated man stood in the dim light, holding a revolver loosely in one hand. He declared that it was a disgrace to be "knocked down for the first time in his thirty years." Moses himself was ready to leave quickly, awaiting a cue from Jesse.

Jesse said, "Let's get out of this," and they did. With others they waited in the yard "for gunfire of a mountain feud to break out," but instead peace was made.

That summer, the poet later declared, "I wrote poems as I had never written them before. They came to me in sequences." Before summer was over, he had approximately 152 poems, including the ones written at Vanderbilt that spring with the exception of "Whispering Grass," lost on the way home. In W-Hollow he wrote them "on scraps of paper and on broad [tulip] poplar leaves with a little stick when I didn't have paper." Often he found Red-Horse tobacco sacks thrown away. On the inside paper was space for six sonnet-length pieces. "I saved my ideas this way that would have left me forever if I hadn't recorded them at the moments they came."

By the time Will Moses visited Jesse in W-Hollow that summer, Jesse had written many of what Moses termed "quasi-sonnets" that would find their way into *Man with a Bull-Tongue Plow*. The time would come when the poet would guide visitors curious about his work through the bucolic haunts of his youth, and by the rolling hillside pastures southwest of the Stuart house. On one occasion he would say, "I wrote some of the sonnets . . . right here . . . some of those sonnets on the light under-neaths of poplar leaves and copied them when I got home from plowing before the leaves shriveled." Eyeing his visitor's response, he would then declare with a typical innocent openness, "A lot of people don't believe me when I tell them that." Will Moses attests to the inscribed leaves of that remarkably creative summer:

> He [Jesse] had been writing . . . that summer, frequently composing during solitary walks in the woods. At least occasionally, they oc-curred to him when he had no writing materials along. He hit on

the device of gathering large sycamore [sic] leaves and, on the pale under-surface, literally incising with a splinter of wood one sonnet on one leaf. Of course he would bring the leaves home and transcribe. When I was there, he had in his room—had just neglected to throw them out, I guess—a few such leaves, dry but with the writing still legible. The whole procedure, I am sure, had been unselfconscious. It represented at once his allegiance to the established tradition of poetry (however much license he allowed himself with the sonnet form), and his closeness to, his use of, the things of his own Kentucky mountains.[7]

That summer the table upstairs in his room "was filled with odd kinds of paper with sonnets written on them." He even used envelopes of random letters on which to write. "The poems just flowed to me. I was the happiest man in the world." Moses found Jesse in "a buoyant, burgeoning mood about his writing . . . and he was beginning to get acceptances from good magazines of poetry." Three publications appeared in rapid succession. His poem "Dreams of an Empty House" was published in the May issue of *Letters.* "Portrait of a Mountain Boy," a biographical piece on his good friend Don West, was printed in the regional *Cumberland Empire.* In "Brother to the Dust," which appeared in the Summer 1932 *Prairie Schooner,* Jesse reflected upon his experience in the steel mills five years earlier. This metrically concise Shakespearian sonnet forcefully juxtaposes images of industry and nature—"long-drawn curses black as winter oaks / From shouting pilots of the zooming cranes," the "air hammers' mighty strokes," "the furnace heat in blistering pains"; but since that time of brotherhood with the dust, "The years like lazy cattle have walked by / And steel I polished once has turned to rust."

Since Harrogate, writing, teaching, farming, and education had held the upper hand in his life. Now, land, home, the deep sense of place and belonging in it and being with his people increasingly dominated his personal feelings and work, forming the bedrock of his personal agrarian vision. Contrasted against the hill people and the land that fed them was the symbol of the city—unnatural, harsh, artificial, "unreal" in the Eliotic sense. Yet, in hollow-stippled northeastern Kentucky, industry was on the march. Industry was essential to America, but its very aura was dehumanizing to the poet's convictions. So he looked upon Nashville streets as barren places where he had walked, a natural man seeking menial work with no success, leaving memories of "her dirty bricks and loose-strung wires," of "pigeons flying down / Between the sooty stacks and sharp-pointed spires," and of "wandering penniless through her streets / With hunger in my guts and trying to find / Some work to do (washing windows, cleaning streets)," until he had actually discovered a kind of Yeatsian triumph in dispassionate irony, "believing hunger was a state of mind."

The places of industry were anathema to both physical survival and creative expression. Using music as a metonym for all life, and for art especially, he had written,

And if I follow the cold streets of stone
And listen to the music in the street;
Cold notes that do not touch the heart of one;
And interrupted by the tramping feet—
Yes, music's cold upon a street of stone.
There is no music there—all is a grind.
There is no place for one to be alone.
There is no beech top for a violin.
Ah, once, I tried the city and its ways.
It would have been better if I had been dead.
I could not ghee-haw to the city's ways.

And so he had turned away from Nashville and to the place of his birth and nurture:

And I came back where there is poetry
Among the streams and hills and skies I love;
And I came back a brother to the tree;
My home the roof of flying clouds above—
I came and threw myself upon the ground.
I put my hands upon green growing weeds.
And then I said: "At last, my life I've found.
For this is all my hungry body needs."
Who doomed my body for a steel machine
And patterned it for dollars and for cents?
This brain cannot forget when weeds are green.
This brain cannot forget the body will be spent.
But last the call of earth I have obeyed.
I found life in the heart of earth and stayed.

The curriculum of his new "university" was by no means limited to the genre of poetry only. He decided to ignore what Kroll and others had taught him about the need "to follow a skeleton" in writing short stories. That was to Jesse a poor analogy anyway, not at all suggestive of the life that should inhere in the story, suggestive rather of "white bones dangling in the wind without flesh on the body, without blood in the veins, without life, color, love, dreams." In this new university, he made the story "my thought," not thought inspired from other literary sources. "It was a slice of life lived by my own hill people. . . . I would write as they had lived to be honest about it." His ideas came as readily as those for poems. Seeking the privacy of the log smokehouse, which was then located just behind and close to the back of Mitchell Stuart's house, he wrote. Among the early stories was "Battle Keaton Dies," modeled on the life of his own Grandfather Nathan Hilton, who wanted to be buried comfortably in a tieless shirt and long underwear, "just like I lay down in my bed."

That summer Jesse's father brought him a letter from the Riverton Post Office, "a thin letter" from the *American Mercury*. It was a check for twenty-five dollars, the first poem he had actually sold for money and what was to be his first recognition in a periodical with nationwide circulation. His surprise was genuine, for he had forgotten about sending "Elegy for Mitch Stuart" to the magazine, following Donald Davidson's advice in the spring. He proudly showed the check around to his friends. On August 6 he penned a card to Barnie Greene Hutchens, telling her "to watch in the *American Mercury* for a 3-page poem of mine. It is one of the biggest American magazines I have crashed into." By now his college records had reported his birthdate as 1907, and having habituated himself to it, he wrote, "I reached it two days before I was 25." He felt so good he added, "I would love to revisit Sneedville and to see my friends there. It's a good place after all." Though James would be seventeen within a week, he continued, "My brother James, 16 yrs. old . . . will be a rather fine looking student at L.M.U. in December. I want him to visit Sneedville and your father and mother." He gave "my very best regards" to Ernest before signing "Stuart," and then decided to add, "My wife is going to be Elizabeth Hale of Nashville, Tenn. You have heard Theron Hale and his daughters sing over WSM Saturday nights. She is one of them. She teaches in Nashville, has taught 5 schools [and] has played over WSM for 7 years. She is 24." Indeed, his thoughts were very much on Elizabeth Hale. Though he still owed money to a Greenup bank, he went to nearby Ashland and spent sixteen dollars on a new blue serge double-breasted suit, then bought "a pair of friendly-five shoes," shirts, underwear, socks, and handkerchiefs. At last he could throw away the old brown suit that had been donated to him after the Wesley Hall fire at Vanderbilt last February, the suit "I never liked to wear because it had been given to me." Seeing firsthand the example of his brother's literary success, James Stuart declared he would follow

Jesse's example and send the story of his Berea experience to Mencken's magazine.[8]

With what was left of the twenty-five dollars, Jesse hitchhiked to Nashville to see Elizabeth and such friends as Lacey Reynolds and Walter Sharpe; the latter he found writing music and collecting antique furniture. On the way south he was robbed of sixty cents by men who had picked him up. Had he not had three dollars "tucked away in my shoe" they would have taken it all. Before leaving Nashville, he "went broke" and much as he hated to do it, "borrowed one dollar from Elizabeth Hale to come home on," although she would have lent him more had he not been too proud to take it. He regretted his judgment in spending the dollar too quickly and "nearly starved" before he got back to "the hills of Greenup County." While in the city, he saw again the "old gray-headed son-of-a-bitch that arrested me on the outskirts of Nashville," the same man that had treated him and Elizabeth "so unjustly—the one that threatened my life out on the hill that night." He wrote Clem Carson, "If it had been one of the younger constables I intended to walk up and try to knock his head off his shoulders with my fist." He mentioned the incident at the close of a letter to Donald Davidson, too: "He looked at me and I looked at him. We never spoke. . . . That is one deal I'm not over yet. It cuts me deeply. . . . I'm sorry to end the letter like this. The looks of this man nearly spoiled my trip."

Jesse's hostility toward constables percolated over into the *Bull-Tongue Plow* poems, one declaring, "My friends, a constable is too low down / For mountain men to touch when he is dead." He clustered his general hatred about the Greenup County counterparts of the Nashville constables he so detested, for the victims of these local authorities were dirt-poor hillmen whose meager livelihoods of moonshining had been as repeatedly preyed upon as had been Nashville couples. Poetically at least, Stuart mercilessly murdered one "Bill," a constable, and left his mortal remains "stiff and cold" and clearly unmourned:

> They said his mouth would make a trap for flies.
> One laughed and laughed and said: "God-damn his soul—
> He's snooping for the Devil—telling lies—"
> We want the hungry hounds to bury him.
> We want piss-ants to come and eat their share.
> The wind and briars can sing the funeral hymn. . . .

Concerning the Nashville incident Stuart recalled, his voice yet edged with disgust, "You couldn't get a couple down there at Vanderbilt to go out and sit down on a settee or anything. The constables made for them if they was well dressed. The constables arrested them and got a small fine out of 'em. It was a racket. . . . You were always in 'misconduct,' and that was the word. And these people would rather have paid their fine than be accused of something like that." On the local constables' victimizing of back-country farmers who moonshined, he was nearly as vehement, "Constables preyed on them. [The farmers] were just pitiful."[9]

Whether Elizabeth Hale visited Jesse Stuart in W-Hollow before or after his trip to Nashville that summer is not clear, but visit him she did. He wrote Donald Davidson,

> Elizabeth Hale came to visit us. She honestly enjoyed the visit. I dreaded, somewhat, for her to come. But then she came. She was infatuated with Mama. We went out and found her picking raspberries and smoking her pipe.

According to Elizabeth Hale's brother-in-law, Edward K. Hardy, she made the visit with two close friends of hers and Jesse's, Carrie Louise Benz and Marvin Smith, who were later married. As a result of Elizabeth Hale's visit that summer, a ten-sonnet sequence poured fourth, beginning, "You came too late to see us, my Elizabeth / Wild roses by the rocks have lost their bloom." She was too late to see the "blood-root," or percoon, those "white blooms along the worm rail fence corners," but she was there "to see the wild larkspur," the "wild wind-loved jonquils," and "goldenrod . . . turning on the hills." And, the poet wrote, "I am glad you came."

During evening walks "under the night trees," his persona carries her "across the swollen streams," and he wonders how she likes the natural intimacies of W-Hollow, the "smell of leaves," "the nighthawk screams" as they "step from shadow woods to white moonlight" and "sit upon a pasture stone." Alone together they walk the pasture fields where "the sky is high" and "Only young rabbits are a-passing by," and if two people alone kiss, well, "Tonight the things we do are our business." The poet knows "a place where Mother seldom goes," "a knoll where a soft night wind blows," a secret place of "the ramble rose, / Smothered by brush, sawbriars and wind-leant pines / By honey-suckle and blackberry vines," surely the actual site of the old Byrns place where the poet's mother first kept house. Here they will stand and "ask the wind for secrets Mother knows."

One evening they sat "on a rotted log," and "smelled the young corn and the pine trees' breath," listening to the night sounds while

> The wind blew your fine hair down on your face
> And played the harp and viol in the young corn.

Have you forgotten then our long embrace
And how we left when stars had set for morn?
Do you remember how you were afraid
When blighted hickory nuts fell through the trees,
And when you heard the popping night corn-blades
And foxes tramping through old last year's leaves?
We heard the sobbing in the dark night-time
Like some old tune or half-forgotten rhyme.

After she left, her presence haunted him:

And when you went away, I went around
Under the pine-trees on our pasture hill;
And there among pine cones and grass I found
The slender footprints of your slipper heel.
I went the same path, Elizabeth, we took;
Down in old W-Hollow filled with mists;
I walked along the singing pasture branch
By wild rose stems where we had stopped and kissed.
I saw the gray owl on a starry limb
So wisely talking to the bright full moon;
The jar-flies and fox-hounds were mocking him—
The trees and wind were sobbing some old tune.
My Elizabeth, I could have told the wind
That you could beat him on your violin.

Elizabeth Hale was received hospitably by Jesse's family in W-Hollow and friends in Greenup. James Stuart remembers her as "pretty and small, a true musician. She talked to all of us." Neither too shy nor too talkative, she impressed James as "about a midpoint in between." The only negative criticism of her, he recalled, was that his sister Mary thought she was "a little too doll-baby-like." Elizabeth Hale remembered that she and their two good friends enjoyed their visit, "the beauty of the countryside in W-Hollow and places of inspiration for Jesse's writings." Especially she singled out "our visit to a service at the dear little country Baptist Church" as "nostalgic and memorable." That was Plum Grove Church. She "did love the beauty of many of his poems and descriptions of his beloved home surroundings in the Kentucky hills." She acknowledged that since she was not a violinist, Jesse "could have transposed my sister's musical notes on the violin which she played." As to the literalness of the poetry, her view is that, "like many writers," he "used poetic imagery and beauty of lines, [but was] not always factual."

In the remaining five sonnets of the *Bull-Tongue Plow* sequence, the poet writes of something in Elizabeth Hale "of finer clay than you find in this man":

Something is in you that is in a rose:
Something is in me that is in a stone.
The wind loves you, all things that smell the breath
Of wind love you—I know they love a rose . . .

The poet, by contrast, is "a gray stone lying in the grass," and over him "night wind and grass make moan," and "the writhing blacksnakes pass," yet he senses "wild rose roots" beneath him—the stone—and he knows that "winds can't shake it from its pasture earth." The stone is transmuted into a man of the mountains. The stone, like the man, will stay where it belongs and, ultimately and perhaps unexpectedly, "show its worth." If there be any doubt that this poem was written to Elizabeth Hale, the poet's letter to Carleton Wells confirms the obvious with his phrase, "Written for Elizabeth Hale."

Clearly during this period of his life, Elizabeth Hale was the poet's primary love and inspiration, though by no means the only one toward whom he was attracted. Their mutual friends attest to the deep friendship of the two during this period; they also acknowledge admiration for Jesse Stuart's high moral character and for Elizabeth Hale as "the virtuous young woman" she was. Despite obvious cultural, philosophical, and religious differences, as she remembers, they shared "some similarities of opinions on many subjects, such as morals and clean lives, high ideals and such." Further, "his willingness to work his way along with his determination to finish his education was a quality which I, and also others admired very much." What she termed their "non-formal engagement to each other" was to last through their "financially lean years."

Sonnet #329, perhaps the most personally revealing of the sequence, begins, "I've loved no one as I've loved you, Elizabeth," and he details the traits he cherishes in her:

Your eyes are colors in the green Spring timber;
And you are slender as the wild phlox stems;
Your hair is blond grain straws in damp November;
Your fingers are the shapely percoon stems.
I know, my Elizabeth, you'll be my bride;
I know, my Elizabeth, I'll be your groom.

And in our lives we shall lie side by side
At death lie down together in the tomb.
Remember, I shall keep the best of you
And let the cold earth have the rest of you.

In mid-summer 1932, eventual marriage seemed natural and inevitable to them, yet neither was ready for this step. Perceptive of his
own Kentucky hillman's heritage and sensitive to the many differences
in their backgrounds, he wonders in #330 if all will be the same when
they are married—if "white flying clouds and moon, / And purple hills
(Where youth is partly buried) / Will be the same." Keenly aware of
mutability, the poet projects their youth together into the metamorphosis
of time: Will their youth spent together "pass on silently into old dreams"?
Under the relentless foraging of Time, will spring crabapples "blossom
white on thorny limbs for you," and will "brown-breasted thrushes . . . sing
/ As sweetly as they used to sing for you"? Will she, indeed, "care to hear
the whippoorwill, / Like we loved in our youth on pasture hills"?

The last two poems of the sequence look back on time and into the
future. Now they have known each other for two years—through youth's
eyes a seeming lifetime. By the time *Man with a Bull-Tongue Plow* would
be published, more than four years of their' "deep friendship" would
pass. In a tone both factual and confessional the poet generalizes, "We've
lived our youth together," and "have gone with many other loves," ex-
periencing severed relationships, only to find themselves "in the
end . . . again together." Amid images of her lips, hair, teeth, and voice
the poet leaps to the passionate conclusion: "These lives of ours are most
too brief for love," leaving serious thoughts to reveal their dilemma of
joy and sadness. He juxtaposes the eternity of their love with the sure-
to-come eternity of their deaths; to the poet love seems to be composite
of youth, as uncertain as the synecdochic "cloud above," and although
the precise moment is uncertain, Time portends "that we must sever, /
And lie with Death forever and forever."

Yet, neither doubt nor death will weaken the poet's resolve, and
the lover's cry for decision in the midst of both negations bestirs him to
aver, "I know where we shall make our marriage bed," a "log shack
where pinks and larkspurs blossom," not far away, on "the Sandy River
bottoms," where they will "hear the river's monotone / And see white
water flashing over stone." They will live "in this shack" and see "the
moon rise high above the white-birch tree / And July corn green-
blanketing the bottoms— / A broad brown blanket made of tassel blos-

soms." He has no doubt they can make their food "from soil, / For I am strong enough to stand the toil," and though such food "will not come easily," the living will be honest.[10]

As important as his "very deep friendship" with Elizabeth Hale was, and despite the fact that the two had an understanding of informal engagement, Jesse first and foremost considered himself a committed writer. Without professional achievement and practical economic success such matters as marriage would remain in the future. From the spring of 1932 into the spring of 1933, he would frequently poeticize his longing for a lover. Although Elizabeth Hale received primary emphasis at this stage of his literary development, many others, including the essentially symbolic Lydia Doore, had entered and would enter into his expression. Often "Elizabeth" merges with "Jean Elizabeth" in *Man with a Bull-Tongue Plow*, and she appears not only in the ten-sonnet sequence, but also in at least nineteen other poems. The spirited and colorful Quadroon Mott, apparently related to Edith Greene, his childhood sweetheart, but containing more—something of a universal extension of every young man's temptation, the dark woman of primitive nature and passionate allure— though now reduced to memory, persistently lingers to haunt him. The rhyme and rhythm of Wilma O'Shean, the subject of Sonnets #341– #346, nominally suggest Barnie Greene, his college sweetheart at Harrogate. Wedded and gone from his life, she yet stirs his unforgotten love. He castigates her for marrying too soon—"Why were you in a hurry?"—and observes that her hasty example has taught him that "love in the flesh is greater than the mind." The poet takes consolation in the present relationship with "my Elizabeth" however, and addressing Wilma O'Shean tells her Elizabeth "has eyes as blue as you," and "she is fair as you." Indeed, "you cannot pair with her," for "you are not rare as her." Lydia Doore tempts him again as they walk by the Sandy River, and he declares, "my Elizabeth Hale's in Tennessee / And Lydia Doore's by this Kentucky stream." He compares Lydia to the elemental "running water" and frankly tells her the sun "has shown down on much fairer girls than you / . . . Girls pretty as young sycamores." Even so he cannot forget how "we danced the whole night through together," and how his poetry "will not express our living for one night," but when he leaves her on this occasion he vows, "I shall return no more."

On July 2, 1932, the photogenic senior girl who had stood next to him in his Greenup High School picture six years earlier, Kyon Pauline Murray, died; she was buried at Riverview Cemetery in Greenup. A four-sonnet sequence, marked by a dialogue of friendship between the two, reveals the slow certainty of her dying. In the final poem of the group the poet walks "upon the earth a man alive," while "Kyon Murray . . . has left her mountain home." There are also a Mabel with whom he long ago carved his initials on a schoolyard tree, one whom he keeps "forever young . . . in the rough lines of a sonnet," and a Lucy who received the tribute of a plowboy's love when both "were young lovers, eager, lithe and free."[11]

And there is, of course, Jean Torris, whom he is "proud to walk beside," who is "straight and beautiful," "as pretty as a willow tree / When its sharp leaves turn silver in the wind," who has "auburn-hair . . . naturally . . . curled," and whose eyes are likened to "dewdrops in the early morn, / The sun left hanging to the blades of corn." Conscious of her, admiring her, he kisses her "not too close the house," for he fears "the barking dog will rouse your mother," and she will discover them. It is a philosophical kiss on this April night, accompanied by the poet's conjecture that older people forget how they, too, kissed when they were young. Perhaps even he and Jean will become forgetful someday when each has married another, and her "small daughter" and his "tall son" meet on such an April night and kiss. Jean Torris' name is remarkably like that of Deane Norris, or Naomi Deane Norris, the young Greenup woman who would, in seven years, become his wife. Sonnet #449 in the sequence opens with a lullaby of the night wind, white stars above gleaming "through fingers of the dark pine tree," the songs of katydid, whippoorwill, and swamp frog as the two would-be lovers walk and the poet is inspired to sing:

"Go out tonight, you young, and love tonight,
For lovers fine as you are under clay—
Go out tonight and drink of the starlight
For soon all hearts are silent under clay."

A fourth poem written to his future wife is basically consistent with the imagery and content of the Jean Torris sequence. The scene depicts a poet living in the highlands, and he will go "down to walk with Bonnie Jean, / Wherein the sun the pale-green meadow lies." Hearing "the wild bird cries" and seeing the meadow "clothed in light April green," he is "proud to walk . . . with Jean." Time goes so swiftly. "She walks as nobly as an April Queen, / She steps as softly as a silver shadow / . . . Upon the velvet carpet of the meadow." Jesse Stuart wrote Carleton F. Wells concerning this poem, "For Jean Torris—a girl who lives in Greenup. Not her real name." In the years to come, as his informal engagement to Elizabeth Hale bloomed only to wither, he would become increasingly conscious of Naomi Deane Norris. Ingenuously frank in his relationships, he had already begun to speak often and admiringly of her, even to Elizabeth Hale, "as his favorite teacher friend, beautiful and queenly," but until 1938 his compulsion to establish himself as a writer and his drive to free himself from debt, to secure his land and achieve some kind of economic stability in his life, would take precedence over all other desires.[12]

It was an eventful summer for the poet in every way. Even the drought that came was so dry "that the rabbits died and the quails for want of water." On a Saturday afternoon in July, so he later wrote in *The Thread That Runs So True*, three members of the Greenwood County Board of Education paid him a call as he was "lying on the parched yard grass under the shade of a bushy-topped poplar whose broad leaves were now wilted pods drooping in the sun." He was "observing light and shadow crisscross and intermingle on the brown-parched grass" when the chairman, Mooner Bentworth, and two other members, William Dawson and Tobias Claxton, approached him with the invitation to become superintendent of the school system. In *Beyond Dark Hills*, the account varies somewhat in emphasis and detail if not in general outline. Jesse receives word through his father that the superintendent, Trevis Blair, wishes to see him "right away," and he accommodates Blair, who tells him the job of superintendent of county schools is open but, "due to hard times," the salary has been reduced to only one hundred dollars a month. Blair is relinquishing the county superintendency to head the Greenup City School system as principal of the high school and supervisor of the grade school.
Beyond Dark Hills depicts Jesse Stuart walking into Greenup for the first board meeting at the courthouse, seeing along the way several friends from county and city who congratulate him, and one old courthouse retainer who, miffed because the new superintendent refuses to buy him a drink, accuses him of "the swell-head." Jesse meets all five board members. The most physically imposing member, newly elected Benton Dangerfield, takes him aside and fills him in on the struggle between the county and city school systems. Under Trevis Blair's leadership the county board had sold its half interest in the Greenup High School building, in the east end of the county. Over one weekend, Trevis Blair changed jobs from the county to the city. The continuing chairman of the county board, Mooner Bentworth, claimed the county board had sold the county's interest at Trevis Blair's urging and that Blair had already hired a new teacher and was prepared to take in all east-end county students, whose tuition would be paid by the county to

the city system. Over the chairman's objection that the move "will wreck Trevis Blair's plans," the county board supports Jesse Stuart's idea to transport east-end county students to McKell High School in the west end, thus avoiding the tuition. In October he gleefully wrote Donald Davidson at Vanderbilt, "We transport right apast the door of the city school—bus loads of students for McKell . . . our own county high school."

The city folks accuse Jesse, who had graduated from the local high school, of hurting the city and having "turned against his own people." Even the Stuarts' family physician, Dr. Torrey, tells Stuart he has "started a battle here." Chairman Bentworth tries to take Jesse's secretary away, but the young superintendent outmaneuvers him by securing the support of Lawrence Loftin. An audit reveals an overspent budget for the previous three years. Much time is taken in explaining non-payment of mounting school debts and in delaying payment to angry creditors, one of whom Jesse offers physically to fight after he threatens to take the debt "out of your hide right now." He strongly opposes the "century-old trustee system" and, hoping to do away with it, urges change and writes articles, but the board members as a unit sit "silently," and the *Kentucky School Journal,* which had published his work previously, rejects his articles. Money from state and property taxes slowly trickles in; to stretch the budget, the school year is shortened. Before the school year ends, the county board is sued thirty-two times, but the city does not win "a single thing." As unpaid teachers and staff press in, so Jesse wrote, "I lied like a dog . . . for the schools must go on!" The summer drought and the havoc of the Depression drive the impoverished to cry for help. Jesse watches long lines of them seeking clothing and Red Cross flour:

> It wore on my nerves so much that once I got the key, went into the storeroom where we kept supplies, and cried as hard as any child. A sturdy race of hill people with farms where they had once raised plenty, were now reduced to hunger and want by a dark depression and the evil forces of the elements.

With a total of $70.00 for expenses to visit, as required by law, eighty-four rural schools dispersed over the county, the young superintendent hires at $3.00 a day "Possum" Larks, Uncle Rank Larks' boy, who owns a ramshackle Chevy coupe. Having been warned Jesse's life is in danger and knowing hostile feelings were running high, the two arm themselves with "settlers of differences," kept handy in the door pocket and under the seat of the Chevy, and set out on the journey. Adhering to the custom of hospitality among the hill people, they break bread with the families of the rural students. Here, in "initial-scarred, dilapidated schoolhouses" the hill children receive "six months of school while the city children got nine," a condition that strikes Jesse as "not FAIR!"—but only "wind from a cornfield stump" seems to listen. The whole community—county and city alike—is caught up in the destructive path of the Depression. The Greenup Bank collapses. School salaries cease for the whole academic year, but Jesse and the teachers, though not paid, keep the schools going. In late winter the Ohio River floods the community. The old river "Made man mourn for man." Yet it pulls people together; he finds himself wanting to help even people he had disliked. Long on the flood-front, Greenup citizens take the disaster "as a sort of holiday," and the town becomes a kind of "New-World Venice." At Plum Grove Church on a Sunday with his mother, Jesse remains outside and talks with his fellow hillmen. He tells Uncle Rank Larks the situation as he has been fighting it, and in turn is advised, "You know all the rakes and furrows we give this old earth, the green grass in the spring will always hide last year's scars." The conflict wanes as the school year ends, but many are sore at Jesse Stuart and he finds himself deeper in debt. He chooses not to seek the superintendency for the next year and resigns, having put in his application for the position of principal and teacher at McKell High School in the west end of Greenup County. He is unanimously approved by the board members.

In *Beyond Dark Hills* Jesse uses the actual names for Greenup County, Greenup, Greenup High School, and McKell High School, whereas in *Thread* he designates these respectively as Greenwood County, Landsburgh, Landsburgh High School, and Maxwell High School. Whereas the historical superintendent was Robert J. Nickel, as noted in Chapter V, he is Trevis Blair in *Beyond Dark Hills*, and becomes Robert Anderson in *Thread*. Possum Larks of *Dark Hills* becomes Lester Larkes in *Thread*, where his character is more fully delineated. Both are based on Charlie Sparks, the son of the Stuarts' Academy Hollow neighbor Frank Sparks (the fictional Uncle Rank Larks). Like Big Aaron Howard, Charlie Sparks once pitched for Plum Grove, but Big Aaron "couldn't touch Charlie Sparks." Dr. Torrey is the thinly disguised Dr. Henry Morris, and Elmer Heaberlin's father, Charles, whose actual surname is used in *Dark Hills*, emerges as Chad Hoskins in *Thread*, Jesse's auditor, personal friend, and financial adviser.

Perhaps the most revealing illustration of how closely Jesse's prose is shaped to follow even the most subtle contours of reality can be seen in the nearly one-to-one relationships between the names and characters of his schoolboard members and their historical prototypes at the center of the conflict. Mooner Bentworth of *Dark Hills,* Chairman of the Greenup County Board of Education, retains the same name in *Thread;* the character points to the real chairman that summer, George Belford of Nonchalanta. The two board members who accompanied Mooner Bentworth in calling upon Jesse in W-Hollow in the earlier book, Lawrence Loftin and Talburt Hauflin, compare nominally and substantively to William Dawson and Tobias Claxton in *Thread;* these characters' factual counterparts are suggested by William F. Lawson of Fullerton and B. C. Holbrook of York. The two new board members who were opposed to Stuart's predecessor and favored Stuart so strongly, the big man, Benton Dangerfield in both books, and Josh Montberry in *Dark Hills* (Manley Warburton in *Thread*), parallel in many respects the two new members of the board during Stuart's tenure, John Beverly of South Portsmouth, in the west end of the county, and Joe Montgomery of Oldtown. Stuart himself wrote, "Every person in this book is a real, not fictitious character even though personal names have been slightly changed." Thus the matrix of actions, characterizations, and themes of *Dark Hills* and *Thread* treating the 1932/1933 school year of his superintendency may be considered, if not always wholly and purely true, certainly of biographical significance.[13]

Meanwhile, outside his educator's world, in August and September Jesse wrote most of the 250 poems to be published in the second section of *Man with a Bull-Tongue Plow.* He stayed at home and continued to help with the farm work. Impressed with Jesse's new position, his father said, "I told you son . . . if you quit writin' over everything on the place you would amount to somethin'." From the troubled beginning of his new job, he returned home "to forget the day," and "sketched rough bits of poetry." Sometimes he walked into the late evening and at night through the black oak trees behind the Stuarts' barn. With these lines he reflected on his father's love of practical work and view of writing as "a lot of damn foolishness":

> Sometimes I've hid in corn-fields making rhymes
> And had Dad looking everywhere for me—
> My Dad could see no good in silly things
> Like scribbling down some crazy poetry.
> Trying with words to mock a bird that sings,
> Trying to speak of sunlight on a tree—
> The best thing Dad could see for me to do,

Since I was strong, was wield the fastest hoe,
To hoe my row and help the others through
And never leave a weed in any row.

From time to time he walked over the ridge path, "over the old hills that stood by me as faithful friends," and helped with the chores. He took night walks, heard again "the loneliness of the night wind in the pine tops," and after a night reviewing the problems of the school, returned to the work in which he was trapped:

Who in this world would give their life to this?
Cooped in a room . . .
. . . .
Where another youth shall waste his mortal flesh,
Where he must age and slander be his doom.

Already an authentically practicing Agrarian in a personal sense, he longed for the work he loved:

I think of pasture lands, wild fern and phlox,
White evening clouds behind the swaying pines,
A chimney corner filled with hollyhocks—
I dream of things forever close the soil;
I don't want office work, but I want toil.

Sometimes he took advantage of office typewriter and paper and typed the poems he had been writing during the summer and autumn. He sought refuge from teachers and staff members wanting their checks by slipping into the bathroom and there writing many sonnets, there cogitating upon his responsibility, sometimes stoically, sometimes indignantly:

And if I stay here long I shall be dead.
My feet are never patient on this floor.
This mind goes blank at questions all day long.
These ears hate hearing knocks against the door.
These ears would rather hear a wind-grass song.
But I must stay until my debts are paid.
And I must serve the PUBLIC while I'm here,
Go forward, clean, unwelcomed, unafraid—
I'll serve this PUBLIC only for one year.
Some buzzards crave this carrion meat I have.
Let them have it and vomit to their grave.

Many a rainy and snowy night he stayed in Greenup at the Columbia Hotel or at the houses of such Greenup friends as Scott Kenner and Frank Warnock, but even in the winter he often slogged out to W-Hollow. He found that the *American Mercury* had, indeed, accepted James' article on Berea College and paid the youth seventy-five dollars; furthermore, James was receiving fan mail from as far away as France. With the money James had bought guns and shells and, when Jesse asked, could loan him nothing. Sometimes the ridge path home was so dark he nearly had "to feel my way." When he returned in the morning "to thaw the ice out of my hair," his secretary told him, "This will kill you, Mr. Stuart." In response he showed her pages of sonnets wet where the falling snow had blurred the lines.

One winter evening he telephoned Naomi Deane Norris from his office and made arrangements to show her a "surprise." There were two front doors by which one could enter the Norris residence, one through the living room where the family would be gathering, and one through the parlor, where he would not meet the family. Hostilities had run so high that he often carried one or two revolvers for self-defense, as he had done in visiting the schools throughout Greenup County. Under the circumstances Jesse Stuart understood that, in receiving him into the parlor, Naomi Deane welcomed him but her family had at least some reservations. She was delighted to see him and, without hesitation, he showed her the freshly typed manuscript of poems he had been putting together. She began to read through them, and he watched her pretty face and expressive blue eyes, reading happiness and sadness in them as she read the poems. Once she looked up to say, "Jesse, I've always thought you had something in you. . . . I've read poems in the big magazines not any better than these!" Another time she said, "It wouldn't surprise me that you don't have a book here." They talked and had some of her good green apple pie and coffee, then returned to the poems. He played records on her Victrola. Both had records of Schubert's "Serenade." He wound the Victrola and played the record as she read the poems of winter aloud, discovering a harmony of sadness between the music and the poems; for he had repeatedly played the same record on his own manual phonograph while composing the very sonnets her voice intoned. It was midnight when he left, but "this was the time for me to leave."

There was no end of surprises that winter. After a long day of work he left his office, stepped out into the darkness, and stumbled over a coffin. It had been left at the courthouse for someone out in the county to pick up. The next day, he discovered that it was part of a shipment of pauper coffins purchased at reduced rates for the public.

"The fluffy green grass of spring" returned and he took up his old habit of walking in the woods. He found himself once again in the Plum Grove Cemetery, where he had earlier been inspired by an inscription on a tombstone:

Remember me as you pass by,
As you are now so once was I;
As I am now, so shall you be,
Therefore, prepare to follow me!

All through the long winter he had been "in a firing-line," and he was "weary of fighting . . . of madness . . . of it all." Writing was not so much work as "a recreation" to him, born out of the conflict and fatigue of routinized administrative work. The summer before, he had written most of the Don Davidson sonnets to appear in the fourth section of *Bull-Tongue Plow,* and now as then at Plum Grove he fully identified with his subjects. Letting the dead "speak for themselves," he literally lay on the ground. "I put myself among the dead as one of their midst and I speak back about the joys and sorrows of my own, and the people around me. I lie asleep and wait for the Spring." In a characteristic burst of honesty he confessed: "I would lie down on my back and imagine myself in the grave and then I would write. I went out to the grave yard at night and did this. One is crazy to act like this isn't one?"

His "Elegy for Mitch Stuart" came out in the January 1933 issue of the *American Mercury,* along with an "Editorial Note" providing a vigorous outline of his life up through his Vanderbilt experience; in the piece he gives Donald Davidson and Robert Penn Warren credit for having urged him to send his poems to the *Mercury.* To Clem Carson he had written in the fall that H. L. Mencken "has most of a letter I wrote him in his editorials." Jesse's reaction to seeing the published poem soon subsided, and by March he wrote Davidson, "Of course I loved to see 'Elegy for Mitch Stuart' in the American Mercury—I'm rather tired of it."[14]

Since August Jesse's *Dark Hills* manuscript had been in Boston under consideration for publication. After talking with Professor Mims, Davidson had got in touch with Theodore Morrison, a Harvard professor who taught with Davidson at Bread Loaf, Vermont, during the summer. Morrison in turn wrote Edward Weeks, urging the *Atlantic Monthly* editor to consider the manuscript. Weeks then wrote Jesse, enclosing a dollar for postage, and requested that he send the manuscript to him. Jesse obliged him and there it had lodged. Perhaps most writers would think that, with a book under consideration by a major publisher, a published poem in a distinguished national magazine, and a mounting pile of sonnet-brimming manuscript, a tyro writer would be fairly well emptied if not written out, at least temporarily. Davidson, who had seen a "sheaf of sonnets" Stuart had sent to Vanderbilt and was favorably impressed, put the question to him, relating it to the *Dark Hills* manuscript: Had it not used about all the material he had?

By way of response Jesse had written Davidson as early as October 1932, mentioning "a strong plot for a novel," giving the planned title "The Tree of Heaven," along with some further details, including his intention of concentrating upon the work the following summer. The sonnets, of course, had taken precedence; then in February 1933, while the river of poetry that flooded into *Bull-Tongue Plow* was just beginning to crest, he picked up an old family photograph album and, turning "the pages . . . to see the people in poetic word pictures," conceived the idea of "these characters going through this album of destiny." He would later entitle the result of an eleven-year-long endeavor "to cover the sweep of humanity upon this earth in 444 poems," *Album of Destiny*, "for there was no other title for it," but now it was a clearly projected book of verse. Through the 1932/1933 school year he had been caught up in the school fight. He had "fought a ring of small time politicians and people agitated by them. . . . Everything that opposed me . . . I have fought them like a Copperhead and by hell I'll be fighting them long as I am here." The year had been "far harder than any year of school work I have ever done," but there is one overriding consolation: "I'm getting a book from this experience." His emotion, anger, frustration, and creative fervor would continue through the summer when he would produce a 640-page manuscript entitled "Cradle of the Copperheads." There was also the novel, tentatively entitled "Magic Moonshine," that would remain unfinished and unpublished. Altogether by the spring of 1933, he had, as he wrote Davidson, "five new books growing in my mind," though he doubted that Davidson would believe him. He also had "material to back them up—I really have—They live right in my mind and I'll not be satisfied until I write them—all I need is the time—." In addition to these creative projects burning in his mind for expression, he had been having "great fun" writing stories and seeing "the living people I had known in words."

By April 4 he wrote Davidson, who was at Marshallville, Georgia, of the differing climatic conditions between Greenup and the deep South. Here, he observed, "a few willows have begun to put forth green leaves along the small streams and the birches have little fine leaves enough to make them look like green wind (if there be such) when the wind blows through their tops. I wonder if you have ever noticed in the very first tinges of Spring how black tree tops change so suddenly when only buds are bursting! The wind above them (close to them) it seems to me, looks very green. I got a couple of sonnets out of that the other day." He had indeed. In what was apparently one of the last of the sonnets to find its way into the *Bull-Tongue Plow* manuscript, the poet had welcomed spring:

> Something to Spring about the whip and stir—
> Green blotches on the pasture and the blur
> Of soft green leaves in a slow blowing wind.

He rejected three titles, "Boy with a Silver Plow," "Man with a Root-Cutter Plow," and "Man with a Cutter Plow," deciding on the ultimate title, for "didn't we use the big bull-tongues on the old root-cutter plows?" He had not thought about publishing it. He "wrapped an old hand-towel around" the "huge bulk of poems." There were a great many things in the book: life, land, rivers and home; love and passion; pride, self-sacrifice, law, murder, violence, war and weddings; anger and frustration; defeat, death, escape, nature and flora and fauna; the seasons, the cycle of life; dozens of characters including poets and politicians; ambition and determination; philosophy, the durability of words and poetry, human conflict, drink and drunkenness; farming and plowing, harvest, soilmen and the mountain earth; the local color of his country and town, Greenup and Nashville; the pioneers, the old people, and the hunts; friendship, betrayal, infidelity and faithfulness; honesty, hunger, rich images of the sky and senses; religion, thievery, and trees; satire and storms and Jesse Stuart himself; the search for self and the journey motif; loneliness; wind images and work; mother and father; music, courage, fighting, dancing, freedom; and Kentucky and America. He laid the manuscript away in his dresser drawer upstairs. He had written most of it during an eleven-month period, a small part of it in Nashville, Harrogate, and other places, but the great balance of it in W-Hollow and Greenup. Six of the sonnets had been published in *Harvest of Youth* in 1930, and the earliest of these, #225, "My loves will remain when I have passed," was "the first sonnet I ever wrote."

Sometime that spring he went into the kitchen and told his mother, "The damn thing is done now."

She said, "What are you talking about?"

"That book."

"I didn't know you was writing a book."

But she did know. Once when he was outside under the oak trees typing the poems from handwritten copies, he had set a rock on the stack and taken a break to go swimming. A wind blew up scattering them and storm clouds gathered, but Martha Stuart got out there in time to pick up the white typewritten sheets and save them from the rain.[15]

9

"A Modern American Robert Burns"
1933–1934

———◇———

That summer he went to Nashville, where he lived downtown at the YMCA. He paid two dollars a day for his room and, "to conserve my dollars," lived on two meals a day. There he rented a typewriter and "poured out my anger" in *Cradle of the Copperheads,* a manuscript which, when retyped and revised forty years later, totaled seventeen chapters and 945 double-spaced pages.

It is the story of his year as superintendent. The book opens with Jesse Stuart/Shan Stringer's return to his native county of Wonder. Times are bad, for the county is in the very pit of the Great Depression. Not only is the county broke, but the 1932 drought has created a "soup house" at the school building for children and a bread line for the poor. Jeff Larmer, a kind of local shaman, reads strange signs like "spit under rocks and signs in the sky." The people say "God Almighty warns him," and they believe him as he predicts a bad year to come with the resignation of the former superintendent and the hiring of a new one. The protagonist, Shan Stringer, becomes the new superintendent, maneuvered into the position by the antagonist, Ace Ruggles, who "is a bag of tricks." When Shan meets Ruggles, the superintendent says, "Looks like you have been working out in the fields."

"Yes, I have been plowing this summer and making a little fence."

"Well I got something in mind that you won't have to get out there in the sun and get black as you are. You'll fair up and look like a white man. . . . I am going to see that you get a job."

Vivid pictures of Jesse's mother and father appear throughout the manuscript. In the first chapter, Shan rides with his mother in a horse-drawn wagon out the now-vanished ridge road as they talk of the past and the old people. Typically, Mr. Stringer is proud of his son's new position, though impatient with his writing habit: "Son you ain't never goin' to do nothing settin' around with a pencil and paper writin' them old poems! What the hell do you think they'll amount to? Galavantin' all over hell and half of Georgia! You can do a lot of work and you are a good farmer. And you got a head to cipher with and not write them damned old poems. . . . You don't have to go away to school and live on one meal a day anymore. You know enough to cipher, read and calculate now. The office of county School Superintendent is a big office. . . . Fred Westbrook said you would be a peach of a man for a Superintendent. I want you to quit that writin' around over everything. You know that is crazy damn stuff to me."

Shan tries to explain writing to his father as "an urge" that came to him. "I could not help it. Yet my father went on all the time about my fooling with paper and pencil. I guess he was right since this had never benefited me financially. Writing had erased my moods on many occasions. I got something off my chest."

Board members speak monologues in the third chapter of the manuscript. The issue of transporting children to the county school so as to avoid city school tuition payments by the county is treated, as previously discussed, and is detailed in the fourth chapter of *Cradle of the Copperheads*. More school issues follow in the fifth chapter as the auditor digs out the spendthrift facts of Ace Ruggles' policies. The routine of administrative schoolwork is counterpointed by Shan's fresh human insights into the local color about him. So rich and varied are the colors and textures of human personalities that the author entitled his chapter "Patches on a Crazy Quilt." He tells the story of Rodney and Lucinda, two teenagers who slip away to live together in a pine pole shack, causing the young superintendent to reflect upon his own inmost elemental stirrings:

> Sometimes the passions surge in the human body. They surge like the water surges upward from beneath the earth. And even in the child there is passion, a native, natural, water se[e]ping from under a hill when the land is hot and dry! There is water surging just before a rain from under the hill—deep from the bowels of the earth something there is. . . . I can tell something of it. I remember the Sunday School cards we used to get had a man with a cloth around his hips and the rest of his body was naked. I remember he was nailed to a cross and the Sunday School teacher told us he was the Savior and she went on to explain a lot I don't recall now—or else I never did remember. But I remember the girl

who was much older than I. I was six. She must have been ten. But I would see her on this cross without her clothes except the cloth tied around her hips. This is why I don't remember about the Savior I suppose.

But this girl, she haunted me until she left the school. I was never so much fascinated with a girl. I wanted to play with her. I never knew why then, I think I know since I have grown older. It is all very strange. The same as a person has teeth and hair I suppose. Yes, there is the passion in the human flesh that is akin to a groundswell in the earth. The water rises from the earth like passions rise up from the flesh. There is beauty in this. There is primitiveness in this. There is the naked rose vine too. It is pretty in the wind. It is pretty when it blooms in the early Summer and the late Spring. . . . I know there must be a groundswell of the human passion in the stem of the rose.

He satirizes the "patterns" by which people live their lives, whether a pattern for a new dress, for smoking a cigarette, for knowledge, or for a school system; he believes people have thereby lost genuine expression for life. Specifically he attacks modern education, declaring, "If you were to throw the pattern away altogether, education would be new, fresher and better!" Taking his inspiration, perhaps, from *Sartor Resartus*, a work he mentions in Chapter X, he continues the pattern motif. "Nearly everybody would wear a new dress! It may be the color of the sassafras and the shape of a hickory. It may be a willow in the wind with thin lilting leaves kissed by a silver April wind." It is the human being that is absorbed with patterns, "one for this and one for that. That pretty sweet American girl—if one says now here is a pattern: You smoke a slim white cigarette. Everybody does it. It is a pattern. You paint one lip and let the other side remain skin-colored. It is a pattern. And she will do it. She follows the pattern of living. There is one cut pattern and little variation. People are very strange to me. I am among them and I want to leave all patterns. But where shall I go—make my own patterns and follow them?"

Shan certainly sets a novel pattern for himself as a county school superintendent. With unrelenting honesty he describes a kind of symbolic scene of what he does in his job, crumbling the ostensible dignity of the position:

I sit on a leather chair and it works on a wheel and turns over and up and around. It is a very fine chair where I can turn to face the people in the room and sit there and answer their questions. I don't like this damn chair—not at all, I don't! My pants are worn slick and thin in the seat. I don't like the questions I have to answer but I can answer them all right. I always manage to get by with them. . . . I don't see anything gigantic to do except eliminate all the little petty red tape stuff connected with it.

It is the people that interest him more than the work. "I like the crazy things they say. They are patches on a crazy quilt. . . . And they are from all kinds of different cloth . . . a different shade of color and a different make of garments. This is more interesting to me than all the school patterns." In this situation he reasons,

> I do not know whether to tell people to take a spoonful of this kind of learning and try it or a spoonful of another kind of learning and try it. I do not know what to tell them. I just say: "Here is a crabapple for you. Sourwood for [you]. Green persimmon for you. Buckeye for you. Shoemake for you, and so on." I don't know whether this is right or not and I don't give a damn. They want prescriptions and I am the educational doctor. I issue these prescriptions with my eyes closed for I am not quite sure they do not have their eyes closed when they get them. And I sit on my leather chair and whirl around and issue them rapidly. I issue them so rapidly I don't know how I am able to do it.

Education could be the most inert of subjects without the originality of Jesse's approaches to it. He interweaves a host of colorful character sketches and a steady chorus of voices around the courthouse bringing rumor and fact to the reader's consciousness as if filtered through the artist's mind for greater purity, but with no discernible residue of conscious artistry to adulterate the result. Such local color proliferates in scenes of square dances and weddings. In the night Shan listens to the fiddle and banjo and the dance calls. He watches boys swing their partners, hears old Kentucky dance tunes, the fiddle and banjo tunes like "Birdie" and "Waltz the Hall," hears "hard leather heels hitting against the rough oak planks . . . [and] the tappings of the slipper heels." Nature speaks through tree and flower, cloud and sunset, season and book and living creatures that know no patterns save what they intuit. Educators, the writer observes, do not seem to be aware that "too much schooling washes the body clean of all the red original there is in it."

He records the jealousies, cursing, fights, revelations of incest, and political chicanery. The reader learns of the antics of Lottie Graham, a Turkey Branch teacher who likes to direct pretend weddings with her students and "put boys under her desk" to punish them while she sits at it. The author always returns to his theme of education and its abuse, his love of the land against the self-absorbing concerns of thickly thronging people at the courthouse and the countless worries of his office. At one point he expresses his personal conflict between what one is taught and what one truly believes and loves:

> I am going to say a farewell to schools . . . the way they are taught. I see no need for all the public expense to teach the philosophy they teach. They destroy the beauty of literature. They knock all the originality out of students with a sledge hammer! If a student with original thoughts survive[s] the school system . . . [it] is a severe test. They teach students that work is something that only uneducated people do. Let me go back to life! Let me live close to the soil—forget I've ever gone to school.

In the midst of educational theorizing and political manipulation of the schools, Shan remains the soul of common sense. He visits the schools out in the county and at one sees a little boy run out of the schoolhouse in a hurry to a willow patch where "he pulled down his pants and deposited there in that patch of willows . . . in plain sight of the road." Others came and went in the next few minutes to this "open air privy." Dogs clustered about the school. He later discovered that the teacher and the children tried to keep them away with rocks and sticks, but "we just can't run them away!" In this situation he sets out to have new outdoor toilets built throughout the county for the school children and eventually succeeds in accomplishing this task.

The most powerful chapter in the book is the ninth: "Dark December: I Remember," which recounts the hardships of the people from December 1932 to April 1933. Situated on the second floor of the courthouse, the second door to the right at the top of the flight of stairs, between the Red Cross Headquarters and the government's Reconstruction Finance Corporation (RFC), Jesse Stuart's office was in the very core of the Depression crisis. On the same floor was the storeroom, where he talked privately with people; next to the storeroom were the toilets and hallway benches. Coffins for paupers were kept in a long dark hallway running back over the clerk's downstairs office beyond a glass door. The homeless and penniless often slept in the hallway on the benches and "on the rough greasy floor." As Jesse worked at night he heard their snores "like dragging logs over rocks with a yoke of cattle." Handouts were daily occurrences until "it got to the place my wages would not have given money to those who begged me for money." Through the RFC, men signed up for road work. "Sign away your birth right," they called it. All winter the people came up the flight of stairs "like cattle comes where one throws out straw in the winter time on the snow. . . . I saw them fuss over their places and quarrel like children among themselves over some small things."

Jesse's only escape was to get away to W-Hollow for the weekend or a night when he got a chance, there to "write about green briars and fodder blades," his love for "the rough hills where the people have to fight the soil for food to keep their bodies going," for the people and for the land. "I am in love with the trees and the music of the wind among the trees. It is sweet music to my ears. I just have to leave all my troubles and come to the hills. Something there is above the hills that is consoling to me." He had loved the hills and he had hated the hills. One could be sustained by the natural goodness of the land, and one could be buffeted by natural disasters as well. The harvest could be bountiful, or the flood could sweep it away. Drought could desiccate the land. He wrote,

> I have seen the primroses and I have seen the stones. And I shall sing of them. I shall sing in a different way but not to say, I have sung in a different key. I shall sing in a different key because I know a different tune. Not one single bard has sprung from the hills to sing of the hills. They go there after they begin to sing and hunt for songs.

The school war goes on, lawsuits accumulate, the politics and gossip flourish, and Shan determines he will beat Ace Ruggles. In the dark winter he sees the underprivileged come and go. Many women get their Red Cross flour sacks, each imprinted with a large red cross on the side. Some with pride turn the sack cross and try to hide the cross "against their bodies" as they leave the courthouse. Many others have little food, wear shabby clothing, and are unable to pay their taxes. There is something in the faces of the long lines of people. "When poverty keeps pounding at a door and the elements are against a bread winner who has battled with not only the rugged land for his food but land thin and sterile as well—then won't the marks of poverty leave a picture on his face the color of the drab winter hills?" In the face of such suffering the school fight seems petty, yet he is more determined than ever to "whip" Ace Ruggles. For every day of battle he seeks an hour of escape, sometimes slipping away to the toilet or down to the riverbank to write a sonnet.

It had been a hard trial to keep the schools going. (December was the last month he drew a check until years after the budgetary crisis was over.) When Christmas break comes, Shan catches a day coach for Nashville, riding for part of one day and all night. During this interim chapter, he seems to search for something in the past, significant yet nameless and undefinable; in a more practical sense, of course, he is trying to find "five to seven days of peace!" He rooms and boards at the YMCA on Church Street. Hot breakfast could be had for twenty cents, and a "good big meal of plain food (very well cooked)" was fifty cents "when and if I wanted to splurge." Once more he walks through the fog and mist of familiar Nashville streets in December, but this time he feels much better. Temporarily disaffiliated from Greenup, he thinks of Nashville as the "hometown" he would choose if he could choose one. On the Vanderbilt campus near Science Hall where Shan had been janitor four hours each day only a year before, he sees Professor Mims. They talk again and Shan realizes, "I liked him even if I did write Beyond Dark Hills as a term paper for him and never got a grade." They agree to meet later for lunch. He then runs into Dr. Randall Stewart, who though teaching at Brown University is on campus to see his "old buddy and classmate, Robert Penn Warren!" In a short time, Warren approaches and greets them. "Typically Red Warren," Shan observes, "he'd not shaven his face clean. Who gave a damn? I didn't." As Shan Stringer's thoughts turn within him, he ventures: "As a writer I thought I might be able to equal if not surpass Warren for he was overweighted by Oxford University and Vanderbilt University and his originality might be sapped. Critics of the past dictated his writing now and would dictate his work in the future." Making his departure, the young superintendent avoids Allen Tate, who had come to the campus from Paris, Tennessee. All these men were friends. "I was slightly younger and certainly less well-known and didn't belong to their circle. So I left them. I only dreamed of writing. They were, so I thought, established writers." Later at lunch, Mims discerns that his "strange" student is coping with a superintendency and in addition to *Beyond Dark Hills* has written a manuscript of poems called *Man with a Bull-Tongue Plow;* furthermore, he has another book in mind, and "if it is a book," he tells Mims, "I'll call it *The Cradle of the Copperheads*. I'm working in a den of human copperheads right now!"

Finally Mims says, "I didn't pass you Stringer. I'm sorry about this. But you are genius and you will write. . . . I know others around here don't believe this. Don Davidson does. Have you seen him yet?"

"No, I've called but there's no one home!" As the two part, Shan thanks Mims for the cafeteria lunch.

The rest of the action in Nashville is taken up by an all-day visit to

Peabody campus, with educators A. L. Crabb and J. E. Windrow. On the way he is somewhat startled to be propositioned by a homosexual and is accosted for handouts by several bums. He returns to the Vanderbilt campus, remembering old friends, football games, the Wesley Hall fire, and his English classes. He strolls over the frozen ground of other Nashville campuses. He remembers the uncomfortable evening when he did not feel welcome at Warren's home because of his Republican politics. He visits bookstores and reflects on his lonely Christmas in Nashville. He had come there to escape school problems in Greenup; but now he questions his choice. "Was I kindred enough to the people I wanted to see to make a trip here on my Christmas Holidays to see them?" Had he chosen the right college after all? Would it have been different if he had instead chosen the University of Virginia "where I had wanted to go," or Harvard, "where I had really wanted to go!"? Apparently, "I was trying to attach myself to Vanderbilt University . . . or to Peabody College," and he finds himself mulling that old question over as he walks "the cold gray streets" in search of an answer.

His most enjoyable night in Nashville is at the Grand Ole Opry, where he can see Elizabeth, Mamie Ruth, and their father perform on national hookup. He knows many of his friends at Vanderbilt and Peabody condemn country folk music, but he differs: "I say it is the natural music born of the people." He reasons, "Back home it is this way. My brother and I like fiddle music, guitar and banjo—dulcimer, mandolin and bass fiddle. We like to hear the dance tunes and dance to them. Sometimes we go and dance all night." Linking his own cultural background to such music, he makes the jump to what he considers artifices and pretenses of education; for had not others, rural teachers and college graduates alike, thought he should be above "anything so low" as folk music and square dances? He takes his stand:

> And this is why that I say so many of our educational attitudes are all wrong—that our square dances (folk dances) and our folk music just naturally came into being—that it is our heritage—that it will live for it is a part of us—that it is immortal. . . . And who are they to condemn that of our heritage and that which is a part of us [?]

The next day—Sunday, New Year's Day, 1933—he catches a train to Greenup by way of Louisville and Ashland. Refreshed from his vacation, he determines to work with "a greater zeal. I will be unmoveable . . . solid as one of my mountains."

In his remaining months in office the young superintendent reluctantly cuts one month out of the school year because of the lack of funds.

He reflects on the tactics of the opposition. A young woman comes to his office and sits and smiles at him, letting her dress ride above her knees. He does not know whether she has been sent or not. Another one comes and sits and says nothing for nearly an hour. "She would then walk up and show me a book of rough jokes and vulgar pictures." He hands the book back to her and tells her he is busy. As for the first woman, he writes, "I am glad I let her go her way" and "never had anything to do with her." He feels little nobility about not succumbing to their invitations. Indeed, he thinks, had he not been a man with "a dream" and an "idea," and had he not used his spare time for writing and poetry, "I might have become involved."

His dream, of course, is to whip Ace Ruggles, the personification of what he hates in public education and in politics. He enlists Uglybird Skinner, based on Jesse's neighbor Alf Sinnett, "a grave digger . . . water witch and fighter," to help fight fire with fire and tell Shan Stringer's story to the people before the election. Stringer is walking in the woods when he is shot at. He falls and remains still. After hugging the earth three hours and feigning death, he manages to slip into the woods and evade the would-be killer. Ironically, one of Stringer's strongest opponents dies in the middle of a lightning storm. A supporter tells him, "He just curled up and died like a snake when its head is cut off with a hoe. . . . He just curled up and died!" Stringer thinks, "A copperhead has gone from the swamp . . . one less copperhead to fear." About him, "the land is awakening to Spring," and he writes five sonnets bidding his "farewell to winter."

The bank fails. He discovers that more people than he had expected are opposed to Ruggles. He links Ruggles to the natural lesson learned watching "the big minnows" in the creek "whip the little ones," for "every gang has to have its bullies! Someone has to torture the others! Ace . . . is just a big minnow among so many small minnows." He visits his parents and his brother James, and on April 1, 1933, writes sonnets celebrating spring; "April is here and peach trees are in bloom!" Openly he writes, "My heart trembles like the tender leaves do in the wind when I come back home and find the peace of this farm."

Meanwhile, in town he finds the county people are on the move against Ruggles and all he represents. But he also hears criticism of himself as "that damn young bird [who] . . . started all the trouble. . . . He thinks he's a runnin' this place!" Ace "ought to have kept that god-damn big fart out of this city and county." Stringer releases an article to a county paper that presents the issues as clearly as he can. When Stringer's "new board" wins over the old, his reaction is direct:

"I am the happiest man that ever walked." The school war is over. The remaining action is comical and touching as Stringer wanders into the corner drugstore, borrows a dollar, draws "Broker's Tip," and wins the Kentucky Derby pot of twenty-odd dollars. Repeated encounters with his father counterpoint politics with the rich humor of contrasting points of view. "I don't know what to think of you," the father tells his son. "I did think you were about to get over all that writing business. Tob Keen said he caught you out in the privy one day settin' right on the stool writin' poetry. He said he stood there and watched you a long time singing it off and makin' a lot of rhymes."

The father and son also have a row over cutting trees on the land. His father wishes to cut pasture trees to sow crops. Shan was glad his father loved the soil, but just as his father did not understand about writing, "you don't understand about the trees either. You never will. You are a pioneer. You don't know it. That is why you hate the trees. You can't even stand to have one in the yard. . . . A hickory tree is dear to me as an apple tree."

"Don't start about trees!" his father responds.

By taking over payments on the land, the son manages to save the trees. "He was a fine dependable father," he reflected. "We just differed over trees."

A choric outpouring follows after the young superintendent turns his position over to Wingo Blair, a good friend of Stringer's, based on Jesse's friend Fred Maynard. The two friends are both reluctant to take the position. They see much alike in educational matters and both have been victims of Ace Ruggles' policies, which they oppose in no uncertain terms, so they flip a coin over who will take the superintendency. To Stringer's relief, Blair wins. Although the real Jesse Stuart had worked out an arrangement to become principal of Greenup County's McKell High School across the river from Portsmouth, Ohio, the author leaves this detail untreated. He rather deepens the drama by having his protagonist pack his suitcase and go away to write a book. But he will return in autumn and find again that deep identity with his land, home, and place, along with the artistic vision to encompass and express them; and so, with mythic harmony, not unlike Antaeus of old, he apostrophizes his "great Mother," Earth:

> Farewell to you my great Mother. I am going away from you for a little while. I shall come back to you and crawl upon your spinal column like a flea. You will hear my feet rustling the dead autumn leaves. You will see me gathering wild grapes and playing in the

sand. Perhaps, you will find me playing along one of your small streams of autumn-dwindling water. . . . Yes, I shall come again to you! I shall come back to you again and again. You are not my flesh and blood Mother but you are my Great Mother! . . . my mother's mother! And so on for mother and mother on down as far as time's beginning. . . . Let me return to you—something I know about. You too will confide my secret. I am going away to stay a little while. I shall be back to you when the dead leaves have covered your backbone . . . your big all powerful clumsy form that lets me crawl on your back like a flea and you don't try to shake me off. . . . Yes. . . . I shall come to you someday and lie closed under your strong ribs where you will take me back for a long sleep. I shall lie closed up there like a lizard lies close to the green bark on a tree—a lizard the color of bark. I shall lie there and the dead leaves shall fall season after season over me—and make many bright quilts to cover my [bed]. But I shall lie snugly there. As a child lies in the womb of its mother—I shall lie there asleep—and asleep forever, too. You are my kind mother. You will protect me. . . . The roots of your trees will go down and drink my blood and hold my dust down so the four winds of the earth won't sweep it to the four corners of the earth—so the wind will let me lie with you my Great Mother— the hills.[1]

So he had come to Nashville to tell the story of the past year, to write *Cradle of the Copperheads*. In telling most, he had not told all. He did tell about stealing the French novels, "gray books trimmed around the edges in gold." "I must steal this set of books," he had thought, seeing them over and over in the superintendent's office where no one ever read them. "It was a joke to leave them there where dust had covered them." He took them home and gave them a good reading, and he believed James "would give them another. . . . All twenty-four of them, which would make two readings they would have had in the past seven years." He had written James Still about it, too, in late May. "I had a load of stolen books," he wrote, "—all I could carry on the left shoulder . . . for a distance of four miles . . . all by French writers. I've gotten away from a lot of the writers I used to be fond of—I'm getting wild about Balzac and Zola." About the books he admonished Still, "Say nothing. . . . I'll steal books—can't help it." He wrote also about how he had rallied at Vanderbilt the previous year to make a strong showing at the end, but he was also forthright about what a hard time he had endured. Frank with his friends, he advised Still to let his hair grow out "a little longer" so he could hide his "prominent ears," then complimented him for "the finest looking brown eyes I've ever seen." He criticized himself, too, for though "strong," his eyes were "blue up-turned slits." He congratulated Still on "getting a good brain . . . something I'll bet you are not proud of for you look for the things that you have not gotten. You should be proud of yourself."

Neither had he written about his return trip to Nashville in April during spring break. Nor, years later in the 1970 revision of *Cradle of the Copperheads,* would he allow much of what he had written about Elizabeth Hale to stand. He would in retrospect blend his aborted love for and plans for marriage to her into his living love for and very real marriage to Naomi Deane Norris. It was, perhaps, natural that he should do so. Yet, in 1933, the goal of marriage was already much on his mind, even though writing was more urgent and dominant. "I do know I want to write my novel 'The Tree of Heaven' before I am married," he said in a letter to Donald Davidson. "I cannot see the beauty in the mountain girl (backbone of the story) if I am married to Elizabeth. Therefore I have some fear." He thought he could write the book and get it off to a publisher by September, but he required "a couple of months on it" without interruptions. He explained that the Tree of Heaven "is the *[ai]lanthus* tree. It looks a little like a shoemake—the compound leaves and dotted bark—they are very scarce here in Greenup County." He had been to Nashville during spring break. "The place sorty called me back." He had actually visited Elizabeth Hale and seen college friends as well as Ransom, Wade, Warren, and Tate. He enclosed a picture of Elizabeth Hale. "I want you to look carefully at her face and eyes," he wrote. If Davidson could see her in person, though, "then you would see why she holds me and I am proud she does hold me. And I hold to her." Noting he had taken over payments on a small farm for his father, he explained that indebtedness "is a stumbling block to marriage," but quickly added, "I am not a damn bit afraid of marrying," for Elizabeth, he believed, would "stand by me. . . . Though she is pious and pretty she has a world of pluck." His P.S. read, "Send the picture back and sometime I'll return the postage." Throughout the letter there is no trace of self-pity, not even in portions recounting his hard year of 1931/1932 at Vanderbilt. Indeed, he concluded, "life is just as great to others as it is to Elizabeth and me."

Their informal engagement continued through 1934 and into 1935, after *Man with a Bull-Tongue Plow* was published, and their Nashville friends remember that time as a happy one for both of them. Richard M. "Pek" Gunn recalls being introduced to Jesse Stuart by Elizabeth Hale at the time the poet was writing the *Bull-Tongue Plow* poems and publishing his work in the *American Mercury*. An affable, peppy country boy from Dixon, Tennessee, a promoter and experienced in Tennessee politics, Pek Gunn would eventually become the Volunteer State's Poet Laureate. "I'm a country fellow myself, and Jesse didn't come from any further back than I did." Pek Gunn's wife, Frances, was a Sunday School teacher and good friend of Elizabeth's sister, Mamie Ruth. Ed Hardy and Mamie Ruth, the Hale family, and Pek and Frances all attended the Nazarene Church in East Nashville. Pek Gunn recalls back then that Jesse often went to church with Elizabeth. "Jesse got a kick out of my leading the singing—I went at it like I was killing snakes, you know." He recalled pleasant social evenings out on the lawn on the western side of the church, next to since-constructed Wise Chapel. On one occasion Jesse wore a white linen suit with a blue shirt and yellow tie—"a very handsome young man." The thing he remembers most about Jesse Stuart back then was that "he . . . was writing a book, and I felt sorry for him. He would sometimes read out of his manuscript, but I wasn't far enough along to appreciate what he was doing then, so I'd just listen the best I could." Pek Gunn would respond by reading his own poetry, "funny stuff you know . . . this old corny stuff I was writing back then." He recalled that Elizabeth had a car, a Chevrolet sedan he thought, but neither he nor Jesse had a car. "I would drive the car, and Jesse, Elizabeth and Frances and I would go all around Nashville here together—Centennial Park—everywhere." One Sunday evening after Mamie Ruth and Ed Hardy had moved back to Nashville and were living upstairs at 502 Russell Street, near the Nazarene Church on 510 Woodland Street, the Gunns, Hardys, and Elizabeth and Jesse all had dinner together.

As Ed Hardy recollected, Jesse and Elizabeth's relationship was "very steady during the summer of 1933," and for a two-year period after that. Jesse and Elizabeth often joined Ed and Mamie Ruth at their Russell Street apartment. "They were mutually, deeply in love . . . planning and talking the possibilities of marriage." Once Jesse was reading a sonnet "to her blue eyes" when Ed came in, "and she was so embarrassed." On another occasion he remembered a picnic with Mamie Ruth, Jesse, and Elizabeth when they went out to his father's farm at Goodlettsville and drove all over it in an old T-Model Ford.[2]

Jesse Stuart had heard good things about the 152 sonnets he had sent to Vanderbilt the year before. By March of 1933 he wrote Davidson that John Crowe Ransom's comment was "especially a favorable one," his compliment "great poetry" truly pleasing, although he was quick to express surprise and delight with Davidson's positive response—something he had not expected because of his mentor's preference for "the ballad-verse," and the difficulties Jesse had anticipated Davidson would glean from his work, for "the sonnet is supposed to be a hard verse form to handle." He soon heard from the professor, who "told me I was writing poetry," and Davidson urged Jesse to send the new poems to the *Virginia Quarterly*, the *American Mercury*, and *Poetry: A Magazine of Verse*. Jesse followed Davidson's advice, and Davidson then took matters into his own hands, writing Stringfellow Barr at Charlottesville, Virginia, on June 3, 1933:

> My mountain friend, Jesse Stuart, writes me that he has submitted you a MS of his sonnets. I hope very much that you'll give them serious consideration. If you are looking for an American Robert Burns, Stuart is the man—the first real poet (aside from ballad makers) ever to come out of the southern mountains.

Although Davidson had expected Jesse to develop rapidly, "I was astonished," he wrote, "at what he had achieved in the sonnet series he sent me. He has an energy, intensity and a flow that simply staggers me." Within four days Barr replied to Davidson that the sonnets were "unusually good," and on June 23 wrote Jesse of his acceptance of a twelve-sonnet sequence entitled "Man with a Cutter Plow." While still in Nashville, Jesse sent another group of sonnets to Mencken at the *American Mercury*, and by August 1 he dropped a postcard to James Still noting that he had just "placed 14 [sic] sonnets with the *American Mercury*" to appear under the title "Songs of a Mountain Plowman." Earlier he had written Davidson, "Man cannot live by bread alone," but "man cannot live without bread." Now, "each editor took a sheaf and paid me with real money." For thirty-two poems he received $130. "In those days dollars had value. And these that I received for these poems looked as big as wagon wheels."

He was back in Greenup County as principal and teacher of McKell High School when he wrote Clem Carson that he still had not received his money for the months he had been superintendent in 1933 in Greenup. But he was enthusiastic about Mencken's acceptance of his poems and alerted his Vandy classmate to their imminent publication. Meanwhile, *Beyond Dark Hills* still lodged at the *Atlantic Monthly*. "They are holding it a mighty long time." He was so absorbed in writing that, concerning teaching, he declared, "I do detest it." What he really wanted was "to write and write and write. I can't get it out of my system." On September 26, Carson received a postcard from the editors of the *Virginia Quarterly* announcing "a copy of the October number of the *Virginia Quarterly Review*, as a present from *Jesse Stuart* . . . a token of interest and esteem." Meanwhile, his mail had been delayed and a mixup had occurred over the typewriter he had rented and used at the YMCA in Nashville. He wrote Davidson on September 28 that "I never knew Songs of a Mountain Plowman would be out in the Mercury until the magazine was on the newsstands." Apparently Mencken had written him at the YMCA and the letter had not been forwarded nor the typewriter returned until he wrote Elizabeth Hale, asking her to check out these things and to take care of them for him. Furthermore, he was worried that his ninth sonnet in the *Mercury* sequence had "exactly the same idea in it" as Davidson had in his earlier poem "Litany":

> You remember I came into your office once when Allen Tate was in there with you. I said something about his "Ode to the Confederate Dead." And your poem "Litany"—The idea of the poem struck me and on that idea I built about six or eight sonnets. I only read your poem once and I don't think I imitated it—though that was where I got the idea for the sonnets. I have worried some about it. I have not been able to get hold of your poem and make a comparison. And I vaguely remember now for I only read it once.— That was two years ago.

For the first time since he began *Beyond Dark Hills* at Vanderbilt in late March 1932—a period of a year and a half—he could claim, if only temporarily, "I'm not writing anything now." And he added, "We have the finest crop of corn we've had since 1926."

During this time several publishers were showing interest in Jesse's manuscript of sonnets. "Mr. Knopf has written and asked me for the original poetry MS the sonnets were taken from," he wrote Clem Carson. "I am working altogether in prose now." By early December he received another major acceptance and wrote Still, then at the Hindman, Kentucky, Settlement School, "Miss Harriet Monroe has accepted somewhere between two and twenty sonnets." Although both Knopf and Morrow had expressed interest in the book of poetry, Dutton was the most enterprising of the publishers. When the company inquired about other such poems as those published in the *Virginia Quarterly* and the *Mercury*, Jesse replied, "I have seven hundred and three in that batch." Dutton immediately instructed, "Send them to us if no one else has spoken for them."

"Lord, no one had spoken for them," he thought. On his way with the bulky manuscript over the ridge path to the Riverton Post Office,

James got his brother to stop and sit down long enough to have his picture snapped with a Brownie camera. In a short time, Dutton responded with a contract and letter, which read in part, "This is a great book of poems. It is like a big river with tributaries of life entering it. It is like a symphony of wind." Jesse Stuart first shook his head in disbelief, then exulted, "I walked in the wind for three days." At night he sought out the oak trees. "Just to think, you try to write something to suit everybody and you suit no one. Then you write to suit yourself and be yourself and the people like it." He described himself as "the happiest man in the world."[3]

As noted, Donald Davidson was the first to compare Jesse Stuart with Robert Burns, writing Stringfellow Barr at the *Virginia Quarterly* June 3, 1933, "If you are looking for an American Robert Burns, Stuart is the man." However, Mark Van Doren was the first, though by no means the last, to publish the often-quoted parallel, in the *New York Herald Tribune Books* just over a year later: "Jesse Stuart is a rare poet for these times, in that he is both copious and comprehensible. His book ought to be interesting, even to those who think that they cannot read poetry. They can read Jesse Stuart, if they please, as autobiography—and find themselves in the company of a modern American Robert Burns."

The chorus of reviews ran the scale from lows of rejection to highs of fulsome praise. Imagist poet John Gould Fletcher saw the same defects in the poet's "cohesion of plot, structure or 'story' . . . monotony and blind confusion" that he perceived in Edgar Lee Masters' *Spoon River Anthology* and in the poetry of Vachel Lindsay. Peter Monro Jack in the *New York Times Book Review*, while noting the first poem "begins badly," declared that "the cumulative effect is far finer than any quotation." He pointed to the poet's "fertility of expression, his careless and commonplace rhythms," "the concreteness of character," "his absolute and inalienable merit," and his "universality"; for his "eternal Kentuckian" becomes "eternal anything else." Malcolm Cowley's review in the *New Republic* was divided, devastating yet encouraging. The Jesse Stuart sonnets were not Petrarchian or Shakespearian sonnets. The poet at times "simply parrots what other poets have said"; when he becomes "conventional" he may be "colt-awkward, tangled in his feet," and "at his worst . . . is scarcely better than the Sweet Singer of Michigan." The book evinced "little power of organization" and lacked a "coherent and simple theme," such as "the cycle of the Kentucky seasons." On the positive side Cowley admitted that Jesse Stuart was authentic: "He is speaking in his own words about his own people, and he doesn't know how to lie." Stuart makes us feel "the dooryard, with its 'paths worn bare enough for feet to tell.' " The young poet can "dress the moon in a new epithet—'the sliced muskmelon moon.' " Indeed, "at their best, his poems have the springtime freshness of medieval ballads."

Taking the sonnet as a kind of "poetic mathematics" rather than as a "form of poetic freedom," which the poet had adapted to suit his needs, some reviewers in rejecting his poetry as sonnets came ironically close to rejecting the poetry itself. Most, however, after dealing with their prosodic reservations, like David McCord of the *Yale Review*, turned to other matters: "There remains the indisputable fact that here is a poet of great sensitivity and with a crude but undeniable power. . . . Education has not injured Jesse Stuart. He is one artist, certainly, who has set down place and character with aboriginal freshness. . . . He will be read." The same critic was sufficiently fascinated with the Stuart sonnet to pay Jesse the compliment of parody, published in the *New Yorker* as "Sonnet 965 (Composed After Reading 703 Of Them—And Some Mighty Good Ones—In Jesse Stuart's 'Man With A Bull-Tongue Plow' ")." In a similar vein, Horace Gregory continued in the *New York Herald Tribune Books*, "It is quite unfair to subject his verse to close analysis or jot down annotations on his abuse of the sonnet form. He has taken the general outline of a sonnet and used it as a stanza for a rambling narrative which at times is pure autobiography and at other moments pencil sketches of Kentucky scenery." Indeed, Stuart's book was "among the spectacular events of this season." The *Denver Post* reviewer seconded Gregory: "The futility of technical perfection as an end in itself never was better proved than in Mr. Stuart's impressive book. The test of the matter is whether making the sonnets conform to the proprieties would add anything to their meaning. Most readers will answer 'No,' with vehemence." Regarding the matter of reviewer perceptivity, "It . . . will be difficult for a born New Yorker . . . to appreciate what Mr. Stuart has done. One needs to know the tangy smell of wild grapes in the fall, and the soft sight of fog on distant hills to understand what has impelled a Kentucky farmer to write such a sonnet sequence about himself, his neighbors and their life."

Despite reservations based mainly on such matters as unconventional form and repetition, reviewers all across the country came down on the positive side, emphasizing the highland poet's authenticity, vitality, natural beauty, genuineness, enthusiasm, self-revealing power, and agrarian significance. In the East, Roy Helton of the *Philadelphia Inquirer* declared, "Once in a blue moon a book appears for which there is no precedent. Something so out of line that book critics generally fumble and stall, and wait to see which way the coin falls before they commit themselves. . . . I venture to say nobody in America ever began as an author before by launching such a poetic Leviathan." He continued, "There is more genuine poetry in this book than I can remember in the first volume of any American poet since Edna Millay published 'Rena[sce]nce; and Robert Frost came out with 'A Boy's Will.'" A book critic of the *Des Moines Register,* while pointing to the volume's need of "ruthless editing," acknowledged Jesse's "enormous vitality." Paul Jordan-Smith advised readers of the *Los Angeles Times* not to "judge too hastily," for this book "arouses an enthusiasm that transcends technical criticism. . . . His book embodies the spirit and essence of poetry." As one reads on, "it matters not that the verses are rugged. His story is shot through with beauty and tingles with vitality." The "story" of the book "carries the reader swiftly through its brief chapters to an awareness of romance that is reality and a reality that is romance." Fugitive poet Merrill Moore of Nashville, no mean sonneteer himself, saw the book as "a folk-tale individually told, a personal yet communal record of unusual simplicity and dignity. A soul has put itself on paper. . . ." Charmed and delighted with the book, Dr. Edwin Mims wrote a twelve-hundred-word review recognizing Stuart's sensitivity to "the vast panorama of natural beauty and splendor" and the poet's "own radiant personality." Confidently he stated, "I do not hesitate to call it one of the most significant volumes of modern American poetry." Later, having lectured abroad at Trinity College at Dublin as a visiting Carnegie professor, he wrote graduate student Lee Oly Ramey, then at work on a thesis on Jesse Stuart's life and work, that "A E" (George W. Russell) said that *Man with a Bull-Tongue Plow* "is the greatest book of verse to come out of America since *Leaves of Grass.*" In the *Atlanta Journal,* Walter Paschall linked the poet's achievement to the Agrarian movement, writing, "Nothing that may be born out of that important southern movement will reflect more credit upon the agrarians than Stuart's work." Further, "the sonnet-form which Stuart uses is elastic and free and altogether suited to his style."

Throughout the country reviewers saw reason to link Jesse Stuart's name and work with those of such widely divergent poets as John Masefield, Edgar Lee Masters, English farmer-poet John Clare, Sandburg, Baudelaire, Stephen Vincent Benét, Robert Frost, A. E. Housman, Chaucer, Shakespeare, Elizabeth Madox Roberts, Piers the Plowman, James Thompson ("The Seasons"), Omar Khayyam, and Robert Browning. While noting that Stuart broke from the formal sonnet tradition and that more judicious editing would have improved the volume, most reviewers saw such consistent, overriding merits as authenticity, originality, honesty, power, and the rare ability to create a book that fascinates as one reads. His work "may be artless but it is as rugged and vigorous as life," Henry E. Christman observed in the Sunday Book Page of the *Knickerbocker Press*, discerning that "in its very artlessness there is a greater art."

Combining praise with faultfinding, the *Chicago Daily News* reviewer commenced, "Jesse Stuart . . . seems to write poetry as naturally as he breathes," then waxed colorful: "His half-rhymes take more liberties with the conventions than a shoe salesman with a party girl. But he's an honest-to-God poet, with more gusto and vitality than any American lyricist has evinced since Stephen Vincent Benét." Isabel Ackerman of the *Lexington Herald* found "among the collection sonnets flawless in their beauty." Further, "the raw material, the spirit of poetry is in the man with a bull-tongue plow," and "they are more essential than fastidious workmanship." Writing that "Mr. Stuart makes no fetish of elegance," John Chamberlain of the *New York Times* pointed to the poet's "ardor and earthiness," and noted "Sometimes he can be startling, as when he speaks of lightning making a sound like 'popcorn over hell.' " W. B. Ward, editor of *New Day*, saw *Bull-Tongue Plow* as a "new and epoch-making book." He found "the tang of the earth" in the poet's personality. "In his heartthrobs one feels the rhythm of humanity. In his mental sweeps glimpses of the universe shuttle in and out. . . . Here is another Bobby Burns who can both sing and plow."

In early August, Jesse Stuart received his first copy of *Man with a Bull-Tongue Plow*. He took it home and said, "Here it is Mom . . . here's my book." She held it and fondled it "like it was a baby." His father took it and looked at it. "I never thought you had a book in your head. I want you to read that book to me sometime when we're not so busy with the work." His mother proudly showed it to other women in the neighborhood. "This is Jesse's book," she said.

Jesse Stuart was back in Greenup County as teaching principal for his second year at McKell High School when a letter came in October from Morton Dauwen Zabel, acting editor of *Poetry: A Magazine of Verse*, announcing that by a vote of its editorial staff the publication had decided to award him the prestigious 1934 Jeannette Sewell Davis Prize for his group of poems "Young Kentucky," which had appeared in the May 1934 issue—since reprinted in *Man with a Bull-Tongue Plow*. Enclosed was a check for one hundred dollars. *Poetry*'s November issue, which reprinted two of the sonnets from the prize-winning "Young Kentucky" sequence, mentioned that among those poets and works in the competition receiving "Honorable Mention" were Ezra Pound for his "Canto XXXVII," William Carlos Williams for "That's the American Style," John Gould Fletcher for "Elegy as Epithalamium," and Paul Engle for "New Times on the Plains." Later, Dr. Henry Seidel Canby would place *Man with a Bull-Tongue Plow* on his list of *The Best One Hundred Books Written in America*.[4]

House where Jesse Stuart was born. Stuart as a young man is visible at what remains of the front door.

Jesse's father, Mitchell Stuart, his mother, Martha Hilton Stuart, and his sister Glennis at home in 1932. Mrs. Stuart is reading the Bible aloud. (*Photo by James Stuart*)

The earliest known photo of Jesse. He was eleven years old and is shown here (far right, front row) with his Plum Grove School classmates. His sister Sophia is in the center of the back row.

"JS" spent August of 1923 at the Citizens Military Training Camp at Fort Knox, Kentucky, in what he mistakenly hoped would be a prelude to a West Point appointment.

The Mitchell Stuart family home, which Jesse and his grandfather Nathan
Hilton built with the help of a carpenter in the spring and fall of 1921.
The bunkhouse to the right and behind was added in the 1930s so Jesse
and James could keep later hours than their father allowed in the main
house.

The 1926 Greenup High School class. Jesse is standing one step down at
the left end of the back row, wedged into the corner of the building. Some
of these classmates have remained his lifelong friends.

Jesse Stuart's senior picture in *The Railsplitter,* Lincoln Memorial University's annual yearbook. The year was 1929.

Why he was sitting in a field of daisies at Lincoln Memorial University, Harrogate, Tennessee, ca. 1926, nobody is quite sure, including Jesse himself.

About 1932 Jesse and his friend
Elizabeth Hale posed for the camera in
Nashville. Elizabeth was with the Grand
Ole Opry; Jesse was a student at
Vanderbilt University. (*Elmer Heaberlin
Collection, Wurtland, KY*)

On a Guggenheim in September 1937,
Stuart more than fills the doorway of
Robert Burns' birthplace at Alloway, just
outside Ayr, Scotland.

The favorite student hangout on the
Lincoln Memorial University campus was
The Hunkstand. Jesse paid a return visit
to it in 1940 shortly after his first novel,
Trees of Heaven, was published.

Newlyweds Naomi Deane Norris Stuart
and Jesse, standing in front of
Portsmouth High School where he had
taught the previous year. (The
Cincinnati Enquirer, June 5, 1940)

Jesse with daughter Jane and Naomi, backed by the Capitol, on a cold December 9, 1945, in Washington, DC. (*Photo by Lt. Art Schoni*)

Shortly after his marriage, Jesse went west on a lecture tour. Here he is at an all-purpose store at a whistle stop in Colorado.

An art shot of Jesse with his pipe and a broken wagon wheel at W-Hollow in 1953. (*Photo by Earl Palmer.* Scenic South, *vol. 10, no. 10* [*October 1953*])

Recuperating at home from his 1954 heart attack in late winter of 1955. (*Photo by* The Courier-Journal, *Louisville, KY*)

October 15, 1955, was declared "Jesse Stuart Day." Here, he addresses his friends and neighbors from a platform set up in front of the courthouse in Greenup, with his favorite Leslie's Drug Store in the background. (*Photo by Billy Graham*, The Portsmouth [Ohio] Times)

Most people don't live to see the monuments erected in their honor. Jesse did, and is here admiring (with Naomi and daughter Jane) the granite shaft on the Greenup County Courthouse lawn. (*Photo by Billy Graham*, The Portsmouth [Ohio] Times)

With Dave Garroway, on whose *Today* show he appeared, broadcast from Huntington, West Virginia. (*Photo courtesy of WHAZ-TV Art and Photography Department*)

On February 13, 1958, Jesse was honored on *This Is Your Life*. With Jesse (left) are Ralph Edwards, host, and Robert A. Thornbury, director of the Kentucky Heart Association. (*Photo courtesy of National Broadcasting Company*)

Celebrating old times at Vanderbilt University, Jesse, Randall Stewart, and Robert Penn Warren have a campus reunion.

The Stuart family on horseback (the camels must have been on their lunch break) in front of the pyramid of Cheops, spring 1961.

Playing tug-of-war with a young resident of Lahore, Pakistan, in December 1962.

Looking like a pair of aging Green Bay Packer linemen, Jesse and August Derleth take time out for a laugh during a writers' conference at Rhinelander, Wisconsin, in July 1967.

Rotarians are a worldwide brotherhood. Here Jesse addresses the members of the Seoul, Korea, club on February 6, 1963.

Whether it was his first or his sixteenth, Stuart received honorary doctoral degrees as if they were new toys. Here he receives his twelfth from Acting President William F. Ekstrom of the University of Louisville, May 13, 1973.

Jesse seldom sat for "studio" portraits, but if compelled, he was cooperative. He and Naomi liked this one, made in 1971, and bought it. (*From the studio of George Hoxie, F.P.S.A., Oxford, Ohio*)

The Stuarts have, at W-Hollow, a semi-tame ground-hog whom they have named "Sugarlump." His (her?) favorite tidbit is melon of any kind. Here Jesse passes a slice to her in mid-summer of 1977. (*Photo by Steven R. Farley,* Ashland Daily Independent)

Christmas at W-Hollow in 1977. Naomi and Jesse with their grandsons Erik and Conrad. (*Photo by G. Sam Piatt*)

The only picture ever shot of the five surviving Stuart children together is this one from James Stuart's collection. In order of their births, they are, left to right, Sophia Stuart (Keeney); Jesse; Mary Stuart (Nelson); James Mitchell Stuart; Glennis Stuart (Liles).

Stuart being interviewed by H. Edward Richardson on the front porch at W-Hollow in May 1979. He had suffered his first stroke nearly a year before and was largely confined to the house and backyard. (*Photo by G. Sam Piatt*)

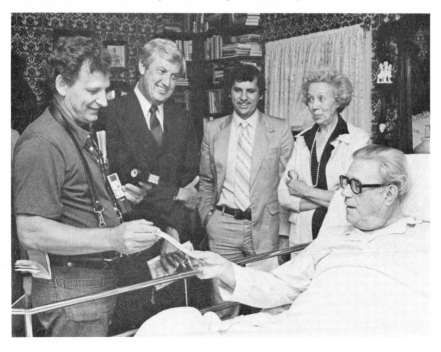

Sam Piatt and Jesse share a joke, as Piatt hands him a check for $600,000-plus for the purchase of Stuart's land as a nature preserve. (*Photo by Rich Sunley*)

In the sunset of life—in April 1980—Jesse still enjoyed not only his favorite month of the year, but a good cigar to go with it. (*Photo by G. Sam Piatt*)

10

Stories to Market
1933–1937

——————◇——————

After Jesse returned from Nashville to his duties at McKell High School in late summer 1933, he first lived at the Crawford Hotel in Southshore or Fullerton, Kentucky, just across the Ohio River from Portsmouth. Within the year he sought "a quieter area" and found it at the large brick colonial house of Forrest and Lillie King located nearby on an Ohio bottomland farm. Here he and other teachers roomed and boarded in what would be his home during most of the next six years. The Kings were old enough to be his parents, and they took more than a casual interest in him, on several occasions signing his notes at the bank and later giving him the benefit of their financial advice. The Kings' home, Jesse wrote, "was as fine a place as I have ever lived in my life. It was a house people drove by Sundays just to see," especially Lillie King's flow-erbeds season in and season out, for she had not only a green thumb but a landscapist's eye. There were four upstairs bedrooms—one in pink, another in green, one in blue, and the fourth in white. Ethel and Maynard Bush lived down the hall from Jesse, who occupied the white room, where he had his clothes, record player, typewriter, small radio, and books. Ethel Bush recalled, "Everything in the room was white, and Jesse slept on this old-fashioned iron bed that was painted white."

During the winter of 1933/1934 when he was snowbound at the Kings', he typed three stories soon accepted for publication. "Battle Keaton Dies" went to Whit Burnett and Martha Foley, editors of *Story,* which paid him $25; "Three Hundred Acres of Elbow Room" brought $125 from Paul Palmer at the *American Mercury;* and he received $75 for "Head o' th' Hollow" from *The Yale Review.* He was doing the story "the way I wanted to . . . a slice of life lived by my own people." However, "Kentucky Hill Dance," which appeared in the May 1934 issue of the *New Republic,* was his first story published in a magazine with a large national circulation, and "Mountain Poor House" followed in the same magazine in November. "Mom," a clearly autobiographical article rather than a short story, made its appearance in the May 1935 *Household*. "Woman in the House," accepted under the editorship of Robert Penn Warren, was published in the *Southern Review* that same month. July 1935 saw "Battle Keaton Dies" in *Story* and "Snake Blue" in the *New Republic* followed by "Head o' th' Hollow," and "Three Hundred Acres of Elbow Room" in September in the *Yale Review* and *American Mercury*, respectively.

As he had the year before, when summer came he was on his way again, this time to eastern Tennessee where he lived close to Gap Creek, a mile from where it emptied into Powell's River. A quarter of a mile up the creek was an old water mill, to which farmers in the area still brought their grain for grinding. The miller was old enough to remember "guns booming over around Cumberland Gap at the beginning of the Civil War," Jesse reported for the readers of his column "Fragments from Nothing" back home. He got to know the miller well that summer, and watched him "feed cracked corn to his pet fish and tell neighbors that hens can swim." Earl Hobson Smith recalled that during this period he saw Jesse carrying groceries and working on his novel *Trees of Heaven*. The LMU professor thought he likely got the name from a row of ailanthus trees that grew little more than fifteen feet from the Smiths' campus cottage, acting as a green and purposeful curtain running down the side of the girls' dorm. The backwoods cabin Jesse inhabited that summer was that of Mme. Eppinger, his LMU German teacher, who had given him the use of it that summer—a remote getaway where he could write. His motivation was high in June, for Merton S. Yewdale, editor-in-chief of Dutton, wrote him early in the month that the copy-reading of *Man with a Bull-Tongue Plow* was under way and "after a second reading I feel more than ever the remarkable vitality of your poetry and its power to live. You have written an immortal work and men of the future will know your name as well as the men of today know that of Robert Burns—for the sinews of eternity are in your poetry."

Extended days of rain and swollen creeks dampened his initial enthusiasm almost as much as his own cooking did. He left no record of how much work he accomplished that summer, but he did enjoy revisiting the Lincoln Memorial campus for the first time in four years. Breakfast was "so good here this morning," and "the biscuits were fine— the cereal, bacon, eggs and gravy." He mused in his column, "The Professors have gotten thicker in the middle despite the Depression and hair on their head[s] has turned in many cases from salt-pepper-gray to egg-shell-white." A desire to resist the compulsion to write rose up: "Somehow it just seems to me that no one hurries here, and it is all so peaceful, so quiet here." He liked to watch the students pass carrying books, talking and laughing, going to classes and the library. "I think of this being the best place to let time slip quickly by I have ever seen. I want to lie down on my back and forget about everything and just let the time pass over. Why not?"

Despite the opportunities to relax, "living here wrapped up among the hills" and roughing it soon got old. "Autumn is not going to find me in the East Tennessee mountains washing my face three times a day in the same creek and cleaning my teeth there and shaving too; nor is autumn going to find me burning my fingers over the cook stove . . . and taking a bath in the mill pond every night—I'm heading for a different civilization."

He was in Nashville in time to celebrate the Fourth of July. Advanced reviews of his new book had been released and the *Nashville Banner* ran a handsome portrait along with a news story and the caption JESSE STUART, POET, IS PRAISED HIGHLY AS MODERN BURNS. The piece linked his career to Vanderbilt and attributed his "discovery" to Nashville friends. While there he read proof for *Bull-Tongue Plow*, commenting in his new column back home, "It took me two half days and two whole days." He added, "The book is advertised as a book of sonnets. I p[re]fer to say they are not sonnets but they are just small fragments that make a continuous poem. They can be called sonnets, songs or anything one pleases to call them." During July and August he sent bits and pieces of local color and customs back to his paper from Louisville. The spirited Fourth was "in full swing" in Nashville, but "it was not half as joy[ful] and colorful as the celebration always is in Greenup." Many in Nashville shunned "the hot noisy streets to spend a quiet Fourth in the countryside," which he well understood for "the shade of the beech trees and the flowing of still waters are soothing to their ears . . . even for a day." "This is Dixie Land here, not Yankee Land." Although southern soldiers had resented being called "Yankees" during World War I, Stuart found the Tennessee people "the most patriotic . . . in America today." All stand at attention when the national anthem is played, but when Dixie is played, "it is hard for Southern[ers] to stand at attention. They can't keep their feet still." He found Tennesseans "the most religious group of people," and agreed with Mencken's having called the South "the Bible-Belt"; for "they are churchgoers," so much so that "the streets are deserted . . . from nine till twelve" Sunday mornings.

Among the friends he saw and visited that summer, of course, was

Elizabeth Hale. Even though he had written Donald Davidson some months before that "I'm going to dedicate a book to you," he dedicated *Man with a Bull-Tongue Plow* To ELIZABETH.

Ed Hardy remembered that when *Man with a Bull-Tongue Plow* appeared, Elizabeth Hale was pleased. His own reaction was one of "unbounded enthusiasm and joy for a friend who had succeeded." When the book first came out, he recalled, "The Hales' reaction was the same— proud, joyful, happy." Nor were they especially surprised at the dedication, for they had heard Jesse say that his first book would be dedicated to Elizabeth. "Nothing on the horizon had appeared that would change it."[1]

Once again he was back into the routine at McKell High School, an autumn made especially memorable by the release of his new book. By December, he wrote James Still concerning the upcoming Christmas holidays. He would definitely go either to New York to see his publishers or to Nashville, probably the latter because of Elizabeth Hale's being there. Dozens of reviews had come to his attention. Originally he had wanted them, but "now I do not. . . . Some are kind. Some praise. While many are sarcastic and plenty of them like *Time* are cute." Cowley he had "appreciated," for the man "has a good understanding of the hill country as he visits it often." The *Nation*'s reviewer, Eda Lou Walton, had written,

> Stuart is like Burns in . . . that he seems to have loved a great many girls and all of them because they were young, sweet and pretty; because, like the land, they indicated a fragrant spring. He wants to live with all of them and he wants to lie in the grave with all of them.

"But the *Nation*'s review was cute," Jesse thought. He had come to the conclusion that reviews "matter little after all. I don't read them." In the spring of 1935 he visited Nashville again and found that already the dogwoods had shed their blossoms. In late May he took his first journey to New York City where his trip was thoroughly reported. The *Saturday Review of Literature* featured a Robert Disraeli photograph of the Kentucky poet in suit, vest, and tie with a dimpled knot as he looked up at New York skyscrapers. He registered at the Prince George Hotel, put down twenty dollars, and said, "My name is Jesse Stuart, from Kentucky. I've come to stay four days." The *New York Times* observed, "Mr. Stuart is not a pale and languid poet. His features are regular and bronzed by the sun and wind. Strong-limbed and weighing 202 pounds without showing it, he seemed to bring the fresh tang of the Kentucky hills and the flesh-and-blood of his sonnets of that rugged country." Quizzed about his travels, he was quoted, "Of course I have traveled some in my life-time. I've been as far south as Birmingham, Alabama, as far north as Springfield, Ohio, and as far west as Louisville, Kentucky. But never as far as this." Jesse did not mention nor did the reporter write that just a few weeks before he had been in Washington, DC, with a senior class of McKell students. The *Herald Tribune* carried a feature story captioned "Kentucky Poet Finds N.Y. 'Big But Distasteful.' " The story is filled with colorful biographical bits and some notice of his smoking cigars. In explaining his new habit he also recorded for posterity the origin of his short story, "Bellin' of the Bride," to make its first appearance the following year in *Head o' W-Hollow:*

> "I was at a bellin'—I guess you say a serenadin'—after a marriage," he explained parenthetically. "We went round to the young people's house, a lot of Greenup County fellows together, and there was the usual shootin' of guns and ringin' of bells and shoutin'. You know, to sort of welcome them to their new place. And, of course, after it was over they asked everyone in to have a drink and a cigar, and one of the fellows dared me to smoke and I did."

A *New York Post* reporter seemed vastly amused at the poet's interest in St. Paul's and Trinity churchyards. Learning that New York stenographers used the tombstones as benches and tables for lunch breaks, Jesse was quoted by the reporter, "I think it's the awfullest thing I ever heard of . . . to sit there on the stones and eat lunch. But maybe they have no other place to eat." The article carries the caption GRAVEYARD BARD TO HAUNT STENOGS.

The most revealing of the New York news stories is headed "Jesse Stuart, Full of Eager Energy, Wears Down the Dwellers on Asphalt Trails." He visited Merton S. Yewdale at Dutton on Fourth Avenue, and declared his intention of seeing such people with whom he had corresponded as Malcolm Cowley of the *New Republic*, Frederic Lewis Allen of *Harper's*, Miss Marion Ives of Charles Scribner's Sons, and Martha Foley of *Story* magazine. "His amazing vitality is matched only by his utter sincerity," the reporter observed. "Ingenuous, earnest, bubbling over with life, he seems an extension of the soil he loves and writes about." A few biographical facts are woven through the article, along with reports that he "was seriously considered for the Pulitzer Prize award this year," and his *Beyond Dark Hills* manuscript "was a runner-up for the coveted *Atlantic Monthly* $5,000 prize."

He left New York at midnight, May 30, and crossed Connecticut and Rhode Island to Boston, spending a sleepless night on a train coach seat. At the offices of the *Atlantic Monthly* he met Edward Weeks and Ellery Sedwich. As an overnight guest of associate editor Sedwich and his family, Jesse was much impressed with their home "over looking [sic] the low heavy-wooded Massachusetts hills," and noted that the "old southern plantation home" had been "moved from Charlestown [sic] South Carolina by boat—each piece being carefully numbered and wrapped." Of their hospitality he wrote, "I was treated by Mr. and Mrs. Sedwich, as if I were their own son." He visited Salem and Concord and saw where the Alcotts, Hawthorne, Emerson, and Thoreau had lived. "I stood in the tower where Hawthorne did his writing." He visited Sleepy Hollow cemetery and saw the great New Englanders' graves, recording, "Their books are their real monuments." On Saturday morning, June 1, he took a bus up the Atlantic coast to Maine, noticing "lilacs at every farm house in Massachusetts." The white birches of New Hampshire stood out among the "still pines and tiny farms with rock fences." He could "understand now why Robert Frost wrote the poem 'Birches' and why Amy Lowell wrote the poem 'Lilacs.' " Maine he found "the prettiest of all the New England states." He stopped at Portland for a few days and wrote, "The air is very chilly as it blows from the sea. Certainly there is not the noise here as in New York City. I love the state of Maine." He could see the Atlantic Ocean really for the first time, clear of fog, and thought, "I'll cross some day when I get the money. The Old World lies beyond. All of our ancestors, though near or distant, sprang from there."

Returning to New York Jesse had lunch on June 6 with columnist Franklin P. Adams. Under the antic stylistic spell of Samuel Pepys' diary-keeping, the columnist of "The Conning Tower" noted, "So to luncheon with Jesse Stuart, and he mighty interesting, with his tayles of school teaching and how he wrote 'The [sic] Man with a Bull-Tongue Plow,' and many things of Greenup, which is in Kentucky." In New York he spoke frankly with one of the reporters about his future plans, including marriage:

> For himself, Stuart wants only to continue to live in his beloved W Hollow. He plans to marry soon—Elizabeth Hale, who is the subject of several of his sonnets, is "sort of engaged" to him. Elizabeth is a school teacher in Nashville, Tenn., and is "real mountain folks," too.
> Yesterday Stuart confessed that the white buckskin oxfords he bought to wear in New York were pinching a bit. But he settled his gray tweed coat a little on his broad shoulders and straightened the

light blue tie that matched his socks. After all, just before he started for his first view of the big town hadn't Elizabeth given him counsel concerning his behavior?

"Keep your hair slicked back, your pants pressed and your shoes clean," Elizabeth said. "If you do that you'll get through all right."

By August of 1935, Jesse Stuart was back in Nashville pressing his suit with Elizabeth Hale, as he had been for nearly the whole of the last year. He found the city "smokey as ever, hotter than ever before." On the east side of Nashville where Elizabeth Hale lived, he joined "a party of old friends" at the Green Lantern and the theater. The success of *Bull-Tongue Plow,* along with the rapid appearance of other of his publications that year in *The Saturday Review of Literature, Scribner's* magazine, *Household,* the *New Republic, Story, Literary America,* the *Southern Review,* the *Yale Review*—and those forthcoming the following month in *Harper's,* the *American Mercury,* and *Scholastic*—had made her see things in a different light. Contrary to what people might have thought about one of the most personable of the Grand Ole Opry stars, Elizabeth Hale, unlike her sister Mamie Ruth, was not fond of being in the public eye. "She never liked that," Jesse Stuart said, "and surprising as it may seem, she didn't like the kind of music they [the Grand Ole Opry] did." Her brother-in-law said that the suddenness of Jesse's success forced her to reexamine their differences. Jesse's roots were in Kentucky, and she finally realized that was where he would be. "She envisioned traveling and meeting people all over the world, and . . . I think [perhaps] prejudged the thing. [It] scared her more than any one thing." Marriage became a critically immediate question between them. An August wedding was seriously discussed, or so Jesse thought. "He wanted her to be up there in New York with him and share his success; and he pressed the question of marriage." Pek Gunn recollected that Elizabeth Hale was a "very practical sort of person and still is, [but] she was swept off her feet by all this." In addition, there were religious differences that came to the fore. From her teens, she had been a devout Nazarene; and although Jesse Stuart could scarcely be typed as an orthodox fundamentalist, Ed Hardy remembered that during this period Jesse "was seeking. 'I'm open-minded,' he would say. 'I believe in a Superior Being,' but he was saying he did not 'know' for sure." Jesse Stuart had often attended Baptist services at Plum Grove with his mother, and considered himself "a Methodist in a sense—just because I grew up in that Community." Ed Hardy thought of him at the time as "a seeking agnostic . . . a man seeking for the truth."

Further, her parents intervened. Mrs. Hale had accepted the courting, Ed Hardy remembered, but when their relationship came down to the issue of love and marriage, Mrs. Hale was opposed. Somewhat as Livy Langdon's parents of Elmira, New York, had questions about their demure daughter's marrying the robust Westerner Mark Twain, Nashvillians Theron and Laura Hale raised their questions with Jesse Stuart also. "They didn't trust me," Jesse believed. "They wanted to iron me out and make a business man out of me. All they talked about was the regular type of man . . . who could make money. That's all Mrs. Hale talked about." Despite all the publicity his poetry and prose were achieving, "I wasn't having any real [financial] success then." Yet he could not give up writing to sell floor wax, as Mr. Hale did after leaving the Opry in the 1930s, nor could he bring himself to forsake W-Hollow for Nashville. It was apparently not the first time he had experienced a basic conflict between himself and Elizabeth. Prophetically, one of the *Bull-Tongue Plow* sonnets addressed the conflict:

> The hills are calling me:
> > "Come back my son;
> Don't waste pure blood on artificial places
> Where men must toil with hungry haggard faces;
> Come live with us until your race is run."
> My lover's voice is calling louder still:
> "Dear Lad: I've known the city all my days;
> Flicker of light, her strange illuminous ways;
> My dreams are not a cottage on your hill."
> Dear hills: Your woods are dark—your rocks
> > are cold;
> I know your ragweeds grow around my shack;
> I hear your voice and Lord I'm coming back.
> Dear girl: The hills keep young. Woman grows old
> Before her time and torturous to kiss.
> I choose the hills mindless of what I miss.

Elizabeth Hale would not share his life, after all.

In the autumn of 1935, he wrote James Still a kind of summary confession, "Now let me tell you another little secret. I went with a girl five years. I was supposed to marry her in August . . . , [but] the whole affair went on the rocks when I went to New York and New England . . . last June." After returning from Nashville in August, he wrote in his newspaper column, "I have found that the old stomping grounds around Nashville are not quite the same. The old crowds have gone.

Friends are a little older and changing their impressions about life and they don't seem quite like they used to seem." He did "but little writing." Then, for a time, "I did a lot of cussing and pining. But hellsfire—that wouldn't do. I started taking in the dances and living like Jesse Stuart used to live—kindly wild and kindly free. I got to feeling better." Not long after, Charlotte Salmon of Ashland, Kentucky, came to the Kings' to interview the author. She found "in an untidy bedroom upstairs . . . scattered copies of . . . conservative highbrow magazines, any one of which many an aspiring intellectual with literary ambitions would mortgage his soul to get into, all with stories or poems by Jesse Stuart." Still on the mantlepiece was "a tinted photograph" of Elizabeth Hale. "She has a sweet, old-fashioned face," the reporter observed, "and is the only girl Jesse ever came near marrying, but her parents thought he was too impractical."[2]

For more than a year now he had accepted dozens of speaking engagements. In addressing such organizations as the business women's clubs, junior women's clubs, and university women's organizations at nearby cities such as Lexington and Ashland, he soon made known the distinctive personality that would for decades fetch audiences throughout the country and the world. On the evening of November 20, 1934, he was "enthusiastically acclaimed" at his appearance before the Business and Professional Women's Club of Maysville for being "as simple and unspoiled as his poems." Here his friend Lena Wells Lykins Voiers, of Vanceburg, introduced him. The poet explained that "his characterizations are drawn entirely from the people he has known." The reporter found him memorable for "his refreshing youngness and simplicity." He was particularly sensitive regarding questions about the concluding lines of Stuart Poem #703 in Bull-Tongue Plow, "Now if there is a Resurrection Day / I shall be one that's taken by surprise," and "vehemently denied any atheistic tendencies," declaring that "it would take a false construction of his poems to make them appear in such a light. . . . On the contrary, he testified to a conviction that poetry and religion are closely akin." Such early speeches earned two and five dollars each, but soon he was getting twenty-five dollars, the sum he was paid for giving an assembly lecture at Eastern Kentucky State Teachers College at Richmond on February 15, 1935. There he read poems, including "Sonatas of Spring," to be published in Scribner's magazine in June. "With no sweep of oratory or consecrated air," college reporter Lois Colley wrote, "something new in poets strode lustily into our midst Friday at chapel— a poet of the soil, of the mountains in autumn, of the farmer busy with nature's thoughts as he guides his homely plow, of sturdy people living their lives in simple contentment." While narrating his life, the speaker was capable of "smiling at himself but never losing his detached view of himself," and "he told with complete naturalness and lack of effort the lively story of his varied life." She was impressed by "this startling young man. . . . A broad humor livened his narrative, the humor of a native son who sees the incongruity of composing odes to the breath of spring with his typewriter nestled by a pile of onions in the family smokehouse." Perceiving the harmony between man and work, she summarized, "His poems are like himself, forceful, sure, easy to understand, unaffected, and they bring a clean, virile message as refreshing as the breeze from one of his own mountain tops." Of this early appearance, Jesse Stuart later wrote,

> It would have been easier for me if I hadn't stopped at the bulletin board before I went into the college chapel. Here I stood before a little notice on the bulletin board which read: "Jesse Stuart, farm boy and schoolteacher from (Greenup) County, will read some of his farm rhymes." Some husky football player stood beside me and read the bulletin same time I did. "Hell," he said, turning to me, "if Eastern can't furnish us with a better chapel program than this, I'm not going, are you?"
> "Hell, yes, I'm going," I said. "I have to go. I want to see what this is all about."
> This Eastern student, who thought I was a student also, and I walked into the chapel together.
> "We'd better grab a seat," he said, as the chapel started filling up.
> Just then President Donovan walked over to me.
> "Are you ready?" he asked.
> "Much as I'll ever be," I answered, while the fellow I'd met at the bulletin board looked strangely at me.

Jesse followed the president onto the stage "where I faced a sea of approximately 1,700 faces in Hiram Brock Auditorium." The president gave him a "full thirty minutes." The applause and laughter were so frequent and the pleasure of the audience so obvious that he went on for "eighty-seven minutes," and when he concluded "I was hot, and wet with perspiration." It was one of his early distinctive successes, from which a distinguished lecturing career was to follow. Even so, he was constrained to write James Still that, although he had "turned public speaker," he would talk "only to select crowds and not often enough to hurt me."

He was energetically writing again by Christmas vacation of 1935, when he made his second trip to New York City, once more registering at the Prince George Hotel because it was "one of the quietest hotels in the city." At the Dutton offices he saw and later lunched with Merton S. Yewdale, the editor of *Bull-Tongue Plow*, to whom he would dedicate his forthcoming collection of short stories, *Head o' W-Hollow*. Yewdale wanted to know if W-Hollow were "thickly populated." Jesse told him, "Ten houses . . . about five miles long and a road passable to automobiles about four months out of the year." At the *Mercury* offices he met editor Paul Palmer, who puffed on "a long-stemmed pipe." Later he went over to Scribner's at 527 Fifth Avenue and had a nice talk with editor Alfred Dashiell and associate editor Marion Ives, from Stamford, Connecticut, who invited him to her home for a Christmas turkey dinner. While at Scribner's he saw "a tall man" walk in. Jesse spoke to him, "Thomas Wolfe, aren't you?"

"Yes," Wolfe said.

He had been deeply impressed with Wolfe's *Look Homeward, Angel* and *Of Time and the River*.

Of their conversation Jesse later wrote, "We nearly tore up the place for a while. He is an enormous man of six feet six. He has done two of the greatest novels produced in this country. . . . His book of short-stories 'From Death Til Morning' has just been published. I did like big enormous Tom Wolfe[.] I came up even with his shoulders." The two met again one day in front of Scribner's. Wolfe said, "Jesse, I've just read your book, *Man with a Bull-Tongue Plow*. I think it's one of the greatest books that ever came out of America."

Jesse wondered if Wolfe were kidding him. "I knew him well. He was older than I and, of course, I looked up to Tom in two ways, in height and in writing. I thought he was the greatest writer that I had ever met—in fact, I knew it. He liked the death sections of *Man with a Bull-Tongue Plow*—and he would. Tom should have been a poet. He was, really, a poet." After a busy day he had dinner with the president of Dutton, Colonel John MacRae, and his son Elliot, at their apartment overlooking the East River. Before he left New York, he talked with editors of the *North American Review* and the *Pictorial Review*. He walked back to the Prince George Hotel "through streets filled with thousands of strange faces." Finding New York "so big, so masculine, so powerful," he was obliged to write, "Kentucky hills, valleys and her little towns mean far more to me than all New York City. I shall be glad to return."

When *Head o' W-Hollow* emerged in 1936, *Time* nearly atoned for its earlier cuteness:

When homespun Kentucky Poet Jesse Stuart sat down and wrote a big stack of "sonnets" . . . a few critics sat up, called him a modern Bobbie Burns. Others just laughed at his unconscious, bull-tongued humor. Last week Poet Stuart made the scoffers scratch their heads over a book of stories that were partly funny, partly serious, in the main tantalizingly good. These tales of Kentucky farmers were written in racy Kentucky dialect, with a wild-eyed, straightforward outrageousness that reminded readers more than once of Erskine Caldwell, at times of the ingenuous slyness of Chekhov. Readers who liked to laugh with a clear conscience, however, were still puzzled by author Stuart's refusal to make the most of his Munchausenish humor. But in spite of a preoccupation with death and burial that will seem to many a reader adolescently morbid, some of his yarns were well worth inclusion in any anthology-of-the-year.

Mark Van Doren in the *New York Herald Tribune* pointed to Jesse's skillful "manipulations of word-order, grammar and syntax" by which "he succeeds in giving the flavor of a remote and special speech," and went on to declare, "the stories in themselves are strange and powerful; a great deal happens in W-Hollow, even if the world has been ignorant of the fact. But now the world may know, possessing as it does at least seven short stories of the very first order." As did many reviewers, William Rose Benét wrote that "this second book is better than the first." Further, "his stories are fuller, for the most part, of his own idiom; and his descriptive phrase, so fresh and forceful in his best sonnets, is quite as good in his prose. There is a firmer fibre and richer variety in this book." Ralph Thompson of the *New York Times* found the book "one of the most appealing collections of short stories I have ever read. . . . A lot of water will go over the dam before Kentucky, or any other State, develops another writer with the art that is this 28-year-old farmer-poet-school teacher's." Closer to home, Elizabeth Hardwick of the *Lexington Herald* perceived a craftsman of "deep sensibilities" at work: "Everything is written from the point of view of his people. You have lines of description such as, 'Her hair was like brown sealing wax you put around fruit jars . . . ,' and 'she has a smile prettier than a hound dog's bark that has run a fox to the rocks.' " Of the stories, reviewer Margaret Trotter of the *Courier-Journal* found "some of them are in their way, Homeric— the kind of story which, told from generation to generation, grows and takes on rich form, and we accept it all as it is told, because it comes to us in the simple language of poor people." In his annual lecture, delivered at Pointe Aux Barques, Michigan, William Lyon Phelps featured *Head o' W-Hollow* among ten fictional works, noting its "amazingly original stories."[3]

Throughout 1936 Jesse was publishing at a furious pace. In addition to the twenty-one stories in *Head o' W-Hollow*, he also published eight more stories in the *Southwest Review, American Mercury, Harper's,* the *Partisan Review and Anvil, Scribner's* magazine, and three stories in *Esquire.* Sixteen new poems appeared in *Southwest Review, Saturday Review, Progressive Farmer, Scribner's,* the *New Republic, Poetry,* and *Esquire,* the last-mentioned containing "The Ballad of Lonesome Waters," a forty-one stanza poem fully illustrated with tempera paintings by Eric Lundgren. At least eight of his poems were reprinted in textbooks and such periodicals as *Commonweal* and *Southwest Review.* In February he published an essay in *Scholastic* on English and creative writing, and in August another in *Country Gentleman* dealing with his purchase of a farm. Articles appeared on Jesse and his work in *Southwest Review* and *Mercury,* while scores of approving reviews of his new story collection trumpeted his name to general and scholarly audiences alike.

One of his stories accepted that year was both a "lived" and "told" story. In the spring a handsome blue-eyed blond woman, whom Jesse gave the name of Mary Frazier Jordan, entered his office. Something was on her mind, there were tears in her eyes, and during the ensuing hour in his office she told him of her frustration in trying to write the story of her family. The story involved the tragedies of marital infidelity and a double murder. "Mr. Stuart," she told him, "you can write the story yourself. If you sell it for money you can take all of it. I don't want money. I have all the money I need and want. I just want this story written and published like it happened."

Jesse thought it was "a great story." She gave him the details and he took notes. When he asked about any possible family repercussion she said:

I don't care if there is. . . . But I don't think there will be for so many years have passed since my father killed Jim Hailey and brother Hilton was killed by Lester Shy. My dear brother, as fine-a-looking man as ever was born in Kentucky—big, tall, broad-shouldered, handsome—died at twenty-eight. My mother, now an old woman, was twenty-eight when my father killed Jim Hailey over her. Jim Hailey was only thirty-one. They were young people then with lovers' troubles. Young people, too, when brother Hilton was killed over his wife. I guess there will always be trouble of men getting killed over beautiful and attractive women.

As Mrs. Jordan told the story, she continued to weep loudly. "I felt a little disturbed [at] having her crying aloud in my office when I was the only person in the office with her," Jesse recorded. "Weepingly, she told me the story of her people, how they have lived on the Big Sandy and the Ohio Rivers all their days—more than a century. They had been pioneers on the Big Sandy and had lived there when 'the gun was the law' and now on the Ohio River where guns were used but they were not the law. . . . The way she described the feelings she had when her father Big-Sandy Bill killed Jim Hailey over courting her mother—I couldn't forget. I was deeply stirred. I began to shed a few tears myself. . . . She had given me the story and it was my story now. She told me about seeing the blood on the floor and smelling the gunpowder when her father killed Big Jim Hailey and about smelling the gunpowder when Lester Shy had killed her brother Hilton in his own home."

It was a story of "river people," boat people, and "all were from well-to-do or wealthy people as compared to others around them. . . . And the ones I knew personally of Big-Sandy Bill's descendants were intelligent and handsome people who went to horseracing in Kentucky and Ohio, bet on horses, and as far away, in earlier years, as Las Vegas to gamble." As she talked with Jesse, Mrs. Jordan frequently interrupted herself to insist, "And, Mr. Stuart, you know we are a good family. We have pride. We live well. We're respected. We're intelligent. And we have integrity." He wanted to say, "Yes, Mrs. Jordan, but stories are lived by the people in top families as well as those on the lower rounds of the human totem pole. Stories are everywhere among all people who live, breathe, eat, drink, and propagate their species." He could have said this and more, but he remained sympathetically silent in order to get the facts down for fictional use.

That night he went home and began writing the story, taking time out to eat a delicious evening meal prepared by Lillie King. He pecked away at the typewriter in his room, on into the night, and finished the story about four in the morning. The most significant change he made was in point of view: "I let a son, Don, tell the story instead of their daughter Mary. . . . I thought it would be more effective if a son told it, then I wanted to disguise the story all I could and protect Mary should the story be published and read by people in this area." He called it "A Land beyond the River," and sent it off to *Esquire*.

In late July that year, although the temperature was 104, Amy Vanderbilt and Morton Clark hiked over the ridge path from Greenup to visit Jesse in W-Hollow. By this time he and James were living in a bunkhouse built over the outdoor cellar a few feet away from the eastern side of the house, allowing the boys more privacy and later hours than Mick Stuart permitted inside the house. The two New York society members had been writing a series on the Kentucky mountain region, and this article, datelined Riverton, Kentucky, July 29, described the young man at home as friendly, powerful of voice, outgoing, and cheery. "He is 5 feet 11, square, brown, and tough." In their tour of the Stuart land, Vanderbilt and Clark "admired with him two Red Durock brood sows bought with the $12 proceeds of a sale of three love sonnets to Poetry Magazine." They visited Jesse in the bunkhouse, the " 'bungalow' over the creamery," as the city slickers described it. They talked with him frankly, discerning that "he drinks wine, doesn't like the taste of beer, never touches hard liquor and began his addiction to black cigars only last year. He's 28 and the rudder of his family . . . [a] principal . . . some 18 miles from home." Jesse took them through his hills of corn and lowlands of sorghum cane. Later, they joined him at the supper table and while he plowed into "a heaped plate of spring chicken" got him to talk about poetry. "You know," Jesse said, "there's twice as many intellectual poets as need be. Poetry needs an upliftin'. You know, I don't send all my stuff to *Scribner's* or *Esquire* and the *Mercury*—I let a lot of it go to the country journals. I want farmers to read poetry." He told them of seven hundred poems in his trunk still untyped and thirty-five hundred still unpublished. "You know for years I just wrote them and salted them away. I thought those magazines were for other people."

As Jesse told the eastern twosome, he was working on a master's degree. During the 1936 summer session at Peabody in Nashville, he enrolled for seven hours of classwork, for which he received one A and three Bs. James went with him and they stayed at the Sigma Chi house that summer. According to one reporter, during this period he used his spare time to "read twenty-nine novels . . . write seven short stories and fifty poems," one of the stories initially entitled "Resurrection." The writer admitted that his Uncle Martin Hilton was the foundation for the idea, his desire to have everybody buried—Sheltons and Powderjays (Hiltons and Stuarts) in the same place so on Resurrection Day, they would all get up and know each other. "Yeah," he agreed, Uncle Martin "had it all worked out. I wrote that for Dr. Crabb. He wanted a paper from his students in education, and he wanted each of us to give our philosophy of education. I told him 'I don't have any, and I can't give it, but I've got an uncle who read the *History of the Decline and Fall of the Roman Empire* and let the weeds take his corn.' "

"He sounds great to me," Dr. Crabb said. "Write about him."

Later, Jesse was questioned about the powerful lyric throughout the story, that life-cannot-die motif commencing, "But we speak not all— the ghosts of us light as the wind and the wind with the identity of us stamped invisible—laugh to the wind . . . in the April sky—we laugh and speak to each other on the same old mountain paths. We cannot die. You cannot take a club and kill us. You might beat off our husk but the real of us is here—it will not die—not even when the smell of summer— the ripened corn and the heading cane with its white-dotted stems . . . the luscious sweet tang of scented wind from the growing summer and the creepy night of the sheepbells tinkling on the hills will mingle with the ooze of night wind in the green weeds and the foxglove on the bluffs . . . we who have been dead so long and sleeping on the hill . . ."

After a pause the poet remarked, "Well, it was read in class, and they liked it. The class cried." He went on to recall, excitement twinkling in his blue eyes and rising in his voice, "I sent it to *Esquire* and I didn't more than get it off than I got a letter back that had a $200 check. I told James, oh, boy, we'll have food until tomorrow. And you ask James about this because you won't believe it . . . that little machine you put a nickel in and beat it everytime and got our meals . . . I'd get food for both of us with a nickel. It was 1936." Later, Tennessee reviewer George Scarbrough wrote of "This Is the Place" as "a tender, understanding story of the beauty and the ending of life, of the timeless faith of man that not all of himself will perish."[4]

Even though Jesse had very much wanted to complete a master's degree, he "never had time to write a thesis," for he was "too busy with creative efforts." That summer at Peabody proved to be fortuitous in other ways. Concerning his romantic life, the summer had in his own mind—to adapt the language of his education professors—"finalized" his break with Elizabeth Hale. He had enjoyed solid academic success; he had done a huge amount of reading and creative work; and Professor Crabb had advised him to apply for a Guggenheim Fellowship. Jesse developed a formally declared fellowship plan: "An effort to discover existing similarities in the highlanders of Kentucky and Scotland—Certain surviving traits as indicated in the poetry and song in the Kentucky Highlanders of Scottish ancestry." Further, "I want to do two novels, a play and rework a book of verse." Excerpts follow from what must be the most original of letters of application ever composed for a Guggenheim or any other fellowship:

Dear Guggenheim Foundation:

This is the first time I have ever asked for a scholarship of any sort. I have debated a long time before I have done it. . . . All of my life I have done things myself and made my own way. . . . I have always done what I started out to accomplish. If I didn't do it at first I went back and did it later. Now, I am going to Scotland if I have to work my way over on a cattle boat. I know why I have to go and I'm going. Scotland holds some things for me that I want. My people are Scotch—the Stuarts—and we have been in the mountains of Kentucky and Virginia a long time. . . .

I ran away from home and went to college. I hitch-hiked to Tennessee. I went there on $29.30 and I didn't know anybody. In the meantime I wanted to write. . . . I just love to write. I love to make living people I know move for me on paper. I wrote poetry all the time I was in college—all the time I was in the mills where there were clouds of smoke by day and pillars of fire by night. Believe it or not I made a good blacksmith. I could temper steel pretty well for an inexperienced man. . . .

At the present I have thirty-five hundred unpublished poems. I don't know how many unpublished stories and manuscripts I have—but six or seven manuscripts. I want to do better work and not more of it. That is why I want to leave school teaching of a winter and farming during the summer. I want to get away—go to Scotland where I can get the background for a long novel I intend to do. I am interested in the hill people there, the Burns Country— and my own people.

I honestly believe if I go to Scotland I can accomplish what I have set out to do. Listen, if I get the scholarship I'll work. I'll show you at the end of the year what I have done. . . . It would be hard for me to tell you all I want to do. What I want is time, and I want this time in Scotland. I am hell-bent on going to Scotland to do it.

In June of this year I was broke. . . . I borrowed money from Leslie's Drug Store in Greenup, Kentucky to mail my stories to the markets. I started writing and farming. I was not doomed. . . . While at Peabody this summer I wrote stories and I studied . . . wrote the story that is in Scribner's now while in Peabody and five others. I wrote 22 stories, 12 articles and 50 poems. I have sold five stories this summer, one article and seven poems. I wrote them this summer. . . . I know this letter is jumbled up and I've said things I shouldn't have said in this application. But they are true. There is no need to pussyfoot about the truth. I say again, I'll try not to make a failure if I get the scholarship. I hope I've filled this out correctly and got it in before the deadline date.

P.S. I had two books published *Man with a Bull Tongue Plow*, E. P. Dutton and Company, October 14, 1934. It is poetry—703 poems (sonnets) now in the third edition. Head O' W-Hollow [sic], April 17th, 1936 by the same company. Another book to be published by them in the Spring. *Beyond Dark Hills*.

Jesse continued to publish vigorously on through the fall and into the spring and summer of 1937. The story mentioned in his Guggenheim letter as being in the October issue of *Scribner's* was "Men of the Mountains," based on an incident "I couldn't have made . . . up." He wrote it because "I couldn't escape it. Not a story like that. A man, my neighbor, and digging his own grave." Every month from January through September he published a short story in *Esquire*, and seven more in *Scribner's*, *Globe*, *Household*, *American Prefaces*, and the *New Mexico Quarterly*, but only about five poems during the same period in *Harper's*, *Scribner's*, and the *Pictorial Review*. Commencing in June he would revive his column "Fragments from Nothing," too, in the *Greenup News*.

These publications were achieved in spite of the fact that he was heavily involved with his duties as a teaching principal in a difficult year at McKell High School. In January, the worst flood in memory inundated the Ohio Valley and marooned Jesse in the school building where he taught. For seven nights he slept on a cafeteria table. For seventeen days he did not receive his mail. Railroad fills were washed out. When the waters receded, they left a "tract of desolation." The frogs, terrapins, and snakes—all cold-blooded animals—had known it first and abandoned their hibernation, moving instinctively to higher ground and up the trees. While he was moated in at McKell, "I rowed a boat under trees and reached up with my oar to knock down clusters of snakes hanging to the barren boughs of trees before I dared go under them." By February 11 he had developed "a terrible cold."

In the midst of this natural disaster, it was typical of him to find a rift of light and hope, and he wrote, "I appreciate the cooperation of the people of America. They didn't wait for us to ask for anything— they came to us. You appreciate this when you are in trouble fighting an army of waters. I was eating a sandwich in Greenup, Ky., and looked to see where it was from; it was from North Carolina. Airplanes flew over at Greenup and dropped food." At this time the *New Bedford* (Massachusetts) *Standard* published a news story headed, "Kentucky Poet Wins Acclaim of Book Critics," noting that he had received honorable mention for a Book-of-the-Month Club Fellowship, the winners being James T. Farrell, Katherine Anne Porter, Robinson Jeffers, and Paul Sears.

Good news came in March with announcement of the award of the Guggenheim Fellowship he had sought. The *New York Times* carried his picture with the notation that he would go to Scotland "to continue his creative writing." The *Nashville Evening Tennessean* of the same date emphasized his purpose of studying the kinship between "the Scotch-English highlanders and their American prototypes."

Jesse's reaction was exuberant: "Not even a book acceptance has meant so much to me!" To his new friend Wisconsin writer August Derleth: "I'm really pleased. . . . It gives me a chance to get away—leisure time for writing." He thanked Carleton Wells for "helping me get the Guggenheim Fellowship.. . . . I'm walking on the wind!" Then he broke loose wildly at the letter's end: "I'll be going to Scotland in June! 'Whoopee! Hold her Newt—She's heading for the barn!' 'I got her Pappie by the old crumpled horn!' "

That spring he somehow found time to give several lectures, two in April at state teachers colleges at Slippery Rock and California, Pennsylvania, then another at Princeton University. By May, Don West, his old friend of LMU and Vanderbilt days, "dropped in out of a clear sky" to pay him a visit, a reunion that would be published the next year in *Beyond Dark Hills.* Detailed profiles appeared in the *Louisville Times,* the *Portsmouth Times,* and the *Huntington Herald-Advertiser.* The caliph of the short story, Edward J. O'Brien, included Jesse's "Hair" in *The Best Short Stories* of 1937 and, as Ralph Thompson noted in the *New York Times,* O'Brien in his "Index" singled out the Kentuckian as having "published the greatest number of first-rank stories during the year—seven in all."

Meanwhile, in January "A Land beyond the River," the story Mary Frazier Jordan had come to his office and told him nearly a year before, had appeared in *Esquire.* By early March "all hell broke loose." One of the Frazier men, formerly a good friend of Jesse's, wrote him a disturbing letter. "Why had I resurrected old family tragedies that had lain dormant these many years? Why did I blow breath into their nostrils to make them live again? He also warned me against even stepping on any of the property his family owned." Mrs. Jordan "looked sadly at me but never said anything." Copies of *Esquire* sold out and newsstands ordered more. The story became the talk of the community. Amateur historians commended Jesse on his accuracy, though daily he tried to escape involvement. The flood had helped distract people a little bit, but not much. One man, vengeful toward the proud Fraziers and "in love with Hilda Thombs, Hilton Frazier's widow," smilingly informed the author that he had bought fifty copies of *Esquire* to distribute "to people who count"; for, he declared, "I want to wreck that overbearing Frazier family."

He knew he would have no peace until the ungentle spring ended with the school year and he went abroad. Perhaps then, three thousand miles from home, he could clear his mind of the furor. "I never had one of my stories to cause so much trouble and talk." On June 11 his friends gathered at Fullerton for a farewell party for Jesse, attended by, among others, Oscar and Ann Sammons, Nancy and Bill Curry, and Naomi Deane Norris, with whom he had enjoyed four dates that year. Before he left, he made sure to pack his portable Victrola, a few records, and books, especially his copy of Robert Burns' poetry, actually the third copy he had owned since Mrs. Hatton had given him the first one his junior year in high school. He had literally worn the others out. Now he thumbed through it and placed a sprig of early Kentucky goldenrod between the pages before he packed it away. He made a quick lecturing trip south, first to Nashville, then on to the Atlanta area, returning to entrain June 22 on the *George Washington* at South Portsmouth to New York. The last thing he saw in Portsmouth was "a bright row of lights out Chillicothe street, then the hills above Fullerton, the floodlights above the Portsmouth athletic field . . . the McKell High school building where four years had been spent . . . Greenup . . . then a longing glance at the hills back toward home—dark and silent. The train whipped on."[5]

In New York City he saw his publishers and visited Scribner's, where he met Marion Ives, the young New England woman who had "criticized . . . severely and praised . . . highly" his short stories. She had also always encouraged him. Jesse had high esteem for her professionalism and apparently enjoyed her company as well, for he spent the Fourth of July in Stamford with her and mutual friends—Bill Fletcher, a native of Scotland, and his wife, Marjorie, Marion's niece. Bill's sister, Pearl, had landed a few small parts in Hollywood pictures and was then modeling fur coats in New York. She was there with her fiancé, Arnold Anderson, who owned a valuable strip of Connecticut beach. Jack MacDonald's party was there, too, some of whom Jesse had met at Slippery Rock, Pennsylvania, during his lecture tour. Like Jesse's, MacDonald's work had appeared in *Esquire,* under the name Alan MacDonald.

They took a dip in the cold salty water and went sailing until they were thoroughly sunburned. In the following days, waiting to embark, he continued his vacation in New York, taking in Chinatown and the Radio City Music Hall where he watched the enactment of the *Blue Danube Waltz* on stage, "a beautiful spectacle."

After two interviews, he kept a date with Charlotte Salmon Wednesday evening, July 8, at "the star lit roof garden of the Waldorf-Astoria where we danced to the music of Guy Lombardo and his Royal Canadians." After her article on him in the *Southwest Review* the previous year, the two had had several dates. His poem "Love in Autumn" sang of her as "lithe, blue-eyed with golden wheat-straw hair," and he had written,

> Come with me, Love, we two have worked together.
> Charlotte, this golden summer has been ours.
> You, clean a girl as ever trod shoe-leather,
> You, fairest of our mountain wildwood flowers . . .

They had enjoyed life together, but

> Our stay can't be forever and one day,
> Our lives must break, our lives must break too soon.

For all things were uncertain, and he was going far away:

> All might be over in a little while,
> The love of living and the dawn of age;
> We walk Time's corridors in single file,
> We take Life's book and scan it page by page.

The next day he had his visa stamped, met an interviewer from the *Philadelphia Public Ledger,* made a brief visit to Scribner's, got his letter of credit from the Guggenheim Foundation Fund, and with Jimmy MacRae running interference met Rudy Vallee and Douglas Fairbanks, Jr., at the NBC studios. Later, he rode the top deck of a Fifth Avenue bus back to the Prince George Hotel. On July 9 he sailed at four in the afternoon aboard the *Samaria,* bound for Scotland.

Up the river Clyde to Greenock on the ninth day out, the ship anchored. Jesse was soon in front of the customs inspector and set his luggage over. "Is Stuart your real name?" the inspector asked.

"Yes, why do you think I'd change it?"

The inspector returned his luggage without opening it and said with a respectful bow, "You're coming home, sir."

The doctor took one look at him and waived the required medical examination. "You look all right. Just go ahead." Jesse walked toward the depot to catch the Glasgow train. Divided into a section for first-class and a section for third-class passengers, with no "second class" as he soon discovered, "the depot made me laugh." He was used to the big Mallies on the C&O tracks along the Ohio, and the engine that pulled up, supposedly a "crack train," caused him "to laugh louder," for "the whistle of the train was like a toy whistle." Up the River Clyde he saw ships being built and "small stone houses with gardens back of them," neat, clean, well-kept yards of emerald. "The hills that overlooked the Clyde River were just as green as the Blue Grass section of Kentucky in late April. Due to heavy rains, it stays green all summer." Exhilarated by his entry into the country he had so long dreamed of seeing, he recorded the details in his "Fragments from Nothing":

> We pass over some of the prettiest country I have ever seen. Honest it was a paradise. Green hills and stone fences to the tops of hills. Maybe there would be a little cluster of trees someplace on the hill. Maybe there wouldn't be. Certainly, there wouldn't be a weed patch or a patch of sprouts. All the land was in grass or in cultivation. We passed through little towns—all the houses made of stone. I never saw a single house of wood. The whistle would scream. And I'd have to laugh and wonder how the George Washington would act on this road.

He went north through Perth, Dundee, Aberdeen, and on up the coast of the North Sea through the county of Caithness to Wick. In place of Kentucky corn along the way, he saw fields of Irish potatoes and turnips that served as food for man and feed for sheep and cattle. "Do you want white coffee or black coffee?" a Dundee waitress inquired. "I want black coffee," he said, not ever having heard of white coffee. He could not take the black coffee and pushed it back, ordering tea. The waitress did not charge him for the coffee. In Dundee he saw "my first Scotch soldier" wearing a colorful tartan and asked, "What do you wear under one of these skirts?"

"In time of peace we wear clothes under them but in time of battle it is a disgrace to wear anything under the tartan for a Scotch soldier."

He had left ninety-five-degree July weather in New York and found it about sixty on his way to Aberdeen by bus, "where they shoved the top back and threw the windows up." Crossing the Atlantic he had worn his topcoat most of the way, "and I could have stood mine on the bus," but the people around him kept talking about the warm weather. The Scots girls had natural color in their cheeks—"not a girl with her lips painted nor her cheeks rouged." They were "a healthy sort and so are the men." Many things seemed strange to him. He had not seen any stop signs and he had to watch out for the tiny automobiles, for "they whip past you like bullets sometimes" and from the opposite way an American expected. Indeed, riding along he kept anticipating accidents. The money, too, was something of a knot he had not yet untied. At Aberdeen he gave the hotel keeper a five-pound note and got the change back. This he had done several times, later figuring what the service had cost, computing it on the basis of the shilling equaling an American quarter. As a result his pockets were soon bulging with silver and large pennies. When the hotel keeper asked if he wanted "tea," Jesse replied, "I had 'tea' in Dundee." He did not know what the proprietor meant just then. Hungrily he went out looking for a restaurant but found not one. Back at the hotel he inquired, "Say, how about a little something to eat here." The keeper looked up. "You do want 'tea' then, don't you?" Stuart told him, "In America we call it supper—some call it dinner."

He would never forget busy, clean Aberdeen, the city "of white granite blocks" at the mouth of the Dee. On a July evening he was talking with the Aberdonians and listening to their famous stories of Scotch thrift, waiting for the evening to get a little dark. "Eleven o'clock came and it was still light. I was told at the hotel that they can see to play tennis until eleven o'clock at night." It was daylight again by three A.M. But in mid-winter it would reverse—"eighteen to twenty hours of darkness." Another difference, one that saddened him: The Great War everywhere, it seemed, had affected people more deeply than in America. Often he saw women in black—mothers, he believed—at the monuments reading over the names of those who had given everything in the Great War. In Aberdeen he met Jessie Henderson, a Scottish lass six feet tall. She took a liking to the bright golden cellophane wrappers on his San Felice cigars and asked for them to make "some kind of a band for her hair." He removed cellophane from a dozen cigars, "much to my regret, for they dried out and crumbled before the end of the oncoming journey." Their quality was nearly irreplaceable, and then only at Scotland's dear price—about a shilling each. Jessie Henderson teased him about American women. He defended them as the "prettiest women in the world," but she returned, "American girls—booh! Make their husbands wash the dishes!" He wanted to say, "They make good coffee though—a biler of black coffee at midnight if you want it." But he refrained, laughing, for he had been told the Scotsman was master of his home. Here, so he heard, were three women to every man; the same in England, and in

Norway and Sweden "there are seven women to one man." When he left Aberdeen after one night, "it was like leaving a family I had known a long time."

North and south of Wick, the rugged coastlines caught his eye, and the old gravestones were "thicker than stumps in new ground." Here in the north, nearly to Pentland Firth, there were no apple trees to be seen. Suddenly, "it looked like the edge of the world." The season was too short for apple trees, and he could hardly understand the language. Somehow the fishing town of Wick did not appeal to him at all. At the end of the train line, in the last northern city in Scotland, he resolved to return south. Just then the fellow at the station came up and asked if he were there for a holiday. "Yes, I'm here for a long holiday," he replied.

"How long are you going to stay?"

"In Wick, as long as Pa[dd]ie stayed in the army."

The fellow did not know what Jesse was talking about. Handling some baggage at the station, he inquired, "How long did Pa[dd]ie stay in the army?"

"They tell me he went in, didn't like it, lit his pipe and came out a-smoking. And soon as I light this cigar I'm getting out of Wick." He asked the man to put his baggage back on the train south.

The resort city of Inverness was crowded, but Jesse eventually found a room at the Hanover Hotel "about big enough to whip a cat in." Washing up for dinner, he heard "the wildest, weirdest noise . . . coming up the river Ness, a beautiful shallow river of blue cold water that rippled in front of the hotel." There were twelve pipers and seven drummers, and the wild music of Scotland was suddenly invading his ear for the first time: "the scream of the pipes and the wind in the fir trees—the rippling of the water—all music to one." As the procession passed in precision along the River Ness, a Scotsman said the music "got his heiland [sic] blood up." The next day a young man, a minister named John MacDougall from the Isle of Skye, took him for a ride in his motor car. It turned into a wild ride when Stuart said, "Turn this thing loose. Step on the gas."

"Fast did you say?"

"I say faster." They zoomed right up along the River Ness, and despite a minor accident, had a great time. Later, MacDougall took him to the train depot. "You know what I like about the Americans?" he said. "They are so full of life. I've never seen people in Scotland like them." Stuart told him he would like to be in his congregation "every time you preached." As the train pulled out they said their farewells and Stuart "gave him one of his good American San Felice cigars."

He rode third-class to Edinburgh, passing Culloden Moor and along the splendid range of Cairngorm Mountains. At the small village of Aviemore on the Spey he could look up and see snow on the mountaintops and "sheep . . . grazing in the green straths below." Trees were few, more often just heather covered the ground, "and the bell heather was in bloom." Down in the valleys were white birch, beech, and fir trees, and in many places the mountain slopes were set in spruce trees. He shared his compartment with a young University of Edinburgh student, and they arrived together at about four in the afternoon at the university grounds. Sightseeing, he heard four women talking—"older women"—and said, "Hello, Americans." They laughed and invited him over. They were from Washington, DC, and gave him a directory to help him locate a room. Shortly after that, he met a young man about his own age on the campus, Dr. Hamish Brown, who helped him find a room just across the parklike "Meadows" from the university and the Royal Infirmary at 8 Viewforth Gardens, not far from Lolith Road, which led down to Princes Street. It was an ancient gray stone building where a narrow recessed entryway with a shallow lintel led into a stairwell with two apartments on each floor. Jesse was soon comfortable in the little room with a fireplace, work table, typewriter, Victrola, and "a place to hang my clothes." Now he could receive mail directly from home. On July 21, he sent a postcard to Deane Norris, who was in college for the summer at Morehead, Kentucky: "Having drifted from north of Scotland down to Edinburgh where I expect to stay the winter." For the better part of a year this would be his home away from home.[6]

11

Scotland: Walking in the Wind
1937–1938
————◇————

From his headquarters at 8 Viewforth Gardens in the year to come he would study Edinburgh, Scotland, England, Wales, Ireland, and twenty-five countries of Europe. Lothian Road to Princes Street brought him into the heart of the historic city and to such memorable landmarks as West Gardens, Edinburgh Castle, the Cathedral of St. Giles, John Knox's home, Holyrood Palace, Sir Walter Scott's Monument, and Greyfriars Churchyard. Almost casually one evening, he ran across Thomas De Quincey's tombstone at St. Cuthbert's Churchyard, and his high school reading of *Confessions of an English Opium Eater* came alive for him again. He visited the eminence of Arthur's Seat and Craigmillar Castle, the latter a favorite residence of Queen Mary. At Arthur's Seat, he wrote in his column "Fragments from Nothing" for the folks back home, centuries ago John Knox was preaching against Mary Stuart and men fought and were killed; but now "life goes on ever so quietly," and "about the castle, and over the mountainside, are just friendly sheep to greet you."

In August he took his first trip to the Trossachs. On the way he paid homage to "the home of the Stuart kings of Scotland" at Linlithgow, the place of origin, he believed, of his father's people. He continued to Stirling Castle and saw the famous site of the Battle of Bannockburn, a struggle that took place more than a century before Columbus discovered America. By letter Jesse recorded the story of the admiring English tourists who remarked to a bystanding Scotsman, "Nice wheat you have here," to which the native responded, "Yes, it ought to be nice wheat for there's enough English blood in it."

Jesse was impressed with Loch Katrine, the source of Glasgow's water supply, and the mirrored image of Ellen's Isle, recognizable to all readers of "Lady of the Lake." He visited the popular resort town of

Callander and walked a winding mountain trail through the heather; proceeded to Doune Castle and gazed upon its fine old baronial architecture. As with most of these grand relics, he noticed that the sheep and cattle now grazed contentedly about the ruins. These highland cattle "were big boned and lean" and had hair that "must have been at least five inches long and . . . tremendous horns."

He was having a hard time getting down to work on the final chapter and revision of *Beyond Dark Hills* and took a break by making his first trip to London on the impressive *Coronation Scot,* which covered the distance of 392 miles in six hours. At Yorkshire along the way, he recalled what he had heard in family lore of the Hiltons' origin from the area. In London he inquired of a policeman the way to the Bonnington Hotel, wiping his brow with a large handkerchief—too large, he noticed, for it was the napkin from the *Coronation Scot* he had unconsciously put in his pocket on the train. But policeman or no, he was not embarrassed. "Picking up a napkin is just an old American custom," he explained.

On this trip to London he saw such sites as St. Paul's, Dickens' Old Curiosity Shop, "the place where Dr. Samuel Johnson used to go for bread and cheese," Oliver Goldsmith's tomb, Buckingham Palace and St. James Park, the House of Parliament, and Big Ben. Westminster Abbey, the "one place most of all I wanted to see in London . . . was closed for repairs." He was particularly taken with the great stone British lions guarding Nelson's monument at Trafalgar Square and the old manuscripts at the British Museum, where he saw the "original hand writing" of more than twenty of the great English writers from Addison and Steele to Dickens and Kipling. At 14 Waterloo Place he found Edward J. O'Brien, who for nearly a quarter of a century had collected and published annually the "Best Short Stories" in the English language on both sides of the Atlantic. O'Brien was also a top executive for MGM Studios in Great Britain.

O'Brien took him in tow on a personally guided tour up the Thames River to Oxford, where at that time O'Brien's family resided. At O'Brien's home Jesse found a library of twelve thousand books. There one day he met Geoffrey West. From Oxford he went through A. E. Housman's Shrewsbury to Chester and, "because of the name," registered at the Washington Hotel; it proved to be "a fairly good hotel with bed and breakfast for 10/6 ($2.62) per day." Fascinated by the old Roman wall of the city, he wrote home, "You can walk on top of the wall, for it is wide enough for a good street, and it is fenced so you can't jump off or fall over." In Chester he wrote Oscar and Ann Sammons that he had just finished a story, a satirical piece with its genesis in the 1937 Ohio

River flood. Ann Sammons had told him a few months before of a coffin lost in the Greenup flood. Out of that he had just built a short piece O'Brien had read and enjoyed. "I changed it from Ann's point of view," he explained, "made it funny and never mentioned the coffin in the story. Had the coffin talking like a man, mad at everybody around there for bringing him in such a place." Apparently there were enough facts in many of his stories, perhaps even in this one, that he added the postscript, "My worst hobby is writing up friends. Oscar, I can't help it." The next day he wrote Naomi Deane Norris a postcard from Flintshire, noting that he was spending a few days in Wales. "This sea-coast town is very pretty," he wrote of Rhyl; and of Wales in general, it "looked more like Kentucky to me than any place yet. . . . Many of the places are grown up with weeds and sprouts and have that appearance of natural wildness which is unlike both Scotland and England."

Up along the Irish Sea the "windblown hawthorne trees" seemed to him to be "nearly rooted out of the ground," but even so, "the countryside . . . is really beautiful." Passing through Liverpool and Preston, he toured Windermere and the Lake District, visiting Wordsworth's grave in an old churchyard, Dove Cottage, and Coleridge's small house, too, beneath a cluster of trees and nearly on the road. In his column, he wrote that Wordsworth had argued with De Quincey and Coleridge, and then left the group, for "he refused to take 'dope' with his friends. At this refusal, he lost these friends." Stuart looked for what Wordsworth had seen in the Lake Country, a simple thing, and recorded his impression: "The sea gulls are thick almost as flowers in this scenic region. Their snow white wings against a dense heavy green foliage in the mountain sides make it one of the most scenic spots in the world. There isn't any wonder William Wordsworth wrote the finest nature poems in our language. Take a look at his country and you can see why."[1]

After Jesse changed trains at Kilmarnock, two Scotswomen told him that Robert Burns' fellow citizens "prosecuted him and persecuted him." Indeed, he could not go to a church for "the ministers took their texts on him." But now, they said, "Ayr brings in thousands of pounds . . . from the tourists from all over the world paying homage to the world's greatest poet." Ayr struck Jesse as "the poorest city I've seen in Scotland and the quaintest old city," right down to the lack of running water and "a single dim gas light" in his room. He also had to watch where he stepped because of the roaming dogs; "But I honestly don't see how the Lord could make better people," he wrote. At Alloway, just outside Ayr, he went through the thatched stone cottage that is Burns' birthplace. Only one of the four doors could accommodate Jesse's height, and "one door

I had to tilt my shoulders to one side to enter." At Alloway Kirk Stuart found the burial place of the poet's parents, a single grave. To the left of the site rose the fluted Corinthian columns of the Burns Monument surrounded by flowerbeds, an impressive scene that made the Kentuckian think, "What if the ministers of the Alloway Kirk could have seen this in their day?"

Everywhere in the Burns country Jesse carried his copy of the Scottish poet's poems with him. After two days in Ayr Stuart visited Tarbalton, where Burns was inducted into Freemasonry, another kinship that drew the Kentuckian to the Scotsman. The old Masonic Hall was in ruins, with "weeds and oats . . . growing from the thatched roof." At Maunchline he found the small room of the humble cottage in which Burns and Jean Armour began housekeeping, and here he could relate Burns' poems to some of his contemporaries buried in the churchyard. Now their graves were of interest chiefly because the poet had written their lives into durable poetry. Jesse thought, "Maybe some people living today would have greater prospects for immortality if the possibilities for libel against writers were reduced." Jesse learned that Burns' original name was "Burness," but his father had shortened it.

Returning to Kilmarnock by train, Jesse visited another Burns monument, then backtracked to Dumfries on the River Nith, where he found a room and three meals a day, tea and biscuits at bedtime, for eight shillings and sixpence, about $2.12. Here in his day Burns had eventually come, driven by his poverty to take a job as an excise man, and here he had died in 1796, although Jean Armour lived on in the house until 1834. This was the "most respectable" of his homes, Jesse wrote, but "it wasn't anything to brag about." The Kentuckian took time to ask the tour guide in Dumfries, "Who's that good-looking girl out there?" She replied, "That's my daughter." Thus he met Olive MacDonald, a University of Glasgow student, and "one of the 'bonniest lassies' I've met in Scotland."

Everyone in Ayrshire seemed to have something to say about Burns. One man on the street "living off the dole" told Stuart, "Bobbie was a man of the people. Poor Bobbie, if he was only alive today he'd fight for us to have better wages. He was a man of the people," and then he quoted the Ayrshire ploughman's "For a' That and a' That." In the Dumfries churchyard at that mausoleum of Grecian design, so much grander than anything Burns had ever known in life, Jesse paid his respects. Then again later, after he told Olive MacDonald goodbye, "I stole silently back to this old churchyard at night to get my last glimpse at the tomb of the man to whom I owe more than I can ever say." The iron gate was locked, but Jesse climbed it as easily as an apple tree and approached the monument. Muirhead writes of Peter Turnerelli's sculptured group as "the Muse of Poetry finding Burns at the plough," but the Kentuckian perceived the scene differently. There was "the statue of Burns with his cap in his hand, the other hand is on the handle of a plow. Above is the Angel Death with a white shield over his arm. Burns looks toward this Angel Death. He must face the inevitable. This statue is white and it gave a strange appearance in the darkness. . . . I spoke to him in the Scottish night while a bright moon looked down on St. Michael's." Then he took the book of Burns' poetry and opened it. He removed the pressed Kentucky goldenrod he had brought from the other side of the world and dropped it on Burns' grave. "This little tribute," he wrote years later, "I could pay the man who had changed my life."

After he returned to Edinburgh, he wrote Deane Norris on September 10, describing the inside of the Burns Monument and enclosing two snapshots, one of the mausoleum. "The other is of myself," he wrote, "in my new tailored plus-fours." Before signing "Goodnight," he added, "My fire is burning a little low but the red glow of the embers is very pretty in this semi-dark little room."[2]

By early November he had toured twelve European countries and written a column or more on his experience in each one. On a brief sightseeing trip to London, the amiable O'Brien was once again his host, and here Jesse was approached by a director in British movies who "liked my looks, my voice, and accent." When offered a tryout, Jesse was not interested. "I was a writer, not an actor," he reasoned. "At least I thought and hoped I was a writer."

In Copenhagen he visited the home of Gurmild Neilsen, called "Neila," a fetching Danish dance instructor whom he had met the previous summer in the United States. From Denmark, he went on to Oslo and Stockholm. At the Hotel Continental in Stockholm, he helped himself to an elk steak dinner, and wrote Oscar Sammons on October 20, "Tomorrow, I journey to Finland." He flew from Helingsfors, Finland, across the Baltic Sea to Tallinna, Estonia, where he never forgot the "broken masses of humanity." Even the horses in the marketplace "were small, poor, skinny, ready for the boneyard. . . . Men staggered about drunk [on vodka]." Latvia was more prosperous. In Riga he had the strange experience of getting a haircut from a female barber. "I honestly believe it was the quickest and best hair cut I ever got in my life. . . . She didn't use lather but dry shaved my neck." In Kaunas, Lithuania, women were "sweeping the horse manure from the streets." It irritated him to see three more women "washing the windows of the train with mops . . . while about them trampled the country's pride—soldiers in gay uniforms—officers with shining spurs and silver plumed helmets!" He sympathized with Lithuania, however, a tiny republic between communist Russia and fascist Germany. Waiting for the Berlin Express at Kaunas, Stuart had a good meal of ox-tail soup, steak and fried potatoes, carrots, green beans, runner beans, asparagus tips, black coffee, and squash pie, for the equivalent of about thirty cents in American money.

In East Prussia he stayed at Königsberg, then took a bus to visit the farm country where he found cows pulling cars of milk cans to market. It seemed to him "hardly fair that the cow should produce the milk, then have to cart it away to the railway station." The Prussian girls in their wooden shoes and "blousy skirts," their hair plaited "down their backs," were "not as snappily dressed as the American girl," but he quickly acknowledged that "in case of a tussle she could pick the average American up and spin her around a few times with ease." He found the Prussians along with the Danes and Finns the "finest looking and certainly the cleanest" of the continental people.

To Jesse Stuart, Germany was a strange mixture. The people were "the nearest to the Americans and English of any people I have found," certainly "the most hospitable," and yet, as he wrote in his column, "I cannot connect the German Government with its people." He wrote of the persecution of the Jews and something hidden in the Berlin atmosphere:

> Not a song written by a Jew is allowed to be played by a German orchestra. How can anything be so absurd? Not any book written by a Jew is allowed in Germany. It is pathetic to visit the German book stores and look at their window displays. When the Jews were forced to leave Germany many of the finest brains left the country. . . . Jewish stores are boycotted, their windows broken, and they do not have any police protection. . . . There is a feeling of suppression in the very air of Germany. Despite their kindness toward you, it seems there is something they want to hide. I can feel a suppression here that I have not felt elsewhere. . . . We stand up in America and holler about a Dictator. We don't know what a Dictator is.

Mussolini had left a wreath at a Berlin war memorial with a little tag inscribed "Anno 15," which at first mystified Jesse. He soon learned the date marked a celebration of El Duce's 1922 "march on the 'Eternal City'—Rome," and commemorated the birth of Fascism. Now Mussolini "and his co-partner, Adolph Hitler, have turned back the clock. Instead of 'Anno 37' it is 'Anno 15.' " The general spirit of war flourished and massive war memorials adorned *Unter den Linden*, further symbols of "a militant spirit . . . not by any means crushed in modern Germany." Perceiving such matters, he wrote for his column, "How would you like to greet a fellow man by saying: 'Hail Roosevelt!' or 'Hail Hoover!' or 'Hail Harding!' or 'Hail Wilson!' The Americans would often forget. In fact I don't believe they'd remember." He pointed to a danger paralleling Germany and his own country, "when the hearts of the people sank in gloom and despair and they put the government gladly into the hands of the President and implored that he save the country. The German people did the very same thing." On a train he talked with two German Catholics. "My American friend," one of them explained, "Germany was a place where we had to choose between Fascism and Communism," a statement causing Stuart to recall an American college president's declaration that, given such a choice, America would reject both extremes and "pursue a middle ground of liberal Democracy."

One evening in a Berlin cafe he met a young woman researcher, Dr. Irma de Arlandis, recipient of a Rockefeller Research Fellowship, and a recent Princeton graduate, Bradford Cochran. Together they listened to German waltzes and applauded loudly when the orchestra played several Stephen Foster melodies, including "My Old Kentucky Home." Brad Cochran, a little tipsy on good German beer, Jesse thought, was so impressed that he had the waiter take "a bottle of the best port wine" to the orchestra with his compliments. In the course of the evening Jesse learned that Dr. de Arlandis was originally from Alsace-Lorraine, her maiden name was Irma Becker, she wrote fluently in Spanish, German, English, and French, and had three books in print. Some time ago she had left her husband in Spain and did not know if he was dead or alive. The threesome drank beer until they found it necessary to rush Dr. de Arlandis to the station to catch her train for Brandenburg on her way to London. Afterward, the two young men rambled over Berlin together, seeking out the former home of the old Kaiser; and still later were "chased up the street by a policeman" for opening a forbidden gate to an art gallery. "He was old and fat and we easily outran him," Jesse wrote. The two ran into another Princetonian, Bob Janney, up from Monte Carlo. In their ensuing conversation the name of Dean Christian Gauss of Princeton came up. Stuart casually mentioned he had once stayed the night at Gauss' home, causing Janney to comment, "You know, I'm a reader of *Esquire*. . . . There's a Stuart that writes for it from Kentucky. Do you know him?" Jesse recorded that Janney "remembers characters that the author doesn't remember." The three new friends drank more good German beer and finally parted about two in the morning.

On a dining car between Hanover and Cologne a young waiter sought Jesse's help in getting to America, for he feared war was soon coming. Three times he came to Stuart's compartment, finally writing on a snapshot, "Don't forget me." Perhaps all the gathering turmoil of Europe could have been avoided, Jesse thought, if Woodrow Wilson's fourteen-point treaty had been accepted. At least it seemed that Germany was "slowly gaining back what Wilson wanted them to have," but as for Wilson's dream of "democracy"—what he had really been "fighting for," being "the idealist that he was"—Jesse was sure that "if he could only be alive today and see, he would not believe." He sent Deane Norris a postcard depicting Hitler smiling under his mustache, benevolently it would appear, holding a little blonde German girl by the shoulders. Jesse's message read, "Bought this card in Germany. . . . You can find all kinds of these cards in Germany picturing Hitler smiling and playing with little children. It is quite a different story over there." Later he would write, "I have seen a lot. If a few people could see Germany they'd wonder which way America was headed. I wish all Americans could see Germany—be there as I've been."

He returned to England through Holland and Belgium and took ship at Oostende. There on the wharves among racks of drying fish he was again impressed with women at work and the generally prevailing absence of men. He put the imminence of war aside and loaded up on cigars, which cost only a trifle, stuffing his pockets full and removing one from a box so the inspector could see the box had been "used." Soon Oostende became "a tiny speck as we toss about on the Channel," he wrote. "The wind is rough and the boat goes up and down like it is going over green hills. Often it looks like a wave will swallow us." As the rising wind threatened to sweep some of the passengers from the deck, people shouted, "Storm! Storm!" But Jesse Stuart sought a writing pad. "I knew there was something about a storm lodged in my mind over many, many long years. Storm! . . . I didn't like to think about it! But now I had to write that story." Then there they were, the "chalk cliffs of Dover." "Yes," he thought, "I can almost bow my head and weep to see England again—England, a land where children can grow up in individual freedom."

By November 1, he was at the Bonnington Hotel in London, where he wrote Ethel Bush in detail about his European trip, remarking that "I had to keep the women shoved away—pretty women too," assuring her that "a traveling man on his own and this far from home takes but few chances unless he's a fool." He planned to keep his health, "the best . . . in all my life—slender at the waist and over 200 pounds—face a robust color—no [Coca Colas] anymore or coffee—plenty of rest and not so much tobacco." He was still deeply interested in the Greenup County elections, and so serious about his expectations of a Republican victory, particularly for Maynard Bush and Oscar Sammons, that he wrote of the possibility of moving to Louisa, Kentucky, or perhaps to Virginia or to Tennessee if his party lost badly again. So sensitive was he about political machinations back home that he wrote of the September publication of "Uncle Fonse and the Starlings" that "I was scared fartless over that Esquire story—afraid they'd try to figure out and start something and use it for political purposes." By way of explanation he wrote that it was a story built around Mrs. Forrest King's "joke about the starlings," to which Ethel Bush may have been privy. To Deane Norris he wrote of the story that he had been "scared to death about" it; but he wanted her to understand that kinships in the story were not intended to be literal. "Not all stories with 'Pa' in them is my father," he put it. "I love to handle older-men characters. I like to call them Pa."[3]

Edinburgh again. His writing and publication continued to flow. He had firmly stamped his mountain identity with his poem "No One Has Sung for Us" in the July *Harper's*. Even as he had arrived in Scotland in July, stories appeared in *Esquire, Globe,* and *American Prefaces*. W.W. Wabnitz did an equivocating scholarly piece on Jesse's short stories for the *New Mexico Quarterly Review,* in the same August issue in which Jesse published another story, "Zeke Hammertight." Poems followed in *Scribner's* magazine that month and in the *Pictorial Review* in September. "Uncle Fonse and the Starlings" came out in the September *Esquire,* a short story in the October 30 *Collier's,* and six poems in the December *Esquire*. Carol Bird published a colorful profile on him, "Give Me the Hill-billy Life," in the *Denver Post* magazine section in October; and Herman Stresau translated his story "One of the Lost Tribe" under the title *"Einer gegen alle"* for the German publication *New Amerika*. Commencing June 11, 1937, and continuing through February 10, 1938, thirty-two travel essays appeared in his "Fragments from Nothing" in the *Greenup News*. However, the editor of the paper did not carry through as Jesse thought he should with their agreement that, in turn for submitting regular copy, Jesse would receive a copy of each column as it was published. Therefore, the poet shifted papers and published the last nineteen travel essays in the *Greenup County Citizen* edition of the *Russell Times,* commencing March 25 and continuing through August

12, 1938. In addition to a total of at least fifty-one local columns, most of which were written along the way of his travels, three retrospective essays would appear in the *Portsmouth* (Ohio) *Times* from May through July. His personal story, *Beyond Dark Hills*, would be released April 18, 1938, to the accompaniment of a huge chorus of reviews throughout the country, most of them carrying notations of his travel abroad as a Guggenheim Fellow. From February 1938 until his return to the United States in July, Jesse's publications would appear in *Progressive Farmer*, *Harper's*, the *New Mexico Quarterly*, *Esquire*, *Collier's*, the *American Mercury*, and *Household*.

Meanwhile, in his little room at 8 Viewforth Gardens, he had temporarily wearied of travel. "I'm tired out—tired—tired—tired—ten foreign countries on this trip." What he truly hungered for was one of Russ Zachem's steaks back in Greenup, with fried potatoes, "tomato catchup," and "a good cup of American coffee and cornbread and butter." He found himself fighting homesickness through much of his Guggenheim year. His loneliness was aggravated by the writer's self-imposed confinement. Craving exercise, he recalled, "I'd get out there in the evening . . . just leave off my heavy clothes . . . and just run over the city."

He carried a small notebook in which he occasionally jotted down ideas for short stories. One night that winter of 1937/1938, his mind reached back across the Atlantic to his homeland. It was a long dark night because "Scotland is on a latitude with Alaska and the shortest day of the year in Scotland has about 22 hours of pitchblack darkness and two hours of light and then darkness again. . . . I couldn't sleep all of these long nights. So, I wrote about . . . the ideas I'd jotted on paper, even if I didn't think too much of them." One of his entries had to do with a salesman of school supplies who had come by his office and told him a story "about high school boys climbing a cherry tree and splitting a branch from the tree and the high school principal's keeping them after hours because he didn't have money to pay the farmer for his tree." What had excited the salesman most, he remembered, was "how the boy's father came to the high school with a pistol to shoot the principal over keeping his son after school." That was something to think about— "a father who didn't believe in microbes until they let him look into a microscope at some tartar he had taken from his teeth. This convinced the father that teachers and the principal . . . were right and he was wrong and behind the times." He had never planned to write the story, really, because it did not seem "colorful or compelling enough" to set down on paper; but now he did it. He called it "Split Cherry Tree," not really valuing it much. He was a bit surprised when Miss Penny, an elderly Scottish spinster who did his typing, did like it.

By early December he came down with a bad cold. "All this week I've been housed in," he wrote Deane Norris. "My face looks like it's been beaten. Dark circles under my eyes." It was a winter such as he had not known in Greenup County. Daylight was down to a few hours in the twenty-four, and the Scots "had to dig the flocks of sheep out of the snow!" On December 15 he sent Deane a scarf for Christmas, and he was well enough to plan a Christmas celebration of his own in London, confiding to Oscar Sammons, "There's a little Dane waiting down in London for Poppie Christmas time! But afraid she'll have to shed her tears and wait." There was a slight language barrier in their relationship, but the young Kentuckian wrote triumphantly that "Poppie and she managed to convey their thoughts to one another . . . crossing the North Sea to her native Denmark!" Perhaps realizing the Sammonses were close friends of Deane's, he admonished Oscar, "*Mum* is the word on all transgressions of the flesh and spirit." Clearly he had Deane in mind in advising such confidentiality, yet he was up to that time uncertain about any future developments in their relationship. He had written of Deane to Ann Sammons, aware the young women were close friends, "I quite agree with you. She's a grand looking girl and a very fine girl! I've known her from a child—grew up with her—have dated her off and on all these years."[4]

Since his parting with Elizabeth Hale two years before, he had resolved to recapture his independent, carefree, and youthful self—or that self he considered himself to be, and so had written James Still, within three months of that breakup, of his sudden meeting of "a beautiful blue-eyed blonde" who "walked up the aisle and shook my hand" after he had spoken in Portsmouth, Ohio. "She was Italian full-blooded," a girl from Pennsylvania. "We fell for each other right there." He wrote of their late evening drive "in her car to Plum Grove Graveyard." Though he was gentlemanly vague about her name, he was specific about the results. "I've gone back to writing with new fervor. . . . I'm in love head-over-heels with her." Within a year of his final breakup with Elizabeth Hale, he professed a romantic identity with Burns: "I too have had my love affairs and many of them—more than Burns I imagine."

Of course the affair with the young woman of Italian extraction was no more enduring than his other temporary infatuations. In May of the following year he wrote to Carleton Wells at Ann Arbor, "I believe

I'm in love"; then to James Still he insisted that he was "in love and it's genuine." This time his affection had turned to Charlotte Salmon of Ashland, Kentucky, the young woman who had interviewed him for the *Southwest Review*. "I've been making my home at her home here lately," he wrote Still, "what time I'm not digging postholes and making fence. We've been taking in the dances. Having a grand time. . . ."

According to Judge Sammons, "Jesse got to courting pretty heavily" during these years, although he had not done very much "real courting" up to that time, for he had always had to work so hard. "Now Jesse was smart in a lot of ways, but 'not knowing'—gullible, you might say. He would believe just about anything anyone would tell him. And he would tell almost anything that happened to him if he was talking to one of his friends. Ann and I were his friends, and he would come here at night and stay over so he would not have to walk up over the Academy Branch path in the dark, or in the rain, snow, or mud." On one occasion, so Judge Sammons recalls, Jesse went to Ashland to meet Miss Salmon, who was attired in a lovely full-skirted evening dress for the dancing. Having no car, Jesse took her to the dance on a bus, and she had some difficulty maneuvering in and out of the bus doors. A hospitable young lady, she invited him to stay the night at her family's home. "Well, you know Jesse," Judge Sammons narrated. "He didn't have so much as a toothbrush with him. And no pajamas either. He slept in the nude. There was no air-conditioning in those days. The Salmons gave him a nice room that opened on the hallway just as theirs did. He shut the door and went to bed with the windows up. Well, the next morning when he woke up, the door was *open—wide open,* and the breeze was blowing through the window curtains and across his bed, where he lay, just the way he was born. When Jess told me the story, he said with that kind of innocent surprise, 'Oscar, you don't suppose anyone saw me, do you?' "

Doubtless, it was this kind of local story combined with the Greenup poet's natural innocence and ingenuous frankness that gave rise to Burton Rascoe's piece in *Esquire* triggering this short editorial blurb:

Is Adonis Fooling?

Jesse Stuart can't understand why girls bother with him.

One evening he attended a dance and during the evening met a very attractive Spanish girl from Portsmouth. When she suggested that they go out to a cemetery (it was after midnight), he told her he would take her out the next day when it was daylight so she could see things. She laughed. He still doesn't know why! . . . Whether Stuart was fooling, Rascoe doesn't know and neither do we, but look him up, girls, next Thursday when he lectures here and maybe you can find out.

During the 1937 flood he wrote James Still, confessing that he was not writing poetry. "You know presently I'm a pale man—the color of poetry in me has left. I believe I need to be in love again—walking on the wind." If romantic flings were the catalysts that activated creativity in the remarkable crucible of Jesse Stuart's personal experience, such chemistries had hardly proved to be without explosive dangers. "Twice I've had to hide out and get away," he admitted to Still of that spring of 1937. "I had to hide in the schoolhouse over the week-end. One of my students slipped me food. Damn it I was framed. But brother I missed a big scandal and the woman missed me. She had to get back to Pennsylvania—not the Italian girl—this one was French. I'm still single and ambitious to get married. . . . All of my life . . . I've been in love. Dreamed of a home, children, a farm, books on the shelf and so on. . . . Always something happens."

On the return from his southern lecturing trip the previous June, he had met "a little Danish girl . . . on the train one night coming up through Georgia. We slept in the day coach—She made me a bed from blankets in her suitcase and I slept right across the aisle from her. We talked far into the night. . . . She teaches dancing in Florida. She's really a peach! Walks like a Kentucky thoroughbred." The two had made the trip together across the North Sea to her home in Copenhagen, and he had met her people in early October; and now the two were meeting again in London for Christmas. Having escaped his sticky romantic situation at home in the spring of 1937, by December he could write to the Sammonses of "old Poppie's blighted pages of his womanly career," exulting with astonishing frankness, "Only two women have claimed pregnancy—neither had babies! Very strange after all the scares, the running and dodging—the whooping it up, the old women guessing and the hurrahs!"

In less than a month, his affectionate nature was centering on Mary Hope, the only child of a retired Scottish army captain. She was a good friend of Dr. Hamish Brown, and both worked at the Royal Infirmary. Jesse wrote Oscar Sammons, "Her work is that of medicine. . . . [She has] delivered plenty of babies not her own but other women's." Of "Hope," as friends called her, he wrote, "She's very pretty—large-blue-eyed— hair almost the color of Deane's. She's 25. Brother, she's physically attractive too. She climbs these mountains right by my side. She can walk down most men." By March he reported to Sammons that he had been a guest at the Hopes' eighteen-hundred-acre farm outside Dunbar, Scotland, overlooking the scenic North Sea. A thousand sheep grazed the meadows. "Hope and I together under the peace of a Scottish Heaven, we walked among the stems of heather. The blue waters of the North Sea were below us, Oscar. I walked in the wind yesterday . . . though I die tomorrow." That March he viewed her as "an ideal woman since she knows the value of a man when she sees one and knows how to treat him." He admitted that "ever since I've been in Europe I've been torn between two women, but now Gudrun [sic] has gone back to Denmark." Apparently, Sammons had questioned Jesse's constancy in affairs of the heart; but whether he did or not, Jesse responded, "Oscar how can you condemn me for loving more than one woman in any extremely youthful days? My boy, check into your own past. . . . Now that your sealing wax heart has been melted by the affectionate summer sun of womanly love, how can you mistake my actions?" In the same letter he expressed an honest envy of his friend, who had a wife, "a little cottage, home, comforts—even damn it to hell, an automobile." Into this domestic context, then, he began to place himself, but invariably the scene was set in Kentucky rather than in Denmark or in Scotland. Meanwhile, he had heard that Charlotte Salmon was engaged to someone else, but he optimistically hoped that Deane Norris would be there when he returned home. "We'll not mention Scotland or Denmark," he wrote her. By May he was enthusiastically looking forward to his return home and was as tired of on-again-off-again relationships with the opposite sex as he had been of rapid travel through a dozen European countries the previous October. He wrote Ethel Bush that he was planning to see that a road to his W-Hollow home was built "if we ever get a Republican Judge." If not he would build a private road himself, for his plans were set and "my dreams have been long calculated. I know what I'm going to do and am going to do just that." Further, "I shall then get a cage built and get me a birdie in it and hatch a nest of young birds."

That his attention seems to have been turning to Deane Norris even as he went through another romantic conflict in Scotland and England is evident in several innuendos in his letters to the young Greenup woman. In January he wrote her of his desire to have "a wide open fireplace in a home of my own someday pretty as this one," though he realized "that is only a dream. I see it in the fire and dreams so readily vanish!" He concluded, "I must say 'goodnight' my love to you, a kiss to you." He shared his anxiety about the impending publication and reception of *Beyond Dark Hills* with her as well. He would miss spring in Kentucky, but looked forward to his return. "What a time that will be! . . . Shall we Dance, my Dear?" he finished. By the end of February he was urging her to "go out home in April" and "have my Dad take you over the farm. I want you to see it then. See it for me." He complimented her correspondence and wrote, "You are a good person—a lady, allow me to say."

Meanwhile, Ann and Oscar Sammons decided it was past time for Jesse to settle down before he made some kind of impulsive mistake, and they could see no more lovely solution on the horizon than Naomi Deane Norris. Jesse and Naomi were their very best friends, after all, and Oscar and Ann wanted the two to get married to each other in the worst way. "I boosted her to him," Judge Sammons said, "and Ann was on the other side, for the most part." The problem was the "things appeared to have been happening so fast for him," he explained. "Just every girl was 'the one' for Jesse then." Ann Sammons added, "Naomi was very fond of Jesse, and she recognized his ability. But at the time, he just didn't seem to fulfill what she expected of a husband." Still, when Deane planned to spend her money on antiques, Ann told her, "No, Naomi, spend it on clothes . . . for Jesse! You need clothes." So the two went with other friends to Cincinnati where Naomi purchased "a four-piece, rust-colored suit, a nice suit with a fur collar." Deane next wrote Jesse from Cincinnati, a fact that did not escape his notice even in Scotland, where he saw the postmark. At Easter he sent her a box of chocolates and wrote, "You are tall and handsome and should look grand in your new Easter outfit."[5]

The long winter, not without eventful moments, was over. As he explained in another letter to Deane, he yearned to get "down to the warm South" and "dodge these tremendous drifts of snow." He was in London in time for columnist George Buchanan to meet and talk with him in January of 1938. Impressed by "short-story connoisseur" Edward J. O'Brien's high rating of the young American's work, Buchanan wrote in the *News Chronicle* that Stuart emphasized the fact that "he was 'from the soil,' " and "unlike former American authors, he does not look to Europe for inspiration, but to his own region and his own worker people." And "no wonder," for Stuart was a native Kentuckian: "Kentuckians are the most home-loving people in the world; their homesick songs are famous; for example, 'My old Kentucky home.' " Buchanan noted Robert Burns as the poet's "chief inspiration," and detected that Stuart was already looking homeward where "he will resume work on a farm, writing between-whiles."

Both the *Manchester Guardian* and the London *Times* carried news stories of Jesse's appearance before the distinguished gathering of the

P.E.N. Club at Pagani's Restaurant on Tuesday, February 1. Three of the group's presidents up to that time had been H. G. Wells, J. B. Priestley, and Henry W. Nevinson—the current president—and among members of its Council and Executive Committee were Somerset Maugham, Edward J. O'Brien, Victoria Sackville-West, Alec Waugh, Rebecca West, and Humbert Wolfe. O'Brien introduced Jesse, relating him to an "English tradition . . . being preserved in certain parts of America," noting "it was from the Kentucky Hills that Mr. Jesse Stuart, our guest, had come. He was a true folk poet, in the high tradition of Burns," with "a large amount of fine work to his credit and his future work would be watched by all lovers of good literature." In likening Stuart to Burns, O'Brien emphasized that Stuart was "the most worthy representative of the English spirit which you have lost and which is preserved in America." The *Guardian* reporter wrote:

> After that came Mr. Stuart himself, a veritable element of nature in this highly civilised assembly. He spoke of his family—Scots on the one hand, Yorkshire on the other, his grandfather, who could neither read nor write, and himself, the first of the family to be a university graduate. "Just as other people of my country took to the gun, the bottle, so I took to poetry. It was my escape." . . . He concluded: "You have a wonderful civilisation here. Sometimes I think it has gone too far when I step on someone's toe and he apologises to me, not I to him."

Things had got off to a wonderful start for *Beyond Dark Hills* with the *New York Times Book Review* devoting its entire front page to the book, with the heading "JESSE STUART'S HOMESPUN STORY—*His 'Beyond Dark Hills' Is Written With an Earthy Vigor.*" J. Donald Adams took the occasion to praise all three of Stuart's books as "vital, sincere and sensitive . . . all written out of a passionate love of place." The editor of the *Maysville* (Kentucky) *Daily Independent,* however, seemed to go out of his way to editorialize not so much upon Jesse's book as upon his writing beautifully "so easily" and being "much too young." The greater weight of national reviews, though, was coming down solidly on the side of his originality, honesty of stance, authenticity, and lyrical genius.

Meanwhile, he had received several letters with the signature "Nancy Astor," all inviting him to London to visit her. Not recognizing her name, he had simply ignored them, until she wrote demanding to know whether or not the Kentuckian was "coming to see me?" When he showed the letters to Mrs. Hastings she eyed her renter closely. "Who do I have staying with me?" she wondered aloud. She said she had never received a letter from "Lady Astor" in her lifetime, even though they belonged to the same party. Realizing no one was trying to blackmail him, Jesse wrote accepting her invitation. In London he took a taxi to her home at 4 St. James Square, where he spent his last days in England. She impressed him as a busy woman, strikingly dressed, and "very attractive for an older woman." Lord Astor he described as "a handsome man, about six-four, who wore tweeds."

He had read in leftist papers that she was pro-German. "I heard that you've already heard I'm a Fascist," the Yankee-born peeress said. "It is not true." Many earlier rumors had it that she was communist in her leanings. Such stories Jesse dismissed, finding Lady Astor "a remarkable human being" with a quick mind and "original and astonishing" wit. He was given a room previously occupied by the German tennis star Godfried Van Cramm. He also had a key "that wasn't an inch long" which "opened a thick door just about the size of . . . a room." Looking at the great entryway, he wondered "how they ever got hinges to hang a door like that," and how that little key opened that big door.

He had his own personal butler during the two weeks of his stay at Lord and Lady Astor's. The butler drew his bath, brought him his suit freshly pressed each morning and his shoes shined. His shirt was laid out with an appropriate necktie, and "socks were turned and ready to slip on my feet." The butler would ask, "Breakfast in bed, sir?"

"Not for me. I'll eat in the dining room."

Each evening a fire burned in the big fireplace, the windows were adjusted, his pajamas laid out, covers turned down, and bedroom slippers readied. In the days that followed he got to know all the butlers and talked some with each one. One of them said that Jesse reminded him of a man from America who was once a guest there, and got around and talked to all the butlers.

"What was his name?"

"Will Rogers," the butler replied.

Lady Astor was a Langley from Virginia, Stuart discovered, and the Virginia Stuarts and Langleys were related. "It was distant, but still kinship." The good meals, especially the breakfasts, tended to make him feel at home. "They had cooked oatmeal, milk from their farm, and yogurt." One morning at breakfast, Jesse asked Lord Astor, "Are you in any way connected with the Waldorf-Astoria Hotel in New York City?"

"Not now," he replied, "but my father built the old Astor Hotel and my cousin built the Waldorf beside it. They were later combined as the Waldorf-Astoria." Lord Astor no longer had an interest in it, but did tell Jesse, "I sold the land where the Empire State Building now stands in New York City."

One evening Lady Astor said, "Jesse, I have two tickets here to the theatre. You can invite a girl and take her."

"But I don't know one in London to take."

"Take one—invite one," she insisted, handing him the two tickets. Later her chauffeur took them to Parliament where Lady Astor got out and paused. "You'd better give me one of those tickets back. You might not get the right girl." The chauffeur took him on to the theatre, where his seat was close enough to Queen Mary "to hear the words she is saying." Noticing the price on the ticket, he was surprised that Lady Astor had paid the equivalent of $10.50 for it.

During the two weeks he was a guest at Lord and Lady Astor's home, he managed to get out for several sightseeing jaunts, one to Stoke-Poges in Buckinghamshire where he sought out the grave of Thomas Gray, and there, "far from the madding crowd's ignoble strife," he walked through the yew-clustered site of Gray's inspiration for "Elegy Written in a Country Churchyard." He went to Stratford-on-Avon and visited Ann Hathaway's cottage, and along the Avon found the ancient church where Shakespeare lies buried. Jesse's eye did not take in the flatrock simplicity of the bard's resting place, but rather turned to the "boat loads of lovers" plying up and down the waters of the Avon "under the spreading branches of the giant yew trees and elms."

One day as he breakfasted with Lady and Lord Astor they wanted to know what he missed most in England that he enjoyed in America.

"A good cigar," he answered.

"Just a minute," Lady Astor said, got up, and soon returned with two large cigars, which she handed him. "Cigars Mr. Winston Churchill left here," she explained. "Try these, Jesse."

Before his stay was over he joined Lord and Lady Astor for a few days at their larger country home at Clivedon on the Thames "for more parties." He did not own a tuxedo but wore instead his dark suit. "I looked all right," he wrote, "and I felt at home with some of the guests, especially beautiful Lady Astor, whose sons were older than I." He took advantage of the visit at Taplow to see the family's dairy—the 160 cows, 400 head of cattle, and 30 thoroughbred horses; and he saw something, of course, of about 460 people who worked there and in the houses. It was a wonderful two weeks, and he was invited to return whenever he visited England again.[6]

Before he left London he again called on Edward J. O'Brien. This time Martha Foley of *Story* magazine was a houseguest of the O'Briens. In late May he crossed the English Channel from Harwich. On May 25, he sent Deane Norris a postcard with a picture of a delft-blue windmill, writing, "Holland is almost too pretty to leave. People are easy going . . . good food—cigars cheaper than in America. . . . You would like Holland."

He continued to Paris by way of Antwerp, Brussels, Flanders, Mons, and Soissons, writing home that the wheat fields on each side of the train were "blotched red with patches of poppies." In the days that followed he toured the battlefields in the vicinity and along the Marne—Verdun, Belleau Wood, Chateau-Thierry. He saw the white crosses of the American cemetery, and a three-minute walk away the black crosses of the German cemetery, then returned through the Marne Valley to Paris. Later he toured Versailles and with American friends took in the Parisian night clubs—Bal Taharin, Moulin Rouge, Odett, and the Folies Bergère—writing for his column, "All we see here cannot be told." With something of a moral stance he wrote Deane Norris that one night club was "vulgar as hell. Homo sexualists dressed up like women," and that "New York is clean as a rose beside of Paris." More tolerantly he informed Oscar Sammons, "These women over here are beautiful," and "American women should send their husbands over here and let them get an education. You can get an education in Paris. I've been attending a few classes. But am presently laid up with a cold."

Leaving his American friends, he proceeded to Switzerland by electric train, finding rain and snow in Berne and the mountaintops of the Alps hidden in heavy clouds. The Swiss were good farmers, he wrote, raising wheat "often five to six feet high and . . . heavily beaded." He admired the "Zurich Sea," a lake, so he was told, which "hasn't any bottom." He found Switzerland a special country "where able-bodied men are not wearing uniforms and where the women are not doing the work of the men."

From Zurich his train wended its way to Salzburg, Austria. In Vienna he composed poetry under the spell of such musical pieces as the "Radetzky March." Johann Strauss' "Tales from the Vienna Woods" was in his mind as he rode a horse-drawn carriage through the Vienna Woods. Whereas in Scotland "there are July, August and Winter," here June was warm and pleasant, and as Strauss' "Tales of the Vienna Woods" played through his head his emotions "rose to the point of ecstasy." From his hip pocket he took his small notebook and wrote the title "Tales from the Plum Grove Hills," which he would use for a collection of short stories seven years later.

By the middle of June he managed to see something of Czechoslovakia, Hungary, Yugoslavia, and Bulgaria. He missed Russia "because his passport said he was a writer," even though that very year *"Paltsy na nogakh,"* a translation of his story "Toes," would appear in the USSR. When Rumanian officials informed him the cost of a visa was ten dollars, Jesse told them, "I don't want to buy the country," and marked Rumania off his list. From Bulgaria he went to Turkey, and would possibly have continued to the Holy Land and Egypt but for the heat and the fact that water was too dear. While sightseeing on his own, he met a young woman, Zobel Ohranian, who could speak English fluently. Together they went to the Museum of Archaeology and then exchanged their shoes for slippers in order to go through the St. Sophia Mosque, after which he made a small donation. Jesse's observation: "I pay about 25 cents for walking barefooted through the church house." He and Miss Ohranian parted at the placid blue Bosporus Strait, but like many others she remembered the Kentuckian. Years later a Michigan professor recalled that he was in Uskudar in June 1938 when a young Armenian secretary came into the American Board for Missions of the Congregational Church talking about a young American writer, Jesse Stuart, whom she had just met on the ferry coming over the Sea of Marmara. "She said he was so excited about crossing over on the ferry just to say he had touched Asia."

Here on the edge of the waters of "The Golden Horn" he had detrained from the Orient Express to climb a hill of cobblestone streets to the Tokatligan Hotel. He painted in words the images of that Near-Eastern world for his column and the people back home:

> Men and women sitting under the wilted shade trees while waiters bring them cold water. . . . A tiny boy delivering bread on a mule, far less in size than a yearling calf. Two huge boxes tied together at the top—and balanced on the ribs of the tiny mule—(known here as an ass). Great round loaves of dry hard bread. Both mule and boy look like they will fall asleep. Fig trees, date trees, palm trees . . . the first he had ever seen. . . . white Mosques with tall spires—minarets against the hot glimmering sky.

He sailed in late June for Italy on the Italian *Palestina* by way of Greece, proceeding down the Strait of Dardanelles toward the Aegean Sea. In places it was no wider than the Ohio River. The ship went by the place where Byron had swum the Hellespont from Sestos to Abydos, a distance of perhaps three miles. Each island seemed to "rise from the blue waters," he wrote, "a huge mass of sun-blistered stone." At the sight of Scyros in the middle of the Aegean, Jesse's thoughts turned in homage to Rupert Brooke, who lay buried there, "one of England's most promising young poets," a casualty of the "ill-fated Dardanelles expedition" in World War I. After disembarking at Piraeus, he and two young English college professors walked the hot distance of eight miles into Athens, Jesse lugging through the hot weather two suitcases, a portable typewriter, and "an all-purpose raincoat."

He began sightseeing immediately, parting with the Englishmen, who were there for the avowed purpose of acquiring Greek wives. He registered at the St. George Hotel and saw firsthand the antique glory he had known only through pictures and words—first the Parthenon and Acropolis, finding a certain peace among "the ancient pillars on this hill overlooking the city." He was moved to write home, "Athens is a beautiful city despite the range of dry barren hills that surround it. There are gardens of trees here, including many palm trees. The houses are made of white stone. The streets are clean. It glistens in an almost tropical sunlight." At first he had planned to stay only a few hours, but he decided instead to let the *Palestina* go on without him to Italy and to catch it on its return trip. He could see why his young English friends had come there—"What beautiful women and handsome men," he wrote. "What wonderful food and music! Why had I never known about Greece? I had found a country which I fell in love with the first three days I was there." In the days that followed he saw Daphni, Corinth, Salamus, Thermopylae; and he ate steaks with gusto, enjoyed the warm Greek hospitality, and basked in the good music.

Yet, in time, there on the edge of the Western world, his thoughts turned homeward to his dark hills again. One day author Jerome Beatty, dressed in white, walked out of his hotel to buy a Paris edition of the *Herald Tribune* when "a strange young man in plus-fours stepped up and said eagerly, 'You're an American?' It was Jesse Stuart, of whom Beatty, strangely, had never heard; and he proceeded to pour forth his loneliness to Beatty's amazed ears. He had written a book and made a little money, and gone out from his native hills to see the world. Seeing the world had left him lonely, which is as it should be. If Jesse Stuart ever ceases to be lonely and talk-flooded, he will cease to be Jesse Stuart, Kentucky writer."

When the *Palestina* returned, Jesse loaded his baggage aboard, adding to it a few Greek records on which he had spent some of his dwindling funds. The ship was small enough to pass through the Corinth Canal and into the Ionian Sea. On July 6, he sailed from Genoa with third-class accommodations aboard the Italian liner *Conte di Savoia,* arriving in New York City July 13. The *Herald Tribune, Post, World-Telegram, Sun,* and *Times* noted his arrival, while dozens more newspapers throughout the country, from the *Nashville Banner* and *El Paso Herald Post* to the *Birmingham News* and the *Providence* (Rhode Island) *Journal,* carried news stories of his return. He had just seven dollars when the ship docked, and he spent and tipped nearly half of that getting to the Prince George Hotel on Twenty-eighth Street. One clipping declared, "Jesse Stuart Home—'Broke,'" and was sub-headed, "Traveled on Fellowship in 25 European Countries."[7] More than thirteen months had passed since his hometown friends had given him a farewell party. The story noted that he had "returned from Europe . . . with scores of manuscripts—hatless, broke and 'tickled to death to get back.'" New York reporters especially had a field day quoting him. About Greece he said, "It's the only country in Europe where a man can get a good steak," and "I like those old bare hills." He looked freshly at England and Norway. "Norway has the best coffee, and . . . is a rest to American eyes because they have wooden houses in Norway. In England you get so tired of looking at stone houses that your feet hurt." Of France, "You know, I'd always heard about French cooking, but you can't get a good steak anywhere in France." However, "France has the best ice cream in Europe."

He expressed honest flattery toward French women: "You can't tell a French woman's age—they know how to dress." Turkish music was something else; it reminded him "of snakes crawling." The German people he loved, a reporter noted, "but their government he detests." May Cameron wrote in the *New York Post* that Stuart all along had "wanted to bump up amongst people to find out what Europeans of his own age were doing and thinking," and his plan had worked. He had met "Peder Jonsen of Chicago . . . singing in the streets of Norway and we went on to Sweden together." In Estonia, "a woman who ran a news-stand . . . married to a white Russian kicked out of Russia was awfully nice to me." He told of the Princetonians he had met in Germany and "always there were girls to introduce you around and to go to dances with." Perhaps the best friendship he had developed that year was with multi-lingual Hamish Brown of Edinburgh, "a shabby young doctor in a mental hospital." In his big car they had explored the Highlands to-gether, gone to art galleries, and attended the ballet and rugby matches; they "had dates together and went to dances, and I did learn the Scottish dances." Brown painted and wrote poetry, which, Jesse observed, "was good," and was learning Hebrew, his seventh language. One day Brown had taken him home for a chicken dinner, and to his surprise Jesse discovered, "my friend was the brilliant son of a wealthy family. He had brought me home for a Thanksgiving dinner. That's Scotch reticence for you."

He was anxious to get home, happy at the prospect, though he frankly said he would need to borrow money from his publishers to get back to Greenup County. "Travel is great, and all that," he said, "but I was lonesome for Kentucky. And how I wish some of the people who are trying to tear down America could go over to Europe and see how it is over there for themselves!" Perhaps Lewis Gannett of the *New York Herald Tribune* best summarized the reporters' reactions with the observation, "They didn't foreignize Jesse Stuart in any or all of those twenty-five countries." Strangely, as good as home seemed to him then, as joyous as the return he anticipated, it would become all too soon a return to exile.

12

Exile, Love, and Marriage
1938–1939

———◇———

Jesse Stuart leaned back against the hawsers along the ship's railing, his elbow on a coil of rope, and grinned at the *New York Post* staff photographer as the breeze from the bay blew his print tie over the lapel of his Scottish tweed jacket, the pleated pocket accented by the tip of a white handkerchief. His eyes squinted against the bright light. The morning before as the *Conte di Savoia* had steamed past the Statue of Liberty, he found it a magnificent sight and declared, "I used to think that was just a statue, but how different now!" He was eager for other sights too—an American newspaper—and for the taste of hotdogs, American cigars, and coffee. Standing at a third-class rail of the ship, the downtown skyline a slowly moving backdrop, he said, "Boy, I'm tickled to death to get back," and recollected his trip to the Big Town in 1935. "When I first visited New York I thought the city was terrible, after the Kentucky hills. But even New York looks good to me now." On board with him were the famous stage designer Jo Mielziner and his wife, returning from their vacation in Rome; Chester Aldrich, head of the American Academy in Rome; and Mrs. George Wadsworth, wife of the American Consul-General in Palestine. Her father, the late Norman E. Mack, had been for many years chairman of the Democratic National Committee. According to E. P. Dutton, however, Jesse Stuart "stole the show from the 'great' in the first class cabins on the steamer," and "just now, his appearance back in New York is creating no little excitement."

In late June Jesse had written Oscar Sammons from Athens, requesting that his friend meet him at the Greenup station upon his return home sometime in late July. He would write more precisely after receiving Sammons' reply at Dutton's in New York City. He also told his friend to be prepared for "[fusillade] after [fusillade] of questions to pop at you." Within ten days from disembarking at New York City, he was home again. After obtaining some financial assistance from his publishers, he detoured to Connecticut long enough to pick up a pure-bred Irish setter and then continued to Greenup, arriving just after noon on July 23, sporting a white suit and shoes, dark tie and handkerchief, and a becoming European tan. His weight was down from 208 to 187 pounds. Oscar Sammons not only was there to meet him, but led a sizable delegation of friends and well-wishers. One of them, Bessie Smith, ran into his pullman where Jesse met her with hugs and kisses. His parents were there, too, but as he tried to hug them, they demonstrated no outward signs of affection. Naomi Norris was on hand, and never forgot that moment of awkwardness between Jesse and his parents. Tall James Stuart was in the crowd, happy to see his long-absent brother, but the first thing Jesse shouted to him was, "James, get my dog out of the baggage coach." Jesse patiently answered reporters' questions and obliged them by posing for pictures with Rusty—a gift for "the folks," he explained.

Later at Bessie Smith's place in Greenup, he was treated to good home-cooked food and declared, "There's no corn-on-the-cob or green beans like these of Kentucky." One reporter observed that among his luggage were eight copies of his new *Beyond Dark Hills*, one to be autographed and presented to Bessie Smith, another to Lady Astor, "another to a pretty teacher in Austria . . . head of a school there," and the rest "to friends and acquaintances throughout the twenty-six countries." That evening he stayed with Oscar and Ann Sammons and visited with many friends who dropped by to shake hands. His plans were to return to W-Hollow the next day, there to spend the remainder of the summer farming and writing. There would be the wheat to get in as it ripened. "There won't be any idle moments," he told reporters.

Jesse was now without a teaching job. Sammons filled him in on the latest political news, and he soon saw the worst open up before him. True, Jesse had received an official leave of absence with the unanimous agreement of the superintendent and the members of the Board of Education of the Greenup County Schools in the spring of 1937, entered in the board's minutes; but now the old superintendent, Fred Maynard, was out, and the new, Tongs West, was in. Jesse's leave was not honored by newcomer West. He had also fired many experienced, conscientious, and well-qualified teachers—including Ethel Bush, Thelma Kaut (one of only two in Greenup County with a master's degree), Lucy Mae Scott Bradford, and Elmer Heaberlin, like Stuart a former principal in the system. Worse, West had replaced them with less qualified personnel from outside Greenup County, including his own secretary, who was from Virginia. At the behest of a friend, Jesse visited West at his office and managed to control himself during their interview long enough to get material for a blistering editorial published in the *Greenup County Citizen*. With his feet on his desk and "a chew as big as a hen egg in his jaw," Jesse reported, the new superintendent "opened his heart to me 'on the situation and his political obligations.' " The result of their interview was a deepening of the poet's anger. West spoke in "soft-mousey words" that "slipped out like grease." There were more than a dozen former colleagues "who got the axe in the pandemonium of terror that has reigned here." For himself, Jesse hotly declared, "I don't want anything Tongs West has to offer. I would see him in the lower regions of the damned before I'd beg him for a job!"

Instead, Jesse Stuart found a job teaching remedial English at Portsmouth High School in Ohio, and resumed occupancy of his old room at the Kings'. Publisher Earl D. Mittendorf lashed out, "Things are coming to a pretty state of affairs when an outstanding school teacher, who has won renown as a writer not only in this country but in others, and who resides right amongst us, has to go to Portsmouth to get a teaching job!!!!" Jesse arranged with Mittendorf to accept the editorship of Mittendorf's small weekly Republican newspaper, the *Greenup County Citizen*, an edition of the *Russell* (Kentucky) *Times*, for he had decided to fight. He served as editor, in his own words, "without pay to build this paper as it is not making money." In his most violent editorial, which appeared Friday, September 30, side by side with his denunciation of Tongs West, Jesse cut loose at the Democratic political boss of Greenup County, Congressman Joe Bates, holding up the mirror of his recent European experience to catch the reflections of fascist images he saw in his own stamping ground:

> Italy has her Premiere [sic] Mussolini, Russia has her Dictator Joseph Stalin; Germany has her persecutor, cold-eyed, consci[ence]less, paper-hanger Adolph Hitler, and Greenup County, Kentucky, has her small dictator, Joe Bates! For the past 16 years [he] has been the virtual Dictator of Greenup County. . . . In person, he is slow-going and physically lazy—but Brother, when he cracks the whip he doesn't mean "Maybe" or "perhaps." He means business! . . . He is as alien as Cyclop's eye to native born Greenup Countians . . . the man with a backbone like a jelly-fish. . . . Who has ever seen Joe Bates except walking slowly across the street, or sitting in a swivel chair in the office—behind closed doors, dreaming and planning and shuffling his cards! . . . Don't send Joe to Congress to get him out of Greenup

County! Beat Joe Bates! Down with this little Dictator who has not the speech delivery of a cold-eyed Hitler, nor the physical tempo of a Mussolini, nor (not quite yet) the 95 percent of the vote of the people like Dictator Stalin of Russia.[1]

Just ten weeks after Jesse Stuart had returned from his Guggenheim, he and his brother, James, walked into Leslie's Drug Store in Greenup during the noon hour. They matched for refreshments. Jesse lost, and James ordered a Coca-Cola while Jesse asked for a chocolate milkshake. As surreal as what was to happen to him must have seemed in the rush of his shock, he would never forget the persistent facts which drove him to stand outside himself and write about them within a week. Something strange and revealing had begun outside the drugstore where Jesse noticed Amos Allen, a deputy constable from nearby Argillite, who had a few months before been indicted for assault and battery, looking at him from time to time and listening to his conversation with local citizens, with whom Jesse always had time for a few words. He thought nothing of Allen's coming in the drugstore behind him either, at first. Pharmacist Sam Leslie was behind the fountain preparing the drinks. Allen inquired of Jesse without any apparent excitement, "Why did you write poor old Joe up in that paper?"

"It's a free country," Jesse replied, "and I've a right to voice my opinion. He owns a paper, so I understand—he can express his views in that."

Allen's voice rose, "He ain't done nothing to you."

"What about the schools?" Jesse said. "Whose hands are they in? Where am I now?" Allen did not answer him. Indeed, Allen said no more, and turning toward the fountain, Jesse put down a half-dollar on the counter.

Then, as he would later write, "Amos struck me when I never expected it—two licks—and the third came more easily, for we clinched. At the first lick I didn't know what had happened. I only wanted to hit Amos Allen in defense. I clinched with him to get close. Blood spurted everywhere, streamed into my eyes—hot blood, and sticky—and it blinded my eyes. If we had been left alone I would have whipped Amos Allen—although he had laid my head open down to the skull in three long lashes with a black-jack loaded with lead and the leather worn from the lead. This is the price I had to pay for writing an editorial about Dictator Joe Bates—the Dictator of Greenup County."

James Stuart recalled that several citizens broke up the "clinched" men. "Jesse had Allen around the neck in a kind of half nelson, with one forearm back of his neck and the other under his chin, kind of like trying to break a possum's neck with a stick—and I think Jesse was trying to break Allen's neck." Next morning the Sunday *Portsmouth Times* carried the story under the caption "Jesse Stuart Blackjacked in Row Over Political Editorial."

Immediately after the attack, the bloodied poet was taken to an Ironton, Ohio, hospital and attended by Dr. William F. Marting, who reported to the press that the patient had received "no less than six severe scalp wounds." Although the physician advised that he remain at the hospital under strict observation for several more days, Jesse managed by late Sunday to get himself discharged. By Monday morning he was back in Portsmouth to teach his classes. Somehow the news got out that the poet-teacher was leaving Kentucky "for good." Several papers carried the story, but nothing could have been further from the truth. Earl Mittendorf reported to the *Ashland Daily Independent* that his "militant editor" had no intention of leaving the state, and "so far as I know, Stuart will edit the edition of the Citizen which is to be published Friday." Further, County Attorney Oscar Sammons announced that Amos Allen had been charged with "striking with a deadly weapon with intent to kill."

Stuart did indeed edit the Friday edition of October 7. In a fourteen-hundred-word editorial entitled "Takes More Than Blows to Halt Jesse Stuart," he lashed back at his political enemies, "Would you citizens who read the Greenup County Citizen doubt now that Greenup County doesn't have a dictator?" Again, "Would you say that a citizen who voices an opinion is safe anywhere in Greenup County?" Further, "I couldn't write an editorial about Dictator Joe Bates without getting slugged in the head." Yet, he wanted everyone to know, "I can whip Amos Allen on less street-space in Greenup than the length of his body. He knows that, too!" Jesse recounted details of the altercation right down to the nature of his wounds. "The gash over the back of my head, over my brain, bled until after midnight at the Marting Hospital." In response to one physician's observation that "he did not see how a man could survive being struck three times over the head with such a weapon," Jesse wrote, "Well, I survived it, and afterwards could have beat Amos Allen's face into the concrete, had we [been] left to fight." He swore, "For every drop of blood I shed—yes, for every red, sticky drop—I shall write 10,000 words in ink to expose this 'gang' work in Greenup County. . . . I shall write— I shall speak the truth—so help me God—as honest and fair as I know how to put it on paper; or I shall be slugged to death, shot to death, or knifed to death—and sleep under the dirt on the hill at Plum Grove. I shall not back, nor retrace, nor take back a thing I have said!"

After expanding upon Amos Allen's violent history, in response to the questions "Why get messed up in this? Why fight it?" he wrote, "My answer is 'I am a citizen of Greenup County. I was born here; my people live here; my farm is here. I love Greenup County and its citizens. I would do anything to help uplift the county.' These are my reasons. It is my home—my everything."

Time magazine reported in November that when a hearing on the assault case came up, the author's brother, James, arrived accompanied by several relatives and friends. When more than two dozen men "filed silently into court," however, "the judge took one look at the two groups, [and] postponed the case." One observer said, "There would have been a little excitement if a firecracker had gone off." Even Jesse Stuart's eighty-six-year-old Uncle Marion offered assistance from Twelve Pole, West Virginia, inquiring, "Have they caught the fellow who jumped you? If they haven't I'll be along presently and help you bring him to justice."

The New York papers followed the story. Under the caption "Black-jacking a Poet," one observed that Stuart's "upscuffle with Constable Amos Allen" evinced more than anything else "that Greenup has never become reconciled to its literary prodigy." The *New York Times* turned ironic: "For a poet to be clubbed by anybody, constable or private citizen, is not rejection but acceptance." It was rare, to be sure, but one had only to look at the examples of Erskine Caldwell, Thomas Wolfe, and Rudyard Kipling to see that a prophet was not without honor save in his own country. "But when somebody gets hurt in a Kentucky quarrel," the editor declared, "it is a sign that he does belong." The editor of the *New York Herald Tribune* was alarmed over stories that Jesse was considering leaving Kentucky. "Where else could he go, and not be lost?" the editor declaimed. "Not to Europe where he traveled, wondering and observing as a Guggenheim fellow, only to be glad to get back to America. And certainly not to New York, the city paved with fool's gold for such a man as Stuart; he could see through the sham of this city at a glance, and Stuart has the eyes of a squirrel hunter. . . . Literary teas, the 'arty' precious talk of the clubs and salons, are not the stuff for this home-grown genius. Kentucky is where he belongs. There is the life he knows, where every wind-blown leaf means something. As one of his elderly well-wishers from his own hills might say to him, 'Keep your shirt on, Jess.' "

On the other hand, Mrs. L. E. Cooke of Richmond, Virginia, urged, "Come out of the dark hills of Kentucky and back to Virginia where you belong," while the alumni secretary of the Vanderbilt University advised, "When you get ready to leave Kentucky for good, why don't you come down here to Tennessee and hang out around Nashville?" And editor Thomas Matthews Pearce of the *New Mexico Quarterly* encouraged Jesse to consider that Land of Enchantment in the West to which many early Kentuckians had migrated: "You might like it, and sooner or later you'll have to see New Mexico."

By late January 1939, Amos Allen was found guilty of assault and battery upon Jesse Stuart. Reportedly, several of the jurors sought a heavy fine and jail term for Allen, but final agreement was reached on a two-hundred-dollar fine and no jail sentence. Even this modest vindication of Jesse Stuart had its drawback. The conflict had reached such a pitch that Jesse's friends advised him "to stay out of Greenup."[2]

Perhaps he was fortunate that his residence was sixteen miles away from Greenup and that his daily teaching duties kept him across the Ohio River in Portsmouth. Aside from weekend trips back to his farm, made remote by natural barriers if not by distance from the county seat, he got away frequently to give lectures at neighboring Ashland, at the University of Kentucky more than a hundred miles down into the Bluegrass, across the Ohio at Ironton and Portsmouth, and at Nashville, Tennessee. These conditions provided a measure of cooling time for the local situation in Greenup. In Nashville he told friends about his trouble but denied that he was leaving Kentucky. "It is my home and they are my people," he explained. "I love 'em." Outwardly staunch, Jesse at times was inwardly uncertain and restless. He took time during a remedial English class to write August Derleth, "The trouble here may blow over. I may leave for awhile—take a rest and write—but I'll return sometime." His days seemed "filled with drudgery" and "going to see lawyers." On Sunday he took walks and tried to relax, but complained, "I can't relax. I've been keyed up all autumn. It is all very petty, August. But I hate to have such men as Congressman Joe Bates to send his henchmen against me and stay in the clear."

And yet, as the New York papers had reported, he was "in exile" now. Most of the time, certainly, he was away from W-Hollow and immersed in teaching and all the duties that went with it. He had less and less time to devote to writing, it seemed, and more to everything else; and the frustration of not having time to write and the consequent seeming waste of the days gnawed at him. He was behind in his correspondence and admitted it to Derleth. "An author," he wrote, "should answer all of his letters—even briefly." He also had "about ten books to read" and "just can't find time to read them with pleasure like I want to read them." Time that would not come again was haunting him, and he wrote, "Yet I'm wasting Time."

Since his return from Europe, aside from his editorials and feature stories in the *Greenup County Citizen,* he had by December published five short stories in the *American Mercury, Household,* and *Esquire;* his poems had appeared in *Progressive Farmer, Household, Saturday Review of Literature,* and *Poetry.* Mary Glenn Rose had her M.A. thesis, "Jesse Stuart: Pioneer Writer of Kentucky," approved at George Peabody College for Teachers; and along with the local and national news coverage of his trouble in Greenup, he had been written up twice in *Time.* Through the winter and into April 1939 came publication of seven more stories and eleven poems, including in January what would become his most often reprinted short story, "Split Cherry Tree," in *Esquire,* and his much-praised "Ascension of Autumn: a Rhapsody," in the newly resurrected *Southern Literary Messenger.* As before, he wrote about what came out of his life and the people he knew in the land he knew. "The Poe of this new venture," the *San Antonio Express* reviewer noted, "may turn out to be Jesse Stuart, Kentucky poet, who contributes the leading article.... There the reader hears a new voice singing. He goes with the poet into his own wild scene, comes upon odd phrases, strange and lovely pictures; meets queer, but friendly persons, the mountain folk who are Jesse Stuart's own.... So does that Kentucky bard sing in native strains and use figures of speech as fresh as Homer's own." The editor's following note read, "*The Messenger* wishes that it might claim Jesse Stuart as its 'discovery' but H. L. Mencken and others recognized his genius some years ago. *The Messenger* is proud to carry a candle with his light."

The poem "City Girl" in the February issue of *Esquire* reflected upon a woman who "would not go with me to better clay," and so "I left her standing on the cold-stone street." The poem's persona thinks it "shameful" that "she is there and I am here / And she is missing all this pretty weather." His story "The Crazy Professor" in the April *Esquire* comically treated his Lincoln Memorial memories of Harry Kroll, and his "Moonin' Round the Mountain" in *Collier's* the same month recounted how the long-frustrated romance of a mountain couple is brought to marital bliss through a horse-quart dose of hot moonshine that permanently cures the groom's alcoholism, a story based on real people. They lived in the W-Hollow area, "right back up the road," Jesse said, "but he [Ace] never did quit drinking."

When spring break came in April, he was in New York City again for a weeklong visit, where he conferred with his publisher, E. P. Dutton.

One of the editors, Florence Bowers, took him to the offices of the *Herald Tribune,* where one columnist talked with him about the growing imminence of war and later wrote, "Jesse Stuart . . . looks pretty much as he should—a Kentucky country boy, to whom the world is all new and exciting. . . . He was steamed up over the possibility of war. . . . He was prepared to join the army at once—almost any army. . . . We asked him which country did he mean to fight, and he didn't seem to have made up his mind; almost any country would do. . . . On the whole, we found his attitude refreshing; at least, he didn't blither about 'the democracies,' meaning Russia. . . . He was simply a Kentuckian ready to oblige in a scrap." The columnist's whimsy aside, many of Jesse's audiences had been interested in his observations on Hitler's Third Reich, and he had frankly obliged them. The "German people he loves," an Ironton, Ohio, reporter observed, "but their government he detests." He told a Greenup newsman that "Jews are maliciously persecuted in Germany, Austria and Italy," and to a university audience at Lexington he said, "The people of Germany have sold their freedom," and Hitler was "taking Germany to Hell." Yet within a year he would write to James Still, moderating the initial outrage of his European experience, admitting many of his letters had been "a little crazy. . . . Europe made me write that way. I thought the whole world was going Fa[s]cist."

Meanwhile he had delighted his publishers with the promise of a first novel. Despite inaccurate reports that he had brought one back with him from Europe, the truth was he had not. Before his Guggenheim he had worked on one novel treating the environmental evils humanity suffered from the denuding of forests and subsequent erosion, continuing unregulated timbering operations, and the great flood of 1937. In a fever of inspiration he had entitled it *Immortal Waters,* but it had turned out to be the worst, he believed, he had ever written. Intermittently since 1932, he had continued to work with the manuscript of *Trees of Heaven,* but he was by no means yet satisfied with it. And he had achieved some brilliant patches of writing through the fall and into the spring on a novel he called *Magic Moonshine,* in which he dealt "with whiskey as it prevailed in Kentucky during the 'dry' [era]," but it needed more work, too.

Back home he announced in June that he was leaving the classroom in order to pursue his long-held Fugitive-Agrarian dream of farming and writing; but there was a new slant to his old ambition, making it more practicable, he believed. While in New York he had discussed his plans with several people, including those at Dutton. Because of increasing demands for him as a speaker and the obvious advantages to him as a writer (and to his publishers), he made arrangements with William B. Feakins, a corporation that had handled Sinclair Lewis' lecture tours, to go on a nationwide lecture tour commencing in October. Farming would demand some of his time in the summer; but, he declared, "I'll do more writing than farming."

His exile, then, lasted no longer than the school year of 1938/1939. Back home in W-Hollow, he told *Courier-Journal* feature reporter Rena Niles, "I can't write anywhere except at home," a general rather than a qualified truth. Referring to the house of Oscar Sammons, he elaborated, "Even here in Greenup, at the home of my best friend, I can't do a thing. . . . Yet Greenup should be home to me." He reflected upon his schooling there, his "first store-bought haircut," the first oysters he had ever eaten. "But when it comes to writing, there's only one place where I can get anything done—and that's right up at the head of W-Hollow." There, Niles observed, "he can write with a profuseness that astonishes even himself, with no numerical limit to the number of sonnets he can turn out in a night; no number of pages beyond which he cannot go." The fact was that he continued to publish plentifully. For the remainder of the year more than a dozen short stories, half as many poems, and seven articles appeared in *Esquire, Household, Poetry, Southwest Review, Southern Literary Messenger,* the *New Anvil, Story, Atlantic Monthly, Scholastic,* the *Prairie Schooner,* the *Russell Times,* and the *New Orleans Times-Picayune.*[3]

"What's she doing here?" he had asked James, *sotto voce.* James Stuart remembered his brother's ostensible surprise at Naomi Deane Norris' meeting him at the station upon his return from Europe. Many of Jesse Stuart's friends had met him that day, but that afternoon she joined him at Oscar and Ann Sammons' house overlooking the Ohio River, where the young people enjoyed Italian wine and Victrola records. The next week she saw him again at Ann and Oscar's, and on August 6 she went to Fullerton with him, after which she noted in her diary a "very, very nice time. Lots of mail, Coca-Cola, hamburger." She was with him on August 8 for a picnic in Ashland, his birthday, and gave him a Kaywoodie pipe. The day after she graduated from Morehead State Teachers College, he called to talk with her. Throughout the fall they saw each other an average of once or twice a week, even though his new position at Portsmouth High School had required his move to Fullerton where he took his old room at the Kings' across the river from the Ohio city. On the evening of October 1, the day he was hit by Amos Allen, she was on hand at Marting's Hospital in Ironton. The next day, she joined Oscar and Ann to bring Jesse home, and afterward picked up his books for him in Russell and took them twenty miles to the other end of Greenup County at Fullerton. They saw each other several times in November, and she was a charter member of the Jesse Stuart Literary Club. For Christmas he gave her a lovely pink evening bag, and they saw each other nearly every day of the holidays, including New Year's Eve, when the two met at Ann and Oscar's house, then went alone to the Henry Clay Hotel in Ashland for dining and dancing. She slept late on New Year's Day 1939, and awoke hoarse.

Since the day he had seen her in Dilley's nearly sixteen years before and later was among the boys in high school fortunate enough to carry her books, Jesse Stuart had been increasingly impressed with her presence, although she was later to remark that in those days "we were merely conscious of each other." During the year of his superintendency he had dated her a few times when she was living with her parents, as the Jean Torris poems of *Man with a Bull-Tongue Plow* attest in lyric detail, but he could easily recall in those days that he was "not very welcome at her home." Both had dates with others, although they remained "conscious" of each other through these years. She had been a loyal correspondent during his year abroad, visiting his parents and home in W-Hollow at his request. He may not have been sure himself why he had asked her to do that, but now he was growing more than merely "conscious" of the young Greenup woman, "straight and beautiful . . . as pretty as a willow tree / When its sharp leaves turn silver in the wind." All along she had been a faithful friend through his difficulties. She had expressed interest in his work, she had taken an active part in the literary club that had honored him by making his name its own, and in addition to literary interests and good reading, both were teachers who shared an educational sense of values.

"Though I had known you a long time," he would reflect years later, "I had not found you." It was a strange thing, and although he could not chronologically place it, he never forgot that moment of his love's epiphany:

> You remember the bright-colored flowered dress you wore that you had a long time after we were married; you were wearing that dress and sweeping . . . from your front porch to the [w]alk, your hair was tousel[e]d in the wind, your lips were painted but not too much and I walked up and said several words to you and you laughed and talked.

At that time you were different looking to me than you had ever been and something within me said "She's going to be my wife."

"Suddenly," he would later reflect, "I realized Naomi D. Norris was beautiful! Where had I been all these years when we had dated off and on that I hadn't realized how beautiful she was. But I had problems!" Aside from economic ones—an indebtedness stemming from his year abroad, the purchase of four farms of about four hundred acres that joined his father's farm, his investment in sheep including ewes brought from Montana, and recent legal expenses—he faced more direct familial ones as well. "Her parents would be against our marriage! So I just dated her during the year I taught at Portsmouth High School."

During the summer of 1939 he was back home in W-Hollow, living in the bunkhouse James had built for them and he had paid for, "where we could sit up at night and read and play music." Their father, Mick Stuart, had no patience with such hours; he usually went to bed at eight and was up feeding the stock by four. But Jesse did not write at first, and found himself behind the plow again. In the morning he often milked six cows and did so in the evening as well. He often fed twenty hogs evening and morning, too. There were 120 sheep he had to contain with fencing, for which he purchased twenty-seven bales of barbed wire. He worked with his father, James, Uncle Jesse, and brother-in-law Leonard Darby cutting and setting locust poles in the hard earth on which to string the barbed wire. Every three weeks the herd of sheep had to be driven into the barn where he drenched them for stomach worms.

Then ideas began to possess him for stories and poems, so much that he found himself troubled at night: "I'd get out of bed and jot down notes. I could see processions of men and women, my characters, I knew they were. I could hear them talk. They were alive and living life. I was not writing about them; they were real." He started taking days off from the farm work and writing—ten short stories, and then poetry. In the joy of outward flow, the old question "Can I write a novel?" rose up once more. He had told Dutton he was working on one, and word had slipped out to that effect in New York upon his return from abroad. Not only had his publishers and the critics begun to question him about it, but he had told them he *was* writing one—a partial truth, for he had worked on the three ideas struggling with birth pangs out of his brain and onto paper—*Trees of Heaven, Immortal Waters,* and *Magic Moonshine.* Although word was abroad that *Magic Moonshine* was in the works, he had in fact put it and the 1937 flood novel aside in order to commence work on *Trees of Heaven.* "It was the third time I'd tried to write this book," he would later admit, but "now words came to me. This novel was in my head. It fell onto the paper as fast as I could use my typewriter." Perhaps it was living in the bunkhouse with James again that gave him the notion to try once more to bring the work around. Although he well knew that James had seen himself in the character of Tarvin Bushman, his brother had said little or nothing of it. Later Jesse would write that he began his manuscript on August 8, his birthday. That day he also visited Naomi Deane Norris at her home in the afternoon. They played records together, and later she told her diary, "I'm so happy."

And she was another thing that gave incentive to the new creative surge, a thing that sent him over the ridge path and down into Greenup several nights a week. From the time of his spring trip to New York, ironically while away from Naomi Deane Norris from April 8 to April 16, he knew that he was in love again. He would walk over the bony ridge and along Academy Branch and down the street to her house. As in the past he often brought with him wildflowers of the season; in the spring percoon, dogwood blossoms, buttercups, blue violets, phlox, and pink lady's slipper; in the summer larkspur, field daisies, blue flag, bottle-brush, wild potato vine, and ladies' tresses; and in late summer and fall yellow primroses, foxglove, snakeroot, boneset, Queen Ann's lace, field thistles, goldenrod, and black-eyed Susans. "Here comes your poet . . . coming down the road," Emmett Norris would say, leaning back in his chair on the front porch of the distinctive two-story white wooden house perched atop a hill of his own making to keep it dry in floodtime, its large banistered south-facing porch and awning extending around the sides of the Main Street home. And Naomi would always remember, "There Jesse would be with a newspaper filled with an armful of flowers." Her father called Jesse "the puh-fessor," and he called her parents "The Colonel and his Lady"; but under the surface of civility, the poet knew her parents remained opposed to his marrying their eldest daughter. So she and Jesse just continued to date heavily. Half the nights of August they were together—such motion pictures as Jeannette McDonald and Nelson Eddy in *Sweethearts;* supper at relatives' homes—that of her sister Millie Zachem, whose husband operated their favorite Greenup restaurant; at social affairs such as the Masonic picnic down at the Kings' in Fullerton; with the Sammonses or Maynard and Ethel Bush, or Naomi's sister Nancy and her fiancé, George Curry. They played records at her house, too, talked books like *And Quiet Flows the Don* together, and such arcane farming topics as drenching sheep. They went out to Jesse's home in W-Hollow many times, attended ballgames, shopped at antique and secondhand stores, and often she accompanied him to lectures he gave in the area. He grew to depend on her in countless ways, for she possessed experience he lacked in matters ranging from house furnishings to social devoirs. In August he hurriedly enclosed two birth announcements received from the parents of Lee Burris Sturgill and Orian W. McElfresh, with this letter to her:

My Dear,

Will you buy these babies presents and I'll pay you. You are a good shopper and you go shopping very often. I am not a good shopper and I don't go shopping besides I can't buy presents for babies.

Always,
Jesse Stuart

As she was happy, he was happy, too, walking on the wind and writing like a house afire on *Trees of Heaven*. He was seeing her almost daily now, and a strange, new thing began to happen to him. Familiar things did not look so good to him at home anymore. "Not even the paper on our bunkhouse walls," he would later write. Again he walked over the ridge path, this time taking his typewriter and manuscript along, and stayed in the back room of Oscar and Ann Sammons' cottage on the river. There he pounded his typewriter all day with one consoling thought adding to the satisfying fervor of creative outpour: "I was close to Emmett Norris' residence where I could see his daughter each evening," just across the swinging bridge.

But one morning he got up and tasted Ann's coffee. "Something's wrong with this coffee," he said.

"Same coffee I had yesterday morning," Ann Sammons said. "I made it the same way. You taste of it, Oscar."

Oscar tasted the coffee. "I can't find anything wrong with it!"

That day Jesse packed anyway and moved to the downtown Callihan Hotel. Voices haunted him. "*He* can't write a novel. He never will!" Even Oscar had needled him. "I got after Jess that he couldn't write a novel. Poetry, short stories, yes—but *not* a novel." He and Ann would later recall that Jesse got so upset he said he would never set foot in Oscar's house again. But it was only talk, for he had done so much on the novel that he was encouraged to go on with it.

More than ever before, he and Naomi Deane talked about marriage. Could it be that Fate had reserved them for each other? Here they had lived most of their lives with only two miles of mountains and valleys between them. They had so much in common. Why had not each chosen another? Certainly both had been involved with others. Indeed, each had nearly married another, yet neither had. Now they were "conscious" of each other in deep, new ways that had begun to change their lives day by day. They would, they agreed, marry—but not too quickly. They would wait until April of 1940, when the school year would be over. That would give them nearly three seasons to do all they needed to do beforehand. More frequently now she went to antique shops and second-hand stores to find the furniture they would need. Their lives increasingly overlapped, and she was with him when he received a telegram from composer Sidney King Russell requesting permission for Nelson Eddy to sing on a nationwide radio hookup the lyrics of Jesse's poem "By Sandy Waters," which had appeared a few months before in the *Saturday Review of Literature.* Jesse wired back his permission to 612 North Rodeo Drive, Beverly Hills, California. On Sunday evening, September 3, he had supper at the Norris' home, and the family tuned in to listen to Nelson Eddy sing on the "Chase and Sanborn Hour":

Much have I roved by Sandy River
Among the spring-bloomed thyme,
Where love and life go on forever
And where I've spun my rhyme.

Much have I loved by Sandy River
Girls with the light brown hair;
I thought love would go on forever,
Spring be forever fair.

The spring for mountains goes forever
But not for us who fade
In love and life by Sandy River
Before our dreams are made. . . .

It was a satisfying evening, and of the moment Naomi wrote in her diary, "Beautiful." In his pleasure Jesse sent Eddy two inscribed books. One of them was *Beyond Dark Hills,* and the famous singer replied, "I sat right down and read about stout Mitch—then the chapter on steel. It's great stuff. Did you ever pay Mattie back that $2?" and signed, "Gratefully yours, Nelson Eddy." Jesse entrusted the letter to Naomi to put in her scrapbook with the many other items she had begun to keep.

Already the sad music of autumn winds played through the leaves now coloring brilliantly, and a few golden beech leaves had already shivered down to haunt him with foreshadowings of mutability. Sitting under the apple trees on the back lot behind Naomi's house, walking downtown, riding in her car to the foot of the hill along Academy Branch below the ridge path from where he could jog-walk home in twenty minutes, he had urged her to move their wedding date closer, first to Christmas and then to Thanksgiving. Any earlier date seemed out of the question, for her sister Nancy and George Curry had already scheduled Sunday, October 15, for their own wedding, a large church affair. *Trees of Heaven* was nearing completion and he was confident about the manuscript's possibilities. On Wednesday evening, October 11, he had ridden up to Ashland in Naomi's car. He still had not bought a car of his own. In fact, he could not drive one then. He was to be guest of honor at the home of the Palmer A. Hiltys on Montgomery Avenue at an informal party. Ann and Oscar met them there, where Jesse read "Eternal Destiny," a poem recently accepted by *American Mercury*. He interpreted the thirty-five-dollar sale as a good omen, and that evening Naomi wrote "Lovely time" in her diary. The next evening she and Jesse were again riding toward Ashland in her car, ostensibly to see a movie in Ashland, but they both knew better. They were driving along the overpass when he abruptly turned to her. He had already told her she was the oldest of Emmett Norris' daughters and should be married first. She had not disputed his logic. He said directly—meaning *now*—"Will you marry me?"

"You've asked so suddenly," she replied.

In a way they were both still hesitant. All kinds of excuses presented themselves. The answer to their own desire to marry at last, in light of the imminent wedding of her sister and George Curry, seemed to be to marry in secret, especially if they were to be married right away. It seemed the only way.

"We've been conscious of each other for 17 years now," he pressed on. "Look at the autumn leaves the winds have carried to this overpass. Time is flying. You are thirty-one and I'm thirty-two."

"When," she asked, "will we get married?"

"Tonight if we can," he said.

They did not go to the movie; instead they drove to the county seat of Boyd County, Catlettsburg, near Ashland, and Jesse telephoned the county court clerk at his home, for the courthouse was closed. They motored out to Chestnut Drive and bought the marriage license at the clerk's home. To their amusement, he thought they were runaways. Jesse later wrote, "He must have thought our actions strange for teachers as old as we were." It was too late to get married that evening. They drove back to Greenup and went to their separate homes. Rehearsal for Nancy and George's wedding required their presence in Ashland Friday the thirteenth, and that evening they dined in the Blue Room after fulfilling that duty. Although they still had time to get married in the late hours that Friday, they believed the date was too minatory. "We wanted our marriage to last," Jesse reasoned, so they waited until just past midnight—the fourteenth. Their marriage took place at the home of the Reverend Frank J. Richardson. Oscar and Ann Sammons met the couple and, along with Naomi's sister Nancy and George Curry, Jr., stood up with them. They were pronounced man and wife at 12:25 A.M., and that night returned to Greenup where Jesse told her, "You go to your home. I'll go to my room in the Callihan Hotel."

The next morning he was back to a stint of writing on *Trees of Heaven*, while Naomi stayed home all day. On Sunday, as scheduled, her sister Nancy married George Curry in a beautiful, formal ceremony. But shortly afterward, Naomi and Jesse were together at Ann and Oscar's house, alone in long-awaited bliss, where their marriage was secretly consummated. For more than another month they would be man and wife in secret.[4]

Jesse Stuart finished the manuscript of *Trees of Heaven*—143,000 words in about seventy-five days. He decided to go to New York to take it to Dutton personally just ten days after his marriage; he borrowed a hundred dollars and, on the same day that Naomi purchased an elegant, ornate Lincoln bedroom suite at Vanhoose's Furniture Store, the two had supper at the Norrises. Although she helped him pack and took him to Ashland to meet his train, her parents seemed none the wiser to the fact that their daughter was now Mrs. Jesse Stuart. The next day she came directly home from schoolteaching and then went to Leslie's Store to see about a mattress and springs for the big new bed. That night she played Jesse's records and wrote in her diary, "Miss him very, very much." The next night she wrote, "Miss Jesse dreadfully," and the next, "So lonely without Jesse."

His first letter to his wife, sent airmail October 26 from Dutton's at Fourth Avenue in New York City, echoed their difficult parting at the Ashland Station. "My Dear Deane," it began. "It was hard to leave you the other night":

I saw you, Oscar, Ann after you had crossed the tracks and were walking toward the car. You didn't see me. I pounded the train window and waved to you. It was hard to leave you and it's going to be terrible to stay away from you. —I'm in love with you—even, more than you think; more than you dream—more than you know! I'm out to make a living for two just now and I feel proud to do so. Life means more to me; it is richer and fuller. . . . I'm proud to have married you. I feel like shouting it to the wind instead of trying to keep it a secret.

Things happened quickly in New York. To save money he took a room at the YMCA, across the street from the old Chelsea Hotel. Within three days Louise Townsend Nichols and other readers agreed with Elliot Beach MacRae that Dutton should publish *Trees of Heaven*, and scheduled the book for spring release. With money Jesse sent her, she went down to Vanhoose's and paid for their bedroom furniture. By November 4 he had sent her his signed contract and two checks, one of them an advance on the novel for $250. However, he had to stay on through November working on the manuscript and lecturing in the East on a new tour arranged by the Feakins Corporation. The tone of his letters was avid, deeply committed. She had asked if he truly loved her, and he wrote,

> . . . Love you? What do you think? You ought to know whether I love you or not. You ought to know. I know myself well enough to know that when I think enough of a girl to marry her that I have to love her and love her deeply. There is not any foolishness about it. To get married is something that means everything and I regard marriage as something sacred if there be anything on earth sacred. And I regard my wife first among all human beings I know on this earth. . . .

About other women and concerning the slow maturation of their love he wrote,

> Deane, I never see another woman. I don't know another woman. I am honest. I am sincere. My feet are planted solidly on the ground. I know what I'm doing. Deane Norris is the only girl in the world that exists as far as I'm concerned. My only regret is, I didn't marry you years ago. . . . Never in my life did I want to hurt you. You were so silent I didn't know—but I believe I have hurt you a few times in the past—and for all this I'm sorry. If I am the man you always wanted—you got me. So, that is recompense—despite the fact, I don't know why any woman would want me. But I do know honestly that others did and you know it. Had you only shown a few signs of jealousy before you did, I would have known you better.

I used to think that I was just somebody for you to be with. If signs of jealousy are properly shown, they are compliments for a man.

Emphasizing his constancy, he added a page to his letter of Nov. 16:

> Honey:
> When I am out like this—I'll never betray you, or cheat on life with you. You can trust me. I know if I should or you should, the foundation of our marriage is wrecked. . . . That trust would be broken. . . . I'm not built like that. From the time I married you, I became yours. I want either to be married (and really be married) or not to be married. I'm not going half way. I have always said when I married and if I knew I loved my wife and we'd get along, this would be the way I'd stand by the marriage vows I'd taken. If not, I'd ask for separation and let her marry a better man and I'd go back a single man. This is the only way I can see marriage and others see it this way if they'd only confess. At least, the majority feel this way about it. If this is Puritanical, then I'm a Puritan.

Her love had touched his proud masculine image of himself. She represented that ideal toward which he believed their marriage should reach, by which it would be inspired and through which it would endure. He wrote in late October,

> I think of you all the time. I'm in love with you beyond words— and I fling myself on you and to you and with you with all the force and gusto that is in my body and spirit. Honey, you have married a man and this is not egotism. You have not married a piece of a man. And my wife, I have always thought must be a woman above reproach—a woman with beauty in her body, heart, spirit and mind— a woman that is respected—and I have that woman. I have found her. I love her and I love her deeply as any man can love a woman. I shall stand by her through thick and thin—until death parts us.
>
> > Always,
> > Stuart.

Of their most intimate moments he spoke with a bold tenderness and passion whetted to a sharp anxiousness by his absence:

> My dear wife:
> Don't let me disturb you in my wails of homesickness. I'm homesick only for you. . . . Before we married, I wondered about you—and I loved you. I desired you. I wanted you. I couldn't wait

until April 1940 to get you—so, we just married. Maybe, you didn't have to marry but I did. I had to marry you. . . . You said that I made you realize you were a woman. I hope I did. I wanted to be that one for I want to give myself to you—all of me, not a part. When I touched you—the day we went to O's and A's (Sunday) is an experience I'll never forget. It is the greatest experience I've ever had in my life. . . . I can't realize I have the type of woman I always wanted for a wife. You know what I told you—I wanted you as you are. . . . I'm so eager to be with you again—I can't wait— Yes, I will love you and love you plenty. You have no need to fear me—Oh no, never . . . and I believe you are as eager for me to love you as I am eager to love you. . . .

Again he would temper passion with common sense, uncertainty with faith, and physical absence with spiritual presence:

Your picture on my dresser has meant more to me than it has ever meant. It was in Scotland with me—through Europe with me— now in New York with me—and it smiles more pleasingly on me now—a surer confidence, trust, a greater love. It can't tell me to eat regularly and get to bed at regular hours; to stop reading and to stop work. No, it doesn't speak. But it is here with me—and not this image but the Deane beyond the picture is here with me in spirit. I know it. I feel the surety of her—always—

And always,
Stuart

Away and looking back over months and years, he tore away all veils of vanity and leveled with her:

My dear wife:
. . . I began to realize that I wanted you but somehow—despite all my blab—it was hard for me to ask you to marry me, for I thought that you might want to marry a man with more conservative viewpoints about politics, religion and everything in general. I knew we'd practically grown up together—that we knew each other— and your attitudes toward my people were honest attitudes—not just a put-on because you dated me. I knew you were from the same stock of people practically—that you were a sweet and at- tractive girl—but somehow you were Deane, a sister and a friendly type—I really didn't know you. . . . I've never thought deep down in any woman's heart she wanted to marry me—meet, part, maybe

kiss—and this be all. It seemed like this to me—that I'd go with the girls and the other fellows marry them—and it seemed that this would go on and on forever—for I wouldn't tie myself to any girl and not date another until that urge or whatever you call it—left me freely—not that I had to force it. . . . You did tell me if I ever dated again, you'd be through with me! I don't blame you for saying that. I admired you for it.

Deane, I was almost afraid to marry. I didn't know about it. And soon as I was married I wasn't afraid. I'm certainly not afraid now. I even thought that you might not be happy . . . with me and all sorts of such ideas came into my mind. . . .

Oh . . . if you can be as much in love with me as I am with you; if you can be just as serious and sincere about marriage as I am; if you will stick by me as I plan to stick by you; give to me as I'll give to you—all I can give and so unselfishly—you'll see that we'll be the happiest couple in America—the long hard fight of life will be won at last. . . . Darling, I'm so in love with you and my staying here has measured this to me. . . .

Neither one of them had been sure about marriage. "My family," she said years later, "opposed and discouraged it. He was surprised when Mother accepted it later, for he was primed for opposition . . . expected he wouldn't be accepted. You know, I think he was somehow . . . scared of marriage, but he changed and was truly happy."

On November 22, he addressed her, "My Darling," and expressed his pleasure in "your brief sweet letter." He knew that she would "have that bed fixed. It pleases me so much—and to think only a few more days and I'll be in it with you." He would kiss her tender smiles and they would play their favorite records over and over.

You don't know how happy I'll be to see you. I'll not tell you on paper but I'll show you when I come. Just to think of sleeping and waking with you! I can't realize that that will be true! No fright, suspense, fear—but calmly lying beside you
        "pulse to pulse and breath to breath—
        where hushed awakenings they are dear—"

He would have to make one more lecture tour in the spring, and then he figured, "You'll be with me about every place I go." In the depth of his longing he admitted, "I don't know what I'm doing. This is going to be a new life for me." But he was sure of one thing. "I am the most married man in America."[5]

13

War and Peace
1940–1946

And so Jesse Stuart fell in love never to fall out of love again. He wrote to James Still, confident his old classmate "would like her. . . . She's 6 feet tall, has curley brown hair—hazel eyes—weighs 120 pounds. She has modeled some clothes—She is very well read, loves poetry (some of it is a little too sentimental for me) is an excellent cook (loves to cook), goes well-dressed—is fairly good in music. . . . Her mother used to play a dulcimer. It was washed away in the '37 flood. My wife is the least in size in her family . . . 3 sisters and two brothers. Look how large my people are! If we have children, they should be robust ones. I am telling you this because I think you might be interested. Soon as we get out in a house of our own, we want you to visit us."

When Naomi Deane finally told her mother on the evening of November 16 of her and Jesse's marriage and asked if they could stay at the house for awhile, Mrs. Norris was simply furious. "I just cried," her daughter remembered.

"You'll have to ask your father," Mrs. Norris said. Naomi asked him, and, as she wrote to Jesse, "He acted up," refusing to give her a direct answer. Finally, Emmett Norris relented. "My father told Mother, and she told me. That was the way they did things." By Jesse's return from New York in November, she had mailed the wedding announcements. On December 1, the Huntington paper carried his picture and announcement of marriage, and the next day her portrait appeared, a large-eyed, oval-faced young woman with a fetching cameo brooch at the lacy throat of her bodice.

The holidays were a busy time, and they spent most of her Christmas vacation from schoolteaching together in the bunkhouse at the Stuarts', where they worked on proofs of *Trees of Heaven* and contemplated a new life for each of them. Their joy together had not come easily, that was certain. Even in small ways, so it seemed to them, objections to their union had risen. There had been the long courtship and gradual evolution of their love. There was the question of her younger sister's wedding that had, perhaps in subtle ways, influenced their own. When the big Lincoln bed had been moved into the Norris home, they literally had to raise the roof to get it in. And then in January, when she went off to school each day, Jesse walked her up the street to Riverton, then returned to their room each day to write, read, and type. "Of course, my parents thought that I was working and he was sitting upstairs at home." The truth was that her parents had never approved of any of the boys she had gone with, and Jesse was no exception at first. By January and February, however, he showed Mr. and Mrs. Norris some of his checks received for publications, those months when a dozen short stories and poems were published in such magazines as *Southwest Review, Esquire, American Mercury, Progressive Farmer, Scribner's Commentator, Household,* and *American Prefaces.* Another lecture tour was planned soon, from which, he explained, he would make some money. Slowly he began to win their approval.

Although Emmett Norris' place in Greenup would be their official address from Jesse's return from New York in November 1939 until June 1940, the desire for a personal home soon emerged as the overriding problem for the new bride and groom. Naomi Deane felt this urgency as much as Jesse, and by the frequency with which he mentioned it she knew how strongly he yearned for a home of their own. Not long after Lady Nancy Astor had mailed Jesse and Naomi a card of congratulation and wish for happiness, the new bride surprised her husband by saying, "Let's take some sandwiches and walk out to your farm today."

Even though it was a cold February day, her words elated him, for he had missed the winter scenery of somber old broom-sage fields and the familiar barns. Furthermore, he would be leaving soon on a lecture tour and it was a chance for them to be together, away from other people who always seemed to be around.

Up the ridge path they walked past Academy Branch and along its highland tributary where "snow-melted water trickled over the blue slate rocks" and "made a purring noise." Along steep slopes winter ferns leaned almost to the blue cold water. Through the woods and out onto the upland pasture, they saw crows winging high in the icy air and cawing to one another. A rabbit darted from a nest in the brown broom-sage. The winter hills were "dark, bleak and forsaken. . . . The barren, dead-leaf-covered hills looked like ugly monsters, and gaping cliffs looked like their mouths. It was a wild, fierce beauty." They found a place to spread their lunch and eat.

"I can see why you write poetry here," she spoke. "This place is lonely, but it is poetry."

"Poetry is already born here," he said. "I do not have to create it. All I do is record it. . . . Away from home . . . in the city . . . I get so I can't write a line. All I have to do is to come back here to the things that belong to me. I start writing poetry again. It just comes natural to me." They talked on and then stood silently for a while. From the ridgetop they watched a belled ewe lead the sheep into the barn for their four-o'clock feeding. In the distance Jesse's father was a slight, bent figure moving along a crooked path beyond the familiar white house on the hill of green pines of the Stuart homeplace. The February wind swept over the wide field of brown broom-sage between them and the white house. "This is a picture I can't forget," she said. "I want to move to this farm."

In answer he held her close to him and kissed her warmly in the February twilight.[1]

By late February his lecture tour had taken him through Slippery Rock, Pennsylvania, and on to New York City where he spoke at Columbia University, the first of many lectures he would make at that school. He was surprised to discover that the Feakins Bureau had him scheduled for appearances in California in early March, even though, as he wrote home, "I didn't bring enough clothes." He was optimistic in reporting that Annie Laurie Williams hoped to sell the movie rights to *Trees of Heaven* for twenty-five thousand dollars, and then jauntily told Naomi, "Honey, stay sweet" and "don't forget me," adding, "sleep on my side of the bed," assuring her, "I long for you—I love, love, love you!" On February 29 his pen mourned that its holder would "never be able to write you another letter on February 29th for four years." The ensuing absence drove home his deepening love for his wife. "It is said that the newness of marriage wears off . . . in six months or so," he wrote. "I don't believe it. For me it wears on. . . . You know, I love you more than anyone in the world and I need you. I wish to God your curley head was on my shoulder. It will always be your pillow," he averred. More typically than not, the ubiquitous writer in the lover had the last word as he gave her detailed instructions on preparing his short stories for typing, submitting, and mailing.

To save expenses he rode tourist rate from Chicago to California. "I'm not allowed back in the observation car where I can hear a radio. I got back there today and was chased out—not only that but escorted to my seat in the tourist car by a cranky old white-mustached conductor—the Devil!" But there was good news: While in Chicago he had sold three stories to Arnold Gingrich, editor of *Esquire*.

Crossing Nevada, he discovered "a land where houses are seldom seen. Scarcely a tree here . . . just a few . . . set along the streets in a tiny town that comes along about every 50 miles. This country is what I'd call a wasteland—just treeless mountains and hard rocks looking at you from all sides." But when he crossed the Sierra Nevadas he encountered more than six feet of snow which the train tunneled through, and then they came down from the mountains into Sacramento Valley where

> palm trees were growing in people's yards—the grass was green—apple orchards in the grass was [sic] green—apple orchards in bloom and weather warm as it is in early May in Kentucky. I've never seen so much difference in a few hours train ride—from ar[c]tic winter to tropical springtime.

Glad to detrain, he wrote, "It's a long bleak streak from here back to New York City—well over 3000 miles." His stationery declared that he was staying at the Hotel Senator, but he was leaving it right away. "I'm sneaking out to a cheaper place—the Y.M.C.A."

Though apprehensive about the Western audience, by March 6 he communicated to his bride the kind of happy response that would recur at many of his major lectures both in the United States and abroad in the years to come: "The first ordeal is through—yesterday, many women came forward and said the talk was the best that has been given this year. The Tuesday Club is composed of about six or seven hundred women—ages from 40 to 70, nearly all are college graduates. It is one of the most intelligent audiences I've spoken to yet." Meanwhile, he had moved from the "swank Senator Hotel," where he had paid three dollars a night, to the YMCA, where the rate was fifty cents. "All I have," he wrote, "is a cot and dresser—not even a desk to write on." His weight was down to 185 pounds and he wrote hungrily, "I'd like a good meal at your house now tell your mother."

His yearning for their own place insistently returned: "I want to get in a house alone with you—just we two—so we can work, plan and build together—so we can go places together. I sure as hell hate to be away from you. . . . Deane, I love you more than anyone on earth—and I'll love you more the longer I live with you." She had inspired him, and he had sold seven stories—"$1100 worth"—which he had revised "while at your house—upstairs in our little room." He foresaw "many more good prospects too." Somehow their love and his creativity were part and parcel of something fine. In his distinctive language of pride he pointed to the sacredotals of his stories and exulted in the language of his heart, "Oh, . . . life is great with you! It is a new wonderful life. How can I ever love you enough? How can I tell you how much I love you . . . how much I have missed you?" Closing, he added another page, careful to underline *"Please tear up"*:

> I've lived the hours over with you since I've been away—you with your head on my shoulder—your curly hair touching my arm—and then you turn to me and I to you in the night.
>
> The feel of your body against mine—and even in sleep—unknowingly, I turn to you—I'll find you—oh the love of you, Deane—the enjoyment of our brief months of married life together—how sweet you are. How you set my whole being to ecsta[s]y! I need you now! It will be hard for me to wait to see you. I could love you to death. Oh Deane how I do love you, dream of you, worship you. . . .

She did not, however, tear up the page.

That March he spoke at the University of California at Berkeley, electing "gate receipts" over a guaranteed fifty dollars. Rather than nurse his loneliness, he often sat up until three-thirty in the morning talking with "these boys," smoking pipes, discussing their mutual lives and marriage or its imminence. Daily observing Californians and their ways, he commented, "There is more laughter, beauty, vice, flowers, whitestone buildings, automobiles, places of amusement, bums, cut-throats and panhandlers here than any state in the Union—more poverty—more riches—more artificial life. It is a world to itself—people have freer minds yet . . . more nuts, more crank religions than anywhere I know." One evening loneliness was setting in when he went to the gym to see a bowling match at the "Y," where "there was only one woman there—one of the bowler's wives—and she sat beside her husband and drank a Coco Cola [sic]. It made me want to be with you—almost a sudden terror seized me and I got so lonely I had to leave. I thought and thought about you."

Before returning, he left Sacramento for Stockton and Pasadena, then Claremont and Pomona College. "You know Deane," he wrote, "that we need to be alone and together. . . . I get along all right with your folks—but your mother who is nice to me—still directs you—and you are going to rebel. I've been scared of this all the time and I don't want it to happen. If you were in a home of your own that attitude would change overnight. We must get out. You know that. And you want out—and desperately too! Well, you're going to get out!" The living he was making would provide their solution, and by April they would be looking realistically toward "a little cottage" together. By bus he went to Alhambra, where he took the Southern Pacific Railroad for St. Louis, Missouri. In Missouri he took time to speak at Flat River Junior College and autograph a few books through arrangements made by teacher-book reviewer Charles E. Bess, whom he told, "I want to plant a few books in Missouri." Later he wrote Bess of his visit as "a great experience . . . among you people who are the backbone of America."[2]

In May he made a return trip to New York and veered south for a brief lecture tour in and about Atlanta, Georgia, addressing Naomi Deane with the diminutive taken from the heroine of his strange mountain love story "The Last Round Up," to appear in *Esquire* in December. "And you little 'Totem,'" he wrote, "you tried to fool me. You put a *Clark bar* in my pajamas (you know I don't like a Clark bar), I have never seen your like. You know how to touch me. When I found that bar of candy—such simple little thing—I shed tears." En route from New York to Atlanta on *The Crescent* and "crossing over the green hills of Virginia on the train that Thomas Wolfe loved," as he wrote, he told her of having met Sidney King Russell and having heard him play in person "Sandy River." He had seen "puggie-beer drinking H. L. Mencken," too, who "has the bluest eyes I've ever seen." Jesse had purchased a new summer suit, size 44, evidence of his pleasure with both strong sales and reviews of his *Trees of Heaven*. From the Ansley Hotel in Atlanta he wrote of his desire to take her on long trips over the country and of their upcoming New York City jaunt. "Honey, how you'll like New York— To me, it's a cage—and will always be—To you, it will be a gotham. You'll love it from start to finish and you'll like Connecticut!"

By early June they had arrived in New York and registered at the Prince George Hotel. He took her with him to Dutton's and to the Aberdeen Hotel to see Ed Cross. Saturday, June 8, they spent sightseeing and had lunch with Jesse's lecture bureau boss, William B. Feakins. That night they went to Harlem. "Scared a little but lots of fun," she wrote in her diary. Artist Woodi Ishmael and his wife, Gwen, joined them for lunch on Sunday; later, Jesse and Naomi saw Grant's Tomb, and took the ferry to Staten Island, seeing the Statue of Liberty and Ellis Island. That week they visited the offices of *Collier's* and *Harper's*. On Wednesday they saw movie agent Annie Laurie Williams and short-story editor Martha Foley. They lunched with Mrs. Bowers of Dutton and J. Donald Adams and his wife at Town Hall. The next day they went to the World's Fair with Mr. Bowers, and were later houseguests of publisher Jimmy MacRae on his birthday in Connecticut. They also met John Vassos, and

Naomi was impressed enough with Connecticut hospitality to write in her diary, "Lovely home and grand people in to see us." In New York again on Friday, Jesse went on to Philadelphia while Naomi rested and slept. That evening she had dinner with the Adamses on Park Avenue. She shopped over the weekend on Fifth Avenue and had lunch at Jack Dempsey's. "Met him," she wrote in her diary. Together she and Jesse left the jeweled city she had, for a little while, held in her hand; they went on to the University of Indiana, where Jesse lectured on June 18 and they were luncheon guests of the president. Jesse gave another lecture on June 21, which Naomi thought "splendid," and they met the radio people afterward.

By the time they came home through Indianapolis, they had made their decision to change their residence. They would go to the Kings', in South Shore, from where they planned to supervise the reconstruction of a log-cabin home they hoped to complete at the head of W-Hollow. The move forced Jesse to face up to the need for immediate transportation and, with Naomi's approval, he bought a car, a black Plymouth from the local Meadows boys. As excited as Jesse and Naomi were, she never forgot how "Jesse made them take off one extra gadget after the other until he got the price down to the money we had to pay for it." They dubbed the car "Fronnie," after Jesse's faithful, dependable character in *Trees of Heaven*. Naomi drove the car, for Jesse had not yet learned how to drive, although he vowed he could and would.

These decisions had not been easy, especially the selection of a home. After they had walked over nearly every foot of the farm, Naomi Deane said, "I'll tell you what I want. I want to remodel one of the old log houses on this farm. You have two houses standing. We can remake one of them." They had rejected the little log house on the middle prong of W-Creek that had been his second boyhood home because it was already rented by people who wanted to stay there, and instead selected the old house of yellow poplar logs, the third home where he had lived from about 1916 to 1918. Although it had been scoured up as a temporary meetingplace for the Jesse Stuart Literary Club after his return from abroad, for the greater part of recent years it had been used for cattle and the storage of hay. Still, Naomi was enthusiastic about its location and possibilities. To Jesse this was the lonely place of that dark winter "when bread was scarce," a time of bleak sickness and the birthplace and deathplace of his infant brother, Martin Vernon. He was not pleased, but her excitement and bubbling plans struggled with his reluctance. Naomi was intent. Her face sparkled as she talked of a new well and a sweep, too, of chimney repair and bookshelves on each side of the old living room fireplace. "We will leave the rafters in the ceiling just as they are and paint them white," she said as Jesse glanced up at them a few inches above his upturning, half-ducking head. She overrode all his objections and banished his doubts, so there was nothing to do but go to work on her remodeling plans, right down to the heavy, thick doors she wanted with old Williamsburg latches and iron-rim locks.

He borrowed four hundred dollars in Flemingsburg, using his sheep for security. They bought all the doors she wanted for less than a dollar apiece in Portsmouth, Ohio, at a wrecking business. By September the work was going full tilt, although it had to be done slowly to do it correctly. Ivan Nelson and Lin Darby did much of the work, and the rest was job-contracted. Finding three partially decayed yellow poplar logs, originally set about 1844, they removed them and replaced them with tough white-oak logs from the Stuart land. Mick Stuart cut oak trees in the dark of the moon, rived oak shingles from them while the moon was light, and then put them on in the dark of the moon so that they would not "cup," as he said, and in so doing he assured the young couple that both the roof shingles and clapboards would remain "flat as pancakes." Through September and October the workmen underpinned the house, rebuilt the chimney, and put in new subflooring for a knotty-pine-plank floor. They extended a new bedroom west of the original log room, sealed on the inside with plasterboard and protected on the outside with storm sheeting and layered twenty-four-inch oak clapboard, overlapping sixteen inches with eight inches showing. The original 1844 room became their new living room, its ancient logs left unshingled to show from the front. Inside, its charming unbanistered stairway led up to the original "loft room," refurbished and snug beneath the inverted-V roof. Behind the living room, in place of the old dog trot, was the new dining room; then came the kitchen. In back of the house was the privy, which in the spring to follow Naomi would decorate with a latticework front covered with vines and flowers.

Ivan Nelson rebuilt the well so that surface water could not leak into the twenty-foot-deep underground pool. An oak bucket was fastened with a chain to a long locust sweep. Naomi painted the windows, ceilings, and doors white. She found the black iron thumb-latches she sought and had them put on the doors. By mid-November, racing with approaching winter, they hired a truck to move their furniture from storage in Greenup. They wrapped the Lincoln bed and Naomi's antiques so they would not be damaged over the rough W-Hollow roadbed, and made the final move at dark. The total cost of the work was eight hundred dollars, most of it for labor, for nearly all the reconstruction had been of native materials—rock, lumber, the white-oak shingles. About the only new thing they had to buy was a cookstove. The morning after their move, eight inches of snow lay on the ground.[3]

Late in 1941 Jesse and Naomi toured the West with his former high school principal, Lena Wells Lykins Voiers, and her husband, Gus, a haberdasher in neighboring Vanceburg. All through Jesse's life, it seemed, especially at significant turning points, she would turn up with that "big 'howdy' smile" that lit up her whole face. The year before, when his name had appeared in *Who's Who in America,* she had written him a long letter. Now, Jesse's lecture tour through the West was coming up, and Gus had a new Chrysler. The merchant and his wife were always happy to get away on a trip, and proposed that they go along together. Gus would take his Chrysler and do all the driving. The offer was too good to turn down, but before they left, Naomi Deane said, "Gus, I want you to take Jesse down to the store and put some good clothes on him, and dress him up so I won't be ashamed of him." The single-breasted dark blue tailored suit they settled on cost fifty dollars, and along with accessories of shirts, ties, underwear, socks, and belt, the bill ran to one hundred dollars, which Jesse agreed to pay at the rate of five dollars a month until the bill was satisfied. Together they left the approaching winter weather of Kentucky and enjoyed the western tour enormously, particularly the Pacific Coast. In Los Angeles, Jesse went as a guest to a breakfast club to hear another well-known speaker, who failed to show up. At length, Jesse was called upon to substitute impromptu. He started with a poem, according to Lena Wells, and when he finished three hundred men were on their feet cheering him. Among the enthusiastic well-wishers that shook his hand was, Jesse thought, a familiar face. "Seems like I've seen you somewhere before," the Kentuckian said. It turned out to be the famous actor Frederic March. With the Voiers, Jesse and Naomi met other well-known people on the trip, too, including Edward Everett Horton and his sister Hannabelle, in Hollywood; and they were amused that her gestures, laughing, talking, and moving about all over the house were pretty much the same as those of her brother.

On the return trip from the Coast, the foursome drove through Arizona and New Mexico into Texas and stopped for the night at El Paso. There the manager, learning of their desire to see a bit of old Mexico, urged them to bypass the border town of Juarez and instead continue south toward Chihuahua City, where a more authentic atmosphere could be savored. The next day, November 24, they were motoring along about a hundred miles south of the border. Gus was at the wheel driving at a good clip and Lena had just tuned in some good music on the radio when a rear tire blew out and flipped the car off the road. It somersaulted seven and a half times, throwing Gus a hundred feet away from the place at which the car finally came to rest. Jesse was thrown clear, too, but the women were still in the car. Suffering from cuts and bruises, Jesse pulled Naomi out of the car first, then took Lena and the seats out as well. Naomi was chilled and in shock, so he placed the seats in the sunshine and laid the women on them. Later he found Gus wandering deliriously on the highway and managed to get him under control. When Naomi regained consciousness, she heard the radio playing and smelled the odor of dripping gasoline. Lena seemed the most seriously injured. Jesse took off his shirt and began to wave it at passing motorists. Finally, he flagged down a woman in a truck filled with children. "You know, this is against the law," she said, "but I'm a Catholic and I can't stand to see anyone suffer."

She took them to nearby Moctezuma, but no doctor was available. They were eventually taken on thirty miles to Villa Ahuamada, where they received emergency treatment from a medical missionary, Dr. Jose M. Acosta, who soon arranged for their transportation on a freight train back to El Paso. While Jesse and Naomi returned to Kentucky, Gus and Lena remained in a hospital for ten days, until they mended sufficiently to make the trip home. Both women had suffered fractured vertebrae and were required to spend several months in casts. To make matters worse, Mexican officials had in the meanwhile confiscated Gus' new Chrysler and would not permit him even to return to the site of the accident to look at the demolished vehicle, nor was he ever allowed to collect the insurance on the automobile.

The Stuarts had a new cause for happiness despite their troubles, a happiness often connected with Lena Wells' risible and risqué tale of "the California earthquake." Throughout their trip, Jesse and Gus had by turns negotiated with desk clerks for the couples' respective rooms, Gus always requesting twin beds consistent with his and Lena's wishes, and Jesse requesting double beds as he and Naomi chose. This good-natured contention got to be a comedy among them; but when their rooms were rocked by a genuine California earthquake one evening, and, as they subsequently learned, Naomi had become pregnant during these days, Gus and Lena joked with the Stuarts: "If you hadn't got up during that earthquake, Jesse, Naomi wouldn't have been in this fix!" She lay in her cast all through the winter and into the spring, nursed by Jesse's youngest sister, Glennis, who by now had returned home from

Lincoln Memorial and received nurse's training at Marting's Hospital in Ironton, Ohio.

By May, as Naomi's pregnancy advanced normally, she exchanged her cast for a brace. Despite the difficulty imposed by a crushed twelfth dorsal vertebrae, she never worried about her condition. "My mother was horrified because I would laugh about things, and would sing. And she'd say, 'Oh, Deane, in that condition how can you?' But I read and Jesse played beautiful music on the Victrola, and I just had the best time. I sewed. I lay there flat on my back. I couldn't have my head on the pillow. I pieced little quilts. I crocheted. . . ." Meanwhile, the news story went out that her back was broken and she would never walk again. Through this ordeal, however, they knew they were going to have a child in August, and were happier than ever. When Gus and Lena teased them over the earthquake, Jesse and Naomi just laughed; and Jesse said, "I wish I could have four instead of one!"

In many if not in all ways, it had been a good year. Twenty-one of his short stories and twenty poems, an average of more than three publications a month, continued to appear in *Southwest Review, Story, Prairie Schooner, Educational Forum, American Mercury, Saturday Review of Literature, Commonweal, Household, Atlantic Monthly, Voices,* and *Progressive Farmer,* among other periodicals. *Esquire* alone had published eight of his stories and poems. His new short-story collection, *Men of the Mountains,* had been released and the reviews were good. The *American Mercury* thought that "Mr. Stuart serves a high quality of mountain brew, distilled from spicy hill lore and honest dialect." The *New Yorker* declared that "these short stories have unity of place and atmosphere, distinction of theme, and great skill in the telling." The *Fort Worth Telegram* saw him as "a consummate artist," who "knows his locale and . . . his people. Probably no other contemporary writer has depicted his section with so much skill and understanding." The *Worcester* (Massachusetts) *Telegram*'s critic said that "everything he writes is tremendously viril . . . His prose . . . [is] often as poetic as his verse, full of lines that are striking and beautiful, but never merely pretty," while the *Montgomery* (Alabama) *Advertiser*'s reviewer perceived in his work "the epochal drama of which classics are made" and the *Oakland* (California) *Tribune* saw in his work "a marvelous picture of the hill people" and for him "a place alongside Mark Twain, Bret Harte, Joel Chandler Harris." Milton Rugoff of the *New York Herald Tribune* thought his work "as authentic as a cornfield in August, as crude as a lean-jawed farmer sweating behind his plow, as fresh as a mountain stream." With such wide critical acceptance, it was small wonder that he had also received the annual award of the American Institute of Arts and Letters at Carnegie Hall, where Stephen Vincent Benét presided as chairman. The award carried a five-hundred-dollar honorarium.

His name and work were growing more familiar to American literary scholarship, too. Lee O. Ramey successfully defended a 271-page M.A. thesis on Jesse's life and work at Ohio University, while at the University of Virginia Blair Dickinson completed a lexicographical master's thesis on the vocabulary of Greenup County as set forth in *Beyond Dark Hills*.[4]

Now the war seemed always with him. In February of 1941, he had received a card from England reading,

Dear Lodger,
Come over soon and help us weather the war . . . Jess Stuart. Best wishes from us both.

Nancy Astor

That same month he had learned that Hamish Brown was stationed as a medical officer at Stromness out on the Orkney Islands; according to his Scottish friend, Hope was now serving as a military nurse. He had both personal and professional reasons for grief when he heard that his good friend and former host, short-story editor Edward J. O'Brien, had died that month following a London bombing raid. Now with the recent Japanese bombing of Pearl Harbor, the war simply came home to him with an official finality. But no matter how much he yearned to get into it, just then he could do little more than think of enlisting; for Naomi's condition took precedence in his life. If their marriage was a beautiful day, having only just begun, it was now threatened by a dark, minatory cloud. By early summer of 1942 he wrote his Vandy classmate Clem Carson, now a private at Keesler Field, Mississippi, on his new stationery as superintendent of the Greenup Independent School District, a job he took for the 1942/1943 school year, explaining, "Our first child will be born in August. . . . That is one reason I've not enlisted in the Army."

Through it all, when he was not farming, lecturing, or running a school, he had kept at his craft. Back in the winter as Naomi had lain abed at the nadir of her condition, over in his corner of the room he had cut loose on the typewriter to revise and complete a richly imagined, partially factual story about their two dogs, the aristocratic Rusty from Connecticut and the spirited fice Jerry-B, who had run away from the Stuarts to live for a while with a nearby moonshiner and partake of his mash. For six and a half days Jesse's typewriter clicked away. An earlier draft of the story had evoked the plaudits of no less an editor than Maxwell Perkins of Scribner's, where Marion Ives, who had been consistently interested in Jesse's work, had continued to read manuscripts. Tactfully navigating through the uneasy waters of publishers' priorities and contractual obligations, Perkins wrote Jesse that "now the problem is what kind of arrangement we can make,—for . . . a publisher cannot do rightly by an author if he has only one book, and nothing to look forward to. If he takes on one book, which is to be followed by others, the situation is altogether different," for then a publisher "can feel that he is 'investing' not only in this one story, but in the author's future, and can act with more foresight." He then put the question directly, "Could we, if we publish this book, hope to publish your later books?" He urged Jesse to write him about this "general matter," assuring him that he had "greatly enjoyed . . . 'Mongrel Mettle.' " Although the two exchanged several letters that year, Jesse with some reluctance decided to fulfill his contract with Dutton. Perkins wrote again, "I knew that you would be loyal . . . and it would be most discreditable on our part if we should try to beguile you . . . or . . . interfere with a mutual confidence presumably existing between you and [Dutton]." Perkins hoped they could see each other in New York on Stuart's next trip, and in November Perkins wrote again, sending him a copy of Scott Fitzgerald's *The Last Tycoon* "because I thought it would interest you to see how he went to work." He hoped that Jesse would come to New York "again before long." Although the letters show that Scribner's desired to do everything honorably possible to bring Stuart into its stable of such distinguished writers as Fitzgerald, Hemingway, and Wolfe, six years would pass before Jesse would break away from Dutton and publish a book with Scribner's.

Among other important literary figures to perceive Stuart's genius was Edgar Lee Masters, in his early seventies when the two became friends in the fall of 1939. "Jesse Stuart blew in on me," he later reminisced, "like a breeze from the hills. He is as full of life as a young colt, and as normal as earth. . . . I have such confidence in him that I would turn him loose in Boston for the rest of his life without any fear that Boston would ruin him." Masters lived in the Chelsea Hotel right across the street from where Jesse usually stayed when he came to New York in those days, at the YMCA located at 215 West 23rd Street; the two got together often when the Kentuckian was there. Masters had a New York girlfriend then, Alice Davis, whom he addressed intimately as "Hen." Before Jesse left New York in November, just after *Trees of Heaven* had been accepted, he confided his and Naomi's secret marriage to Masters and Miss Davis, who responded with an amusing congratulatory card of

Oriental design in a thick envelope; the card depicted a proud rooster with a prominent red comb and wattle stepping out protectively under a tree with his hen. In the elder poet's hand it read,

> For Jesse Stuart and his wife
> We wish a long and happy life.
> Alice Davis
> Edgar Lee Masters
> N.Y.C, 1939

It was to be a happy friendship of mutual admiration, producing a rich correspondence. In late 1941, after Jesse's "New-Ground Corn" was published in *Men of the Mountains*, Masters read the story and wrote that it had given him a definition of genius:

> Genius is a bend in the creek where bright water has gathered, and which mirrors the trees, the sky, and the banks. It just does that because it is there and the scenery is there. Talent is a fine mirror with a silver frame, with the name of the owner engraved on the back.

Masters concluded his letter simply: "I hope you will do lots of stories. They are out of the soil."

Jesse canceled a southern lecture tour in order to be with Naomi until February 1942, while she was still in her cast, but gave three talks in order to pay his way to New York to see his publishers. In New York by early February, he missed Jim Putnam, Maxwell Perkins, Frederick Allen, and Marion Ives, but did see Edgar Lee Masters, Annie Laurie Williams, artist Woodi Ishmael and his wife, Gwyn, and Whit Burnett and Martha Foley. He paid a call on the *Harper's Bazaar* editors, who would publish his short story of snakes and love, "Dawn of Remembered Spring," in their June issue. He broke the news of Naomi's pregnancy to a few New York friends. "It's good news," he wrote Naomi, underlining "*good*" eight times, "so why not?"

It took the birth of Jessica Jane Stuart to get him behind the wheel of their car, Fronnie. He simply had to drive the Plymouth because Naomi was not able to. Proudly he wrote August Derleth of the nine-and-one-half-pound baby, born August 20, 1942, at King's Daughters Hospital in Ashland. She was twenty-one inches long, he boasted, "one of the tallest babies born there in some time." Characteristically self-revealing, he added, "It is a strange feeling to be a father. I drive every day to Ashland to see her."

When Jesse learned the following year that Derleth and Marcia

Masters, Edgar Lee Masters' daughter, were planning to marry, he wrote Augie, "If everything goes through and you marry, if you don't have children I'll be terribly disappointed. It takes a child to make a home." He urged Derleth to read his nine-stanza poem to appear in *Commonweal*, "Poem for My Daughter," revealing the depth of his experience as a father keeping watch over the baby, snug in her quilt, "as if she were percoon in spring / About to burst from earth's warm loamy sheath." The baby is a "daughter of this mountain earth/ For she was born with April in her eyes," and "she is perfect as the leaves." He prays, "Let her know rugged beauty inwardly, / Not artificial beauty second-hand; / Let her be free as the mountain wind is free / To know, observe, and love her native land." Hoping she will have "world and time wherein to dream," he yet realizes, "Too soon she'll know of greater storms than this / When she must be awake to know of life." Ahead he sees her maturation, and expresses what must be the feeling and hope of all caring parents of daughters who ever lived:

> You'll know the joy and sting of love's embrace
> Before your travail on this earth is done.
> Rest now, young brain, in tender brittle growth!
> Be still, small hands, do not clutch for the wind!
> Rest now, for many dreams will come with youth!
> Be frugal with the life you have to spend!

In the same letter he told Derleth that he was 1A in the draft and expected to be inducted by Christmas of 1943. Instead, he would serve as superintendent of the Greenup City Schools until March 1944, when he was sworn into the Navy at Local Board No. 55 in Greenup. Until his induction, for convenience to their work he and Naomi moved with their new daughter into a two-story white frame house on East Main Street in Greenup. There he continued to write upstairs. A new story absorbed him. Long before he wrote *Trees of Heaven* he had known the family to whom he gave the name of Tussie, a prolific tribe of backwoods, fun-loving, dancing, singing mountain folk. He had heard the stories around the Greenup County courthouse, and he had heard such friends as Oscar and Ann Sammons and Opal Rice McKee talk about "the Tussies" and their antics. Opal Rice McKee had heard some of the same stories from World War I on through the 1930s. Her mother owned the Rice Grocery Store near Wurtland, where the family she thought Jesse's stories were based on got their groceries on credit. During World War I, the family had a son in the service, too, and they ran up a bill of more than five hundred dollars. Whenever Mrs. Rice questioned the rising amount, the prototype of Mrs. Tussie always said, "Now, Mrs. Rice, you'll get your money just as sure as God made little green apples," but Mrs. Rice never did get her money.

The talkative Mrs. Tussie had a daughter-in-law, Bessie, who lived with the family; the family, sometimes by the dozens, all lived together. Opal McKee once hired one of the Tussie women for fifty cents a day to do housework, and the woman sang so loudly Mrs. McKee almost brought herself to shut all the windows so the neighbors would not hear her. The head of the family was one George Washington ("Wash") Tussie, who would bring his wife and let her work while he waited outside until she got through. On one Saturday Nannie Tussie brought all the children and her mother as well, and gave them all a bath at Opal McKee's home. Wash as usual was waiting outside for them when they left. "Wash would have had a bath, too," Judge Sammons recounted the story, "but that was too alien to him. The only time he ever got a bath, I think, was when he went swimming."

Near midnight of December 31, 1942, Jesse finished the first draft of a manuscript he called *Inherited Indolence* and stacked up the pages to take downstairs to Deane. "The bells were ringing," he recalled, and "I was crying. I handed it to Deane . . . and Deane read it and laughed."

"I laughed and laughed," she later admitted. "I thought it was funny."

Subsequently Jesse discussed the manuscript with Huntington newswriter Raymond Brewster, who told him that *Inherited Indolence* was a poor title. With the war uppermost in everyone's mind, he suggested instead *Taps for Private Tussie*, and so the book was titled. Its selection as a Book-of-the-Month in 1943 was the incentive for Dutton's throwing Jesse a big party in New York on October 14, when everyone ended up at the Stork Club at three o'clock in the morning, the only time Jesse was ever in the Stork Club. In the years ahead *Taps* would appear in more than fifteen republications, several of them with the distinctively gaunt, angular, shovel-handed mountaineer sketches of Thomas Hart Benton. *Ladies' Home Journal* published a condensed version early in 1944, and copies of a 318-page Armed Services edition were to be found in the libraries of American servicemen all over the world. A three-volume edition in braille was published in Cincinnati, and Geoffrey Bryan read for a seventeen-record issue for the American Printing House for the Blind in Louisville. A condensed pictorial version of F. R. Gruger was distributed to several newspapers by the King Features Syndicate. Softback printings were published by Pocket Books in 1946, by the Paperback Library in 1962, and by Ballantine Books in 1973. Peter Huston

Publishing Company printed an edition in Sydney, Australia, in 1946, and translations appeared in Czechoslovakia, Denmark, Norway, Argentina, and Sweden up through the 1960s. It became the best seller of Jesse's works, and as late as 1978 he commented that he believed he had through the years received from its various sales perhaps as much as a quarter of a million dollars, most of it through the 1940s from the time he went into the Navy until he came out after World War II. On a subsequent lecture tour in California, he and Naomi Deane visited a motion picture set where they met Barbara Stanwyck, Clark Gable, and director Clarence Brown. MGM studios purchased the motion picture rights to *Taps* for fifty thousand dollars, and they were discussing it when Stanwyck told Jesse, "Write some for women," and again, "Write something for me!" During the time Stanwyck was there, as the Stuarts heard, the motion picture people were trying to get together on filming *Taps*. One problem never resolved was the Army's refusal to admit even the possibility of a mistake in identification concerning Private Kim Tussie's body, as Jesse had written it. One current report that got out at the time was that the movie rights had sold for one hundred thousand dollars, but Jesse later denied the accuracy of the figure. "They always give a much bigger figure in the newspaper than the writer ever receives. And after taxes it's much less. . . ." Even so, the overall profits were large that year; he later acknowledged one of his "biggest checks going out in taxes—$86,000."⁵

When he was inducted into the Navy in late March 1944, Jesse was asked in Louisville to appear on a radio program with several other inductees, including an attractive WAVE. A *Courier-Journal* photographer posed Jesse and the WAVE for a candid human-interest shot. He and the WAVE were instructed to smile at each other as if she were proud to put a seaman's cap on his head. Jesse later wrote Naomi Deane, "I was to smile because I was glad to be in the Navy—You'll probably see this picture in the *Journal*."

She certainly did see the picture. Nearly everyone in Greenup saw it because the postmistress, Bessie Morton, known for her inquisitiveness, had clipped the photo out of the paper and put it up in the Riverton Post Office. Miffed at Jesse's seeming familiarity with the WAVE and some thoughtless ribbing at home, Naomi at first refused to write him. When he finally did hear from her April 9, he wrote back reassuringly, "Don't ever get the idea in your head that you are not first in my life . . . above everybody else. I could love you forever." Aware that she had taken a good deal of razzing over the picture, on April 10 he wrote again, "I'm sorry about the picture." He would have objected to it, he explained, but "the extent of my vocabulary at present is "Yes Sir, No Sir, and Aye-Aye Sir." Later in the same letter: "What burns me up about the whole thing is, that people around you, people you have known, would try to tease you and to intimate that the Navy is a place of love—a place to meet women and all of that. The idea is crazy as hell." He then urged her to "tell me for once in a letter how you feel toward me?" As if to provide an object lesson, he wrote,

> I feel that you feel pretty deeply about me—you can be a little jealous and that is a good sign—however, I never want you to be—I just want to live with you, to love you as long as I live. . . . Look at you and get as excited as I did at first and that is the way I am and you know it! . . . And when I see you I want to go straight home with you and see you and then see others later. I love you Deane. And I always feel deeper than I write. . . . Do you love me as I love You[?] Tell me.

By return mail he received four letters from her and replied right away, "I am happy as a lark."

He had been even more homesick after his first leave. Naomi, complaining of insomnia and missing his arm to sleep on, wrote out her feelings; but he refuted her with a lover's protest that spiritually she *always* slept on his arm at night, so he wrote, "You're telling something that is not so for I know that you are no matter where the War Department places me." In moments of epistolary intimacy, he often allowed his words of love to meld with gustatory images producing a synesthesia as striking as, though perhaps more impromptu than, that of Henry Fielding's *Tom Jones:*

> All your wild honey, your wonderful jellies, your good canned peaches, which are wonderful appetizers to this man, cannot take the places of your kisses and your love. My appetite for your love and your kisses is much greater for I'm hungrier for them than . . . for the wonderful jellies you make, the good coffee—the good breakfasts that you prepare. But remember these foods must come with love, so all will work well.

After completing his basic training at Great Lakes and being commissioned Lieutenant j.g. he was sent to Washington, DC, to assume his new duty, listed officially as "Training Literature, D.C.N.O. (Air)." He and other specially assigned members of the "Writers' Unit" were to prepare pamphlets for apprenticed seamen in training, officers, and other personnel for the Navy and armed services in the United States and abroad. John Bird, editor of *Country Gentleman* and the *Saturday Evening Post,* recalls meeting the famous Kentucky writer shortly after Jesse's arrival in the capital city. Returning in the fall to Washington after being stationed some months at Pensacola, Bird had driven through the Appalachians, ablaze with autumn coloring, and reported for duty when his skipper, Larry Wadkin, asked about how the trip went.

"Fine!" he replied. "The mountains were beautiful. They looked just like Jesse Stuart writes about them."

Wadkin grinned and pointed to a stocky Lieutenant j.g. whom Bird had not seen before, then said, "John Bird, meet Jesse Stuart. He's just joined our unit."

The "bullpen," Bird recalled, "was a den of satirists and cynics," writers like Robert Taylor of the *New Yorker,* who possessed "a biting, sometimes cruel wit"; Roark Bradford of *Green Pastures* fame, who asserted he was "the best horse-tail braider of the Confederacy and practiced on the Venetian blind cords"; and Hannibal Coons of Hollywood, "who believed in numerology."

Jesse found Washington crowded and the food poor. Apartments were so scarce he had to delay plans to bring Naomi and Jane; instead he watched papers and enlisted his friends in looking for him as well. He wrote Naomi, "An apartment here is as hard for me to get . . . as it is for me to write a novel." Repeatedly he wrote her of the problem, but her responses caused him to enter in his daily journal, "I think she doubts me in my letters."

For nearly a month he looked for an appropriate apartment, and finally found one in a new complex in Greenway, across the Anacostia River, complete with a grassy treed area for small children, a playground of scooters, slides and swings, "a small city within a large city." On September 29, he took a brief leave to go to Greenup and get Deane and Jane. They returned to Washington in their Plymouth, "old Fronnie," over mountainous Highway 60 through the country around White Sulphur Springs and Lewisburg, West Virginia, where the sunless sky of the Blue Ridge Mountains reminded him of Scotland. When they reached their new home in Washington, among the things Jesse unloaded from their car were ten pounds of sugar, four pounds each of bacon and butter, nine dozen eggs, one ham, five pounds of onions, one bushel of apples, an electric iron, an alarm clock, four cans of tuna, ten cans of baby food, four cans of Eagle Brand Milk, one can of mushrooms and one of fruit juice, many seasonings, one bushel of Irish potatoes and a half-bushel of sweet potatoes, twenty-six quarts of peaches, six quarts each of blackberries, beets, canned pork sausage, and tomatoes, six pints each of raspberries and cherries, four pints of blackberry jam, four quarts of sweet pickles, six bottles of tomato relish, fourteen glasses of wild plum jelly, eighteen glasses of blackberry jelly, thirty-four glasses of peach jelly, and dishes and silver for six. All these vegetables, fruits, and jellies had come from their farm, where Deane had canned them. When he got the last of it into their apartment he sat down and mopped the sweat from his brow.

The next evening Deane welcomed Jesse home to a clean apartment. "I think this is a beautiful spot," she said. "I'm glad to be here." Then they sat down to a delicious supper of fried ham, mashed potatoes, hot tea, good salad, jelly, butter, and hot rolls. The savory food brought back memories of W-Hollow. The next day they drove up into Maryland and found "a few wild flowers and autumn-coloring leaves" to bring back to their apartment. And they discovered

little roads all along the highway leading back into a dense undergrowth . . . back to sand pits and timber woods I figured . . . yes, back to a few lonely shacks. . . . And we found a Maryland country schoolhouse that appealed to us since it looked like so many schoolhouses in Kentucky . . . battered paintless sides with siding nailed across one paneless window. Thought: It's not only in Kentucky. It's in many of the states where people put more premium on public privies, barns, garages than they do schoolhouses. . . . A schoolhouse where people send their children . . . to obtain a little knowledge is the place for sad neglect in so many of our states. This is something, above all buildings that should be made inviting to the youth of America.

That fall he saw Robert Penn Warren again. In September Jesse visited him and his wife, but "Cinina" was in bed. "I didn't ask her what was wrong," he wrote in his journal, instead reflecting on the couple's hospitality at Vanderbilt, "the many good steaks we had eaten in [their] cottage together . . . twelve years ago." Time had changed all of them but he thought it had changed Red the least. "If anything, he looked younger and in better physical condition than I had ever seen him." A few days later he and Warren met in the Library of Congress where Jesse spent an hour in a recording session reading "Three Hundred Acres of Elbow Room" and thirty-two poems, about fourteen of them from his forthcoming *Album of Destiny*.

On Thursday, October 5, Red Warren picked Jesse up at 19th and Constitutional Avenue, and they drove off for lunch at the Willard Restaurant. They drank a glass of beer apiece. For a short time they joined a dark-complexioned Purdue English professor, Herbert Muller, who had done a book on the modern novel, but returned to their table when their lunches were ready and began talking about the old days at Vanderbilt, figures of their mutual past, and short stories. During their conversation they discussed Jesse's new volume of poetry, *Album of Destiny*. Warren observed, "It's the better of your two books. It's decidedly better and shows vast improvements." In their long conversation following, Jesse seemed to think that Warren "forced me into the lead in conversation and drew me out." He told Warren many things, but "many things I didn't tell." Jesse was an hour late returning to work, and Warren insisted on taking him back to the Navy Building. "No," Jesse insisted in turn, "I'll catch a taxi," but Warren's persistence won out and he dropped Jesse off within a few blocks of his destination.

He read Kay Boyle's *Avalanche*. Like Edward J. O'Brien, Jesse had always been "a great admirer of her work"; but this time he found she had crafted "a very weak ending for [the] novel." He was downcast to learn that his Uncle Jesse was leaving the farm back home. The situation worried him with only his mother and father left to take care of the farm; neither was able to do any kind of rigorous farm work. James had left schoolteaching in Michigan and become a gunnery officer in the Navy. He wrote Jesse from a motel in San Diego, where he was preparing to embark for the Pacific Theater—first to Pearl Harbor, then, he guessed, to "somewhere in the Marianas." Concernedly he ended,

> Let me give you some advice. If you want to get to sea it's very good but remember there has to be several officers on the land too. They're needed there. You've got a little girl, a wife and Mom and Dad depend a lot on you besides. Just don't be too hasty. Put in a little time at a shore station to see how you like it before thinking about sailing. Keep that desk and typewriter for awhile. I have proof that you're still adept in the mastery of music and thought of works in the form of poetry. I've read the first 20 pages in *The Album of Destiny*. . . .

In the months to follow James would see enough action for both of them—at Guam, Bougainville, Tacloban, Lingayen Gulf, and Okinawa. Gunnery officer aboard an LST-625, his crew would be credited with downing three kamikaze planes—one in Lingayen Gulf and two at Okinawa. Jesse would remain ashore and do his part, producing in a dozen ways. On October 16, for example, he donned flying gear and parachute and with Commander Winston flew to Winston-Salem, North Carolina, where he took part in a war fund drive. Their hosts were Jim and Mollie Hanes, and in the large sitting room of their mansion Jesse took a glass of wine and reflected on the fact that "I could have told [them] that I had worn and I suspected Comdr. Winston had too, underclothes made by Jim Hanes' mills." During the flight Jesse closed the cover over him "due to the terrific beating I was getting from the wind." High in the air he saw Commander Winston "rock himself on his seat and shake the plane and get my attention . . . then . . . point to something below and smile. He was like an eagle that ruled the skies. I've never seen a man as happy as he was." On December 13, Jesse spoke on poetry before nearly a hundred people at the Coolidge Auditorium in the Congressional Library, encountering the worst lighting arrangements of his career, which "nearly put my eyes out." Meanwhile, he had difficulty writing "the Navy way," as John Bird recalled. "It always came out Jesse Stuart." In late November Jesse's superior, Captain Hollingsworth, called him into his office and complimented *Taps for Private Tussie*. "You have a good style and instead of our trying to convert you to our regular style, we['re] going to convert the Navy's style to your style." Jesse was "amazed," but went to work on his new character Uncle Kim Tussie. By January 22, 1945, he saw the first product of his labor in the *Naval Aviation News*. For the first time in months he experienced "a tiny feeling of accomplishment." Then "the feeling surged in me until I walked proudly up and down the hall."

On his own time he worked through an early draft of *Daughter of the Legend*, then titled *Look Down from Heaven*, but when he took it with him to New York in November Dutton's rejected it. He did not seem greatly concerned, but others wanted his work. Hallie and Whit Burnett took him to dinner at an Armenian restaurant around the corner from Whit's office at 432 4th Avenue. Both editors liked his story "Thanksgiving Hunter," to appear in Whit's anthology *Time to Be Young*. Jesse had revised it eight times, thinking he may have "taken the sap from it with too much revision," but Whit said, "It just fits the picture." A few days later Lena and Gus Voiers visited them in Washington and together they toured the capitol, where they talked with Senators Alben Barkley and "Happy" Chandler. Chandler played with Jane, although she would not let him kiss her.

In late November Jesse had represented the Navy in Boston. It always seemed to rain when he was in Boston, and that time it stormed. He was a guest of Henry Lee Shattuck, up twelve stories high on Beacon Hill. Shattuck was the noted philanthropist who had financed the college educations of five deserving students Jesse had recommended to him, after the Harvard-connected Bostonian had read and been impressed with Jesse's own example in *Beyond Dark Hills*. While Jesse read Irish poetry from Shattuck's collection, thinking, "I never heard such a wind blowing as . . . whipped around the top of this building . . . the sound of the wind and the Atlantic," he heard his host come in out of the cold. Glad to see Jesse, Shattuck brought out a bottle of seventeen-year-old whiskey. "He was cold and I was cold . . . ," Jesse recorded, "so I took a swig with him before I went to bed." The next morning Shattuck had breakfast sent up to the apartment, where they ate scrambled eggs and bacon at a card table. Afterward they sat, talked and smoked while waiting for the storm to diminish, then together walked out across the Commons, where Jesse caught a taxi to the Copley Plaza. There he spoke to "a very intelligent book group" of about four hundred women and was "called up for applause 5 times." The next morning before catching the 8:45 train to New York, Jesse was Mr. Shattuck's breakfast guest at the Union Club.

By March 1945, he was transferred to the staff of the *Naval Aviation News*, not even having to change his office in the process, continuing work on his column as well as on other assignments through the duration. As the war began to wind down in August, the staff of the house organ was reduced. One of Jesse's remaining duties was to attend the Boston Book Fair in October and to take part in the program. There Jesse looked up his good friend Shattuck at his office on Federal Street, and nothing would do the man but to be host again. Shattuck had to be at his brother's place to help entertain the Chinese ambassador, but "he gave me the key to his apartments and sent a note down to the Union Club where I was to eat." After breakfast the next day with Shattuck at the Union Club, Jesse went on to Symphony Hall, where he spoke along with Clifton Fadiman and Donald Ogden Stewart. Jesse got to know both men and the latter's wife, Ella Winters, who impressed him most as the former wife of Lincoln Steffans. He also met Andria Locke Langley, author of *A Lion Is in the Streets*, whom he found "full of life and real." Upon being questioned concerning the nature of his reception in Boston, Jesse answered his commander ingenuously, "I got more applause than anyone." In early November he received the blessing of his superior, Commander Ron Richardson, to substitute for ailing J. Donald Adams before the Virginia Poetry Society at Lynnhaven, Virginia. Later that month he swung energetically into what proved to be his favorite assignment as a Navy writer, a special project entitled "Recovery of Submerged Aircraft," which would absorb most of his remaining work days in Washington.

Great historical events, of course, stippled Jesse's seventeen months in the capital city. Often heavy casualties of battles were reported daily on the radio—for Iwo Jima, Jesse noted in his daily journal for March 16, 1945, "4,189 killed, 19,938 wounded." On March 25, accompanied by Deane and Jane, he saw the Washington cherry trees in bloom and was haunted again with mutability: "By next Sunday the blossoms would be gone. A shame they couldn't last all summer. But all beauty must fade." In young April their neighbor Mrs. Hefron rushed in without a greeting, announcing, "The President is dead." Commentators spoke of Roosevelt's death, Jesse noted, "then would follow dirges of wailing music . . . old religious hymns. Negroes marched and sang. Women fainted." The Hefrons came again to their apartment, then such friends as the Lavines, "whose faces were pale as chalk over the shock of F.D.R.'s death." The next day, Friday the thirteenth, he remarked "wild stories floating over Washington . . . how a negro had seen F.D.R.'s ghost not far from the White House." Although he recorded "Washington in hysterics and confusion over F.D.R.'s death," he observed with purposeful emphasis "Americans in the outskirts of Berlin." By late April, Mussolini was shot, "dragged in the streets, hung by the heels like a hog swinging from a scaffold," and Hitler was reported dying. "More good news," Jesse exulted. Washingtonians received word on August 6 that the atomic bomb had been dropped on Hiroshima, and the next day the newspapers were filled with details of devastation the world had not previously known. That Tuesday evening Jesse and Naomi went to the Allies Inn for dinner and saw *Valley of Decision* at the Loew's Theatre. In one more week the final peace announcement came from President Truman, and Jesse reverted to his natural present tense: "Washington goes wild; Train whistles blow . . . automobiles hon[k] their horns to an incessant roar. People kiss on the streets. Officers' bars are torn from their shirt collars! And children parade all over Washington . . . bands of them with a drummer and a flag bearer in front. Mrs. Hefron gives Jane a drum and she beats it and joins a little children's parade." The writer on all occasions, he added to his daily entry, "Sold a story, Battle of Bees, to *Tomorrow*."

While most of the bullpen found the Navy mindset an "appalling waste of manpower," devotion to rank at the very least "distasteful," and made their objections known to each other, Jesse, at least in the beginning, "came on as a super-patriot, respectful of authority . . . and a bit naive." Such was the sardonic misreading of his open nature, uncomplaining in the face of difficulties, and his natural enthusiasm and self-confidence. In fact, Jesse complained repeatedly of the dullness of his Navy duties, but silently, as his journal reveals. Rather than gripe out loud, he offset much of his frustration with his own writing projects, skillfully salvaging time for them under the noses of his superiors. In time the bullpen came to know him. Jesse entertained them "hugely with his stories of his own adventures, told with his innocents-abroad slant." Once he was telling about "the scare some of the people down home got when the great northern lights came to that section for the first time." Lieutenant Commander Watkin "started laughing and laughed all the way up to the office. He thought it was the funniest thing he'd ever heard." Jesse had never thought of it as being so funny, but the incident put him to work on a novel in March 1945. He took time out from developing the characters of this tour de force he would call *Foretaste of Glory* to write an introduction for poet Byron Herbert Reece's *Ballad of the Bones and Other Poems*. Jesse was optimistic about his own work, and in early April wrote his Missouri friend Charles Bess that he had three books to be published—the story collection *Tales from the Plum Grove Hills* and the novels *Hie to the Hunters* and *Foretaste of Glory*. Meanwhile, he received a $200 check from a piece on Grandfather Hilton for *Reader's Digest*'s "Life in these United States." The "northern lights" characters fascinated him so much that he worked on them whenever he could during his Navy time. Once he was nearly caught, but did not lie. He scrambled to a drawer and grabbed a copy of an Uncle Kim Tussie column he had handy and told the commander, "Sir, this in the type-writer is not finished. This is a finished product I'm showing you." He worked on *Foretaste* nearly every remaining day of March and into early April, revised it through May, and then wrote the opening chapter on June 15, the most difficult of the chapters to write—indeed "the hardest of writing I have ever tried to do," for it had been five years since he had seen the northern lights. His mood was one of gloom when he mailed the manuscript to Dutton June 21, for he had "a very depressed feeling about the whole affair, time wasted and energies spent for nothing." By late July he decided to require pay for reprinting of his stories in an-thologies, whereas formerly he had let editors reprint them free of charge. The matter was made clear to him by his experience with "Uncle Fonse Laughed," for which *Esquire* had originally paid him $125; now reprinted in *The Bedside Esquire* on the basis of a 1/101 of the earnings, he had received in two years over $800 in royalties. By the end of the month, he had planned no fewer than five novels.

Dutton accepted *Foretaste of Glory*, and by late October he was at work on the proofs. During this time he received a letter from Governor Willis asking him, so he wrote in his journal, "to come to Kentucky and accept the Presidency of Murray State Teachers' College." The offer stirred him as had other opportunities: that of the British movies in London back in 1937, later a BBC program offer, and a radio program offer after a trip to Hollywood. About the time *Taps* was published, as he later wrote, "I was offered a thousand dollars a week to be a script writer in Hollywood." He managed a brief return trip to Kentucky, and after seeing his folks went on to Frankfort, where he was an overnight guest in the governor's mansion. He was served "a wonderful breakfast with plenty of bacon" in his room.

Governor Willis and he discussed the college presidency in Willis' office, where Jesse looked over the list of applicants. Before he was through talking with the governor he had decided against accepting. "It is for someone else to bicker in petty politics and not for me," he wrote in his journal. "With two Republican regents and two Democrat regents and the Supt. of Public Instruction the deciding vote," he saw himself in a holding position inevitably to be ousted by the caprice of politics. Furthermore, "I didn't like the idea of living in the Mississippi Delta Country. Give me high ground." He would also be offered a creative writing position at Columbia University, where he had lectured, but even though he was interested in accepting it, "my native land . . . pulled me back every time I tried to escape." Behind these opportunities he wisely perceived that his country was "my fountainhead, my source, my inspiration, my everything. These people didn't want me. They wanted my land through me." He later wrote, "I could not exploit my heritage."

During the Washington months he and Naomi Deane kept their personal and family lives with Jane comfortably regular and active in their home away from home, despite the demands of a busily involved social life as well. They often went to the National Theatre to see such live productions as *The Student Prince,* Burl Ives in *Sing Out Sweet Land,* the musical *Marinka,* and *The Late George Appley.* They entertained several times each month and took such visitors as George and Nancy Curry to plays like *Dark of the Moon.* Jesse's favorite of the year was Ralph Bellamy and Ruth Hussey in *State of the Union,* "as good acting as I have yet to see at the National." In early March they went to Greenup to spend a rainy furlough visiting relatives and friends, and the last day of February Jesse drove by Shower's Jewelry Store to pick up a diamond for Deane, in time for her to wear it home. Jesse "had always had in mind to get her one, because she wanted it, when I got the money." Before they left Washington, he received in the mail two twenty-dollar checks from *Saturday Review* and *Progressive Farmer,* likely for his poem "Alien Atolls" in the former and his article "Sheep Are Great Sprout Killers" in the latter. Near-flood conditions spurred their return to Washington, where they were "glad to be back . . . after all criticisms," at home in their little apartment in Greenway, unpacking wet clothes. It was a leave they would never forget. About a month later his piece of homespun satire, "Washington Is a Swell Place," appeared in the *Southwest Review*. The day after seeing Burl Ives in *Sing Out Sweet Land* on May 14, they left sweltering Washington with picnic basket in hand and found "quietness of the green natural wooded hills where the ivy was in bloom." Jesse later wrote, "Enjoyed the wind in the leaves more than I did some of the music in *Sing Out Sweet Land*." In June they toured the Mellon Art Gallery, where they enjoyed the old English and Dutch paintings, "and many of the American paintings . . . especially those done in the 19th and 20th centuries." After peace came, they missed the new musical *Oklahoma* at the National Theatre, where a thousand people on the streets were waiting for the remaining tickets, and instead went to the Museum of National History "and didn't regret it."

As autumn began Bill and Elizabeth Moses visited Jesse and Naomi, and together with Jane they went to Annapolis to see the sights. Jane got carsick, but all in all "it was a good day." They invited their friends to dinner, and Moses recalled that "the meal was delicious," especially the W-Hollow sweet potatoes, a "medium-sized" variety, Moses recalled; he could not testify "that the variety in question" was "superior to all others, but Jesse thought it was . . . and had . . . a supply . . . from Kentucky." Moses remembered, "We had cocktails . . . of the kind that come prepared in a bottle, Jesse professing ignorance of cocktail mixing."

That October of 1945 they explored antique shops, among others those in Fairfax, Virginia, where, Jesse observed, "the countryside was honestly beautiful." In one shop Naomi purchased a glass pitcher. As they dined at the only restaurant open in the town, the fond parents watched their three-year-old as a cat came through the window. "Jane fed the cat and laughed at her red tongue." Jesse and Naomi smiled at Jane, dined, and listened to Roy Acuff's records on the jukebox. In less than an hour they were back in their apartment. "It had been a wonderful day."

In the midst of life's simple and profound joys occurred a simple and profound tragedy. After Jane, they had wanted more children. By August that year the hope had seemed realistic. "Jesse thought the war was going to end," Naomi recalled, "and we knew I was older and we shouldn't wait." They had sought the advice of "a good Navy doctor"— a Dr. Jacobs, as Jesse recollected. When Naomi Deane was about three months pregnant, she began having difficulty and called the doctor. With doctors in short supply, the receptionist gave her an appointment "in two or three weeks, and until then they wouldn't let him see me." Instead, she went to her neighbor's doctor, and through him to his wife's gynecologist, a Dr. Quinn, who had her admitted to George Washington Hospital. As in her previous pregnancy, Naomi's sister-in-law Glennis was on hand to see the crisis through. Jesse returned from a lecture at the Virginia Poetry Society, a commitment he had accepted for an ailing J. Donald Adams, just in time to receive the news that she had hemorrhaged heavily and was unconscious. Her life would be saved, but the baby was lost. The bad news "threw me into a state of despondency," he recorded, but he busied himself with the nearest duties. Daily he made fifty-minute trips back and forth across Washington to visit his wife. Once he took along Jane who had been fretting to see "my Moma," although Jesse was not supposed to. "I took her up to see Deane and she cried and Jane cried." When he brought Naomi home to an immaculate apartment on November 25, thanks to Glennis and Jesse's earlier hard work in cleaning it, "Jane went wild" and "didn't want anybody to talk to Deane." In the next hours and days friends came too often and stayed too long, and the phone rang far too much; but Glennis saw them through it all until she herself fell ill. By early December, however, both were well enough to prepare dinner; and by December 9 Jesse took Deane and Jane to the Capitol Building where Lieutenant Art Schoni directed them through a picture-making session with their daughter, despite the very cold weather.

The last Christmas in Washington was happy because people were leaving the Navy Department all day with bags packed for home and the holidays, and that meant Jesse's turn would be coming at any time. Even the weather for driving home looked better than they had hoped. On Thursday, December 27, he received a call to pick up his orders. Typically, he worked until midnight to finish a final bit of Navy work on the salvage article he had begun for Commander Richardson. The next day he went early to the Separation Center. By one in the afternoon he was out of the Navy, but did not escape "the dry lecture about what to expect when returned to civilian life." The next day he expressed twelve boxes home and had the car serviced. On December 30 they packed old Fronnie to capacity, bade their neighbors Ed and Ellie Hefron farewell, and started for Kentucky. When they drove down familiar old Minnesota Avenue for the last time as residents of Washington, DC, Jesse noticed that "Deane shed a few tears."[6]

After seeing friends in Greenup, they drove Fronnie home to W-Hollow. "Lucky for us the ground, though it was plenty rough with deep chugholes and ruts, was frozen hard enough to hold the car up and I drove all the way home." It was "home again in mid-winter. And the hills were dark, bleak and cold." They found the house molded and moth-eaten. They cleaned and kept fires going. He had to walk over the ridge path to Greenup and bring a load of groceries home; he hurried to beat the darkness of the short winter day. The next day they cleaned and dried the books in front of the living room fireplace. Receiving his first mail in a long time from the Riverton Post Office on the tenth of January, he found that "Nest Egg" had sold in England for eight guineas and two shillings. Showers of winter rain, he wrote, "whipped the dark, desolate barren timber on the hills around us with an unmerciful lashing." In the weeks to follow during that first winter when the war was over, the roads were "slick as freshly peeled pawpaw bark," and the W-Hollow Road was slickest of all.

With friends like Bob Hillman to help him, he went to work in Coonden Hollow and in the middle of January cleared about one acre of sprouts. He cleaned the powerhouse and recharged the batteries to supply the house's electricity. A foxhunt passed within ten yards of him and he saw a beautiful chase of thirty or more hounds. Among the hunters were such old friends and denizens of the county as Charlie Bates, Glen Hilton, Kenneth Harper, Ed Howard, Ivan Nelson, and George and Ralph Alexander. In late January he avoided, as usual, the winter hog butchering, admitting in his journal, "I'd seen the hog, had known it, fed it and I didn't want to see it killed."

By February 1946 he was lecturing as far north as Michigan. There he discovered Owosso, near "rich dark onion lands . . . one of the prettiest towns I'd yet seen." And there he found James Oliver Curwood's home, whose books he had read in high school, and Thomas Dewey's home "on the top floor of an old garage or store . . . not anything very sumptious [sic] but certainly a palace compared to my one-room birthplace." The next day he received "a great ovation" at Thomas Dewey's old high school. Later, at Lake Odessa High School, he autographed about two hundred books until "my hand got very tired." He went home again by way of Kent, Ohio, where he renewed acquaintance with old Navy friend Nickie Cerri, who had lived in the apartment under the Stuarts in Washington. Cerri was now teaching in the language department of the university there.

An eastern trip with Naomi Deane through Washington to New York followed with lectures, conferences with publishers, and more plans with the Feakins Lecture Bureau. He lunched as the guest of William B. Feakins at Town Hall on February 20, and his boss talked about how hard he had worked all his life, "said he'd never take a vacation." In

Washington Jesse had taken Naomi Deane back to the Navy gynecologist, Dr. Jacobs, who ran tests and then told her that in all probability if she had not had the accident in 1941 and lain in a cast during a large part of her pregnancy, she would not have carried Jane to birth.

Soon Jesse was back home writing again, busy on stories, including "Lap of Destiny" and "More Fun Than a Circus." In early March he received a fifty-dollar check from *Saturday Review of Literature* for his essay "Lesson in a Liberal Education." By St. Patrick's Day Deane and Jane were hunting trailing arbutus, the first spring flower to bloom, along the steep hill across the creek from the house. He was farming, doing a dozen chores—he trimmed cedar, cut brush and piled it, and carried off dead broom-sage. He paid men to grade the road, while he burned brush, checked fields, and with his father and Uncle Jesse de-horned castrated cattle. He worked on a story he called "The Muddy Road." He spent time with his financial adviser, Calvin Clarke, in Portsmouth, Ohio, and stopped by Martings Bookstore to autograph books. On March 28, he received surprising word of Mr. William B. Feakins' death and took time to marvel that he had eaten lunch with him at Town Hall in New York City not much more than a month before. Sorry at his passing, Jesse speculated, "Now, he will take a vacation . . . a long vacation, with or without pay."

Jesse planted potatoes and sugar corn in the garden. He moved earth, a hundred wheelbarrow loads, to open a cellar and fill in the yard and raise the low ground by the creek. He worked so hard on the farm that his legs were very stiff and his hands were sore—"I can hardly touch the typewriter keys."

In late April he and Deane took a trip through Harrogate, Tennessee, visited Lincoln Memorial University, and continued to the Book Fair at Atlanta, Georgia. His chapel talk at his alma mater got "a wonderful reception," he thought, and he enjoyed talking with President Robert Kincaid and his college speech teacher, Earl Hobson Smith. At Miller's Bookstore in Knoxville, he autographed over a hundred copies of *Foretaste of Glory* and other books, and in Chattanooga relished the pleasure of seeing college chum and fellow writer and athlete Nick Carter and his wife, Gillie, once more. In Atlanta he met novelist James Street and "Low-Man-on-the-Totem-Pole" H. Allen Smith, both "quite a pair of small men." He was impressed by Street and soon grew fond of him, but did not think Smith was nearly as funny as his publisher thought. Jesse appeared on the platform with such speakers as John Mason Brown, and he met such personages in the publishing world as bridge expert

Ely Culbertson, finding him "like the article I had once read about him in the *American Mercury*, an ego-maniac."

He began writing again in mid-May, working on stories: "How Sportsmanship Came to Carver College," "Old Alec," and "Tackie." Proofs of *Tales from the Plum Grove Hills* arrived on May 18, and that fall when the book was published, he wrote in the first advance copy,

At Home

Sept. 25th 1946

To Deane: You will remember that you and I in our happy days together have gone over these stories, dammed [sic] them, laughed over them and sent them away hoping. . . . Half of these titles you've given the stories herein—And while we sit before this open fire, listening to good music, living in and loving this little house that you have Dammed [sic], it is more than a pleasure to write these words for you.

Woo! Woo!

Jesse—

In the accolade that followed the book's publication in September, one response that probably meant most to Jesse was Donald Davidson's, who commended him for succeeding

in your own way, which asks no odds of anybody, and which comes from a kind of knowledge and belief that are sadly lacking in many writers nowadays. So much of what I read, here and there, leaves me with the impression that the authors have been buying literary vitamins to try to make up for their lack of either knowledge or beliefs. But all you need to do is to let your bucket down into the old Kentucky well, the well that never runs dry, and up comes the stuff of life again; plenty of it; and the vitamins don't need to be added.

Davidson praised the volume, writing, "and your opening story. 'Another April' is unbeatable. You have wrought better than you may realize in that story. It belongs at the top." Davidson later included "Another April" in the third edition of his widely known college text *American Composition and Rhetoric*. Whit Burnett also reprinted the story in his 1942 collection of outstanding stories. Reflecting on the piece inspired by Grandfather Hilton, who had just before his death developed the habit of talking to an ancient turtle, the author said, "This sort of a thing haunts me when a ruthless dynamic sort of a human being . . . is calmed enough by the passing of time to sit and talk with a wrinkled-neck terrapin. Furthermore, there is something to man's associations with earth and the trees, plowing the rugged soil for a scanty livelihood—these are enduring things . . . as solid and substantial as stone."

Especially since the publication of *Foretaste of Glory* the year before, conflicts with local people had risen from time to time, eventually causing him to write an article, "My Book Made My Town Mad." By the late spring of 1946, while Naomi Deane was shopping on the mezzanine of Parson's Department store in Ashland while Jesse was waiting down on the main floor, three young women looking from the upper floor to the author below pointed him out as "the man who had ruined Kentucky." Deane was upset, but Jesse told her "to pay no attention to all this nonsense coming from three silly girls. What the hell did they know about writing of Kentucky[?]"

Through June he tried to begin a novel, but farm work and the need to settle his taxes took most of his time. He figured that he was a thousand dollars in the red on the farm and got nothing from it but the joy of working on it. Yet "everytime I started talking about selling," he jotted in his journal, "Dad started getting red in the face. Farm certainly in the red. Disgusted."

With maps in hand Jesse and Naomi took Jane with them on his July lecture tour that year through Ohio to Claire, Michigan, and then into the upper peninsula for "a beautiful brief voyage across the sky-blue water" to Manistique. Driving along Lake Superior toward Marquette, they camped along the way and had a fine lake-trout dinner cooked on an open fire under the tall pines; in his journal he painted the scene: "the constant sweep of wind in the tall pines, a swish-swish music akin to the lapping of lake water along the shore. . . . And it was good to hear." He spoke through Iowa, and they returned through Detroit on July 19 and drove over the Ambassador Bridge into Canada to Chatham, a pretty town where they got in for the night just before a hard thunderstorm came. At Windsor they ate inch-thick steaks and later, as he wrote, "we rejoiced to start for the States below us." At rest in a tourist home in Sandusky, Ohio, he recorded, "I dreamed about home in the night."

Agent and friendly critic Marion Ives continued to sell stories for him, and upon his return he made the pleasant discovery that "How Sportsmanship Came to Carver College" had sold to *Esquire* for $300 and "Old Alec" to *Country Gentleman* for $400. Folding back into life in

W-Hollow, he sometimes dropped his mother off at neighborhood Baptist churches, while he and Naomi Deane fell into the pattern of attending the Greenup Methodist Church. Sometimes he attended Sunday School as well; yet in time he would feel, as he would put it, "*beyond* members in my own church. Maybe that isn't right, but that's the way I feel. I don't mean to down-rate anybody. I think Martin Luther got beyond his church; I think people can rise *beyond* the church." Self-chidingly, he would add, "*I try my best to be dogmatic, but I can't be!*"

The farm was always with him, and when he was not farming or lecturing, he wrote. Yet he took time to visit with relatives and friends, usually at his home rather than at theirs. In early August 1946, he and Naomi drove over the county, picnicked, and stopped by James and Betty's place on Raccoon Road, not far from W-Hollow; the birth of their first child was imminent, and they talked an hour before Jesse and Naomi went on home. At home Jesse wrote in every room in the house—there were books in every room, too—but he preferred as weather allowed to get off by himself in the smokehouse facing Shinglemill Creek where he kept his growing files of correspondence, stacks of publications, and no small part of his library. A check for $150 came from *Household* for "The Muddy Road," a story Marion Ives neither liked nor had been able to place. He did not expect anyone to mention his birthday that year, but at the dinner table August 8, Deane gave him a box of candy, Jane presented a tobacco pouch, and long-time friend Bob Hillman produced a pipe and can of Prince Albert pipe tobacco. And so another birthday came—his fortieth—to him "a constant and grim reminder" of the brevity of life, which haunted him when he wanted to do so much and live so long; life seemed simply all too short to build the kind of heaven on earth of which he believed himself capable.

The remainder of that year of peace was largely farming, road work, and lecturing, although he did more significant writing than he thought. He purchased pipe for the W-Hollow Road and paid for much of the repair himself, since his good Republican friends had told him the county was without road construction funds to do the job. Repeated frustrations with the project led to his composition of the short story "Road No. One," published the next year in *Pic*. Jesse repeatedly experienced the conflict of wanting to write but being too distracted to do much of it. "Couldn't write a poem though I had moods to do so," he explained in his daily journal. "Too many things to do on this farm . . . destroyed all poetic moods." And there were too many uninvited visitors dropping by. One weekend he yearned to put pen to paper, but Lawrence Bowling, an English instructor at Yale, was waiting for him at the gate one evening. Because the hour was late, Bowling stayed overnight, and the next day, perhaps unwittingly, he got caught in the eye of Jesse's stormy frustration. "Wherever I went . . . and how I did want to write . . . Lawrence was with me. He'd suggest things that he planned to write and asked me my opinion and when I'd tell him they weren't any good, then he would argue. If he hadn't been my unexpected guest, I would have asked him why he asked me in the first place. And I wanted to tell him there was the man that always talked about writing something . . . and there was the 'doer' who didn't talk about them but did them and that I was one of the fellows. . . . I talked after the story was written . . . did it and talked. A very miserable day . . . and Lawrence went on to Wurtland."

In late August he wrote in rapid succession "a hot article" entitled "Land of the Sacred Fox" and short stories "Slipover Sweater" and "Going Down the Mountain." Then for days he was too restless to sit at his typewriter and so continued to work on the farm. "Couldn't write a line no matter how hard I tried," he noted on August 17. "Found myself in a mental depressive state. Worked on farm." Yet things were still moving in the literature and in the land that had become the twin cores of his life. The electric line for W-Hollow was surveyed in early September by the Kentucky–West Virginia Power Company's crew to bring light into the valley darkness. "How glad we were to see them," he wrote. Marion Ives sold "Tackie" to *Woman's Day* for $500 and "When the End Comes" to the new veterans' magazine *Salute* for $200. In late September, Henry Lee Shattuck arrived at W-Hollow in time to see the "pasture fields . . . beautiful in their autumn colors." Little more than a year before Jesse had written the Bostonian thanking him for his hospitality and asking permission to use a Shattuck family anecdote as a basis for a short story. Shattuck had replied right away, recapitulating the family story of the 1830s and how his grandfather, probably a medical student at the time, had delivered a body by sleigh from Boston to Hanover, New Hampshire, where there was an extreme shortage of cadavers for dissection—an unusual present from one surgeon to another. Jesse had immediately written and revised the story, but had not yet been able to place it. Now having a chance to return something of Shattuck's generous hospitality, Jesse took him first to Greenup High School and the Plum Grove hills on a tour of his poet's world. The next day, with Naomi and Jane along, they picnicked at Anglin Cemetery, went up Lost Creek and over to Keyhoe, then progressed down to Tygart to Warnock, stopping to spend a little time with James and Betty on Raccoon Road. From there, they drove along the winding course of the Little Sandy, turned in at Womack Hollow and came full circle to the Stuarts' home, where they had supper before Jesse took Shattuck to his train in Ashland. Within the week James dropped by to announce the wonderful news that Jesse's nephew, James Stephen Stuart, had arrived at 8:30 P.M. on Thursday, October 3. And then James spent the night.

The autumn slipped away into a long November lecture tour. In Springfield, Illinois, he signed many books at Coe's, a fine old bookstore he would never forget; at the Vachel Lindsay home he met the poet's sister. He visited Lincoln's tomb and Lindsay's grave, where his stone, with birth and death dates, read simply, "Poet." In his journal Jesse entered, "How much that word 'poet' meant." Back in Greenup he talked Deane into a belated seventh anniversary celebration, and they picked up Ann and Oscar Sammons and drove to the Club Continental in Southpoint, Ohio, for an evening of dining, dancing, "good music," and talking and laughing with their old friends. By early November he was away lecturing in the East—Brooklyn, where he reflected on the correctness of Thomas Wolfe's view that only the dead knew the place; New Jersey; Laconia, New Hampshire; Boston; Columbia University; in New Jersey again at Trenton where after his talk, so he wrote in his journal, "I was chased by an insane woman." Lecturing his way through Pennsylvania, at Easton he followed Randolph Churchill at the podium of the National Dinner Club. On November 15, he crossed Bucks County and got to Philadelphia just in time to call on friends and editors—John Bird, Bob Reed, and Ben Hibbs at the *Country Gentleman* and *Saturday Evening Post* offices. Jesse was booked at the Art Alliance on Rittenhouse Square. John and Katherine Bird attended his lecture, and their hearts sank when they saw the audience, made up of "prim and proper Main Line ladies." Bird had known the misfortune of speaking to a similar group of "the coldest, least responsive of humans ever encountered," but now he could only shudder in sympathy. "I can't remember exactly how he did it," Bird recalled, "but in about three sentences with some anecdote from his boyhood in the Kentucky hills he had them where he wanted them; the whole speech was a great success. The Main Liners had never heard anyone like him."

Returning home moved Jesse deeply. Something having to do with his happiness to see Kentucky again set him down on Friday, November 22, to write 220 lines of a poem he first called "Heart of America." He had first written it in prose, then reasoning that it was "poetic prose," he broke it up into free verse, seeking "a new form and a new departure." It began:

> Kentucky is my land.
> It is a place beneath the wind and sun
> In the very heart of America . . .

He defined its boundaries and then wrote,

> Within these natural boundaries is Kentucky,
> Shaped like the mouldboard on a hillside turning-plow.
> Kentucky is neither southern, northern, eastern or western,
> It is the core of America.
> If these United States can be called a body,
> Kentucky can be called its heart.

And he speculated upon his own life in this place,

> I didn't have any choice as to where I was born,
> But if I had had my choice,
> I would have chosen Kentucky.
> And if I could have chosen wind to breathe,
> I would have chosen a Kentucky wind
> With the scent of cedar, pinetree needles,
> Green tobacco leaves, pawpaw, persimmon and sassafras.
> I would have chosen too,
> Wind from the sawbriar and greenbriar blossoms.

He sang of his own beloved W-Hollow and his steady awakening to the land's beauty, and of Poetry choosing him to write what he lived as naturally as he breathed:

> When I was compelled to put poems on paper
> They wrote themselves for they were ripe
> And ready for harvest
> As the wild berries, the persimmons and the pawpaws
> As the yellow leaves and nuts falling from the trees.

He compared Kentucky to each region of the United States in turn— the canyoned cities of the East, the softer-voiced, more slowly paced South, the "doers" rather than talkers of the West, and the industrialized North—finding his homeland not these,

> But it was the heart of America
> Pulsing with a little bit of everything.

He named Kentucky's "even tempo," "mild traditions" of "horse racing" and of "ballad, song, story and folk music," its "pioneer tradition of fighting men, fighting for America / And for the soil of Kentucky," a soil

> That is filled with bluegrass beauty
> That is not akin to poetry
> But is poetry. . . .

And so Kentucky would not ever leave him, not even when he left it:

> And when I go beyond the border,
> I take with me growth and beauty of the seasons,
> The music of wind in pine and cedar tops,
> The wordless songs of snow-melted water
> When it pours over the rocks to wake the spring.
> I take with me Kentucky embedded in my brain and heart,
> In my flesh and bone and blood
> Since I am of Kentucky
> And Kentucky is part of me.

The following May, in 1947, "Heart of America" would be accepted by *Country Gentleman* for $500, the most he had ever received for a poem; it would later be reprinted as "Kentucky Is My Land," in his poetry volume of 1952 to which the poem would give its name.

In that December of the first full year of peace he wrote a "story about a man wrestling with a bear," which he would entitle "No Hero." Through the early part of the month he was moving earth on the W-Hollow Road and around his house to eliminate a bridge in front of his garage, but he paused to admire the simple, peaceful scene before him. "Jane played in the beautiful December sunlight . . . one of the prettiest winter days ever to come this late in winter." Beauty, poetry, and the land. He thought about them. There had been no time for the land in wartime, a time as demanding as farming, though with a different reaping. There was yet something nurturing in the land, something life-giving that complemented his time of song. When he tried to write and could not, he instead revised or wrote letters, or as he had done all year, swung into the farm work. Back in September he and his hired hands had worked long hours to finish hauling soybeans from the long bottom and had shocked the Korean clover on the flat. One day by himself he had thrown eight and a half wagon loads of soybeans up from the wagon into the barn loft. Hauling from the long bottom had set him to thinking about "the sweat I'd shed on this bottom . . . from days as early as I could remember." And in the flat where they had shocked the soybean hay, "I could remember when a child of nine, I used to hunt turkey nest[s] among the giant trees that stood here, dig rabbits from the waterseaps in winter and haul big logs with old Fred in the winter of 1917–18 for wood. This was the earth that I knew as well as I did my own arm, leg, hands or fingers."

Always his thoughts flew home whenever he had gone away, when he had gone to the Navy and became a thwarted warrior who would rather have piloted a ship than a Washington desk; but whether away in one place or in another seemed not to matter. Regardless, he held in his mind cherished images of home, as he had written in "Last Leave,"

> Of redbud coves in fiery flakes of bloom,
> Curve of Naomi's lips, her handsome face,
> Jane's playing with blocks in our living room.

Now he was back living those images again, something to be thankful for; and they had reasons to be thankful. The war was over, peace had come, and they were in their W-Hollow home again preparing to send out 250 Christmas cards to some of their closest friends. One evening just before Christmas, little Jane returned thanks at the supper table: "God bless our home. I am glad the war is over so children can have bal[l]oons. The men had to have the plastic. Amen."[7]

14

Valley of the Shadow
1946–1954

◇

One of the Stuarts' Christmas cards just after the war, depicting the exposed log section of the front of their house, went to James Still, who had written Jesse, complimenting him as "a national possession." Yet during those first months of peace, Jesse experienced a letdown in his writing; he had difficulty getting down to work, and replied to his old LMU classmate, "Never a day passes but what I think I'm through as a writer. I don't like anything I've written but *Album of Destiny*. . . . I don't have any book coming out or any ideas for one." It was the second time a creative drought had struck, the first having come in 1943, when he had turned to Harry Kroll for advice. "Your creative life, once you catch your second wind, is all ahead of you," Kroll had written him, for he had been through writer's drought, too. "I think your job is to keep on plowing and hoeing and give your soul a chance." After all, no man could write "when he was frantic," so "just keep writing, and discipline yourself not to be too badly hurt, too disappointed; and somehow, because you are a writer, you will get your second grip. I can't tell you how to do it; no one can. It's one of those things you have to work out yourself." Specifically he had counseled Jesse "to look back into your pioneer stuff and dope up a rattling yarn. . . . use *idiom* instead of too much dialect, and let that carry along the genius of your style." Within six months Jesse had written *Taps for Private Tussie*, his most lucrative success.

Doubtless his postwar drought was aggravated by an intermittent eight months of remodeling on the W-Hollow home. He and Naomi contracted and supervised for their house a new foundation, a reconstructed kitchen, a new living room, a bathroom, and a new bedroom for Jane. A new chimney and hearth were mortared into place by a local mason with the appropriate name of "Mr. Brickey." Between lectures in the spring, Jesse revised and wrote additional portions of *Magic Moonshine*, but was not satisfied with the manuscript. There was the farm to contend with as well as the continuing problem of the W-Hollow Road. Distracted and overworked, seeking a change, he wrote one friend in the middle of 1947, "I get hungry to get back into the school room." Although his lecture calendar was full for September and October, he was cutting down after that, explaining lecturing "takes too much time and I need it for writing." The year before he had been in every state in the country east of the Mississippi River except two, Maine and Louisiana. He had slept in hotel lobbies and traveled by bus, rail and plane. His lecture tours in the fall of 1946 and spring of 1947 "nearly got me down." Definitely, once he finished his lecture tour in the East, he would return home and write.

Despite his complaints, Jesse's river of publication for 1947 flowed along unabated with twenty different pieces appearing in such periodicals as *Collier's, Salute, Household, Pic, Esquire,* the *Courier-Journal Magazine, Author and Journalist, Farm Journal,* and *Country Gentleman.* Just before Christmas he received "one grand" from *Woman's Home Companion* for his short story "Slipover Sweater," $100 going to his agent, Marion Ives, and $900 coming to him—the "largest check ever for a short story." At the beginning of the year, Joe Creason had pointed to Jesse's astonishing reservoir of material, dubbing him "a literary King Midas," and at the end of the year Margaret Shelbourne's spirited piece, "Jesse Stuart: Young Man of the Mountains," appeared in *Holland's Magazine.*

In early January 1948 he sat down to work on a book concerning his teaching experiences, using as a basis an old manuscript he had begun before the war, *The Odyssey of a Country Schoolteacher.* "Plan to call finished product, if ever finished," he wrote in his daily journal, "The Needle's Eye." As if it were a good omen, the next day he received through Marion Ives a check from *Country Gentleman* for $950 in payment of "Love beyond the Law," the most he had ever received for a story. The following day carried another "nice surprise"; after rejection by "every large slick magazine in America" where his agent had sent it, the distinguished literary *Virginia Quarterly* accepted his story "Governor Warburton's Right Hand Man." Jesse swung into *The Needle's Eye* and worked steadily through the winter.

At the outset he tried to write it as a novel, but put aside the first thirty-nine pages because he believed the story had to be as wholly true as he could make it. He had always respected his teachers and valued education, but in his lectures all over the country to students, teachers, and other educational and professional groups, his conviction that teaching was the most important of all professions had deepened to a certitude. "A teacher teaches every other profession," he later explained to his audiences. "Teaching uplifts humanity. All the great Greek thinkers were teachers, who lifted up their students." Later before university groups he would declare with typically unabashed enthusiasm, "I love teaching, everything that went with it—the glory, the fights, the ball games. I liked my students. A teacher is the thread that holds a school together, as thread holds a bound book together."

Enthusiastically, he wrote August Derleth in late April that he was at work on a nonfiction book that he hoped to finish in May, adding, "I couldn't get back to the swing of writing," but "I will soon have written my first full length Ms since I . . . returned from the Navy."

Once he had decided on a definite nonfiction form, the book came nearly as naturally as it reads. It was the story of his life again, but his life in schools as a teacher, commencing his junior year in high school in the summer of 1925, with his first teaching job at Cane Creek Elementary School, Lonesome Valley in the book, where he had to whip twenty-year-old first-grader Guy Hawkins in a knock-down-drag-out nearly as soon as he organized thirty-four students from grades one through eight into fifty-four classes a day; but in the process Hawkins was transformed into an ally of education. As Jesse watched the school children play a favorite recess game, singing "The needle's eye that does supply, / The thread that runs so true . . . ," he reached a metaphorical conclusion: The schoolteacher was the needle's eye and the thread that ran so true was work and play. Yes, "their work should be play," he grasped, in the inspired moment in much the same spirit that Albert Einstein later expressed in his "On Education," that the love of learning was a greater motivation for attaining knowledge than fear of failure, that there was in learning that thing akin to play, and that he had known children who preferred schooltime to vacation.

The author's schema is a keenly original use of the six lines of the children's song. Part I focuses directly upon Jesse during his teaching days at Lonesome Valley when he perceived himself as "The Needle's Eye That Does Supply" the work and play of learning. Part II, "The Thread That Runs So True," following his parent-influenced decision to teach for less money in Winston High School rather than to work for more in the steel mills of Aukland (Stuart's fictional name for Ashland), focuses upon his experiences at one-room Winston High School, actually in the nearly landlocked valley of Warnock some twelve or thirteen miles southwest out Raccoon Road from Greenup. Part III, "I Stumped My

Toe and Down I Go," commences with his father's expression of pride in his son's becoming, after a summer of graduate work at George Peabody College in 1930, principal of Landsburgh High School, in reality Jesse's high school alma mater. Despite a year of successful teaching, administrative and community work, Jesse "stumped his toe" when he asked for a modest raise and Superintendent Larry Anderson, based on Robert J. Nickel, and his board did not rehire Jesse at all. "Many a Dark and Stormy Night," the title of Part IV, is the author's apt rhetorical figure for his Vanderbilt experience and his lawsuit-ridden year as Superintendent of the Greenup County Schools, when he fought the educational wars with one hand and grabbed 703 pieces of starlight out of his W-Hollow homeland with the other, lyrically recorded in *Man with a Bull-Tongue Plow*. Jesse's creative, pedagogical, and early lecturing experiences during the Maxwell (actually McKell) High School years from 1933 up to his receiving the Guggenheim Fellowship in 1937 are treated in Part V, "Many a School Have I Let Go"; and the concluding Part VI, "Because I Wanted You," chronicles his return to exile, his violent editorial career when he carried a .38 pistol to protect his life and warred against political corruption in the schools, his teaching year at large Dartmouth (Portsmouth) High School in Ohio, his continued courtship of Naomi Deane Norris, their elopement and decision to live in W-Hollow on the land where he would farm, raise sheep, and write. He still loved teaching, "the greatest profession under the sun," he wrote. "But I'm leaving it because it's left me."[1]

In late February he took the first two parts of the manuscript with him to New York, where Dutton's initial editorial response to the material was positive. But in time the editors told him, "We don't want that kind of book."

"Why?"

"It's about schoolteachers and schoolteaching and the subject is cold."

He believed the Dutton editors had not known he had been a schoolteacher. "If schoolteaching is cold I'm crazy," he said. "It's the warmest subject in the world. You deal with people—human minds and human hearts."

"It will fall flat," they predicted.

Determinedly, Jesse put the manuscript into the hands of Marion Ives. She in turn showed it to her two sisters, both schoolteachers. They read it and reported to her, "It's wonderful, even if he is from Kentucky." Encouraged, she took it to Scribner's where John Hall Wheelock, poet and editor, read it and wrote Jesse optimistically, "It's going to be a classic."

In November of 1948, Jesse had lunch at the Gotham Restaurant in New York City with Marion Ives and Lonnie Coleman, the latter of *Ladies' Home Journal.* Coleman liked Jesse's *Thread* and had recommended it for publication in condensed form by the *Journal;* if accepted, the *Journal* would pay seven to eight thousand dollars. The same day Jesse met for an hour with Scribner's editor John Hall Wheelock, who recommended some detailed changes. Meanwhile, Wheelock assured Jesse there would be no problem with a prior magazine sale to the *Journal;* indeed, the editor hoped that the *Journal* would take it for he believed the advanced publicity would help the sale of the later publication by Scribner's.

Jesse also got together with Annie Laurie Williams, who still saw in his books strong possibilities for motion pictures and for the new television medium as well, for TV seemed to be here to stay. From her he heard the sad story of John Steinbeck, who, having enjoyed a huge success with *Grapes of Wrath,* bought property, paid his first wife off, and married a second. This much younger wife, so Annie Laurie told Jesse, had demanded a cook, housekeeper, jewels, clothes, and furs, "and went wild over night life." She told John she no longer loved him and would not let him work in the house the author had recently purchased for them. He worked instead in Annie Laurie and Maurice Crain's apartment at the Bradford for a month, but had difficulty writing. According to Annie Laurie, Steinbeck had returned to California "a broken man in finance and spirit." Though he had once made a million, now he was living in a small house in Pacific Grove where a sister was looking after him. Reports of heavy drinking followed, whereas before he had never done anything like that, having only a glass of wine before a meal. Steinbeck's ex-wife, having returned to New York only the night before from Reno, had thrown a cocktail party and invited all Steinbeck's old friends. And so it was "another New York story," Jesse thought, and it was "silly and . . . tragic." Annie Laurie did not think Steinbeck would make a comeback.

On the way to his hotel room at the Prince George, Jesse mulled over the Steinbeck story. It was rainy and gloomy, and a mist covered the city. His thoughts flew homeward to escape an old loneliness that struck him. In his room he sat down, began his letter, "Dear Deanems," and wrote of the busy day, his hopes, and his agent's sad story of John Steinbeck. If such a tragedy had happened to Steinbeck, could not it possibly happen to him? At length he cut through all fear and artifice shrouding such comparisons of the human condition, and exposed himself in flowing words of dark blue ink to the woman he loved:

> But Deane I stand. I will stand too. I will always stand with you with me. I know what I want. I have two written books and four more to write besides the stories. Someday I have to get an honor in writing—like the Nobel Prize—but I don't guess I'll ever make that. . . .
>
> I love you Deane. Love you more than I can say—I'll stick by you always for I love you.

Ladies' Home Journal did indeed accept and publish the condensed version of *The Thread That Runs So True* in May 1949. He and Naomi took a notion to go to Europe for the summer with their good friends, Lena and Gus Voiers. Before leaving New York on the *Queen Elizabeth* Jesse was assured by John Hall Wheelock that *Thread* in book form would be out before they returned from the continent, and the editor would see that an advanced copy, according to publication schedule, would reach him by the time their itinerary took them to Switzerland.

The ship proved to Jesse to be a vacation in itself, with fourteen decks and somewhere between seventy and a hundred elevators to deliver him to sumptuous dining rooms. It was good to see England again, to have tea on the trains, partake of meals at five shillings, and behold colorful gardens between the railroad tracks. Signs of the London bombings were everywhere visible, and there was a sugar shortage—only a half-teaspoonful for tea, and no candy. They toured Scotland, Norway, and Sweden, where in Stockholm they got their first steaks, melons, and large salads. Food was still being rationed in Denmark. Jesse found Bremen and Hamburg now in a shambles and saw Germany as "a tragic land." Holland was not what it was before the war, Belgium he found most comparable to the United States, and France reminded him of a drunk man still reeling from his losses. At Switzerland there was no book from Scribner's awaiting him—a bad omen—and in his disappointment he told Naomi that Dutton might have been right after all and the book indeed might have "fallen flat." Perhaps a book on teachers and schools might not go in America, where everything seemed to be business and politics. In America, he thought, we put up big statues to political leaders, while in some other countries they put up big statues to their poets, artists, and teachers. When he returned to New York, though, he found the publication of *Thread* had merely been delayed.

It was published September 26, 1949, and the reviews were hearteningly positive. Measuring the book against Jesse's first autobiography some eleven years earlier, *Beyond Dark Hills*, Harriette Arnow found it "just as readable and entertaining." Worth Tuttle Hedden in a fifteen-hundred-word review for the *New York Herald Tribune Weekly Book Review* pointed to the book's rich local-color details, romantic interludes, nuts-and-bolts educational substance, and the author's justified, often eloquent outrage against political corruption and penny-wise-pound-foolish educational shortfalls. He observed the book was dedicated to the school-teachers of America, then qualified, "but it is every American's book," and concluded it was "as indigenously epic as the Paul Bunyan saga and with a hero possessed of brains as well as brawn." J. H. Jackson of the *San Francisco Chronicle* read it as an autobiographical testimony of "a teacher at heart, a man who believes in education, and some of his most eloquent passages are those in which he expresses his faith in the profession in which he made his start." Jack Conroy in writing for the *Chicago Sun* saw Stuart's style as "simple, strong and direct," and observed, "His joy for living illuminates each page," while the *Nation* reviewer saw *The Thread That Runs So True* as "an entertaining book by a born story-teller."

The editor of the *N.E.A. Journal*, Joy Elmer Morgan, wrote, "It is a truly great book—the kind that comes but once in a generation, a book that will live to entertain and inspire new readers as Eggleston's *Hoosier Schoolmaster* has lived to be read decade after decade." He continued, "As 'the most important book of 1949,' we name 'The Thread That Runs So True' by Jesse Stuart because it is concerned with the unique institution which gives strength to all other institutions in American life." The book is "good literature" for "it records life throbbing with energy, aspiration, conflict, and love. It is full of suspense and vivid imagery—difficult to lay down until one has finished, the kind of a book that keeps people up beyond the usual bedtime. It appeals to a wide range of readers, young and old, city and rural, teacher and layman, the little and much schooled." Morgan pointed to the book's historical significance: "It reveals the immense lifting power of our free public schools and tells of an experience that in various forms has been repeated on one frontier after another as our country has swept westward and forward." Morgan found in the book something of Ruel E. Foster's later reading—"a song, a poem, a manifesto, a hymn to the profession of teaching"—and tied it emotively to the stuff of epics, which "exalts the aspirations and ideals by which our people have risen rapidly to national and world greatness."

Jesse would later declare, "I lost a publishing house on *The Thread*

That Runs So True." In truth he had simply decided to find another publisher when Dutton turned down the book, and in the process he left Dutton for a more amenable publisher. He had, since Maxwell Perkins had invited him to come to Scribner's, looked forward to the possibility when and if conditions were suitable. Yet he was not to remain there long. The other book he had written at the time Scribner's accepted *Thread* was *Hie to the Hunters*, a Twainian idyll of the city boy, Did Hargis, accustoming himself to the natural agrarian world of a Huckleberry-like "Sparkie" Sparks. Whit Burnett was pleased with the "backwoods information" that the boys encounter, "a team a little reminiscent of Tom Sawyer and Huck Finn." The head of Scribner's junior department believed it was not a junior book. "It's for adults." Wheelock thought otherwise: "This is for boys, a junior book," and there the two Scribners' editors stalemated. The impasse was resolved when Ed Kuhn, a bright young Dartmouth graduate whom Thomas Wolfe's editor, Ed Aswell, had brought with him to McGraw-Hill from Harper's, read the manuscript and said, "It is a junior book for adults." McGraw-Hill accepted the manuscript and published it May 1, 1950, under its Whittlesey House imprint. By 1976 the book had gone into seventeen printings.

That same year McGraw-Hill's publication of a collection of twenty of Jesse's short stories, *Clearing in the Sky*, met with a litany of critical praise. To Charlotte Capers his "ballad-like stories of the hills of home" were evocative of a "last remnant of eighteenth-century life." E. P. Nichols of the *Library Journal* saw them as "more superb tales of . . . mountain folk by a superb craftsman." The *San Francisco Chronicle*'s J. H. Jackson commended "his marvelous ear for the dialect of his people," while Kelsey Guilfoil of the *Chicago Sunday Tribune* declared, "Here is Jesse Stuart at his magnificent best, telling his well loved tales of the Kentucky hills"; and Coleman Rosenberger of the *New York Herald Tribune Book Review* found them "tart, full-flavored, immensely readable." In the title story, Jesse's father is clearly the undisguised hero, as Jesse is the narrator, following Mick Stuart up "a pretty little footpath under the high canopy of hickory, walnut, and oak leaves" to a clearing of fertile land. Here, Mick Stuart tells him, "something goes back. Something I cannot explain. You go back to the places you knew and loved." Jesse later identified the W-Hollow locale of the story, saying the clearing lies "about midway between here [the Jesse Stuart house] and Bud Adams' [place]. Dad went up in there . . . and that garden can be found right now. There's wire around it . . . fenced to keep the cattle off it . . . nailed to a piece of wood, nailed to the tree (so the tree would not grow around the wire)." Consistently, Jesse wrote Carleton Wells, "the story in there about Dad, I wrote as an article. It is not part truth but all truth about my Dad—just what I have in the story."[2]

In January 1950 Jesse read Joe Creason's *Courier-Journal* piece "The Author Who Writes So True," which emphasized the factual basis of *Thread,* especially his realistic handling of the depressed conditions of so many schools. Jesse thought Creason's article was "very, very good." Years later he would write of his book as "heartfelt" and of his "Characters in the Flesh," identifying his beaten-up sister as Sophia Stuart Keeney; the provincial genius at Warnock, Budge Waters, as Charles Rice; teacher-coach Bill Hadden as the real William Harrell; Lonnie Maxwell as longtime friend and fellow teacher Lewis McCubbin; Chad Hoskins as auditor Charles Heaberlin, father of Jesse's close friend Elmer; Charles Manson as Superintendent Fred Maynard; Coach Charles Meyers as the future father-in-law of his daughter, Jane, Charles Juergensmeyer; sixty-nine-year-old sophomore at Maxwell High Martha Binion, as McKell adult student Nina Mitchell Biggs, ninety-seven at the time Jesse's article appeared. The remedial student with a fine voice at Dartmouth was Portsmouth student Robert Tucker, who became a radio commentator; and Lydia and Forrest Kingston were, of course, Lillie and Forrest King.

After a mid-American tour in March of the Chicago and St. Louis areas, then Kansas and Iowa, Jesse caught a Constellation flight from Chicago to New York where he met Ed Aswell, Ed Kuhn, and Sonia Levinthal at Whittlesey House. In February Jesse had returned a call from Walter Wanger on the West Coast, who wanted him to write a book to be published in a magazine, possibly *Ladies' Home Journal,* and then Wanger was to make a movie of it. The idea had excited Jesse; but when he had dinner with Marion Ives and Ed Kuhn at Chinatown Charlie's on Tuesday evening, March 14, they talked over Wanger's proposition and agreed against it. The next forty-eight hours went in a social whirl. On Wednesday evening a cocktail party was given in Jesse's honor at Sonia Levinthal's apartment on Park Avenue. There he met many of the newspaper book reviewers and thought it was a good party. "It was hard for me to believe that such would be given me," he wrote frankly in his journal. "It was a long way from a one-room log cabin in the Kentucky hills to a cocktail party on Park Ave." Then he added, "Much as I appreciated this honor I'd take the log cabin." The next evening Ed Kuhn helped get Jesse into the editor's tux, the first one Jesse had ever worn, and he went with Sonia Levinthal and Harold McGraw to the Waldorf for the National Book Award Dinner, where he heard

Eleanor Roosevelt, Senator Paul Douglas from Illinois, and Frederick Lewis Allen speak. "It was a great evening," he noted in his journal, one of many highpoints in a year he would label "a milestone!"

Meanwhile, back in W-Hollow, more and more fans and other curious people dropped in to visit him. He was fond of company and good conversation, but when visitors came too thick and fast he became frustrated because he could not get his work done. By August *Country Gentleman* was paying twelve hundred dollars for a Stuart short story; that month he went to a hilltop sproutfield and started work "up high in the wind," thinking, "Company couldn't compare to this. I got back to the thing I did with my father and mother when I was a child. I wrote two poems." He read when he could snatch a spare moment such random works as Henry Reston's *Northern Farm* and Maxim Gorki's short stories, after walking "the sunny streets of Chicago" during a break in his October lecture tour. By the end of the month he was wondering why he worked so hard: "And for what? I have one child and wife to keep and a few dependents. But I could live peacefully in a small cottage and do more writing. I would, perhaps, live longer and I wouldn't give an extra day of life for the best short story I've written."

In November T. M. Longstreth of the *Christian Science Monitor* reviewed Jesse's new collection of stories, *Clearing in the Sky*, praising his "freshness of plot, the gusto and savor and genuineness of matter and manner, which left the sum of Jesse Stuart's work up against the literary skyline like one of his mountains"; yet Longstreth had earlier admonished the reader, "One may tire of the same locale." Perhaps it was such a qualification that caused Jesse a few days later to cut loose and write August Derleth:

> You and I write of the people we know. We write what is called regionalism. I wonder what will be the future, how long they are destined to live . . . the books on sex, on war and on things that are timely for awhile and then are gone forever—whereas, the little things are immortal and are with us forever—such things as natural love, landscapes, rivers—stories of simple people—people who are the backbone of America. I hope to write of these things.

Altogether in 1950, he traveled and lectured in thirty-nine states, made seventy-five talks, and spoke to over a hundred thousand people. In addition to *Hie to the Hunters* and *Clearing in the Sky*, he also sold and published eight short stories, four poems, and four articles. Nor in the midst of all these activities had he stinted on farm work: Under his direction and with his own labor nearly two miles of the W-Hollow Road had been built, the bottomland pasture had been made and several more pastures developed, along with other improvements in his land. Looking back on the twelvemonth at mid-century, he summarized it in his daily journal as "a year lived and loved and cost me a lot of sweat."[3]

All his achievements in 1951 were starkly overshadowed by a profound sadness that was never wholly to leave him. Off and on for over a year Martha Stuart's health had been failing. On Thursday, May 3, Jesse took her to Ashland to an optometrist. Surprisingly her humor was good, and they laughed and talked the fifteen miles along the way. They smoked together and talked about his father and the grandchildren. When she tried to pay the doctor with her own money, Jesse would not hear of it, and both of them laughed again. Then when he tried to pay for her new glasses, she said, "No, Jesse, let Mick pay," and they laughed at that, too. Altogether, it was "one of the nicest trips I ever had with her."

The next day, his father came down the hill and reported that his wife was not well. "It's unusual for your mother to lie in bed. She has been a woman of great strength without a lazy bone in her body. It's not right to see her in bed in the daytime." Later Jesse called on his mother, found her asleep, and let her rest. As he walked back down the hill he thought of her: "She gave me life, nursed me when I was a baby, taught me to work. She gave me great strength." It rained the next morning, and suddenly the rain stopped and the sun came out. By afternoon it was dry. His father came down and talked with him. "Jesse, it's your mother," he said. "Everything has suddenly got very strange up on the hill. I can't figure it out. But I believe the spirits of her people have come for her."

The next day when he visited her, his mother did not know him. "Mom can't get over this," Jesse thought, but did not tell his father. He returned home and told Deane she was dying. In the days that followed the whole family gathered and sat with Martha Stuart, although she did not recognize them. Deane sat up all Sunday evening with her. On Tuesday Jesse arranged at the doctor's recommendation to have her taken to the hospital in an ambulance. Martha Stuart rallied sufficiently that her gray eyes followed her children's movements when they were close, then late in the evening she lapsed again into unconsciousness. Just a week after her and Jesse's happy trip to Ashland, her condition was so grave that Jesse stayed by her bedside through the night. He went home the next morning but could not sleep and returned to the hospital by noon. All afternoon he sat by her bed and held her pulse. Both the doctor and nurse commented that her strong heart kept her alive. Jesse had one hand on her shoulder and held her hand with his other when her last breath went. All the children were there.

A horrible day followed. Overcome with fatigue as well as grief, they selected a casket. Faithfully Jesse wrote in his journal, "This was hard. We got a steel casket and it didn't look like the right kind of bed for Mom." The ambulance took her back to the homeplace, where the windows were shaded and she was placed in the dining room. "The house was filled with people—the yard was filled—but it was my mother dead and I understood her so well and felt this loss so deeply. And knowing how she fought death like a row of corn, I couldn't stay in the house. I had to get out under the stars."

The morning of her funeral Jesse did not go up the hill to the homeplace. "I don't know what I did," he later wrote. In the afternoon, "I went up and looked at Mom." He and his father were, in fact, the last to look upon her. "Think," Jesse wrote, "she was leaving The Hill forever." Then he spoke softly to her, "Goodbye, Mom."

On Mother's Day they buried Martha Stuart in the Plum Grove Cemetery.

That night after the funeral he returned to Plum Grove and "stood in the starlight and looked at her long grave which was in the very spot where the old Plum Grove School used to be." He thought of how she had sent them all to school and urged them to get educations, how she had worked with her hoe, and sent them dollars from her butter-and-egg money. "And the good earth she believed could restore her to health by working in it again, now held her eternally. I couldn't adjust myself that she was gone."

Before Decoration Day in late May, because Mitchell Stuart wanted it that way, Jesse's father selected his wife's epitaph, culling the possibilities read aloud to him from *Man with a Bull-Tongue Plow* and *Album of Destiny*. "Not like your mother," he would say. Then Deane read to him,

> A will to work—one unafraid of life—
> One that loved life and gave her seven life;
> Now, unafraid, she's gone to meet new life,
> Beneath white glistening beauty of a star.

His father said, "That's it. That's your mother."

In late May as Jesse hauled the leftover stone-studded clay from beside Martha Stuart's grave, "Strange thoughts of her death returned." In his mind's turning he contrasted her valiant struggle to live with the fact of her death "and how after she was gone a little muscle kept flicking on her right forearm." A smothering old anger nagged him. "Now in this Plum Grove clay is not the right place for Mom," he thought. "Hers should not be a house of clay!" The year's end brought him little retrospective pleasure in the shadow of his sorrow. "I lost this year, the greatest friend I had on earth—my mother—and I'm the man without the mother complex." He had been reading in *Tomorrow Magazine* about Maxwell Perkins and Thomas Wolfe and what he took to be "Tom Wolfe's mother complex. But my mother's loss gets under my skin, takes my breath when I think about her in the Plum Grove clay—that place where all of us—a red-blooded family—must someday lie."

He found no consolation in books but felt stirring within him the old kinship to the earth about him. "Do not read any second hand poems from books," he wrote in his journal. "Not when my world about me is one great poem. Not when the leaves on the trees are the most prolific crops of leaves I've ever seen—so much rain—and spring so late. When I hear night winds struggle to get through these leaves I stand and listen to this fresh, strange and weird music. I cannot get as much satisfaction out of the reading [of] the best of poems by the greatest English and American poets [old and new] as I can this sort of thing and I probably should never record this but it is true." For a time life possessed his thoughts, concrete life and real people. "Hell, I feel like sometimes I could turn a hill over to see what's under it—that I could meet a thousand people and ask each a thousand questions about himself and what he gets from life."

He would write again but it would have to be something close to the magic earth. Through July, August, and September, he completed and partially revised a manuscript he called *Laurel Ridge*. By year's end he was disappointed not to have had a book published in 1951, although he had published six short stories, eight poems, including one reprint, and four articles during the year. Even though his "What America Means to Me"—which appeared in the May issue of *The American Magazine* and in which he "gave my country credit for the little I've done" in a most selfless, generous, and convincing essay—won him an American Freedom Award at Valley Forge, Pennsylvania, and the editor described the author's story as "a simple and powerful story of faith and fulfillment," Jesse nevertheless recorded at the end of his journal entries for 1951, "I seriously doubt I've written one single thing that will live." As midnight of New Year's Eve approached, he went out into the yard and looked at the stars—"a beautiful night with a sky full of stars and a warm wind blowing over the earth." Out of the requiem of desolate weeks and months, his thoughts turned once more to what he was for. He resolved "not to make any resolutions but to work slowly and cautiously and try to finish one or more books in 1952." Strange, life even with all its grief was good. "This year 1951, I hate to see go, not that it's been good for me but another year of my life is gone. I hate to see them go."[4]

The first day of spring in 1952 was a reflection of what it should be, Jesse thought:

The sky, high and blue and the wind blowing over full of sunshine and a little chill which made it good to breath[e]. The wind full of wild birds; wings and grass greening here and there. And our weeping willow with long light-green fronds leaping and playing with the wind! Another spring with something magic which made my heart rejoice.

In April he wrote about old Op (Theopolis) Akers riding the devil, another chapter for the manuscript he began to call *The Good Spirit of Laurel Ridge.* Jesse had bought the Seaton Ridge acreage from Op's prototype, George Alexander, a woods-wise old man who continued to inhabit the land. Later the author would speak of the transaction, "I had a deed recorded in the county court records . . . but Old Op Akers had a deed for it in his heart."

He worked on the proofs of *Kentucky Is My Land* in late July. During the year he published seven stories, ten poems, and three essays. Three masters' theses on his life and work appeared, one each at East Texas State Teachers College, Western Kentucky State University, and the University of Southern California. Fulfilling his plan to finish one or more books during the year, *Kentucky Is My Land* was published by September 21, and the reviews of this sandwich-thin volume pointed up the regional richness of his work and "a handful of poems exceedingly choice," especially "Elegy for Mitch Stuart," which the *Saturday Review* critic found "a gem of concision," and "The Ballad of Lonesome Waters," "a folk myth, lusty, indigenous and veined rich with images, flavored with provincialisms." Continuing, the reviewer praised "By Sandy Waters," "The Last Leave Home," and the eleven-page, free-verse "The Builders and the Dream" as containing "certain excellences achieved with the sure touch of craftsmanship." This last poem was also singled out by Russell MacFall of the *Chicago Sunday Tribune,* who perceived it to be "one of the few poems in praise of forest conservation that is really readable." *The San Francisco Chronicle* reviewer thought the volume "the best kind of regional record" and "a portrait of a happy man at home." One critic termed the book "disappointing," lacking the spontaneity of Stuart's earlier poetry, whereas Donald Davidson wrote that the poet "has steadily become more solid and selective," and that the poems of *Kentucky Is My Land* "show the mature Stuart."

The early fifties were of a pattern into which he wove his writing, farming, and lecturing, producing the homespun fabric of his, Naomi's, and Jane's W-Hollow life. Their happiness was full during these years, yet daily activities were not always a consistently pleasant counterpoint to his writing, and sometimes fragmented into small daily frustrations. One day, for example, Jesse took Jane to school in Greenup and hurried home, where he worked on *Good Spirit*. Then he worked in the yard and returned to Greenup to pick up Jane. The twice-a-day trip to Greenup simply "ruins the day for me." Briefly he contemplated a move to Greenup, but evaded the issue by turning philosophical. "The longer one lives the more involved little details become to rob him of time," he entered in his journal. Visitors continued to take his time, too. On a Sunday in late July, no fewer than thirty-five people called on the Stuarts in W-Hollow. Home for Jesse was always the better place, but to make it so was a matter of frequent and loving labor. To plan, contract, and oversee installation of a hot-water heating system required much of his time intermittently from August through December, and in the process necessitated the construction of a garage and utility room, costing $5,000.

He continued a heavy correspondence and speaking schedule. Lecturing at Morehead State College in July, he espied a short familiar figure and looked again quickly. "I was mortally shocked to see James Still, my classmate," he recorded. "I'd not seen him for 23 years." The two ate at President Spain's that evening. After Jesse had spoken and conferred with several students, "James Still came and went shyly," he observed, "as in the days at L.M.U. He hadn't changed much." It was a pleasant reunion. Donald Davidson had good news. The forthcoming edition of his textbook *American Composition and Rhetoric*, Jesse learned, was to feature his "Another April," along with James Joyce's "Araby," the only stories to appear in the section on narrative writing. Jesse was pleased that his former professor wrote, "I think your story is definitely better, on all counts, than Joyce's much admired little piece." Davidson went on to say that when Robert Frost had walked up the road with his collie dog to pay the Davidsons a visit at Breadloaf, the Vanderbilt professor had taken the occasion to read him "Another April."

For years Jesse and Naomi had attended and contributed to the support of the Methodist Church at 607 Main Street in Greenup, located on the eastern end of the downtown area. The structure is distinctive in that the four-sided tower of brick serves at its base as the front entrance and vestibule. The tower rises harmoniously up to its spiring roof, at which point a white tower of wood continues to pierce the sky. The Stuarts often entered the Williamsburg-style door, accented by a small brass knob, crossed the vestibule beneath the tower, and walked into the squarish auditorium with its high wainscoting of golden oak, blending with pews and twin pulpits of a corresponding grain and hue. Shortly after his forty-sixth birthday, August 24, 1952, Jesse made up his mind "to be on the inside looking out in[stead] of on the outside looking in," and joined "the church of my father's people." The decision was his alone. "No one, not even my wife, knew I was going to join." He was even attending Sunday School fairly regularly in 1954 when, well prepared one Sunday, he drove over to the little brick church and went to his class, then later jotted in his journal, "I do hate to answer all the questions while others sit in class like so many wooden men."[5]

In 1953 he continued to improve his land and to increase his W-Hollow acreage, his largest acquisition being ninety-two acres purchased from Newt Baldridge for $3000. He finished an outdoor furnace on the hill just above the north side of the house, complete with steps leading uphill to the patio area, rebuilt and roofed his toolshed, repaired a barn and finished a cabin on the ridge, and repaired the old Collins barn, which commanded the large open valley near the entrance to W-Hollow from Highway 1.

More than forty of his stories, poems, and essays were accepted, published, or reprinted that year. By May 18 he finished his final revision of *The Good Spirit of Laurel Ridge,* and he received his first advance copy in the mail October 13. He had also begun a junior book somewhat reluctantly at the suggestion of editors by expanding a ten-page short story, "Christmas in the Valley," into ninety pages. "I'd been trapped into writing it," he complained, and could find no suitable title until Deane came to the rescue with *The Beatinest Boy.* Exclusive of other book royalties, he listed payments for publications and reprint fees in his daily journal totaling $3932, although this figure by no means included all his income from new sales.

It was a busy year for Jesse on the lecture circuit, too, in the spring speaking in such places as Adrian, Michigan; Huntington, West Virginia; Spartanburg, South Carolina; Franklin, Indiana; and Breadloaf, Vermont. In the fall his lecture tour took him north, east, midwest, and south to Bedford, Pennsylvania; Goshen, New York; Battle Creek, Michigan; Galesburg, Illinois; British Columbia, Canada; Muncie, Indiana; Columbus, Ohio; Oklahoma City; Hattiesburg, Mississippi; Ruston, Louisiana; Madison College, Tennessee; Huntington, West Virginia; Des Moines, Iowa; Wayne County, Michigan; and back to New York to Syracuse. Exclusive of travel time, he spent about fifty-two days literally on the stump. His lecture fees varied from a high of $1,000 to a low of $25. He listed $5,000 in lecture fees that year, although he did not list all amounts paid directly to the lecture bureau; a conservative estimate of his lecturing income that year would seem to have been closer to $10,000 than $5,000.

During the early 1950s several memorable tours took the Stuarts to Miami, Texas, Canada, and Jamestown and Williamsburg in Virginia, but none was more enjoyable than their trip to New England and New York City in July 1953. They had planned it a long while back, and on July 8 they packed and were on their way to Breadloaf School of English in Vermont, where Jesse had accepted a speaking engagement. Part of the agreement was that he would get to meet Robert Frost, who had been one of Jesse's literary heroes since his Greenup schooldays when he had first read Frost's "Mending Wall." An added incentive was Donald Davidson's presence, a longtime summer teacher there during regular-semester respites from Vanderbilt. Using an AAA map Davidson had mailed them, the Stuarts drove by way of the northern lake country of New York State. From Erie, Pennsylvania, they motored to Canandaigua, New York, into the Finger Lakes district. At the L. W. Singer Book Company they were cordially received and hospitably treated to lunch by the editors. In Adirondack country, they toured Fort Ticonderoga, then crossed Lake Champlain on a little ferry into Vermont, continuing to Middlebury and Breadloaf.

There they were met by Reginald Cook, a pleasant director known as "Doc," who showed them around Breadloaf, "an isolated spot in the Green Mountains," so Jesse recorded his first impression of the place, "miles of timber in all direction[s]—a most beautiful spot for a school, not a store, gas station, near." They got settled into a big room with a fireplace and plenty of wood, for though it was midsummer, they had to have a fire. Naomi felt chilly and was coming down with a cold. There they were delighted to renew their friendship with Donald and Theresa Davidson. Soon Jesse was taken out a narrow lane and up a hill to a cabin to meet "Mr. New England," as he later referred to Frost in an essay he had to put down on paper. Jesse was as deeply impressed with Frost as he had expected to be; "a nice-looking man," he observed, who "wore tweeds and did not smoke. You'd take him as a businessman." Although professors like Davidson often found Frost "cautious and elusive" and "given to speaking . . . in riddles," to Jesse he seemed friendly and warm.

During their conversation Frost asked Jesse what he thought about "schools of modern poetry." The Kentuckian was slow to respond with what he actually did think, but Frost was not slow in relating his opinion to Jesse. "He laughed," Jesse reported, "at why a group of men's minds should unite in a school of art." In this, as in other ways, the two possessed a common viewpoint, for both were of an individualistic turn of mind. Frost explained himself metaphorically: "If there was a grove of oaks growing in the forest, each would reach approximately the same size. If only one grew there, an individual oak, it might be a giant. It would be larger than any one of the grove." Then Frost laughed again.

As they talked Jesse sat up close to Frost and looked into the New Englander's blue eyes, descried his physique, studied his face and hands. Watching him, Jesse reckoned Frost had composed over six hundred poems and, he thought, all but perhaps a half-dozen of them were about people. "There's not one of his poems that doesn't have character," he mused as Frost talked. "After listening to him," Jesse wrote, "I thought I had found the same character in this poet which I found in his poems." Teir conversation went on until midnight. Jesse asked Frost "if he liked to get out and walk over the hills at night, sit on a stone or the roots of a tree and write poems," a penchant Jesse had detected in Frost's work. "Then his face was aglow," Jesse wrote. Later, Donald Davidson confirmed that Frost was "a night owl."

Jesse was scheduled to speak the next day, and as he prepared to leave with Donald Davidson, he was surprised when the New England bard remarked, "I don't go to talks."

That suited Jesse, although he did not tell Frost so. Outside Davidson explained, "Frost almost always *avoids* lectures."

The next day, July 13, Jesse spoke to about 150 people at Breadloaf. Among those in his audience in addition to Cook and Davidson were Theodore Morrison from Harvard, Elizabeth Drew of Smith, Carlos Baker of Princeton, Jewett Joyce from Dartmouth, Robeson Bailey of Yale, and a select group who, in the main, were creative students and college teachers from all over the country. "I dreaded this talk," Jesse later acknowledged. Naomi was not present, having remained with a cold in their cabin. Jesse walked to the front of the auditorium, where sat Mr. New England himself. "Look, Doc," Jesse said to Cook. "There is Robert Frost."

"You can pitch to him," Cook said. "Many a young baseball pitcher has had to pitch to his hero."

"But I'm pitching to Babe Ruth," Jesse groaned. Yet pitch he did. Later he wrote in his journal with undisguised elation, "Greatest reception I ever received. Doc's wife[,] Anita, went to tell Deane." And Cook told Jesse: "It was the greatest talk ever given at Breadloaf. You've pitched a no-hitter." Even Frost, not given to complimenting others, "told Mrs. Morrison something to this effect." Jesse also fetched Frost's presence at the informal session afterward in "the barn." Davidson later wrote Jesse, "I have heard many people here comment on . . . how very much Frost was delighted with the whole evening's performance. . . . I don't think Frost ever *moved* this audience as you did." Davidson was revealingly concrete about the power of his former student's talk:

> I was "carried away"—moved not only by the truth and force of what you were explicitly saying but by all it implied, all that it called up in the way of memories reaching far back beyond the time when I first knew you. There were voices speaking in your voice that I haven't heard since I was a boy, some of them very beloved to me. You weren't trying, outright, to speak for them, but you couldn't help doing so. Whenever a Southerner speaks in the manner native to him, as you do, he is always speaking not only with his voice but with the voices of his foreparents. That is one of the big differences between being a Southerner and not being one. Very likely I was the only person in that room who could know, out of full experience, somewhat like yours, what was back of your utterance. . . . The present generation of teachers and professors really know little about education, since they never lacked it, never had to work or even fight for it, but indeed were too well provided, have had an excess of books. . . . I've heard the old men speak, as you have, in the old way, in the voice that lifts you out of your seat. They could speak. I mean they could carry you from laughter to tears and from tears to laughter. What is the use of getting up to speak if you can't do that? They didn't "lecture." You didn't. You don't need to, because you can *speak*—and besides you are a poet.
> . . . I will add that, while you had me in a trance, I managed nevertheless, now and then, to look around out of the corner of

my eye and see what was happening to my colleagues of the Bread-loaf faculty. I can't tell you how much good it did me to see Arthur Jensen, of Dartmouth—high-powered "liberal" and intellectual that he is, and ignorant of the South—completely captivated by you. So were they all.

Following his talk many of the faculty members came around and spoke with him. He was impressed with Professor Carlos Baker and his family, especially with his daughter of fourteen, who, though older than Jane's eleven, "was very kind to Jane." Jesse later wrote Davidson, "I had imagined before going there everything and most everybody would be scholarly, stiff and cold. But all these thoughts were dispelled. And all my thoughts had been illusionary ones."

From Breadloaf the Stuarts drove through the Green Mountains into New Hampshire's White Mountains. They visited Dartmouth at Hanover and went on to Portland, Maine, where they stayed at the Graymoor Hotel and ate at Boone's Seafood place. There Jesse found Longfellow's birthplace. At Boston he sought out Whittier's birthplace, thought about *Snowbound,* and mulled over "a great writer now slightly forgotten." Later, they visited the homes of the Concord group and their graves in Sleepy Hollow: "The simple stone of Hawthorne—the resting sacred earth that held Emerson at last. We loved Concord, but at a late hour drove on toward Boston and got into the tremendous eddying steams of traffic." Jesse drove on to Raiders Village. They also toured Providence, Rhode Island, "a city we love"; there Deane bought antiques. In New Haven they "looked at the mossy [buildings] at Yale University," and Jesse recorded, "They looked antique too."

In New York they cancelled a fifteen-dollar room at the Taft Hotel, taking instead an eleven-dollar one at the smaller Plymouth and saw *The King and I, The Bandwagon,* and the Rockettes at Radio City. Naomi and Jane did some sightseeing and shopping at Macy's and Altman's, while Jesse met his editors and publishers: Ed Kuhn, Mrs. Fry, and Sonia Levinthal at McGraw-Hill, and George McWhorter and Wallace Meyer at Scribner's. He went by the *Scholastic Magazine* offices and, later, joined by Naomi and Jane, he saw Louis Untermeyer at the Decca Building. He and the Stuarts dined together at an Italian restaurant. Unfortunately a waiter spilled a bowl of soup in Untermeyer's lap, ruining not only the anthologist's suit but also splattering Jane's new Altman's dress and Jesse's suit as well. "Some experience," he commented in his journal. The high-point of the New York trip was talking ideas with Ed Kuhn and the Stuarts' visiting Ed and Polly Kuhn's home in Chappaqua, New York, where they were overnight guests and ate a good breakfast at seven in the morning. With the continuing success of *The Thread That Runs So True* yet in the atmosphere, Kuhn was impressed with the possibilities of another educational work. They checked out of the Plymouth and transferred their luggage to their own car at 54th Street near the pier where the *Queen Mary* and *Queen Elizabeth* docked, and Jane got to see many of the big liners. Then they drove under the Hudson, across the speedways of New Jersey to the Pennsylvania turnpike, where he pointed their car homeward.[6]

Growing up in W-Hollow and Greenup County where he had, as he wrote, "read the landscapes, the streams, the air, and the skies," he had always had time to live and to think and to write. He had developed a terrific pride in his body from the time he had realized "in a pinch," as his father said, that he could do the work of two or three ordinary men, whether plowing eight acres of new ground or cutting in one day eighty-eight shocks of corn twelve hills square on a steep hillside. Then had followed the work at ARMCO, LMU, and Vanderbilt, the teaching, writing, and lecturing to leaven the farm work and to help him to bring his agrarian dream of writing, farming, and teaching to harvest. Back in 1935 he had laughed to see people walking so fast in New York City. "Even the dogs," he thought, "walked sidewise to keep from flying." But long since he had begun to change, had learned to "save time" by doing more work more intensively. Increasingly he had found himself living by schedules and watching clocks. "America is my lemon," one of his friends had said. "Brother how I love its juice." This was the way Jesse had begun to feel; and he was moving faster and doing more, writing and buying more denuded and farmed-out hill acres, endeavoring through land enrichment and forestation, like Ben Tuttle in his poem "The Builder and the Dream," "*To build, and live, and never to destroy.*" The first week of January 1954 opened with a flurry of lecture trips to Cleveland, Cincinnati, Chicago, and Dallas and Waco, Texas; at the latter he spoke at Baylor University to a thousand who paid to hear him talk. "I gave them a talk, too," he recorded, and signed dozens of books. The next day after a flight to Columbus and similar affair at Ohio State University, he returned home to join Deane and to go over his books with Calvin Clarke, his tax attorney and financial adviser. "I'd spent as much as I'd made and I felt very badly about it. Deane and I came away after seeing facts and figures, disgusted with ourselves." On the twenty-sixth, he was off to Chicago on a three-day lecture tour of the midwest, during which he spoke so vigorously in Ernest Hemingway's hometown of Oak Park that his clothes were wet with perspiration. Returning home on a 7:15 flight from Chicago, as the plane arose he "saw distant clouds of red and then the sunrise. Beautiful in winter. Coffee and a sweet cake for breakfast." At Cincinnati he indulged his old habit and visited Acres of Books and the Ohio Bookstore before continuing to Greenup in the early afternoon. The next week he was back in Cincinnati and Chicago again. At the Book and Author Luncheon at the Blackstone Hotel he met Bergan Evans at the speaker's table, where he sat beside Mrs. Adlai Stevenson. Evans spoke, then Jesse—"one of my best," Jesse judged, "made it hard on other speakers. Sorry for this. I never got away from the speakers' table. They carried my books there for me to sign."

The following week of Lincoln's birthday he was at his alma mater in Harrogate, Tennessee, where he renewed friendships with Hazel Fulton Davis, Roland Carter, President Kincaid, Earl Hobson and Myrtle Smith, and later saw Ida Shifley at Ewing, Virginia. Back in W-Hollow the last day of February, he, Naomi, and Jane went to church. "Then we came back home, the best place of all, to spend the day, woods very bleak and hills very da[rk]. Yet, I enjoy the bleakness of winter and moan of February winds up this valley."

As early as February 2, he had "got up not feeling too well." In mid-February a fire broke out close to the old Collins house, and Jesse fought it with over forty others. He complained that he "tired easily, even while fighting fire." He had had to lie down and rest before he could get up and fight fire again. So he went to Dr. Charles Vidt for a checkup and found his "heart was skipping beats" and his blood pressure "was not right either." The physician put him on a diet of twelve hundred calories, and soon he was losing a pound a day. "I am glad the doctor told you to 'slow down,' " Donald Davidson wrote from Nashville. It was another thing when he was young; "then, after a while, you don't bounce quite as readily. Nobody knows, except writers, how much writing takes out of a man, especially when he's doing other things in addition . . . like lecturing."

By mid-March his weight was down to 199 and his clothes were too large for him. He felt lighter on his feet but also weaker. "If anything was wrong with my heart, I didn't know it. I couldn't feel it. I felt fine except for my being weak," and he complained of growing "tiresome too soon." He knew, though, he was not up to par—"not up to the capacity of real work and this hurt me." By March 17 Dr. Vidt found Jesse's blood pressure normal and lifted his diet from twelve hundred to sixteen hundred calories a day. In early April he worked and supervised the setting of twenty thousand seedling pines. His father and he were later looking at the alfalfa when he got sick with a migraine "and suffered hell. I did much vomiting."

It was a strange year. Honors came heavily, yet they did not come easily. On March 18 he reluctantly went to the state capital "to show reason why" he should be selected "Poet Laureate of Kentucky." He was so offended at the backhanded compliment that at first he did not want to go to Frankfort at all, but after talking on the telephone with his friend, H. L. Donovan, President of the University of Kentucky, who advised him to "take it" even if he had to share it, Jesse made the trip. In fact, the Legislature had deadlocked over Jesse and Edwin Carlisle Litsey, in Jesse's view "an unimportant writer—even locally." The aging Litsey read a poem before the Legislature. Then Jesse read "Kentucky Is My Land," and the affair was over. With something less than genuine enthusiasm he wrote in his journal, "Kentucky I suppose [is the] only state in the Union with two poet laureates." He had published only two short stories and one essay up through June that year; his essay "Character and the American Youth," appearing in the university publication *Baylor Line,* was a condensation of his first university commencement address. He had spent long hours preparing his address. "I must not fail," he wrote in his journal. "Writing a talk and writing fiction are entirely different. I never cared to write a talk. But to be forced to write one, then I could do it." During the final week of May, President and Mrs. White and Professor Hudson Long guided him through a maze of receptions, media interviews, academic and theological gatherings, luncheons and dinners. On May 28 he spoke to ten thousand people in the Baylor stadium, after which he received his fourth honorary doctoral degree, his first having been granted at the University of Kentucky in 1944 when he had appeared on the platform with Milton Eisenhower. (Others had followed at Lincoln Memorial University in 1950 and at Marietta College in Ohio in 1954.)

Before 1954 was out, five more stories would appear in such publications as *Ladies' Home Journal, Progressive Farmer,* and *Esquire.* His junior work *A Penny's Worth of Character* was published as his seventeenth book in late October and *Taps* appeared in translation under the title *Hurra for soldat Tussie* in Stockholm. Baylor English Department Head C. E. Bryant's article "Kentucky Is His Land" was printed in the *Christian Herald.* Even Allen Tate, who had never cared for Jesse or his work, was obliged to include him in his Library of Congress publication *Sixty American Poets.* During the summer Jesse made trips to attend the twenty-fifth reunion of the Class of 1929 at LMU in June, to speak at Northwestern University in July, and with Deane and Jane to Washington,

New York City, and the Williamsburg–Yorktown area for combined professional and vacationing purposes. They returned in early September by way of White Sulphur Springs and the Hawk's Nest, West Virginia, over what must be one of the most sharply winding mountain highways in America.

Jesse was cutting grass with the electric mower when a pain struck him in the chest. He went to the porch, but the pain was so sharp he could neither sit nor lie down. Deane got him an Alka-Seltzer but it did not ease the pain. Dr. Conley, a local osteopath, gave him two glycerine tablets, which immediately produced relief; he thought it was definitely Jesse's heart and advised him to go to Ashland. There Dr. Paul Holbrook checked him out with an EKG, and brought in Dr. Winnans, a heart specialist, to confer on the case. Jesse was worried, but more EKGs failed to reveal any definite heart damage. Still, Jesse did not feel good; he did not sleep well and often could hardly get his breath. Dr. Holbrook told him on September 24, so Jesse recorded in his journal, "how people often thought they had something wrong with their he[arts] and all [that] was the matter was the thoughts in their minds. He intimated that the whole idea was in my head." He may have experienced "acute indigestion." Jesse told the physician, "I had a feeling that a muscle had been strained over or near my heart. It felt like something torn." He kept telling the doctor "about this strange feeling," but the doctor "only looked strangely at me and smiled." Though uncertain of his condition, Jesse mowed grass the next day and resumed his schedule. Two days later he had just got up from his writing when "strange feelings" swept over him. "I almost fell in the floor." Deane rushed him to Dr. Conley's who hurriedly administered glycerine tablets, as before bringing him some relief.

On September 27 he entered King's Daughters Hospital for a rest and complete checkup. Following EKGs and X rays the next day he reviewed his case history with Dr. Paul Holbrook: "I told him the pain was over my heart, that the pains, very light[,] went down my left arm to my elbow and that I felt like vomiting—that the pains bent me almost double. He said the fact the pain was over the heart was a sign that it was *muscular* instead of *heart*. I argued with Paul that his machine couldn't record pain. And the pains I'd had were terrific. He said to me: 'Too many people get it in their heads they have something wrong with their hearts when there's not anything wrong with them.' " The next day Jesse smoked freely in his hospital room, "now that Dr. Paul had the feeling my trouble was muscular." Dr. Winnans also talked with Jesse, and both physicians went over his EKGs. Neither could find anything wrong. "So they came to the conclusion my trouble was muscular." Jesse was a happy man, and that afternoon Deane drove him to the new high-level dam below Greenup, where Jesse joined other such dignitaries as Senator John Sherman Cooper and Congressman Bruce Spence for the ground-breaking ceremonies. On the last day of September, a jubilant Jesse sent telegrams that he would, after all, be available for his strenuous autumn lecturing schedule. This was a financial relief, too, for he would soon be making two talks a day at five hundred dollars each. "I'd been given a clean bill of health and I was proud of this."

Jesse had written Donald Davidson about his worry over his heart and his decision made by September 21 to cancel "all planned visits and autumn lectures." His former professor replied, "You are lucky to have Nature's warning. . . . Undoubtedly you have been pushing yourself *much* too hard for a long time. . . . And you are no longer 25 years old! . . . For heaven's sake, and your own sake, and all our sakes who cherish you so much, do be careful and restrain your enthusiasm for swinging scythes or moving boulders and logs—and for sticking all night at a typewriter on coffee and tobacco." Yet, as human as anyone else, Jesse tended to believe what he wanted to believe, and on the first day of October cel-ebrated his "clean bill of health" by mowing the grass just before he ate supper. Then suddenly, "I was almost overcome with deep chest pains . . . had to lie down on the divan." The pains continued for an hour and a half. "This *muscular* pain," he wrote in his journal, "was terrible." He called Dr. Holbrook, and the physician asked him to come to Ashland for heat "therapy" for muscular pains, and Jesse obliged him. In fact, the next day when, as Jesse believed, "the muscles in my chest were giving me trouble," he reasoned, "if I worked and got hot I could relax my muscles and, perhaps, get rid of the pain." So he cut grass again, while Deane got out and worked in the flowers. The next day he did not feel well and stayed home from church, getting a little exercise by typing an article on one-room schools, which he mailed to *Reader's Digest.* He would soon be leaving on his lecture tour, and he believed himself fortunate that his trouble was muscular and not his heart. Pre-paring to leave W-Hollow the next day, he wrote in his journal, "I didn't have a sure feeling of myself." The next morning, Thursday, October 7, he awoke with pains in his chest, applied the heat pad he had pur-chased for his therapy, felt somewhat better and arose and packed. Naomi took him to the airport, and he flew to Paducah, Kentucky, where college official Marvin O. Wrather met him. He spent the night in the Wrathers' home following a social evening, but he did not sleep well.

Friday morning he sat around upstairs at the Wrather home for a while, and then he and Ann Wrather walked to the Murray State College auditorium where President Ralph Woods introduced him to Murray students and to thirty-five hundred teachers from the First Kentucky Educational District. Jesse gave a typically good talk, but extended it for an hour. Dr. John Minton, Vice-President of Administrative Affairs at Western Kentucky University, was sitting up front in the audience then and noticed that when Jesse got to the end of his speech he was perspiring and obviously laboring. The audience was not aware that anything was wrong. A Mr. Henson guided Jesse through the crowd on his way to catch a chartered plane to take him on to Flora, Illinois, for an afternoon talk. Just outside the auditorium, down he went, his feet higher than his head. *"I will not die,"* he told himself as he collapsed. "I will not die," he told himself as he went out.

Mr. Henson and a college student got him into a car and took him to the Wrathers. Vaguely he managed to ask for glycerine tablets, and someone found two, he later recalled, "which perhaps saved me." As a result of the coronary occlusion, his shattered heart was beating 250 times a minute, forcing its way seepingly around the double-infarction blockage.

Four days later he regained consciousness long enough to speak briefly with Dr. Woodford B. Troutman, a heart specialist from Louisville who had been called in on the case by the Stuarts' family physician, Dr. Charles E. Vidt of Ironton, Ohio, with the concurrence of Dr. Hugh Houston of Murray, the local attending physician. Jesse found himself under an oxygen tent. Among other medications, Jesse was administered Hedulin, an anticoagulant. Deane was there, too; it was the evening of their fifteenth anniversary. Whereas before his lecturing schedule had rarely allowed them to be together on their anniversary, this year they ironically were. Dr. Houston roused Jesse and introduced him to Dr. Troutman. "Do you drink?" Dr. Troutman inquired.

"No," Jesse replied.

"What about smoking?"

"I smoke incessantly but never inhale," he said. That was the extent of their conversation. Jesse was still in the clothes he had collapsed in, and he had not shaved since that Friday morning.

A week later Nurse Edith Meeker McDougal was attending him in the darkened room when Jesse awoke and asked her to open the window high and let the fresh air and sunlight in. He had no way of knowing she had been instructed by the doctors to keep the room dark, to make it more isolated. Jesse began talking about his Grandfather Hilton and how they used to cut timber in the hills. "I loved the out-of-doors," he continued, "and can't stand to be shut in too long." He went on talking, "I love life and never want to die." Then he noticed that she was averting her head toward the wall. She wiped the tears from her eyes and gave him a sedative, and Jesse went back to sleep.

On October 16 he received "a check for a few hundred dollars" from Marion Ives. This made him feel "very, very good to know I was still earning something. It was like a good dose of medicine . . . that does one good. It gave me a lift. I knew I wasn't through." After lunch he requested a radio. The nurses said he could listen to ballgames if he did not have a special interest in one of the teams. Five days later, on October 21, Dr. Houston had the oxygen tent removed. That day, he later wrote, "I felt that I was stepping out of my grave."

Relatives and friends were on hand. Deane, Jane, James, Glennis, and Whitie were there by Saturday, the day after his attack. Deane could not handle all the phone calls coming in from all over the country, so Marvin Wrather arranged to receive them in his office at Murray State College. Flowers came by the hour, and mail and telegrams arrived from all over the country. Wire services, newspapers, radio, and television carried reports, as did Walter Winchell in his column. President Woods and the Murray officials did what they could. By Monday, his father, Sophia, Mary and Orin Nelson, and others came to the hospital. Although he was not conscious of their visits, when he was told of them he wrote in his daily journal, "I later learned I had friends."

He dreamed,

> I was back home on the land with my father and mother. I was getting the cow, Old Gypsy, up morning and night for my mother to milk—just like I did from 9–12 years old. Mom milked her under a white oak tree and I gathered the manure with a shovel and piled it up. I later hauled this manure a half mile and put [it] over our garden. We had only a horse and cow in those days. I was walking barefooted again on the dews of morning and hunting Gypsy for my young parents. We are the food we eat, the air we breathe and we are our ancestry too—in time of near death we go back to them.

Even here on this Delta plain of western Kentucky, the path of his life was W-Hollow, as his imagination had retraced it from beyond the dark hills back to its wellspring. If the kingdom of God were, as he believed, within him, then this was the way he had to go, the way that, as the psalmist had said, had been made straightest of all the world before him.

How he yearned to live, to move out from and back to it again; for in death he feared there would be no remembrance of his beautiful valley. And how could one write poetry from the grave?

He dreamed about W-Hollow:

> I dreamed it was a brother to me in my youth and that it had to be a brother still. I hated to die and leave this land. I was tied to it by a close affinity—so close that I couldn't bear the thoughts of ever leaving it and let my trees be cut, my wildflowers be destroyed by fire and wildlife be destroyed by ruthless boys—boys that could be changed by proper advice. My dream was [so] vivid that I thought of the W-Hollow Valley and my hills as home and an idea for a poem came to me. To contrast W-Hollow features with those in other countries and W-Hollow's were dearer for W-Hollow was home.

Forty-six days after his admittance to the Murray Hospital, November 23, he was released. Naomi Deane and her sister Nancy Curry shared driving the five hundred miles across Kentucky the long way. Sore from his first day of riding, Jesse thought, "The dark trees, blue skies and even cool November rain looked good to me. I wanted to reach out from the car and pull all the bright wind into the car and around me." After a few days in Louisville and further checking by Dr. Troutman, Jesse rode on through the Bluegrass, enjoying it. "Kentucky looked good even if all the leaves were gone." At W-Hollow his father, Mrs. Norris, and George Curry were on hand to greet them. Mick Stuart, now seventy-four and barely half Jesse's size, helped his son from the car. In W-Hollow once more, with his father, Jesse was deeply touched. "Back home again," he thought, "and I was lucky . . . [I] could thank my God for returning."

The signs No Visitors. Doctor's Orders went up at the Stuarts' private drive and on their porch, for Dr. Vidt had determined that even well-meaning visitors caused Jesse's blood pressure to shoot up with the natural excitement of his ardent temperament. For convenience Jane gave up her new downstairs room next to the bath and close to the kitchen for her father, where he lay with thick socks to warm the extremities of his feet and to ease the strain on his heart. From the time he had written "Clearing in the Sky," Jesse had known that his father was seriously ill, that when Mick had cleared that new ground garden on the secret hill, he was going back to something deeply intuitive, to "the land that God left," as he had said, but perhaps to his youth as well, to a place away from pain and further aging. Jesse knew that just a week before Christmas his brother-in-law Whitie Liles had taken his father to Ashland to do Christmas shopping and to see the doctor. On the way back they had stopped so that Mick could get a haircut, and then he had stopped in to see Jesse. "Jesse," his father told him, "the only reason you are alive is because of the prayers of the Christian people. God has so ordered you to live. It's for a purpose. Your work is not done." It was strange talk, coming from his father, Jesse thought. A few days later Whitie stopped in briefly and Jesse asked how his father was. "Not well," Whitie answered. "Not well at all. He has a burning in his chest." Whitie came again two days later and when Jesse asked about his father said, "He's not well, Jesse. He's got that burning in his chest. He tried to go to the barn and we made him come back." Jesse wanted to see his father, but it was not then possible. He stoically reasoned, "But as soon as I got better and he got better, I knew we'd be seeing each other this summer."

The next day, December 23, Jesse was aware of a lot of traffic going up and down the hill to his father's house. He wondered if his father were worse. In a little while, Naomi and Dr. Vidt walked into his room and the physician checked Jesse's blood pressure and listened to his heart. Jesse urged Dr. Vidt when he finished to go up and see his father. "Maybe you can stop that burning in his chest."

Dr. Vidt did not answer, listening to Jesse's heart. Then he said, "I'm going to give you a shot that will relax you. I don't want any tension buildup but I want to keep you relaxed." They talked awhile and Jesse began to get drowsy. "Jesse," the physician said, "I've been asked to bring you some bad news. Your father died at 7:25, which was an hour ago."

"Oh, no, no, no," Jesse said. He turned over with his face on his pillow and shook with grief. A hundred images of the familiar thin, wiry figure with the red face raced through his dazed mind. His father had always been "one of those men who seemed to be an immortal fixture in his natural surroundings as much as a rock, a tree, or a hill."[7]

That October of 1954 a darkness had closed in upon his life. Now in December, another dark, a dark within the darkness, had fallen, too, and there was no deeper darkness than in this valley. Yet for now he must, crippled heart and all, walk through the valley of the shadow.

15

Return to April
1955–1960

———◇———

The day of his father's funeral he got up, staggering. Dr. Vidt and a few well-meaning relatives and close friends were on hand to help him see the day through. His father's dying had borne so heavily on his mind that he wrote in his journal, "For every pleasure in life there are six ills to beset it." There had never been a time in his life when Jesse dreamed that he would not be able to attend his father's funeral. Facing up to it, he characteristically gave full measure and faced the future, too. "What a terrible time to live," he wrote, "but one must be able to endure and one must look forward to health and a new tomorrow."

He would keep his land. "I certainly was not in any mood to preside over the parts of my dismembered farm." In the days following his father's funeral he worked and saw some relatives and friends, including Bob Hillman and Jake and Margaret Lynd. Whitie faithfully picked up and brought his mail. As Calvin Clarke and Irene Earls had come to stay with Jesse and Naomi during the funeral, now Glennis, Mr. and Mrs. Norris, and James dropped by. Jesse's enforced rest periods and sedated naps brought the beginnings of a slow recovery and some freshness to his short working hours. Small successes boosted his morale. Another of the much-desired thin, flat envelopes arrived, a check for his article "Rendezvous with Happiness," and his article "My Father's Fifty Acres" appeared in *Better Farming*.

By the end of the first week of the new year he "got into a story" he first called "The Longest Row of Corn in the World" and soon finished it for Deane to entitle "A Ribbon for Baldy"; it appeared the next year in *Coronet*. Then Jesse received good news of his improvement from his doctor. For months he had worn pajamas, robes, heavy socks, and house-slippers, but on the cold early morning of January 13 he put on his trousers, shoes, shirt, and sweater and "felt more like a man again." He worked on a new story, "Angel in the Pasture," dealing with that personal memory of his mother, their cow Gypsy, and an idyllic day of his boyhood he had recalled in the Murray Hospital under the oxygen tent; it would eventually be published in *Esquire*. By the middle of January he had resumed his prodigious correspondence and for the week's mailing sent sixty-nine letters to the post office. He began to get up early enough each morning to see Jane leave for school. One noon he rode with Naomi Deane to Greenup, a routine run for her but "a wonderful trip" for Jesse. He got back home in time to return to bed for his afternoon nap, after which he revised another story, "Love Is a Quadratic Equation."

On January 20 he ventured outside and walked around the house over the snow when the sun was shining, and then following his afternoon nap he did it again. He could not find his pen, so against Dr. Vidt's advice typed a new short story, "Uncle Jeff Had a Way," which would appear in the *Southwest Review*. One cold January Sunday he and Naomi looked out a frost-silted window to see twelve snowbirds, two redbirds, and two ground squirrels eating birdfeed under the dogwood where they had scattered it for their outdoor friends. Some days he got little work done. One day he "piddled with" poetry, four poems he planned to send to the *Saturday Evening Post*. When the thermometer dropped late in the month, he was up in the dark early morning and went to the porch to see the stars in the blue cold sky and to see how cold it was— six below zero, he found, "and I was delighted." By month's end he felt much better and could look back on a solid stint of original writing and revision, by his own count ten poems, fourteen short stories, and three articles. He had also kept up both his daily journal and a special journal he had begun January 1 in order to provide exercise for his hands, left stiff and sore by his coronary. Naomi had also urged him to write; for she had known all too well, Dr. Vidt's advice or no, that with Jesse "it was write or die." Writing for him, she believed, would prove therapeutic.

Wednesday, February 2, "was a shadowy day for Mr. Groundhog," but that morning Jesse and Naomi drove to Ironton where he saw Dr. Vidt. At noon he ate his first meal of the year outside home at the McArthur Hotel, and "it tasted wonderful," he recorded. Later he enjoyed talking with Joe Creason and Tommy Miller of the *Courier-Journal*, where his essay "When the Percoon Blooms, It's Spring" would appear the following month. He had "a wonderful morning" the next Friday. He had got up thinking it was daylight, only to discover it was four A.M. and the moon "big as a barrelhead was bright as a morning sun," shining low directly over Shinglemill Hollow. He had watched a rabbit play in their yard in the moonlight.

In the mail came two short-story acceptances from *Esquire* for "As a Man Thinketh" and "Sweetbird for Sheriff." On rainy nights he could hear the stream beneath the house "full and roaring," and he began to sleep without sedatives. Some tin cans littered on upland yards along a road he and Naomi drove had taken his eye. The scene beneath imminent snowclouds gave him an idea for a poem he had to write. He took the idea through three sets of words before it emerged the way he wanted it, a solace of winter snow set in his apostrophe to the clouds:

> Move closer, fast, dark, storm clouds over earth,
> Enfold it in a blanket clean and white . . .
> Come, gentle snow, before the winter's over,
> Too long away are legions of green grass;
> Spread over earth your clean and wholesome cover
> To hide with loveliness these scars we pass.

The piece, "Come, Gentle Snow," would appear in the *Colorado Quarterly*.

Spring floods came again, and though they inundated Greenup, in W-Hollow the rushing water only raised the volume of its merry voice down Shinglemill Creek through the culvert under their house, making the house seem snugger and sleep sweeter. He wrote of these things in the new journal. Word came that *Better Farming* was willing to pay "one grand" for his new essay "Suppertime." For recreation he read Emerson, and by May turned a critical eye upon more than a hundred accumulating pages of his new journal, doubting it would "amount to a hill of beans"; yet he continued to record his daily encounters with the natural world he knew so intimately and to which he was relating again with renewed vigor and insight. He would continue to write until, by the end of the year, 1,795 pages had piled up. From this manuscript, editor Ed Kuhn would carve the most Thoreauvian of Jesse's books, *The Year of My Rebirth,* to appear late in 1956 and receive critical praise across the country. In New York its pages would move Lewis Gannett to write, "Words come as naturally to Jesse Stuart as humming to a bee. They bubble out of him like water from a mountain spring." In Chicago, V. P. Hass reported it as a "beautiful, thoughtful, and wonderfully rewarding book," and in San Francisco, William Hogan advised his readers that they "need not be recovering from a near-fatal illness to respond to Jesse Stuart's truths."

Watching a June sunset, his lyric muse transcribed, "The crickets chant under the floor and near our porch. The sound of their drowsy singing softly scratches the silk of evening." He took time again to rest and to live as well as to write. "I didn't sweat over lectures and trouble about the right end for a novel. I had much that was new to see in a new world of ground, tree, leaf, stream, flower, wind, and sky. I didn't think of . . . stories I was going to write this month. Characters for these didn't start kicking up their heels in my mind." He did little things, but they were not unimportant. He shot a rat that was killing ground sparrows and stealing birdfeed, and some of his old fight came back when he nearly stepped on a copperhead, then killed it with a tobacco stick. That month he took time to watch the battle of a hummingbird and an English sparrow.

He wrote August Derleth, "My world is about 5 miles in diameter . . . this farm to the post office. I'm not allowed to drive the car yet." But he kept his depression over his new limitations in check no less than his cholesterol. In July while he and Naomi were sitting at a counter having coffee and doughnuts—Jesse's first cup since October—a fine-looking waiter changed his dollar and left the coffee pot. Naomi passed a note observing the man was blind. Jesse had not caught the detail. "This man's cheerfulness in his corner-cupboard world," he admitted, "made me ashamed." Putting it all together, he wrote "My Heart Attack and I," published next month in the *Saturday Evening Post*.

Though he worked, he rested and frequently went back to the land, the source of his creative substance. He sought remote places, the habitats of the flora and fauna he knew well. At one time in July he reveled in sheer laziness. "I was under the high bullgrass and wild phlox that grew on the banks of W-Branch, away from everybody." There he contemplated the minnows in a water hole. Gradually, each pleasure was becoming his again. Even driving the car excited him, though he doubted most people would believe him if he said so. "But the little things we do, the small pleasures, only seem important when we are forced to stop doing them."

In August of that year he went to Berea College, where he and fellow Kentucky writer Harriette Arnow received Berea Centennial Awards. The Stuarts had decided to make a vacation of their trip to the century-old school located in Madison County, where the Bluegrass meets the Cumberlands. There Jesse saw dramatist Paul Green and attended Green's new summer drama *Wilderness Road*. They went on through central Kentucky and near Springfield visited Elizabeth Madox Roberts' home and saw her grave. At Bardstown, they toured Federal Hill, "my old Kentucky home." They saw Knob Creek Farm near Hodgensville,

Lincoln's boyhood home, and went on into southwest Kentucky, stopping at Guthrie, "where . . . I met Thomas Warren, brother of Robert Penn Warren," and "looked at the places they had lived and where they went to high school." At the beach of Kentucky Lake, they "took a dip in the bright clean waters" and he enjoyed teaching Jane to swim. Back home Jesse went to work with relish, while Naomi and Jane extended their holiday with a final trip to Lake Vesuvius in Ohio. "No one disturbed me," Jesse wrote in his journal. "I wouldn't let them. I was in bed when one carload came. I hid when another came. Our car was gone and they thought we were away."[1]

For some weeks he had known the townspeople were organizing a tribute to him of some kind, and although he was pleased and curious, he said but little. On October 7 he went to a Greenup dentist and while in the chair having his teeth cleaned, so he wrote in his journal, "I watched the workers erecting a memorial to me on the courthouse square." When he left, he drove on the opposite side of the courthouse up the street by the blacksmith shop so he would not be seen close to the monument. "Yet," he admitted, "I'd liked to have seen it." In the days that followed he worked on his speech for the occasion, cooperated by assembling some information and materials to loan for an exhibit, and took hours-long afternoon naps. In early October he recorded pains in his arms and chest, but said nothing. The afternoon before the big day, following a nap, he wrote, "I didn't think much about tomorrow."

It was "The Biggest Invasion in the History of Greenup," one reporter observed of the October 15 celebration. Thousands poured into town, engulfing the courthouse square and surrounding streets. Over their surfaces Jesse had once helped pave, flapping in a brisk autumn wind, were bright bunting replicas of his books, while the parade, replete with six school bands from the area, blared marches behind high-kicking drum majors and majorettes. High school floats depicted such scenes from Jesse's books as six lugubrious pallbearers at the sides of a flag-bedecked casket, toting the representational remains of Private Tussie, while a bugle sounded "Taps." Led by the Lions Club, Greenup County civic organizations had come together to plan the affair. Governor Lawrence Weatherby had declared October 15 "Jesse Hilton Stuart Day in Kentucky." Master of Ceremonies Circuit Judge J. R. Sowards introduced two college presidents who spoke on the occasion. Dr. Robert L. Kincaid told of Jesse's student experiences at LMU and termed its famous graduate the "voice of all youth and old folks of these land-locked hills," a writer who makes his readers "live and love with him the beauty of God's great outdoors." Dr. Herman Lee Donovan of the University of Kentucky paid tribute to Jesse as "one of the foremost literary men in the world," compared him and his W-Hollow to Thoreau and his Walden Pond, and pointed to Jesse's realism, his "true picture of mountaineers." There was something else, too. "No other literary man has had such an honor as has been paid to Jesse Stuart today," Donovan concluded. Then at four o'clock Jesse, Naomi, and Jane walked to the tall draped bulk on the courthouse lawn, and while the Ashland Tomcat Band struck up "My Old Kentucky Home" and Jesse stood biting his lip, thirteen-year-old Jessica Jane unveiled the nine-foot Georgia granite monolith topped by a bust of Jesse facing southward between two granite pilasters. Cut into the Georgia granite shaft below in bas-relief was a bull-tongue plow, emblematic of the land and people of whom he sang, and under that his name with "Poet, Novelist, Educator," and the inscription from Pakenham Beatty:

> By your own soul's law, learn to live,
> And if men thwart you, take no heed,
> If men hate you, have no care;
> Sing your song, dream your dream,
> Hope your hope, and pray your prayer.

Then Jesse spoke that day. He had spoken to many audiences over America, but he told them, "This is the greatest audience I have ever faced." Phantoms of old battles that day held back incipient tears: the lawsuits of the *Cradle-of-the-Copperhead* days of his first superintendency, the old educational wars, his exile after the Guggenheim, carrying a gun during his editorship, the blackjacking, the political isolation, and the furor just after the war about *Foretaste of Glory* when, more than once, he and Naomi had discussed leaving. But these were now at worst only memory's nagging evanescences. "What makes this occasion unique," he said, "is the fact that this tribute is being paid to me in my lifetime. I have not always been a good boy in my home town. But I never was at any time in my life without ambitions and dreams." He spoke of Greenup— and of Greenwood—of Blakesburg—and Honeywell, too—and of his fictional children like the Tussies, Old Op, Shan, and Finn, conjecturing, "Maybe because my friends here knew these people so well is why I am honored today." Education having been the transforming experience of his life, he said, "I have learned that sound teaching, tolerance, and love are the greatest things on earth." Above all, "I rejoice that I am living. . . . I have so many things to be thankful for, of which the greatest is life. Each day, I make myself believe this day will be the finest." He expected to do more books, "as many more . . . as you see jackets displayed over the streets. . . . This rests not only in the hands of my good physicians but in the hands of the Great Physician over all." His eyes met those of the men, women, and children of his audience. "You know, my friends, people must have courage. The young, middle-aged, and old alike must be courageous. We must have the will to live forever. We must have the will to dream forever. We cannot turn back." Briefly he mused upon the simpler past when he recalled only six automobiles in Greenup County, but mutability affected everything and his writing was changing, too. "I have written of the present because I have found it interesting. I like to write of life that is being lived around me. . . . People live dramas so strange and incredible they often have to be changed to be made plausible; then, they become fiction."

He recalled his Plum Grove teachers still living, first among them Calvin Clarke, who had taught him to read and write, then Nora Riggs Scott and Mrs. Earl Kotcamp. He wished two other people especially could be there that day. "They have left many footprints on this spot of earth since the turn of this century, never dreaming a marker would be erected here to one of their children. This was their home town, too." He rose to his peroration: "My home was the strong springboard from which I dove into the waters of life, believing firmly it was my duty to amount to something," and concluded:

It can never be truthfully said that you in my home town haven't been good to me. You and my fictional children are becoming chummier all the time. Minor reforms in education which seemed radical twenty years ago, when I advocated them, have come to pass. Because I have followed my profession diligently, whether I have pleased or displeased you, I am thus honored by you. And for this honor I am grateful from the depths of my heart.

When reporters interviewed Jesse after the ceremony and asked how he felt, he likened himself to the Duke of Wellington after Waterloo and Meade after Gettysburg: "I felt victorious, but battered, too." The next morning the Stuarts went to church, they came home and ate a good lunch, and that afternoon he went to bed and slept four hours. People in cars drove up to his house, seemed to sense his desire for privacy, and turned around and left the Stuarts to an afternoon by themselves. Good wishes came in from all over the country, but two letters that stood out were from Donald Davidson and August Derleth. Davidson had just returned from Breadloaf when he heard of the whole affair and wrote, "Never was a tribute more richly and truly deserved than the one paid you in the 'Jesse Stuart Day' celebration in your honor. It is wonderful that you can have this expression of admiration and devotion from *your own folks,* and have it now. That hardly ever happens. It couldn't have happened to Tom Wolfe. It can't happen to Ransom, Tate, Warren, or me—I would think. And Mississippi is certainly not going to honor Wm. Faulkner in such a way. You have a certain gift that none of these have." The words moved Jesse, but what the lyric poetry professor wrote next touched him most deeply: "In a sense you have restored the *bardic* tradition, which has been thought entirely obsolete and lost." In his reply to Davidson, Jesse repeated Davidson's words on the bardic tradition in his postscript and added: "Gee, I love this statement. How wonderful of you to say this. . . . If I have done anything for poetry and poets . . . I am happy."

From the summer of 1955, August Derleth had not heard from or about his old friend until he received an invitation in the mail to come to Greenup and take part in "a 'memorial' to Jesse Stuart." The Wisconsin writer had been frankly "jolted," as he wrote, "because 'memorials' are usually for dead writers, and for a little while I got to wondering if you had shuffled off, because even if there had been nothing in the milestones column of *Time,* it seemed a remote possibility." But Derleth finally concluded that "what the people in your neck of the woods were doing was a tribute and not a memorial, no matter what they called it, because I couldn't quite believe you could have passed on in utter silence." After Jesse finally wrote Derleth in early January of 1956, the Sac Prairie native responded with visible relief, "It was certainly good to get your letter. . . ."[2]

Mr. Gallion's School summarizes in a fictional dimension many of Jesse Stuart's experiences during the 1956/1957 school year, when he once again assumed the principalship of McKell High School. The argument between Naomi and Jesse over his assuming this rigorous duty after a coronary is recapitulated in the first chapter of the book, at which point of action Grace tells her husband, George Gallion, "You're egotistical," and he replies, "Maybe I am." His rationale is that he is needed in a desperate educational situation, and so differs with his wife. They agree to leave the decision up to Dr. Charles Vinn, of whom the thinly disguised prototype was Jesse's physician, Dr. Charles Vidt; the M.D. agrees to go along with George if George in turn thinks he can handle the job and agrees not to climb stairs. As the prototype of Grace, Naomi was as furious and protective as the fictional wife. When Grace takes her husband to task for being a "do-gooder," George replies, "You wouldn't

want me to be one of our walking dead, would you? How can people
live just for full bellies and soft beds? How can they?" Though still
convalescing from his heart condition, George defends his nearly killing
pace: "We can't live smugly in our shells with a little security. In an
ignorant world, no one is secure."

Though still too weak to climb stairs, the first day he does it anyway,
and "takes on" Kensington High (McKell High), a problem school with
a maddening scope of conflicts: a corrupt political system operated by
a superintendent who can raise thousands to buy votes when there is
not enough in the budget for textbooks; a teacher shortage; overcrowded
classrooms, which even cast-off pre-fabs cannot remedy; a watered-down
curriculum; off-campus hoodlums; spoiled children of indulgent parents; shoplifting students; a dissident group of teachers; more than a
handful of rebellious students who want to be expelled; a petty gambling
syndicate; student riots, and more.

Gallion is a man with timeless as well as old-fashioned values, caught
up in a rebel-without-a-cause atmosphere. As early as October 30, 1955,
Jesse had seen James Dean in *Rebel without a Cause* and thought it "a
terrible movie," which "wasn't finished, [or] solved." He perceived a
direct causal relationship between the cinematic testament of direction-
less youth and the recalcitrance at McKell High that year:

> Very soon we had . . . many boys going around mad about nothing,
> trying to be James Deans. . . . The idea was: Be mad at the world
> for nothing. I have seen many silly pictures, but this was the superior
> silly. Nevertheless, it influenced elementary and highschool stu-
> dents, for they are great imitators in those years. Well, James Dean
> was their image for a time. But he forgot, in his role of make-
> believe, that a high-speed engine could make four wheels leave the
> road. So he's no longer a rebel without a cause. But his movie
> influenced more youth in my school than I wanted to admit.

Gallion seems at times a modern Quixote graced in the strangely
unfamiliar armor of commonsensical decency, not above introducing
prodigal students to a different kind of "board" of education. He somehow manages, in an arpeggio of scenes, to put together a faculty, a
curriculum, a band, a football team, and eventually an esprit de corps
of an exhilarating, yet contradictory nature. Resourceful as his creator,
Gallion has a word to each. It is desirable that a teacher have many sides,
but "until education becomes a passion it is only routine," he tells one
teacher. To another, "You never enter the classroom alone. There is
somebody following you."

"And who is he?" the teacher asks skeptically.

"The man or woman you really are," Gallion replies.

Again, "If the world ends I think I know what will cause its destruction. And that is ignorance." Behind Gallion's epigrams is the wisdom of a lifetime and a depth of conviction that clearly restores faith in youth. Against administrators and teachers too inured to cynicism even to be outraged, he charges cowardly fear. To red-faced school board members and other critics he states that the old world is contaminating the teenagers. Once he reminds a self-righteous judge, "The trouble with adults is that they don't give youth credit for being great imitators."

In artistic balance as well as in substance, Mr. Gallion's school makes such topical educational novels as *Up the Down Staircase, Hickory Stick,* and *Blackboard Jungle* look like the frantic outpourings of novices. For here is a far more believable American high school in trouble, and it is treated through the complex vision of a mature, if idealistic, persona at once active and enigmatic, egotistical and self-giving, unorthodox and imaginative, comic and grave, wise and—not infrequently—powerful. By the end of the novel, Gallion's school has become a citadel of learning, high on a hill "in a world of darkness, bathed in light," emblematic of the human spirit caught in the eternal conflict between good and evil. Gallion is a committed man in an uncommitted world, and he convinces the reader that one human being can make a difference.

When Gallion's blood pressure jumps up and down erratically, and the pressure of his job begins to tell in his excitement, Dr. Vinn responds to Grace's complaint that her husband "won't take it easy" with the adjuration, "He'd better take it easy. If he doesn't he'll be the best teacher in the graveyard." Whereas in the novel, the decision for him to resign is medically decided through George's doctor—"You can't pass your physical this time, George"—in reality Jesse's decision to step down was more gradual and made by Jesse himself after the close of the school year. In truth, Naomi Deane continued to express her fears for her husband's welfare through her opposition to his principalship. Why should they teach when there were so many other things to do now, "so many interests"? She reminded Jesse that the years were passing and he should go to work on another book, "an idea," he admitted, "that might make sense." By March he had grown tired of teacher absences and his own diligence in substituting for them, thus performing double duty as principal and teacher. "Why do this?" he questioned himself. "Why not get back to writing and do a book!" He began to sleep fitfully and there were increasingly frequent hard days at McKell. There were intermittent victories, too. On January 25 he won the Kentucky Press Association's

"Kentuckian of the Year" award, and brought back from Louisville the inscribed silver pitcher for his students and faculty to see; and on April 15 the whole school got out of class to see the NBC Matinee Theatre dramatization of *The Thread That Runs So True.* He also won the *Lyric* magazine poetry prize of fifty dollars that year. Such recognition doubtless stimulated students' desires to pursue excellence on their own. As one student put it, seeing and knowing that Jesse Stuart was "a famous author gave me, and others, a feeling that we had a chance to climb higher." Jesse sensed Naomi Deane's dissatisfaction with their new life as returning teachers when she would not go with him to the annual April meeting of the Kentucky Education Association in Louisville. As the brief spring vacation neared, Jesse admitted his frustration in being "over extended in my work." He was trying to cover not only his educational work, but farming and writing as well—"three fields and not doing either one of these successfully." By the middle of May, "I was ready for this school to close. I was getting tired of school. I'd had enough. I wanted to get off schedule." This admission was due to more than the usual end-of-semester fatigue of teachers. There were too many people who wanted special favors. With work on the farm and writing, the principalship was simply "too much." Yet it was more than a month before he handed in his resignation for reasons he summarized as "outside pressures."

He was more exhausted than he realized, for he had much difficulty in getting back to work writing. "Writing is slow for me." After an arduous year as principal, turning out new work was "most difficult." Yet through June that year, he had managed to see into publication one short story, nine poems, and fourteen essays, eight of them for a special "Under My Sky" series in the *Louisville Courier-Journal.* The topics of this latter group dealt with a wide range of subjects: hot-rodding youth, the "hen's teeth" scarcity of teachers in Kentucky, the joys of nature and being alive, the expense of discipline, blackberry jelly, the first telephone in W-Hollow, an accolade for Kentucky writer Billy Clarke, and love songs of whippoorwills. Again he had found enchantment in April, stirring him to create anew in lofty concept and homely images these nostalgic lyrics:

And where have bright young winds of April gone,
Who lift their songs embedded in each heart?
Where are wild irises on gray sandstone?
Why do they and their blossoms now depart?
The rain-washed petals on the dogwood trees,

Starched by the night, pressed by the morning sun,
Have fallen like rain through eternities
Until each white bough is a barren one.
Why should one grieve to see this April pass
When it leaves history on futile grass?

He had been working hard on the farm, too, as he wrote Dr. Mims, now a long-retired professor in his mid-eighties:

This past year I . . . farmed. . . . Worked when I wanted to and when I didn't want to I didn't work. I steered away from excitement. Farm work and growing things is a very calm business. I have a farm here of 800 acres, valleys and hills and ridges. Have built roads here and reset forests. Then, I have two farms, level as floors, with 70 acres each. One farm is very valuable now since it joins the land from the C & O RR to Ohio River where a hundred million dollars worth of plants are going. So life moves on up here. One time when a meal was hard for me to get, I can get them now but I have to be careful what I eat. That is the irony of life but I love every day of it. Would love to see you. You're a great one and I love you for everything you have done for me.

> Sincerely,
> Jesse Stuart

What Jesse really needed was a good vacation, and a brand new "forward" of fifteen hundred dollars from McGraw-Hill provided him with the reason to go ahead. The middle of August the Stuarts vacationed north through Ohio to London, Ontario, then toured Toronto and Montreal. They continued along the St. Lawrence to Rimouski, heading southeast down the Matapedia to Amherst, Nova Scotia, just east of Chignecto Bay. There they stayed the night after having driven "along coastal waters over a nice country." Once Deane and Jane went down to the beach and gathered shells. Halifax was memorable, to Jesse the "most colorful city in North America." They lodged on Dalhousie Street near the university and explored the old seaport town. Jesse spent time at St. Marks Cemetery and The Citadel, while Jane bought herself a skirt of Stuart colors; later they saw a show together. The next morning the Stuarts left a foggy Halifax and drove to Yarmouth, where they caught "the Blue-Nose Ferry"; it took 160 cars to the mainland, and theirs was the 159th aboard. A westward trip across the Atlantic south of the Bay of Fundy brought them to Bar Harbor, and Jesse wrote, "How good it was to be back on U.S. soil! Canada was fine but it was better here. We ate a good breakfast for less." Later, they walked over the sand dunes of the desert of Maine, and at Portland toured Longfellow's home, "the most interesting of all authors' homes I've ever visited." They drove on toward Concord, Naomi Deane navigating with the map, and ended up at the capital of New Hampshire. Later in Concord, Massachusetts, where they got a room at an Irish-American home, Jesse and Jane "laughed at Deane and teased her a little about her mistake." She had first guided them west instead of south toward Boston and the Concord of Sleepy Hollow, their destination and the final resting places of Emerson, Hawthorne, and Thoreau. Sunday, August 25, they spent in the literary Concord, as Jesse recorded, "thinking of the life that had been here and what this little place had meant to America and to the world."

In three days they were back in W-Hollow, where Jesse had a box of two hundred letters waiting. These he answered religiously, as he always had, although since his heart attack he tried to hold all letters to a single page, usually in his characteristically large, upright script of blue or black ink. He found time that fall to attend the Kentucky Heart Association meeting in Louisville at the Pendennis Club, and to visit with old friends who called on him in W-Hollow, including Paul Dykes of the Class of '29, whom he had not seen since their graduation twenty-eight years before. By September he was hard at work gathering stories for his new collection. Even though he complained that he had "not one outstanding creative thing," that the drought had taken much of his crops, and that the loss of weight of his cattle was due to dry pasture, he was writing again. True, the short-story market was shrinking and he published only one new one that year, but he published ten poems and thirty-eight essays. Nine pieces appeared about him and his work, and one impressive checklist in the May/August issue of the *Bulletin of Bibliography* noted he had published fifty-one stories and poems in *Esquire* alone up through 1941. In addition, three more of his works were translated this year into Spanish, German, and Telugu. In October and November he finished two more manuscripts, and in a topical mood dubbed them Sputnick No. 1 and Sputnick No. 2, declaring that they had been "launched in my small literary sky." The first was his collection of short stories to be called *Plowshare in Heaven*, the second a juvenile book, *The Rightful Owner*. In late November he attended a reception at Georgetown College hosted by Dr. Woodridge Spears, and the next day gave his first talk to an audience of college students since 1954, when he had spoken at Northwestern University. His topic was "Why Write a Novel?" and he received a standing ovation. Now it appeared that he might be permitted to do some selective lecturing in the future. And although his eight hundred acres were expensive to maintain and the farming lost money more often than not, his conservation program on the land was moving toward completion. In late November he saw that lime was spread, and he and his men sowed wheat and rye—then the last of the rye on rough ground that would be "dished under"; and the last of the wheat, rye and winter oats were sowed and dished under in other areas to enrich the pasturage. He even helped haul his tobacco crop to market, using his own truck. One day that fall he lost his glasses. "I had to wear Naomi's glasses because I'd lost mine," but by late noon he had thirty-eight letters ready for posting. He finally found his "specs" when he raised the spare wheel of his truck up in the bed. In December he went to Maysville and, to his delight, saw his tobacco average more than sixty-five cents a pound, an all-time high in Jesse's experience. He was happy for he could pay a few of the bills he owed now—bills for seed and fertilizer, and for Gorden Metzler for clearing land with his hog-harrow.[3]

In the late 1950s Jesse's literary production remained prolific; he also expanded his land holdings and continued his farmwork and conservation program, began to make a gradual comeback on the lecture circuit, and involved himself in educational and community activities, especially volunteer work as a director with the Kentucky Heart Association. By early February 1958, he commenced preparations for a trip to California to give a talk for the Los Angeles County Heart Association, having been selected, so he was told, over other famous personalities, including General Mark Clark and Eleanor Roosevelt, among others, to spark a drive for a million dollars for the association. The trip had many attractive details, among them that all his and Naomi's expenses would be paid. On Sunday, February 9, he and Naomi dropped Jane off at her grandparents' home in Greenup. Wanting to go with them, Jane "acted up," Jesse recorded in his journal, and he told her to calm down, for the time would come when she would ride planes. Besides, he did not want her to miss school. Their Piedmont plane "arrived like an angry wasp" in Cincinnati, where they boarded a TWA Super-6 seventy-two passenger ship for a first-class "voyage through the skies" until they reached "warm and sunny California." It seemed they had "changed worlds," Jesse reported. They had fine rooms in the Town House on Wilshire Boulevard. On Tuesday Mrs. Orenstein, a representative of the Heart Association, came to their suite and briefed Jesse: he would speak to two thousand of Los Angeles County's forty thousand workers in the Association. It was to be a large affair, a tremendous charitable undertaking. Jesse sensed several things were wrong. First, the Association had footed the bill for first-class air tickets for both him and Naomi, and their suite in the Town House was clearly expensive; yet he had received no advance publicity he had been able to detect, and he wondered why. He began to question both the efficiency and extravagance of the Los Angeles Heart Association.

But he had little time to wonder about his questions. It was all he could do to snatch a few minutes to sit down and write two letters to Jane. When Naomi would not assume the chore, it bothered Jesse. He resorted to the consolation of comedy. Naomi had earlier become excited when Marlon Brando's car had flashed into public view for a few seconds, so Jesse let Jane know how her mother acted when she saw Marlon Brando's car. He put the letters aside for posting and went to work on his talk for the large Western audience. In addition he had to prepare his comments for a short publicity video piece scheduled for filming at the NBC studio in Burbank. On Wednesday, February 12, he arose to "a beautiful day . . . sun shining—70 degrees plus—wind stirring the leaves of the palms," as he noted in his journal, adding, "I've always liked California for a soft state." Mrs. Orenstein arrived and took him to meet several officials of the Los Angeles County Heart Association. They looked over his written talk and pronounced it "perfect." Later back at their suite he learned that the filming session, originally scheduled for three P.M., had been delayed, but the studio would be back in touch. Jesse was dressed and ready, his speech in his pocket, when a car came for him at six o'clock. He was whisked away to the NBC studio in Burbank where he was ready and waiting in an anteroom when Ralph Edwards came in and sat down beside him. Not having a television set in his home nor even particularly liking the medium, Jesse did not recognize the famous emcee, but assumed the amiable fellow was one of the directors. But Edwards knew Jesse, even spoke to him and said his name. "I was fooled, really fooled," Jesse later wrote, when Edwards declared to forty million viewers over the land, "Jesse Stuart, *This Is Your Life!*"

Anyone who has ever seen that presentation of *This Is Your Life* will be aware of the total and amusing surprise, even the consternation of the principal, the wide-eyed darting of his glance bespeaking an intuitive awareness that he was somehow missing something yet was alert to all possibilities, impatient to perceive as if sensing something was beginning to happen to him, yet unable quite to define it. Then from backstage and sidestage they came, a deluge of personalities from his past, among them his wife and Jane, of course, his brother James, and his sister Sophia

Stuart Keeney; his old boyhood friend of the "Saving of the Bees," Aaron Howard, now of Owasso, Oklahoma; Professor Harry Harrison Kroll and good friend Roland Carter, Tennesseans of his LMU days; and Marvin Wrather of Murray State College, who had aided Jesse through his crisis on the campus in 1954.

Robert A. Thornbury, Executive Director of the Kentucky Heart Association, was there, too; he had helped negotiate the show behind the show and told many of the little white lies that kept Jesse in the dark. Thornbury had first cleared the project with Jesse's heart specialist, Dr. Woodford B. Troutman, then had visited W-Hollow and enlisted Naomi Deane's enthusiastic cooperation. Jane was "on cloud 9 at the news," yet not only kept the secret but beautifully and truly "acted up" and touched her father with convincing thespian skill. The idea had originated with Hal Marc Arden of the American Heart Association in New York. Thornbury had sent producer Axel Gruenberg a copy of *The Year of My Rebirth,* after which Arden and Gruenberg made the decision to go ahead. Getting Jesse Stuart on *This Is Your Life* had not been easy. Rehearsals had gone on all around him, and while Jesse and Naomi were in the Town House, Jane and the others were a few blocks away at the Roosevelt Hotel on Hollywood Boulevard. A happy reunion party was held after the filming, and the guests got to see themselves on the program and to visit afterward and talk about the nearly seven thousand dollars' worth of prizes presented to Jesse for his appearance, including an original manuscript of a Robert Burns poem and a farm tractor. Later, Jesse was surprised that so many people asked him if the surprise was real or fake. He then wrote, "If ever a man was completely . . . hoodwinked or framed into getting on a program, I admit I was he." Over a month later, reflecting on the often-put inquiry, Did he know he was going to be on Ralph Edwards' *This Is Your Life,* he was even more specific: "Not any question about it. I would not have gone that far to have been in that program had I known what I was going out there for."

That summer he took his family with him and taught graduate courses for the College of Education at the University of Nevada in Reno. He had a full load of teaching, and in addition conducted a creative writing class of twenty-five, while Jane audited classes and Naomi kept things organized and served as their tour guide over the West. In all he read about six hundred papers, including thirty-seven graduate papers. In Reno the nights got down into the low forties, while the day never got over ninety; it was a wonderful, dry climate and he felt fine. "I could work and did with the best of them." Back home in September, he tried to get his farm into shape after the hot summer and had a thousand bales of hay to bale and about seventy acres of corn to pick.

He lectured selectively all over the country that year, first in Kentucky, then in the Midwest, in the North and the West—North Dakota, San Francisco, and Portland, Oregon—and in the South in Pensacola, Florida. In June he wrote August Derleth, "I've been over hell and half of Georgia on the circuit again." In September he wrote his old mentor Dr. Edwin Mims that he still had six or eight lectures to give. "When and if I leave this world, Dr. Mims, I'll have my working clothes on. And, I have no fears of death. I don't want to go of course for I have dreams to realize." It was six years since he had been in Nashville, although he had flown over the city twice. He went on to acknowledge his aging teacher's greatness and paid him a more personal credit, "You pulled the first book from me in your class—Beyond Dark Hills. You certainly did. May God bless you and keep you. We will meet again."

That year Jesse published six short stories, twelve poems, and nine essays in such periodicals as *American Forests* and *Saturday Review,* and eighteen articles and other short pieces, fourteen of these last in the *Courier-Journal,* continuing his "Under My Sky" series. Early in the year he had finished a manuscript about a fourteen-year-old girl and an albino deer he tentatively called "Whitie." In his journal he entered, "I liked my characters and shed tears often over the little girl and the helpless deer." However, his most significant publication was the new collection of short stories, *Plowshare in Heaven,* released September 3, which brought kudos from the critics. Helga Sandburg of the *New York Herald Tribune Book Review* saw "fine expressive prose" in the stories. "Putting down his book," she wrote, "it is as if one had gone visiting in that stark and beautiful land, had accepted a corner chair in one of the single-room cabins, had shivered when the wind moaned under the voice of this teller of authentic tales." The *San Francisco Chronicle* reviewer felt "a nostalgia for a part of the country he had never visited." Outrageous humor aside, V. P. Hass of the *Chicago Sunday Tribune* declared that "the stories have this in common—all have heart." Borden Deal of the *Saturday Review* praised Jesse's memorable characterization and concluded, "Jesse Stuart is one of our finest and truest storytellers."

Through these years the Stuarts continued to lead an active family and social life. Jane was growing into a sensitive teenager, excelling in creative writing and language study, and during her sophomore year she was crowned Basketball Queen at Greenup High School for the 1957/ 1958 season. Whenever Jesse and Naomi got together with the Sammonses, Jane usually was there too and especially enjoyed visiting with Oscar and Ann's sons, Ken and Doug. Sometimes other mutual friends, such as Jake and Margaret Lynd of Bellefonte or Gus and Lena Wells Voiers of Vanceburg, would be there too. Because language study, especially Latin, was not available in the local high school, Jesse and Naomi took Jane to Stuart-Hall, a girls' preparatory school, in Staunton, Virginia, where she would finish her last two years of high school. By Christmas she was back home for vacation, and they all visited the Sammonses together. That late December night was reminiscent of another, two years before, when Jesse autographed a copy of *The Year of My Rebirth* "To Oscar—Who has endured me for 34 years and kept his sense of humor—from your longtime friend—Jesse." A few months before, Jesse had taken with him a presentation copy of *Plowshare in Heaven* for Oscar. On the dedicatory page the formal published italics read: *"To Oscar Sammons / classmate and friend / and story teller."* It was a deeper than usual gesture of friendship, of course, like the naming of a new child for a cherished friend whom one profoundly admires.

Jesse and all poetry lovers as well lost a friend that year. Christmas Eve he wrote Donald Davidson, urging him to read his recently published tribute to Byron Herbert Reece in *The Georgia Review*. That summer while Jesse had been at the University of Nevada, he had been stunned to hear of the young Georgia poet's tragic death. To Jesse, "his poems had a way of entering and penetrating one until the reader wondered why Byron Reece had used an idea the reader had known all his life but hadn't done anything about." Yet, only Reece "could have clothed that idea in his choice of words and phrasing, which seemed so simple to the reader, and that is genius." To Jesse, Reece's poems were as "true, honest, and sincere" as those of Yeats, Marvell, Burns, and Robert Frost. He had taken a sheaf of Reece's poems to Dutton and insisted, "whether profitable or not," that his publisher print them; thus Reece's first slender volume, *The Ballad of the Bones and Other Poems*, for which Jesse had written the Foreword, was published. He had never laid eyes on the Georgia poet, but he had been taken by the ballad "Lest the Lonesome Bird" in *Prairie Schooner,* and then the sheaf of Reece's poems; so, Jesse wrote, "I had seen something that came from his mind and I had felt the pulse of his heart."[4]

By the end of the decade he was busy on the lecture circuit again. He had rejoiced by letter with his old friend August Derleth, when the latter's book *The Moon Tender* was made a Literary Guild selection. On the stationery of the Marvin Hughill Hotel, Huron, South Dakota, Jesse admitted, "I lecture because I need to get out—because it's a little needed money—and quickly earned—but it does tell on a man." The tension of contemporary society disturbed him. "We of this generation and of generations to come, will be subjected to more tension and more pressures. We're not at home unless we get . . . scare headlines in our papers." He boosted Derleth's sagging ego by comparing him to Daniel Defoe, whom "people looked upon . . . in his day as something unusual and not necessarily as a great writer. They even laughed at Robinson Crusoe. Today, the ones who laughed are forgotten." Greatness would come. "It has to come. It's bound [to come] to pass."

Before winter was over he was looking forward to Donald Davidson's moderating the Vanderbilt Literary Symposium in which he had been invited to participate, scheduled for April, but he had mixed feelings about the event. He hoped Ransom would be there, mentioned his friendship with Ransom's sister, Ellene, whom Jesse thought "an excellent person," and declared, "While in Nashville if the plow stands, I've got to see Dr. Mims." But he had mixed feelings about the event, frankly admitting, "I dread being on a panel with 'Red' Warren—we came up in such different worlds. He was educated . . . when I was a wild boy in the woods." Ironically, on the very day Jesse wrote Davidson, his former professor was taken to the hospital with a coronary, where he remained thirty-two days. Davidson's brother, William, would moderate in his place. Donald Davidson later reassured Jesse: "You'll get along splendidly with Red Warren. Have no worries. You are both writers of top quality—and you'll probably find that Red, with all of his 'education,' has a lot of 'wild boy in the woods' in him."

Jesse responded by return mail to Davidson's letter, telling him Randall Stewart, the Vanderbilt English Department Head, had written him of Davidson's heart attack. When Jesse had received the bad news, he dropped the letter on his desk, sat down and stared at the wall in silence. Naomi picked up the letter, read it, and was silent, too. When Davidson wrote, Jesse replied, "Please hold on! Keep your chin up! Randall Stewart knows and understands! So do I!" And then he sent what he called "a longer letter which is in book form . . . *The Year of My Rebirth*. . . . It will show you that you can come back and the best isn't over for you."

His professor's heart attack put his own apprehensions about the symposium into a more proper perspective. At first he had feared that Allen Tate might be there, the niggling pitcher of "New Critical" curve balls that would never let him get on first base. Back in 1950 Donald Davidson had questioned Tate and Caroline Gordon's leaving Jesse's work out of their text *The House of Fiction,* to which Tate responded, "I suppose prejudice explains our omission of Jesse Stuart. His dramatization of himself as the Hill-billy, for New York consumption, has disgusted me for years, and I suppose I can't be fair to his work." Perhaps in a later edition, "we can make changes." But the Vanderbilt English Department by vote determined the participants in the symposium, and Tate, Ransom and other prospects, if indeed they had been considered, lost out to Stuart, Warren, and Flannery O'Connor, each championed respectively by Davidson, Randall Stewart, and Walter Sullivan.

Jesse met Flannery O'Connor on the morning of April 22, when he heard her read "A Good Man Is Hard to Find." Davidson had written Jesse that he did not care for her stories, and the Kentuckian's reaction to this one as noted in his journal was "story didn't end right." Flannery O'Connor reported that Stuart told her that "he didn't know why I ended it that way. Didn't I realize the audience identified with the grandmother? I should have kept it going until the cops got there and saved the grandmother!" O'Connor also wrote she enjoyed the proceedings and that "Jesse Stuart's ego was like the light on the front of a train but as Warren remarked, we probably all have that much but just know how to keep it under cover better." After O'Connor's reading, she, Jesse, Randall Stewart, and Warren had lunch together. Before he spoke, Jesse saw Davidson, and the meeting apparently moved them both. Davidson was too ill to hear Jesse speak that day, but even so when Jesse did speak to the symposium he felt called upon to declare that Davidson was "one of the greatest teachers and poets in America today—one who has not received his proper recognition." Eve Blair, who would publish the first biocritical book-length study of Stuart, was in the audience and recorded Jesse's speech as "impassioned, eloquent." He spoke "so rapidly and so vehemently" that many in the audience of faculty, students, and townspeople feared another heart attack might be imminent. The result was "prolonged, enthusiastic applause that . . . amounted to an unreserved ovation for the man from the Kentucky hills." Kathryn Geny, who had been in Warren's 1931/1932 class with Jesse, was in attendance and remarked, "I wouldn't have missed it for the world. They did not argue the way they did in class, but . . . Warren had a new respect for Jesse Stuart. There was professional respect on both sides." Davidson received a blow-by-blow report on the symposium from his daughter, Mary, and he later wrote Jesse, "How powerfully you wrought upon the Vanderbilt audience, and I have kept thinking about how much I missed by not being in the middle of the excitement." Davidson had in the meanwhile immersed himself in *The Year of My Rebirth,* reading it "*slowly*—every page—all the way through," finding it "almost as great a miracle as the extraordinary recovery you made. It takes strength and insight beyond all ordinary conception to go through the experience you relate, win through as you did, and all the while to keep your shaping mind observant, busy, and, shall I say, full of the savor of life, positively moving and alert, even while the body was limited in its performance. Jesse, I salute you with wonder added to old affection. You are a true poet—and this book shows it as much as if it were written in verse."

Jesse had returned from Nashville just in time to guide Gus Pasquarella about his W-Hollow world. Gus was doing the photography for John Bird's insightful profile "My Friend Jesse Stuart," to appear in the July 25 *Saturday Evening Post*. The woods above Shinglemill Hollow around the Stuart home were still alive with the color of dogwoods, pink and white against the pale spring-green of the trees and valley grass. The *Post* readers would see his place at the time of year Jesse thought prettiest. It certainly had been a full spring. In mid-April he had delivered the annual lecture on Robert Burns at Centre College in Danville, Kentucky, reading his remarks and digressing effortlessly on a favorite topic; his address was "well received," Jesse recorded in his journal, the president and sponsor pronouncing it "the best ever given on Burns there."

He was in Nashville again in late May, lecturing at Peabody College. At home afterward, he reflected with satisfaction on two recent developments. Not only had *Plowshare in Heaven* made the 1959 *Masterplots*, one of a hundred selected from more than twelve thousand American books, but E. P. Dutton had reprinted a paperback edition of *Man with a Bull-Tongue Plow*, which Jesse hoped would permit a mass circulation. Before the year was out a new junior book, *The Rightful Owner*, would be accepted by McGraw-Hill, and he received word that *The Thread That Runs So True* was accepted for Brazilian publication. French and Egyptian translations would follow in the 1960s and a Japanese translation in 1978.

Then as summer came, Jesse felt worse. He had dizzy spells and his heart skipped beats. One morning he nearly blacked out when he got up to go to the bathroom. Dr. Vidt performed a series of tests and then ordered Jesse to stay inside in his pajamas and "to take it easy." He could read and write a few letters with a pen but could not use the typewriter. Medications to lower his blood pressure, Hedulin to thin his blood, and an appetite depressant were prescribed. Again he was not permitted visitors. He had to give up accepted lectures, too, including major ones at Northwestern University and Berea College. His patience and morale plunged, and his journal entry exploded at his plight: "Of course—in a room! In a room! In a room! Lying down! Sitting up!

Disgusted as hell. But what the hell can I do about it? Man, am I disgusted—now, losing and will probably have to lose more or all of the talks I have booked. Well, sometimes, I wonder why I keep on fighting to live." He turned to his pen and wrote Donald Davidson that he was "side-lined." Davidson replied the following week and took him to task for working too hard, especially doing too much physical work on his farm, lecturing Jesse like a son: "I hope you won't do such-like again. And I hope this rest and careful observance of doctor's rules will get rid of that trouble and have you on your feet again."

Davidson's hope was soon fulfilled. Jesse was on his feet again in time to receive an honorary doctoral degree—his fifth—at Morris-Harvey College in Charleston, West Virginia, but his doctors would not permit him to deliver the commencement address. Still, it was "a wonderful day," and he had come out of that "room" again. Dr. Vidt diagnosed a "branch block." Jesse recorded, "A third of my crippled heart was blocked off." Dr. Troutman said that EKGs revealed Jesse had experienced "a silent heart attack."

By the end of the year, Jesse received from Egypt a telephone call from Dr. Raymond McLain, President of the American University at Cairo, who wanted to meet him in Lexington later in the week to discuss the possibilities of his teaching at AUC for a year. Jesse talked the opportunity over with Naomi briefly. Their natural inclinations toward adventure and new places lured them, so they agreed to meet the educator at the Lafayette Hotel in Lexington. In short, Jesse chronicled, "we were impressed with him. He was impressed with us. He told us about American University—gave us his proposition and I accepted." The next day they were both elated over their future plans for spending a year in Egypt. It all depended on his health, of course. His enthusiasm did not abate, and at year's end he wrote August Derleth of the likelihood. The family would go with him, of course, "by boat" in July or August. "The whole thing sounds fabulous," he continued, "at least to us."[5]

It was business as usual that winter of a new decade. He did his bit for the community, directing the canvass for the Heart Fund and setting a record high: In five years of work in this service, he had seen the annual fundraising go up from three hundred dollars in 1955 to over two thousand dollars in 1960. In early March he flew to Amarillo, Texas, where at nearby Texas West State College in Canyon, he addressed students and a large teachers' meeting. To "many fine . . . wonderful people," as Jesse saw them, he gave "one of my finest talks." He signed books "fast as I could," the entry in his journal reads, and "teachers came up—wanted to shake my hand—touch me—said so—as if I were something immortal. I could hardly get to [the] airport. . . . I just about had to leave Amarillo," for the "pressure was too much." He thought he could make St. Louis, but could not, staying the night in an airport motel in Oklahoma City. There his first "Hawaiian supper" may have contributed to an illness following coffee early the next morning, but he could not be sure. "I got so sick—a strange sickness I didn't know whether I would make it home or not." He did make it to the plane and on to St. Louis, and was still sick while changing planes there. "Then something happened. My heart beat real fast when I thought I was going to fall, began to pull out of it and feel better." He boarded his flight and met Naomi Deane in Huntington. He told her of his sickness and "wondered if a clot had passed through or what had happened." Anyway, he felt much better.

Even though the Texas trip "had taken the pep out of me," as Jesse wrote, he rallied for a spirited "Jesse Stuart Day" celebration at the University of South Carolina. There people were standing in the corridors to hear him, and, in the judgment of Eve Blair, he was "at his extemporaneous best." The audience's reaction was "eager, responsive" and "tremendous" as he spoke for over an hour. Then followed a sumptuous English teachers' luncheon, visits to local schools, a television interview, and a motorcade that took him to a reception at eighty-year-old writer Julia Peterkin's fine old colonial home. He was even presented to the South Carolina Legislature. The hospitality of President and Mrs. Robert L. Sumwalt in their campus home pleased Jesse and Naomi, but in Jesse's opinion the party at Eve Blair's "surpassed a New York literary party."

During the cold months he was rolling along on his new educational novel, eventually to be published as *Mr. Gallion's School,* a junior book expanded from his 1954 short story "Soddy," and his biographical collection *God's Oddling,* about his father, Mick Stuart; but he was determined not to risk the plans for a year in Egypt, not to overwork, and to protect his health at all costs, even if it meant taking it easy. Spring refreshed his lyric soul again. "There is not another month of the year as delightful as April in Kentucky," he wrote. "Now, the last of the snow has melted. . . . There is a fresh breath of spring in the warm winds blowing over. Every little stream is filled with blue snow water which flows down the channel singing on its way to larger streams, to rivers and the oceans."

One morning in early April he looked at the old serviceberry tree above the cliff but saw no familiar blooms. The next morning, however, he could hardly believe the oft-repeated miracle of what he had seen as far back as he could remember; "for the tree looked like it was filled with large flakes of snow clinging to the tips of little leafless limbs." This tree was "a joy—a friend—because each spring I had looked forward to seeing the snowflake blossoms come to its boughs . . . the first tree to bloom." Then it would give its fruit too, to be made into "a delicious 'sarvice berry' pie."

This month he decided he would do no more work than he had to do. "Why not take it easy and be a part of the life around me? . . . For whom should I lay up riches when the riches were all around me—the kind that could only be stored in the wind! . . . So, I walked out among butterflies and bees and watched them rivaling each other for the food they found in the few blossoms." He took time to set out one hundred yellow poplar and thirteen hundred pine seedlings in fourteen acres of cleared land, and was amazed to see thousands of spider webs spread over what would someday be a pine forest. The day before he had not noticed any. During the night the spiders had worked and built a city, erecting "tents by the thousands that looked like small white clouds that had dropped to rest on a dark land." One day he enjoyed breathing and listening to the fresh winds and had a delightful time being alone. "I collected the hard core of my thinking . . . and sat so still a squirrel came close to me . . . a wild squirrel which had a nest in a beech near where I sat. A wild bird almost lit on my shoulder. Why? I was getting more of nature's secrets in my solitary rambles." Again, he was as still as the dead log on which he sat and leaned back against a tree. Then "down by the creek in an opening, I saw a deer—a doe—She walked up and stood in this opening . . . took several bites of wild honeysuckle leaves before she walked on!" He made the discovery that wild honeysuckle, so troublesome to farmers who loved neat fencerows, "was wonderful feed for the deer." Further, it had the advantages of helping prevent erosion, and "besides, it had a fragrant smell and its blossoms were very pretty."

Very early one morning he walked up to the toolshed with Charlie Cottle on the way to dig up and reset some pines. "I smell a snake," Old Charlie said. "Do you smell it?"

"What kind of a snake?"

"A bull blacksnake," he said.

"How do you know it's a bull blacksnake that you smell?" Jesse asked. "How does one smell?"

"Like a polecat," Charlie answered. "You don't believe me, do you?"

"I don't know," Jesse said.

"All right," Old Charlie spoke. "I'm looking around here for that snake." He raised some planks in a lumber pile, then turned over some old roofing. He did not find anything, and Jesse smiled. Old Charlie threw aside some sticks of wood, working down the stack. "At the bottom of the stack lay a big blacksnake at least five feet long." Then, Jesse recorded in his journal, "I stopped smiling."

Early that April Jesse found a rabbit killed on the W-Hollow Road, probably blinded at night with car lights and run down. He picked the rabbit up and laid it over on the meadow grass. Two crows had already made the discovery and waited up in a tree. They cawed and Jesse thought they wanted him to leave. He looked around and thought about how the pasture was green all winter under the snows and the parent rabbits had found food. "This was their little world—one which was home." He went on, and when he looked back the crows were flying down to the rabbit.

That was the way death was. It came in the midst of life, even in April. Within the past year it had come to three people close to him in different ways. The Riverton postmistress, Bessie Morton, who had sent away most of his manuscripts to his publishers, had shocked him with her death the spring before. Then in September his old friend Dr. Edwin Mims had gone into a coma and died, not long after Jesse had seen him for the last time in the Vanderbilt Student Union Building. He wrote Professor Mims' daughter, Ella Puryear Mims, "Time will show your Father a giant teacher even among the topnotchers . . . he went a little higher. . . . The better I knew him the more I loved him." Then the first week of January the man who had taught him to read and write, his first teacher at Plum Grove and later attorney, financial adviser, and close personal friend, Calvin Clarke had died. How lively images of the man hung in his mind—how Clarke's "brown eyes flashed with a little excitement." Once the man had told Jesse "about the little boy, Jesse Stuart, he used to know climbing over a fence on his way to school to him." And now what? "He was . . . a part of the world," Jesse wrote, "and now he was gone—something that couldn't happen but it had."

But April was life, and nature was the wellspring of life, to which he turned his thoughts again. The redbuds did not like to be outdone. "Soon their tops would be pink as clouds in a sunset," he thought. "How wonderful to be alive! How wonderful to have enough health to live— to be a part of April in my valley and on my farm for another year. For this I thanked God over and over repeatedly as I walked down the lane where there were more dogwood blossoms, more redbud blos-

soms. . . . And the morning sky was blue. It was too early for the sun—
and mists were ascending from the valley where the creek bottom meadows were as green as young gourds." His aging dog, Birchfield, twelve
now—in human terms, eighty-four—pursued Jesse's heels. "He, too,
was enjoying another spring and, perhaps, thinking as I was thinking
he was glad to be alive in this world which was his world too—glad to
be alive, a part of the beauty and to still share the gift of life."

If April strengthened his hold on life, it also put his work into wiser
perspective. "All my work can wait," he reflected as the month waned.
He did not think this would be his last April, but it might be. "Who
knows when his last days are near? No one in good or poor health really
knows." He could not take a chance. "I must go out today since I have
told myself long before April came, I wouldn't miss living each April
day in my own way." He walked the W-Hollow stream, sat on a stone
near the splashing water, "singing on its way down the valley," and beheld
the bursting dogwoods, rising to song himself as he took in "red and
white sails of blossoms stationary on an unsailing ship—the good earth—
my earth—rugged W-Hollow earth," nor could he cease singing his April
poem with "sentences of blue in the wild sweet williams in the cove near
the oakgrove . . . sentences of white in the percoon that sprang up from
the oakleaf loam . . . sentences of pink in the dogwood blossoms on the
slopes. . . . Dots of blue in violets. . . . Dots of purple in the wild iris. . . . Dots
of red in the whippoorwill flowers by the cliffs," each sentence and each
dot leaving "a memory like an endless stream of blue water," until April
had fled into the byway of another year.[6]

16

Egypt and the World: Man of Letters
1960–1970
———◇———

In the summer of 1960, when Jesse was asked why he was going to Egypt, he replied, "To meet new challenges." Beforehand, there were dozens of loose ends to tie up—a five-hundred-mile trip to Murray State College where he delivered the commencement address, then back across the state again and on to Staunton, Virginia, for Jane's graduation and trip home. Professor Hensley C. Woodbridge, with whom Jesse had worked off and on the year before in W-Hollow, was putting the finishing touches on Jesse's bibliography—279 short stories, 287 poems in periodicals in addition to more than 1,300 already collected in book form, 117 essays and articles, 19 translations of his work into such languages as German, Swedish, Spanish, Russian and Telegu, 18 theses and special studies, and 71 pieces about him by others in periodicals and newspapers. Jesse finished and mailed the 1,520-page manuscript of his new novel, drove down to the Bluegrass where he spoke to twelve hundred people at the University of Kentucky, and along with Naomi and Jane, completed his shots for the year abroad. He came down with lumbago in his back and could hardly move for two days.

By mid-July his thin little collector's item *Huey the Engineer* was published in St. Helena, California. He was reading proof for *God's Oddling* when word came from McGraw-Hill that the new manuscript, then called *The Gifts of Gallion,* was accepted and the contract was on its way. The Stuarts were packing when it arrived, specifying a fifteen-hundred-dollar advance, but Jesse hung up on two details: The publisher wanted him to agree to a two-thirds cut of the manuscript, and further, to put up two thousand of his royalties for revisions since he would be in Egypt. "I boiled on both counts and knew I wasn't signing this contract." Having traded in his typewriter, his "old friend" that had been with him through Europe and on which he had typed most of his books, he had second thoughts and hurriedly retrieved it from the dealer. There was a family get-together at "Sister Mary's," and everyone was in good spirits. Jane and her boyfriend, Julian Juergensmeyer, whom she had known in high school, rode along in his new Renault. The day they left W-Hollow the phone rang incessantly. Jesse's nephew Gene Darby, the prototype for *The Beatinest Boy,* came over with his new German wife, Hilda, to say goodbye on July 24. Old Charlie came, too, Jesse recorded in his journal. "He, most of all, except Birch, hated to see me go. We drove down the valley having a last look."

In New York City they checked in at the American University International office. There Jesse received a five-hundred-dollar advance on his annual salary while Naomi and Jane shopped for lighter clothes. Later, he conferred with his agents Annie Laurie Williams and Maurice Crain, then stopped in at Scribner's, where he was pleased to learn that *The Thread* had chalked up more than 52,000 in sales. It would continue to sell steadily for many years to come, he was told, and was then promised a "forward" on his royalties. All the problems with his contract had been ironed out by the next day when he lunched in the McGraw-Hill Dining Room with Harold McGraw, Helene Frye, Alison Hume, Bob Gutwillig, Gray Williams, Barbara Adams, and Al Potter. Jesse recorded "a good meal" and a "pleasant meeting," after which he signed 125 books and talked some more with the editors. The next day, following a scenic drive up the Hudson River, he discussed a proposed editorial project with a World Books textbook team. On July 30, Jesse signed no fewer than 675 books at McGraw-Hill, got a thousand Egyptian pounds at the American University office, and then with his family boarded the Italian liner *Augustus* at Pier 84, where friends Max Bogart and Nell Brown were waiting to bid them bon voyage.

The upper and lower New York harbors were rough and the Atlantic rougher still. "I never saw so many sick people," Jesse chronicled, "vomit everywhere—deck scrubbers and people trying to reach the deck rails—but just couldn't do it." The Stuarts felt a bit squeamish but endured only mild discomfort. Then the next day, Sunday, the sea was smooth, the sun bright.

The *Augustus,* Jesse objected, had no Protestant services on board. "I remember on British ships when there were few Catholics. Service was arranged for them. For us, there is no church service." But the amenities were first class: talented musicians, good movies (except for one, *The Apartment,* which Jesse thought "vulgar"), excellent meals, a fine captain's party, and lots of shuffleboard, all of which the Stuarts entered into with zest. They passed the Azores and the next day sighted "the irregular, rough shores of Portugal on the North . . . the international zone to the South." A young stowaway was placed in the brig after he had faked an overboard suicide, as a result of which the *Augustus* had altered its course and circled the waters five hours in a "rescue" attempt— until the culprit had finally been discovered in the food reserve with a wine bottle in hand. The *Augustus* "stowed" at Gibraltar and Jesse observed that "they took our proud young American stowaway off—handcuffed—but he put on an act of waving to his audience—who cussed the SOB who had delayed everybody." The next day the ship passed Sardinia, then the Tyrrhenian Sea on Jesse's fifty-fourth birthday. They sighted Capri, and behind it thin clouds of steam issued forth from Mount Vesuvius. "The moon in the blue sky was something," Jesse thought, "and now the lights of Naples." The *Augustus* docked near midnight, and they watched the tourist class disembark first into a crowd of two thousand people. "Old friends met," Jesse marked, "and there was much crying—laughing—rejoicing." That night in Naples, the Stuarts stayed at the Santa Lucia Hotel.

They drank wine instead of water and were careful with what they ate. On the streets, hawkers accosted them as they explored the countless shops, "one after the other like little caves back in the walls." They soon left Naples and went to Rome by train, enjoying the Italian countryside along the coast, through tunnels and across the farmlands; dry areas and "fertile valleys with vineyards" took his eye. The Eternal City amazed them. "We couldn't believe Rome was so beautiful—the railway station so nice. We didn't meet the cheats, panhandlers and beggars at this station." Past fountains and statues and medieval buildings still in use, they proceeded to the Sistine Chapel and there viewed the treasures of Michelangelo and Raphael. He saw the Roman Forum and the Coliseum as "a bit of historical earth," recording "now heaps of broken stone with a few pillars standing, a place that once was a world Center of Control. But what was it now? A place of history and forgotten dreams." He experienced what he remembered from his Latin and history books, then later wrote, "to see the Tiber was something." They took in St. Paul's Cathedral, where the saint's "immortal dust and bones are supposed to be contained in the tomb—whether or not, who knows? I'd like to see in to see." The extensiveness of the catacombs interested him greatly—"125,000 graves in one catacomb . . . and there were . . . over 350 miles of catacombs." They toured Florence and Venice, too. The ruins of Pompeii were "unforgettable—something that impressed me deeply." The scenic Amalfi Drive southeast of Naples "surpasses anything in Switzerland," and Sorrento was "a place where one could stay a week, two or three—and not have time enough"; for "here the quivering palm fronds whispered about the great writers, musicians and world leaders who had been here centuries ago." They sailed to the Isle of Capri, transferred to small boats, and in these found their way into the Blue Grotto. Then by bus they climbed a mountain to a hotel overlooking the Mediterranean, where they ate lunch. Soon his romantic fervor for Capri was cooled, however, and he pronounced it a "typical resort town with prices rigged for American tourists and prices for their own people." Back across the bay he could not restrain his penchant for getting the crooked straight, entering in his journal, "Back in dirty Naples—dirty and dishonest as a city could be."

Before leaving they had time to see Vesuvius, and on Jane's eighteenth birthday father and daughter rode the lift and looked into the crater itself. Later, near Naples, they found Vergil's tomb. Perhaps Jesse identified with the poet's humble, country origins, and with the Mantuan's conspicuousness of frame, dark complexion and, as we have it from Donatus' description, "air of rusticity."

They sailed at midnight and found the sea rough where the Adriatic met the Mediterranean, but despite the fact that the Stuarts were "inlanders," Jesse recorded, "we . . . could stand a tossing ship better than most who lived in countries by the sea. We never missed a meal." They enjoyed being among the people on the ship, with one exception. That was an American from Nevada studying at the Sorbonne, "no doubt smart enough—but if I ever met the perfect snob he was that one. There is the Eastern Cultural snob—and the Southern Subtle Snob—the one I detest [more], not yet determined." The next day Jesse went up on deck "to get a whiff of fresh sea air," and then, "while leaning on the deck rail, looking toward the ship's prow, in the distance over the oval of shining waters I saw an outline of a city." After breakfast they anchored at Alexandria.[1]

From the time he arrived in Egypt, Jesse's writer's eye was keenly focused upon this oldest of new worlds. He would carefully and consistently record the Stuarts' adventures and his own reactions, feelings, conflicts, and thoughts in a 1,502-page manuscript, *The Egyptian Diary*. In time he smuggled it (because it was critical of the Nasser regime) piecemeal out of the country to his agent Annie Laurie Williams in New York City. In a letter to Ed Kuhn of McGraw-Hill, she later said, "Jesse had a very interesting and exciting experience," and Bruno Neumann, one of the readers, was in agreement, describing the manuscript as a "blow-by-blow account of his impressions, observations and meditations, from the day he arrived in Egypt to the day he left." Neumann saw Stuart as "an honest and unpretentious writer" whose senses were "in good working order" and whose mind was "discerning, discriminating, and seeking for perspective." Jesse's heart, he noted, "beats for freedom, liberty, and some little more salvation for the underprivileged." Admitting the manuscript's need for much "judicious editing . . . much cutting, some condensing, a little reorganizing, and lots . . . of attention to spelling and punctuation," Neumann was nevertheless sanguine. "Getting the thing into shape should be a lot of fun: and something of an honor." Since Egypt was in the news "on and off . . . and since Jesse Stuart is Jesse Stuart, there wouldn't seem to be much doubt about publishing the book."

Arriving on the *Esperia* at Alexandria August 24, the Stuarts had been advised not to disembark until their "contact" from the American University in Cairo (AUC) met them. He was late, however, and Raif Jeha, a Lebanese, befriended him as Jesse ventured out to the American Express office to telephone the university. Baggage and ship hucksters were everywhere. Changemakers thronged the "customs . . . madhouse." Back on ship, the AUC contact, Abdul Messiah, a Copt Christian whose name meant "Messenger of God," finally arrived about the time the Stuarts had finally decided to eat lunch aboard the *Esperia,* where they were charged seven dollars for a light meal that would have cost about two dollars in the United States. "Robbery," Raif Jeha complained. "I feel sorry for Americans trying to travel. The reason I wouldn't want to be American is, I hate to be robbed." He argued with the Italian waiter.

"Don't argue with him, Raif. This time we're the pretty Americans and he's the ugly European."

Then there was Mounikan, a leather-faced Egyptian without teeth. Like most Egyptians he wore a soiled gallabiah, or coat, and an ammah wrapped around his head, and hawked money from tourists whose luggage he carried and got through customs. Ostensibly working for Abdul Messiah, on the sly he cadged piastres from Jesse. Their wagon driver hauled their luggage, while Jesse, Naomi, and Jane, walking behind the wagon with Abdul Messiah and Old Mounikan, laughed at the picture they made. "I wish I could have a picture of this," Jesse said. Jesse did indeed slip Mounikan a twenty-five-piastre note while the old port character whispered, "I'll see that Allah will bless you. I can fix this; I'll have it done. You will see." Jesse thought, "He was a liar and he knew that I knew he was a liar but I liked him for he was sort of an honest liar."

They were ripped off to the tune of forty-nine dollars for getting their baggage through customs and up the Nile Delta to Cairo, but without Abdul Messiah and Old Mounikan it might have been much worse.

Going up the Nile it was as if, Jesse chronicled, they "had turned a page in Time's Ageless Book," eight thousand pages, and gone back into a world where civilization began; here "the B.C. world and the A.D. world" were "rolled into one." There was the new four-lane highway running up the rich Nile Delta, but with the speeding cars along the way were carts and mules of the past. Everywhere there were pictures of Nasser, yet on the Nile, sailing vessels with masts for one or two sails plowed the waters with freight, nudging modernity with their quaint antiquity, as picturesque as pottery jugs carried on the heads of the Nile people up and down the 140-mile train trip from Alexandria to Cairo. "The feluccas were going upstream, for this is the way the wind blows constantly," Jesse wrote. "Their sails were spread and full of wind. Other boats came down with the current. Transportation on the Nile, the wind taking the boats up and the current bringing them down, hadn't cost anything as long as there had been an Egypt."

In front of the American University in Cairo was an iron gate. A *bowwab*, or "watcher-of-the-door," came to the taxi, his long gray-striped gallabia sweeping the ground. "You mean you keep the place locked?" Jesse asked him. That night they were house guests on campus and went out under the blue Egyptian sky as the moon shone down through palm fronds. "Here we stood . . . in the center of Cairo, Africa's largest city— which was in the approximate center of the world."

Morland House, an aging five-story *pensione* in which they had made arrangements to spend the year, was "most unattractive" with its peeling paint and dirty front. The elevator would not work. When they entered, a young man at the desk "came to his feet as if he were in the presence of the leader of his country," Jesse observed. "In other countries convenience was placed before such grand manners." The Stuarts got to their flat by climbing a "steep mountain of stone steps" to the fourth floor. There was no bath for each apartment but rather one for the floor, a tub made in Scotland such as Jesse had used in Edinburgh in 1937. "It looked like a large deep coffin. There were dirty outside pipes running all over the wall. The flush box to the commode was up on the wall. One pulled a string and the water poured down. There was also a heater of some kind hanging on the wall near the interlocking and crisscrossing of ancient pipes." It would do. The first nights the August heat lay heavily upon them, though. "I don't know where it comes from,"

Jane said. "When the wind doesn't blow the still air is like a slow fire!" Because of the heat and humidity they opened the back porch doors, even though they had been warned not to sleep with the doors open; but then the music from the orchestra playing on the roof of the Semiramis Hotel across the way rode the breeze to them until two in the morning, so that they could sleep only in the early hours of the morning. Jesse awoke to hear hawks screaming brazenly in tall trees thirty feet away. They were after the little birds feeding on the roof. He wished he had a gun to kill the hawks. He tried to sleep but could not, lying there "listening to the hawks' wild screams as they chased the birds that were trying to feed on the roof below."

Adding to these difficulties was an older Egyptian man who ate in the dining room of Morland House and insisted on presenting Jane with gifts and planning outings to which he invited her. At first the Stuarts thought only good of Mohammed SaKarkin's kindnesses, once allowing Jane to go to the movie with him and his "niece," so SaKarkin said, introducing a young woman "who was dark-olive complexioned, thick and broad across the hips." He liked to watch Jane as he dined. After the Stuarts learned the young woman might not have been his niece, after all, he became known to them as "the Character." One Sunday he invited Jane to the zoo, but she coolly excused herself on the grounds of the day's being their Sabbath and her family's going to church. Another time "the Character," wiping perspiration from his face and murmuring some pleasantry, left a beribboned package of mangoes at the Stuarts' table. Later that evening Jane told her father, "I feel like a rabbit chased by a hound." Meanwhile, Jesse's new Cairo physician, Dr. Guindy, who held a degree from Columbia University, advised that they move to a place with either an elevator that worked or fewer stairs. The straw that broke the camel's back came when Naomi attempted to operate the antiquated hot water heater for her bath and it blew up. She jumped out of the tub, threw her robe around herself, and dashed for the door. "The steam and I went out into the corridor together," she reported, unhurt but "scared to death."[2]

They decided to take an apartment across the Nile on Gezeriah Island, near their new friends Carl and Mary Leiden, with whom Jesse could share a ride most mornings to the university. It was modern, spacious, clean, and conveniently furnished. Socrates Patsalidis, head of maintenance at AUC, helped them move. Although they did not especially want a cook and cleaning man, custom on Gezeriah virtually required the arrangement, so Naomi employed a *sofragi*, a big dark Nubian, Salah Ramadin, who wore a neat gallabiah, sandals, and ammah. Right off he won their hearts with his first meal of roast beef, mashed potatoes, peas, broiled tomatoes, rolls, and fresh fruit—"the best cooked food we had had in Egypt."

Little by little they absorbed the local color and learned the customs of the people. Jesse saw "one youth with a tray balanced on top his head," riding a bicycle through the thronging streets selling bread that looked more like doughnuts. "The tray was four feet square and bread was piled high yet the tray never toppled nor a piece of bread fell off." On a corner, "a woman roasted green corn over a fire in an oven on a cart and sold the roasted corn." Eating grapes became habitual, and he learned to drink black, sirupy coffee by weakening it with water. He finally found cereal and powdered milk for his low cholesterol diet, at the United States Embassy. He grew accustomed to passing Moslem churches where shoes lay on the floor while people said prayers. He saw the political funeral of John Kale of Uganda, held in an outdoor tent, which reminded him of revival tents back home. He had a most difficult time getting used to people running up to look into his wallet, and learned to be careful when opening it. At the Liberty Midan (*El Tahrir*) he got used to seeing people in front of their shops asleep, a soldier near a government building dozing with a rifle over his lap, but never "the poor policemen, wearing coats in this tepid heat," standing at "intersections with eyes half-closed like lizards basking in the sun." He learned that Friday was the equivalent of Christian Sunday, and Sunday was merely another work day in Moslem Egypt. And so one Sunday morning he awoke to crowing roosters and braying donkeys. "I thought we were at home in W-Hollow—back in Kentucky." Their balcony faced the Gazira Sporting Club, and he could see men with carts and donkeys hauling away the garbage along a palm-lined street. "The donkeys that hadn't been fed an armload of green fodder were braying." The crowing roosters, he conjectured, "were perhaps in coops on their way to an early market."

He taught three classes, a somewhat uninspiring one in advanced English composition, a good class in education, and an outstanding creative writing class. He enjoyed the first two faculty meetings, but soon afterward found them boring attempts at indoctrination and generally unnecessary. About the time classes began, he received a hardback copy of Professor Woodbridge's *Jesse Stuart: A Bibliography*, containing a seventy-four-page list of his publications in small type. It thrilled him to hold in his hands the bibliographical facts of "practically all I'd written in a lifetime." It was not the first time he had referred to his literary creations as his "children." Now in the *Bibliography* he held before him, it seemed his "children had gathered for a Homecoming." He proudly showed it to Carl Leiden, a political science and government professor from Iowa, who had known of Jesse's work since reading *Taps for Private Tussie* in the 1940s. The Stuarts and the Leidens became close friends during the following two semesters; the two families often squeezed into the Leidens' Morris Minor car for short trips to such favorite places as the Cairo museums, the City of the Dead, the Giza pyramids, and for visits to the bazaars, to the country, and to each other's and students' homes. Indeed, hardly a day passed that the two colleagues did not see each other and get together to do something or to talk at length.

Jesse impressed Leiden as one who was "happy in meeting students in or out of the classroom," one who wanted to know students and "to share their experiences if possible." And "he was instantly ready to share their burdens." Jesse "had a way of conveying to a student that he, the teacher, was honored by having that particular individual in his class." He was truly "excited about being with students," and sensing this, "students . . . understood what a rare person he was and loved him for it." More than once Leiden and his colleagues saw Jesse and his students "making their way down some sidewalk . . . Jesse in their midst, waving his cigar or pen, laughing, talking, listening." As Bruno Neumann observed that the poet's " 'heart' beats for freedom," so Leiden recalled, "he was always proud of being an American." Yet, Jesse's patriotism was in no way insular. "He had a way of helping foreign students rediscover a new pride in their ethnic backgrounds and in the culture in which he was a guest." He adjured them "to cherish their history, their religion, their art, their family—and he urged them to write about it all, not as an American would write, but as an Egyptian, a Greek or an Italian would write." As in Kentucky, Jesse got next to a culture, up close to it, down into the very soil of it. Leiden discovered in their months of deepening friendship that the mountain chronicler found all life worthy of his vision, and his voracious appetite absorbed it. "Jesse always loves the places that he is in and he quickly establishes with his students or audiences that he is not a superior being who looks down on them but rather one who looks up."

At the outset of the academic year Jesse wondered about how his own upbringing with total freedom would affect his teaching, specifically "how could I teach in a country where newspapers, magazines, publishing houses, radio, and TV were 'nationalized'?" In his creative writing class especially, he encountered a wide range of students from Egypt, Persia, Germany, Greece, Turkey, Kuwait, and the United States. They were multilingual and anxious to learn. Jesse perceived "no distrust or hostility in any of their faces," so the familiar "sense of the missionary teaching zeal that had prompted me to accept the AUC job in the first place came flooding back." The students worked hard, competing for such coveted prizes as an expense-paid scholarship in the United States. The second semester Jane was promoted by her freshman teacher, Mildred Ware from Dublin, Ireland, who also urged more advanced work for her. Compelled to write, she decided to take her father's class, which turned out to be a highly competitive one. Many of the student works of both classes appeared in a new college literary magazine that Jesse sponsored and, upon request, for which he selected the name—*The Scarab*, "a god in early Egypt," Jesse reasoned, and "a symbol of creativity."

In late November he received his first copy of *God's Oddling*, the book he had put together to create and, perhaps, to relive a tribute to his father. President McLain himself had brought it back from New York City by jet, toting a cache of letters and a batch of "fine excellent reviews" with him. Jesse wrote August Derleth of his delight with the book's having made an annual reading list compiled by newspaper critics. He was pleased that "Helga Sandburg, Carl's daughter," writing for the *New York Herald Tribune*, had declared it "a fine piece of Americana," for "it overruns with laughter and with deep feeling for the beauty and ugliness of the countryside, with respect and pride and vigor about the work done on the soil." Fanny Butcher of the *Chicago Sunday Tribune* observed that "the story of Mick Stuart" was also "the story of Jesse Stuart," and "to admirers of that gifted writer, it is a richer book for his own life being so much a part of it."

There was something more deeply satisfying about the book, too. Shortly after the death of Jesse's father that bleak December day in 1954, Donald Davidson had written in consolation and the bright hope of expectation: "Jesse, remember, that though you personally have lost a father in the way of mortality no human being can escape in the flesh, you have made his mortality into immortality in your poems and your prose where he lives and will live for all the world. If from him you had the gift of life, from you he has a gift of life that mounts beyond death. Few fathers, few sons, in this old world, can ever be so joined in affection—the memory that is not only of the person and in the family, the long, long memory of immortal art." Further, Davidson had expected that Jesse would, "when you are healed both of your grief and your physical wounds—as I know you will be—put your hand again, when you are fully well and ready, to the great work of memory that the Lord so clearly intended you to do. As a writer, you are everybody's memory.

People might forget what they ought to remember—and no doubt in their hearts really want to remember—if writers like you did not arise to remind them to remember." It can hardly be a surprise that Jesse had "a wonderful day" after this birth of a special literary child, conceived in despair. He knew the joy of a plan fulfilled, of an inchoate vision melded into shape and completion, and of a tragic loss faced up to and triumphantly transmuted into "everyone's memory."[3]

Despite the undeniable rewards of teaching in a new culture, Jesse had difficulty accustoming himself to restraints upon freedoms he had long enjoyed. In October President Nasser came home from the United States and the United Nations, and loudspeakers blasted music and messages all over Cairo. The noise got so loud that AUC had to suspend classes at ten in the morning. Thousands of man-hours were spent on decorating the capital city. The next day was declared a holiday—"no work"—and everyone's mail lay in the post office while "loudspeakers blasted away" and "people marched and chanted." Jesse exploded in his journal, "What this country needed—even on low income—was a sense of time, being, accuracy . . . efficiency and honesty." Egypt needed to change. "We, the country and I ran cross-grain to each other. Why waste so much time on holidays and celebrations when progress and efficiency . . . were needed so badly here?" The celebration was followed by Moslem "Sunday"—"so, three days and no mail from the inefficient and corrupt Postal Department—filled with political, loyalist followers." In November, when Nasser returned from the Sudan and the noise started again, he chronicled, "I've seen all this so much, so often, I'm sick of it. How many of his pictures have I seen? Thousands and thousands."

Jesse was especially put out with the Egyptian postal service. One day he received a statement in his mailbox informing him that money had been deposited in his name in the Cairo National Bank. He encountered many delays, much red tape, and several trips to the bank before he could even partially resolve the problem. His contract signed with a Prague, Czechoslovakia, publisher had required the publisher to pay him a $150 permission fee. The Egyptian government had taken the check from his personal mail. The bank official explained that checks were removed from letters because of "the economy of the Government."

"Our Government Officials could be sent to prison for taking a check from a citizen's mail," Jesse said.

"You are in another country," the official replied.

"Could I have the check sent back to Czechoslovakia?" Jesse asked.

"No, you can't," the official said. "It must be cashed here."

The bank would not let him have the tourist-rate exchange and paid him the equivalent of only $94.38. "I had lost," Jesse calculated, "over one third of my $150 check from Prague, Czechoslovakia."

He wrote August Derleth that after what he had experienced in more than thirty countries, the "American postal system, under any president, any administration is the best I've seen in the world," and added, "You don't know what some countries can be like." Socrates Patsalidis told him that postmen in Egypt often steamed off uncancelled stamps and resold them in order to supplement their meagre incomes. As a result, ten percent or more of letters mailed did not get through. But in writing his friend, Jesse felt constrained only to hint of the deplorable situation, "Now the postage on this letter, nine piastres (about 23 cents) is more than a man makes in a day here: so sometimes our letters don't get to their destinations. . . . Get me!"

"To work in a police state," he wrote, "where even one's outgoing and incoming letters are opened does something to one. He guards what he says in his letters—he can't tell the truth." Yet Jesse did not hesitate to discuss some controversial issues in his classes, such as compulsory education for the masses as it existed in the United States and as it could exist in Egypt. A young Moslem woman, Laila Enan, took exception to Sayed Rashid's paper, calling his ideas "dangerous," and a spirited discussion followed. If the *fellaheen* were educated, who would do the work in Egypt? Jesse suggested parallels between them and his own background and that of other American youth from the hill country of Kentucky. Sayed pointed to no other than Gamal Abdul Nasser, who had risen from the masses. Jesse suggested mechanization of farms, training of all Egyptians from elementary school through high school, reasoning that even the most abject could learn to farm with tractors and eventually, if properly trained, to repair them. He had been warned not to criticize Egypt or Egyptians in his teaching, but since good teaching involved criticism, he proceeded to put down such anachronisms as the human-powered Archimedean screw in preference to motorized pumps, even simple ones that could be rigged from automobile engines. Sayed and Laila left the classroom that day still arguing, but Jesse felt good, for his students were dealing with a major problem that confronted Egypt. He realized he had flung a problem into the face of Egypt, but justified his teaching methods. "How can I teach a course when I am told what to say and what not to say? I don't follow orders. I can't." Yet there was always that uneasiness, "that fear of what can happen," that possibility of an "Egyptian-paid student in my class reporting . . . what

I say." What chance, really, did even his good students have in such an atmosphere?

He was determined to see that more than one student had a chance, even if it meant putting his job on the line to strike a blow for education and against sexual fascism. Shwiker Elwan, a thirty-eight-year-old young woman, wanted to go to the United States for graduate school; her family would not permit her to go, especially a "dogmatic brother . . . steeped in thousands of years of traditions." Through Carl Leiden, a scholarship at an American university and an air-grant to take her there and bring her back after completing her work, if she chose, had been arranged. One early December morning Jesse met Leiden and they drove up the Nile to El Ma'adi, where they first picked up Shwiker Elwan's friend, Christine Bergener, and then Shwiker Elwan herself. "Carl had [Ms.] Elwan's clothes, her passport money—everything." Then they took a circuitous way through El Ma'adi to the desert road to Cairo, "all this to dodge her brother and members of her family . . . [who would] block her going to America." At the airport they had coffee. The young woman was uneasy for she had never ridden in a plane, had never, in fact, been out of Egypt. They got her aboard an Olympia flight before most of Cairo was even awake. "Soon," Jesse thought, "she would be in Athens, then London . . . then in New York City." It had been an exciting day, but the next morning he was called on the carpet by President McLain for taking the young woman to the airport. "I played silent," he wrote of the event, "but was guilty of all charges. Why not send her to America to further her education?"

Surely Time had forgotten Egypt, Jesse thought, more than once, as he watched the feluccas sailing upstream and drifting downstream on the Nile as they had done for seven thousand years. It was the convenient way, the passive way of acceptance, and Nature supplied the power without cost "as she had done for countless generations that had lived and died and left their histories in hieroglyphics on stone in the cool tanks on the west bank of the Nile where the fertile valley met the Sahara Desert sands." One evening the Stuarts found a Bedouin village with its tents tucked away under the palms. A young Bedouin took them into a large tent of bright colors and gave them chairs while the wild, maddening music of flutes and drums arose and began to accompany the equally wild swaying of Bedouin youths to a mad rhythm. There Jesse saw as strange a ritual as he had ever imagined. Naomi Deane and other women in the group of sightseers were allowed to enter, "for being Christians they were of a foreign religion and lost anyway." The tempo of the music hastened, "and the people weaved more furiously until a few forgot time, place and the world and toppled over on the Holy Ground inside the tent." The swaying youths were exhausted and writhing on the sand, "moaning and kicking," and then the elderly Moslems with long beards took "sticks which were about the size of our tobacco sticks at home . . . [and] larruped their behinds until they took off." Only the sects of the Holy rollers and unknown tongues that had swept Jesse's own hill country long ago could compare with this strange spectacle of religious fanaticism. Later, outside the tent, he asked a minister in their group about the unusual haircuts of the dancers, clipped close except for hanks of long hair on top of the head, and if they signified anything.

"Yes," he whispered, "it very definitely signifies something. Some of these people are so devout they think when danger or death threatens the boy angels will snatch them quickly into heaven."

Outside in the night on the edge of the village someone saw the new American satellite *Echo* streaking across the sky from the north like a bright star. Its orbit scribed the village, and the Bedouin women looked up at the strange omen and "said something to each other under their veils which were darker than the night." Now, Jesse thought, surely they perceived something new. "Wasn't this an omen . . . that the world had changed?" No, for the world had not changed in this place. "It was the same as it had been for centuries."

Despite ever-present problems, as the semester waned the Stuarts knew they had built some beautiful memories together. Jesse, Naomi, Jane, and friends like the German student, Christine Bergener, who had stood by Shwiker Elwan, rode Arabian horses, two silver and two black, through the desert sands around the pyramids of Giza. "Out there it was the sand, the sky and the stars," Jesse wrote, and they had not returned until past midnight. After an American Thanksgiving with the Leidens and a special service at which Ambassador Rhinehard had read a proclamation, the Stuarts had met their Kentucky friends, Mark and Willie Snow Ethridge, at the Nile Hilton; their meeting so far from home had for a little while brought home closer. Out on the road to Alexandria early one morning they had passed the pyramids at dawn and watched the sun rise over the yellow sands, then seen the Roman Museum in the city. They had gone down the Nile to Old Babylon, too, and seen "the church where Christ's mother had hid him for two years—we visited the crypt where he was supposed to have stayed. At least, this spot, He and his Mother and Joseph had once been." There was the trip to the Holy Land on Air Jordan, when they saw the Mount of Olives and the Garden of Gethsemane. Jesse "went down the path," he recorded, "that

Christ had walked from the Mount to the Garden—and then to the old city—through Damascus Gate—and we followed the stations of the Cross from the trial of Jesus to his Crucifixion." Yet the condition of the Holy Land disturbed him: The many different churches, "each sharing and controlling some small part of a 'sacred spot'—a divided Christianity," and the excluded Jews on the other side of the Holy City—"not so holy with a No Man's Land going through it," disillusioned Jesse with the whole situation. There had been the biggest New Year's Eve party in Cairo at Munir Doss's, where Jesse shared his old complaint—"a most distressing thing . . . to see the year pass and [us] grow older." And there had been the boat trip in the moonlight on the Nile to remember, Syria in May, windy Damascus, and their return to Cairo.

And now they were preparing to leave. By late April, "the hours went by rapidly," he wrote, "but they didn't make days fast enough to suit me. Egypt had now begun to have a deadening effect on my mind." He counted the days until they would be leaving. He grew increasingly critical of the educational planners, "wise men," he satirized, who would help spend "nearly two million American dollars . . . to give us the privilege of helping Egypt." In return the Egyptian government would hardly recognize the American University. "No wonder Egyptians think we are crazy. We are."

They planned to leave in June, and by early May Jesse had got most of his *Egyptian Journal* ready at the risk of having Henrietta Nasser, a young Palestinian woman, type it bit by bit through the spring months. Since his own luggage would very likely be thoroughly searched and he did not want to risk confiscation, he took most of the manuscript in his briefcase to United States Information Service official John Slocum, who, in accord with Jesse's instructions, would see that it made its way safely to Annie Laurie Williams in New York City. In mid-May Jesse went to Port Said with Slocum, upon his invitation, and addressed the USIS at that "beautiful . . . clean seaport town." The following week Jesse spoke to about fifty students at the American College for Girls in Heliopolis and "kept them laughing." Then he delivered a commencement address in El Ma'adi, and through John Slocum received an offer to lecture in the future for the United States Information Service, an arm of the State Department, an honor to which Jesse would give serious consideration.

On the way by taxi to AUC "the wind came in at open windows," Jesse reported, "and burned our faces." It was only late May, but the temperature was 111 degrees. His disillusion grew big with the heat when he thought of how he had all year dug into his pockets over and above his lecturing income "for the privilege of teaching, under such conditions, and for being insulted by and abused by the Egyptian Government," and he resolved, "not anymore." The Stuarts carefully completed their packing, hoping to get by customs with little difficulty, then left for Alexandria. Once again Jesse worked with Abdul Messiah and this time Old Mounikan's brother to bribe the luggage through customs. "For one day," Jesse wrote in words that moaned with disgust, "I'd seen the crooked work. . . . Any one or all could be bribed." The next morning, June 12, they boarded the *Achilles,* bound for Athens. They were happy when the ship pulled away. And looking back to Alexandria at that moment, Jesse frankly chronicled, he "wouldn't have cared had it been the mythical continent, Atlantis, that broke apart and fell into the sea."[4]

"What a wonderful feeling it was," he thought, "to be able to express my thoughts out in the open and not behind closed doors." This aura of freedom went with the basics he loved, the clean Greek ship and the good food and the civilized people. After a good night's sleep they awoke to the sea winds, sunshine, and blue Mediterranean water, then passed Crete. They spent several days in Athens and traveled throughout Attica. Jesse walked to Constitution Square right away, where he had stayed twenty-three years before in the King George Hotel, but it had all changed except for the good coffee in front of the hotel and the soaring Acropolis across the way. Athenian museums were a bit of a letdown after the Cairo Museum. With so much to see in southern Greece they had hardly enough sleep. Jesse was up with the cock's crow at five in the morning, keenly responsive to his guide's sparkling eyes that bespoke her pleasure in her work, "a very nice middle-aged woman . . . loved Athens as much as Socrates must have loved this city." One day Jesse, Naomi and Jane drove out "along the Saronic Gulf, where the Greeks defeated the Persians, then south to Argos, through the valley and on to new and old Corinth." Tobacco now grew where there used to be a city. They proceeded to Navplion for lunch and then to Epidaurus and its twenty-four-hundred-year-old theatre. He found the ruins of Mycenae, the wellspring of Homeric legends and the blind poet's epics, and was deeply impressed by the tomb of Agamemnon. "We loved Greece and the Greek people," he recorded; it "seems we were of the same mind in our love of freedom and learning."

On June 18 they flew out of Athens over Corinth, along the Adriatic coast above northern Italy and the Alps to Munich. There they enjoyed a reunion with the Leidens, who had driven up through Italy and Austria, and with their student-friend Christine Bergener and her parents, natives of Munich, in "the Rathskeller where the Germans used to heil

Hitler." Jesse finished the last parts of his *Egyptian Diary*—had to, for "my notes were wearing out," and "my mood, after Greece and now Germany, was changing. And I knew if I didn't finish the last chapters now my Journal would have two moods." The Stuarts entrained to Bayreuth and Jesse felt a kinship with the "city made famous by Wagner and Liszt" and the birthplace of Jean Paul Richter, whose work Carlyle had translated into English; for here Jesse was now in old Bavaria, an American fictioneer with his *Hie to the Hunters* being translated into the German *Kentŭcky-Melodie* by the venerable publishing house of Hestia Verlag, which he visited and came away from with a prized author's copy, translated by Rudolf Roder. Three years earlier his *Good Spirit* had been published by the same firm under the title *Der gute Geist von Laurel Ridge*. Here in Bayreuth they had literal kin, too, and enjoyed the hospitality of Mr. and Mrs. Milleus Eckstein—"wonderful and delightful people," Jesse wrote of the parents of Hilda Darby, whom Jesse's nephew Gene had married. Nothing would do for Jesse but that the Ecksteins join his family for dinner at their hotel, after which they all walked to the opera house on "the green hill" overlooking the city, "the house of music Wagner and Liszt loved and made famous."

A bus took them to the Nurnberg airport, where they caught a flight to Copenhagen via Frankfurt; and Jesse saw again the copper roofs turned green and felt the sudden, bracing contrast of 40-degree June temperatures, chilling their good time at the Tivoli Gardens. Down into the heart of the old Scandinavian city the next day, he stepped out of his taxi at the Gyldendal publishing house, where two of his junior books would soon appear in translation by Hanne Zahle, *Drangen i Dalen* (*Beatinest Boy*) and *Een syvende Pose* (*Penny's Worth of Character*). "I was never treated better," he wrote; nor had he ever enjoyed a publishing-house tour more, for this two-centuries-old concern owned its own printing presses and binderies and employed 150 editors and 400 technicians—a complete and self-contained house. Through Rotterdam and Belgium they proceeded to Paris and took in some of the paintings of the Louvre one afternoon, though they regretted not having a week to spend there. Aware the Romans and Italy had taken much from the Greeks, Jane was "greatly impressed," Jesse thought, even though she observed that if you subtracted "Egyptian and Greek sculpture from the Louvre there would be little left." The next day after coffee, rolls, and marmalade at a small sidewalk cafe, they strolled through Montmartre and enjoyed cool drinks at the Café de la Paix, visited Napoleon's Monument, and he and Naomi dropped in for nostalgia's sake at the Claridge Hotel where they had stayed on their first European tour together twelve years earlier. They took Jane with them to the Moulin Rouge and Folies Bergère, and Jesse responded with enthusiasm, "The house was hot as hell but the show, 40 different scenes, was great. The French can do it. They are originals. No mass culture here."

They journeyed through northern France on Monday morning, June 26, on the boat train, a "nice" area that reminded them of the Kentucky Bluegrass. At Calais they left the train for a smooth channel crossing to Folkestone, quickly passed through customs, and caught a boat train for London, crossing County Kent with its "orchards and hops, wheat and sheep," in time for tea by the Thames. Exploring London and its bookstores, Jesse picked up two volumes written by his old friend Dr. Hamish Brown, now residing in London. Jesse later telephoned him and heard his Scottish brogue for the first time since May 1938. Brown invited the Stuarts out for the evening, and they had a "wonderful time" with Hamish, who had gained even more weight than Jesse, and enjoyed meeting Hamish's wife, Heda, and their daughter, Ann. For the next several days the Stuarts toured London and England. On a morning tour including Westminster Abbey, they encountered Todd Kuhn, his wife, and their son, "Skeeter," and two students, Betty Yates and Kinon Valaskakis, people they had known at the American University in Cairo. "Jane was enthralled," Jesse thought, "to see Oxford University with 35 colleges and less than 9000 students." At a shop near Warwick Castle, two antique glasses fetched Naomi's eye, and she had to have them. Jesse was content to spend a whole Friday wandering through Dickens' Old Curiosity Shop and booksellers "like Foyles," where he bought an edition of Thomas Hardy's collected poems. Later in the day he talked with editors in such publishers' offices as Gollancz, Limited, on Henrietta Street. "His girls" met him and together they saw a French musical that evening, and the next especially enjoyed a British-American production with Van Johnson, *Music Man*, at the Adelphi. Jesse dropped into pubs to hear the English talk, and got around, of course, to a cemetery—the one in which movie star Kay Kendall had been buried about a year ago. Before entraining on the *Coronation Scot* to Edinburgh, they savored another "wonderful evening" with the Browns at their home, where Hamish played the piano with marvelous skill and talked with Jesse about a book on propaganda he had been writing. And Jesse, with his eye for odd detail, observed of Hamish that "he fed the hedgehog in the garden." That evening Jesse wrote in his journal, "This would be the last time, I had the feeling, I'd see Hamish in a long time. His health was none too good."

In Scotland they saw much in four days, beginning with Princes

Street and Jesse's old headquarters more than two wars ago at 8 View-forth Gardens. At St. Giles Church he ran into a pair of old LMU classmates, Grace Jones and a man surnamed Moore, her husband, though Jesse could not for the life of him recall his first name. The Stuarts went on to Patrick Thomson's Department Store, an old favorite of Jesse's. While having lunch, they bumped into the Moores again. On Monday, July 3, the papers were filled with news of Ernest Hemingway's death, an event Jesse captioned in his journal entry that day, commenting, "Really a shock . . . killing himself by accident or suicide." They journeyed on to Glasgow and toured the Trossachs, afterward taking the train to London's Waterloo Station. There they retrieved their stored luggage and engaged the boat train to Southhampton, embarking July 5 on the *New Amsterdam*. Great Britain had truly been enjoyable, yet it was only the prelude to the main attraction of America and home. That old, yet ever-fresh excitement one week later had Jesse up on deck at five in the morning with citizen and immigrant alike taking in the familiar shoreline of his country, goading him to headline his journal page for Wednesday, July 12: GREAT DAY: AMERICA.[5]

As Odysseus' aged dog had survived his master's wanderings until Odysseus returned to rocky Ithaca, so Birchfield survived to welcome the Stuarts home to W-Hollow from their year abroad. It took the cocker spaniel the better part of a day to realize his master and mistresses were home again, and as the realization struck him, Jesse recorded, "he was going wild" and "followed us all over the house." By October Birch was ailing so they took him to the vet's, then brought the old fellow home in a few days when he had showed little improvement. He licked Naomi's face when she carried him to the car, and was happy to get home and go over his old walks again. He ate all his supper and slept on the rug by their bed, snoring a bit before they, too, went to sleep; but two days later their fourteen-year-old pet died of a heart attack. Jesse wrapped him in his rugs he liked to sleep in, and "put his dish and water bowl away." His only note at the end of October read, "Lost Birchfield, a faithful dog. . . . He loved us—We loved him."

They were soon back into the routine, Jesse lecturing, writing, and farming at the end of the season as he could. In one of his many talks he addressed the Ashland Kiwanians, stressing teachers' problems of freedom of speech in Egyptian schools, the outdated, crude implements of the farmers (fellaheen) there, and how "Egyptian students far surpass their American counterparts in desire to learn." One reporter noted Jesse's "rapid-fire manner which held Kiwanians in rapt attention." Outside family and household activities and getting things settled, Naomi taught school, helped Jesse with his lecturing schedule, and took just a bit of time to speak herself at local women's clubs. Jane assisted her father by typing poems but was soon off to college at Randolph-Macon and was more and more caught up in her own work. Before she got away that fall to Lynchburg, Virginia, though, her boyfriend, Julian Juergensmeyer, now a student at Duke University, joined them for a family picnic on Seaton Ridge. Jesse and Naomi would see less and less of Jane as she pursued her studies, eventually achieving her A.B. degree, *magna cum laude*, at Western Reserve University, her M.A. at Indiana University in Greek and Latin, with a minor in Italian, and later her Ph.D. at IU in medieval and modern Italian. She had evinced talent in creative writing, publishing her first book of poems, *A Year's Harvest*, in 1957, and would continue to publish books, stories, poems, and works in translation in the years ahead.

Jesse's and Naomi's was an established routine that would continue at W-Hollow with interruptions here and there, through the 1960s and 1970s. All the while Jesse's reputation as a man of letters continued to grow nationally and internationally, his poetry, fiction, and essays appearing altogether in more than thirty different countries. Honors began avalanching in the 1960s, the one meaning most to him coming while he was in Egypt. The Stuarts had just taken their Holy Land trip and returned by way of Lebanon to Cairo when the news came. After a morning of writing and errands, he was getting a bit sleepy when the Leidens dropped by and Socrates Patsilidis telephoned that Jesse had received a cablegram and had won five thousand dollars. Jesse was skeptical, but Carl Leiden drove him to AUC to get the cablegram and verify the message. It was true. When they went to John Slocum's party that evening Jesse thought it "a gay affair—one of the gayest," and afterward headlined his journal, "RECEIVED ACADEMY OF AMERICAN POETS AWARD $5000." The following day the Stuarts rode out to a favorite spot with the Leidens—the Giza pyramids—and there they "loitered about, taking it easy." A few days later the letter from the Academy of American Poets arrived, signed by Mrs. Hugh Bullock, president of the organization, whose chancellors included such distinguished names in literature as J. Donald Adams, W. H. Auden, Witter Bynner, Henry Seidel Canby, Max Eastman, Randall Jarrell, Marianne Moore, Robert Nathan, John G. Neihardt, Frederick A. Pottle, and John Hall Wheelock. "I was deeply touched," Jesse recorded. "I wept—I felt humble. I couldn't believe this had happened to me. The impact was enough to shake me emotionally." He sat down and wrote out his feelings to Mrs. Bullock until he could write no more. "My, my, I never felt so grateful for the biggest literary award I'd ever received."

"Now, honestly," he pressed Donald Davidson a few weeks later, "did you ever think a thing like this could happen to me?" Jesse thought that Robert Frost, to some extent, was behind the committee's choice. Of course, John Hall Wheelock knew Jesse's work and had edited some of his prose. Robert Hillyer had praised his *Album of Destiny* back in 1944 as "a fine piece of work . . . that will last." He had written, "Stuart's sonnets and variations on the sonnet are beautiful. I could spend days over them. Deep roots and abundant flowering." Hillyer and Robert Nathan, and others who believed that Jesse Stuart deserved more recognition than he had received, had in fact pushed his name. He would go to New York City formally to receive the award, he informed his old mentor.

In early November of 1961 Jesse and Naomi went to Wallingford, Pennsylvania, near Philadelphia, where they were guests of John and Katherine Bird and several of the *Saturday Evening Post* staff at a delightful party hosted by the Birds at their home. Then it was on to New York City, where they registered at the Woodstock Hotel; Jane joined them from Randolph-Macon in Virginia "and there was great rejoicing." On Wednesday, November 8, they went with Eve Blair to the Park Avenue apartment of Mr. and Mrs. Eli Whitney Debevoise, a director of the Academy of American Poets. There they met Mrs. Hugh Bullock, who presided. "And here were my old friends over the years," Jesse observed, "editors from three publishing houses." Jesse was presented with a scroll citing him for "distinguished poetic achievement" and his lifework in the genre. In turn Jesse first read "Hold to a Living Dream," then from *Kentucky Is My Land* the lines

I cannot write tonight for the moon is full
And large as a wagon wheel above the timber.
I must go out, for the world is beautiful,
Must leave the open fire and dying ember.
For what are words upon an ink-stained scroll
When magic moonlight floods this stubborn world?
When wary winds of ruthless winter roll
Over the knolls, and leaves and sedge are hurled
Into illimitable starry space?
I must be out in beauty, hectic, rough,
On mountains big enough for my embrace.
I must be out where I can love enough. . . .

Remember, hills stay young; their beauty keeps
Eternally as seasons come and pass.
They will be here when this admirer sleeps,
Who will not leave his shadow on their grass.

Continuing in an "emotion-choked voice," he concluded with the first poem from *Man with a Bull-Tongue Plow*, commencing, "Sir: I am a farmer singing at the plow . . ." Blair noticed that one of New York's most sophisticated audiences gave Jesse its rapt attention. "So must Robert Burns," she thought, "have held his listeners in the salons of Edinburgh!" John Hall Wheelock was moved to exclaim, "A great poet, a great poet. A fine, sensitive poet!" No mean poet himself, the Scribner editor praised Jesse's poetry as "natural," and the poet as a man in the bardic tradition who could "communicate" with readers "an almost mystical union with the infinite." After this highpoint of poetic recognition for him, Jesse wrote in his journal, "I was deeply touched at the reception and friends of past and present there—and the whole thing. It was a long way for a man from W-Hollow to Park Ave. and a $5000 poetry prize. For me it was over 1600 published poems long."[6]

That trip to New York he spent many hours with his publishers, especially with editors at McGraw-Hill where, if revisions were made on time, three of his books would appear in 1962: the volume of poems, *Hold April;* the *Jesse Stuart Reader*, for which he was writing introductions; and the educational novel, tentatively called *Gifts of Gallion*. When Jesse asked Ed Kuhn, "Do you plan to publish my *Egyptian Journal?*" the editor got up and paced the floor, drawing on his pipe stem as he sometimes did when he was disturbed. "We sure do," he answered, "but when I don't know. You have these books for 1962. You are ahead of us." Jesse had to admit that he was and let the matter stand at that.

Back home in W-Hollow, he finished the proofs for *Hold April* and returned them to McGraw-Hill by late November, but he was irritated because of too many visitors and excessive interruptions. He found himself longing for the old days in W-Hollow, "when the place was without a road—country was a little wild—and in those days I wrote scores of poems—many of which were accepted by the good magazines in America. How I longed for that time again." The phone rang too often, sometimes every five minutes. Then people just came. "They didn't want anything. They came out of curiosity." His good friend Robert Nathan sympathized and wrote, urging him to take a Huntington Hartford Fellowship "where I could go and work for six months unmolested." But Jesse had already obligated himself to make a speaking tour for the

United States Information Service, which would require him to go around the world, concentrating his appearances in the Near East, Middle East, and Orient.

Despite his complaints, he was working consistently and getting a great deal of writing done, along with lecturing; although he had to say no to several requests for talks, by June he would give approximately twenty-nine. Heart pain and flu distracted him in February 1962, but by early March he was well enough to fly to Lexington, where he was taken on to the Eastern Kentucky State College campus at Richmond and enjoyed the hospitality of its new president, Robert R. Martin. At the Student Union Building he signed 530 just-purchased books in addition to old ones his readers brought in, over 600 in all. Former Governor and Mrs. Keen Johnson were on hand to greet him. It was the same handsome old Hiram Brock Auditorium "where I gave my first college talk 27 years ago." The crowd was larger now than before. "I faced over 2000 young faces—and I didn't have a note. They roared. Those standing didn't leave. Time passed, I heard no class bells. When I finished I was called back to the podium three times." He enjoyed similar, highly successful appearances at East Tennessee State College and at Nashville, where he got to visit Vanderbilt and found time enough to fold back into his graduate-school past by sitting in Donald Davidson's class and even taking notes while his old professor lectured. What fun! That month he received a $1,500 check from *Saturday Evening Post* for his essay "Are We a Nation of Digits?" and the usually dependable semi-annual royalty check from Scribner's for *Thread,* this time in the amount of $1,643.19; so now he and Naomi decided to go on with their plans for a new room, as a result of which their W-Hollow home would reach nearly across the opening of Shinglemill Valley to the green, dogwood-stippled acclivities on each side. Now its white bottle chimneys in contrast to the brown oak shingles reached picturesquely into the sky, achieving the design Naomi Deane had long planned.

That summer the interruptions and disturbances of all kinds were rankling more than ever. Working on another of the seemingly endless, mounting pile of scrapbooks of clippings, he questioned himself, "Why was I giving my time to this? . . . So little time left and it should be made (every minute, hour, day, week, month and year) to count for something creative—something more practical—more worthwhile." By July he told himself "that this year, creatively[,] has been one where I have actually done less creative work than any one year since I entered college." There had been "too much 'overseeing' work, too many visitors—and the health problem of humidity and heat." Because of these problems, he wrote,

"I cannot work here—or live here—and be in the right frame of mind. I must go to a new place where my health will be better where there is stimulus for work—an atmosphere for creativity—where people are not wanting to know what I 'make.' 'Damned little,' I could tell them. But I'm disgusted and fed up with here. I won't just talk and write about this but I shall act." One Sunday in early September Naomi and Jane were away from W-Hollow, and wanting to rest after arduous preparations for their now-imminent tour, Jesse closed the front door—locked it. "Cars came, 14 to 20—people got out and knocked on the door. I wasn't home. But I wanted to hear the baseball game, Redlegs vs. San Francisco Giants. I went to the kitchen and turned on the radio." He had the new cocker spaniel, Boswell, in the room with him and was relaxing and really getting into the game. Then, "I looked up and people had come around back and found me."

In Jesse's mood it was just as well that he and Naomi Deane were getting away. Before leaving they attended a party for the fifty-fifth wedding anniversary of Naomi's parents and had a nice evening. They said goodbye to Jane and good friends Ben and Jean Webb. In New York Ed Kuhn's reaction to an old manuscript Jesse had hauled out of his reserve and revised through the summer, then sent to Kuhn for placing in the safe at McGraw-Hill, was positive. They boarded a jet clipper on their way to Paris and Tehran, flying the northern route over Boston, Halifax, and St. Johns. They finished breakfast crossing the west coast of France and landed in Paris at 8:25 on the morning of September 17, having flown just over six hours. From there they flew to Beirut, Lebanon, then across Syria and Iraq into another world, the mile-high city of Tehran where mountains extended all around them.

In Iran they were still sleepy after ten hours of sleep, but talking with the Iranian-American Society Literary Club, Jesse was soon awake, learning from its scholars and literati that "poetry had been and was everything here"; even through an interpreter he sensed "their great respect for poets and poetry." Altogether he would give ten talks before their stay in the land of Firdusi's epic *Sha Nemeh* ended with September. They would travel nearly twenty-five hundred miles by plane, train, and station wagon from the Elburz Mountains overlooking the Caspian Sea in the north to the Persian Gulf in the south, seeing Masshad, Shiraz, the ruins at Persepolis, and Esfahan. In one village they passed a camel train; "rider asleep, camels kept on going—about 20," he jotted. In Masshad at the American Consulate they enjoyed the society of the Franklin Standishes, eight-year veterans in Greece and both schoolteachers. Jesse visited Tus, "where Firdusi, Persia's great poet, lived and worked," now a plain where the old city once stood, marked by "the most lavish monumental monument I'd ever seen in all my travels erected for a writer." They entrained with interpreter Nasser Feisal for a journey that stretched its slow length across the northern rim of the Dashte Kavir Desert: "Night came over the vast desert," Jesse wrote, "and virginal stars blinked in the blue Iranian skies. In the morning at three I woke and looked out at a new moon hanging high like a bright [sickle]." To the south, they enjoyed Shiraz, "a clean and wonderful city . . . capital of Poetry in Iran." Here they visited the tombs of Hafiz and Saadi, and studied out historic Persepolis. The sight of "flocks and herds of the two Great Federations of Tribesmen" along their way "moving south to Persian Gulf with at least 100,000 animals" impressed him every bit as much as the Zorastrian Fire Temple and the tombs of four Persian kings. By Chevrolet station wagon six of them drove over the Zagros Mountains to Esfahan, rugged going over dusty and often unpaved roads, with no facilities along the way. "Naomi, only woman in the group and I," he chronicled, "used a tree-lined ditch at Pasargade," a fact he felt obliged to record with as much emphasis as their viewing of Cyrus' tomb. Jesse left impressed with the Iranian people, who had treated him and Naomi with courtesy and kindness. "Iranians [are] definitely in pro-American orbit," he transcribed with confidence.

John and Eileen Slocum met the Stuarts at Cairo, but even with their marvelous hospitality, it was "strange" to be back in Egypt. Jesse went by the American University where "old students and friends swarmed around me!" and he acknowledged, "I was touched to tears." He spoke at the American University and lunched with President and Mrs. McLain. At a reception hosted by the Slocums for Jesse and Naomi, more than 125 of his former colleagues and students at AUC, members of the American Embassy, and Egyptian teachers from other institutions came, "a great party," Jesse thought, that went on past midnight. During their sixteen days in Egypt, Jesse delivered nineteen lectures on such topics as "Teaching and Writing: Twin Professions," "How to Write a Novel," "Writing Poetry," and "The Short Story." More often than not, however, he spoke on his own life, how he got an education, and on what being an American meant to him. At the huge University of Cairo, then a hotbed of anti-Western sentiment, Jesse filled the seats and aisles and kept the students for fifty minutes. "Applause so great, I never finished my talk," he recorded. "Had invaded stronghold and won." John Slocum complimented him. "This is it right down the middle," he said. "You said the right things." On October 14, after he spoke at Alexandria University, the subsequent question-answer session with English, Scottish, Irish, and Sudanese teachers in his audience became heated, "and maybe [my] replies were a little heated," too. That evening a full-house reception kept him and Naomi from privately celebrating their twenty-third wedding anniversary, but at least on this lecture tour Naomi Deane was with him. Jesse's *Thread*, translated by Fatimah Mahjub with a review and preface by Ahmad Zaki Muhammad, appeared in Cairo that year, and the Ministry of Education held a banquet in Jesse's honor at Shepheard's Hotel, attended by Egypt's "top educators"; he recognized that "this was high rating for an American." With obvious pleasure he jotted in his journal, "Embassy was surprised." In addition to his heavy speaking schedule, Jesse attended eleven social events, five conferences, and three interviews. Most of these Naomi Deane attended with him, yet they still sandwiched in some time for get-togethers with old friends at Geziriah where they had lived, in El Ma'adi where Naomi had taught, and at such familiar haunts as the "Mousky" Bazaar. They even saw Salah Ramadin, their Nubian *sofragi* again, about whom Jesse later wrote, "Had we continued to live in Egypt, we would have kept Salah as long as he lived. The Stuart family became attached to him."

In Greece they had a month, and everything was easier and more fun. Lectures and conferences continued, but there was time to travel extensively as well. Much of the material that would appear in his journal *Dandelion on the Acropolis* found birth in dozens of pages of notes Jesse transcribed during this trip. Cultural attache Bill Curran photographed Jesse and Naomi against the fluted, wind-gnarled Doric columns of the Temple of Poseidon at Cape Sounion, where the Aegean sea winds tousled Naomi's hair and wafted the smoke of Jesse's cigar. He stood on Mars Hill with the limestone eminence of the Acropolis behind him, enjoyed the sidewalk tables on Constitution Square, and photographed Naomi buying flowers from grinning girls on the Island of Aegina. One day they walked around the agora of Socrates where the peripatetic teacher had lived and worked more than four hundred years before Christ was born. Here was Socrates' little world and his jail, too, Jesse observed. "Socrates' Athens and his Greece were not large enough to contain the mind of the man—for it had taken a future world to hold him." They journeyed to Thessaloniki in the north where they were guests of the Consular General, John Folson, and to Olympia in the west where Jesse stood at a market near the site of the ancient games. At Thebes he reflected upon Sophocles and *Oedipus Rex*, and was moved to write poetry at the ruins of Pindar's home, the Greek poet who reminded Jesse of Donald Davidson in that he could not change as his country changed:

The grass and dandelions his yard-green earth
And old Boeotian winds that bend the grass.
These are the only durable things that last
While four-and-twenty centuries file past.

Beyond Thebes at "Ipsalinti" he and Naomi had "two small skewers of broiled lamb and a small bun each," while Jesse reflected on the college at Ypsilanti, Michigan, where he had spoken twice. Then on their tour bus again, they were high in the mountains near Liakoura, between two worlds, "the human and mythological," at the "windy place" of Arachova literally above the clouds. Here they found Delphi, built as a sanctuary to Apollo, the pure god who reigned over the world of Art. Jesse marveled at the huge Delphic urn, the metaphorical "navel" of the world's body, which the young female guide modestly called "the middle of the body." He walked the sacred way through the sanctuary and contemplated the massive stone where Apollo killed the python, as a result of which the Oracle was bestowed upon the young god by his mother, Letho. While the tour bus waited for sightseers to return from the Delphic ruins, Jesse dodged up a footpath under olive trees a short distance away, then descended carved stone steps to Castalia Spring, out of which sacred waters flowed from Mount Parnassus. He was alone. Winds rustled the greenish gray olive leaves above his head, Parnassian winds in cypress boughs, too, perhaps echoes of multiplied sounds reaching back into the past? "Great art is simple art," a male voice seemed to say though it could have been a "more rasping wind in the leaves." Then he heard it again, a male voice speaking of Homer and his living poetry. Perhaps Poseidon, Jesse reasoned. Then a feminine voice spoke of the gold masks from Mycenean times, no doubt Gaea, Mother Earth and the mountains, then Letho, and suddenly what must have been the voice of Apollo, "a soft-wind-whisper as musical as the clear tones of a flute." Or, "could it be that I was dreaming?" Jesse wondered.

"I am still here," Apollo spoke of his people, "a memory in their hearts and minds." Jesse spoke, too, telling the voices of the Oracle that he was of "a dynamic race in the new world," a land of "doers and do-gooders" not unlike the Hellenic Greeks, who were "brothers of the mind." His people, Jesse explained, "are trying to help the world" and believed in four freedoms—from want, of speech, of religion, from fear. This intelligence delighted the voices of the Oracle.

"Tell me how your citizens are conceived beyond your world!"

"In some countries we are put in jail," Jesse answered. "For all the good our minds, hearts, and hands try to give, to help a world, our country is looked upon, generally speaking, very disdainfully."

"You must have risen high among the countries of the world," the flute-voiced god intoned. Then it admonished, "They will destroy you."

"Maybe not for we are young and we have hopes."

Then, the god's words were "soft-wind, musical words that trembled like the leaves on the tree above him," inquiring of Jesse what he did in the world.

"I work with my hands on my land in a western world," he said. "Besides doing this, I am a poet."

"First comes the poet," Apollo abjured. "Then work with your hands."

The goddess Gaea understood. "Ah, so good, and no wonder, you have come to us. I remember the Great Homer and Sappho! You have come to Parnassus, our mountain of inspiration to poets!"

"I need that inspiration," Jesse said.

Apollo was speaking again when Jesse heard—from the end of the footpath beyond the olive trees—the tour-bus driver saying, "Mr. Stuart is missing." Then unmistakably, Naomi's voice: "We are ready to go, Jesse! Come on! Don't keep us waiting. What are you doing up there anyway?"

By Castalia Spring, Jesse heard a fellow traveler answer for him, "Listening to the water." Now the wind rustling the green leaves above him suddenly ceased. The oracular voices departed as "frightened November birds," and he arose slowly "from the ancient stone, chiseled and shaped by ancient hands that were now dead and dust."

A week after the Stuarts had been in Lebanon, Jesse wrote from the Alumni Club in Beirut to the *Ashland Daily Independent* to correct a mistaken reference that he was teaching at the Nazan University in Japan. He would not be in the Orient possibly until February 1963. Despite an average of a lecture a day for his fourteen days in Lebanon, Jesse was holding up well except for a painful toothache, which hurt so much "that I could hardly eat breakfast." Later, the "tooth was killing me," and although he had never had a plate, Jesse "promised God and myself, if this continued I'd have the last ones pulled when I got home and have a set (of) teeth—painless ones—I could depend on." One of their delights was meeting and lunching with a tall, slender young Christian, Emily Nasarallah, whose novel *Birds of September* was all the talk of Beirut. It told the story of the country people of Lebanon, who like the birds, had migrated, most of them to Beirut. Lebanon struck Jesse as a small but "wide-awake and beautiful country, with such hospitable people." Among other places his lectures took him to Tyre, Sidon, Byblos, and Tripoli. One of their most memorable jaunts was over the cedared mountains to Zahlah and "up the beautiful Beka'a Valley to Baalbek . . . Lebanon's breadbasket." He found Baalbek "fascinating—spent hours there" before they motored back to Zahlah and lunched with Said Ahl, "Lebanon's foremost writer." The Stuarts joined the party of American Ambassador Armin Meyer in his car and drove south to Sidon and inland to the village of Ell-Assad for a political picnic attended by about thirty thousand people. "His majesty and our ambassador made speeches while the crowd cheered," and as usual Jesse's eyes missed nothing: "one hundred and fifty barbecued lambs, heads and all were consumed plus other Lebanese dishes, gallons of wine and lavish deserts." Meyer's wife was a Kentuckian from the Lexington-Frankfort area, and Jesse and Naomi "enjoyed them tremendously." Later, at the Beirut Bookshop on Rue Bliss, he signed sixty-seven copies of *Qati al-Ajus*, his *Red Mule*, at his first autographing party on foreign soil, hospitably followed by a party hosted by the American cultural attaché and his wife, Mr. and Mrs. Russell Linch. In his spare time Jesse had been writing; by the time the Linches and other friends saw them off on a BOAC Comet jet to Karachi, Jesse's journal of Lebanon had reached something like 150 longhand pages.

In West Pakistan several things disturbed him. He had been warned that "the freeze was on" toward Americans. The Karachi paper carried a scathing cartoon about the powdered milk CARE had sent to the country, and another satirizing President Kennedy as a "boy scout"; while Jesse granted a partial truth to the caricature, he believed it was "not for them to say here . . . after the way we were helping people here." Even though he was a guest in the country, he had to register with the police, which did not set well. To be sure, when he met the Karachi Writers Group of newspaper and magazine editors, poets, novelists, and dramatists, he was pleased to find them friendly and himself well received. He entered into a whirlwind of appearances, and especially enjoyed meeting Mrs. Maya Jamil, English Department Acting Head at Karachi University, where he lectured, and Miss Aileen Aderton, assistant cultural affairs officer and the Stuarts' hostess for a luncheon with Fulbright Professor and Mrs. Frank McCloskey and Dr. and Mrs. J. Y. Bryan of the American Embassy. By December 8 he was in Lahore, where his heavy work load began to tell. After speaking in the morning at Lady MacLagan Teachers College for Women, giving a poetry reading at a press luncheon, and lecturing at the Writers' Guild at four in the afternoon, he attended a dinner—"a wild affair. Drinking, quarrels"— that lasted from eight o'clock until midnight. "What Price Glory?" he exploded in his journal. "How much could people stand? . . . why ride a free horse to death[?]" There had been no break in his day from breakfast until midnight. "This would have tired me when I was 24 years old and this was saying something." The next morning at breakfast he told the assistant cultural affairs officer, Pat Hogan, that if they kept "squeezing" him he was turning back at the Philippines. The next afternoon he and Naomi went sightseeing in Lahore at the Fort Mosque and the Gardens. Later, at Rawalpindi, they stayed at the Flashman Hotel and toured the ruins at Taxila, an hour's drive away, before he lectured at the Writer's Guild and was interviewed on radio. That evening the Stuarts were entertained in the home of an Oxford man, A. H. Kardar, where they met the members of the Kenya soccer team. The middle of the next day the Stuarts were guests at the home of A. D. Sheikh, Deputy Minister of Agriculture and Food for Pakistan, and there Jesse met "Hafeez," who, Jesse wrote, "was thought to be 'greatest poet of subcontinent.' " Jesse personally found Hafeez "a wonderful man" of sixty-two, who had resisted the overtures of Russia to become a propagandist and had the courage to say that "the heart of man" was poet, not "the machine of Russia." That evening Jesse lectured at the Education Club to teachers "and I turned loose and was myself. I gave them a lecture they wouldn't soon forget." At Peshawar he lectured at the university on poetry and read his poems. The next day they went to Khyber Pass, speckled with plaques marking historic engagements of Scottish, English, and Punjabi troops. Now mountain tribesmen guarded one pass after another on up to the Afghanistan border. On the way back the Stuarts stopped at the Village of Smugglers, then flew in the rain to Rawalpindi and on to Lahore. December 2 was a nice leavetaking after tea at Islamia College, where "on the grassy yard in the sunshine and amid blooming flowers I read poems and lectured to about 75 selected English students."

Old Dacca, East Pakistan (now Bangladesh), was a dervish of people, of rickshaws, buggies, horse-drawn vehicles made "like our old stage-coaches," and of a few autos on streets too narrow for them. "Here," Jesse observed, "people were smaller than in West Pakistan," and the vegetation was different with large banyan trees. Soon Jesse and Naomi were off into the northern wilds to Rajshahi, where their plane landed on a steel strip used by Americans in World War II. Supplied with bedrolls, they slept on cots to the sounds of howling jackals and buzzing mosquitoes, distractions that did not seem to bother others on the scene, Russ Prince of Utah and Betsy Chalmers of Massachusetts, lab-technicians doing their bit in the new Peace Corps. Jesse and Naomi viewed the sacred Ganges, photographing it with a new Leica camera, and Jesse gave "my best talk to the largest audience" at British-built Rajshahi Government College. Back in Dacca on December 19, they learned of the sudden death of Naomi's father from Oscar Sammons' telegram, rushed to them through Dean Rusk at the State Department. Jesse read it first. It was an automobile accident. "Your father is gone," he told her, "and your mother is in critical condition."

"Jesse," she said, "I told my parents I was the oldest and if they ever needed me I would come."

"Do you want to go?"

"The plane that takes me can bring me back," she said. So Naomi decided to go, although it was not easy, for she was deeply concerned about her husband's health. She briefed him on his medications while Jesse reassured her, and in four days managed to make her way back to the other side of the world through the roughest kind of winter weather to Greenup, there to be with the gathering Norrises in their tragic crisis.

The morning she left, though, Jesse did not know whether he could do without her or not. "I had much ahead of me," he considered. "Maybe if I kept busy it would be better." Typically, he began to shape adversity into triumph. He first turned to writing, then lectured at Dacca College to an audience of twelve hundred, even though there had been a strike and he had not expected to speak at all. "I didn't have a note. But I got up and spoke 50 minutes. The teachers had to open a way for me to get out. Never received such ovation."

Among the seven millions of Calcutta he had never seen such poverty, where "500 are [reliably] reported to be picked up dead off the streets each morning." His plane was late. "Most planes here like the countries, ran late." It was worse only in the leper colony just outside Karachi, "human beings shunted off to die—the walking dead with knotted hands and feet. And lying on [the] ground one man blind and without arms—all dying a slow death. . . . 170 here and their children playing around the compound of filth." Hundreds of cows ruminated in the streets of the starving. Exasperated he jotted, "COWS—people never bothered them. So how can you expect anyone who regards a cow as a sacred animal—ever to make any progress!" Tortured India tortured his patience. "This country is a thousand years behind the world!" he wrote, and apostrophized, "Where is their leadership?"

He flew on to Rangoon and found the Bay of Bengal "the most beautiful bay in the world." Bangkok, Thailand, became a favorite city. "People were so much cleaner," he thought, "little brown people who liked to smile." He toured that city of pagodas and temples and Buddhist shrines, then flew by KLM Dutch Airlines eastward over Thailand, Cambodia, Laos, Vietnam, and across the South China Sea to Manila, into "a Christian country in time for Christmas." Lighted Christmas trees bedecked Manila. When his car stopped for a traffic light on the way to his hotel, he saw across the street a park and in it a nativity scene similar to thousands he had seen, though somehow it seemed so long ago. When he registered at the Manila Hotel desk people were humming familiar carols. After the six countries in which he had been traveling since September, non-Christian with the exception of Greece, "it was very strange." He had made the most strenuous journey of his lifetime, absorbing Moslem, Hindu, Zoroastrian, and Buddhist cultures. "I had respected their rights to worship, for their religious beliefs were part of their cultural heritage. But Christianity was my cultural heritage." Since September he had faced new people and different situations—"even where people were hostile to my country, but seldom hostile to me as an individual. I wouldn't let them be hostile to me. While we had talked, we understood each other." Something of his Christian heritage, "an innate something deeply embedded in my heart, mind and soul went to work to remove dark clouds and the so-called immovable objects between their people and my people and our countries."

In January and February 1963, his tour continued through the Philippines and the Orient—Hong Kong, Taiwan, Japan, and Korea. It was the first Christmas he and Naomi had not been together since their marriage, but he took comfort in the fact that she was home with Jane in Kentucky. He worked for "parts of two nights" on a paper to be presented before the Asian Writers Conference Delegates, "The Role of a Writer in a Revolutionary World," then delivered his speech "off the cuff . . . a good talk," he thought. As a writer facing the future, he had during his stint at the American University in Cairo published these lines in a poem entitled "The Poet and Tomorrow":

> A poet can't unite with other minds;
> His is an only path to walk alone.
> His thoughts like surging rivers, blowing winds,
> He hears and understands a voice from stone.
> A poet must escape the petty clan.
> Evade the schools of blowing winds of thought.
> Behind his poem there must be the man
> Himself, sure of the artifice he's wrought
> And proud he reached alone up for the stars
> Despite his knowing he could not reach them,

Contented that he put dream above his cares
And that he puts his lifetime in his dream.

He flew south to Cebu and Dumaguete where he spoke at San Carlos University and Silliman University respectively. Lyle Lane, the American Consul in Cebu, invited Jesse along for a family swimming party. By ferry they left Cebu, Jesse noted in his journal, "where Ferdinand Magellan and ship's crew converted the natives to Christianity in 1521," and crossed over to Mactan Island, where "Magellan was killed by Lapu and his men when he tried to convert them by use of a blunderbus[s]." They ate lunch in a coconut grove but could not go swimming at that spot because of small octopuses; farther down the beach they swam until he and Lyle "got into sea urchins and got spines in our hands." In Dumaguete he met Minnie Palmore, a native of Frankfort, Kentucky, who took him along with other guests to her home for lunch, then saw him off at the airport. In Hong Kong he bought a watch for Naomi Deane, a light meter for his Leica, and a fifth of Scotch "to take evenings before bedtime to make me sleep," then proceeded to Taipei, Formosa. There he spoke at the American School and Soochow University. On his way to Taichung, he was surprised at the modern train, though there was no heat despite the forty-degree temperature. The stewardess "(Yes, on this train) brought us hot tea—I didn't like it but drank some to keep warm." Farms were "neatly patterned along the way. . . . Men and women were working everywhere." He reflected upon what he had observed and "decided the Chinese woman was of a superior breed—surpassing the men." He would later put it into an essay, "By Train to Taichung." In that city he lectured to five hundred young Chinese students at Providence English College, and later saw "the great sitting Buddha—largest in the Orient," the genesis of a story, though he told himself, "I'd probably never write it."

When he received the news on January 23 that Naomi's mother had died as a result of the accident in which her father was earlier killed, Jesse considered dropping everything and going to his wife. He discussed the matter with USIS officer Chuck McGinley, who advised him not to go for two reasons: He could not get home in time for Mrs. Norris' funeral, and a program awaited him in Korea. Jesse reluctantly stayed the course and purchased heavy clothing for "terribly cold" Korea, the last leg of his journey. He arrived on "the frozen tundra" by way of Tokyo across the Sea of Japan, and would never forget his first night in Seoul in the home of native Jim Kim and his wife, where he slept on a bed on the floor and could hear every sound in their room. The next morning Mr. Kim brought him a suit of heavy underwear. "I had to pull it on," Jesse recorded. "It was tight. So he and I pulled to put it over my underwear. Then Mrs. Kim came in and helped. I got it on." He spoke at the Jesuit College and to several other groups in Seoul, lectured at the Korean Military Academy, was interviewed by native Koreans and for the *Stars and Stripes,* and appeared before audiences at the Chongu Cultural Center, after which Jesse and the Kims went to a restaurant "where all officials of the city came in and ate with us" as "we sat on the floor around a low table," while Jim Kim translated their conversation. At Kyhumgi University, where he found the campus "beautiful and cold," he met President Byunghook Koh and renewed his acquaintance with Byungtaik Yang, whom he had met at the Asian Writers Conference on Manila. On one of his typical "hardest days" Jesse sent forty-five letters, attended five events, lecturing at three of them, and could find "no rest between events." Yet he reassured Naomi by letter, "I am watching all things—conserving myself as much as I can for I want to get home to you. I love you. When I get home fix me one of the old breakfasts."

He visited Panmunjom where "two ideologies had divided this land and these people," and chronicled, "Here we saw the Communists and they saw us. This was virtually war—all except there was no shooting." Nearly every evening he was invited out for dinner, one hosted by Ambassador and Mrs. Samuel D. Berger, and another at the home of Mr. and Mrs. William L. Magistretti to honor Magistretti as Deputy Chief of Mission, "a very pleasant evening," Jesse remarked. Another evening he was made an honorary member of the prestigious Pine Tree Club in Seoul, where he also spoke to several civic groups such as the Rotary Club. In the question-and-answer period following his talk, a Korean inquired, "Mr. Stuart, why are so many recent American books obsessed with sex?" Jesse shot back, "Well, Sir, your civilization here in Korea is nine centuries old. America's is an adolescent by comparison and some of our writers have just discovered sex." On the back of a photograph of him at the lectern before the Seoul Rotarians Jesse penned, "Here they laughed. I had them under the tables—even an Englishman and a Scotsman. I did it on purpose. They'll never forget me and my talk here." Indeed, he did such a thoroughly cooperative job for the USIS that he inadvertently overstayed his visa and had to get special clearance before he could leave the country.

Homeward bound by Lincoln's birthday, he stopped over in Tokyo to buy "many presents." He was met by General and Mrs. Ralph Lovett in Honolulu, where between planes they took him on a brief, specially arranged tour. By early the next morning he was near Chicago "looking down onto sheets of snow in the moonlight," but they did not excite him for he was too tired. At O'Hare Airport he "put cold water on my eyes that wanted to remain shut." He breakfasted in Indianapolis, then flew on by way of Cincinnati through rough snowstorm clouds, arriving "into the arms of my wife and daughter—and Ben and Jean Webb. What a meeting!" They drove home to W-Hollow. Boswell, the young cocker, was up on the flat roof of the garage, looking down. "He came down," Jesse recorded, "and he knew me: I was home again."[7]

Despite his frequent complaints that he could not get much work done in W-Hollow, Jesse's record of publication during the 1960s reveals a continued prolific output, including fifteen books: the biography of his father, *God's Oddling* (1960); his new collection of poems, *Hold April* (1962), which Robert Hillyer called "a beautiful book, a rare book, with its own golden place in our too-often shadowy literature"; two novels, *Mr. Gallion's School* (1967) and the richly archetypal *Daughter of the Legend* (1965); and five distinguished short story collections, *A Jesse Stuart Reader* (1963), *Save Every Lamb* (1964), *A Jesse Stuart Harvest* (1965), *My Land Has a Voice* (1966), and *Come Gentle Spring* (1969). In addition he published two new junior books, *The Rightful Owner* (1960) and *Andy Finds a Way* (1961); two revised reprints, *Huey, the Engineer* (1960) and *A Ride with Huey the Engineer* (1966); and as editor participated with others in two works, *Outlooks through Literature* (1964) and *Short Stories for Discussion* (1965). The record of that remarkable decade reveals approximately 108 poems, 98 short stories, 104 essays, 40 newspaper pieces, and 18 translations of his works. Further, 102 articles or other published items and 13 books, theses, and bibliographical studies appeared about Jesse Stuart and his work, among them Everetta Love Blair's *Jesse Stuart: His Life and Works* (1967), based on her doctoral thesis at the University of South Carolina; Lee Pennington's *The Dark Hills of Jesse Stuart: A Consideration of Symbolism and Vision in the Novels of Jesse Stuart* (1967), based in part on Pennington's master's thesis at the University of Iowa; Ruel E. Foster's excellent biocritical study *Jesse Stuart* (1968); and Mary Washington Clarke's *Jesse Stuart's Kentucky* (1968), which examines the original and authentic aspects of his work from an insightful folklorist's point of view.

During this decade Jesse continued his work in civic and community activities, accepting the General Chairmanship of the Kentucky Heart Association Fund Drive for 1964. The national office of the Heart Association arranged for its radio-TV-film director Hal Marc Arden to produce a half-hour sound-and-color film for the nationwide fund drive, to be called *Heart of a Town*. Greenup was chosen, according to one source, because of Jesse Stuart, his *Year of My Rebirth,* and his long-time involvement with the Kentucky Heart Association. Narrated by Edward G. Robinson, himself a heart patient, the film focused on Greenup, Jesse's recovery from his own coronary, teenager Patricia Harmon's progress from a "blue baby" to a normal teenager, and the family of civic leader Joe Mauk, who had died in his forties of a heart attack—in short, the effects of heart disease upon individuals, families, and a typical American community. The film crew arrived September 8, 1963, and the cameras rolled for five days. At one-room Cane Creek School Jesse was before the camera three hours and recorded in his journal, "I didn't know it took so many hours to make an inch of film." At the Greenup Fairview Cemetery up high overlooking the town and the Ohio River, while the camera rolled and he walked among the graves, Jesse meditated: these "stones that disturbed me—people I used to know! The City of the Dead up here was larger than the City of Greenup below. Many of the stones dated back to . . . 1800—So people come and they go—and over a century later a man from their ancest[ry] walked among them and was photographed for a film because he had cheated death." Scenes were shot of Jesse at the home of G. K. Harmon and his family in Greenup, by the Ohio River on friend Dave Kinner's property, of Jesse autographing books at the Greenup County Fair, of the author at home in his backyard walking along Shinglemill Creek "in a meditative mood," and of him entering and working in his writing room inside the "smoke-house."

Prior to the film's release for national television in February, a packed courthouse in Greenup viewed it following a day of festive speech-making. Jesse briefly praised the producers, then told his neighbors that he "would not want to be a movie actor permanently." While other speakers ranged widely and waxed euphoric, Jesse put the purpose of *Heart of a Town* into a nutshell: "If it hadn't been for the Heart Association, Patricia Harmon . . . would have been dead [eleven] years ago and I would have been dead nine years ago. If those who have gone could have had the care we received, they might be with us today." When the drive was over in the spring of 1964, as General Chairman Jesse sent signed letters of thanks and recognition to county leaders of the volunteer workers all over the state whose success spoke for itself: They "broke all previous records in raising funds." Typically, he took time to add personal notes to many of the letters, including one to Mrs. Ward McBrayer in Greenup, whom he had taught in 1930/1931 and who had since become a much-loved principal in the same school in which Jesse had taught her: "Ethel, how wonderful you are! It gives me pleasure to thank you!"

Other achievements and honors followed in the 1960s, honorary doctoral degrees at Marshall University (1962), Northern Michigan University (1964), Eastern Kentucky University (1964), Berea College (1966), Murray State University (1968), and Pfeiffer College (1969). On November 7, 1966, he and Naomi drove to Louisville to attend a reception in his honor and the dedication of a new building and twelve-hundred-student high school in Jefferson County, to be called the "Jesse Stuart High School." After the affair, he wrote simply in his journal, "I was deeply touched to see this school named for me."

Writing, teaching, farming, lecturing—it was the dream he had lived and was continuing to live, and Naomi was with him in the home they had first dreamed and then built together in W-Hollow. Yet their home had expanded in more ways than one. They traveled a great deal now, and Jesse's world had long ago brimmed over his region into America and the whole earth. He had become a self-acknowledged "world citizen," his material becoming all that lay beyond W-Hollow as well as in it. "The world belongs to me," he would write. "I can never get enough of life, of living, breathing the fresh winds in Kentucky, America, the world." The Stuarts spent the summer of 1964 over part of Europe, most of it in Greece; they traveled in Africa and Europe in 1968, and were in France during the riots. The decade had its sad moments, to be sure. In June of 1967 Jesse received word that his old teacher and friend of forty-one years, Harry Harrison Kroll, had died. "Harry Kroll had meant much in my life," he reflected. In April 1968, Donald Davidson's death left him with thoughts too deep for words, and he wrote nothing of his tears. Then in the mid-sixties Jesse himself was in the hospital for eight days for erratic blood pressure, a fibrillating heart, and adjustments in his medicine and diet; by decade's end he was felled by another heart attack, as a consequence of which he was "out of doing" for most of the fall of 1969. Nevertheless, he lived, and with the same spirit in and faith out of which he had lyrically sung following his first near-fatal attack:

I thank God that He granted my stay here
To count the many songs in winds that blow,
When April's spring returns again this year

I'll walk with Him where rivers rise and flow.
I'll stand beneath the graybarked sycamore,
With softer hands I'll feel its scaly bark,
Not any man will ever love life more.
I'll pray as I walk in the April dark.
Death held me prisoner 'til God stepped in
And took me by the hand and gave me breath,
And I was glad this heart was cleansed of sin,
And that I followed Him from arms of Death.
Back to my valley for the blooming spring,
Back to my garden and the wild bird's song,
To shadow, sun and multicolored wing,
The land, God must believe, where I belong.

In July 1967 there had been a happy reunion with his old friend August Derleth in Wisconsin, where they toured Derleth's Sac Prairie country, appeared together at a writers' conference in Rhinelander, and agreed to collaborate on a book with Robert E. Gard. Looking like two aging Greenbay Packer linemen, they posed together laughing for the cameras. "August was at his best describing everything." Four years earlier, Jane Stuart and her high school sweetheart Julian Juergensmeyer, attorney and later professor of law at the University of Florida in Gainesville, had married on her twenty-first birthday. While Jesse and Naomi were yet at Rhinelander, they received news of the arrival of their first grandson, Conrad Stuart Bagner Juergensmeyer. "We couldn't imagine having a grandchild," Jesse reacted. "Now we had one! And we rejoiced. We had entered a new phase of living. Another fulfillment in our lives, another generation had come."

As 1969 waned into the new year of a new decade, Jesse had reason to feel good, too, about more literary birthings of his own. He had a successful new collection of short stories released in May of 1969, *Come Gentle Spring,* from which one had been selected for Whit Burnett's *This Is My Best in the Third Quarter of the Century,* soon to appear. By July of 1969 *God's Oddling* had been translated and published for distribution in France, Algeria, Morocco, Tunisia, the Republic of the Congo, and Senegal; *Taps* had been reprinted the same month in hard cover. In late November he had received his first advance copy of his new autobiography, *To Teach, To Love,* bringing his classroom experiences up through his year at the American University in Cairo, although the book's release had been delayed until February 1970. Only a year before, at the end of 1968, he had counted sixty-two acceptances of books, short stories, poems, and articles—"which isn't bad for a freelancer in his 61st year," he appended. "What I like about this is, I am not through." Indeed, his summary at the end of 1969 listed no fewer than 110 items. Jesse could look back with satisfaction on the 1960s, and ahead to the time that yet remained for him.[8]

17

Twilight: W-Hollow
1970–1980

——————◊——————

Honors came steadily to the man from W-Hollow in the 1970s, including his twelfth doctoral degree, from the University of Louisville on May 13, 1973. He stood in front of the pillared portico of the university's administration building while gowned faculty members adjusted his hood and Rodin's *Thinker* sat in timeless study with his chin on his fist, just visible in the background over Jesse's left shoulder, as the photographer captured the event. Jesse's scholar's cap is tilted back on his head with the casualness of a perspiring baseball player catching a breather. The citation reads:

JESSE HILTON STUART

Son of Kentucky, poet, novelist, autobiographer, storyteller, teacher of students the world over, innovative educator, fabulist of the Plum Grove Hills and your world of W-Hollow, bardic chronicler of Appalachia; from your first book, *Harvest of Youth*, 1930, to such representative works as *Man with a Bull-Tongue Plow*, 1934, and *Beyond Dark Hills*, 1938—through *Trees of Heaven*, 1940, *Taps for Private Tussie*, 1943, *The Thread That Runs So True*, 1950, *The Year of My Rebirth*, 1956—and to *My Land Has a Voice*, 1966, and your most recent novel, *The Land Beyond the River*, 1973, you have shaped an artistic vision of the earth and the human experience at once real and imaginary, fictive and lyric, regional and universal, remarkable for its primal depth and amplitude. American Representative to the Asian Writers Conference, State Department Specialist, Guggenheim Fellow, honored by such distinguished societies as the Academy of American Poets, you honor us today by your presence here. The University of Louisville is proud to make formal its long

standing respect and affection by awarding you the degree of Doctor of Humane Letters (*Honoris Causa*).

The recognition was typical, and through the decade he would receive
four more honorary doctoral degrees, from Morehead State University,
Ball State University, Ohio University, and Transylvania University, making
a total of sixteen by 1978—seven from Kentucky, two each from Ohio
and West Virginia, and one each from Indiana, Michigan, North Carolina, Tennessee and Texas.

There were, to be sure, stones among the primroses. To noted
editor and former Navy buddy John Bird, Jesse posed in September
1973 an enigmatic question. "Can you tell me—?" he began, then dropped
into an emotionally wrought anacoluthon: "I had 58 stories, 2 articles
and 29 poems in Esquire [sic]. Not one of their contributors contributed
as much. Scott Fitzgerald was second to me with 48 stories. . . . Yet in
Esquire's [sic] Fortieth Anniversary [edition], 39 authors were reprinted,
even Leon Trotsky and others with only one publication and I was left
out." One reviewer reported an *Esquire* editor's reason, that Jesse Stuart
was "out of sync" with the magazine's "current and recent New Fiction
policies," then pointed his finger to what, at worst, must have been
editorial ineptitude, and, at best, a contretemps, "Shame on *Esquire*. . . ."
Jesse sent a copy of the piece to Bird, inquiring if he knew the editor,
whose name Jesse thought was "Hayes (or, is the name HAZE[?]) got
fired. Do you know[?]" Then he added, "I care so damned little I've not
bothered to find out." In truth, he was hurt by the snub. "What a letdown!" he penned in his journal. "What can I say?"

But *Esquire*'s stone had not hurt him nearly as much as *Guideposts*'
avalanche five years earlier. That "inspirational magazine for all faiths,"
as it declared itself, had permitted the article "Virtue Is Not a Private
Matter" to get into publication in its November 1968 issue with the name
of the author appearing as "Jesse Stuart." In the article the author confessed to having had a child out of wedlock and marrying a woman other
than the child's mother. The executive editor, Leonard E. LeSourd,
thought the piece "had value and could be helpful to other young people
with a too casual attitude toward sex." Meanwhile, Jesse was receiving
unsigned mail commenting, "We didn't know you had begotten out of
wedlock," asking him, "How is your Baby?" and making other "derog-
atory remarks" in kind. A rash of correspondence followed in which
Jesse scathingly referred to LeSourd's periodical as "TRUE CONFES-
SIONS Guideposts" [sic]. Jesse was outraged, and even after LeSourd
apologized and offered to make the apology public and printed, Jesse

angrily demanded "the real name of this imposter." LeSourd attempted to soothe things by suggesting Jesse submit an article for which he would be paid $300 upon receipt, but Jesse spurned the invitation: "I want no part of Guideposts [sic]. Not under any consideration would I have an article in Guideposts" [sic]. What he wanted was the culprit's name—a young married man, LeSourd explained, who had innocently used "Jesse Stuart" as a *nom de plume*. But Jesse's anger was unassuaged. "I don't care if he is married. I'm married too, very much married for 29 years. And as sure as hell, I have no children out of wedlock and never treated a woman in my life like this man (who took my name for his dastardly act)." The matter was finally resolved with the help of McGraw-Hill editor Ed Kuhn. LeSourd agreed to publish an explanation and apology in the March 1969 issue and to supply Jesse with 100 copies of the announcement right away for his own correspondence. In his journal Jesse wrote of the incident as a disaster "which caused me much trouble. . . ." Even after he had seen *Guideposts'* published "Item of Regret," he typed LeSourd one last letter, declaring that the use of his name "has hurt me worse than anything that has ever happened to me," and added, "When I think of this, I rise up again."

But Jesse kept at his craft, and publications appeared frequently through the decade of the 1970s, totaling approximately 69 stories, 105 poems, 70 essays, 22 newspaper pieces, 22 books, and 3 translations. Before the middle of the decade six collections of short stories were published: *Seven by Jesse* (1970); *Come Back to the Farm* (1971); *Dawn of Remembered Spring* (1972); a French edition of *Come Gentle Spring, Printemps, doux printemps* (1973); *32 Votes before Breakfast* (1974), and a Japanese editon of his short stories, *The Short Stories*, edited and annotated by Kenzo Soneda and Norio Shimamura in Tokyo (1974).

His 1973 novel, *The Land Beyond the River,* is narrated by a teenager, Pedike Perkins, who relates the saga of his mother and father and their brood of fourteen children—the family of a Freewill Baptist mountain couple who believe they should "have more children and replenish the earth." The story takes the Perkinses to "the Promised Land" of Ohio, "the land of milk and honey" beyond the big river. By working hard they enjoy success until Poppie Perkins is "fanged" by a copperhead, and the family goes on welfare. Determined to expose the welfare system's abuses and excesses, the Perkinses' wealthy but tax-tired Uncle Dick expertly guides them through a wide range of "benefits" permitting them access to free housing and, eventually, so much surplus food they have to feed their leftover steaks to hound dogs (one of them named "Birchfield"). In a biting satire on welfare cheating, the author directs his exposé on selling and profiteering on food stamps, free medicine and hospitalization, free school lunches, free dental treatment, free clothing, and high living at public expense with no taxes. "No wonder people come here from South of the Border!" Poppie exults. Yet even as Poppie asserts his pride in being an Ohioan now, a subtle demoralization sets in. The family's motivation erodes, and they give up their truck farming and their own garden. Because of his reputation for hard work and ability with his hands, Pedike acquires a good factory job, but is shocked when he learns that over one-fourth of his pay "goes out" and he never sees it. At the end of the novel he remembers the starlings and cow birds back home, "pillagers" and "parasites," and how the she-birds "laid their eggs in other birds' nests for mother birds to hatch and to raise. . . . Were we not the blackbirds and cow birds?" he asks, determined to break with his past. Of the book Martin Levin in his *New York Times Book Review* column "New and Novel" wrote: "Tucked in among the down-home humor is the suggestion that there may be something wrong with [the Perkinses'] life style. Or rotten in the state of Ohio. Or both."

Reviews were mixed. While the book critic of *Choice* dismissed the novel as "hillbilly schmaltz with an undercurrent of rather vicious satire of welfare programs that turn people into 'liars and cheats,' " it was praised by R. F. Cayton of the *Library Journal* for the " 'purely' accurate poetic dialogue" of the family story. Cayton further thought that "this most naturally artistic of Stuart's many novels will soon be an American classic." It was Jesse's first major novel since *Daughter of the Legend* had appeared in 1965, first begun while he and Naomi were on a three-week Caribbean cruise in February and March of 1971. About midway through their cruise on the *Stella Oceanis*, between Cap-Haitien, Haiti, and San Juan, Puerto Rico, "an idea jelled—a novel I'd rolled over sometime in my mind—an idea rather." Then he was "running wild" as the idea took him into its grasp. At such times "I write in torrents. I run wild . . . whether good or not. I don't think about this. I am really pregnant and this brainchild will be born—when it is born—afterwards—I'll wonder why. After it's revised I'll hate ever to touch it again. And if and when it's ever published, I'll be one never to read it. It will be old and dead to me. So this is the way it works." Of the initial writing he was characteristically evasive, "It's a sequel—only much different to, *Taps for Private Tussie*. It's in the same theme. Setting *not* in Kentucky." On the ship he had grabbed the available stationery, first in his and Naomi's stateroom, then at whatever writing desk he could find; he borrowed more paper from passengers, until they complained they had nothing to write letters with. He wrote across the Caribbean and along the Yucatan peninsula of Mexico. When they disembarked at Port Everglades, he had 205 pages in longhand. By the following June he had 800 pages he had taken through a first revision.

This prolific outpouring is all the more astonishing when one understands that it commenced only about six weeks after his third heart attack, actually a cardiac arrest; and the cruise, supposedly, was undertaken to give him a change and to help his recuperation along. He had been stricken at home on January 11. The Stuarts' guests, Delmar and Mary Hamilton, had arrived at six, enjoyed drinks, and then sat down to a steak dinner, when Jesse passed out and slumped over. Naomi called the ambulance immediately. Hamilton pulled Jesse from his chair and "beat and massaged" his chest until the ambulance arrived. Jesse later credited Hamilton with helping him get his breath back and saving his life. Rushed to St. Mary's Hospital in Huntington, he awoke to what was actually his first day of recuperation, a long day and a lonely one after Naomi left for the evening. Three days later, however, he was revising stories in bed; in two more days Dr. Bray, his cardiologist at that time, dismissed him from the hospital.

In the fall of 1973, Jesse and Naomi made preparations to go halfway around the world to Taipei, Taiwan, for him to attend the Congress of World Poets as an honored guest. They had taken their shots, had their passport photos, and made hotel and airline reservations. It was a chance for him to treat Naomi to that part of the Far Eastern trip she had missed in 1963 as a consequence of her parents' tragic accident; their 1973 itinerary included exciting flights west and tours of Hong Kong, Manila, Cebu, Dumaguete, Korea, and Tokyo, as well as Taipei. On October 13 he had experienced a "bad day" while signing books at Leslie's Drug Store—perhaps even a "light heart attack," although he could not be sure. An EKG and blood tests followed two days later, and then on Wednesday, October 17, he enjoyed an especially good day. The next day he spoke at Berea College and signed 150 books, then took things easy until visitors interrupted his rest on October 20, the day he signed a contract with Ballantine and Mockingbird publishers to reprint a paperback edition of *Foretaste of Glory*. On Sunday, October 21, Dr. Bray, who by now had read Jesse's most recent electrocardiogram, informed him that he had, indeed, experienced another heart attack, and promptly hospitalized him. The cardiologist went further and urged heart surgery, sending Jesse by ambulance to St. Joseph's Hospital in Lexington.

Nothing was left for the Stuarts, of course, but to cancel their trip to the Far East. By mid-week the news broke that Kentucky's poet laureate had been near death in St. Mary's cardiac unit in Huntington. Meanwhile, Drs. Gay and Doud, Lexington cardiologists, went over Jesse's EKGs and could not agree, despite Dr. Bray's diagnosis, that Jesse had actually experienced another heart attack. By October 25 calls were coming in from all over the country, so Dr. Gay arranged a kind of protective isolation for the patient. Fifty baskets of flowers had to be moved with the patient. A nurse reported him for sitting up on the edge of the bed brushing his teeth, shaving, and using the bathroom on his own. Jesse complained, "I was tired of the slow death of lying in bed." By October 29 he was well enough to walk the square of the building four times and to spend an enjoyable thirty minutes talking with visitors Happy Chandler and John Y. Brown. More floral gifts deluged St. Joseph's and Jesse's brother James dropped by to see him. The mail was very heavy. "We can't believe it," he entered in his journal. "People we never dreamed thought anything of me or my books have reacted most favorably." From Bennettsville, South Carolina, came a phone call saying "they were holding a prayer meeting for me." By November 1, Dr. Gay released Jesse from the hospital, and the Stuarts were on their way home with a car full of "green-growing and autumn-colored flowers."

On that "youthful, splendid day," the poet sang happily of his new life and going home again. It was no reflective moment for a brief and tranquil lyric, though. In a surge of joy he wrote not another fourteen-line sonnet, but a fourteen-stanza poem of 196 lines entitled "My Health Is Better in November," a poem remarkable for its autobiographical simplicity, rich classical allusiveness, his identity with that poetic past he had known in traveling and reading, and his melding of the Greek and Roman worlds with his own. Through Lexington speeding east, Naomi at the wheel, immersed in taped sounds of "favorite Beethoven music and free of death," and on through the undulating meadowlands toward the soaring mountains, he takes in the

> Sky indigo-blue bowl, the headdress over the earth,
> Bright splintered sun so far away and yet was here,
> Splashing light fingers on old faded pasture fields,
> And limestone rocks like sleeping sheep dotting the land . . .

Happy to be free from "odors of hospitals," he is hurrying home, seeing

> November's multi-colored leaves against the sky,
> The sourwood, sumac, dogwood, sweetgum, oak and pine,
> The poplar, sycamore, sassafras, wild grapevine.
> My land, beautiful land in autumn's coloring.

He associates this returning with others before, with other "sceneries in other lands" from which he had returned, and other poets:

> Did Horace remember some November First
> Upon the farm where he was born in Venusia . . .
>   the Roman chestnut trees,
> The umbrella pines, the cottonwoods and willows?
>   . . . fields of grain in harvest on his Sabine farm?
> Did he remember November brown with autumn's turning
>   . . . on his beloved land?

And what of "delightful, gentle" Vergil,

> Riding in a chariot from Brundisium to Rome
> Along the scenic wonders of his Appian way?

then home again

> In a chariot then back from Rome to Brundisium
> Where ships departed for the Mediterranean world.

He considers Catullus:

> Did he observe the willows on the Tiber's banks
> In Roman suns and winds two thousand years ago?

Then the Kentucky laureate resuscitates ancient Greece, as he becomes a limner of antiquity:

> Twenty-five hundred years from then until now
> Is long-paced yellowing with passing, passing time,
> As thin vapour thinning on the bluest air,
> Above the Mediterranean, a world within a world,
> The cleanest, bluest air people have ever known.

And Jesse recalls old Simonides, who lived in Athens . . . Pindar in the stone house of his beloved Thebes . . . Sappho "of Mytilene or Eros in Lesbos," that "woman poet for women poets . . . dateless in literary history" in that legended land of her birth.

Jesse's autumn world is turning on State Route One "along the Little Sandy," clearly to him "a river to compare with Catullus' Tiber" right down to the details of "willows, cottonwood and birch":

> This is the road that leads us to our valley home
> Where greenest of green meadows carpet valley, hill,
> Where multicolored leaves on hills beside the meadows

Are turning and November's burning, turning, burning
Sending in each windgust multicolored leaf-drop rain.

And Jesse and Naomi are into W-Hollow once more, Jesse receiving it
"with open arms," this place that gave him birth and "a body of prolific
clay":

This is my Sabine Farm, my Rome, Brundisium,
My Athens, Mytilene and Thebes rolled into one.
November First Nineteen Hundred Seventy-three.
Invisible hands extending from my house greet me.
Since birth I've been part of this immortal land.
By being part of land I'm brother to the tree,
Returning to my own eternal destiny.

On December 19 of that same year, he worked on his correspondence and sent out a fairly typical eighteen letters. After supper he sat
down to listen to the news when he was struck by a "terrific pain that
wouldn't go away." In the ambulance a few minutes later he was "full
of pain all the way" to the hospital, this time to King's Daughters Hospital
in Ashland where Dr. H. Bennett McWhorter, his new cardiologist, relieved his pain with a shot and admitted him to the cardiac unit. The
EKG showed "where I had had another heart attack," he recorded, but
fortunately they could not find any further damage to his heart. Lying
there in the cardiac unit, he heard another patient's conversation with
a nurse—a troubled dialogue—then three hours later listened to the
disturbed man die. Another man was moved in on Jesse's left, who died
within thirty minutes. Then a new man, moved in on his right in place
of the first who had died, was dead by noon. Within twelve hours Jesse
had listened to three men die and watched their bodies removed. Dr.
McWhorter had Jesse moved out of the cardiac unit into another room
that day, and released him from the hospital in time for him to spend
Christmas Eve back home in W-Hollow. Jesse had survived his fifth heart
attack.

In the middle of the decade two similarly titled yet very different
works of Jesse Stuart appeared. J. R. LeMaster, a Defiance College professor, edited an edition of Jesse's poems, *The World of Jesse Stuart*, which
spanned the four decades between *Man with a Bull-Tongue Plow* and
1975, drawing his lyrics together under seven sections: the poet's "self-
singing" poems; his lyrics of the earth and nature; springtime pieces;
those of "Appalachian Desolation"; his world of satire; his poems of such
foreign lands as Greece, Korea, Egypt, Iran and England; and his pieces

treating the themes of universal amplitude. R. L. Brooks of the *Library Journal*, typical of reviewers who thought of the poet-author as more author than poet, declared that "his poetic achievements are remarkable," and pointed especially to the "simplicity of treatment" of the Lyndon B. Johnson–mocking "The President and I" and the "sensitive and touching" Hiroshima sequence; the volume, Brooks believed, would "increase Stuart's poetic reputation significantly." Scholar-reviewer Wade Hall discerned LeMaster's controlling purpose of allowing the Kentucky laureate's work to trace his development "from selfhood to brotherhood" through "the power of his imagination," skillfully expressed "in familiar English words." The poetry Hall found "intensely personal but not private or abstruse," at once realistic and optimistic, as illustrated in the line "Light over darkness has a final power." Recognizing LeMaster's achievement in exhibiting the "scope and strength" of Stuart's poetry, Hall reminded readers of what they might have forgotten—that Stuart's "first calling—and still his first love—is poetry." That same year Jesse's *My World*, published as one of the University Press of Kentucky's Bicentennial Bookshelf projects, achieved in about thirty-six thousand words of autobiographical prose something of what the two hundred-poem volume had done in illuminating that process of bringing the individual world of the literary artist into national kinship and universal brotherhood. Beginning with "My W-Hollow" and "My East Kentucky," the poet-author progressed through six more sections of the Commonwealth, then concluded with "My U.S.A." and "My World," in the last discussing places he had lived and would like to live again, among them Lebanon and Greece. "When I travel," he wrote, "I'm not a regionalist. I'm a world citizen. The world belongs to me. I can never get enough of life, of living, breathing the fresh winds in Kentucky, America, the world."[1]

Jesse thought of his "greatest triumph" in 1976 as avoiding another heart attack. His *The Seasons of Jesse Stuart: An Autobiography in Poetry 1907–1976*, edited and published by Wanda and Terry Hicks in deluxe, limited, and standard printings under the Archer Editions imprint, turned out to be a handsome collectors' item sized for parlor tables. Containing 145 poems arranged under seven chronological headings from youth, struggle, and summer, to success, rebirth, travel, and autumn—each heading containing a brief profile in prose—the book produced the effect of a personal story in poetry, an impression deepened by the poems' being framed on the large double pages by photocopies of each poem in Jesse's longhand, distinctively written with his ink pen in that straight-up-and-down script he compared to "crows' tracks in the snow."

He was honored that year at LMU, where a Lloyd Ostendorf oil portrait of him was placed in the library. His literary works, though fewer now, were still much in evidence in such magazines as *Adena, Southwest Review, Kansas Quarterly,* and *Saturday Evening Post,* where his stories appeared or were accepted in 1976; less than a dozen of his poems were published that year in the *Post, Wind,* and *Scimitar and Song;* and a half dozen essays appeared in such periodicals as *American Forests, Forum,* and *Tennessee Teacher.* He co-authored *The Only Place We Live,* which he thought of as "a beautiful high-level book with Bob Gard and excerpts from our friend . . . August Derleth." In October he and Naomi celebrated their thirty-seventh wedding anniversary. As a gift to themselves, they took that long-delayed Far Eastern trip, touring Thailand, Hong Kong, Malaysia and Japan. On the way to Tokyo they stopped over in Anchorage, where Jesse recorded in capitals, "FIRST TIME TO SET FOOT IN ALASKA. THIS MADE ALL 48 STATES FOR ME." Actually, he meant to write "50."

Jesse was especially pleased that the Gale Research volume *American Fiction, 1900–1950* (1974), compiled by Professor James Woodress of the University of California at Davis, had included him among the forty-four novelists selected for the first half-century on the basis of critical esteem between 1950 and 1973. Jesse wrote in his journal on March 2, 1977, "Only 14 of the writers listed [were] living. Bill Saroyan was the youngest at 67 and I was the second youngest at 68. . . . Thornton Wilder has passed on. Yesterday I read where Edward Dahlberg had died. This leaves twelve of us. . . . We are passing."

The first day of spring in 1977 was warm, but within a few days there were wild snow flurries. High winds were so strong Jesse and Naomi could not keep fires going in the fireplaces. Their "semi-pet" groundhog, fat, glossy-coated Sugarlump, out of hibernation another year, was hungry, so they fed her. Her favorite food was melon, not available until May. That year they would have Gene Darby put a sheet of tin on their back door to keep Sugarlump from tearing the door down at feeding time. Often she just came to the screen door and scratched vigorously, but sometimes she came on in when they held the door open for her, and was specific in declaring her wants—bread, melon, apples, or pecans. Once when there were no nuts for her, she tried to take off the nutcracker. Another time Jesse recorded, "She almost tore the door down coming in and going out. We opened it wide for her. She carried a pecan at [a] time out on the walk and ate it." Reporters from the *Ashland Daily Independent* heard about Sugarlump and came out to get the story, as well as a picture of her coming into the house, standing up on her hind legs and taking a piece of melon from Jesse's hand. "Naomi and I had coffee together while Sugarlump had melon and pecans," Jesse chronicled.

In late March he finished a 125-page manuscript, "Bluetick," and sent it to Eleanor Nichols, editor of junior books at McGraw-Hill; it was his first junior book since his visiting grandson Conrad was a baby, and now the boy was nearly ten years old. Jesse was glad to see April come and in black ink captioned the first of April "MY FAVORITE MONTH." That day he revised a story and two articles, and signed a dozen books for Mona Greene Johnson and Heman McGuire, who had driven in from Elliott County. The next day, Saturday, Al Abrams and his editor, Betsy Scala, arrived with four hundred spanking new copies of the hardback collectors' item *Honest Confession of a Literary Sin,* in which Jesse gave the embarrassing, factual lowdown on the publication of his first book, *Harvest of Youth,* "the sounding of brass cymbals . . . the vanity of youth published by a vanity press." He signed the four hundred, taking only one coffee break, during which they "talked books." Jesse mentioned several in his own prized collection, especially those signed by Thomas Wolfe, Mrs. Roosevelt, Robert Frost, and Edgar Lee Masters. The twosome stayed over until Sunday afternoon, and when they left, Jesse wrote, "I was so tired I sat in a chair and went to sleep and slept two hours," waking intermittently to watch the Reds and Phillies play baseball. On Monday he got up after a good night's sleep feeling rested, though "a bit groggy from too much sleep and rest," and he and Naomi resolved not to have any more guests over the weekend. "We're getting too old for it"; they had no help and, he admitted, "Naomi does it all." They drove in to Greenup where he deposited four checks adding up to "a few dollars less than one grand," then went on to Huntington, where they met "the downpour of rain—a blessed rain, growing rain, falling from the low dark heavens." They ate at Bailey's Cafeteria, purchased a new sportcoat for him at Corbin's, and returned by way of Ashland to W-Hollow, taking time in Greenup to finish the last of their taxes with Ira Smith, their CPA. It was still raining when they got home.

Jesse did not remember what happened that night. On Tuesday, April 5, his mind was in a fog. He was dreaming: "People in a portion of my head began fighting people in another part." The "both sides of my head people turned loose and were engaged." Even his physician, equable Dr. H. Bennett McWhorter, joined in the fracas, "giving injections to a sweaty multitude engaged" in the altercation. Then Jesse vaguely remembered having been in the car with Naomi Deane "before dawn was breaking." They were on U.S. Highway 23 on the way to

Ashland. The few cars going both ways seemed "to be creeping." Naomi ran the red light at Raceland. She ran more in Ashland. Suddenly he was in a wheelchair at King's Daughters Hospital, recalling very little of how he got there. "I knew I endured enough pain to kill a man," he later reported in his journal. And later, too, he would learn that he was in intensive care again, but he could recollect little else, not even his own name. There had been no time for an ambulance. Naomi had rushed him there in their car—about twenty miles in something like twelve minutes.

In the days that followed Naomi could visit with him only five minutes twice a day. Time was disjointed in his mind. He wrote in his journal that Jane visited him for her two five-minute periods on each of several days before she actually arrived from Florida nearly a week later on April 11. Meanwhile, he was in another world, sometimes groggy and sometimes vividly alert, repeatedly in the presence of Mick and Martha Stuart, too, strangely. "I wasn't having any pain and I was with my parents. We were having fun around the old home—talking and laughing and my father and mother looked so young," and yet he could not then remember their conversation. Time seemed an eternity as another day passed in the hospital. "Right now," he later recorded for his entry of April 7, "my parents were the closest to me again. They were ever with me—ever near me—so nicely dressed in their clothes I used to know . . . dressed in clothes like they used to wear. And they were much like they were in other younger years. They were full of fun and laughter." Once they all sat on the ground together and talked and laughed. "The laughter was loud" as they talked of ancestors, "and no end to the fun. . . . Here were the people with whom I belonged." He spent Easter Sunday in his hospital bed, where the day crept by. "But in a mid-afternoon doze the time was very pleasant" because "I was with my mother and father again and we were laughing and talking. We were back at the house where we lived so long together." They were drinking "water from the well in the kitchen yard under the tall sassafras tree. After drinking cool water we sat under the poplar shade in the front yard."

By April 14 Jesse was receiving mild therapy and could walk across the floor of his room without falling. He believed he was "on the mend." The next day Naomi Deane and Jane drove to W-Hollow, and upon their return Jesse was delighted to hear about April in W-Hollow, later writing in his journal, "Jane was full of enthusiasm for her old home-place. The new rail fence had been finished. . . . The valley was green and beautiful and home was an inviting place in April." Two days later he was moved out of intensive care. On April 19, two weeks after his attack, he sent seventeen letters now that he could "separate time" again. The next day Jesse felt he was beginning "to get back to some primary working habits." Naomi stayed over at the hospital with him, twice sleeping with him on his hospital bed, and like him complaining the next morning of soreness and stiffness. How they missed their large Lincoln bed at home!

Jesse was buoyed up at the prospect of receiving an honorary doctorate from Ohio University in June. He began to sleep regularly again at night. His new short story "Nine Bean Rows" was published in the *Saturday Evening Post,* and on April 23 he saw a copy of the issue for the first time with Robert Redford's picture on the cover. McGraw-Hill sent him a handsome floral arrangement; and on the next day, April 27, he was released from the hospital, just over three weeks after his admittance. Now in the car with Naomi driving home, he observed the "trees more heavily leafed. Wild flowers were everywhere in bloom." Acknowledging he "had lost almost all of April in the hospital," he nevertheless recorded, "Everything was beautiful. I'd come home to as pretty a spot as I had known on earth."

While in the hospital, he later set down, his thoughts had run erratically up and down his emotional scale. Having survived the crisis of the first days after being stricken, he reflected on his anticipated birthday—his seventieth "writer's birthday," in actuality his seventy-first. "On August 8 I would be 70," the writer wrote, "and this would about finish my writing career . . . 70 years, 50 books and seven heart attacks old. There couldn't be much beyond this. So it would be over for me." Alert to post-cardiac depression and changing mental attitudes, he wrote down in his journal and underlined what he felt on the morning of the last day of April: *"What do I have to live for? The best is over! Look at the things in life I will be deprived of from now until the end of life."*

Then followed several nights of restorative, unbroken sleep, interspersed with restful afternoon naps. His weight was down to a healthier 197. He began to write letters, some typed, some in longhand, sending out fourteen on May 5, a fairly typical day of correspondence. Altogether in 1977, he would record that he mailed 2,948 letters while receiving 2,864, a drop of several hundred letters from his usual 3,000-plus annual mailings. He exercised regularly, too, walking familiar roads and paths in W-Hollow, and that day went up to the corncribs and back. On May 7, he enjoyed receiving Dr. and Mrs. J. R. LeMaster. Now Director of American Studies at Baylor University, Dr. LeMaster was seeing two books on the W-Hollow poet through publication, including a soon-to-appear collection of scholarly essays and *Jesse Stuart: Selected Criticism* (1978). LeMaster also showed Jesse his manuscript that would be published in 1980 under the title *Jesse Stuart: Kentucky's Chronicler-Poet.*

The crisis had passed, and Jesse began to live again.[2]

By July 1977 he was well enough to put in his seventh summer in a row teaching in the Jesse Stuart Creative Writing Workshop at Murray State University. There on July 26 the poet-author dressed in his blue seersucker suit, white shirt, dark blue tie; he shined his shoes and put on his horn-rims, then went to teach one of his last classes of the three-week session. He had reason to believe something was up and he had prepared to meet it. That day Governor Julian Carroll sent a proclamation making Jesse's upcoming birthday Jesse Stuart Day in Kentucky. In was delivered by Governor Carroll's Director of Commerce, attorney Terry McBrayer, who, many thought throughout the state, would be the next governor of Kentucky. McBrayer was the son of Jesse's friend Ethel McBrayer, a fellow Greenup citizen and former student with whom he had worked for several years in raising money for the Heart Fund. When he strode into the classroom, Jesse was glad to see him. McBrayer carried the gold-framed proclamation under his arm, and made the presentation. It was a proud and friendly moment. Jesse and Naomi Deane had been expecting something, but nothing as big as the event turned out to be—the presentation itself accompanied by photographers and reporters and a lot of well-wishers. "This took much of my class time," Jesse jotted down in his journal, "but we read four stories." A special luncheon followed, presided over by President Curris, attended by many dignitaries, including the mayor of Murray. That evening, much to Jesse's subsequent regret, he attended what he described as "a slow long drawn affair." Returning home from Murray a few days later, he paid the price of the strenuous three weeks of teaching, suffering angina four times on the last evening of July.

Much newspaper publicity followed concerning his seventieth birthday. The evening before he saw several of his old friends at the Jesse Stuart Lodge, including one Plum Grove classmate, Willard Broughton, whose greeting brought back a raft of memories. Willard Broughton had taken little Jesse's part when there had been trouble at Plum Grove School. They recalled Jack Dysard, also known as "Andrew Truitt," who was expelled from grade school for carrying a pistol. The colorful Dysard, with whom Jesse had originally gone to Camp Knox, had become Sparkie in *Hie to the Hunters*. August 8 brought more stirrings of things past. No fewer than forty phone calls came from as far away as New

York, Texas, Connecticut, Oklahoma, and Illinois—and sixty-three pieces of congratulatory mail were delivered. "Terrific rain and thunderstorms" invaded the afternoon, and the "rainfall poured down in vast gray sheets." When it stopped, his friend Sam Piatt of the *Ashland Daily Independent* came out for an interview, and later accompanied him to the Lodge for a birthday dinner with close family members, arranged by Naomi Deane. Coming as it did at the end of a hectic day, Jesse wrote in his journal, "a wonderful rest[ful] occasion!"

And so summer waned and the leaves began to turn in the cyclic pattern he knew so well. It was the August Elvis Presley died. "We're pro-Elvis—not against," Jesse chronicled, then transcended his own feelings to make an observation concerning the "popular American singer"—Elvis the "recorder of 44 Golden Albums—who died at 42." He proceeded to compare and contrast Presley's achievement and demise to those of "a musician's musician who gave music to the world—music to last forever, Ludwig von Beethoven—1770–1827—and this man died in poverty. . . . He left more legacy than ever Elvis Presley has accomplished. But [Elvis] was American! America has a way of snubbing its truly great for the immediate!"

In early September he and Naomi took a break to visit Jane, Julian, Conrad and Erik (born Nov. 5, 1970) in Gainesville. One evening they had the grandchildren with them at the Holiday Inn, Conrad sleeping with Jesse and Erik with Naomi, when Jesse awoke at two in the morning of September 6. He was suffering terrific angina pains and had broken out into a heavy sweat. He thought at first he was having another heart attack, but he toughed out the pain and with the help of eleven nitroglycerine tablets and several Scotches prepared with ice and water by Naomi "escaped the hospital." They made the drive back to Kentucky without further difficulty, and a subsequent EKG showed no further heart damage. He had not had a heart attack, he believed, not even a "light" one. That month Jesse autographed some books for dealers, among them two boxes of *Beyond Dark Hills* for David Helm of Bowling Green, Kentucky, then more for Don Grayson, a bookdealer in Louisville. To his astonishment, Jesse learned that his older books were bringing higher and higher collectors' prices. William Curry sold one copy of the 1950 *Clearing in the Sky* for $275.

In late September Jesse picked up the typescript of *Dandelion on the Acropolis: A Journal of Greece*. He had revised it twice, and it would be published the following year by Archer Editions Press in Danbury, Connecticut. That same day he received and was much impressed with LeMaster and Clarke's *Jesse Stuart: Essays on His Work*, an assemblage of ten critical essays providing more accessibility to his most significant work. Reviewing for the *Nashville Banner,* William Boozer discussed several of the pieces, quoting, for example, Ruel E. Foster's comment, "No other American writer today can call us so delightfully into the outdoor world." Boozer summarized, "This collection of essays acclaims him as an original whose voice will be heard as long as the eye and ear are attuned to nature, the land, the seasons, and the cupidity or indolence, the reaching up or falling down, of people." As a Tennessean familiar with the Vanderbilt tradition of Agrarianism, Boozer perceived the Kentucky poet-author as "more agrarian than any Agrarian," and his work more durable "because he is a keen observer and gifted artist who can turn a rock and find a short story, pick a leaf or listen to the wind and see or hear a poem. He loves life, lives it fully, and shares it generously."[3]

Concerning the Grecian journal, Jesse declared, "I want to get this done and out of mind. I want to go on to something new." Tired as he was, it was his way. At Murray in July, Dr. Jerry Herndon had interviewed him, asking if he believed he had reached his peak. "I didn't understand this question," Jesse later commented. "I couldn't answer it with accuracy. Does an author reach a peak? I think one reaches a reputation, local, national, and international. An author, if he writes quality, should rise in different countries of the world at different times. I think last year I had a good year in Japan having been published in two of their leading textbooks with a number of stories. One was a book of my stories, selected by their editors. . . . I can produce at any moment a publishable manuscript from my reserve . . . which is like a deep bench in baseball. . . . I wouldn't have to write anything to continue my publishing for a while longer, perhaps, for ten years with a book per year. But, I am not content with this. There is something beyond resting on my reserves for me. . . . I'm not happy very long after I get an award until I want a better book published."

Finally, the old, wild feeling of creativity struck again. "I spent all day upstairs working on a MS, Thank God," he wrote in his journal September 28. At first he called it his "Shan Powderjay story," but he had put his hand to *The Kingdom Within.* It would absorb most of his time through October and into November. The action opens with a dream. Shan's New York editor is calling him with the news that he has won the Nobel Prize for literature. "Ah no, my God—no-no-no—" Shan responds and expresses doubt that his often-referred-to "barnyard," "redneck," and "hillbilly" books could win a Nobel. Back in the 1930s people "used to hunt me like they hunted for rabbits and squirrels." They had even "tried to shoot me," and "put me in the hospital once!"

His books had refused to die, but they would not win prizes. It was another angina-induced dream, he supposed. Nitroglycerine tablets and Scotch and water, both prescribed by a cardiologist, failed to stay the attack of "Lady Angina at her worst," a "love-clinging bitch." Shan was, indeed, having a heart attack—his sixth. His wife, Jean, sped him twenty miles to the hospital in twelve minutes. Sedated, he could see himself in the hospital, and out of his head emerged little people that quickly became big characters that fought vigorously. His cardiologist, Dr. Benjamin McAilster, went about in his white coat with a large syringe injecting the fighters and rendering them, one by one, unconscious.

Miraculously, Shan escapes the physician and the characters being born of his own head, walking down corridors out of the hospital and taking an old train of the past back to Riverton. Back over the same ridge path where sulphur from ragweeds used to discolor his pantlegs, he traverses the dark hills, reflecting upon favorite spots all the way back to his high school days when he had sat on a particular stone and written themes for his English class, that first radio he had purchased and brought into the hollow, necessitating his lugging a big battery over the path weekly to have it recharged. At the stile he stops to think again only to discover that he is not at all tired. He has "wonderful legs now," and walks on through the "thin green April wind's eerie light over the pasture fields. . . ."

"His world had good memories," the book reads, and "what he had done in his world was returning to him." At the old homeplace Shan sees and converses with his mother and father, Mollie and Mick Powderjay. Some mysteries are revealed. "It's all a joy, Shan," his father says, "this never ending!" Life is an existence "in borrowed dust," while people are like water, changing form but undying. People do not die, his mother informs him. "They only change into something rich and strange." And so they walk and talk over the homeplace. Shan discusses his parents' appearances, his mother's olive complexion and her being one-fourth Cherokee Indian, and his own books—how he had tried to kill *Harvest* out of shame, and how proud he had been of *Plow,* in which what he wrote was tied to the land. Now imbued with the vigor of youth, he is told by his mother that he must meet the train at Three Mile, the old way station at the juncture of the W-Hollow Road and Highway 1. Unquestioning, he goes, taking in along the way such familiar landmarks as Op Akers' Laurel Ridge, his Uncle Mel's farm, and Peddler's Well. He hears Huey the Engineer's train coming to Three Mile Station, where he had seen his father flag it down with a burning newspaper. Suddenly there it is pulling up, Huey Cranin in his pin-striped cap and overalls and "a red bandanna as big as a shawl around his neck." The passengers step down: Viddie and the numerous Tussies, Shan's *Plow* people, including Georgia Greene, who drank kerosene, Quadroon Mott, Lief McCowan, World War I veteran Fred Sowards, and Jet Fillson and her seven daughters; and on they come, more than thirty of the *Glory* children—Aunt Effie Winston and her knife-wielding sons, and characters from his other books, even short-story characters like Corbie, dancing and playing his harmonica. Many more trainloads and carloads are to come with the *Destiny, Thread, Gallion,* and *Story* people. These people say they are going to their father's funeral. Shan accepts this and continues to Plum Grove where, across from the church to the south, the cemetery now spreads over the very site of the old Plum Grove schoolhouse. All the Powderjays would be buried there, and he plans to be buried there, too, no matter if one or more of the flesh-and-blood people had sworn, "If Old Shan Powderjay is buried at Plum Grove, I don't want to be buried there!" Now the rejection means little to him, even though his critic had been correct in declaring that Shan had written about a third of the people buried there.

Now at the top of Plum Grove Hill he sees a gathering crowd. Both flesh-and-blood people and his head children are waiting to attend Shan's funeral, while more arrivals climb the hill. Many of the flesh-and-blood people had been his characters, too. What all these people buried that day, however, would be Shan's "enriched resignation," his "borrowed dust" as his parents had told him, his "husk" as his Uncle Mel had put it; for the real of him lived and could not die. That familiar dust, "once so much alive with blood flowing through veins like water through the waterseeps of earth," would be "laid back to amalgamate with his mother earth." Shan realizes, "It was all earth, wind, water and spirit in the end," and none of these ever died for "each one was everlasting."

Still, Shan Powderjay's head-birthed children come up the hill, and with them "flesh-and-blood people, walking alive upon this earth"; yet the latter could neither see the poet-author's children nor perceive the hilltop thronging with the characters of his creation. Shan attends his own funeral, in a manner of speaking, looking into the Plum Grove Church through a window, hearing the prayers, songs, and preaching. He is exalted and grateful, for few indeed are those who are privileged to attend their own funerals. On his way back to W-Hollow, he sees his parents once more. They, too, had witnessed the procession. "We knew he was taking your temple of clay," his mother says, "that the real you had been with us." That clay part would "sleep forever under the music of immortal winds blowing from infinity to infinity." Now Shan reflects that life "had been a great adventure from beginning to end," and in life he had discovered his "second self, his Kingdom from Within, powerful and everlasting." Unlike the tower at Plum Grove, he bore no cross; personally, he felt no need to wear it for a symbol. "His was implanted within him . . . invisible. . . . His Kingdom Within him had decided everything he had done." Then, his parents tell Shan he must go back, return through the Gate again to life. Reluctant to go, for Shan knows no pain and his strength has been renewed and he has never been so happy, he nevertheless obeys his parents and returns.

Then he awakens, confers with his doctor and is released from the Kingston Hospital, anxious "to be out in April, the month of resurrection." His wife, Jean, drives as his hungry eyes search with the light of his remembered dream, or whatever it was. Forsythia bloomed, and he is positive he had come this way as he had dreamed, or whatever he had done. Somehow, he thinks, "he had walked this way." They pass the stone railway station in Ashland, they drive on to old Riverton, passing the depot near where once had stood the octagonal post office, the outlet of Academy Branch; and they turn left on Route 1. At the W-Hollow juncture is the site of old Three Mile Station, where Jesse had so recently met Huey and encountered his own head children on the way to their father's funeral. The valley is "an April paradise" with "white sails of blooming dogwoods moved by the wind" and "red sails from the redbuds waving in the wind," for "this was Shan's world and it was his farm." They watch a gold and black terrapin cross the road to the green meadow, rich in red and ladina clover and fescue. Up the Valley Road under the walnut grove "were hundreds of white percoon flowers bending in the wind." The fresh air of April blows into his rolled-down window, and everywhere it seemed "the air was filled with bird wings." They stop on the driveway in front of their house. Sugarlump, the woodchuck, rises on her hind legs to greet them. Jean gets out of the car on her way to feed the woodchuck, but Shan has a story to tell her. "I want to tell you what happened to me at Kingston Hospital! I've never told this story to anyone."

But Jean is on her way to get pecans for Sugarlump. "Don't tell me your story at all. . . . Write your story for me, Shan!"

The device of Shan's attending his own funeral, as Charles E. Bess observed in his *St. Louis Post-Dispatch* review, permitted the poet-author to review his work through focusing on his characterization and his own life as a man-artist reflected in the twin mirror of Shan Powderjay, Jesse Stuart's alter-ego. In what Don Edwards of the *Lexington Herald-Leader* termed Stuart's "most intimate book," the author provided insights into a wide range of subjects—killing, drinking, God and religion, the will to love, youth and lust, the survival of heart attacks, love of the land, reverence for trees, women, vanity, the spiritual dimensions of life, the enduring love of family, death and the nature of oneself. Within the tight circumference of the book's fifty-two thousand words, the recurring landmarks in Stuart's work abound. The oldest ones, like the EK Railroad, taken up in the 1920s, become freshly real here. Even Sam Leslie's Drug Store, now managed by pharmacist David Miracle—where Jesse's books have sold since 1930, where he was blackjacked in 1938 and where his fourth heart attack was precipitated in 1973—emerges as the social gathering place it stubbornly persists in being. But a new note is added to the writer's familiar technique of emphasizing the concrete places of his developmental life, and a worldwide geographical association begins to mark his work. For example, an Ohio River valley panorama recalls the author's memory of another scene of the Communist People's Republic of China seen from little independent Macao; "the elephant and the mouse" is the writer's apt figure. The high pastures of his homeplace remind Shan of the English countryside. The corridor of the hospital in Aukland (Ashland) suggests the corridors of the London tube. Shan's difficulties of exertion at the hospital reflect his exhausting effort to climb the steps of the Temple of Lindos on the Island of Crete; and the hospital elevators trigger a comparison to those in New York City, which took him to the McGraw-Hill offices on the fortieth floor. The windblown silver maple leaves along U.S. Highway 23 paralleling the Ohio River from Ashland to Greenup cause Shan to recapitulate another journey on an Italian train from Rome to Florence, where Shan never forgot "the silver upturned cottonwood leaves on the banks of the Tiber and along the tracks." Even the particularity of Jesse's sense of place, so clearly that of W-Hollow, becomes through association every place in America and the world.

The genesis of *The Kingdom Within* goes back at least fifty-two years to Jesse's high school days, very possibly to his Bible course with Dr. Hatton; for it was during that period that he read and applied Luke 17:21 to himself, as discussed in Chapter 2. The author said as much when he declared, "It stuck with me all my life, and it's the forerunner of *The Kingdom Within*." Although the battling head-children scene doubtless stems from the onset of his sixth heart attack in April, the origin of the Three Mile and Plum Grove funeral scenes can be traced at least as far back as May 1971, when J. R. LeMaster in an interview remarked on Jesse's outstanding characters, and Jesse commented, "I have many of them. If these characters could all come back to my funeral someday, they would fill a hillside. But they won't all be there. Some are mythical and imaginary, although a lot of them are real people whom I have disguised. That is, after all, where a writer gets his real characters—his convincing characters." By November 18, just about seven weeks after he began the Shan Powderjay story, he had finished the manuscript and taken it through a first revision. The final 225-page typescript was ready for mailing to McGraw-Hill by December 20, 1977.

Meanwhile, the grandchildren were in W-Hollow visiting during the Christmas holidays. Three days before Christmas Jesse recorded in his journal "a great morning with Conrad and Erik." The only problem was that time was passing "too quickly," and he knew the boys would be going back to Gainesville soon. Sam Piatt came down from Ashland for a human-interest piece, followed by a busload of Boy Scouts of the Ashland ARMCO Troop 114, who had come to talk with the famous author and to ask him questions "about those poems and stories." Something like twenty-five boys crowded into the middle living room. As the boys "tossed scores of questions" and Jesse answered them, Sam Piatt snapped several pictures, one over the heads of a dozen boys showing Jesse in a favorite easy chair facing the camera, a square-shouldered Conrad to Jesse's right, perched on the chair arm. Erik is in front of Conrad on the floor, his back to the camera, looking up at Jesse and his brother. The photograph is a study in joy, everyone in the room happily engrossed; but Jesse is clearly the happiest of all. The scouts left in a little while. After a steak supper Jesse and Conrad watched TV and then went to bed. About eleven P.M. pains struck Jesse and he broke out in a sweat. He vomited and took "NGs" but they did no good. Naomi called Whitie and Glennis, who hurriedly came. She prepared a Scotch for Jesse and put a robe on him, and they were on their way, arriving at King's Daughters Hospital at 11:40. The next day Jesse awoke to find himself in intensive care for the third time. In the days following, Dr. McWhorter had Jesse monitored closely. On Christmas Eve Naomi brought Conrad and Erik to see him and Jesse recorded, "My grandsons were a little frightened to see my lying there with three wires attached." The next day Naomi got the boys off on a plane to Atlanta, where they rejoined their parents, who were returning from a trip to Warsaw, Poland; from Atlanta they would all fly home for Christmas at Gainesville. The day after Christmas Jesse was out of intensive care and watching football on television. On December 28, Dr. McWhorter released him from the hospital. Since Jesse had experienced no pains after his initial attack, the cardiologist was not sure Jesse had in fact had a seventh heart attack. The physician noted "unstable angina" in Jesse's medical record, however, and told him he may have experienced "intermittent Wolfe-Parkinson-White syndrome," a condition in which blood is conducted abnormally and in which the patient evinces a proneness to abnormal functions that could explain EKG changes in Jesse's case. Indeed, it was possible Jesse had had the condition from birth. Following their discussion, Jesse wrote in his journal, "After knowing about this I wondered how I could have done anything at Lincoln Memorial. . . . No wonder I never won a first place in any race."

He also wrote that it was good to be home again, "wonderful to be here, to sleep in our own big bed . . . great to eat at home and sit before a blazing woodfire." When discouragement came, he was inclined to put it aside by an act of will, and being home in W-Hollow was incentive enough to do it. He decided to enter 1978 "in an ambitious mood, looking forward to the future as I have always looked." But one thing nagged at him, aside from his brushes with death. It was the question of his land. Twice in August G. B. Johnson, an enterprising Ashland banker, had come to see him "with something on his mind," as Jesse wrote in his journal. "He had dreams of what to do with W-Hollow . . . an area of fine homes, keep the valley intact but have a country club and golf course . . . protection of all wild life." This was in a general way consistent with what Jesse wanted to do with W-Hollow someday. Certainly he wanted to preserve it, but as things stood now, nothing had really been done to make preservation a certainty. Sometimes he found himself worrying that when he was no longer around commercial interests would somehow get the land, scoop off the mountaintops, stipple the hills and valleys with condominiums and tennis courts, and cut down his trees and destroy the wildlife. The matter was very much on his mind when he wrote me early in 1978: "Harold . . . I've owned these acres and I'd like to hold them together and pass them on. Remember Italian poets who had farms[?] Now in Italy they're trying to discover them. Mine is here still and I wish something could be done in my lifetime to hold these acres together; preserve and keep them and protect wildlife as I have." He knew the land conservatively was worth $1–1.5 million, "but I won't sell. Dollars are paper. This is land. Whitman was grass. I am land."

He was not sure about his new manuscript or what McGraw-Hill would think of it. "This one is something else," he wrote, recounting his bad time in April with his sixth heart attack. "This book came out of this one—I think it an unusual piece of writing. I've never done anything like it." He seriously doubted that McGraw-Hill would accept it, "a book that goes from life, into life. That is what this is all about." Then he said something as strange as the book itself. "I'll go before the Chief Justice of the Supreme Court and make an affidavit of what happened to me. I know what I know is true. I didn't dream it." The next month he wrote, "Today, Feb. 17th, I got a letter of acceptance. They accepted on Valentine's Day and said it was a nice Valentine's Day present." He added with obvious pride, "I wrote this one after I passed my 70th year."

On Saturday morning, March 18, Jesse and Naomi drove up to Portsmouth, had their car serviced, and on the way back at Greenup picked up the mail, in which he received several copies of *Hari no me wa toru sugu ni nobiru ito wo,* Japanese translations of his *Thread* by Fumi Onoyama. That evening Jesse turned on the television set and Naomi brought in trays for their dinner, for he had especially wanted to see the University of Kentucky Wildcats fight it out with the Michigan State University Spartans in the Mideast Regional. Naomi later recalled, "We were watching the game and suddenly the tray and everything hit the floor. He couldn't speak, or hear." Jesse's "unstable angina" had given way to a cerebral hemorrhage—a stroke. Dr. McWhorter again placed Jesse in intensive care, where he remained for three weeks. "No response at all that I recall," Naomi later said.

He remained in the hospital until May, Naomi Deane close by his side. Then she brought him back to W-Hollow. He was paralyzed on his left side, and Dr. McWhorter prohibited visitors until well into June. A hospital bed was arranged for Jesse in their bedroom, the head of the bed often in a raised position so that he could look out through the south-facing door and window of their bedroom across the yard at the view of W-Creek and Breadloaf Hill.

On the afternoon of June 30, the new director of the University Press of Kentucky, Ken Cherry, and I drove up from Lexington to see him and talk about books. Jesse was neat and clean-shaven in blue pajamas, his thick gray hair well-groomed and his blue eyes alert behind his polished horn-rims. Displayed on a chest close by were the Japanese edition of *Thread* and his most recent honorary doctoral degree from Transylvania University, his sixteenth. Ken Cherry was especially interested in reprinting several of Jesse's out-of-print books, commencing with his first two story collections, *Head o' W-Hollow* and *Men of the Mountains.* Around Jesse's bed, we talked. Jesse seemed nearly like his old self again, minus half of the gesticulations as he spoke, which he did often. In a little while he looked at me, then at Cherry, and asked Cherry, "Do you want him to do a biography on me?"

Cherry replied, "He knows I do."

Jesse looked at me, his blue eyes wide comments of "there now, what do you think of that, Harold?" and "Well, if you want to do it say so!"—but remained silent, anticipating.

So I said to both, "Well, if you want me to, I will." That was the day the decision was made. Jesse, Naomi, and I later worked out the details; and they cooperated in every way, making Jesse's records and correspondence available and assisting in a thousand details. In the next thirty-nine months, forty-two taped interviews would take place in W-Hollow, in addition to as many unrecorded conversations. As many more interviews with Jesse's relatives, former teachers, friends, and classmates would follow, along with hundreds of letters, telephone calls, visits, and other communications—the raw material with all the hues and shades of light that would help to paint the facts, anecdotes, and the rare ana that would bring the canvas of Jesse's life into shape and focus.

For the first several interviews Jesse lay propped up on pillows, but then a more informal pattern gradually developed. Jesse would be up in his wheelchair with his attendant, Richard Prince, at the helm. With all the difficulties of a stroke, Jesse's imagination had not suffered. Although he was not writing, he dreamed and daydreamed a good deal. He named the rooms through which he was wheeled. The bedroom was Athens, the dining room England, the kitchen Scotland, the sunny front porch Egypt, and modest Shinglemill Creek out back the Thames. An inveterate cigar smoker now released from medical restrictions, Jesse always accepted the cigars I brought him. All of us smoked except Naomi, and a kind of custom gradually developed. On Jesse's good days we would go together to "Scotland," where Naomi had a table of piping hot coffee, tasty canapés, and sweet cookies. There, or sometimes out back by the Thames, we smoked and talked about everything from colorful neighbors and the past to farming, politics, sports and, most often, Jesse's life and work. We laughed and snacked a lot, too. At first we sampled a variety of cigars, but then Jesse settled on the redolent Robert Burns Black Watch, which comes in a white tube, as his favorite. It is a big cigar, and he found he could smoke one lightly for a half-hour, "tube" it, and then later light it up again.

In the fall of 1978, the question of his land was nagging at him once more. There were medical expenses, full and part-time nurses, and mounting expenses to meet, including the continuing demands of the farm. Although Jesse did not say so, he was concerned about Naomi's future more than his own. "I've got a buyer for this place," he told me. "And they've got the money to pay for it . . . [a] bank in Ashland . . . close to Ashland Oil. . . . This ridge up here—it's just filled with building sites." Despite the tempting prospect, however, it was not what he envisioned for his land. Since he was a youth he had watched people around him and his family "butcher timber, burn land over to kill snakes, and let their soil erode," but he had bought his acres and improved them. Some had thought his motivation was greed; others had thought him foolish. Piece by piece he had brought twenty-six parcels together into one 730-acre farm, uniting all the farms his father had share-cropped and all the places the Stuarts had lived in W-Hollow, with the exception of the peripheral birthplace. Now the pastures were enriched, large portions reforested, and the erosion ended. People from urban areas drove to W-Hollow to fill their flowerpots and planters with the leaf-rot topsoil, for his timber had built new topsoil for years. Jesse let them have it for there was so much of it. He had never made money from the land; indeed, it was "a failure" from the financial point of view, but he had known all along what he was doing, writing in *The Year of My Rebirth,* "I am taking care of this land for those yet to be born."

Now he worried about the old stands of timber and pasturelands teeming with wildlife. With no more lecturing, writing, and farming, life seemed to be drawing about him. One day he told me, "As you know now . . . my world is the bed." He went on to say that he wanted this land to be preserved for all time as it was and is. Naomi felt as Jesse did, and I agreed to go to work on a long-range plan for preservation. With Jesse's advice and that of other friends, such as John Demos, Dean of Libraries at the University of Louisville, who worked with me in drafting the initial plan, and Don Harker, Director of the Kentucky Nature Preserves Commission at Frankfort (whose office opened the way for federal and state matching funds), we organized, with the legal assistance of B. Hume Morris II, the Jesse Stuart Foundation. On June 6, 1979, I signed as incorporator of the public, nonstock, nonprofit Foundation, composed largely of university presidents, deans, government, industry and business leaders, and others interested in Jesse's life and work. The twenty charter directors and first officers selected were A. D. Albright, Highland Heights, Kentucky; Paul G. Blazer, Jr., Ashland (Vice-Chairman); Constantine Curris, Murray; John T. Demos, Louisville; John Dryden, Ashland; Donald F. Harker, Jr., Frankfort; G. B. Johnson, Ashland (Treasurer); Donald Lyons, Frankfort; Ethel McBrayer, Greenup; John D. Minton, Bowling Green; B. Hume Morris II, Louisville (General Counsel); Morris L. Norfleet, Morehead; J. T. Norris, Ashland; J. C. Powell, Richmond; Edward F. Prichard, Jr., Versailles; Frank G. Rankin, Louisville; Harold E. Richardson, Louisville (Chairman); Otis Singletary, Lexington; and Jesse and Naomi Deane Stuart. In the remaining months of 1979, working together diligently in common cause, the other directors and I raised approximately $1.2 million, half of the amount donated through the value of his land by Jesse. As of 1980, the Foundation succeeded in preserving for posterity the actual 730-acre physical world of W-Hollow that Jesse had, for half a century, transmuted into enduring poetry and prose. On January 17, 1980, Jesse assigned by contract publication rights and titles of his literary works, both published and unpublished, to the Foundation for management by, and benefit to, the Foundation and its many purposes and activities, as well as to the Stuarts as long as both or either lives. Thus by 1980, both the physical and literary worlds of Jesse Stuart were preserved in an active sense.

During May 22–25, 1980, the Foundation presented *Jesse Stuart and the Greenbo Sessions, A Weekend In "Stuart Country,"* an academic and cultural event in celebration of the preservation of W-Hollow for the people of Kentucky, the region, and the nation. The nine sessions of the program included Jesse Stuart and the land, his literary achievement, the folk tradition of his work, the life and work in biographical relationship, bibliography and special collections, criticism and humor in his work, Jesse Stuart as educator, readings and commentaries on his work, and a tour of W-Hollow and of Greenup County. Scholars and teachers such as Harry M. Caudill and Thomas D. Clark of the University of Kentucky and others from nearly every university in the state took part in the sessions. Distinguished professors and writers from outside the state also participated, including Wilma Dykeman, University of Tennessee; John T. Flanagan, University of Illinois; Ruel E. Foster, West Virginia University; M. Thomas Inge, then of Virginia Commonwealth University, now of Clemson University; Frank H. Leavell and J. R. LeMaster, Baylor University; Frederick B. Shroyer, California State University; Hensley C. Woodbridge, Southern Illinois University; and T. D. Young of Vanderbilt University. A total of twenty-one colleges and universities were represented at the sessions attended by more than 244 persons from nine states from California to Virginia and Illinois to Texas.

On Saturday afternoon during the Greenbo Sessions over a hundred symposium participants took the W-Hollow tour. Afterward most of them walked down the hill from Glennis and Whitie Liles' and the bunkhouse to Jesse and Naomi's house, where several of Jesse's old friends had gathered on his front porch to reminisce. Judge Oscar Sammons moderated and read a letter from Bill Harrell, who had taught science when Jesse was principal of Greenup High School in 1930. Thurman Darby, Eunice Mitchell Harper, and Earl Hobson Smith were there. University of Texas Professor Carl Leiden was prevented by illness from participating, but sent along his reflections on their days together in

Cairo, Egypt. Meanwhile, Richard Prince had wheeled Jesse out into the sunny backyard by Shinglemill Creek. Then Naomi announced to the delighted people that they could come around or through the house and see Jesse out there. An informal reception line quickly formed and for nearly an hour Jesse met and talked with former students, old friends, and other visitors, including Glen Taul of Frankfort and Sturgis, his LMU protozoology classmate Lucille Jordan Palmer of South Carolina, novelist-painter Charley Robertson of Louisville, and two-time Fulbright scholar John T. Flanagan, who complimented Jesse's "strong voice." Western Kentucky University Professor Emeritus Addie Hochstrasser thought Jesse's inquiry about a friend's granddaughter was a "super" feat of memory, and answered him through her astonishment, "She's a junior at Smith." And so the fleeting hour went, Jesse recognizing dozens before they had a chance to re-introduce themselves. Only once did his memory seem to hang fire. "Where is that boy who's writing my biography?" he asked. I stepped forward. Jesse looked up and blinked his eyes in the sunlight, then said, "Harold, give me a cigar."

"This is one time you've caught me empty-handed, Jesse."

Fortunately, another nicotinic samaritan came to the rescue and thrust forward a cigar. Taking it, Jesse said impishly, "It's not a Black Watch, but it'll do." Morehead English Professor Don Cunningham offered his Cricket lighter, and in short time Jesse was lit up and puffing away, enjoying the smoke, the people, and talking in the sunny May afternoon.

In a little while Richard Prince began to ready him to go back into the house. Obviously pleased with the whole affair, Jesse declared, "If they'd have said at Vanderbilt that something like this would happen someday, nobody would've believed it." Jesse's wheelchair began to move down the walk. "Out of that class in the novel, I'm the only one who wrote a novel." Journalist Bill Boozer was moved as he watched the poet-author's leavetaking. "It is time to go," he later wrote of the moment. "The eye is filled with seeing but not the ear with hearing this man who had Warren for teacher and came home to write his novel."

That year *Trees of Heaven* was reprinted with a Foreword by Wade Hall, who noted it contained some of Jesse's "most skillful writing—a spare, sinewy prose that can be as direct as a twelve-gauge shotgun or as lyrical as August corn tassels blowing in the warm wind." A collection of sixteen essays, *If I Were Seventeen Again,* followed upon a similar volume of twenty essays published the year before, *Lost Sandstones and Lonely Skies and Other Essays,* which had been the first volumes of essays to mine the thick vein of the author's nonfiction prose pieces. In 1979, Robert

Penn Warren wrote the Foreword to the new edition of *Head o' W-Hollow*, a publication quickly followed by a reprint of *Men of the Mountains*. Hensley C. Woodbridge's newly revised Stuart bibliography also made its appearance in 1979. The year ended dramatically when Governor Julian Carroll visited Jesse's bedside on Friday, December 7, to participate in the dedication ceremonies of the Jesse Stuart Nature Preserve. Directors of the Foundation found themselves shifting positions to allow television crews to move through the two living rooms to Jesse's bedside, where the conversation of the two men was recorded on video tape. Among the distinguished guests present that day was Jesse's editor, Lou Ashworth, who had flown in from New York to represent McGraw-Hill at the affair. Yet it would be June 25, 1980, before another Kentucky governor, John Y. Brown, Jr., would send his emissary to W-Hollow to make the Commonwealth's official presentation of a check for $601,750 for half the value of the land, the amount settled upon after final surveying figures had come in. The agreement provided that Jesse and Naomi retain their home and fifteen acres of surrounding acreage as agreed, and resulted in an official total of 715 acres for the Jesse Stuart Nature Preserve itself.[4]

In the fall of 1979 Clem Carson, Jesse's old Vanderbilt classmate, wrote Jesse from Tifton, Georgia, "Well, here are we! Both of us are old men! My, how time slips away. Although my health is excellent, I have feelings that the winter can't be far off." It was true, the signs were everywhere around them. By summer of 1980 Jesse had begun to talk about his life's end. Of the forty-four major novelists in Woodress' 1974 list, now there could be no more than three surviving—he could not be sure—Caroline Gordon, Erskine Caldwell, and himself. During the 1970s he had lost so many close friends such as "Augie" Derleth, with whom he had corresponded since 1936. "A big and energetic author of 120 [sic] books, living on 10 acres of wooded land in a house his father built [sic]," Jesse had once written of the man so like himself in so many ways. Derleth had died July 4, 1971. That same year his good friend Henry Lee Shattuck, whose philanthropy Jesse, through the power of *Beyond Dark Hills*, had moved in remote Boston nearly as long ago, had died, too. Lewis "Mac" McCubbin, the Ag teacher at Greenup High when Jesse had been principal, the man who had sent him a suit in the dark Vanderbilt days after the Wesley Hall fire, had died September 15, 1973. Affable Jake Lynd had paid his debt to nature in 1977, and Jesse had watched Lena Wells Lykins Voiers physically deteriorate until she was "bent double"; yet, he discerned her spirit to be great—so like the marvelous woman's history. Longtime friend and pharmacist Sam Leslie, who had perhaps seen Jesse on a regular basis more frequently than even the poet's closest friends, and sold Jesse's books in his drugstore for forty-seven years, had died October 3, 1977. Now in June of 1980, Jesse found the ranks of his friends decimated by the merciless reaper again, and he was nearly unable to reconcile himself to the passing of Elmer Heaberlin. Details were sketchy, but Naomi had heard Elmer had experienced several heart attacks—Oscar Sammons said five in a single week—and had been shocked back to life each time. Then pneumonia had so weakened him that with the last onset he had died. Jesse wept openly as his thoughts reached back to their 1926 graduating class at Greenup High. "The class will go to the funeral," Jesse said, "and I want to go and sit with my class." Jesse had always thought of Elmer as having the finest mind in their class. Naomi went to the funeral in Jesse's place. For days he relived their high school adventures and college years at LMU, where they had been roommates. Jesse recalled Elmer and Scottie's young son Mac, who had died in January 1947, and how he and Naomi had gone out the frozen W-Hollow Road and on to Wurtland for the boy's funeral. Jesse and Elmer had been together the previous Christmas, too. Elmer had bent to him just before he left and in a soft voice told him he would not be living much longer. "I'll be going soon," Elmer had confided to their mutual friend Oscar Sammons. When Naomi returned from the funeral and told Jesse everything, he said, "Well, Elmer's with his son now." Then he and Naomi continued to talk for a while. Jesse said, "Isn't it wonderful to have another life? That promise of eternal life?" He seemed suddenly relieved. "I can't wait to go."

Naomi chided, "Better not go and leave me."

"Well, I'll be looking for you."

"Don't go without me," she said.

More directly than Whitman in "Passage to India," less symbolically than Tennyson in "Ulysses," Jesse faced the inevitable as an adventure, rich with the plight of God's troth. "The promise of Eternal Life is so wonderful! And isn't it awful you have to beg some people to make that decision?" As Naomi recalled their conversation, her eyes shone brightly with a wondrous sadness.

Later that evening in June, I offered Naomi a hand in bringing the supper trays in to the bedroom from the kitchen, so we could eat together while we talked. Naomi had prepared a cream of chicken soup with just a little curry, producing a symphony of flavor, not uncommon with her dishes. A peanut butter sandwich on thin white toast followed, then dishes of baked apples and fresh strawberries, the last of the late spring crop from Glennis and Whitie's farm up the way. They talked about such things as the Greenbo sessions and how many good things had come out of them. Naomi read a portion of a letter from Hensley Wood-bridge aloud, recounting Woodbridge's "strangest meeting . . . with [Frederick] Shroyer." Back in 1939 the California professor had a note in the *Saturday Review* that caught Woodbridge's attention—something in utopian literature or science fiction. So they had started a brief correspondence forty-one years ago. Shroyer told Woodbridge that his letters were so literate he assumed Woodbridge was a member of the College of William and Mary faculty, when he was only a freshman just out of high school. "When I saw the program," Naomi read on, "his name rang a bell and sure enough here we were forty-one years later meeting at Greenbo Lodge." Life could be strange, we mused. The topic turned to sports, Jesse's favorite television pastime, then to travel and trips. I was planning to go up soon to Madison, Wisconsin, to see Jesse's letters to August Derleth in the collection of the state's Historical Society, where the Sac Prairie author had placed them before his death; and Jesse talked about the 1930s when they were young together and Derleth, having trekked to W-Hollow, "told me I was great . . . that I had a future out there before me . . . [if] I remained true to my land and people." Jesse's words echoed his fourteen-stanza tribute "Letter to August Der-leth," published in the *Wisconsin Academy Review* in August 1973.

Naomi looked over Jesse's shoulder out the back window into the lengthening shadows of Shinglemill Hollow. "Oh, look!" Two gray bea-ver-like animals moved across the backyard toward the walk. "Oh, those cute little baby groundhogs are out there," she said. "I have to feed them," she added, and excused herself.

Jesse was quiet for a while, then spoke to me, "The greatest trip I'll ever take will be the last one." He looked straight at me. "I will visit God and be judged, and I'm not afraid of that." Then his gaze moved obliquely to the south-facing window, toward the sun-gilded green grass of W-Hollow stretching to shadowy Breadloaf Hill in the golden twilight of the dying day. "If you want to know, I will visit with my old friends, and I'll have some eons to talk with people I've never got to talk with long enough. It will be a great day."

Naomi returned, a little breathless. "They'll find it," she said.

"What did you feed them?" I asked, rising, for it was time to go.

"Betsy Ross Bread, five loaves for a dollar," she said. Over Jesse's shoulder, out the rear window two happy animals trundled back across the grass, each with a slice of Betsy Ross Bread.[5]

Epilogue: Naomi's Watch

During the fall of 1981, the Kentucky Media Award was presented, as the plaque reads, "to the Works of Jesse Stuart," at the annual conference of the Kentucky Library Association on October 9. Jesse and Naomi had asked me to represent them at the Louisville meeting and to accept the award in Jesse's name, which I was glad to do. I mailed the plaque to them, and Naomi took time to reply graciously, although the week had been a busy one with Jane and the family visiting. An English class from Rose Hill, Virginia, arrived unexpectedly and were disappointed when Jesse was not able to see them. Naomi pinch-hit for him and "did my best." Then forty fellow members of the Greenup Methodist Church came for a Sunday afternoon vesper service Jesse had requested, after which they walked on the newly cleared nature trails along Shinglemill, Coon Den and Ralph Hill Hollows, and Seaton Ridge. By now, a No VISITORS sign had gone up over the front door. "Jesse is too tired," Naomi said, "too weak to meet everyone who comes and wants to meet him. So, he sees only family and friends he wishes to see—briefly."

In November Jesse had to go to the hospital again as the result of several angina attacks and recurring pains. His physician prescribed Nitrostat and Isordil; after eleven days Jesse rallied and was permitted to go home. By Christmas he was inquiring, "What about the books?" concerned that he did not have a new book to give for presents. "When am I going to see one?" By January 1982, I completed and mailed the last of the copy for the forthcoming *Best-Loved Short Stories of Jesse Stuart* to McGraw-Hill, containing my commentaries on thirty-four of Jesse's short stories and an Introduction by Robert Penn Warren. The distinguished teacher-poet, reflecting on their friendship at Vanderbilt, recalled Jesse's "remarkable and strangely eloquent" book, *Beyond Dark*

Hills, and those "glimpses of . . . the inner world [Jesse] carried with him," his being so "physically proud," and his "gripping anecdote and strange poetic turn of phrase." Rereading the stories had stirred the three-time Pulitzer Prize–winner to summarize, "Jesse Stuart knows the beauty, virtue, and romance of his world. But he knows its bestiality, too." Lou Ashworth, the in-house editor of the project, wrote the Stuarts in W-Hollow, "We believe we will have a fine book, fall of '82." Meanwhile, Dr. Jerry Herndon of Murray State University had also been putting together a collection of Jesse's short stories selected to appeal primarily to a whole new generation of middle and high school students, *Land of the Honey-Colored Wind*, a project funded by the Jesse Stuart Foundation, which would appear in 1982.

When asked, Naomi kept her remarks about Jesse's condition general, referring to "a few areas of concern—but so far we are managing." His nurses and Richard Prince were still "faithful," and the family visited often, but "not so often as they did." She was pleased that her sister Millie Zachem had moved back to Greenup County from California; in the months ahead Millie would become Naomi's "strong right arm." Things were as "stable" as could be expected.

Then on Wednesday evening, May 19, Jesse was outside in the backyard, where he had snacked on cheese, crackers, apples, and coffee. He wanted to sit out a bit longer and smoke his cigar. When he was brought in for his nap at five o'clock, Sam Piatt was there; after their conversation Jesse managed to autograph a copy of *Kentucky Is My Land* for him. Sam, Naomi, and Jesse then had a prayer together, to which Jesse said, "Amen." Sam left, and Jesse dropped off to sleep. Sometimes Naomi, too, would lie down to rest before preparing dinner, as she did that evening. Later, when she tried to wake Jesse at about seven, there was no response. She held up his good right arm, but it was lax and dropped lifelessly. He was breathing but unconscious. After his first stroke four years earlier they had feared that another was imminent. Jesse had told her then that if and when it did come, he did not want to return to the hospital again. He preferred to live the rest of his time in W-Hollow, even at the risk of impending death. So true to their understanding, Naomi waited. Jesse did not wake up and he did not die. Then she recalled a question she had put to him sometime after their agreement, "Well, Jesse, what would you do about me in such an instance?" and his reply, "Why, I'd take you to the hospital." That gave her at least a technical out, she reasoned; so after watching him suspended between life and death for some forty minutes, she decided to take him to King's Daughters Hospital. She decided not to lose him, agreement or not. Dr. McWhorter examined Jesse, diagnosed a bilateral stroke—cerebral hemorrhage—and recorded his condition as "comatose." From the beginning the unified opinion of examining physicians was that there was absolutely no hope that Jesse would survive the stroke. Dr. McWhorter said that he did not expect Jesse to live a week. The family members began to arrive in small groups, sometimes one by one.

Naomi commenced her vigil. Once when she was watching over him, the nurses advised her that she should not be alone with Jesse. "Why?" she asked.

"Because he can slip away at any time."

During those days and nights following his stroke, Glennis, Whitie, and Mary stayed with him, sometimes over several nights. Then the nurses who had helped Jesse the past years put in rounds of duty. And the days of attentive watchfulness stretched into weeks. Because he could not swallow, he had to be fed by a tube inserted through his nostril and leading down to his stomach. His lungs were "suctioned" to rid them of excessive fluid. But oxygen and all other life-support systems were gradually removed. On June 28, Jesse was discharged from the hospital to the Jo-Lin Health Care Center in Ironton, Ohio. His brother James visited him on July 17, and although he did not tell Naomi, thought he looked "emaciated." He said, "Jesse, how you doin'? This is your brother, James." But there was no response. James thought Jesse's cheekbones had lost their natural tint and had "a gray cast." Naomi meanwhile wrote friends, "Jesse's condition remains unchanged. No doctors have encouraged me that Jesse will regain consciousness. I remain optimistic and hopeful. Oh yes, hopeful."

Alert to any signs of progress, Naomi kept her watch in Ironton now. Each day she drove the fifteen miles over the Ohio River to 1050 Clinton Street to share most of the day with Jesse—usually four to five hours. Sometimes she stayed the night on a cot, but more often she drove back to W-Hollow for sleep before returning the next day. She was advised not to bring him home as long as the paralysis prevented his swallowing on his own and required regular four-hour liquid feedings. Even though Jesse did not respond or speak, she believed that he heard what she said. Often she took letters, inquiries about his health from concerned people, information about recent reprints of his work and publications about him to relate. In July she advised me to help with promotion of the forthcoming *Best-Loved Short Stories*, for "don't you think Jesse would want you to? I do. He would want it to get off to a good start and sell well." She often combed Jesse's hair and groomed him as she spoke to him. "I talk to Jesse and tell him many things," she said to one reporter. "No one *knows* for sure that he does not hear and understand. The nurses tell him when they turn him and feed him. I never tell him of any problems—only happy, cheerful things."

On August 3, Lou Ashworth called me from New York City wanting to know if it were true that Jesse Stuart had died that morning. I immediately telephoned James Stuart in Greenup, who said, "No, I would have been notified immediately," although he added that it had been five days since he had seen Jesse. I then called Lou Ashworth back, and she explained her urgent inquiry. *Publishers Weekly* had called that morning with the question, for somehow the staff had received news of Jesse's death. "We'll hold the presses to get an obit in if it's true," she was told.

Later in the month, my wife, Toni, and I drove up from Louisville to Ironton to see Jesse and Naomi. Expecting to find him pale and motionless, we were both surprised. His thick gray hair was neatly combed above a still ruddy complexion. His head propped up in bed, he seemed to be striving to look out under his eyelids that from time to time partially opened. He seemed uncomfortable, yet tolerant of the tube that ran through his nostril and down his esophagus. He wore his usual freshly pressed blue pajamas, and on his bed was a lap-size quilt, mostly baby blue in color, with sixteen of his titles pieced in, crafted by his sister Mary Stuart Nelson the year before. I spoke for a while to Jesse, and although he did not respond verbally, he did manage to turn his head on his pillow and open his eyes several times. I held Jesse's right hand and said, "Jesse, this is Harold. I've come to see you. If you can hear me squeeze my hand." I was sure I felt the faintest pressure, but when I tried again, the pressure was so faint I could not be sure I felt it at all. After our visit Naomi took a break and had dinner with us. In November promotion of *Best-Loved Stories* would require us to be back in Ashland, so we planned to get together again.

But when November came and we were in Ashland as planned, Naomi was unable to meet us when we arrived. She was in King's Daughters Hospital herself! That Friday morning, the nineteenth, Naomi had left W-Hollow and joined Jesse as usual at his bedside. She had eaten a light breakfast and near lunchtime felt what she took to be pains of indigestion that crept up into her chest and throat. Medication did not ease the pain, and when she took a second dose and the pain did not abate, she called Dr. McWhorter. He promptly admitted her to the hospital. She did not wish to leave Jesse, but gave in to the physician's wishes that she undergo monitoring and a series of tests. Once in the hospital, she realized that she had apparently suffered an onset of angina, which she had experienced before, yet the pains soon subsided. Toni and I were relieved to find her in good spirits, sitting up on the side of her bed and planning to get back to take care of Jesse within a few days. After visiting, we went over to Jo-Lin to see Jesse again.

It was a rainy trip across the river and down to Ironton, one of those November weekends in Kentucky after the leaves have fallen and before winter sets in. The temperature hovered in the fifties beneath a light gray, clouded sky. As if asleep Jesse lay in his blue pajamas with white piping on the collar and lapels. This time his pajamas were wrinkled, his head back on his pillow, his mouth open. The nurse gently shook him and his eyes fluttered, then rolled as he tried to move toward consciousness. But the effort was very hard. He breathed more quickly around the clatter of his feeding tube, as if struggling for breath. Again his eyes moved. His hands clenched in half-fists, and he moved his mouth as in greeting. I stayed with him for some little while, and held his right hand as before. This time Jesse's hand relaxed somewhat as I held it. Before leaving I spoke to Jesse, said a prayer, and looked at him a bit longer, lying there quietly, seemingly stoical if not contented in his silence. I fancied he missed Naomi, was resolutely awaiting her return, and I thought of his sonnet to her:

> I cannot sing forever like spring grass
> For you when passion in this brain is done;
> I'll die much quicker than the wind in grass,
> My words be darkened like the noon-day sun
> Obscured by mountains of dark rolling cloud.
> I cannot sing forever like the wind,
> Naomi Deane the wind for you sings loud
> And soft, sweet music of the violin.
> But I can sing for you this timely hour
> While white heat deeply stirs this mortal brain;
> Sing songs as fragile as a woodland flower,
> And sing and sing while powers of life remain.
> If you should pass, eternity-faithful friend,
> If you should pass, I fear this song would end.

The reception of *Best-Loved Short Stories* was highly favorable. John Patterson in the *Pittsburgh Press* recalled Jesse's early contemporaneity with Thomas Wolfe: "Oh, these two could paint word pictures that shut you away from all distractions." He found this book "a cornucopia, a bountiful literary harvest." William Boozer of the *Nashville Banner* declared, "One wishes that . . . Stuart could hold the book in his hands and admire and be proud of it as only he could." Stating "without reservation, a truly lovely book," Beaufort Cranford of the *Detroit News* wrote, "Though in spots as rough-hewn as clapboard, Stuart's stories have the inborn persistence of a hickory hoe-handle, the fresh ebullience of crows in a cornfield, the conviction of a Slab Baptist foot-washing, and the quiet joy of Christmas around the hearth." The *Milwaukee Journal*'s Norbert Blei saw in the tales "the highest storytelling art" belonging with the best American writers "like Twain, as almost any story in this book will illustrate." Giving news of Jesse's coma, he concluded, "but writers of Stuart's caliber never die. They leave stories like these. They come out whole." New reviewers like Morton S. Corwin of the *Miami-Herald* discovered Jesse's work for the first time in the volume. Among other good things he wrote, "Though rooted in Stuart's native hills of eastern Kentucky, these works—of which the 34 gems in this collection are but enough to whet the appetite—transcend origin in their universality," and in giving the stories a thorough read found that "whether macabre or tender, Stuart never mocks or dehumanizes his characters." Then Corwin did something unusual in a book reviewer of any time. He wrote Mrs. Stuart a personal letter: "I must admit that before reviewing the book I was totally unfamiliar with Mr. Stuart's work," he said. "However since then, as reflected in the review, I have gained an intense appreciation of his literary contributions. I only regret that I never had the opportunity of actually knowing the man." Novelist Katherine Paterson in reviewing for the *Washington Post* wrote that "Jesse Stuart's prose has so much poetry in it that he often seems to throw away great lines," but his prose "rolls with the rhythm of the Psalms and lights up with bursts of Shakespearean imagery." When Naomi, soon out of the hospital and visiting Jesse daily again, received word that the book had received another one of Jesse's nominations for a Pulitzer Prize she responded, "How exciting that the book has received a Pulitzer nomination! I told Jesse in a very excited voice and I hope he understood. He just must. I'll tell him each day when I go."

More good news had come during 1982, recognition singular in any literary artist's lifetime. As early as 1980 one of the Foundation directors, Frank G. Rankin, commenced a concerted effort to get the Jesse Stuart home in W-Hollow on the National Register of Historic Places. For a time, the nomination was held up because the policy of the National Register was not to accept properties associated with living persons. As Chairman of the Kentucky Heritage Commission, Rankin exerted the weight of his own office and marshaled the influence of senators, congressmen, and governors until the keeper of the Register finally assented to the exception. The *Courier-Journal* carried news of the

placement of the author's home on the Register June 8, 1982. President
Reagan sent a letter to Naomi Deane "expressing concern about the
author's health and wishing him a speedy recovery."

Jesse's condition remained continuously stable during the winter.
Naomi wrote that she was "on a limited routine schedule now," but in
truth she was soon resuming daily trips to see Jesse. "I am so thankful
that he has no problems," she wrote just before Christmas, which she
spent with him at Jo-Lin. During the holidays she recalled that only once
had they been apart, and that was when he was in the Philippines for
the State Department in 1962 when she had returned on that sad, con-
solatory journey of loyalty to bury her father and to help her mother
die. She spent Christmas Eve at the health care center, catching a little
sleep on a couch in the TV lounge near Room 129, where Jesse lay.
That Christmas he had received a Swiss music box that played "Little
Drummer Boy." She played it for him. "I played it over and over for
him. . . . Jesse loves it so much." She ran her fingers through his thick
gray hair and discussed the Christmas cards and well-wishing messages
with him. "How should I answer this one, Jesse? What do you think I
should say?" Jesse did not speak, yet as if he had, Naomi opened a
stationery tablet on her lap and commenced writing. Sometimes Jesse
opened and closed his eyes. Sometimes there was a facial expression,
but he did not speak. He had not spoken since May 19, when doctors
had said he could not survive "more than a few days." When Sam Piatt
interviewed her she told him, "I believe he can hear me, and that he
understands." To those concerned about her own health and the constancy of her watch, she could say, "He is my strength. It doesn't tire
me coming here each day. Just seeing him, holding his hand, keeps my
strength up."

What did take her strength, Piatt reported, was answering the huge
correspondence that arrived daily—from Kentucky, the country, and
abroad. "He gets so many letters from people we don't know," Naomi
said, "and I can't possibly answer all of them, though I do the best I
can." Part of the problem was that so many of those writing were not
even aware of his condition. Requests for lectures and public appearances continued to roll in. "I don't know how Jesse did it," she said to
Piatt. "He would try to answer every letter, especially if they were from
students." Naomi opened two batches totaling a hundred greeting cards
from sixth-grade Louisville students and fifth-grade Paducah students
while Piatt continued his interview with her. Recently she had received
requests from book and autograph collectors in England and Yugoslavia
for an original manuscript and "a specimen of one of your handwritten

letters and a photograph of you with your authentic signature." The Executive Director of the Library of Congress in Washington, John Y. Cole, invited Jesse personally "to attend a luncheon celebration for the 40th anniversary of the Armed Services Editions, which reprinted several of his books," including *Taps for Private Tussie*.

In January 1983 Andy Mead of the *Lexington Herald-Leader* interviewed Naomi at W-Hollow. She wore a red sweater out into the thin January sunlight to show the reporter around the house and outbuildings where Jesse had often walked and written. Once more she recounted the circumstances of Jesse's stroke, his surviving and subsequent condition at Ironton, his neither responding nor speaking, but her believing that "he hears what I say. And he sometimes opens his eyes, but not always on demand." Still the doctors held out "no hope" for Jesse's recovery or improvement. While unsure of what was going on in his mind, they told her that he was probably "unaware of his surroundings." But Naomi knew better. For a long time after she began visiting Jesse at Jo-Lin, she would come into his room and kiss him, telling him she *brought* him a kiss, but that she also *took* a kiss. Then, "he used to squeeze his little mouth up . . . when I said that, but now he doesn't." Yet from time to time there *were* responses when she told him things and read to him. "I tell him what is going on around the house—who has come to cut the grass, that sort of thing—and tell him what has come in the mail." In late February she wrote, "Now I sit with him four and five hours each day for I continue to need the closeness I feel when here. Jesse remains fairly stable." But then she had suffered with the flu "or whatever" for a whole week, and she could not risk infecting Jesse. It had been a difficult enough winter, but now "spring is on its way and everything will be better."

Contrary to expectations, he made it through March and into April. Jesse's attending physician at Jo-Lin, Dr. W. Rex Duff, spoke to Naomi of her husband's being "just an unusual physical specimen." Somehow Naomi knew he would be all right in April. How he had sung of his favorite month his whole life! Years ago he had captured its transient beauty spun of threads of wind and apple blossoms, rain and streams and wild birds and bees woven into the fabric of a sonnet, and tailored into a garment of lyrical images and intense loveliness:

Hold on to April; never let her pass!
Another year before she comes again
To bring us wind as clean as polished glass
And apple blossoms in soft, silver rain.

Hold April when there's music in the air,
When life is resurrected like a dream,
When wild birds sing up flights of windy stair
And bees love alder blossoms by the stream.
Hold April's face close yours and look afar,
Hold April in your arms in dear romance;
While holding her look to the sun and star
And with her in her faerie dreamland dance.
Do not let April go but hold her tight,
Month of eternal beauty and delight.

At the end of April, Jesse lay half turned on his left shoulder, his head back on his bunched pillow, asleep with his mouth open. When I moved to the edge of his bed and spoke, Jesse's eyes opened and flickered, and his mouth moved slightly as if in suggestion of his usual, courteous greeting. When I told him, "Jesse, the biography is nearly completed to the Epilogue," his eyes flickered again. Then I told him about how W-Hollow had looked on the last day of April—the apple-green valley running up to the lines of the tall trees bordering the pastures, the white dogwoods and redbuds like clouds amid the pale green of the trees—and a slight "Ah-ahh—" more like a little boy's than a man's, in awe and wonder, emanated from his mouth. And somehow he seemed to gesture his feelings with his mouth, too, something unspoken but welling from the deep of his emotional reservoir. Thus, we communicated a little more, and then Jesse relaxed and started to go back to sleep, all but a smile on his face, as if he were turned toward some recalled magic day of his youth in W-Hollow when life would last forever.

He survived the long dry summer, too, and came to his seventy-seventh birthday August 8, 1983. That month fellow writer James Still called on him. "Jesse, this is old Jim," he said. "I've come by to see you. You look good." Jesse's eyelids moved, but he did not open his eyes. More than a half-century had passed since they were classmates at LMU. With Naomi at Jesse's bedside, Still talked of the long ago, Jesse's poetry, books, and manuscripts. It was a good day.

In late September, when multicolors of Naomi's snapdragons, geraniums, liriope, marigolds, salvia and dusty miller along the front walk in W-Hollow were still bright in the cooling weather, we returned and with her drove to Jo-Lin to see Jesse again. Naomi bent over his bed and spoke softly, "Jesse, here's Deane girl . . ."
His eyes opened and fluttered.

"I brought kisses," she murmured, bending closer to him, while his eyes kept moving. Then, "Harold and Toni are here."

We moved to him. "Hello, Jesse." Even though his cheek was pressed to his pillow, we could see his color was good. His eyes opened more widely until we could see the blue. I told him the biography was complete up to the present date. His eyes began to flicker, almost to bat, and he began making facial expressions. Sensing excitement, I asked him to close one eye if he could understand me. As if in answer, he scrunched his face deeply into the pillow, cheating and hiding one eye that way. "Very good," I said. Then we told him how W-Hollow looked with the dogwoods just starting to turn to that purple plum color. He seemed attentive and content. Nurse Davidson came in to remove an intravenous tube and to turn Jesse from his right side to his left. We went out for a short time.

When we later returned, Jesse was in a sitting position in a chair beside his bed. Therapy included keeping him in a sitting position part of each day. In a little while the nurses asked us to go out again while they put him to bed. He was resting comfortably when we left, his color still ruddy, his feet bedecked in blue crocheted booties made by Mary. He rested beneath a lightweight quilt of blue and white tones, lettered in dark blue thread:

My basket songs are woven from the words
Of corn and crickets, trees and men and birds.
I sing the strains I know and love to sing.

October came, for Jesse "the best autumn month . . . and of all the months, second only to April." He had explained his preference: "There is great beauty in the changing colors of the leaves." He had written, too, that October was a woman, and "she is a beautiful killer. October kills so gracefully that she stirs the imaginations of poets to write about the beauty of death on the land."

October died herself, but so beautifully she seemed to live right into November. The wind smelled of frost. Flaming orange, yellow and red, the trees were torches against the blue and graying November skies. Hosts of varicolored leaves eluded killing frosts and rioted into November above the yet greening grass, colorfully silhouetting stark white birches and sycamores across the hollows and meadows of the Kentucky land. Flowers, dead or dying, lent their paler hues to the stronger tinctures of gumtree leaves, persimmons and sumacs, whose leaves were falling now, as Jesse had written, "like drops of red rain." Now "yellow leaves tumble gently and softly from the tall poplars. Warm-brown leaves fall from the oaks, orange-red from the short dogwoods. Everywhere there is color. Everywhere there is a grace, beauty, and gentleness in death."

Then winter came once more, the time "of narrow valley and the frozen stream," of "dark brooding oak broomsedge and leafless vine," of that "upheavaled white world where the cold stars shine/And long tree shadows break the white moonbeam." Through most of it his condition continued "stable." In February 1984, he suffered a bladder infection followed by a virus. The day after Valentine's Day Naomi could see that, although the antibiotics Dr. Duff had ordered had helped, the virus had taken its toll. She knew by Jesse's actions that his stomach was uneasy. All the signs were there; his breathing changed. She alerted the nurses and they were ready when he vomited. Naomi had seen him sick with vomiting many times before, but this time it was worse than it had ever been. The nurses could not understand and declared that he had vomited much more than his intake. But he rallied afterward and by Friday, February 17, had in the judgment of his nurses "the best day in a month's time." Caroline Brown, the nursing supervisor, reported her new hope to Naomi. "Old Blue Eyes," the nurses called Jesse now, had opened his eyes and they had flirted with him.

"Well, what I want to know is," Naomi inquired anxiously, "did he flirt back?"

"Of course he did!" And they laughed together.

Meanwhile the Reverend Julian Hammonds from the Methodist Church had come and stayed a long time. He had difficulty completing his prayer, Naomi thought, and then he said, "I could not finish my thoughts to you." It was strange, as strange as the expression Naomi could read so well on her husband's face when he was "listening to voices that caught his attention." Jesse would catch his breath so that he could hear them better.

A little after 4:00 that afternoon she left Jo-Lin to drive back to W-Hollow, stopping for a sandwich at Murphy's along the way. At 4:40, as nearly as the floor nurse could tell, Jesse died very quietly, as if slipping away. At first the attendants thought he was asleep, until they tried to turn him. Dr. Max Wheeler, who was in attendance at the time, said there had been "multiple strokes" and "multiple coronaries," that "He just sort of wore away." The virus had been "the straw that broke the camel's back." The technical cause of Jesse's death, he said, was "intractable heart failure."

Meanwhile, Naomi was driving home. When she turned up from the W-Hollow Road to the long common driveway to the house, she could see two cars, then James and Glennis and her daughter Melissa. Naomi drove on into the garage, thinking they had come to help with arrangements for graveling the driveway, stippled with the usual chuckholes from the winter weathering. The farthest thing from her mind was Jesse's well-being. But the staff at Jo-Lin had called Glennis, and she had quickly called James.

Naomi got out of the car as James spoke to her from the driveway by the garage. "The worst has happened," he said.

"What?"

"Jesse passed away."

"It can't be true," she said. "I've just left him. I know it's not true." For the longest time she stood there over the car and cried. Nothing they could say or do assuaged her shock and grief. She insisted on going back to see for herself. They went in James's car, violating the speed laws, avoiding all the stoplights through Ironton that they could. At Jo-Lin Naomi went over to Jesse while James and Glennis stood by. She grasped Jesse's hand and wept. It was a controlled emotion, but she was dying inside. James was outwardly stoical, but inwardly crushed; yet he had been calm enough to call undertaker Eddie Riggs in Greenup.

In a little while Riggs was there with the Chevrolet ambulance. It was time to go. James moved toward his car and the passenger door, but Naomi said, "No, I want to go home with Jesse." She got into the front seat of the ambulance, and James and Glennis followed in the car. At the funeral home in Greenup where the Stuarts had now gathered, Naomi got out of the ambulance and then rode home with her husband's people. James looked at her distraught face and blinked. "Deane," he told her, "we're all for you and all with you. No one could have done more for Jesse than you. You are part of the family. Anything we can do now, just ask. We are *all* family. And we'll be with you always." James's words touched her.

That night when she went to bed she remembered Jesse's saying to her nearly two years ago, before the voice-impairing stroke of May 1982, "Oh, Deane, what is this doing to you?" And she had replied, "What it's doing to me is what I want." The tears welled as the memory and convulsing events of the day and that grim paradox of Jesse's having had the "best day in a month's time" combined and overwhelmed her. The tears broke as she riddled something else: Jesse had waited for her to leave before he slipped away, so she would not see.

Late Sunday afternoon, February 20, the sun was falling in the west, casting our shadows over Jesse's freshly dug grave. The rocky yellow clay dirt was piled high on the northern side, beyond which the Plum Grove Church stood in solemn simplicity. To the east along Shack-lerun Road in the valley below were the multicolored houses of Plum Grove. Closer, two cedar trees rose into the sunny blue sky. Above them fluffy white clouds floated over the distant hills beyond the road, the hilltops jagged with the brown fringing of winter trees. Just to the south was the grave of Herbert Lee Stuart, Jesse's little brother who had died that winter seventy years before—then in a continuing line the graves of Martin Vernon and Martha and Mitchell Stuart. Jesse had once said that he would be buried on the very spot where the recitation desk of the old Plum Grove School had stood, but James thought, as best he could remember, that Jesse's grave was located just outside the site of the vanished one-room school's western window.

Clad in a navy blue suit, Jesse's "enriched resignation," as he had long ago envisioned his lifeless body, lay in a long bronze casket that Sunday evening at the Riggs Funeral Home. His white-on-white shirt was accented by a navy blue tie with red and gray cross-stripes. Tiny proud lions, suggestive of the British tradition of which the highland royal Stuarts had been a prominent part, romped in the navy blue background. Jesse's familiar horn-rims were perched on his well-shaped nose. Everyone said he looked amazingly good considering his long illness. More than four hundred people came and went, and his friends of older, happier times gathered and talked and smiled, although a few were pensive or quietly grieving. Misty-eyed, Naomi stood nearby Jesse from 6:00 to 9:00, alert to many, sometimes smiling bravely, knowing that this was what Jesse wanted. Why shouldn't friends gather with the remains of a lost one and remember him in joy as well as in sorrow? Was not his funeral to be a celebration, too, and had they not planned it that way? Some spoke of Jesse's recent book, *The Kingdom Within,* in which he had written so expansively and sensitively of the death of Shan Powderjay, his familiar alter ego. If people applied what he had written so con-vincingly in that book, then what lay before them, flower-flanked at the head of the great room, was hardly Jesse at all, but only the "well-used husk" of the man-artist; the "real" of him now, his spirit, knew only joy. The talking, smiling friends, after paying their respects to Naomi, Jane, James and the other family members, moved into the outer hall, pre-ferring to remember Jesse alive and walking on the wind.

Many more came and went the next morning before noon, paying their last respects to the man from W-Hollow. The funeral was held in the same little brick Methodist Church he had been a member of since

1952. Facing the pulpit, the Stuarts' pew was up front on the right, where he and Naomi had sat so many times; but this time Jesse lay in bronze solemnity several feet away at the head of the church, placed there above a red carpet in front of the rows of light oak benches. The "dust of his enriched resignation" was flanked by white lilies to the left, and an equal-sized bouquet of purple iris, yellow snapdragons and white calla lilies to the right. The characteristic shock of gray hair—once dark as a crow's wing—fell carelessly over the right side of his forehead, as if the wind had blown it. Behind him was the pulpit, and back of it the oak-paneled wainscoting ascended steeply to a peak, suggesting the front view of a hip-roofed barn. On the barn's pediment was the Christian cross in dull gold.

Before the service began Eddie Riggs removed Jesse's horn-rims, tucked him in and closed the lid to the light of the cooling February Monday. Now the long bronze top glowed in the light's reflection through stained glass windows arching to a peak on each side, admitting blue, terra cotta, pink and gold light to the interior. The organist played "I come to the garden alone." Governor Martha Layne Collins was there with other dignitaries and the gathering friends, waiting and absorbed in quiet meditation. Then the Stuarts entered under the tower, through the foyer and into the church, Naomi and her family going to their pew in the front and the other Stuarts, Norrises and remaining relatives following, filling the whole right side of the church. The Reverend Hammonds led the call to worship, and the congregation stood and sang "A Mighty Fortress Is Our God." Following Beethoven's anthem "Preludio Religioso," Dr. Robert Wood eulogized Jesse in "The Celebration of Triumph," recalling that he was "a warm and outgoing person, and to know him a while was like knowing him a lifetime." Once he had interviewed Jesse and, to his surprise, found the author putting *him* at ease rather than vice-versa. The Reverend Hammonds spoke directly to his and Jesse's neighbors, "You people from Greenup County who are here, I hope you'll know what a treasure you had among you." He remembered not only the "songs of beauty" and "What a talent he had!" but also how the mountaineer had always been "available and approachable" to people of all walks of life. He urged them to "go out under the trees and read his books again." Following the "Canticle of Conquest over Death," during which the congregation read responsively, and such scriptures as "Let not your hearts be troubled" and "In my Father's house are many mansions," the Reverend Hammonds delivered the benediction, and the congregation rose to the lofty strains of Gloria Patri.

Outside, Governor Collins, wearing a long white coat, walked to her official car and stepped inside. Earlier she had told reporters, "Jesse has made a tremendous contribution to Kentucky and was internationally known. This is a real loss to Kentucky." The ever-lengthening funeral procession quickly formed, guided by the Greenup County sheriff's deputies. In the minutes that followed, the cortege grew so long that it took more than five minutes to cross the four-lane U.S. Highway 23 and move southward down Kentucky Highway 1 toward W-Hollow, while the deputies held back the thickening traffic going up and down the Ohio River. By 3:00 the lowering sky had turned pearl gray—what Jesse had once described as "February winter shawl-cloud weather"—and the earlier springlike temperatures were dropping into the forties. Car lights brightened the W-Hollow road sign as the procession continued past the site of the old Three Mile Way Station where Huey the Engineer had throttled his train on the vanished T-rails above the still visible bed of the old EKRR. The cortege angled off onto the gravel-and-dirt Shacklerun Road and made its way through the Plum Grove hills. Another mile and it climbed the steep cemetery hill. Somehow the parking areas and fields in front and along the sides of the Plum Grove Church, and the road itself, managed to absorb the mile of automobiles of every make and model from an old International Harvester truck to a sleek new Jaguar sedan.

The family was seated in a green tent before Jesse's grass-green bier. His multitude of friends formed a huge crescent around the top of the hill. Dr. Wood opened the simple graveside ceremony with the reading of the first stanza of "What a Friend," then other verses, and in what seemed too brief a time those familiar words from *The Book of Common Prayer,* "Earth to earth, ashes to ashes, dust to dust; in sure and certain hope of the Resurrection unto eternal life." Then momentary silence. The wind was rising and chilled the mourners. The Reverend Hammonds prayed the benediction and shook hands with the family. For a few moments Jane's composure broke and she sobbed into her clenched hand. Naomi rose from her position between Conrad and Erik, who stood staunchly on either side, then stepped to the coffin and gently placed her right hand on it, hesitating. Touching it ever so lightly with her left hand she spoke softly, "Goodbye, Jesse," and walked away between her grandchildren. Of her counterpart in *The Kingdom Within,* he had written words perfect to the occasion: "She had the stateliness and the dignity of a queen." Jane followed with her husband, Julian, then James, so like his brother in so many ways. Asked his reaction to Jesse's death, James had told reporter Shirley Williams, "We didn't just love each other, we liked each other."

It was over. A hundred cars parked awry and pinched in over lot, field, and road began to back and pull and turn, first clearing space for the family's car to go down the hill. Others followed one by one, down and out Shacklerun Road. The pallbearers, old friends who had brought him comfort, especially in his last illness—Oscar Sammons, Thurman Darby, Sam Piatt, William Harrell, Richard Prince and Dr. Charles Conley—lowered Jesse's "enriched rented dust" into the grave he had desired and lyrically foreseen a half century before:

And I am glad I will be left to lie
In Plum Grove many a long and lonesome year
Under the sun and stars in Plum Grove sky,
Where my own black-oak boards will cover me
While I sleep at Plum Grove eternally.

Now his prayer had been answered, that the "Creator of the Universe" would "let me lie back in the heart of it in the end . . . the land that has cradled me."

And he had written, too,

It is not long until the winter's over;
Just February, March, and then green April.
Of all the months I choose April my lover—
Blood-root, wind-flower and the daffodil . . .

And of death and April, "Everywhere the wind whispers that the time of sleep between death and resurrection will be brief." True of October, it was more immediately true of February. "Death is made all the more beautiful by the knowledge that green April awaits to resurrect the dead."

That was the way of April.

"There is not a month in the year as fascinating as April," when, Jesse had thought, "I can put my ear down against the earth and hear sounds like the slow beating of a heart." Although one must not presume, one could hope. "I feel confident—I have faith—" Jesse wrote, "that when man, the seed of God, is planted in the ground, though his husk will go back to the earth, he will be resurrected into a new life . . ." There was a way in spirit if not in body, he knew.

For April came always with the reassertion of its old pattern of birth and rebirth. First the serviceberry trees would bloom like thin clouds against the barren twigs, then the dogwoods like white and pink sails of ships on the pale green ocean of spring leaves and grass. The trailing arbutus and then the percoon would follow along the fence rows, pied with white Dutchman's-breeches and blue phlox Jesse often called "Sweet Williams." As his literature spoke from the durable leaves of his books, his land had a voice, too, and would call him back to "my world of the visible and invisible . . . from which I cannot escape," where he had lived in five different places from birth, whose every square acre of arable land had known the plows and hoes of the Stuarts, and before them the others back beyond the days of Harrison, Cleveland and McKinley into the pale of time when the pioneers moved through the Appalachians into the great Transylvania Colony of the West.

There were the ever-living invisibles of Six Hickories, too, those wraiths that dug the ore for the old furnaces, and the old people from another century he remembered as a child, living into his own time— Old Op Akers, Grandma Collins and hunter and imbiber Warfield Flaugherty, Uglybird Skinner, Charlie Deer and his brood of beautiful daughters, Uncle Mel Shelton with his mining cap just living for the resurrection, and Peg and Arn Sparks in their hug-me-tight behind old Gunpowder on W-Hollow Road just *clip-clopping* it along. Jesse would never leave nor could he escape this place where his real and fictive worlds merged into indistinction and endured, for he was of them and had learned long ago where he belonged. "Like the spider's strong gossamer threads, anchored to the weed and flower to secure his food, make him a home, where he has dreams, a country and clime," Jesse had written, then moved from local color to universal amplitude, finishing, ". . . maybe these same invisible gossamer strands of love have tied each of us to our valley forever."[1]

April would come again, *yes*. Somehow he would be there.

Abbreviations, Works, and Interviews

AD	August Derleth
AS	Ann Sammons
CC	Clem Carson
CW	Carleton Wells
DD	Donald Davidson
EB	Ethel Bush
EH	Elmer Heaberlin
HER	Harold Edward Richardson
JAS.	James M. Stuart (JS's brother)
JS	Jesse Stuart
MB	Maynard Bush
NDN (S)	Naomi Dean Norris (Stuart)
OS	Oscar Sammons
STILL	James Still

These abbreviations and those following have been used in the notes in order to save space. For convenience of reference, the remaining abbreviations and shortened references are arranged in four listings: (1) separately published works by Jesse Stuart, including a summary by genre; (2) other works by JS, including essays, manuscripts, newspaper columns, and daily journals; (3) interviews with JS and with others about JS by HER; and (4) works by others about JS. Abbreviations and shortened references not included in these four groupings are clarified upon first usage in the notes themselves.

The notes are arranged by chapter following the four groupings of abbreviations.

(1) ABBREVIATIONS USED FOR SEPARATELY PUBLISHED WORKS BY JESSE STUART

AD   *Album of Destiny* (poems). New York: Dutton, 1944.

AFW   *Andy Finds a Way* (junior book). New York: Whittlesey House, 1961.

AL   *Autumn Lovesong: A Celebration of Love's Fulfillment* (poem). Kansas City: Hallmark Editions, 1971.

BB   *The Beatinest Boy* (junior book). New York: Whittlesey House, 1953.

BDH   *Beyond Dark Hills: A Personal Story.* New York: Dutton, 1938. Repr. with a Foreword by Jesse Stuart, New York: McGraw-Hill, 1972.

BLSSJS   *The Best-Loved Short Stories of Jesse Stuart.* Ed. and with commentaries by H. Edward Richardson. Introduced by Robert Penn Warren. New York: McGraw-Hill, 1982.

CBF   *Come Back to the Farm* (short stories). New York: McGraw-Hill, 1971.

CGS   *Come Gentle Spring* (short stories). New York: McGraw-Hill, 1969.

CIS   *Clearing in the Sky & Other Stories.* New York: McGraw-Hill, 1950.

CTMT   *Come to My Tomorrowland* (junior book). Nashville and London: Aurora, 1971.

DOA   *Dandelion on the Acropolis: A Journal of Greece.* [Danbury, CT]: Archer Editions Press, 1978.

DOL   *Daughter of the Legend* (novel). New York: McGraw-Hill, 1965.

DRS   *Dawn of Remembered Spring* (short stories, poems). New York: McGraw-Hill, 1972.

FOG   *Foretaste of Glory* (novel). New York: Dutton, 1946.

GO   *God's Oddling: The Story of Mick Stuart, My Father.* New York: McGraw-Hill, 1960. Repr. as *Strength from the Hills,* adapted by Elizabeth Chamberlain, New York: Pyramid Books/Ladder Edition, 1968.

GSLR   *The Good Spirit of Laurel Ridge* (novel). New York: McGraw-Hill, 1953.

HA   *Hold April: New Poems by Jesse Stuart.* New York: McGraw-Hill, 1962.

HCLS   *Honest Confession of a Literary Sin* (essay with a Foreword by Jesse Stuart). Detroit: W-Hollow Books, 1977.

HE   *Huey, the Engineer* (an Esquire railroad story). St. Helena, CA: James E. Beard, 1960.

HOWH   *Head o' W-Hollow* (short stories). New York: Dutton, 1936. Repr. with a Foreword by Robert Penn Warren, Lexington: University Press of Kentucky, 1979.

HOY   *Harvest of Youth* (poems). Howe, OK: The Scroll Press, 1930. Repr. with an Introduction by Marc Crandall, Foreword by Hargis Westerfield, Berea, KY: Council of the Southern Mountains, 1964.

HTH   *Hie to the Hunters* (novel). New York: Whittlesey House, 1950. Repr. with a Preface by Jesse Stuart, Chicago: Scott, Foresman, 1968.

IIWSA   *If I Were Seventeen Again and Other Essays.* [Danbury, CT]: Archer Editions Press, 1980.

JSH   *A Jesse Stuart Harvest* (short stories). New York: Dell, 1965.

JSR   *A Jesse Stuart Reader: Stories and Poems.* Foreword by Max Bogart. "Author's Introductions" by Jesse Stuart. New York: McGraw-Hill, 1963.

KML   *Kentucky Is My Land* (poems). New York: Dutton, 1952. Repr. Ashland, KY: Economy Printers, [n.d.].

LBR   *The Land Beyond the River* (novel). New York: McGraw-Hill, 1973.

LHCW   *Land of the Honey-Colored Wind* (short stories). Ed. Jerry A. Herndon. [Morehead, KY]: The Jesse Stuart Foundation, 1982.

LSALS   *Lost Sandstones and Lonely Skies and Other Essays.* [Danbury, CT]: Archer Editions Press, 1980.

MGS   *Mr. Gallion's School* (novel). New York: McGraw-Hill, 1967.

MLHV   *My Land Has a Voice* (short stories). New York: McGraw-Hill, 1966.

MM   *Mongrel Mettle: The Autobiography of a Dog* (novel). New York: Dutton, 1944.

MOM   *Men of the Mountains* (short stories). New York: Dutton, 1941. Repr. with a Foreword by H. Edward Richardson, Lexington: University Press of Kentucky, 1979.

MW   *My World* (autobiography). Lexington: University Press of Kentucky, 1975.

MWBTP   *Man with a Bull-Tongue Plow* (poems). New York: Dutton, 1934. Repr. Dutton Everyman Paperback, 1959, with 622 of the original 703 poems.

OB   *Old Ben* (junior book). New York: McGraw-Hill, 1970.

OPWL   *The Only Place We Live* (poems), with August Derleth and Robert E. Gard. Ed. Mark E. LeFebvre. Madison: Wisconsin House, 1976, pp. 119–147. Wood engravings by Frank Utpatel.

OTL   *Outlooks Through Literature*, as editor, with Robert C. Pooley, Lillian White, Jay Cline. Chicago: Scott Foresman, 1964.

PIH   *Plowshare in Heaven* (short stories). New York: McGraw-Hill, 1958.

PWC   *A Penny's Worth of Character* (junior book). New York: Whittlesey House, 1954.

RM   *Red Mule* (junior book). New York: Whittlesey House, 1955.

RO   *The Rightful Owner* (junior book). New York: Whittlesey House, 1960.

RWAC   *Rebels with a Cause* (commencement address). Murray, KY: Murray State University, 1967. Delivered May 29, 1967.

RWHE   *A Ride with Huey, the Engineer* (junior book). New York: McGraw-Hill, 1966.

SBJ   *Seven by Jesse* (short stories). Indiana Council of Teachers of English. *Indiana English Journal*, vol. 5, pt. 2, nos. 2–4. Terre Haute: Indiana State University.

SBJS   *Stories by Jesse Stuart* (stories and poems). Adapted by Laurence Swinburne. New York: McGraw-Hill, 1968.

SEL   *Save Every Lamb* (short stories). New York: McGraw-Hill, 1964.

SJS   *The Seasons of Jesse Stuart: An Autobiography in Poetry 1907–1976*. Selected and introduced by Wanda Hicks. [Danbury, CT]: Archer Editions Press, 1976.

SSFD   *Short Stories for Discussion*, as editor, with Albert K. Rideout. New York: Scribner's, 1965. Includes a story and an essay by Stuart, pp. 349–365, 450–458.

32V   *32 Votes Before Breakfast: Politics at the Grass Roots as Seen in Short Stories by Jesse Stuart*. New York: McGraw-Hill, 1974.

TIM   *Time, a Story*. Cincinnati: The Little Man, 1939. Subsequent editions include one with a Foreword by Jesse Stuart, Cincinnati: W-Hollow Books, 1967.

TKW   *The Kingdom Within: A Spiritual Autobiography*. New York: McGraw-Hill, 1979.

TOH   *Trees of Heaven* (novel). New York: Dutton, 1940. Repr. with a Foreword by Wade Hall, Lexington: University Press of Kentucky, 1980.

TPGH   *Tales from the Plum Grove Hills* (short stories). New York: Dutton, 1946. Repr. with an "Author's Foreword" by Jesse Stuart, New York: Ballantine/Mockingbird Edition, 1974.

TPT   *Taps for Private Tussie* (novel). New York: Dutton, 1943. Repr. several times, including an edition illus. by Thomas Hart Benton (as was the original), New York and Cleveland: World, 1969; and New York: Ballantine, 1973.

TSS   *The Short Stories*. Ed. Kenzo Soneda and Norio Schimamura (4 short stories in English; annotations, notes, and biographical summary in Japanese). Tokyo: Aratake Schuppan, 1974.

TTRST *The Thread That Runs So True* (autobiography). New York: Scribner's, 1949. Repr. several times, including Scribner's, 1958, 1961, and 1968; also a special edition commemorating the centennial of Eastern Kentucky University, with essays by Thomas D. Clark and Wilma Dykeman, Lexington: University Press of Kentucky, 1974.

TTTL *To Teach, To Love* (autobiography). Cleveland: World, 1970. Repr. Baltimore: Penguin, 1973.

UHFL *Up the Hollow from Lynchburg.* With photographer Joe Clark. Introduction and descriptive text by Jesse Stuart. New York: McGraw-Hill, 1975.

WJS *The World of Jesse Stuart: Selected Poems.* Ed. and with an Introduction by J. R. LeMaster. New York: McGraw-Hill, 1975.

YMR *The Year of My Rebirth* (autobiography). New York: McGraw-Hill, 1956.

SUMMARY OF
JESSE STUART'S SEPARATELY PUBLISHED WORKS BY GENRE

Short story collections (some with poems included)		18
Poetry collections		8
Novels		9
Autobiography, autobiographical fiction, and biography		8
Junior books		8
Short volumes		
Stories	2	
Essay	1	
Address	1	
Subtotal	4	4
Essay collections		2
Co-authored works		2
Edited works		2
TOTAL SEPARATELY PUBLISHED WORKS		61

(2) ABBREVIATIONS USED FOR OTHER WORKS BY JESSE STUART

"Autobiographical . . ." "Autobiographical Reminiscence." *University of Kansas City Quarterly,* vol. XXVII, no. i (Oct. 1960), 57–59.

"Can She?" "Can She Milk a Cow?" *Saturday Evening Post,* vol. 213, no. 48 (May 31, 1941), 34, 104, 106, 108, 110.

COC *Cradle of the Copperheads.* Unpub. novel MS. (copy), JS Collection, University of Louisville, Louisville, KY.

DJ JS's *Daily Journal* (1943–1947; 1950–1955; 1957–1977). Notebook and calendar vols. typed and handwritten, W-Hollow, Greenup, KY, JS Collection, University of Louisville, Louisville, KY.

"E.P." "E.P." *Today's Education* (Kentucky ed.), vol. 59, no. 9 (Dec. 1969), 48–49.

ED "Egyptian Diary," unpub. MS. (orig. typescript of first 351 pp. of 1502 pp.), JS Collection, University of Louisville, Louisville, KY. Another copy, complete, in the JS Collection, Murray State University, Murray, KY.

"FFN"   "Fragments from Nothing." JS's first newspaper column, begun in 1934 for the *Greenup News;* most available in the JS Scrapbooks, JS Collection, Murray State University, Murray, KY.

"JS's   "Jesse Stuart's Characters in the Flesh." *Courier-Journal Magazine,* Oct.
Characters . . ."   27, 1963, pp. 30–34.

JSSB   *Jesse Stuart Scrapbook* (followed by a colon and the number of the scrapbook). In the JS Collection, Murray State University, Murray, KY.

"Kentucky . . ."   "Kentucky: My Source of Song." *Scholastic,* vol. 27 (Sept. 28, 1935), 6–8.

"My Teachers   "My Teachers at L.M.U." MS., unpub. except for portions used in
at L.M.U."   *TTTL;* in box labeled "THE TEACHERS WHO TAUGHT ME . . . LINCOLN MEMORIAL . . . ," JS Collection, University of Louisville, KY.

"Naomi"   "Naomi." *The Peabody Reflector,* vol. XLV, no. ii (Spring 1972), 28–31.

"Notes"   "Notes on My Poetry," in *poems from the hills.* Ed. William Plumley, Charleston, WV: Morris Harvey College, 1970, pp. 69–72.

"Place"   "A Place for Poetry: Jesse Stuart Becomes an Editor." *L.M.U. Alumnus,* vol. XXI, no. ii (Winter 1972), 32–34.

"The Professor"   "The Professor Who Didn't Like Me." *The Peabody Reflector,* vol. XLIV, no. iv (Fall 1971), 98–99.

"There Shall   "There Shall Not Be Left One Stone upon Another." *Filson Club History*
Not Be"   *Quarterly,* vol. XXI, no. ii (Winter 1977), 221–233.

"What   "What Vanderbilt University Meant to Me." *Vanderbilt Alumnus,* vol.
Vanderbilt"   53, no. 2 (Nov.–Dec. 1967), 17–21.

"WJSA"   "With JS Abroad." JS's newspaper column after "FFN," pub. beginning ca. March 25, 1938, in the Greenup, KY, *County Citizen* edition of the *Russell Times,* clippings from which are most readily available in the *JSSBs* in the JS Collection, at Murray State University, Murray, KY.

(3) CODES USED FOR INTERVIEWS WITH JESSE STUART AND WITH OTHERS ABOUT JESSE STUART

Interviews of Jesse Stuart conducted by H. Edward Richardson in W-Hollow, Greenup, Ky., unless otherwise noted. In the notes, interviews are referred to by "I" and the number indicated:

#1. Sat., and Sun., Nov. 19 and 20, 1966. This interview served as a basis for an address, *"Beyond Dark Hills:* The Archetypal Themes of Jesse Stuart," to the faculty and students of the College of Arts and Sciences, Founders Hall, University of Southern California, Los Angeles, July 3, 1968; then, with other changes, as the primary source for H. Edward Richardson, "Stuart Country: The Man-Artist and the Myth," in *Jesse Stuart: Essays on His Work,* eds. J. R. LeMaster & Mary Washington Clarke, Lexington: University Press of Kentucky, 1977, pp. 1–18.

#1A. Stouffer (Louisville) Inn, Louisville, KY, with Sylvia Gibbs, May 25, 1969, 9:45 P.M.

#2. July 9, 1978, 2:50 P.M.

#3. July 15, 1978, 4:15 P.M.

#4. July 16, 1978, 3:45 P.M.

#5. Aug. 19, 1978, 2:30 P.M.

#6. Aug. 20, 1978, 10:30 A.M.

#7. Sept. 2, 1978, 1:50 P.M.

#8. Sept. 3, 1978, 1:00 P.M.

#9. Sept. 15, 1978, 1:00 P.M.

#10.   Sept. 16, 1978, 10:30 A.M.
#11.   Oct. 7, 1978, 2:30 P.M.
#12.   Oct. 8, 1978, 3:30 P.M.
#13.   Nov. 3, 1978, 2:45 P.M.
#14.   Nov. 4, 1978, 10:00 A.M.
#15.   Nov. 17, 1978, 4:15 P.M.
#16.   Nov. 18, 1978, 2:05 P.M.
#17.   Dec. 29, 1978, 11:00 A.M.
#18.   Dec. 29, 1978, 2:05 P.M.
#19.   Feb. 9, 1979, 6:00 P.M.
#20.   Feb. 10, 1979, 1:50 P.M.
#21.   Feb. 11, 1979, 10:30 A.M.
#22.   April 1, 1979, 3:00 P.M.
#23.   May 4, 1979, 4:00 P.M.
#24.   May 23, 1979, 4:10 P.M.
#25.   June 16, 1979, 2:00 P.M.
#25A. June 17, 1979, 1:45 P.M.
#26.   Sept. 1, 1979, 3:25 P.M.
#27.   Sept. 2, 1979, 1:48 P.M.
#28.   Oct. 19, 1979, 3:30 P.M.
#29.   Dec. 6, 1979, 3:27 P.M.
#30.   Jan. 16, 1980, 5:00 P.M.
#31.   March 18, 1980, 2:45 P.M.
#32.   March 19, 1980, 2:30 P.M.
#33.   May 8, 1980, 4:00 P.M.
#34.   May 9, 1980, 10:00 A.M.
#35.   June 17, 1980, 5:15 P.M.
#36.   Aug. 8, 1980, 1:30 P.M.
#37.   Aug. 9, 1980, 11:30 A.M.
#38.   Sept. 19, 1980, 2:00 P.M.
#39.   Sept. 20, 1980, 7:30 P.M.
#40.   March 21, 1981, 4:45 P.M.
#41.   Sept. 15, 1981, 2:00 P.M.
#42.   Sept. 17, 1981, 11:54 A.M.

Interviews with others about Jesse Stuart, conducted by H. Edward Richardson. In the Notes, interviews are referred to by "I" and the number indicated:

#43.   Lou Ashworth, New York City, March 18, 1981, 3:37 P.M.
#44.   Paul G. Blazer, Jr., Ashland, KY, Sept. 19, 1980, 10:30 P.M.
#45.   Ethel Bush, Greenup Co., KY, Feb. 10, 1979, ca. 4:30 P.M.
#46.   ———, Greenup Co., KY, Oct. 19, 1979, 4:30 P.M.
#47.   Grace Hilton Carter and Essie Hilton Roland, Greenbo Lodge, Greenup Co., KY, Sept. 2, 1978, ca. 10:20 P.M.
#48.   William and Irma Collins, Muncie, IN, May 27, 1981, 10:00 A.M.
#49.   Dr. A. Leland Crabb, March 17, 1979, Nashville TN, 9:30 A.M.
#50.   Thurman Darby, Greenup Co., KY, Nov. 5, 1978, 10:00 A.M.
#51.   J. Paul Davis, Southshore, KY, March 19, 1980, 2:45 P.M.
#52.   Dr. Edgar H. Duncan, Vanderbilt University, Nashville, TN, March 17, 1979, ca. 3:30 P.M.
#53.   Dr. Ivar Lou Duncan, Nashville, TN, Oct. 25, 1979, 10:30 A.M.
#54.   Kathryn Geny, Nashville, TN, Oct. 26, 1979, 11:00 A.M.
#55.   DeRoy Givens, Nashville, TN, March 17, 1979, ca. 10:30 A.M.

#56. Richard M. "Pek" Gunn, Nashville, TN, March 16, 1979, 5:30 P.M.

#57. ——, Nashville, TN, March 17, 1979, 8:30 A.M.

#58. ——, Nashville, TN, April 13, 1979, 8:00 P.M.

#59. Edward K. Hardy, Hendersonville, TN, March 17, 1979, 4:30 P.M.

#60. ——, Madison, TN, Oct. 25, 1979, 2:00 P.M.

#60A. Eunice Mitchell Harper, Greenbo Lodge, Greenup Co., KY, Sept. 2, 1978, ca. 10:00 P.M.

#61. Robert E. Hatton, Louisville, KY, Nov. 12, 1978, 11:00 A.M.

#62. Elmer Heaberlin, Wurtland, KY, Dec. 29, 1978, 4:00 P.M.

#63. ——, Wurtland, KY, Feb. 9, 1979, 8:30 P.M.

#63A. Everett P. Hilton, W-Hollow, the Jesse Stuart home, Greenup, KY, Sept. 3, 1978, 11:00 A.M.

#64. Bill Clay Holmes, Portsmouth, Ohio, May 9, 1980.

#64A. John W. Howell, D.D., Louisville, KY, Jan. 4, 1979, noon.

#64B. Mrs. Ernest O. Hutchens, (Barnie Greene), Knoxville, TN, July 10, 1979, 4:30 P.M.

#65. Sophia Stuart Keeney, W-Hollow, Greenup, KY, Nov. 18, 1978, 3:10 P.M.

#66. ——, W-Hollow, Greenup, KY, March 19, 1980, 9:00 A.M.

#67. Maud King, Southshore, KY, May 9, 1980, ca. 2:30 P.M.

#68. Glennis Stuart Liles, W-Hollow, Greenup, KY, July 16, 1978, 11:50 A.M.

#69. Ethel Brown McBrayer, Greenup, KY, May 9, 1980, ca. 5:00 P.M.

#70. Opal Rice McKee, Judge Oscar Sammons, and Ann Sammons, Greenbo Lodge, Greenup Co., KY, Oct. 8, 1978, 2:30 P.M.

#71. Mrs. T. L. McDonald (Winnie Palmer), Cumberland Gap, TN, July 19, 1979, 11:30 A.M.

#72. Dr. H(oward) B(ennett) McWhorter (telephone interview), Ashland, KY, March 31, 1983, 3:00 P.M.

#73. Catherine Mims and Ella Puryear, Nashville, TN, Oct. 26, 1979, 9:00 A.M.

#74. Mary Stuart Nelson, and James M. Stuart, W-Hollow, Greenup, KY, Nov. 18, 1978, ca. noon.

#75. Lena Nevison, Greenbo Lodge, Greenup, KY, Sept. 21, 1980, noon.

#76. Lucille Jordan Palmer, Greenbo Lodge, Greenup, KY, May 24, 1980, 9:52 P.M.

#77. G. Sam Piatt, Ashland, KY, March 19, 1980, ca. 11:00 A.M.

#78. ——, Greenup and Southshore, KY, May 9, 1980, ca. 1:30 P.M.

#79. Judge Oscar and Ann Sammons, Greenup, KY, Sept. 2, 1978, ca. 10:15 P.M.

#80. ——, Greenup, KY, Sept. 15, 1978, 5:30 P.M.

#81. ——, Greenup, KY, Oct. 8, 1978, 11:00 A.M.

#82. Judge Oscar Sammons, Ann Sammons, and Opal Rice McKee, Greenbo Lodge, Greenup Co., KY, Oct. 8, 1978, ca. 2:30 P.M.

#83. Judge Oscar and Ann Sammons, Greenup, KY, Nov. 4, 1978, 5:30 P.M.

#84. Professor Earl Hobson Smith, Lincoln Memorial University campus, Harrogate, TN, April 8, 1979, ca. 1:00 P.M.

#85. ——, Cumberland Gap, TN, July 18, 1979, 9:00 P.M.

#86. James M. Stuart, Greenup, KY, W-Hollow and ridge path tour, Nov. 4, 1978, 10:00 A.M.

#87. ——, Greenup and old Riverton, KY, tour, commencing in W-Hollow, Nov. 4, 1978, 1:10 P.M.

#88. ——, Plum Grove, Cedar Riffles, and W-Hollow, KY, Nov. 18, 1978, ca. 10:30 A.M.

#89. James M. and Betty Stephens Stuart, Executive Inn, Louisville, KY, Jan. 13, 1979, 8:00 P.M.

#90. James M. Stuart, Raccoon Hollow Rd., Greenup Co., KY, Oct. 19, 1979, 6:15 P.M.

#91. ——, Raccoon Hollow Rd., Greenup Co., KY, March 18, 1980, 8:00 P.M.

#92. James M. Stuart and Sophia Stuart Keeney, W-Hollow, Greenup, KY, March 19, 1980, 9:00 A.M.
#93. James M. Stuart, Howard Johnson Motel, Shelbyville Road, Louisville, KY, Nov. 11, 1980, 10:00 P.M.
#94. Naomi Deane Norris Stuart, W-Hollow, Greenup, KY, Aug. 20, 1978, 12:15 P.M.
#95. ——, W-Hollow, Greenup, KY, Sept. 16, 1978, noon.
#96. ——, W-Hollow, Greenup, KY, Oct. 7, 1978, 1:30 P.M.
#97. ——, W-Hollow, Greenup, KY, Oct. 8, 1978, ca. 5:30 P.M.
#98. ——, W-Hollow, Greenup, KY, Oct. 18, 1978, 9:15 A.M.
#99. ——, W-Hollow, Greenup, KY, Nov. 3, 1978, ca. 4:00 P.M. Also in I#13.
#100. ——, W-Hollow, Greenup, KY, Nov. 4, 1978, 1:30 P.M. Also in I#14.
#101. ——, W-Hollow, Greenup, KY, Dec. 29, 1978, 2:30 P.M. Also in I#18.
#102. ——, W-Hollow, Greenup, KY, Feb. 10, 1979, ca. 2:30 P.M. Also in I#20.
#103. ——, W-Hollow, Greenup, KY, Oct. 19, 1979, 2:30 P.M.
#104. ——, W-Hollow, Greenup, KY, Oct. 20, 1979, 10:20 A.M.
#105. ——, W-Hollow, Greenup, KY, June 17, 1980, 6:00 P.M.
#106. ——, Jo-Lin Health Care Center, Ironton, Ohio, Aug. 17, 1982, 5:30 P.M.
#107. ——, Kings Daughters Hospital, Ashland, KY, Nov. 20, 1982, 4:30 P.M.
#108. ——, W-Hollow, Greenup, KY, April 30, 1983, 5:00 P.M.
#109. ——, W-Hollow and Ironton, Ohio, Sept. 23, 1983, 11:00 A.M. and 2:00 P.M.
#110. Horace "Choppy" Thomas, Greenup, KY, Nov. 4, 1978, 7:30 P.M.
#111. Virginia Monroe Tippett, Louisville, KY, Oct. 11, 1980, 10:15 A.M.
#112. Lena Wells Lykins Voiers, Vanceburg, KY, Nov. 5, 1978, ca. 4:30 P.M.
#113. Robert Penn Warren, New Haven, CT, March 19, 1981, 11:00 A.M.
#114. ——, New Haven, CT, March 19, 1981, 1:25 P.M.
#115. J. E. Windrow, Nashville, TN, April 13, 1979, ca. 11:30 A.M.
#116. Kenneth Wright, Southshore, KY, March 19, 1980, noon.
#117. Professor T(homas) D(aniel) Young, Nashville, TN, March 17, 1979, noon.

(4) ABBREVIATIONS OF WORKS
BY OTHERS ABOUT JESSE STUART

(alphabetized by title or by name)

"Addendum" H. Edward Richardson. "Addendum: The Jesse Stuart Bibliography of the L.M.U. Years: 1926–1929." *Jack London Newsletter*, vol. XII, nos. 1–3 (1979), 79–82.

"An Appreciation" William Boozer. "Jesse Stuart: An Appreciation." *The Kentucky Review*, vol. III, no. 1 (1981), 54–69.

EMcSB *Ethel McBrayer Scrapbook*. Greenup, KY.

Fain and Young *The Literary Correspondence of Donald Davidson and Allen Tate*. John Tyree Fain and Thomas Daniel Young, eds. Athens: University of Georgia Press, 1974.

Fugitive Group Louise Cowan. *The Fugitive Group: A Literary History*. Baton Rouge: LSU Press, 1959.

FYD Naomi Deane Norris (Stuart). *Five Year Diary*. Begun in 1937 and continued through portions of 1940. W-Hollow, Greenup, KY.

GSLSB *Glennis Stuart Liles Scrapbook*. W-Hollow, Greenup, KY.

"He Visited" August Derleth. "He Visited Jesse Stuart." *News of Books and Authors* (May–June 1939), 8.

"Inquiry"   Lee Oly Ramey. "An Inquiry into the Life of Jesse Stuart as Related to His Literary Development and a Critical Study of His Works." Unpub. master's thesis, Ohio University, Athens, Ohio, June 1941, 271 pp.

JLN   *Jack London Newsletter*. Professor Hensley C. Woodbridge, ed. Carbondale, IL: Southern Illinois Univ. (Source of bibliographical information and scholarly articles on Jesse Stuart.)

JS   Ruel E. Foster. *Jesse Stuart*. New York: Twayne, 1968.

"J. S."   Charlotte Salmon. "Jesse Stuart." *Southwest Review*, vol. 21, no. 2 (Winter 1936), 163–168.

JSB   Hensley C. Woodbridge. *Jesse and Jane Stuart: A Bibliography*. Murray, KY: Murray State University Press, 1979, 3rd ed. Includes also *Jesse Stuart: A Bibliography*, Harrogate, TN: LMU Press, 1960, which contains essays by Roland Carter, Lawrence Edwards, H. H. Kroll, E. H. Smith, and Jesse Stuart. Includes also a 2nd (1969) ed. All references are to the 3rd (1979) ed. unless otherwise specified.

JS:EOHW   *Jesse Stuart: Essays on His Work*. J. R. LeMaster and Mary Washington Clarke, eds. Lexington University Press of Kentucky, 1977.

JSK   Mary Washington Clarke. *Jesse Stuart's Kentucky*. New York: McGraw-Hill, 1968.

JS:KCP   J. R. LeMaster. *Jesse Stuart: Kentucky's Chronicler-Poet*. Memphis, TN: Memphis State University Press, 1980.

JS:LW   Everetta Love Blair. *Jesse Stuart: His Life and Works*. Columbia: University of South Carolina Press, 1967.

"LCJS"   Frank H. Leavell. "The Literary Career of Jesse Stuart." Unpub. doctoral dissertation, Vanderbilt University, Nashville, TN, Jan. 1965, 240 pp.

Man   John R. Gilpin, Jr. *The Man . . . Jesse Stuart: Poet, Novelist, Short Story Writer, Educator*. Ashland, KY: Economy Printers, 1977.

"My Friend"   John Bird. "My Friend Jesse Stuart." *Saturday Evening Post*, vol. 232 (July 25, 1959), 32–33, 79, 81–83.

Rayford   Julian Lee Rayford. "Jesse Stuart: Kentucky's Immortal Chronicler." *The American Book Collector*, JS no. (Sept. 1958), 5–7.

ROJS   Dick Perry. *Reflections of Jesse Stuart on a Land of Many Moods*. New York: McGraw-Hill, 1971.

"Stuart   H. Edward Richardson. "Stuart Country: The Man-Artist and the
Country"   Myth." *Jesse Stuart: Essays on His Work*. J. R. LeMaster & Mary Washington Clarke, eds. Lexington: University Press of Kentucky, 1977, pp. 1–18.

"Student and   Earl Hobson Smith. "Student and Friend." *Jesse Stuart: A Bibliog-
Friend"   raphy*, compiled by Hensley C. Woodbridge. Harrogate, TN: Lincoln Memorial University Press, 1960, pp. xx–xxii.

Notes

———◇———

Faced with a plethora of references, I have sought to compromise between a superscript-studded text, referring to individual notes for each source and fact, and a paginal system that arbitrarily divides notes by text page rather than thought. The result is notes that correspond to sections of text; where they are lengthy, paragraph breaks denote subject shifts in the text. The preceding list of codes, in "Abbreviations, Works, and Interviews," allows the notes to be condensed so as to give the fullest references possible for a work of this size.

CHAPTER 1

¹The man in the photograph is JS, Stuart Photograph Collection, W-Hollow, Greenup, KY. This notation in his hand appears on the back of the photograph: "Birthplace— / Jesse Stuart / Born here Aug. 8th 1907 [sic] / House destroyed by a / forest fire in 1956 / House on a high hilltop overlooking W-Hollow on / one side, Shackle Run / Valley on the other." I#7. The name of the watercourse on the southern hill is Cedar Riffles, noted with other facts in *BDH*, pp. 26, 30; also see pp. 229–230; and in *MWBTP*, pp. 62–66, including sonnets 120 ("This is the tumbling shack where I was born"), 121 ("And I would love to speak unto this house"), 122 ("I ask where are the ramble rose vines now?"), 123 (The house is silent now—the folks have gone"), 124 ("My boy, stand here beneath the August skies"), 125 ("The wind beat high up here when autumn came"), 126 ("Somehow the years recall—I do not hear"), and 127 ("Stand in your ruins, you tumbling mountain shack"). Every published biographical source to date lists 1907 as JS's year of birth, including *JS:LW*, p. 3; *JS*, p. 13; and *Man* (p. 7 of unnumbered pages). However, his employment record at American Rolling Mills, Ashland, KY, listed "8–8–1906" as his date of birth. In 1926 the space labeled SIGNATURE is handwritten "Jesse H. *Stewart*" whereas the 1927 signature space shows "*Stuart*", indicating that the poet was still in the process of changing the spelling of his surname from *Stewart* to *Stuart,* a change begun when he came under the influence of Mrs. Robert E. (McFarland) Hatton and her penchant for the Scots. (For further details, see Ch. 2.) In I#86, the author's brother James M. Stuart confirmed that JS's year of birth was 1906, and further explained that by Jesse's college

years the 1907 birthdate was part of his school records, and so it has remained. Some inconsistencies can be resolved by the 1906 date of birth, although the author chose to apply the 1907 date generally. When I asked JS about his birthdate, he did not deny being born in 1906, but responded, "I'll be . . . slow to admit it" (I#23). Most of his age designations in the autobiographical writings are tied to a 1907 birthdate and, consequently, may be most consistently understood by readers in that context. Although Martha Stuart retained "Hylton" as the spelling of her maiden name, most of the family now spell the name "Hilton."

²*BDH*, pp. 30–31.

³"Vacation in Hell," orig. pub. *Esquire*, vol. 10 (July 1938), 70–71, 184–186; repr. in *MOM*, pp. 266–282. The "coal buggy" or "jump the track buggy" in *BDH*, p. 229, appears in *MOM*, p. 267. JS said in I#6 that the story was based on his father and a man with whom his father used to mine. "It happened. One of the men hurt in that was a Garthee. He lived right up here on the hill, on this farm. He had his back broken. . . . In those days you couldn't do much about it. When I came on as a boy, a lot of people remembered him. I wrote that story in Scotland, on my Guggenheim. Lefty Weaver was a Garthee. He was the biggest [man]. . . . [The cave-in] . . . scared them all to death about going under the ground, naturally. My dad was even scared, and hell couldn't scare him." Asked about the character Sall, JS said, "That would have been Mom. It is just . . . right around the hill [close to] . . . my birthplace. We've burned coal out of there about every year, until recently."

⁴*YMR*, p. 78.

⁵*Man*, p. 7, states, "When his father left the coal mine, he moved his family into a three-room log cabin down in the valley [of W-Hollow] where he became a tenant farmer." Despite this move there seems to have been little improvement in the economic and living conditions of the family, except for more rooms and a fireplace. Gilpin continues, "JS spent his early childhood where the Stuarts worked hard to eke out a scanty living from the stubborn soil." JS recounted the move from his birthplace at Cedar Riffles to the first W-Hollow farm and the location of "our new destiny" in *BDH*, pp. 32–33. However, in I#7 he said that house "was not on the *tip* of the prong; it was on the *center* of the prong. I want to correct that [in *Beyond Dark Hills*]." Mrs. Stuart added in agreement, "Because up where Mary [Stuart] Nelson is would be the tip of it." While the Stuarts lived at Jesse's second home at the center of the middle prong of W-Creek, the family "increased three new members" (*GO*, p. 19). These Stuarts were Herbert Lee (b. November 2, 1909), Mary (b. August 7, 1912), and James Mitchell (b. August 11, 1915).

⁶*BDH*, pp. 31–32. I#1A. Some twelve years after this earlier conversation, in I#2, he answered my question "What are your earliest memories?" by replying, "I set the house on fire."

⁷I#1A. Also see *JS:EOHW*, pp. 8–9.

⁸I#65. *BDH*, pp. 352–353. I#2. Dr. Henry Morris was the Stuart family doctor throughout JS's childhood and youth.

⁹This second home is owned by Mr. and Mrs. Roy Abdon, the poet laureate's nephew and niece (Mrs. Sophia Keeney's daughter and son-in-law), and is rented to the McClure family. *YMR*, p. 51; for Peddler's Well, pp. 186–188.

¹⁰*YMR*, pp. 197–198. Mr. and Mrs. [Granny Lydia] Collins are buried at Three Mile Cemetery in an iron-fenced lot: Nathaniel Collins (b. Sept. 5, 1837; d. May 31, 1911); Lydia Collins (b. October 23, 1852; d. October 13, 1928). In reality, the event took place in 1911, not 1910, as JS wrote.

[11]*BDH*, p. 28; "Whose Land Is This?" first pub. in *Esquire*, vol. 18, no. 3 (Sept. 1942), pp. 36–37, 173–175; repr. in *TPGH* (1946 ed.), pp. 35–46; (1974 ed.), pp. 17–25. Sonnet 137 in *MWBTP* (rev. ed., 1959), p. 75; 148 in orig. 1934 ed., where line 4 reads, "I got up four at morn to feed the cattle" (p. 76).

[12]*JS, GO*, pp. 51, 246; "Author's Introduction" to "Nest Egg," *JSR*, p. 3; *YMR*, p. 57; *TTTL*, pp. 18–19.

[13]*BDH*, pp. 13–14, 24. I#8: JS said his mother's mother, Violet Pennington Hilton, was one-half Cherokee Indian, making his mother one-fourth and himself one-eighth Cherokee. *BDH*, pp. 24–25; also *GO*, pp. 53–55. Baptist or no, Grandpa Hilton liked his "Honorable Herbs" and "fragrant weed." He also provided Jesse's model for "Grandpa Birdwell's Last Battle," orig. pub. *Esquire*, vol. 16 (Sept. 1941), 58, 123–124, 126; repr. *TPGH* (1974 ed.), pp. 77–86. "Another April" was orig. pub. *Harper's*, vol. 185 (Aug. 1942), 256–260; repr. most recently in *BLSSJS*, pp. 362–369. Nathan Hilton [also Hylton] was born Oct. 29, 1851, and died Feb. 8, 1943, at ninety-two (see note 22 below). *JSR*, p. 188; *GO*, p. 20.

[14]The source of JS's paternal ancestry, *BDH*, p. 14. However, he told me, I#2, that the Stuarts, he thinks, originally came from Linlithgow, Scotland, close to the Firth of Forth, about ten miles west of Edinburgh. *BDH*, pp. 13–23, Raphy and Mitchell Stuart. Jesse's grandfather Mitchell Stuart's first wife was Cynthia Meade, a first cousin, by whom he had eleven children, the last being JS's father (p. 13). He had eight children by his second wife, a younger woman with whom he was reported to be "having trouble" (p. 22). When JS asked his father "how many men Grandpa had killed besides the men he killed in the war," Mick Stuart's answer was, "Don't ask so many questions, son. Little boys don't need to know too much" (p. 18). I#9.

[15]*BDH*, p. 14. *GO*, p. 252 (courtship and marriage of parents). Mitchell Stuart was born June 17, 1880, and died Dec. 23, 1954, at seventy-four. Martha Hylton [Hilton] Stuart was born Aug. 1, 1882, and died May 11, 1951, at sixty-eight.

[16]"The Storm," *Household*, vol. 41 (Jan. 1941), 4–5, 9; repr. in *TPGH*, pp. 51–58, most recently in *BLSSJS*, pp. 1–9. For the genesis of the story see esp. *BLSSJS*, pp. 1–2, also I#2 and *GO*, p. 9. I#25 (parents' temporary decision to separate).

[17]*GO*, pp. 35–36 (corn story); *TTTL*, pp. 224–230 (nature as teacher); *YMR*, p. 55. Pawpaw, persimmon anecdotes, *GO*, pp. 39–40.

[18]*TTTL*, pp. 18–19, 23; *BDH*, p. 33. Mary Stuart Nelson was born Aug. 7, 1912. *ROJS*, p. 75.

[19]*TTTL*, p. 23; *BDH*, p. 34; *TTTL*, pp. 19–24; I#9.

[20]*GO* (JS's resentment of sister), pp. 42–43; *BDH*, pp. 33–34.

[21]*TTRST*, pp. 5–6; "Kentucky," p. 6.

[22]*BDH*, p. 39 (Herbert Lee's death); *GO*, p. 19 (father's grieving). Herbert Lee's gravestone (b. Nov. 2, 1909; d. Jan. 12, 1914). *GO*, pp. 19–20 (first gravesite); *YMR*, pp. 120, 116. *BDH*, pp. 37–39 (Herbert's funeral). "Brothers," *Household*, vol. 38 (Dec. 1938), 4–5, 12–13, 15, 18, 25; repr. *TPGH* (1974 ed.), pp. 54–72.

[23]*GO*, p. 21 (swimming incident); "Brothers," *TPGH*, p. 32; I#47.

[24]"Brothers," *TPGH*, pp. 31–32; also *GO*, pp. 20–21 (John becomes Herbert).

[25]*YMR*, pp. 78–79; author writes that years later doctors in both Scotland and America told him that his stomach "was slowed by typhoid fever." Other details, p. 45.

[26]GO, pp. 21–23; "Brothers," TPGH, pp. 32–33. In fact, James Mitchell Stuart was born Wed., Aug. 11, 1915, at about 10 A.M. "Mrs. Collins delivered me. . . . The doctor got there about 1:00 [in the afternoon] . . . I was already dressed and doing well" (I#89). Young JS had likely been out playing when he saw the doctor riding his sorrel horse up to the house.

[27]JS, "Nest Egg," Atlantic Monthly, vol. 173 (Feb. 1944), 85–89; repr. in TPGH, pp. 164–172. Asked if the story were true, JS replied, "Right in that yard still stands the white oak, in the backyard where old Nest Egg was killed" (I#9). The "white-oak roost" is located, according to the story, "between the barn and the house." Today W-Creek is gradually washing the soil from around the roots, endangering its life. Also see JSR, pp. 3–4; BLSSJS, pp. 10–11.

[28]"Angel in the Pasture," Esquire, vol. 51 (June 1959), 49–50; my source is the italicized version in YMR, pp. 11–14.

[29]TTTL, pp. 20–24, gives additional background on Calvin Clarke, who went to Washington, DC, was employed by the US Tax Department, attended George Washington University, finished college and law school, became an attorney and, ultimately, a millionaire in Portsmouth, Ohio, before his death at sixty-five. Nora Riggs finished three months of the term Clarke commenced, apparently JS's third term (p. 34).

[30]GO, p. 25; TTTL, p. 28.

[31]TTTL, pp. 28–32. I#65.

[32]JS's plan for revenge is recounted in TTTL, p. 31, but "their secret" eluded him. I#9 ("It may have been Grace"). I#47 (green apple anecdote).

[33]In GO, pp. 22–23. I#9. I#7. Sophia Stuart Keeney thinks she was twelve when the move occurred, between Sept. 3, 1915, and Sept. 3, 1916 (I#65). Adding to the problem of dating the move to the third house is the author's statement that he lived in this house from his ninth to twelfth years (YMR, p. 67: MW, p. 7). The 1906 birthdate points to an Aug. 8, 1915/Aug. 8, 1916 period for the move, consistent with Mrs. Keeney's memory, often relied on by JS.

[34]BDH, p. 82 (shoes). TTTL, pp. 34–35 (Elta Cooper Kotcamp). I#5 (amusement at Mrs. Kotcamp's memory of him as "just wild"). GO, pp. 42–43 (JS's rapid academic progress). The photograph is in the JS Collection, W-Hollow, Greenup, KY. Author's notation reads: "Top row left to right: Tinnie Runnell, Rhetta Jordan, Sophia Stuart, Chester Broughton, Willard Broughton. Second row left to right: Polly Jordan, Edna Dials, Esther Dials, Katherine Carter, Mannie Thompson and Hilda Broughton[.] Bottom row left to right: Harlan Broughton, Everett Sennett, Charlie Dials, Morris Sennett and Jesse Stuart[.]" Across the right end of the back of the picture is "oldest picture ever made of me." Mrs. Elta Cooper Kotcamp, letter to me from Birmingham, AL, Sept. 28, 1978. TTTL, p. 35.

[35]MW, p. 7. I#7. GO, p. 53 (the land).

[36]BDH, pp. 38–40 (description of winter 1917/1918). I#4 ("murrain," i.e., the "scours"). Note JS's statement, BDH, p. 38: "Another brother was born there the spring after we arrived" (Martin Vernon Stuart, b. Feb. 11, 1918; d. Apr. 17, 1918). The locale of both stories is clearly the third farm, then the head of W-Hollow. "Spring Victory," orig. pub. Commonweal, vol. 37 (Nov. 20, 1942), 111–115; repr. TPGH, pp. 135–146. Also see "Dark Winter," HOWH, pp. 67–92. Cf. "Brothers," TPGH, pp. 31–44. Note "Greenwood" (p. 139) becomes "Greenup" on the next page, a rare slip into fact that may serve as a kind of signature to the authenticity of the substance of the story. MOM refers to "two graves under the plum tree in the garden" (p. 34), which may symbolize the deaths of the

author's two brothers. It may be revealing to compare JS's use of names for the two deceased brothers, as well as the name of his surviving brother, James Mitchell, in these five separate works:

(Actual Name)	FIRST BROTHER (Herbert Lee)	SECOND BROTHER (James Mitchell)	THIRD BROTHER (Martin Vernon)
Beyond Dark Hills	Herbert Lee	James	"my youngest brother"
"Dark Winter"	Not mentioned	Finn	Mitchell ("tiny")
"Spring Victory"	Not mentioned	James	"big fine brother" in March
God's Oddling	Herbert	James	Lee ("so little")
"Brothers"	John	James Mitchell	Lee ("so little")

[37]"Dark Winter," *HOWH*, pp. 67–92; repr. *BLSSJS*, pp. 20–41.

[38]JS observed in I#4 that "Dark Winter" was autobiographical in many ways, specifically saying that the baskets were made "in that old living room right there," referring to the original log living room in the present JS home, a room around which cluster many memories and events transmuted into his fiction, e.g., "Grandpa Birdwell's Last Battle" (cf. note 13, above). *BDH*, pp. 38–40.

CHAPTER 2

[1]I#5. Cf. also "Thanksgiving Hunter," orig. pub. in *Household*, vol. 43 (Nov. 1943), 26–27; repr. most recently in *BLSSJS*, pp. 386–392. Also see JS, "The Builders and the Dream," *CBF*, p. 106. *BDH*, pp. 42–43, gives these and other details of young JS's work for Daugherty.

[2]*TTTL*, pp. 35–37 (the contaminated water bucket).

[3]*BDH*, p. 43. I#81: JS and his father at that time cultivated the corn "along the Riverton bottoms right through this property." The Sammonses live, at this writing, at 1204 Riverside Drive, formerly Riverton but now part of Greenup. JS said that the Bates house was "a mansion to me" in I#12.

[4]JS mentioned his wartime work and "Wilburn Crump, a negro," in *BDH*, pp. 43–44. In I#7, the author told me, "He was a black man. . . . When I wrote that story . . . [I] did all these things to try to black my face and try to be like him. And my mother told me we were two races. . . . I sent it to *Atlantic* . . . and they wouldn't take it because I'd done that. And then I took the story back . . . took all the color off it and placed the story." Wilburn Crump nursed the family "right here in this house" (the JS home). The Crumps lived on an adjoining farm toward Greenup and the Academy Branch ridge path. "And, you know, we helped to take care of his old man. . . . He had a broken back. We were good to those people and helped them." "Wilburn" was published in *MOM*, pp. 170–181. JS treats his yearning to return to Plum Grove School in *TTRST*, pp. 4–5.

[5]As of this writing the spring, below the steep bank of the driveway, is covered with rock, soil, and old leaves. Jesse's sister, Mary Nelson, a teacher who writes and paints and is a mother of seven children, lives there. I#74. Also I#91.

[6]*GO*, pp. 49–51. *BDH*, p. 44. In an introductory note to an excerpt from *GO*, reprinted in *JSR*, Signet ed., 1966, p. 194, JS writes, "Finally in 1920 my father was able to buy some land of his own."

[7]*GO*, pp. 53–55, and *BDH*, pp. 44–45, deal with JS and his grandfather's building of the first Stuart house.

[8]JS has written of the social, political, and religious conflict between his parents and their families several times, but most pointedly in the short story "Two Worlds," orig. pub. in the *Georgia Review*, vol. 21 (1967), 449–456; repr. in *CGS*, pp. 12–20—the quotation is from pp. 17–18. Of the quarrels between his mother and father stemming back to his early memories, including those events giving rise to "The Storm," JS told me in I#25, "It shook me. I cried."

[9]I#68. JS, I#9, remembers his youngest sister's birth. "Mother was milking," he said, and "barely got home and Glennis was on the way." Mrs. Liles believes she and her mother moved to the new house when she was "only a month old." Whether the move actually took place in October or November 1921 is not clear, but apparently the house was not completed at the time of the move.

[10]"The Builders and the Dream," *CBF*, pp. 105–132; quotations, pp. 109, 111–112, 113. JS I#11, recalled his mother's saying, "Love the Lord and beat the Hiltons."

[11]I#11. JS also noted positive aspects of Martin Hilton's personality: "He's the same uncle who's in 'This Is the Place'" (*MOM*, pp. 315–331, and *BLSSJS*, pp. 393–406). I#9. I#12. His uncle liked books, raised peaches and apples, and sold apple cider for ten cents a gallon. He also "reared a fine family." JS's memory of his first cousins is mellow in I#9, and of their father: "He was a very bright man . . . read [*Decline*] *and Fall of the Roman Empire* and let the weeds take his corn." JAS., I#88.

[12]*TTTL*, pp. 36–37. I#63A. Also see JS, "E.P.," pp. 48–49.

[13]*YMR*, pp. 141–142 (JS's friendship with Howards and Glen Hilton).

[14]"Saving the Bees," orig. pub. *Esquire*, vol. 13 (Jan. 1940), 104–105, 108; repr. in *MOM*, pp. 226–247, and in *BLSSJS*, pp. 55–71. Concerning the Howard family, in I#13 JS said he had a novel in his upstairs study called *Magic Moonshine* that "I could spend a month on and finish. . . . It's [inspired] by the Howards. . . . [The characters] used to live around here and moonshine." The story "Tradelast" first appeared in *Progressive Farmer*, vol. 67 (April 1952), 84, 86–88, 90, 92; repr. in *JSR*, pp. 183–198. "Coming Down the Mountain," *CIS*, pp. 147–159.

[15]Zetta Sturgill Stephenson, letters to *HER*, March 5 and 20, 1979.

[16]I#11. *BDH*, p. 47 (JS's wage, hours, and work on Greenup streets).

[17]*TTTL*, pp. 38–39; JS mentioned his twenty-two months of learning at Plum Grove in *MW*, p. 8; he averaged no more than perhaps five months of attendance each year during his first four years, achieving in Elta Cooper Kotcamp's class of 1917/1918 an advanced eighth-grade standing. His subsequent attendance in Claris [not the real name] Brown's class was sporadic at best; in his own view he received very little "learning" in her class as did other students; and it was not until his final two months of training with Everett Hilton during the 1921/1922 school year that he was again making progress. Everett Hilton exhorted him, "Your first goal is to finish the eighth grade. Your second goal is to enter and finish Greenup High School" ("E.P.," p. 48). Jesse resumed his education at Plum Grove then, and only for a period of two months—hence, the twenty-two solid months of formal education. I#11. For the "turning point" in the author's life, see *Man* [unnumbered p. 9].

[18]The observations on the family rivalry are in I#9 and I#11; Martha Stuart's pride in Jesse in *MW*, p. 10; his father's admiration of Everett Hilton in *TTTL*, p. 42; also see JS's tribute to Everett Hilton, "E.P." The attraction toward his schoolmates and his personal

desire to dress like them and look like them are in *TTTL*, p. 42; see further *BDH*, p. 48. In his unpublished MS "Walking into My Ninth Seven Year Plan," JS writes, "From fourteen to twenty-one my plan was to finish high school and write a book," and continues, "I fulfilled these two ambitions under great difficulties" (p. 1). During his freshman year he discussed with his principal and algebra teacher, Lena Wells Lykins (Voiers), his ambition of writing a book (*YMR*, p. 303). Having failed algebra at least once, he apparently retook the course and received an A.

[19]I#86; I#11; I#14. Also JS, "My Heart Told Me This Was the Place," *Household*, vol. 47 (March 1947), 9, 55; and, most recently, a vivid rendering of his memories of the ridge path in *TKW*, pp. 48–62.

[20]All grades of JS mentioned in this chapter are from his record on file at the Greenup County Board of Education, Office of the Director of Pupil Personnel, US Highway 23, Greenup, Kentucky. The incident of Miss Lykins' going over the ridge path to talk JS into returning to high school is in *TTTL*, pp. 44–45; *YMR*, p. 301. Also Lena Wells Voiers, letter to *HER*, Oct. 10, 1978; I#112; JS, *BDH*, p. 49; and Sophia Stuart Keeney, I#65.

[21]JS, letter from Paris, France, to OS, June 1, 1938; I#80; *BDH*, p. 52; I#8; I#10; I#15.

[22]I#62. For more information on the Heaberlins see "JS's Characters . . . ," p. 32.

[23]*TTTL*, p. 45; *BDH*, pp. 50–52.

[24]*BDH*, pp. 50–54; *TTTL*, pp. 45–48. In *YMR*, p. 282, JS wrote that he missed an appointment to West Point because of being a Republican in a predominantly Democratic state.

[25]In the Camp Knox annual, *The Mess Kit* (Chicago: Military Training Camps Association of the United States), vol. II (1923), his name appears as "Stewart, Jesse" of "Riverton, Kentucky" (p. 74); the group picture is on p. 72; for activities of the personnel see "Daily Impressions," by Dall, pp. 75–76. The minimum-age rule is published on p. 12. JS would not have been seventeen until August 8, 1923, which suggests that he probably either "stretched" his age, or the officials overlooked the thirteen days he lacked being seventeen. The picture of JS at his first CMTC in 1923 is from the family collection.

[26]*TTTL*, pp. 46–49; *BDH*, pp. 52–54.

[27]*BDH*, p. 54; *TTTL*, pp. 48–49. I#7; I#86; I#80; I#70.

[28]*BDH*, pp. 54–55, and *TTTL*, pp. 48–50, treat the corn-cutting episodes; for the hunting of opossums and skunks (for the latter he received from one to seven dollars for each hide) see *BDH*, pp. 55–57; *TTTL*, pp. 50–51. NDNS, "How I Met My Husband," as told to Jan Weyl, *Ladies' Home Journal* (March 1950), p. 70, indicates that the boy had hunted skunks during his freshman year also, when he then wore kneepants or knickers.

[29]I#111. JS, letter to Virginia Monroe Tippett, April 24, 1967. Although JS wrote that he was "only twenty," and "I was a boy too of 15, 16, and seventeen when you left Greenup," the then Miss Monroe, born Nov. 19, 1901, was twenty-one and twenty-two during her year at Greenup; and JS was actually seventeen during that academic year, although his published writings, following a 1907 date of birth, make him sixteen. The letter is a characteristic illustration of the author's generally adhering to fact while refusing to be tied altogether to it. Mrs. Tippett wrote of her memories of her year at Greenup High School and JS in "My First Teaching Position," *Second Spring* (Lexington, KY: Council on Aging, 1977), pp. 7–8. All JS's grades are listed in his school record, on file at the Greenup County Board of Education, Office of the Director of Pupil Personnel, Greenup, KY. *TTTL*, p. 43.

[30]I#111; also see Tippett, "My First Teaching Position," pp. 7–8. I#61. Also see the yearbook *Echoes from R. C.* (1905), from Mr. R. E. Hatton's library.

[31]I#61; also Mr. Hatton's letter to HER, Frankfort, KY, November 24, 1978. He remembers, "Greenup had an old academic heritage," a fact that did not go unnoticed by JS. Mrs. Hatton followed her husband in teaching at Greenup High School. Apparently, Dr. Hatton later "left Greenup in 1926 to teach in Philadelphia at a business college"; then, "in 1928 or 1929 Dad and Mother went to Wurtland [KY] to teach." Dr. Hatton had a stroke in March 1930, after which his son returned from Yale Law School "to help care for him and to take his place at Wurtland." Mrs. Hatton continued teaching through the 1929/1930 school year in Wurtland and died suddenly in September 1930. Dr. Hatton, after six years as a stroke patient, died in July 1936. Both are buried in the Catlettsburg, KY, Cemetery.

[32]*TTTL*, pp. 52–55; *BDH*, pp. 57–58.

[33]*TTTL*, p. 53; *BDH*, pp. 57–58; *TTTL*, p. 55. "Nest Egg" was first published in *Atlantic Monthly*, vol. 173 (Feb. 1944), 85–89, repr. in *TPGH*, pp. 164–172, and *BLSSJS*, pp. 10–19. Also see "I wish I had written the 'Cotter's Saturday Night' by Robert Burns," in E. J. Woods, *I wish I'd written that . . .* (New York: Whittlesey, 1946), p. 293.

[34]*YMR*, pp. 228, 318. Mrs. Bud Adams also commented on JS's study habits, "sometimes till four o'clock in the morning," in *ROJS*, p. 129.

[35]I#2; *BDH*, pp. 59, 228.

[36]I#80.

[37]I#80.

[38]I#80, I#61.

[39]I#82; I#7. Robert E. Hatton, letter to HER, Nov. 24, 1978. Regarding Luke 17:21, the commentary of the Reverend C. I. Scofield, DD, editor of the Scofield Reference Bible (New York and London: Oxford University Press, 1945), p. 1100, reads, "The kingdom in its outward form, as covenanted to David . . . and described by the prophets . . . had been rejected by the Jews; so that, during this present age, it would not 'come with observation' (lit. 'outward show') but in the hearts of men. . . . Meantime, the kingdom was actually 'in the midst' of the Pharisees in the persons of the King and His disciples. Ultimately the kingdom of heaven *will* come, with 'outward show' (as the following verse Luke 17:24 indicates)." John W. Howell, DD, I#64A, indicated that "the basic meaning is applicable to every person who has the faith, self-insight, and perception to appropriate it." Indeed the truth of such a stanza may involve a synthesis; or, in Dr. Howell's words, "The truth may be an assimilator of many sides, nor can the whole truth always come through highly reasoned translation. One should not gainsay an intuitive awareness of the presence of God, nor can the statement be defined or interpreted in a totally complete or absolute sense." Even the original Greek word *entos*, while often translated "in the midst," may also be translated "within you," as the King James Version renders it. JS's *TKW*, in which the hero, Shan, like JS, has suffered six heart attacks, was pub. in 1979. Although the "Kingdom Within" idea recurs through the book, JS partially explains the title as a living force within him in the reference to the Plum Grove Church, which has a spire and cross on the front: "There it was, the cross, a symbol, his symbol. He never wore a cross in his life. He didn't have to wear one for a symbol. His was implanted within him. His was invisible. The Kingdom was within him. A cross didn't have to be worn to show who he was. His Kingdom Within him had decided everything he had done" (p. 113).

[40]See note 18, above. JS, "Notes," p. 69 (*HOY* poems "written between the ages of 15

and 22"). Based on the 1907 birthdate, this would mean the poems were written from 1922 to 1929, evidence indicating he had begun writing poetry as early as his freshman year, one year prior to his sophomore instruction under Miss Monroe, 1923/1924, when he was certainly writing poetry, consistent with his inscription on a copy of *HOY* inscribed to Mrs. Virginia Monroe Tippett. Similarly, *ROJS*, p. 174, notes two of his stories, later published as "Victory and the Dream" (*Boy's Life*, vol. 57, no. 2 [Feb. 1967], 18–24, 41–43; repr. in *CBF*, pp. 55–57) and "A Ribbon for Baldy" (*Coronet*, vol. 40 [Sept. 1956], 140–152; repr. in *JSR*, Signet ed. [Nov. 1966], pp. 151–154) were written, quoting JS, "one time in high school." Also see *JSR*, pp. 151–152, in which JS terms the piece a "factual article, which became a story," given its title by NDNS. Originally the piece was written for his general science teacher in high school, Dr. Robert Hatton (*TTTL*, p. 55), although Hatton could hardly have taught the class until January 1924, after his official duties commenced. JS expresses his fondness for the Hattons in *TTTL*, p. 52. The source of his response to "The kingdom . . . is within you" is I#11.

⁴¹*BDH*, pp. 57–58; *TTTL*, pp. 51–55. "Victory and the Dream," cited in note 40, above. *BDH*, p. 52. *ROJS*, p. 174.

⁴²"Victory and the Dream," pp. 55–57, 66; cf. *GO*, p. 246; *BDH*, pp. 58–59.

⁴³The memory of the Burns lyric poem is treated in JS, "Straths in the Green Valley Below," *American Forests*, vol. 74, no. 8 (Aug. 1978), 12–15, 52–54; the relation of Scotland to the Ohio River Valley is on p. 12. The quotation is from Ralph Waldo Emerson's "Nature," in *Masters of American Literature*, eds. Leon Edel et al., vol. 1 (Boston: Houghton Mifflin, 1959), pp. 293–294. I#4. Dick Perry in *ROJS*, p. 180, inquired of Mrs. Hatton's influence, "But suppose you didn't have a teacher like that?" to which JS responded, "I would have gone on writing anyway." The earthy motivation for writing specified as the "loneliness of sounds" is in *BDH*, p. 57.

⁴⁴*BDH*, pp. 61–62.

CHAPTER 3

¹I#16; *BDH*, p. 63; *TTTL*, p. 59. I#48. Although Mr. Collins remembers several "scraps," he cannot recall this specific incident. William Collins, letter to HER from Muncie, IN, May 18, 1981, adds, "This does not mean it didn't happen." In I#48, he further commented, "It's not like Jesse to hatch up something like that and tell it. He must remember that pretty well." *BDH*, pp. 63–64; *TTTL*, p. 59. Whereas JS recalls an EK train up to Carter County, Mr. Collins thinks they walked most of the way and hitchhiked part of the way. I#80; I#81; I#82. I#50; I#17. NDNS, "How I Met My Husband," as told to Jan Weyl, *Ladies' Home Journal*, March 1950, p. 70. For JS's nickname, "Poppie," see I#18. I#48. I#62. *BDH*, p. 69.

²*BDH*, pp. 67–78; *TTTL*, p. 62; *TTRST*, pp. 1–62. I#86. I#17.

³JS, Greenup High School Record, 1922–1926, Greenup County Board of Education, Office of the Director of Pupil Personnel, Greenup, KY. *BDH*, p. 69; I#17; I#7; *BDH*, pp. 101–107 (Maria Sheen). I#86. I#50. For further possible imaginary significances of Maria Sheen, see Ch. 8. I#70. JS, letter to AD, Nov. 17, 1936, wrote of his love for a Catholic girl in high school. "She told me about the religion," he wrote, and "I thought it was very beautiful as I still do." I#79; I#80. I#17 (Rose Bergmeier and her father). I#60A. I#62; I#63. *The Old Fashion Days Gazette*, Greenup, KY, Oct. 1972, p. 7 (Callihan's Restaurant). Photo Album of JS, W-Hollow, Greenup, KY. I#80, I#81; I#82. I#9 (Rose Bergmeier as model for JoAnne Burton). I#17 (Edith Greene). JS's "The Slipover Sweater"

was orig. pub. in *Woman's Home Companion*, vol. 76 (Jan. 1949), 25, 52, 54; collected in *CIS*, pp. 76–90, and most recently in *BLSSJS*, pp. 148–158. I#48 (Mr. and Mrs. Collins were members of the Greenup High School Class of 1927, and she knew Rose Bergmeier well during their high school days).

⁴*BDH*, pp. 69–70; *TTTL*, pp. 63–64. Regarding the "self-assertion" vs. "submission" conflict, I wish to credit both Herbert Read, "The Creative Experience in Poetry," from *The Forms of Things Unknown* (London: Faber and Faber, 1960), pp. 130–131, and Maud Bodkin, *Archetypal Patterns in Poetry* (London: Oxford University Press, 1965), pp. 22–25. *BDH*, p. 7; *TTTL*, pp. 64–65. "Cole's Field" was the real name of the old carnival grounds in Greenup. I#17. *BDH*, pp. 107–112; *TTTL*, pp. 63–65. I#93. *BDH*, pp. 118–120 (poetry excerpts).

I#18 (Jack Dysard as model for Sparkie). I#62. *The Mess Kit* (Chicago: Military Training Camps Association of the United States), vol. V (1926), pp. 36, 38; EH is listed on the roster of Company K, 11th Infantry, p. 67, and appears to be in the top left-hand portion of the photo, next-to-last row, the youth with prominent ears under a big hat (p. 66). I#17. Photo Album of JS, W-Hollow, Greenup, KY; *BDH*, pp. 120–133 *passim;* *YMR*, p. 282.

⁵I#62; I#63. *BDH*, Ch. 6, pp. 134–170. "Stuart, Jesse. American Rolling Mill Co. Employment Record," Ashland, KY. His name is spelled "Stewart" in 1926, "Stuart" in 1927; his height is "5 Ft. 11 In.," his weight "145 lbs." in 1926, "152 lbs." in 1927.

I#18; *BDH*, "over-21" story, p. 135; other anecdotes, pp. 144–154 *passim*. In I#8, Jesse Stuart identified Floyd Berry as the prototype of both John Findlay and Ruddy Flannery. Also I#7; *BDH*, "weedmonkeyin' " episode (pp. 162–164); fight (pp. 158–159); JS's poetry (pp. 160–161). I#62; I#63. I#89. *BDH*, talks with his mother (p. 58); his departure to college (p. 170).

⁶*BDH*, pp. 171–177 *passim;* appearance of a fierce Indian, pp. 150, 139, "a reddish-brown, the color of burnt bacon . . . a fire tan." I#3. Old KY Highway 388 is now KY Highway 627; old US Highway 227 is now KY 388. JS, Transcript, Lincoln Memorial Univ., lists his date of matriculation as Sept. 20, 1926. Also see Earl Hobson Smith, "Student and Friend," p. xx. I#76. The girl in the registration line was Lucille Jordan (Palmer) (See Ch. 4). JS, "Place" [32] states that he had $29.30, although this source does not clarify the amount he paid on his tuition—probably as little as $10.00, for he specifies $10.00 as all he could pay on his first quarter of college work at LMU in both *BDH*, p. 176, and *TTTL*, p. 73.

CHAPTER 4

¹*BDH*, pp. 177–221; *TTTL*, pp. 71–134 *passim*. I#4. For his LMU work experience see *BDH*, pp. 177, 181, and "Place," 32. The work "gang" of the summer of 1926 is depicted in *The Mountain Herald*, vol. XXIX, no. viii (Oct. 1926), 14–15; pictures of the stone quarry are in vol. XXX, no. v (July/Aug. 1927), 3. I#85 (Earl Hobson Smith).

JS in I#21 recalled that Professor Trosper, who lived nearby and did not share Mrs. Grannis' penchant for dogs, gave him a loaded pistol and told him, "Go over there and shoot the s.o.b. I'll stand behind you." But Mrs. Trosper's good sense intervened. Jesse took "special care" of her flowers. "She used to give me a dollar every time she could because she knew I needed it and I did. That's where I got my spending dollar."

"JS is Editor-in-chief" was announced in *The Mountain Herald*, vol. XXXI, no. v (Autumn 1928), 28. *TTTL*, p. 120 (Smith as JS's speech teacher). Also see Smith's "Student and Friend," p. xx.

²I#76. Also I#26. JS, Transcript, LMU. I#71.

[3]"To Muddy Waters," *BDH*, pp. 205–206; *TTTL*, p. 110; the poem was pub. in *HOY*, p. 54; as Sonnet 223 in *MWBTP*, p. 116; and in the 1959 reprinted ed. as Sonnet 202, p. 108. Woodbridge, *JSB*, lists it under *MWBTP*, p. 10; *HOY*, p. 4; and *BDH*, p. 22, but gives no earlier pub. Nor does the sonnet appear among the 42 JS poems pub. during 1927 through 1929, including 13 titles not listed in *JSB*, although the record of these publications is by no means complete. See "Addendum," pp. 79–82. For further information on Kathryn Howard Wells, see *TTTL*, pp. 110–113. See also *BDH*, p. 206. "Place," 32–33 (Kroll's advice on writing; JS's quest for the editorship). In I#19, JS identified his editorial predecessors as Mabel Adams West and Edith Jones Schoocraft.

For the three poems see *The Blue and Gray*, vol. XI, no. i (Oct. 15, 1927), last p. of 4-p. fragment in the Winnie Palmer McDonald Collection, possibly p. 6 and final p. of the issue. "Addendum," p. 79. I#76 (Kroll's advice, "Crank 'em out . . . ."). JS, "Foreword" to *Tim* [unnumb.] (Kroll's thirty thousand-word assignment). I#62: "It was nothing to write thirty thousand or forty thousand words a quarter" in Professor Kroll's English class; further, Kroll encouraged Jesse "to write about home . . . the steel mills . . . things like that." In *Lyrics from Lincoln Memorial University,* pub. under the direction of Harry Harrison Kroll (no place or publisher given); JS's photograph, a biographical note, and four poems, "Morning (Bugle Call)," "Tennessee Roads," "Six Hickories," and "Things I Have Loved," appear on pp. 10–15. "Foreword," *Lyrics . . . ,* p. 3; see p. 30 for picture of journalism class. Kroll, "Stuart the Student as I Remember," *JSB* (1960 ed.), pp. xviii–xix. See "River Railroad Man," *The Blue and Gray*, vol. XII, no. xiii (May 28, 1928), 6, noted in "Addendum," p. 81.

[4]For titles and other facts of publication, see "Addendum." JS, "Foreword," *HCLS*, pp. 7–15. Despite the poet's hostility toward his first book, *HOY* survived and was reprinted in 1964. As with most first books of writers who later become important, some parts are amateurish, but others anticipate the writer to come; hence, it records an essential part of the man-artist's development (see Ch. 5). "Place," 33 (poet's mood of excitement at Harrogate).

[5]Jesse Stuart's copy of *The Railsplitter* (1929) [pp. 91, 60]. For Edith Gertrude Jones (Mrs. J. Elmer Schoocraft), see the 1929 *Railsplitter*, p. 40; for the Student Volunteer Band, see the 1928 *Railsplitter*, p. 70 (JS listed as secretary), and note Don West and Mabel Adams' photos in a row below Stuart's (they became Mr. and Mrs. Don West). *BDH*, p. 179 (field of daisies). Lawrence Edwards, "Jesse Stuart at Lincoln . . . ," *JSB* (1960 ed.), p. xvi. I#62. *TTTL*, p. 78.

[6]I#76. JS, "My Teachers at L.M.U.," p. 35. *BDH*, pp. 214–216. I#19 (factual fight); I#26 (bullied girls' gratitude); JS recalls the matron as Mrs. N. C. Rose, but Lucille Jordan Palmer recalls Mrs. B. B. Huntzinger (I#76). Kroll, "Stuart the Student," p. xviii; letter to JS, Dec. 7, 1959. I#19; *BDH*, p. 215.

[7]Edwards, "JS at LMU . . . ," p. xvi. I#19; "How Sportsmanship Came to Carver College," *Esquire*, vol. 26 (Dec. 1946), 111, 321–326; reprinted in *PIH*, pp. 127–137; "My Teachers at L.M.U."; also *TTTL*, pp. 102–109. I#21.

[8]*TTTL*, pp. 77–83, 113–119, 120–126. *BDH*, pp. 218, 221; *YMR*, p. 262; "Place," p. 33. Also see Kroll, "Stuart the Student . . ." (in *JSB*), pp. xviii–xix. I#62. Harry Harrison Kroll, *The Mountain Singer* (New York: William Morrow, 1928); quotations are from pp. 100, 206, and 214.

TTTL, p. 117 (Kroll's book at LMU). I#21. Kroll, letter to JS, Jan. 1, 1953, in Leavell, "LCJS," who says that Kroll denied that *The Mountain Singer*, as JS wrote, was the cause of his discharge; rather, the " 'housecleaning' was the backwash of the president's [John Wesley Hill's] frustrations and failures," noted in fn. 3, p. 48. *TTTL*, pp. 78–79 (two feuding teachers), p. 118 (power of creative writing).

[9]I#17. I#84. I#64B. Barnie (also Barney) Greene of Sneedville was JS's most consistent campus sweetheart during 1927 and 1928. Mrs. Ernest O. Hutchens corroborates their courtship of these years, although she pointed out that both "Stuart and I dated others, too." I#84. I#64B. JS, "Autobiographical . . ." "Mountain Funeral" originally had two more stanzas (see *HOY*, pp. 22–23), but the poet J wisely excised them, intensifying the simplicity and artistic purity of the lyric. Woodbridge, *JSB*, lists seven publications of the poem, including *KML*, p. 28, and *New York Times Book Review*, Oct. 19, 1952, p. 2. I#64B.

[10]*BDH*, pp. 179–180. I#76. *TTTL*, pp. 80–81. Ida Shifley's photo is in the 1927 *Railsplitter*, p. 25. I#17. I#71. Paul B. Dykes is listed under "Staff," p. 8, as Editor-in-Chief of the 1929 *Railsplitter;* his senior picture and biographical note are on p. 35. I#62. I#76. *The Blue and Gray*, vol. XII, no. xiii (May 28, 1929), 4, col. 3. I#76. For a photograph of Jesse with the twinkling eyes and expression of comic anticipation, see the front page of the May 29, 1969, ed. of the LMU *Blue and Gray*. I#71. Smith, "Student and Friend," p. xxi. *BDH*, p. 219. The sonnet was pub. as "To Edith" in *HOY*, p. 49; in *MWBTP* as Sonnet 236 under the title "B. G.," p. 122. The Beta Kappa banquet story is in *The Blue and Gray*, vol. XII, no. xiii (May 28, 1929), 8, col. 1, under "Jesse Stuart Wins Honors"; the faculty vote on honorific student categories, p. 2; Jesse's specialties are listed: "Kentucky, poetry, short story, one act play, editorials, special articles, essays and criticisms"; his farewell editorial, "Finish," is on p. 4, cols. 3–4. I#76; the sonnet "Margaret," *HOY*, p. 52, was inspired by Margaret Brooks of Birmingham, Alabama. JS, letter to STILL, Sept. 20 [1929]. JS also dated Nellie Gray from near Chattanooga, TN, and Audrey Ausmus of LaFollette, TN. I#25. I#71. The multi-faceted description of Battle Keaton's beard is in "Battle Keaton Dies," *Story*, vol. VII, no. xxxvi (July 1935), 57–72; repr. *HOWH* (1979), pp. 150–192. I#64B. I#71. I#84. *The Blue and Gray*, vol. XII, no. xiii (May 28, 1929), 8; cf. the closely parallel incident in *TTTL*, pp. 124–125, in which the class, on a technicality, voted Jesse out of the second-place award. The track photo is in the 1929 *Railsplitter*, p. 102. *BDH*, p. 178. *The Mountain Herald*, vol. XXXI, no. vi (Winter 1929), 18 (Women's Club piece). JS's invitation to commencement, June 4, 1929, is in the JS Collection University of Louisville, file drawer IV, 4, folder labeled "Very Important Varied Letters"; his transcript lists the date of conferring his BA degree. "L. M. U. Walkways," *Railsplitter* (1929), p. 14. Maxwell Anderson and Laurence Stallings' popular *What Price Glory?* had been produced in 1924, pub. in 1926. JS's senior picture and biographical note are in the *Railsplitter*, p. 39; Still is listed as "Senior Editor" on an introductory p. under STAFF.

[11]"My Teachers at L.M.U."; *BDH*, pp. 177–178; with Willis, pp. 215–216; the challenge of the student critic in "Place" [p. 34]. I#17. I#62. *TTTL*, bad canned beef, pp. 99–102; Woodward, pp. 82–83; Kroll and Smith, p. 134. *BDH*, pp. 217–218; the West incident, p. 217; in *TTTL*, p. 131, the author calls Don West "Ron East." For the voting incident, see *TTTL*, pp. 128–130. See Ch. 3 for more information on JS's work at ARMCO, esp. June 2–Sept. 10, 1927. In *YMR*, p. 162, $300 saved. The barrel incident is in I#18. Cf. "32 Votes Before Breakfast," *Esquire*, vol. 28 (July 1947), 83, 180, 185–190; reprinted in *CIS*, pp. 91–104; *32V*, pp. 314–347.

CHAPTER 5

[1]*TTRST*, p. 67; his arrival home after hitchhiking from LMU on a "Sunday in August" (p. 65), assuming he had received his degree on the date of its official conferring, would of necessity have been on Sun., Aug. 25, the last Sun. in Aug. 1929. "Sin," *American Poet*, 1 (Jan. 1929), 5; repr. in W. S. Braithwaite, *Anthology of Magazine Verse for 1929* (New York: Sully, 1929), p. 351, and in *HOY*, p. 65. "Desire," *American Poet*, 1 (April 1929), 11. "Hurt Not the Proud," orig. pub. in "Quatrains," *The Blue and Gray*, vol. XII, no. viii (March

12, 1929), 3; repr. in *American Poet*, 1, (April 1929), 13, and in *Hoy*, p. 65. "Like a Strong Tree," *American Poet*, 2 (June 1929) [unnumb. p.]. "Mountain Farmer," *Bristol Herald-Courier*, July 14, 1929, sec. 2, p. 4. "My Mountain Home," *Sonnet Sequences*, II (Sept. 1929), 74; repr. in *HOY*, p. 50. JS, letter to STILL, Sept. 20, 1929. *BDH* (p. 399): "I walked in the wind" is JS's favorite metaphor for expressing joy. For three versions of his return trip to Greenup from LMU, see *TTRST*, pp. 65–67, *BDH*, pp. 220–221, and *TTTL*, p. 134. In *TTRST*, p. 66, the door of the church in which he spent the night is unlocked; in *BDH*, the door is locked, p. 220 (1972 ed., p. 177). As tradition has it, the genesis of LMU is traceable to a meeting between Lincoln and General Otis Howard, noted in Mildred Shumate, *A Brief History of Lincoln Memorial University* (booklet) (Cumberland Gap, Harrogate, TN: Lincoln Memorial University Press, 1972), p. 1. *TTRST*, p. 66; *TTTL*, pp. 65–67; *BDH*, pp. 220–221. Of his grades at LMU, JS wrote in *BDH* "something like a B average," which "I never stopped to count . . . up," p. 220; in *TTRST* he wrote, "I had made better than a B average," p. 67; in *TTTL* he wrote, "I had made something like a B average," p. 133; in "Place," "I finished college . . . with a 2.2 out of a possible three, for I was in a hurry." His transcript indicates that, if an A for the school paper credit voted by the faculty is assigned a grade-point value, he achieved a 2.5 grade-point standing in English, and approximately a 1.73 overall. Unpub. MS "The Word and the Flesh, by Jesse Stuart," JS Collection, W-Hollow, Greenup, KY. "Word and the Flesh" was orig. pub. in *HOWH*, pp. 129–149, most recently reprinted in *BLSSJS*, pp. 247–264 (Ceredo-Kenova experience). *BDH*, pp. 187–202; his return, spring 1927, pp. 206–214. I#18. *BDH*, Brother Tobbie, pp. 206–207.

²I#48. *BDH*, pp. 222–224. I#12 (Bealer/Wheeler). *BDH*, pp. 225–227 (ridge path, reflections). I#4 (religious doubt). Decision to teach: *BDH*, pp. 227–228; *TTRST*, pp. 66–67; *TTTL*, p. 138.

³Part II, *TTRST*, pp. 65–104. For JS's conflict with Robert J. Nickel, see Ch. 8. JS's unpublished MS, *Cradle of the Copperheads*, later abbreviated *COC*, details the 1932/1933 year of conflict with Robert J. Nickel and others (see Ch. 9). *TTTL*, pp. 138–139; *TTRST*, pp. 68–69. JS contends that most of *TTRST* is factual; see his article, "Jesse Stuart's Characters . . . ," pp. 30–34; Warnock sources esp., pp. 30–32. I#89: Betty and JAS. do not recall such a vehicle precisely as the author describes it in *TTRST*, pp. 69–70; but JAS. does recollect an "R. E. Olds" truck, which could have been called a "Reo Speed Wagon," that belonged to Burt Kenner, a grocer in Greenup. Betty Stuart recalls a truck used for the mail line, which took mail, passengers, chickens, eggs, and groceries in and out of Greenup from Warnock. Mr. Ron Bradford, as she recalls, carried the mail then on horseback. Cf. the author's description in *TTRST* of the mail carried on horseback by Wid Mattox from the "autumn rains" to "next May or June, depending on the condition of the roads" (p. 80). JS, "The Value of Well Kept Yards," *Home Circle*, vol. 20 (April 1930), 2. *TTRST*, p. 104; *YMR*, first sale, p. 162. For the Taylors/Baylors in Warnock, see *TTRST*, pp. 70–71. For a 1977 picture of this home and the author's comments on it, see JS, "There Shall Not Be," p. 228. I#89. *TTRST*, pp. 78–80. JS, letters to STILL, Sept. 20 and Oct. 27, 1929. *TTRST*, pp. 83–90, the winter survival scene. I#1; I#24. I#60A. I#89. "Greenup Hi School News," *The Republican*, Greenup Co., Fri., April 11, 1930, clipping in *GSLSB* [p. 32]. *TTRST*, pp. 97–101, the contest. JS, letters to STILL, Oct. 7 and 28, 192[9]; the sonnet referred to is "My Mountain Home," *Sonnet Sequences*, II (Sept. 1929), 74; repr. in *HOY*, p. 50, and in *MWBTP* as Sonnet 232, p. 120. "Boon," *International Poetry Magazine*, vol. 7 (Oct. 1929), p. 27; "Mountain Funeral," p. 24 (Ch. 4, note 9). "North-East Kentucky," *Kentucky Folklore and Poetry Magazine*, vol. 4 (Oct. 1929), 14–15. "Sleep Spell," *The Poet's Scroll* (Nov. 1929), p. 235; repr. in *HOY*, p. 69. Two other poems by Jesse to appear in *Sonnet Sequences* that year were "To Louise: a Lover of Earth," vol. 2 (Nov. 1929), p. 137, repr. as "Louise" in *HOY*, p. 57; and "Sleep," vol. 2 (Dec. 1929), p. 163, repr. in *HOY*, p. 24. "I Have a Path" appeared in W. S. Braithwaite's *Anthology of Magazine*

Verse for 1929 (New York: Sully, 1929), p. 351; repr. in *SJS*, p. 129. JS, letter to STILL, Oct. 28, 192[9]. This letter is dated "1927," but internal evidence clearly shows this to be a typo, which should read "1929." JS, "There Shall Not Be," p. 227. I#89. "Heaven Enough," *The Spring Anthology* (London: Mitre Press, 1930), p. 433; repr. in *HOY*, p. 54. JS, letter to STILL, Oct. 7, 1929 (social dating). "Foreknown," *Montclair* (NJ) *Times*, June 18, 1930, p. 9; repr. in *HOY*, p. 63. "The Higher Type of Mountain Ballad," *The Kentucky Folk-Lore and Poetry Magazine*, V (Winter 1930), 3–7.

⁴*TTRST*, p. 109 (Peabody); *HCLS*, pp. 7–24 (pub. of *Hoy*. In all likelihood, Hartsock's little book was *Narcissus and Iscariot* (Atlanta: Bozart Press, 1927), 79 pp. (Cf. form, wording of "ACKNOWLEDGMENT" and "CONTENTS" to those of *HOY*). I#13; I#23; I#24 (*HOY*); letters to STILL, Jan. 6, 1930, and Sept. 20, 1929. I#13. Fourth sec. *HOY* [pp. 61–80]; "Tennessee Farmer," p. 75; "Fug[i]tive," p. 78. Stephen Vincent Benét, "The Ballad of William Sycamore (1790–1871)," in *The Stephen Vincent Benét Pocket Book*, ed. Robert Van Gelder (New York: Pocket Books, 1946), pp. 386–388. JS, "My First True Love," *HOY*, pp. 66–67; "My Peoples' [sic] Prayers," p. 69; "Carver Life," pp. 70–71; "Harvest of Youth," p. 63 (lead poem, sec. four).

First sec. *HOY* [pp. 11–24]. Re the influence of Henley's "Invictus," also see Foster, *JS*, p. 53; Blair, *JS:LW*, p. 670; and Hargis Westerfield's "Foreword" in *HOY* (1964 ed.) [p. vii]. Lee Pennington, in "Jesse Stuart: His Symbolism and Vision" (M.A. thesis, State University of Iowa, Iowa City, Iowa [July 1965], p. 2), wrote "Out of the Night" is "appropriately and symbolically" apt, for death is the dominant theme throughout the section. However, though the young JS recognized and repeatedly faced up to death, he was even more interested in "what comes out of death," what comes out of that darkness that is of human significance. *BDH*, pp. 228ff; "What There Is to an Old House," *HOY*, pp. 14–16; "Free God," pp. 16–20. That JS was influenced by Emerson in his reading of the Concordian's essays and poems is clear in I#4: "He walked beside me. He lived with me. He walked up that ridge with me . . . a great influence." JS, "Epitaphs," *HOY*, pp. 20–21, including "For Elmer Heaberlin." I#62. "Consider the Poet," *HOY*, p. 22; "Poet," p. 20; *TKW*, esp. p. 119; "Mountain Funeral," pp. 22–23 (Ch. 4, note 9); "I Know the Gypsy Wind Too Well," p. 21; "Last Lover," p. 21; and "The Winner," p. 24.

⁵Second sec. *HOY* [pp. 25–44]. JS, "Sandburg, My Hero," *Lincoln Herald*, Sandburg Memorial Issue, vol. 70, no. 1 (Spring 1968), 40–43, abbreviated hereafter "Sandburg." Sandburg, "Cool Tombs," in George McMichael et al., eds., *Anthology of American Literature*, vol. II (New York: Macmillan, 1974), p. 1114. Echoes of Sandburg can be heard in JS, "Does Abraham Lincoln Remember?" *Mountain Herald*, vol. XXXI, no. vi (Winter 1929), 30. Also see *BDH*, pp. 141–142. In addition to the 1922 *Collected Poems*, the works of Sandburg JS may have read in the 1920s include *Chicago Poems* (1916), *Cornhuskers* (1918), *Smoke and Steel* (1920), and *Slabs from the Sunburnt West* (1922). JS, "Sandburg," pp. 40–41. For the line from "Grass," "Shovel them under and let me work—," see George McMichael, *Anthology of American Literature*, pp. 1114–1115. JS, "River Railroad Man," *HOY*, p. 27, orig. pub. in *The Blue and Gray*, vol. XII, no. xiii (May 28, 1929), 6; "Fantasy in Black," pp. 27–28. "Six Hickories," *The Blue and Gray*, vol. XI, no. ii (Oct. 29, 1927), unnumb. frag., repr. in *Lyrics from Lincoln Memorial University*, pp. 13–14. "Steel Gang," *HOY*, pp. 38–40, is a reworking of "Six Hickories"; "My City," pp. 40–44.

JS, "Silhouettes," *HOY*, p. 32; for JS's study of Pound and the Imagists, see his "What Vanderbilt," p. 18. At this early time, he may have had occasion to read such collections as Amy Lowell's *Tendencies in American Poetry* (New York: Houghton Mifflin, 1921), which includes the work of such poets as Robinson, Frost, Masters, Sandburg, H. D., and John Gould Fletcher. Foster, *JS*, p. 54 (imitating the Imagists); also see Foster's helpful introductory analysis of *HOY*, pp. 52–55. JS, "Undulated Season," *HOY*, pp. 28–31; *BDH*, pp. 261–262. One may observe an e. e. cummings influence in "Undulated Season," esp. the seventh stanza, p. 30, which includes a lowercase i. Cf. the interpretation of Lee Pennington in his thesis (see note 4, above), pp. 10–11. JS, "Vagabond Houses," *HOY*, pp. 32–33; "Black April," pp. 33–37. For a discussion of "Dark Winter," see Ch. 1. Sylvia Salem Gibbs' M.A. thesis, "The World of W-Hollow: Jesse Stuart's Cyclic Vision," University of Louisville, Louisville, KY (June 1970), pp. 31–35. JS, "Up the Branch," *This Is the South*, ed. Robert West Howard (Chicago: Rand McNally, 1959), p. 221; motivating forces behind settlement of pioneers; their being a "Last Original Type" in the mountains (pp. 221–228).

⁶Third sec. *HOY*, pp. 45–60. Hargis Westerfield, "Foreword," *HOY*, [p. ix], states that he found five *HOY* sonnets in *MWBTP;* Foster, *JS*, p. 54, note 10, and pp. 156–157, also notes the same five sonnets. Both apparently overlooked "Silent Earth," which emerged as Sonnet 240 in *MWBTP*. "Harvard or the Sea," *HOY*, p. 57; repr. in *BDH*, and discussed in Ch. 3; letter to STILL, Sept. 20, 1929; "Loneliness," *HOY*, p. 47, orig. pub. in *The Blue and Gray*, vol. 12, no. 13 (May 28, 1929), 6. I#64B. JS, letter to STILL, Sept. 20, 1929 (his visit to Margaret Brooks' home in Birmingham): "Margaret," *HOY*, p. 52; "My Loves Will Remain When I Have Passed," p. 47; "August Night," p. 48; "Clean Fingers Sloped in Farewell," p. 50; "To a Georgian Lass," p. 51 (re Elsie West, see Ch. 4). Also I#13 (Don West's sister). "Returned," *HOY*, p. 52; letter from Nashville to NDN, Aug. 4, 1931 (discusses Warnock). I#89 (radio & Delco battery); I#86. Charles K. Wolfe, *The Grand Ole Opry: The Early Years, 1925–35* (London: Old Time Music, 1975), esp. sec. "The Hoe Down Bands," subsection, "Theron Hale & His Daughters," p. 93; see their picture on p. 18 with other members of the Opry cast. JS, *HCLS*, pp. 7–8. I#76 (her inscribed copy of *HOY*).

Chapter 6

¹*BDH*, pp. 290–291; orig. pub. in *The Gypsy*, vol. 7 (Dec. 1931), 11.

²JS, Official Transcript, George Peabody College for Teachers, Graduate Student Record, copy dated 2/22/79, Nashville, TN, hereafter called "Peabody Transcript." *TTRST*, p. 141; I#13; I#17; "What Vanderbilt," p. 18; "Foreword," *BDH*, 1972, ed., p. xii; "Notes," p. 69.

³Hensley Woodbridge, ed., "More on the Mohr Copy of *Harvest of Youth*," *Jack London Newsletter* (hereafter *JLN*), vol. 8, no. 2 (May/Aug. 1973), 91–92. JS, *HCLS*, pp. 20–21; I#13; *TTRST*, pp. 117–128, *passim*.

⁴*TTRST*, pp. 128–132. I#89. I#17. *TTRST*, pp. 110–11, 133–137; "JS's Characters," pp. 30–34; letter from Nashville to NDN, July 25, 1931.

⁵*TTRST*, pp. 141–142; "Foreword," *HCLS*, p. 8; Peabody Transcript; letters from Nashville, TN, to NDN, n.d., both postmarked July 15, 1931. I#89. JS, letter to DD, April 4, 1933 (first meeting with Elizabeth Hale); *COC*, pp. 394–397 (Grand Ole Opry). I#59; I#60. Elizabeth Hale, letter to HER, April 16, 1979. I#56; I#57. I#22.

⁶I#89. JS, "The Professor," 89; letters to NDN, n.d., postmarked July 25, 1:30 P.M., and Aug. 19, 1931; card postmarked Aug. 28, 1931. I#26. JS, "What Vanderbilt," p. 18; I#27; Peabody Transcript (other grades included Agriculture 3050—Problems, 2 hours, B; Greek Literature in Translation 405, 4 hours, C; English 442, History of Literature for Children, 2 hours, C; English 471, Modern Poetry, 2 hours, B).

⁷*BDH*, pp. 281–327, treat Ch. 9, "A Stranger Was Afraid" (see esp. p. 282); I#26; I#27. *BDH*, pp. 282–284 (Don West); JS's letter in "People—Poet-Novelists," in *Letters*, vol. 2, no. 26 (Dec. 23, 1935), 6. Rayford, pp. 5–6. JS, "Portrait of a Mountain Boy," *Cumberland Empire*, vol. 3 (July 1932), 35–38 (contains photo of West). CC, letter from Tifton, GA, to HER, postmarked June 25, 1980. JS's 1931 pubs. include "When all the splendors," *Sonnet Sequences*, vol. 3 (Jan 1931), 218; "A Dollar a Smoke," *Kentucky School*

Journal, vol. 9 (March 1931), 42; "The Yarb Doctor," *Kentucky Folklore and Poetry Magazine,* vol. 6 (March 1931), 4–10; "Requiem for a Playboy," *Echo* (Spring 1931), p. 1; "To Ernest Hartsock, 1903–1930," *Sonnet Sequences,* vol. 4 (Sept. 1931), 86; "Nig," *Echo* (Fall 1931), p. 1; "Savings Brains," *Kentucky School Journal,* vol. 9 (Nov. 1930), 25; and "Courage, Be with Us All," *The Gypsy,* vol. 7 (Dec. 1931), 11.

[8]Harry Harrison Kroll, *The Cabin in the Cotton* (New York: Ray Long and Richard R. Smith, 1931), 289 pp. *New York Times,* Nov. 15, 1931, p. 18; and Books, Nov. 15, 1931, noted in the *Book Review Digest* (1931), p. 596. Allen Tate, "A Mississippi Dreiser" (review), *The Nation,* vol. 133, no. 3465 (Dec. 2, 1931), 614–615. I#19; "Harry Kroll as I Knew Him," *The Peabody Reflector,* vol. XL, no. iv (July/Aug. 1967), 180. Rayford, p. 6. William R. Moses, letter to HER from Manhattan, KS, June 30, 1979. JS, "What Vanderbilt," p. 18; *BDH,* pp. 287–289, 312; I#23; *YMR,* pp. 301–304 (Voiers' visit in late summer or early fall, 1931).

[9]*BDH,* pp. 284–285, 311. CC, letter to HER, Feb. 5, 1980. JS, "Notes," p. 69. I#71. *BDH,* p. 314.

[10]*BDH,* pp. 290–310 *passim.* Even though JS writes that he caught a ride home on Jan. 4 and spent "Monday, January 5th . . . in Greenup" (p. 291), my calendar shows that the first Monday in 1932 was not Jan. 5, but Jan. 4. Assuming my calendar to be correct, it would appear that Jesse caught his ride home on Sunday, Jan. 3, arrived at and spent most of Mon., Jan. 4, in Greenup, and returned to Nashville Tues., Jan. 5, arriving there early Wed., Jan. 6. A simple explanation for JS's dating is that he may have relied on a 1931 rather than a 1932 calendar. JS calls the fiddler "Blind Hartley" in *BDH,* p. 93; "Blind Frailey" in *MWBTP,* pp. 67–69. Charles Wolfe, letter to HER, May 11, 1981, notes two fiddlers: "Ed Haley . . . and an old fiddler named Fraley . . . father of modern fiddler JP Fraley," in Ashland. JS, letter to DD, undated (ca. Oct. 3, 1932), describing a similar Monday "salesday"; "JS's Characters . . ." pp. 33–34 (possible allusion to Forrest and Lillie King and note at the bank).

<h2 style="text-align:center">CHAPTER 7</h2>

[1]*BDH,* pp. 311, 310. Jesse Hilton Stuart, Transcript, "Dept. of Graduate Instruction— Vanderbilt Univ.," hereafter "VU Transcript." Allen Tate's description of the youthful Warren is in Louise Cowan, *Fugitive Group,* pp. 106–107, note 24. Charles H. Bohner, *Robert Penn Warren* (New Haven: College & University Press, 1964), p. 13, gives Warren's age (b. Guthrie, KY, Apr. 24, 1905). Warren is approximately fifteen months JS's senior.

[2]DD, *Southern Writers in the Modern World* (Athens: Univ. of Georgia Press, 1958), p. 55 (background on Warren). I#114 (Jesse called Warren "Red" in their closer, "face-to-face" relationship). Don Kington, "Pulitzer Prize Winner Robert Penn Warren and His Fort Knox 'Nugget,' " *Louisville Courier-Journal* mag. sec. June 3, 1979, pp. 20–23 (Warren at Camp Knox).

[3]I#54. I#114.

[4]*TTTL* (JS's hunger at Vanderbilt), p. 152. *BDH,* pp. 311–313 (hunger in Warren's classroom). I#18.

[5]Rayford, pp. 5–6. Allen Tate, letter to DD, March 7, 1927, in Fain and Young, pp. 193–195; Appendix G, p. 431 (Hirsch, Fugitives). Also see *Fugitive Group,* on Hirsch, pp. xvii, xvi (Fugitive poets and their distinction from the Agrarians; Ransom, DD, Tate and Warren common to both groups); Tate's reaction to Hirsch, pp. 34–38; Hirsch's distinctive

middle name, p. 17. DD's memory of Hirsch is in his *Southern Writers in the Modern World,* p. 12.

⁶Rayford, "Jesse Stuart," pp. 5–7. JS, *BDH,* p. 323.

⁷*BDH,* p. 323. *Fugitive Group,* pp. 17–18 (Hirsch as a world traveler, acquaintance with celebrities).

⁸*BDH,* p. 310 (low grades), p. 313 (DD); "What Vanderbilt," pp. 17–18 (Davidsons). T. D. Young and M. Thomas Inge, *Donald Davidson* (New York: Twayne, 1971), p. 13; DD was born in Campbellsville, TN, Aug. 18, 1893, so he was in his thirty-eighth year when he taught JS; for information on Theresa Sherrer Davidson, see note 25, pp. 151–152. The information on DD's literary page is in *The Spyglass: Views and Reviews, 1924–1930, by Donald Davidson,* ed. John Tyree Fain (Nashville, Vanderbilt University Press, 1963), pp. xiii–xiv; photo of p. about the time JS began reading it, p. 239. JS, "Foreword," *BDH,* 1972 ed., pp. xi–xii (information on the Fugitives and Agrarians). I#13 (reading of DD's literary page "every Sunday" in *Knoxville Journal* while at LMU). DD, *The Tall Men* (Boston: Houghton Mifflin, 1927), pp. 4–17. For JS's "Tall Figures of the Earth," see *BDH,* pp. 13–25. It seems possible that the teacher's lead poem, celebrating the pioneers of Tennessee, gave incentive to JS's soon-to-be-written first chapter of *BDH,* "Tall Figures of the Earth," which treats his own pioneer ancestry and echoes DD's title and concluding line, "The bones of tall men lie in the Tennessee earth." Concerning DD's role as prime mover behind *I'll Take My Stand,* see Young and Inge, *Donald Davidson,* p. 132. I#27 (description of DD's eyes); *BDH,* p. 313, JS's conference with DD.

⁹*TTTL,* p. 154; *BDH,* p. 313 (DD's advice); "Foreword" *HCLS,* p. 10. CC, letters to HER, Feb. 5 and June 25, 1980. JS's poem appeared in *Sonnet Sequences,* vol. 4 (Sept. 1931), 36. Ernest Hartsock, "Roses in the Desert," *Sewanee Review,* vol 37 (July 1925), 33, noted in Young and Inge, *Donald Davidson,* p. 121, note on p. 160.

¹⁰I#26; I#27.

¹¹*TTTL,* p. 154 (DD's advice, the "natural poems"). DD, "The Vanderbilt Literary Tradition," *Vanderbilt Alumnus,* vol. 41, no. 4 (May/June 1956), 8.

¹²DD, letter to Lee Oly Ramey, "Inquiry," p. 59. *BDH,* pp. 314–315; I#7. Frank H. Leavell, "Jesse Stuart at Vanderbilt" (hereafter "JS at V"), in *JLN,* vol. 10, no. 2 (May/Aug. 1977), who credits his personal interview with DD, April 24, 1963, on pp. 88, 93.

¹³*HCLS,* p. 9. CC, letter to HER, June 25, 1980, suggests two conjectural prototypes, "both intellectuals in [DD's] Lyric Class," Walter Paschall of Atlanta, connected with the *Atlanta Journal* and a newsman on WSB radio, and Walter Sharpe of Nashville, who possessed musical ability and collected antiques. Both are now deceased. Will Moses and Randall Jarrell were also among the best students in the English Department with whom JS may have discussed his *HOY.*

¹⁴Rayford, p. 7.

¹⁵JS, "Notes," p. 69; *BDH,* p. 313; "What Vanderbilt," pp. 20–21; letter to DD, Feb. 23, 1934 (Tate's rejections of JS's work). Tate's letter to DD, Jan. 15, 1932, and DD's letter to Tate, Feb. 11, 1932, are in Fain and Young, pp. 268–269.

¹⁶*BDH,* p. 313; "What Vanderbilt," pp. 20–21. I#113: DD had been Warren's teacher at Vanderbilt before Warren graduated in 1925. Concerning DD's ability as a teacher, Warren said, "I never had a better. I learned a vast deal from him, a man of great kindness and humanity."

¹⁷*BDH,* p. 318. Fain and Young, pp. 268–269. Rayford, pp. 6–7.

¹⁸Rayford, pp. 6–7. The "smart funmaking . . . young minister" was named "Sharpe"; Rayford neglected to mention that Stuart was angry with him for striking Sharpe while Sharpe was sitting down, and "Rayford backed off" from a fight with Jesse. JS, letter to DD, Nov. 14, 1958.

¹⁹Robert A. McGaw, *The Vanderbilt Campus: A Pictorial History* (Nashville: Vanderbilt University Press, 1978), n.p., contains a photograph of Wesley Hall in flames dated Feb. 19, 1932, 5:15 P.M. *BDH*, pp. 315–316; "What Vanderbilt," p. 21. That JS had in his possession a well-studied picture of "Miss Hale" is clear in his letter to DD, May 4, 1933. Also see Charlotte Salmon, "J. S.," p. 165. See also Ch. 10, esp. last part of note 2.

²⁰JS, letter to DD, May 4, 1933. *BDH*, pp. 315–316.

²¹*BDH*, pp. 316–317; I#6; "JS's Characters . . . ," p. 32 (Lewis McCubbin). I#62. The photograph is in EH's collection. I#27.

²²Elizabeth Hale, letter to HER, April 16, 1979. Her married name does not appear in this book because of her request that it not be used. I#56. I#59. W. R. Moses, letter to HER, June 30, 1979 (Jesse and Elizabeth Hale). Hardy, I#60, emphasized the "many times" JS walked to the Hales' home in east Nashville to save streetcar fare. JS, letter to DD, May 4, 1933 (JS's eating at Elizabeth Hale's home); also see *COC*, p. 693; further, letter to CC, ca. Oct. 17, 1932; letter to DD, April 4, 1933 (JS's eating scraps from restaurant tables).

²³*BDH*, p. 316. "Autumn Potency" and "Four Sweethearts Go to Bed with Death" first pub. in *Muse and Mirror*, vol. 6 (Autumn/Winter, 1931/1932), 7. I#60 (Marvin Smith was then engaged to Elizabeth Hale's "best friend," later became an engineer with South Central Bell Telephone Co.; according to Hardy, this couple accompanied Elizabeth Hale to W-Hollow to visit JS in the summer of 1932). See also Ch. 8, esp. note 10.

²⁴Tate's letter to DD is in Fain and Young, pp. 269–270, the excerpted paragraph on p. 270. Allen Tate, "Horatian Epode to the Duchess of Malfi," orig. pub. in *The Fugitive*, vol. I, no. 2 (Oct. 1922); repr. in DD, *Southern Writers*, pp. 24–25. JS "Elegy for Mitch Stuart," *American Mercury*, vol. 28 (Jan. 1933), 30–32; "House in the Wind," *Yale Review*, vol. 23 (June 1934), 748–750; letter to DD, Feb. 23, 1934 (Tate's rejection of JS's poems, their subsequent acceptances). DD, letter to E. L. Blair, dated March 27, 1953, in *JS:LW*, p. 149, compares young JS to a flowing river.

²⁵DD, interviewed by Frank H. Leavell, April 24, 1963, in Leavell's "JS at V," p. 89. *TTTL*, p. 154. DD, letter to E. L. Blair, April 19, 1954, in *JS:LW*, pp. 149–150. DD, interviewed by Leavell in "JS at V," p. 88. DD, letter to Jesse Stuart, Oct. 28, 1955 (the "*bardic* tradition" in JS's poetry); his modest questioning of his own influence on JS in "The Vanderbilt Literary Tradition," p. 8.

²⁶JS, "VU Transcript"; *BDH*, p. 318 ("a new Vanderbilt" attitude).

²⁷"What Vanderbilt," p. 18. Fain and Young, Appendix F, pp. 424–425. The capsule review of *Penhally* appeared in "Check List of New Books," *American Mercury*, vol. 25 (Jan. 1932), xxiv.

²⁸Cowan, *Fugitive Group*, opposite p. 104; also cover, *Vanderbilt Alumnus*, vol. 41, no. 4 (May/June, 1956), and p. 6, for photos of Tate showing some of these traits and details. JS, "What Vanderbilt," p. 18; "House in the Wind," *Yale Review*, vol. 23 (June 1934), 748–750 (Eliotic influence in rat images, waste places); also *BDH*, p. 252 ("rat prints . . . waste land" and "desolation"). See Foster, *JS*, pp. 24 (imitation of Eliot), 59 (Pound influence stemming back to "Personae" in *HOY* [1930]). For further influence of Eliot and Pound see J. R. LeMaster, *JS:KCP*, esp. pp. 19, 35, 110. JS's interest in Greece and Rome are

evident in such works as *DOA* (journal) and "My Health Is Better in November," *New York Quarterly*, no. 20 (Winter 1978), 44–47 (poem). Also see Chs. 9, 16, and 17.

²⁹JS, letter to DD, Sept. 28, 1933 ("Litany"); letter to DD, Feb. 23, 1934 (remarks on Tate). DD's "Litany" was pub. in *Fugitive*, II (Dec. 1923), 187; also, *Fugitives: An Anthology of Verse* (New York: Harcourt, Brace, 1928), p. 7, and DD's *The Long Street: Poems* (Nashville: Vanderbilt University Press, 1961), p. 77.

³⁰JS, "VU Transcript." I#73 (Mims was born May 27, 1872). JS, "What Vanderbilt," pp. 19–20. I#27 (did not do the memory work). "Mims" (brochure pub. by the Office of Alumni and Development, 308 Kirkland Hall, Vanderbilt University, Nashville, TN 37203, n.d.). Note photos of Mims and mention of JS, *BDH*. "I knew he was a genius when I read it," Mims is quoted. Cowan, *Fugitive Group*, p. 16 (DD's recollection of Mims' dynamic teaching).

³¹*BDH*, p. 317 (difficulty in writing papers for Mims); also *TTTL*, p. 158, p. 155 (Carlyle paper); *BDH*, p. 314.

³²*BDH*, pp. 317–318, and *TTTL*, pp. 158–259 (paper for Mims, written late Mar., finished "about the first of April"); letter to DD, Feb. 11, 1938 (11 days to write *BDH*, "and I attended classes too!"), evidence showing JS probably worked on the MS. from about Mar. 21 to Apr. 1, 1932. *BDH*, pp. 318–319 ("Blindly I've beaten . . .").

³³I#1 (origin of title *BDH*). Also see HER, "Stuart Country," p. 8. *BDH*, pp. 315–316; *COC*, p. 66, and *YMR*, p. 273 (Katherine Atherton Grimes). I#27. *BDH*, pp. 317–318, and *TTTL*, pp. 158–159 (West, who becomes East in *TTTL*).

³⁴*BDH*, pp. 319–321, and *TTTL*, pp. 160–161 (Mims' reaction to *BDH*, JS's reactions). I#23. *COC* (writing and "over-enjoyment"), p. 659; *BDH*, p. 312 (Stuart sonnet). I#54.

³⁵JS, letter to DD, Feb. 11, 1938; "What Vanderbilt," p. 21. I#113. Rayford, p. 7. Leavell, "LCJS," p. 65.

³⁶DD, *Southern Writers in the Modern World*, p. 52 (Wade). JS, "What Vanderbilt," p. 20; "VU Transcript" (shows for 3 quarters, C, B, and A in Wade's classes). *BDH*, p. 324.

³⁷"What Vanderbilt," p. 18 (the Ransoms). Fain and Young, "Appendix G," pp. 430–431. I#117. I#113; I#114 ("furtive tear"). The four books of Ransom JS could have read: *Poems about God* (1919), *Chills and Fever* (1924), *Two Gentlemen in Bonds* (1927), and *God without Thunder* (1930).

³⁸"What Vanderbilt," pp. 19–20. I#117 (Mims anecdote). *Fugitive Group*, pp. 16–17. I#13 (JS's praise of Mims). Also I#4; I#6; I#14. Further, see JS's interview with J. R. LeMaster, W-Hollow, Greenup, KY, May 31, 1971, pub. in *Indiana English Journal*, vol. 8, no. 4 (Summer 1974), 7–8, 21 (notes Mims as first man ever to call him "a genius"). I#73 (Mims's racial views).

³⁹"Mims" (brochure). JS, interviewed by J. R. LeMaster, *Indiana English Journal*, p. 8. JS was unaware then and later that Mims and Warren did not get along well. I#113.

⁴⁰I#73. I#54. I#113.

⁴¹"What Vanderbilt," p. 19. Warren, "Foreword," JS, *HOWH* (1979), p. x. *BDH*, p. 320; "Notes," p. 70. I#13 (writing on *MWBTP* sonnets before he left Vanderbilt, intensity of the writing period); also see JS's interview with J. R. LeMaster, *Indiana English Journal*, p. 7.

⁴²"What Vanderbilt," p. 19 (Warren visit); "Foreword," *BDH* (1972 ed.), p. xii ("Their farming was on paper."). Also see Leavell, "LCJS," p. 62. I#113; I#114. I#73 (Warren's

cottage life). I#28 (Stuart's political differences with Warren); "One of the Lost Tribe," *HOWH*, pp. 266–287.

⁴³*BDH*, pp. 323–324.

⁴⁴I#23 (the arrest). I#60.

⁴⁵"VU Transcript." *BDH*, pp. 316, 318, 321–326; JS's letter to DD, Feb. 11, 1938; "Foreword," *BDH* (1972 ed.), p. xv ("never cut a class and I lived on one meal a day"). I add parenthetically "perhaps . . . an erasure" in the apparently blank column of the third-quarter grade space of Warren's class because my photocopy of Stuart's transcript appears to be lighter, with a palimpsest of a letter or serif, as if a letter had once been put down, then later scratched out or removed—thus raising a doubt as to whether or not the column was, indeed, intended to be blank. Unresolved, this question, too, is part of the mystery. Warren, "Foreword," *HOWH* (1979 repr.), p. x (friendship with JS). I#4 (JS's friendship with Warren); "Love" (short story); repr. in Brooks and Warren, *Understanding Fiction*, 2nd ed. (New York: Appleton-Century-Crofts, 1959), pp. 293–295; also in their *The Scope of Fiction* (1960), pp. 241–251. JS, "Woman in the House," orig. pub. in *Southern Review*, vol. 1 (July 1935), 139–150; repr. in *An Anthology of Stories from the Southern Review* (Baton Rouge: LSU Press, 1953), pp. 16–27, and in Warren's *A Southern Harvest* (Boston: Houghton Mifflin, 1937), pp. 269–281. I#27 (Mims grade "deserved"); "Foreword," *BDH* (1972 ed.), p. xi. I#113: Warren said, "I don't remember details of the grades"; "might be a *B* under there"; and "I don't remember anything about it." Mims' letter to JS, Sept. 29, 1943. The correspondence between the two reveals a mutual admiration and deep affection. "Mims" (brochure) notes "Old Central," his home on campus. I#73. I#4 (Mims' mention of JS as "a genius").

⁴⁶*BDH*, pp. 324–325 (listings). *TTTL*, p. 162 (not being ready for Vanderbilt).

⁴⁷*BDH*, 1972 ed., p. xv (scholarships). *BDH*, 1938 ed., pp. 321–322 (homing "dreams"). *TTTL*, pp. 162–163 (DD's parting advice). *BDH*, p. 325 (one suitcase). JS's interview with J. R. LeMaster, May 31, 1971, *Indiana English Journal*, p. 7; "What Vanderbilt," p. 21 (DD's advice, wish for "million readers"). *ROJS*, p. 154.

⁴⁸JS, "Foreword," *BDH*, (1972 ed.), pp. xi–xii; in "Kentucky . . . ," p. 7 (one meal a day from March 19 to June 2, 1932). JS meant to write Feb. 19 (instead of March 19), the day of the Wesley Hall fire. "What Vanderbilt," p. 21 (personal vision as writer rather than a group vision); letter to DD, Oct. 3, 1932, is an example of his seeking criticism and advice; in his letter to DD of March 3, 1933, he mentions Ransom's "especially . . . favorable" reading of a "sheaf of sonnets." JS, letter to DD, May 4, 1933 (JS's return trip to Vanderbilt in April 1933); letter to DD, Feb. 23, 1934 (differences with Vanderbilt group, individual stance in writing); "What Vanderbilt," p. 21 (what VU did for JS).

⁴⁹JS, "Foreword," *BDH* (1972 ed.), pp. xi–xii; *TTRST*, pp. 141–142; "What Vanderbilt," p. 17 (Kirkland's hoeing). CC, letter to HER, Feb. 5, 1980 (loan of two dollars to JS); cf. *BDH*, p. 325. W. R. Moses, letter to HER, June 30, 1979 (Moses' visit to W-Hollow). JS, letter to DD, April 4, 1933 (Elizabeth Hale's visit to W-Hollow); see sonnet sequence in *MWBTP*, Sonnets 323–332, pp. 166–170. See also Ch. 8 of this book. *BDH*, pp. 325–326. Rayford, p. 7 (ice cream parlor scene). I#53 (Candy Land).

CHAPTER 8

¹*BDH*, pp. 329–331; I#24. I#89: JAS. said his brother's weight had been 150–170 pounds until 1932, when he returned from Vanderbilt weighing over 200 pounds.

²*BDH*, pp. 150, 331–336; letter to CC with "Jesse Stuart, Superintendent" imprinted on the letterhead, ca. Sept. 1932.

³*BDH*, pp. 332–333. JAS., "A Freshman at Fishbone," *American Mercury*, vol. XXVIII, no. 110 (Feb. 1933), 153–157.

⁴*BDH*, pp. 333–335; "A Mother's Place Is with Her Son," *Ball State Teachers College Forum*, vol. 5, no. 2 (Spring 1964), 33–37; repr. in *MLHV*, pp. 98–106, quotations from pp. 99–100.

⁵*BDH*, pp. 338–339. Sonnet 1, *MWBTP*, p. 3.

⁶*BDH*, p. 336; Sonnet 220, *MWBTP*, p. 114, and Sonnet 233, p. 121.

⁷I#27 (Moores). W. R. Moses, letter to HER, June 30, 1979. I#93: JAS. commented that the "fight" Moses recalls may well have been a "put-up job," a typical prank of the young JS. The twelve-line excerpt is from Sonnet 312, *MWBTP*, p. 160; also see Sonnets 309–311, 413–416, 699, and 700. The "Jenny" (Virginia) poems may also have been inspired in part by Virginia Moore; cf. Sonnets 12, 381, 382, 417, 420. JS, "Notes," p. 70; *BDH*, p. 339; I#13 (wrote "about 30" of the poems while at Vanderbilt, after finishing *BDH*). Moses, letter to HER, June 30, 1979 (leaves with poems incised on them). Also see "Stuart Country," *JS:EOHW*, p. 4. Charley Robertson, letter to HER, June 20, 1980: After a visit to W-Hollow, novelist-painter and JS buff Robertson sent me such a poplar leaf inscribed with a personal note. Though dried, the leaf remained easily readable more than a year later.

⁸Moses, letter to HER, June 30, 1979. *BDH*, p. 339; "Dreams of an Empty House," *Letters*, vol. 5, no. 19 (May 1932), 42; "Portrait of a Mountain Boy," *Cumberland Empire*, vol. 3 (July 1932), 35–38; "Brother to the Dust," *Prairie Schooner*, vol. 6 (Summer 1932), 263; sonnets from *MWBTP*, 209 (p. 109), 242 (p. 125), and 243 (p. 126). *BDH*, pp. 378–379 (ideas on short story). "Battle Keaton Dies," repr. in *HOWH*, p. 162. I#9 (model for Battle Keaton). JS, card to Barnie Greene Hutchens, ca. Aug. 6, 1932.

⁹JS, letter to DD, ca. Oct. 17, 1932; letter to CC, ca. Oct. 17, 1932; Sonnets 421 and 422, *MWBTP*, p. 215; I#30 (*Magic Moonshine* MS).

¹⁰JS, letter to DD, April 4, 1933. I#60 (Hardy was in doubt as to the spelling of "Benz," and recalled the family used to be in the jewelry business). See Ch. 7, esp. note 23. The orig. *MWBTP* (1934) was dedicated "To Elizabeth," and the ten sonnets quoted in sequential order are 323–332, pp. 166–170. I#86–90, esp. I#90. Elizabeth Hale, letter to HER, April 16, 1979. JS, letter to CW, Nov. 22, 1935. I#59–60. I#56–57 (courtship of JS and Elizabeth Hale). I#10 (their friendship "a very deep one"). I#59: Hardy notes, from the spring of 1932 to about 1935, until their breakup, "They were mutually, deeply in love . . . planning and talking the possibilities of marriage . . . seriously considering marriage." Also I#56–58. Most internal evidence of the sequence, while not consistent, suggests a late June or early July 1932 dating of her visit to W-Hollow.

¹¹Among the sonnets that refer to "Elizabeth," "E. H.," "Elizabeth Hale," or to "Jean Elizabeth" in *MWBTP* are 161–166, pp. 83–85; 172, p. 88 (indirectly); 205, p. 107; 238, p. 123 (Elizabeth Hale); 248, p. 128 ("E. H."); 308, p. 158; 323–332, pp. 166–170; 362, p. 185 (Elizabeth Hale); 412–413, pp. 210–211 (Elizabeth Hale); 699–700, p. 359. Among the refs. to Quadroon Mott in *MWBTP* are those in Sonnets 45, 198, and 441–443. JS, letter to CW, Nov. 22, 1935, links the two Quadroon Mott Sonnets, 45 and 198 to "an old sweetheart of mine. I wrote this with her by the Little Sandy River in April" (Sonnet 45), and "with her at her home on the Little Sandy River" (Sonnet 198). I#8: JS said, despite his use of "Quadroon," she was not a quadroon but was dark-complexioned; further, she was "fiction—all fiction," a substitute "for real love . . . genuine love . . . something . . . for

what I'd like to have and didn't have." Cf. Ch. 2 (further details on literal and symbolical uses of "Quadroon Mott"; also the possible origin of the sobriquet in *BDH*, pp. 102*ff*. Charlie Greene and his family lived close to Put-Off Ford on the Little Sandy River a few miles south of W-Hollow, as did Maria Sheen and her family).

The Wilma O'Shean (Barnie Greene) sonnet sequence is 341–346, pp. 175–177, in *MWBTP*. Also see Sonnet 236, "To B. G.," p. 122. The Lydia Doore sonnets or sonnet variations referred to here are 412–416, pp. 210–212. The Kyon Murray sequence: 363–366, pp. 186–187. Greenup High School Class booklet, *GHS* [p. 17], provided to HER by Class President Eunice Mitchell Harper, 1979 class reunion at Greenbo Lodge, Greenup, KY, n.d. Kyon Murray after high school was in the nurses' training program at Marting's Hospital in Ironton, Ohio; she never married, and her last given address was in Greenup. Sonnets 247, p. 128, and 441, p. 226 (Mabel and Lucy).

¹²Jean Torris sonnets, *MWBTP*, 447–449; several other sonnets include refs. to "Jean"; examples are Sonnets 150, p. 77, and 114, p. 59. JS, letter to CW, Nov. 22, 1935. Elizabeth Hale, letter to HER, April 16, 1979. Also see JS, "Naomi," 28–29.

¹³JS, "Kentucky . . . ," p. 7 (summer drought, 1932); *BDH*, Ch. X, pp. 346–377 *passim*, and *TTRST*, Pt. IV, pp. 139–218 *passim* (events of 1932/1933 school year of JS's superintendency). *The Kentucky School Journal*, e.g., had pub. JS's "Saving Brains" in vol. 9 (Nov. 1930), 25; and "A Dollar a Smoke" in vol. 9 (March 1931), 42. "JS's Characters . . . ," pp. 30–34. JS, letterheads, letters to DD, ca. Oct. 3 and Oct. 17, 1932 (school board members' real names); statement on reality of characters in *TTRST*, introd. ed. note in JS, "JS's Characters . . . ," p. 30. Also see this book, Ch. 5, note 3.

¹⁴JS, "FFN," the *Greenup News*, clipping in *JSSB*#4 (ret. from Nashville ca. Sept. 3, 1934). *MWBTP* was released Oct. 15, 1934. *BDH*, pp. 348, 353. *MWBTP*, Sonnet 219, p. 114. *BDH*, p. 359; "My Father Is an Educated Man," orig. pub. in *Esquire*, vol. 22 (July 1944), 39 and 160; repr. in *TPGH*, Mockingbird ed., 1974, p. 29. Sonnets 395, entitled "County School Superintendent's Office, and 396, p. 202, *MWBTP*, are excerpted here. I#17 (staying at friends' houses in bad weather). *BDH*, pp. 369–371. *TTRST*, pp. 205–210 (visit with NDN): While substantially factual, this chapter compresses into a dramatically effective but earlier time frame subsequent, deeper aspects of their relationship that actually were to follow his return from Europe in 1938. In reality at this time, of course, the poet had a serious understanding, an "informal engagement" with Elizabeth Hale. Also see JS, "Naomi," p. 28 (school board's ban on intra-faculty dating). NDS, "How I Met My Husband," *Ladies' Home Journal*, p. 70; also *BDH*, p. 366; p. 372 (coffin incident); pp. 373*ff* (return of spring); letter to DD, April 4, 1933. "Editorial Note," *American Mercury*, vol. 28 (Jan. 1933), x, xii; "Elegy for Mitch Stuart" appears on pp. 30–32. JS, letters to CC and DD, ca. Oct. 17, 1932.

¹⁵Ramey, "An Inquiry," pp. 189–194 (pub. history *BDH*, Theodore Morrison, Edward Weeks). JS, letter to CC, ca. Oct. 17, 1932; letters to DD, March 8, 1933 (plentiful material); ca. Oct. 17, 1932 (*TOH* and strong plot); Oct. 3, 1932 ("sheaf of sonnets"). Note the early gestation of *TOH;* Wade Hall, "Foreword," *TOH* (1979 ed.), p. 7, quotes JS to the effect that the novel was suddenly commenced Oct. 14, 1939. Also see JS, letter to STILL, June 4, 1940: "I told that I started the book in Scotland, but I didn't. I don't want Dutton's to know how long I had worked on it."

BDH, p. 375 (*MWBTP* poems completed Feb. 1933, after 11 months); "Notes," pp. 70–71 (genesis of *AD*); letters to DD, March 8, 1933, and Sept. 28, 1933. I#13: *Magic Moonshine* MS (inspired by Howards, "could spend a month on it and finish it"). *BDH*, pp. 378–379; letter to DD, April 4, 1933. *MWBTP*, Sonnet 104, p. 54; see also Sonnet 200, p. 102. *BDH*, pp. 374–375. For six poems in *MWBTP* pub. in *HOY*, see this book, Ch. 5, esp. note 6. *BDH* includes Sonnets 236, p. 219; Sonnet 232, p. 326 (pub. earlier in *Sonnet Sequences*, vol. 2 [Sept. 1929]), 74; Sonnet 223, pp. 205–206; and Sonnet 224, p. 161. JS, letter to CW, Nov. 22, 1935, makes these comments on Sonnet 225, adding "Took poetry prize at L.M.U. in 1928. Got $5. Later was accepted by H. L. Mencken for American Mercury (1933)." JAS., "Alumni News," *The Blue and Gray,* n.p., n.d., clipping in *JSSB#2,* p. 17 (ca. Oct. 28–Nov. 4, 1934), is the source of JS's telling his mother that *MWBTP* was finished.

CHAPTER 9

¹*MW,* p. 14; *HCLS,* pp. 10–11. *COC* (MS): Jeff Larmer, p. 1; Ruggles, esp. pp. 57–58; father's objections to Shan/Jesse's writing, pp. 58–59; the passions, pp. 249–250; patterns, pp. 251–252; superintendent's work, pp. 258–259; local color, pp. 287–288; originality in education, p. 532; Lottie Graham, p. 301; "farewell to the schools," p. 476; boy in willow patch, pp. 504–505.

COC, Ch. IX, pp. 571–664; Shan's office and hallway, p. 581; quarreling, p. 604; hills as consolation, p. 609; "primroses . . . stones," p. 612; Red Cross flour sacks, "thin land," pp. 641–645; Tennessee, pp. 657–703 *passim.* Professor Charles Wolfe, letter to HER, April 21, 1982.

COC, temptresses, pp. 893–895; violence, pp. 843–878 *passim;* Shan's opponent's death, pp. 845–852 *passim;* sonnets to spring, pp. 855–859; bank failure, pp. 861–863. Minnow analogy and April 1 poems, pp. 883–888; repr. in *MWBTP,* pp. 135–138, 70–71, 81 (Poem 157).

COC, criticisms of Shan/Jesse, pp. 896–897; election, p. 899; Broker's Tip, pp. 901, 918; father and trees, pp. 918–920; Wingo Blair, pp. 919–930 *passim* (JS states in "JS's Characters . . . ," p. 33, that Blair was based on his real friend and fellow educator Fred Maynard; also see photo); apostrophe to the earth, pp. 335–337.

²JS, *COC,* pp. 940, 915–916; letter to STILL, May 24, 1933. Orig. copy, *COC,* contains cover sheet: "written summer 1933: revised and retyped August–September 1970." JS, letters to DD, April 4 and May 4, 1933. For JS's hard time at Vanderbilt, see Ch. 8. I#56. I#59.

³JS, letter to DD, March 8, 1933. "Inquiry," pp. 67–69; notes 1–3 also provide dates of letters noted. JS, postcard to STILL, postmarked Aug. 1, 1933; letter to DD, Oct. 3, 1932. Also see *BDH,* p. 380. "Inquiry," pp. 190–194 *passim.* JS, "Notes," p. 70; letter to CC, Sept. 15, 1933, and postcard, postmarked Sept. 26, 1933.

JS, letter to DD, Sept. 28, 1933; letter to CC, Sept. 15, 1933; letter to STILL, Dec. 3, 1933. "Inquiry" mentions Morrow's interest, p. 70. JS, *BDH,* p. 387. JS Photograph Collection; *BDH,* pp. 387–388.

⁴DD, letter to Stringfellow Barr, ed. *Virginia Quarterly,* noted in "Inquiry," pp. 67–68; note 1, p. 68. Mark Van Doren, *New York Herald Tribune,* vol. 12 (June 12, 1934), 31. John Gould Fletcher, "Kentucky Georgics," *Poetry: A Magazine of Verse,* vol. XLV (Jan. 1935), 217. Peter Monro Jack, *New York Times Book Review,* Oct. 21, 1934, clipping in *JSSB#2,* p. 5. Malcolm Cowley, "Man with a Hoe," *The New Republic,* vol. LXXX (Oct. 31, 1934), 342–343, clipping in *JSSB#2,* pp. 4–5. Robert Nye, ed., *A Book of Sonnets* (New York: Oxford University Press, 1976), p. 31, writes in his Introduction that "having summarized the rules, it is only fair to add that the sonnet is not a piece of poetic mathematics but a form of poetic freedom," my source for the figure here. David McCord, *The Yale Review* (Winter 1935), p. 393, clipping in *JSSB#2,* p. 69; for a copy of McCord's eighteen-line parodic "Sonnet," see *JSSB#2,* p. 49.

Horace Gregory, "A Farmer Singing Behind His Plow," *New York Herald Tribune Books,* Oct. 14, 1934, clipping in *JSSB#2,* p. 13. "Sonnets Catch Kentucky Air," *Denver Post,* Oct. 28, 1934, clipping in *JSSB#2,* p. 16.

Roy Helton, "JS Anointed Poet of Mountain Men," *Philadelphia Inquirer*, Oct. 27, 1934, clipping in *JSSB#2*, p. 26. Clipping from the *Des Moines Register* in *JSSB#2*, p. 27. Paul Jordan-Smith, "Spirit of Kentucky Hills Alive in Farmer's Verse," *Los Angeles Times*, Oct. 21, 1934, clipping in *JSSB#2*, p. 30. Merrill Moore, quoted in "Poetry Notes," clipping (source unidentified) in *JSSB#2*, p. 63. Edwin Mims, "Man with a Bull-Tongue Plow" (review), source unidentified, clipping in *JSSB#2*, p. 22; Mims' letter to Lee Ramey, dated Dec. 2, 1939, is included in Ramey, "Inquiry," p. 73, note 1, my source here. Walter Paschall, "Man with a Bull-Tongue Plow" (review), *Atlanta Journal*, Oct. 28, 1934, clipping in *JSSB#2*, p. 42. A sampling of the clippings in *JSSB#2* associates JS and *MWBTP* with the following poets and concepts: Robert Burns (pp. 3, 10, 23, 46, 52); Omar Khayyam (p. 5); A. E. Housman (pp. 8, 46); William Blake, John Clare, Oliver Goldsmith, William Wordsworth, Chaucer, and Edgar Lee Masters (pp. 9, 52, 53, 23, 46, 66); Robert Frost pp. 22, 23, 26); Edna Millay (p. 10); Walt Whitman (pp. 15, 22); John Masefield (p. 64); James Whitcomb Riley (p. 18); Baudelaire (p. 20); Rudyard Kipling (p. 22); Julia Moore, the Sweet Singer of Michigan (p. 25); Carl Sandburg (p. 26); Stephen Vincent Benét (p. 31); Browning (p. 31); DD and the Agrarian group (p. 65); Shakespeare (p. 52); Homer and the children of the cabin, Abraham Lincoln, Aesop, John Greenleaf Whittier, Edwin Markham, James Whitcomb Riley, Edgar Guest (p. 52); and Old English poetry (pp. 36, 53). Henry E. Christman, "Poet Looms Powerfully in 'Man with a Bull-Tongue Plow,'" *The Knickerbocker Press*, Oct. 14, 1934, clipping in *JSSB#2*, p. 24.

"Farmers Make the Finest Poets," *Chicago Daily News*, Oct. 10, 1934, clipping in *JSSB#2*, p. 31. Isabel Ackerman, "A Sonneteer Sows in Kentucky," *Lexington Herald*, undated clipping in *JSSB#2*, p. 36. John Chamberlain, "Books of the Times," *New York Times*, Dec. 28, 1934, p. 19, clipping in *JSSB#2*, p. 51. W. B. Ward, *New Day*, clipping in *JSSB#2*, p. 52.

JS, *BDH*, p. 393.

Morton Dauwen Zabel, letter to JS, Oct. 20, 1934; both the letter and envelope are in *JSSB#2*, p. 6. The "Young Kentucky" group of poems published in *Poetry: A Magazine of Verse*, vol. 44 (May 1934), 61–65, included I, pp. 61–62, repr. in *MWBTP* as 677, p. 348; II, p. 62, repr. in *MWBTP* as 295, p. 152; III, pp. 62–63, repr. in *MWBTP* as 371, p. 190; IV, p. 63, repr. in *MWBTP* as 349, p. 179; V, p. 64, repr. in *MWBTP* as 299, p. 154; VI, pp. 64–65, repr. in *MWBTP* as 662, p. 340; and VII, p. 65, repr. in *MWBTP* as 680, p. 349. *JS:LW*, pp. 72–73, 39.

CHAPTER 10

[1]JS, letter to CW, Aug. 16, 1935; "There Shall Not Be," p. 229: *TTRST*, p. 247. "The Best Years of Our Lives," *Ball State University Forum*, vol. 9, no. 3 (Summer 1968), 35–42; repr. in *CBF*, pp. 89–104 *passim*. See the end of Ch. 6 of this book (Kings as financial advisers). I#45.

JS, "The Snow Storm," *Amer. Book Collector*, vol. 16, no. 6, spec. JS no. (Feb. 1966), 16–17; *BDH*, p. 378. "Battle Keaton Dies," *Story*, vol. 7, no. 36 (July 1935), 57–72; repr. in *HOWH* (1979), pp. 150–192, and in Whit Burnett, ed., *Firsts of the Famous* (New York: Ballantine, 1962), pp. 178–194. "Head o' th' Hollow," *Yale Review*, vol. 25 (Sept. 1935), 169–188; repr. as "Head o' W-Hollow" in *HOWH* (1979), pp. 3–5. "Kentucky Hill Dance," *New Republic*, vol. 79 (May 16, 1934), 15–16. "Mountain Poorhouse," vol. 81 (Nov. 21, 1934), 42–43; repr. in *HOWH* (1979), pp. 118–121. "Mom," *Household*, vol. 35 (May 1935), 24, 29. "Woman in the House," *Southern Review*, vol. 1 (July 1935), 139–150; repr. in *HOWH* (1979), pp. 54–66, and in *BLSSJS*, pp. 208–218. "Snake Blue," *New Republic*, vol. 83 (July 24, 1935), 304–305; and "Three Hundred Acres of Elbow Room," *Amer. Mercury*, vol. 36 (Sept. 1935), pp. 27–37, repr. *HOWH* (1979), pp. 6–22.

JS, "FFN," *JSSB#4*, p. 19, letter from Merton S. Yewdale repr. here, a column JS commenced ca. June 1934, cols. generally undated except for what internal evidence provides. See "JS Makes Bow as Columnist," *JSSB#*4, p. 1; his apparent first col. locates him, p. 2, in eastern TN; also see clipping dated June 15, 1934, re editor Jack Kinner. I#85.

JS, "FFN," *JSSB#*4, clippings on pp. 2–4, 6–7; letter to DD, Feb. 23, 1934. I#59.

²JS, letter to STILL, Dec. 12, 1934. Eda Lou Walton, "Sonnets of a Mountaineer," *The Nation*, clipping in *JSSB#*2, p. 8. JS, "FFN," clipping in *JSSB#*4, p. 44. "Visiting Authors et al (Smith)," *Saturday Review of Literature*, June 8, 1935, clipping in *JSSB#*2, p. 85. Clipping with caption "Full of Eager Energy" in *JSSB#*4, p. 54. " 'Big But Distasteful,' " *New York Herald Tribune*, clipping in *JSSB#*2, p. 86, with photo by Zerbe. "Graveyard Bard," *New York Post*, May 28, 1935, clipping in *JSSB#*2, p. 87. "Full of Eager Energy," clipping in *JSSB#*2, p. 85.

"Inquiry," p. 193: most judges "agreed that the MS was the most original of the contest," but eventually decided "it would take too much revision to be awarded the prize," which went instead to Frances Winwar for *Poor Splendid Wings*. Edward Weeks continued to hold the MS and to urge its publication. JS, *BDH* (New York: Dutton, 1938); "JS Takes a Backward Glance on His Trip Abroad," the *Portsmouth Times*, May 1, 1938, clipping in *JSSB#*17, p. 69. Franklin P. Adams, "The Conning Tower," *New York Herald Tribune*, June 8, 1935, clipping in *JSSB#*3, p. 20. "Full of Eager Energy," clipping in *JSSB#*4, p. 54.

JS, "FFN," clipping in *JSSB#*4, p. 50. I#22. I#60. I#56. JS, letter to AD, Nov. 17, 1936. I#59; I#60: Theron Hale did sell a well-known self-polishing floor wax, e.g., at Cane Sloane's in the Bellemeade area. Dressed in costumes of the gay nineties, the Hale family of Grand Ole Opry fame were depicted on labels on the cans of wax with the trade name "Hale's Success Wax." Hale successfully marketed the wax, but the secret formula died with him (1950s). JS, Poem 172, *MWBTP*, p. 88.

JS, letter to STILL, Nov. 13, 1935; "FFN," *JSSB#*4, p. 50; letter to STILL. Charlotte Salmon, "J. S.," pp. 164–165.

³"Prominent Poet Is Guest Speaker Here," *Maysville* (KY) *Public Ledger*, Nov. 21, 1934, clipping in *JSSB#*2, p. 33. JS, Poem 703, *MWBTP*, p. 361. Other clippings noted are in *JSSB#*2, pp. 61, 62, 71, articles undated. JS, "Sonatas of Spring," *Scribner's Magazine*, vol. 97 (June 1935), 356–357. Lois Colley, "The Man with the Bull Tongue Plow Visits Campus," *The Eastern Progress*, Feb. 22, 1935, clipping in *JSSB#*2, p. 67. JS, *TTRST*, pp. 249–250; letter to STILL, Jan. 28, 1935.

JS, *HOWH;* "FFN," *JSSB#*4, pp. 74–75. "Stuart Country," in *JS:EOHW*, p. 17. JS, interview with E. L. Blair, March 27, 1953, in *JS:LW*, p. 39, note 4.

"Kentucky Home Brew," *Time*, October 15, 1934, clipping in *JSSB#*1, p. 11. Mark Van Doren, "The Good Speech of a Ky. Hollow" (review), *New York Herald Tribune*, May 3, 1936, clipping in *JSSB#*3, p. 7. William Rose Benét, "Hill-Man of Kentucky" (review), *Saturday Review of Literature*, May 2, 1936, clipping in *JSSB#*3, p. 3. Ralph Thompson, "Books of the Times," *New York Times*, April 18, 1936, clipping in *JSSB#*3. Elizabeth Hardwick, "Head O' W-Hollow Symposium of Life in the Kentucky Hills . . .," *Lexington* (KY) *Herald*, May 3, 1936, clipping in *JSSB#*3, p. 15. Margaret Trotter, "Mountain Poet's Prose" (review), clipping in *JSSB#*1, p. 40. William Lyon Phelps, "Phelps Looks at Literature," clipping in *JSSB#*1, p. 37.

⁴JS's short stories pub. in 1936 include "Before the Grand Jury," *Southwest Review*, vol. 21 (Jan. 1936), 169–176, repr. in *PIH;* "Vacation in Heaven," *Harper's*, vol. 172 (May 1936), 667–673; "Pockets Full of South Wind," *Partisan Review and Anvil*, vol. 3 (June 1936), 14–16; "Hair," *American Mercury*, vol. 38 (July 1936), 311–320, repr. in *MOM* (1979) and in *BLSSJS;* "Men of the Mountains," *Scribner's Magazine*, vol. 100 (Oct. 1936), 57–61, repr. in *MOM, BLSSJS;* and three stories in *Esquire:* "Uncle Fonse Laughed," vol. 6 (Sept. 1936), 32–33, 182, 184, 186, reprinted in *GO, BLSSJS;* "Uncle Joe's Boys," vol. 6 (Nov.

1936), 56–57, 221–226; and "This Is the Place," vol. 6 (Dec. 1936), 54–55, 300, 302, 305–306, repr. in *MOM* and *BLSSJS*.

The poems "A Lark Is Flying," "Mule Heaven," "My Land Loves," "November Day," "I Watch the Clouds," "Three Poems: 'Before the End,' 'Mountain Graveyard,' 'Elegy for Jim Turner,'" "Amos Larkin," "Mountain Mother," "Spring Rain," "From a Trilogy," "The Ballad of Lonesome Waters," "Hill Farm," "Youth in Spring" (three sonnets), "Corn Will Shoot Stalwart," "Three Poems," and "Drought, W-Hollow: 1936" are listed alphabetically with bibliographical details in Woodbridge, *JSB*, pp. 89–123 *passim*.

JS's articles and pieces published about him in 1936 include "Teaching Creative English in High School," *Scholastic*, vol. 28 (Feb. 1, 1936), 7–8; "I Buy a Farm in 'W' Hollow," *Country Gentleman*, vol. 106 (Aug. 1936), 10–11, 31. Charlotte Salmon, "J. S." Thomas Burke, "The Short Story in America," *American Mercury*, vol. 39 (Sept. 1936), 102–105.

JS, "A Land beyond the River, by JS," MS in the JS Collection, W-Hollow, Greenup, KY, in part since pub. in HER, "About the Story," *BLSSJS*, pp. 73–75.

Amy Vanderbilt and Morton Clark, "Adventurers Find Kentucky Hill Billy Poet Is Dirt Farmer as Well as Man of Letters," clipping in *JSSB#1*, p. 56. Pickney R. Allen, *Louisville Times*, June 11, 1937, clipping in *JSSB#3*, pp. 42–43. JS, "This Is the Place," repr. in *MOM* (1979), pp. 315–331, and *BLSSJS*, pp. 393–406; also see HER, "Men of the Mountains: An Interview with JS," *Adena*, vol. 4, no. 1 (Spring 1979), esp. 21–23. George Scarbrough, "Fine, Enduring Work" (review), *Chattanooga Times*, March 23, 1941, clipping with photo of JS smoking pipe in *JSSB#7*, p. 10.

[5]JS, "The Professor," pp. 98–99. I#10 and I#93 indicate that by summer 1936, JS's break with Elizabeth Hale was final. CW, a University of Michigan English professor, had written JS on Dec. 9, 1935, suggesting the possibility of a Guggenheim Fellowship. JS, letter of application (copy) quoted here is in TN State Library and Archives, Archives and MSs Sec. Ac. no. 1239, Nashville, TN.

JS, "Men of the Mountains," *Scribner's Magazine*, vol. 100 (Oct. 1936), 57–61; repr. in *MOM* (1979), pp. 13–26, and *BLSSJS*, pp. 93–103. I#5.

JS's short stories of 1937 include "A Land Beyond the River," *Esquire*, vol. 7 (Jan. 1937), 36–37, 166, 168, 171–172, 174, 176, repr. in *PIH, CGS*, and *BLSSJS*; "The Blue Tick Pig," *Esquire*, vol. 7 (Feb. 1937), 36–37, 200–203, repr. in *JSH, MOM*, and *SEL;* "One of God's Oddlings," *Esquire*, vol. 7 (March 1937), 36–37, 192–193, repr. in *MOM;* "Sunday Afternoon Hanging," *Esquire*, vol. 7 (April 1937), 48–49, 200–202, repr. in *PIH* and *BLSSJS;* "Whip-Poor-Willie," *Scribner's Magazine*, vol. 101 (April 1937), 19–27, repr. in *MOM* and *O'Henry Memorial Award Prize Stories of 1937;* "Fast-train Ike," *Esquire*, vol. 7 (May 1937), 44–45, 194, 197–198, 200, 203–204; "Against the Sunset," *Globe*, vol. 1 (June 1937), 17–22; "Goin to th' Buttin'," *Esquire*, vol. 7 (June 1937), 48–49, 242–247; "Pa," *Household*, vol. 37 (June 1937), 8–9, 18–19, 21; "Color of the Wind," *American Prefaces*, vol. 2 (Summer 1937), 174–176; "The Faded Flag," *Globe*, vol. 1 (July 1937), 84–86; "The War and Cousin Lum," *Esquire*, vol. 8 (July 1937), pp. 36–37, 201–206, repr. in *CGS;* "Zeke Hammertight," *New Mexico Quarterly Review*, vol. 7 (Aug. 1937), 161–182, repr. in *PIH;* "Uncle Fonse and the Starlings," *Esquire*, vol. 8 (Sept. 1937), 40–41, 202–206; and "Little Giant," *Collier's*, vol. 100 (Oct. 30, 1937), 16–17.

His poems of 1937 include "Sonnets of Summer," *Harper's*, vol. 174 (Jan. 1937), 190–191; "Mountain Funeral" (reprint), *Progressive Farmer*, vol. 52, no. 5 (May 1937), 9; "No One Has Sung for Us," *Harper's*, vol. 175 (July 1937), p. 167, repr. in *Poems Editors Buy: A Textbook of Verse Marketing*, ed. Edith Cherrinton (Pasadena, CA: Press of Star-News Pub. Co., 1939), p. 28; "Mountain People," *Scribner's Magazine*, vol. 102 (Aug. 1937), pp. 46–47; "Girls of Yesterday," *Pictorial Review*, vol. 38 (Sept. 1937), 69; "Six Poems of Mountain People," *Esquire*, vol. 8 (Dec. 1937), 80–81.

JS's "FFN," 1937–1938, listed with pertinent bibliographical facts in Woodbridge, *JSB*, p. 144.

JS, *YMR*, pp. 58–59. JS, letter in "A Glimpse of Ky. Floods," clipping in *JSSB#1*, p. 120. JS, letter to STILL, Feb. 11, 1937. "Ky. Poet Wins Acclaim of Book Critics," *New Bedford* (MA) *Standard*, Feb. 7, 1937, clipping in *JSSB#1*, p. 144.

"Guggenheim Fund Makes 61 Awards," *New York Times*, March 29, 1937, clipping in *JSSB#3*, p. 5, carries his picture with the news story. "Stuart to Eye Mountaineers of Scotland," *Nashville Evening Tennessean* of the same date, clipping in *JSSB#3*, p. 5. JS, letter to STILL, April 7, 1937; letter to AD, April 5, 1937; letter to CW, April 7, 1937.

See "Young Kentucky Author to Address Student Body in Chapel, Thursday," *Hammer and Tongs*, California State Teachers College, California, PA, April 9, 1937, clipping with photo in *JSSB#3*, p. 22, and p. 47. JS, letter to AD, April 5, 1937; *BDH*, pp. 395–397 (West's visit). "Mountain Writer Gives Autobiographical Talk," *Princetonian*, p. 35, clipping in *JSSB#3*, p. 35. JS, letter to STILL, May 6, 1937, notes the Princeton trip's being "fine," as well as Don West's recent visit. The profiles: Pinkney R. Allen, "Guggenheim Winner 'Mountain' Climber: Amazing Energy Outstanding Asset of Youth Who Aspires to Become 'America's Greatest Poet,' " *Louisville Times*, June 11, 1937, clipping in *JSSB#3*, pp. 42–43; Nancy Grimes, "Candidly Clocking Kentucky's 'Bobby Burns,' " *Portsmouth Times*, clipping in *JSSB#3*, pp. 30–31; and Raymond Brewster, "An Appraisal of JS," Huntington, WV, *Herald-Advertiser*, clipping in *JSSB#3*, p. 32. Ralph Thompson, "Books of the Times," *New York Times*, May 28, 1937, clipping in *JSSB#3*, p. 33.

JS, "A Land beyond the River, by JS," MS quoted in HER, "About the Story," *BLSSJS*, p. 75.

NDNS, *Five Year Diary*, entry under June 11, 1937. JS, *YMR*, p. 161; two cols. "FFN," clippings in *JSSB#5*, pp. 3–4, treat his lectures in the Nashville and Atlanta areas; also see "JS Takes a Backward Glance on His Trip Abroad," *Portsmouth Times*, May 1, 1938, p. 20.

6JS, "FFN," clippings in *JSSB#5*, pp. 5–7; "Love in Autumn" (poem), clipping in JSSB#1, p. 63. John Egerton, "JS: Ky. Is *His* Land," *Louisville Courier-Journal and Times* mag. Sec., May, 28, 1967, pp. 29–31. JS, "FFN," clipping in *JSSB#5*, pp. 8–12; "JS Takes a Backward Glance . . . ," *Portsmouth Times*, p. 20; postcard to NDN, Morehead, KY, July 21, 1937; postcard to EB and MB, postmarked July 24, 1937. I#8. Allen Engle, via Dr. Fred A. Engle, Jr., photo and letter to HER, Aug. 22, 1979. Frances Street, letter to HER, May 1983.

CHAPTER 11

1JS, "FFN," clipping in *JSSB#5*, p. 12; letter from Edinburgh, Scotland, to OS, Aug. 1, 1937; "FFN," clipping in *JSSB#5*, pp. 13, 15, 16 (trip to Canterbury), 17 (trip with O'Brien to Oxford). JS, letter from Chester, England, to OS and AS, Aug. 29, 1937; "The Latest Thing in America," *Kansas Magazine* (1966), pp. 38–44; postcard from Flintshire (Rhyl), England, to NDN, Aug. 30, 1937; "FFN," clipping in *JSSB#5*, p. 19 (Wales); p. 20 (Wordsworth's Lake District).

2JS, "FFN," *JSSB#5*, pp. 21–22 (tour of Burns country); *YMR*, p. 160 (copy of Burns' poems); 161 (tribute); letter to NDN, Sept. 10, 1937; clipping in JSSB#17, pp. 32, 50–51, a scrapbook NDN kept prior to their marriage.

3JS, letters to NDN, Sept. 27 and 30, 1937; *YMR*, p. 263. JS gives "8 Waterloo Place" as O'Brien's London office, but in his earlier column gives "14 Waterloo Place"; here I am relying on the earlier evidence—14 Waterloo Place. JS, "The Kentucky Poet Takes His First Trip to the Continent," *Portsmouth* (Ohio) *Times,* July 17, 1938, clipping in *JSSB#*17, p. 86 (June 1937, meeting of Gurmild [also Gunnild] Neilsen [also Neilson], or "Neila," on a train from Macon, GA, to Cincinnati). JS, letter from Stockholm, Sweden, to OS, Oct. 20, 1937; the snapshot, mailed later, is dated Nov. 1, 1937, and notes, "taken last month." JS, "FFN," clippings in *JSSB#*5, pp. 29–31. Commencing March 25, 1938, JS began a series of approximately twenty columns pub. in the *Greenup County Citizen* ed. of the *Russell Times* under the title "With Jesse Stuart Abroad" ("WJSA" hereafter), which continued to appear until Aug. 12, 1938. The first of these, describing his meal in Kaunas, Lithuania, in Oct. 1937, was pub. March 25, 1938, p. 2; clipping in *JSSB#*5, p. 32. JS, letter to NDN, Feb. 8, 1938 (change of col. to *Greenup County Citizen*); "WJSA," April 1, 1938, p. 2, clipping in *JSSB#*5, p. 33 (East Prussia); in the same scrapbook, clippings on pages indicated, he wrote of the Danzig Free State, April 8, 1938, p. 34; of Germany in three subsequent columns with the following descriptive captions: "Jesse, in Berlin, Welcomes Letters from Back Home . . . Says Persecution of Jews Both Absurd and Pathetic," April 15, 1938, p. 35; "In Berlin, Jesse Hears Fine Music, Is Chased by Cops, Meets Brilliant Young Woman, Doing Research Work," April 22, 1938, p. 36; and "Jesse Finds Germans Have Faith in Hitler as Leader; Recalls Post-War Days and Woodrow Wilson's Treaty," April 29, 1938, p. 37 (parallel danger, potentially, between U.S.A. and Germany). He identifies the college president remarking on the ideological conflict as H. L. Donovan of Eastern State Teachers College, Richmond, KY.

JS, "WJSA," May 6, 1938, *JSSB#*5, p. 38 ("In Belgium, Jesse Finds Women Working, Men Fishing; Mighty Glad to Cross the Channel Back to England"). HER, "About the Story," *BLSSJS,* pp. 1–2. JS, letter from Bonnington Hotel, London, to OS, Nov. 1, 1937; photo inscribed "Gunnild Neilsen of Copenhagen, Denmark . . . taken last month" was orig. contained in this letter. JS, letter to EB, Nov. 3, 1937, postmarked Edinburgh, Nov. 6, 1937. JS, letter from Edinburgh to NDN, Nov. 4, 1937 (*Esquire* story, nonliteral aspects of his "Pa" characters).

⁴JS, "No One Has Sung for Us," *Harper's,* vol. 175 (July 1937), 167; for a copy of this poem see the clipping in *JSSB#*17, p. 78. JS, "The War and Cousin Lum," *Esquire,* vol. 8 (July 1937), 36–37, 201–206; "The Faded Flag," *Globe,* vol. 1 (July 1937), 84–86. W. S. Wabnitz, "JS and the Old and New in Short Stories," *New Mexico Quarterly Review,* vol. 7 (Aug. 1937), 183–188. JS, "Zeke Hammertight," in the same source, pp. 161–182; "Mountain People," *Scribner's Magazine,* vol. 102 (Aug. 1937), 46–47; "Girls of Yesterday," *Pictorial Review,* vol. 38 (Sept. 1937), 69; "Uncle Fonse and the Starlings," *Esquire,* vol. 8 (Sept. 1937), 40–41, 202–206; "Little Giant," *Collier's,* vol. 100 (Oct. 30, 1937), 16–17; and "Six Poems of Mountain People," *Esquire,* vol. 8 (Dec. 1937), 80–81. The poems are listed in Woodbridge, *JSB,* p. 114. Carol Bird, "Give Me the Hillbilly Life," *Denver Post,* mag. sec., Oct. 10, 1937, p. 10. JS, "*Einer gegen alle,*" trans. by Hermann Stresau in *Neu Amerika,* ed. Kurt Ullrich (Berlin: S. Fischer, 1937), pp. 380–410.

Woodbridge, *JSB,* p. 144, lists twenty-six columns entitled "FFN," commencing June 11 and continuing July 2, 9, 16; Aug. 6, 13, [19] 20; Sept. [2] 3, 10, 17, 30; Oct. 15, [21] 22; Nov. 4, 11, 18, 25; Dec. 2, [8] 9, 16, 23, 1937; Jan. 6, 20, 27, 1938; and Feb. 3 and 10, 1938.

JS, *JSSB#*5, correlated with *JSSB#*17, indicates that all columns listed by Woodbridge are preserved in these two scrapbooks except that of Jan. 27, 1938, which I was unable to locate or place in my photocopies. Further, the dates noted in brackets above appear to be accurate ones rather than those Woodbridge lists, errata accountable through occasional Thursday rather than regular Friday publications of "FFN." In addition, *JSSB#*5, correlated with the dated columns in *JSSB#*17, reveals seven columns more than those listed by Woodbridge. These seven are a column Stuart wrote in preparation for his

Guggenheim year abroad, undated (*JSSB#5*, p. 2); a Fourth of July piece, Stamford, CT, while Stuart awaited embarkation (*JSSB#5*, p. 6); a column on Aberdeen, Scot., Aug. 26 (*JSSB#5*, p. 10); Edinburgh–London trip on *Coronation Scot*, Sept. 24 (*JSSB#5*, p. 14); Stuart's London–Canterbury trip, Oct. 7 (*JSSB#5*, p. 16); his Finland trip, undated but in context Jan. 13 seems a likely if approximate publication date (*JSSB#5*, p. 28); an undated "FFN" piece on Riga, Latvia, and Kaunas, Lithuania (*JSSB#5*, p. 31). *JSSB#5*, p. 40, contains a Feb. 10, 1938, "FFN" column, "Notes on Scotland," which is not in my photocopy of *JSSB#17*. Together *JSSB#5* and *#17* provide clippings and datings of publication of thirty-two of JS's "FFN" columns, rather than the twenty-six noted in Woodbridge, *JSB*, p. 144. Taken together these scrapbooks provide a thoroughly insightful, if perhaps not complete, record of the first half of JS's Guggenheim year abroad, especially his October 1937, tour of northern Europe.

Woodbridge, *JSB*, p. 144, lists twenty published columns entitled "WJSA" in the *Greenup County Citizen* edition of the *Russell Times:* March 25, 1938; April 1, 8, 15, 22, 29; May 6, [13], 20, 27; June [3], 17, 24; July 1, 8, [15], [22], 29; Aug. 5 and 12. I was able to find clippings of all except the bracketed datings in *JSSB#5* and *#17*. However, four undated clippings of "WJSA" are in my incomplete photocopy of *JSSB#5*: "Jesse Takes Auto Trip in Scottish Highlands, and Visits Historical Scenes, Including an Old Cemetery," p. 39; ". . . Trip to London, Attends a Party, Visits Broadcasting Offices, and Even Makes Address at the London P.E.N. Club as a Guest of Edward J. O'Brien, Who Introduced Him," p. 41; "Game of Rugby, and Ballet Dancing, Attracts Jessie [sic] . . . Enjoys Visit to Large Farm of a Friend in Scotland," p. 43; and "Year Over, Jesse Starts Home in Round-About Way; Finds Irish a Friendly People; Then Goes to London," p. 44. Quite likely, these four undated travel essays may be those among the missing ones in bracketed datings noted above in Professor Woodbridge's list.

Of JS's travel essays for his Guggenheim year, then Woodbridge lists twenty-six "FFN" and twenty "WJSA," a total of forty-six travel essays. I located thirty-two "FFN" and nineteen "WJSA," a total of fifty-one travel essays. Further sources are JS's reflective pieces published in the *Portsmouth* (Ohio) *Times:* "Jesse Stuart Takes 'A Backward Glance' on His Trip Abroad," May 1, 1938, clipping in *JSSB#17*, p. 69; "Jesse Stuart Surveys 'England and Robert Burns' Country' and Writes of His Trip," May 8, 1938, clipping in *JSSB#17*, p. 80; and "The Kentucky Poet Takes His 'First Trip to the Continent,' " July 17, 1938, clipping in *JSSB#17*, p. 86.

Clippings of approximately fifty or more reviews of *BHD* are in *JSSB#6*. *JSSB#9* contains as many or more. The April 24, 1938, edition of the *New York Times Book Review*, sec. 7, featured a full-page review of the book by J. Donald Adams; clippings in *JSSB#9*, pp. 6–7. Representative reviews in *JSSB#6* (scrapbook page nos. given below) are from the *Columbus* (Ohio) *Dispatch*, May 8, 1938, p. 7; the *Washington Post*, May 8, 1938, p. 8; the *Jacksonville* (FL) *Times-Union*, May 8, 1938, p. 9; *San Diego Union*, May 1, 1938, p. 10; *Nashville Commercial-Appeal*, n.d., p. 13; the *Galveston Daily News*, May 8, 1938, p. 18; *Milwaukee Journal*, n.d. p. 25; the *St. Louis Post-Dispatch*, n.d., p. 26; the *Columbia* (SC) *State*, May 29, 1938, p. 27; the *Detroit Free Press*, n.d., p. 28; the *Oakland* (CA) *Tribune*, n.d., p. 34; the *Kansas City Star*, n.d., p. 36; and the *Akron Press*, May 8, 1938, p. 37. In *JSSB#9* (scrapbook page nos. given below), from *The New York Times*, April 18, 1938, p. 13; *Time*, April 18, 1938, p. 15; *Saturday Review of Literature*, April 23, 1938, p. 17; *Huntington* (WV) *Advertiser*, April 24, 1938, p. 18; *San Francisco Chronicle*, April 17, 1938, p. 19; *Boston Transcript*, April 19, 1938, p. 24; *Los Angeles Times*, April 17, 1938, p. 23; the *Lewiston* (ME) *Journal*, April 16, 1938, p. 25; and *New York Sun*, April 22, 1938, p. 26.

JS's publications from February through July included among others "February Wind," a poem in *Progressive Farmer*, vol. 53 (Feb. 1938), 27; "Creator of the Universe," a poem in *Harper's*, vol. 176 (Feb. 1938), 245, and "His Autumn-Colored Face," another poem, *Harper's*, vol. 176 (March 1938), 355; stories "When the Foxes Flirt," *Esquire*, vol. 9 (May

1938), 52–53, 160–161; "Vacation in Hell," *Esquire*, vol. 10 (July 1938), 184–186; "Love in the Summer," *Collier's*, vol. 101 (May 14, 1938), 12–13, 54–56; "Gallons or Bushels?" *American Mercury*, vol. 44 (June 1938), 194–207; and "Eustacia," *Household*, vol. 38 (July 1938), 2–3, 12, 15, 18.

The *Providence* (RI) *Journal*, July 3, 1938, *JSSB#6*, p. 58, lists these countries. JS, letters to NDN, Nov. 4, 1937 (post-tour fatigue), and Nov. 14, 1937 (homesickness). Church program, Edinburgh Methodist Mission, Central Hall, Tollcross, in *JSSB#17*, p. 33 (hymn list, meal receipt from cafeteria at 63 Princes St., Edinburgh). JS, letter to MB, Nov. 20, 1937. I#8 (running to assuage loneliness). HER, "About the Story," *BLSSJS*, pp. 135–136. JS's "Split Cherry Tree" was orig. pub. in *Esquire*, vol. 11 (Jan. 1939), 52–53, 99–100, and has since been credited with more than thirty reprints, including French and Israeli editions. For further information, see Woodbridge, *JSB*, pp. 78–79. JS, letter from Edinburgh to NDN, Dec. 10, 1937 (illness); letter to AS and OS, Dec. 14, 1937 (Scottish winter, delayed date in London). Declared value of the scarf was four pounds, noted in *JSSB#17*, p. 46. JS, letter from London, to AS, Nov. 1, 1937 (complimentary remarks concerning NSN).

⁵ JS, letter from Fullerton, KY, to STILL, Hindman, KY, Nov. 13, 1935. I#45 (meeting with young woman in Portsmouth). EB recalls JS's spirited conversation with her and her husband about the incident: " 'This woman came up to me and she put her hand over there on me and, boy, children! It was like a bolt of lightning went right through me. I never saw anything like it in my life! . . . She's *got* it!' Jesse would sit right up with his friends and tell you about it just like old wives' tales." JS, letters from Fullerton, KY, to CW, Sept. 16, 1936 (his "love affairs" compared with Burns'); May 28, 1936 (his admission "I believe I'm in love"). Also see Charlotte Salmon, "J. S."

JS, letter from Riverton, KY, to STILL, re Charlotte Salmon, June 18, 1936. I#80. I#79. Burton Rascoe, "*Esquire* Five-Minute Shelf: An Impression of Jesse Stuart and Incidentally, of the Old Dying-to-Be-Picturesque South," *Esquire*, vol. 7 (March 1936), 104, 184, 186; source here, "Is Adonis Fooling?" is in a clipping in *JSSB#3*, p. 2. I#10 (Olive Nicklin). JS, letters to STILL, Feb. 11 and Sept. 8, 1937 (hiding out to avoid "a big scandal"). Also I#45 (JS's romances in the mid-1930s).

JS, letter from Edinburgh to CW, Sept. 29, 1937 ("Danish girl," trip to Copenhagen). JS, letter from Edinburgh to AS and OS, Dec. 14, 1937 (youthful romantic escapades); letter to OS, Jan. 10, 1938 (friendship with Dr. Hamish Brown, new interest in Mary ["Hope"] Hope of Edinburgh and Dunbar, romantic conflict between her and Ms. Neilsen); also letter to OS, March 21, 1938. JS, letter to EB, May 11, 1938 (marriage plans and W-Hollow home); letters to NDN, Jan. 11, Feb. 8, Feb. 28, and April 1, 1938 (growing awareness of and attention toward NDN); also his letter of April 20, 1938 (her handsome appearance in her new Easter outfit). I#80.

⁶JS, letter from Dublin to NDN, May 6, 1938; letter from Bonnington Hotel, London, to EB and MB, May 9, 1938. George Buchanan, "Present Company," *News Chronicle*, Jan. 18, 1938, p. 6, clipping in *JSSB#6*, p. 2. "A Poet from Kentucky," *Manchester Guardian*, Feb. 29, 1938, clipping in *JSSB#6*, p. 3. "An Austrian Author's Tribute" (clipping notes Dr. Karl Federn and JS as guests of honor at the P.E.N. Club), *Times* (London), clipping in *JSSB#6*, p. 4. "London P.E.N." (program) in *JSSB#6*, p. 5.

JS, *BDH*. J. Donald Adams, "Jesse Stuart's Homespun Story—His 'Beyond Dark Hills' Is Written with an Earthy Vigor," *New York Times Book Review*, sec. 7, April 24, 1938, clipping in *JSSB#9*, pp. 6–7. Other clippings in *JSSB#17*, pp. 74–76, and a May 20, 1938, clipping from the *Greenup County Citizen*, p. 77. "Autobiography of a Youth" (editorial and review), *Maysville* (KY) *Daily Independent*, clipping in *JSSB#9*, p. 20. For a representative portion of these numerous reviews, see *JSSB#6* and #9. Also note 4 above. JS, "WJSA," *Greenup County Citizen* ed. of the *Russell Times*, June 17, 1938, clipping in *JSSB#17*, p. 75 (Lord and Lady Astor). I#9; *TTTL*, pp. 205–206. Also see Clip Boutell, "Lady Astor's Butler Liked Him," *New York Post* "Daily Magazine," March 8, 1946, p. 45.

[7]JS, "WJSA," *Greenup County Citizen* ed. of the *Russell Times*, June 17, 1938, p. 2, clipping in *JSSB#*17, p. 75; also June 24, on p. 81. JS, postcard with "Nederland" stamp to NDN, May 25, 1938. JS, "WJSA" ("Jesse Visits Flanders Field . . . with Three Other Americans, Checks Life in Paris"), clipping in *JSSB#*17, p. 82. JS, letter from Paris to OS, June 1, 1938; postcard to CC, June 6, 1938. JS, "WJSA" (Jesse Visits Switzerland . . . Clean People, Good Farmers"), clipping in *JSSB#*17, p. 83. Lewis Gannett, "Books and Things," *New York Herald Tribune*, clipping in *JSSB#*5, p. 55. JS, "Author's Foreword," *TPGH* (1974 ed.), pp. v–vi. These countries and others are mentioned in a clipping from the *Raleigh* (NC) *Observer* in JS, *JSSB#*6, p. 58. Lewis Gannett, *New York Herald Tribune*, p. 55. JS, "Paltsy na nogakh," trans. P. Okrimenko, *30 Dnei*, no. 6 (1938), 71–79 (Russian trans. of "Toes").

JS, "WJSA" ("Jesse Visits Turkey and Finds It Greatly Modernized; Terms It Strange Country, with Its Music Very Weird"), clipping in *JSSB#*17, p. 93. Professor John Orr/ HER, interview, Twentieth Century Literary Conference, University of Louisville, Louisville, KY, Feb. 26, 1981. Excerpt here is from JS's col. on Turkey noted above, *JSSB#*17, p. 93. Also see JS, *DOA*, p. 1. JS, "WJSA" ("Hot Weather Forces Jesse to Change All His Plans; Visits Greece, and Has Warm Spot in Heart for Greeks"), clipping in *JSSB#*17, p. 95. JS warned readers to expect mistakes in his column, but "don't blame it on me," rather on his "almost unreadable hand" ("FFN," *JSSB#*4, p. 1); further, "Please do not question the way it is written for it's liable to be thrown on the page in awkward sentences" ("FFN" *JSSB#*5, p. 1). Thus, one column reads "Ekyros" for "Skyros" or "Skiros" (*JSSB#*17, p. 95). JS, *DOA*, pp. 1–10, *passim* (reflections on first trip to Greece). Lewis Gannett, "Books and Things," *Boston Transcript*, May 16, 1940, noted Jerome Beatty's meeting in Athens with JS, recorded in Ramey, "Inquiry," pp. 236–237. JS, *DOA*, pp. 2–3 (departure from Greece, journey to Genoa, Italy, and to New York City). Also see the *Providence* (RI) *Journal*, July 3, 1938, clipping in *JSSB#*6, p. 58; and "Poet Ends Tour of 25 Countries 'Flat' but Happy," *New York Herald Tribune*, July 14, 1938, clipping in *JSSB#*6, p. 56. New York newspapers carrying stories of JS's return to the United States included the *Herald Tribune*, July 14, 1938, clipping in *JSSB#*6, p. 56; the *Post*, "Young Kentucky Author Returns," in *JSSB#*17, p. 96; the *World-Telegram*, clipping in *JSSB#*6, p. 57; and the *Times*, clipping in *JSSB#*6, p. 58. Among other clippings in *JSSB#*6 are those from the *Nashville Banner*, July 20, 1938, p. 58; the *El Paso Herald Post*, May 21, 1938, p. 58; the *Birmingham News*, n.d., p. 63; and the *Providence* (RI) *Journal*, July 3, 1938, p. 58.

"JS Home—'Broke,' " clipping in *JSSB#*17, p. 84. NDN, *Five Year Diary*, June 11, 1937, notes the farewell party. Lewis Gannett, "Books and Things," *New York Herald Tribune*, clipping in *JSSB#*6, p. 55. " 'American Women Are Fortunate,' JS Tells Local Group," clipping in *JSSB#*6, p. 74. May Cameron, "JS, Kentucky Poet and Guggenheim Winner, Returns Home," *New York Post*, July 16, 1938, clipping in *JSSB#*6, p. 50.

CHAPTER 12

[1]Henry Beckett, "Europe's Ahead of U.S. on Graveyards, Nothing Else, Says Kentucky Hill Poet," photo by Stein, *New York Post*, clipping stamped July 13, 1938, *JSSB#*6, p. 49; clipping, p. 51; and clipping from the *New York World-Telegram*, marked July 13, 1938, p. 52. The remark on the Statue of Liberty is from the *New York Herald Tribune*, "Poet Ends Tour of 25 Countries 'Flat' but Happy," clipping stamped July 14, *JSSB#*6, p. 56. Editor's Note in the *Huntington Herald-Advertiser*, clipping in *JSSB#*6, p. 59.

JS, letter to OS, June 26, 1938. Unsigned article, "JS Is Back Home and Broke," clipping in *JSSB#*6, p. 60. "Greenup Plans Saturday for Stuart," clipping dated July 21, 1938, clipping in *JSSB#*6, p. 60. Chet Anderson, *Huntington* (WV) *Herald-Advertiser*, July 24, 1938, clipping of article and photograph in *JSSB#*17, p. 90. Unsigned article, "JS Is Back Home and Broke," clipping in *JSSB#*6, p. 60.

See copy of this unanimously approved motion in *JSSB#3*, p. 65. JS, "My Conversation with Tongs West" (editorial) and "We Have Our Own Dictator—Joe Bates!" (editorial) in the *Greenup County Citizen* ed. of the *Russell Times*, Sept. 30, 1938, clipping in *JSSB#17*, p. 105. [Earl Mittendorf], "JS Is Now Editor of This Paper," *Greenup County Citizen* ed. of the *Russell Times*, Aug. 19, 1938, clipping in *JSSB#17*, p. 97. "JS to Teach Here," *Portsmouth* (Ohio) *Times*, Sept. 11, 1938, clipping in *JSSB#17*, p. 98. Unsigned editorial, dateline Russell, KY, Sept. 16, 1938, clipping in *JSSB#17*, p. 101. JS, "JS Makes His Bow As Editor" (editorial), the *Greenup County Citizen* ed. of the *Russell Times*, Sept. 16, 1938, clipping in *JSSB#17*, p. 102.

²JAS./HER, Interview, Louisville, KY, April 5, 1982; I#100. "JS Blackjacked in Row Over Political Editorial," *Portsmouth* (Ohio) *Times*, Oct. 2, 1938, clipping in *JSSB#17*, p. 106. JS, "Takes More Than Blows to Halt JS" (editorial), the *Greenup County Citizen* ed. of the *Russell Times*, Oct. 7, 1938, clipping in *JSSB#17*, p. 113.

"JS in Hospital After Slugging," Louisville, KY, *Courier-Journal*, Oct. 2, 1938, and "Hurt in Political Row, Poet Leaving Kentucky 'For Good,' " Huntington, WV, Monday morning, Oct. 3, 1938, clippings in *JSSB#17*, p. 107. "Editor Not to Leave, Is Said," *Ashland* (KY) *Daily Independent*, Oct. 4, 1938, *JSSB#17*, p. 108. JS, "Takes More Than Blows to Halt . . ."

"Greenup Poet," *Time*, Nov. 7, 1938, pp. 62–63, clipping with photo in *JSSB#6*, p. 72. "86-Year-Old Uncle of JS Offers to Come from 12 Pole, W. Va. To Help Bring Assailant to Justice," *Greenup County Citizen* ed. of the *Russell Times*, Nov. 11, 1938, clipping in *JSSB#17*, p. 128. "Better Stay, Jess" (editorial), *New York Herald Tribune*, Oct. 4, 1938, and "Topics of the Times," *New York Times*, undated, clippings in *JSSB#6*, p. 76. *Time*, Nov. 7, 1938, clipping in *JSSB#6*, p. 72. Clippings from the *Greenup County Citizen* ed. of the *Russell Times*, Oct. 14, 1938, and Jan. 26, 1939, in *JSSB#17*, pp. 117, 135.

³JS, *JSSB#6*, pp. 75, 61, 73–74, 78; letters to AD, Nov. 14 and Dec. 8, 1938. JS's short stories, "Gallons or Bushels?" "Eustacia," "Vacation in Hell," "Brother Spencer Takes a Bride," "Brothers," published from June through December 1938, are listed alphabetically with bibliographical information in Woodbridge, *JSB*, pp. 51–87; JS's poems, September through December 1938, included "Goldenrod," "Return," "The Ballad of the Bride," "Ridley Donnell," "Old Christmas," pp. 89–123. Mary Glenn Rose, "JS: Pioneer Writer of the Kentucky Hills," M.A. thesis, George Peabody College for Teachers, Nashville, TN, 1938, 165 pages. "Greenup Poet," *Time*, vol. 36 (Nov. 7, 1938), pp. 62–63, and "Blackjacked Poet" (letter), *Time*, vol. 32, no. 26 (Dec. 26, 1938), pp. 4–5.

JS, "Ascension of Autumn: A Rhapsody," *Southern Literary Messenger*, vol. 1 (Jan. 1939), 16–27; "Split Cherry Tree," *Esquire*, vol. 11 (Jan. 1939), 52–53, 99–100. Woodbridge, *JSB*, pp. 78–79, lists approximately twenty-seven reprints including French and Israeli editions. HER, ed., *BLSSJS*, p. 136, note, notes a total of more than thirty reprints of the story. In addition to these, "One, Two, Three, Four," "The Basket Dinner," "The Crazy Professor," "Of Yesterday," and "Moonin' Round the Mountain" appeared by April 1939. See Woodbridge, *JSB*, pp. 51–87, for further bibliographical information on the short stories; on the poems of this period, "By Sandy Waters," "City Girl," "Tim Lawthorne," "Munford Sowards," "Hester Trimble," "Bee Moore," "Mountain Woman," see pp. 89–123. JS's remarks on "Moonin' Round the Mountain" were made in I#7. In recognition of JS's "Ascension of Autumn," see "Melange," clipping in *JSSB#6*, p. 81; Albert Goldstein in the *New Orleans Picayune*, p. 82; the *Saturday Review of Literature* notation, clipping stamped Jan. 14, 1939, p. 82; especially the *Watertown* (NY) *Times*, Jan. 11, 1939, p. 82, noting "Ascension" as "a rhapsody of the Kentucky hills and valleys, instinct with nature. Alive it is to every flower, bird, and small animal, to wind and sun and color of the leaves." The quotation from the *San Antonio Express* is dated Jan. 10, 1939, clipping in *JSSB#6*, p. 83.

New York Herald Tribune, April 11, 1939, clipping in *JSSB#6*, p. 84. Also see clipping dated April 9, 1939, in *JSSB#*17, p. 136; also clippings on pp. 61, 74, 96, and 97. JS, letter to STILL, Jan. 3, 1940.

Raymond Brewster, "An Appraisal of Jesse Stuart," *Huntington* (WV) *Herald-Advertiser,* 1937 clipping otherwise undated, *JSSB#*3, p. 32. "JS Hitch-hikes to Ironton for Speech" (to Business and Professional Women), caption reads, "Now Working on Novel Moonshine Magic . . . ," *Greenup County Citizen* ed. of the *Russell Times,* Oct. 14, 1938, clipping in *JSSB#*17, p. 118.

"Stuart Leaves Students for Lecture Stage," "Stuart Quits Teaching," clippings in *JSSB#*17, p. 142. Rena Niles, "Poet and Farmer with Big Cigars," *Courier-Journal,* mag. sec., June 25, 1939, clipping in *JSSB#*16, p. 144. NDN, *FYD,* notes Jesse left on his New York trip April 8 and returned April 16, 1939.

From May through December JS published these stories: "He's Not Our People," "Not without Guns," "Sallie's Hired Girl, Minnie," "Uncle Java Buzzard," "Sour Grapes," "Betwixt Life and Death," "Turn of Corn-meal," "Brother-in-law Eif Tongs," "Rich Man," "Charles," "Eyes of an Eagle," and "Election," alphabetically listed with full bibliographical information in Woodbridge, *JSB,* pp. 51–87; plus these poems, "For Archie Wren: Traitor," "We Smoke Cigars," "Alien Hills," "Mountain Church," and "Land I Love," also in Woodbridge, *JSB,* pp. 89–123; seven articles listed in Woodbridge, *JSB,* p. 149.

⁴I#89. NSN, *FYD,* July 23, 30, Aug. 1, 6, 8, 20, Oct. 1–2, Nov. 6, 11, 12, 16, 25, 27, 30, Dec. 21, 24, 25, 26, 27, 30, 31, 1938; Jan. 1, 1939. "New Literary Club Formed," *Ashland* (KY) *Daily Independent,* Nov. 20, 1938, and *Portsmouth* (OH) *Times,* clippings in *JSSB#*17, p. 129. JS, "Naomi," 28–31; Poem 447, *MWBTP,* p. 228; letter to NDS, July 21, 1944; "Naomi," p. 28; "JS on Himself: A Soliloquy on the Writing of His First Novel," *News of Books and Authors* (Jan./Feb., 1940), p. 12, clipping in *JSSB#*8, p. 50. I#9; I#10. NDNS/HER, Conversation, W-Hollow, Greenup, KY, Oct. 7, 1978. NDN, *FYD,* Aug. 8, April 8–16, Aug. 3, 5–8, 13, 21, 19–20, 24, 26–29, 1939. Millie Zachem's nickname is "Tillie." JS, letter to NDN, Aug. 28, 1939; "Naomi," p. 29. I#80.

JS, letter to Charles E. Bess, Aug. 31, 1939. NDN, *FYD,* Sept. 3, 1939. "Nelson Eddy to Sing Song Written by JS, on Radio Sunday Night," *Russell Times,* Sept. 1, 1939, and *Portsmouth* (Ohio) *Times,* Aug. 31, 1939, clippings in *JSSB#*17, p. 146. JS, "By Sandy Waters," *Saturday Review of Literature,* vol. 19 (Feb. 25, 1939), 5; text here is from *KML,* p. 35. Nelson Eddy, letter to JS, Sept. 13, 1939, in *JSSB#*17, p. 147. "Group Hears JS," *Ashland Daily Independent,* Oct. 12, 1939, clipping in *JSSB#*17, p. 148. NDN, *FYD,* Oct. 10, 1939.

I#9 and #10. NDNS/HER, Oct. 7, 1978. NDN(S), *FYD,* Oct. 3–15, 1939 *passim.* JS, "Naomi," p. 29. "JS Takes Bride," *Ashland Daily Independent,* undated clipping ca. Nov. 1939, in collection of OS and AS, Greenup, KY.

⁵ JS, "JS on Himself . . .," clipping in *JSSB#*8, p. 50 (completion of *TOH*). NDNS, *FYD,* Oct. 16–27, 1939, *passim.* JS, letters to NDNS, Oct. 26, 29, Nov. 15, 16, 1939, also undated letter postmarked Nov. 16, 1939. NDNS/HER, Conversation, W-Hollow, Greenup, KY, Sept. 16, 1978. JS, letters to NDN (*sic*), Nov. 19 and 22, 1939.

CHAPTER 13

¹JS, letter to STILL, Jan. 3, 1940; clipping in letter from *Huntington* (WV) *Herald-Dispatch,* Dec. 2, 1939 (Naomi's portrait). NDNS/HER, Conversations, W-Hollow, Greenup, KY, Oct. 7, Sept. 16, Aug. 20, 1978. NDNS, *FYD,* Nov. 16, 17, 29, Dec. 1, 2, 26–30, 1939; and Feb. 8, 1940. I#4 (including NDNS). JS, "Can She Milk a Cow?" (hereafter "Can She?"), pp. 34, 104.

²JS, letters to NDNS, Feb. 26, Feb. 29, March 2, 1940 (from New York); March 4

and 6 (from Sacramento, CA), March 8, 14, 20, 1940. JS, letters to Charles E. Bess, March 11, May 2, 1940.

³JS, "The Last Round Up," *Esquire,* vol. 14 (Dec. 1940), pp. 84–85, 239, 281; repr. in *CGS,* pp. 130–142. JS, letters to NDNS, May 18, 19, 1940. NDNS, *FYD,* June 7–22, 1940. JS, "Can She?" pp. 106, 108, 110; "Naomi," p. 30.

⁴I#112. JS, letter to CC, July 1, 1942. NDNS/HER, Conversation, Nov. 4, 1978. JS, *DJ,* Sept. 1, 1944 (Hollywood visit with Hortons). "Woman's Back Broken in Crash on Mexico Road," *El Paso Herald-Post,* Nov. 26, 1941, and "JS's Wife Learns Her Back Broken . . . ," *Huntington* (WV) *Herald-Dispatch,* Dec. 3, 1941, clippings in *JSSB#8,* p. 16.

JS's 1941 publications in these representative periodicals included the following short stories (other publication facts given in *JSB,* pp. 5–87 *passim*): "The Twelve-Pole Road," *Southwest Review;* "The Champion," *Story;* "Death Comes to Nicodemous," *Prairie Schooner;* "Little Briar," *Educational Forum;* "Chapter from a Last Novel," *Commonweal;* "Wild Honey," *Household.* Also the following poems (other pub. facts given in *JSB,* pp. 89–123 *passim*): "Sonnet: Sweep On, You Wind," *Saturday Review of Literature;* "Song of Spring," *Atlantic Monthly;* "Long MacKinnon," *Voices;* and "Country Types: Steve Powers," *Progressive Farmer.* Stories in *Esquire:* "For the Love of Brass," "Rain in Tanyard Hollow," "When the Hen Crows," "The 'Fitified' Man," "Freeing of Jason Whiteapple," and "Grandpa Birdwell's Last Battle"; the three poems in *Esquire,* "Deserted Mine Town," "Mortal Song," and "December Moon," appeared under the collective title "A Group of Poems." An article, "JS's Life Story," was pub. in *Progressive Farmer,* vol. 56 (March 1941), 30–31; his short story "Saturday Holiday" in the same issue, pp. 7, 36–38.

Reviews of JS's work mentioned here are contained in *JSSB#7* (unless otherwise indicated), and page nos. are from this scrapbook: *American Mercury* (May 1941), p. 8; *New Yorker* (March 22, 1941), p. 9; *Fort Worth Telegram,* p. 10; *Montgomery* (AL) *Advertiser,* p. 12; *Worcester* (MA) *Telegram,* p. 16; *Oakland* (CA) *Tribune* (March 30, 1941), p. 17; Milton Rugoff, *New York Herald Tribune* (March 16, 1941), p. 22. Felicia Graffen, Western Union telegram from NYC to JS, informing him that Walter Damrosch, President, and Henry Seidel Canby, Secretary of the National Institute of Arts and Letters, "beg you to attend the ceremonial and the institute will gladly pay your expenses to New York in order to present you with their grant on Saturday evening January Eighteenth at Carnegie Hall," in folder marked "*MOM/*1941–1945," in JS Collection, University of Louisville. Also see "Stuart Receives Literary Award," *Portsmouth* (OH) *Times,* p. 27. Ramey, "An Inquiry." Blair Dickinson, "A Lexicographical Study of the Vocabulary of Greenup County, Kentucky, Set Forth in JS's *BDH,*" University of Virginia M.A. thesis, 1941, 71 pp.

⁵The Card from Viscountess Nancy Astor is in an envelope dated Feb. 12, 1941, the return address reading "Cliveden, Taplow, Bucks." Hamish Brown, letter to JS, June 29, 1940. Clipping in *JSSB#8,* p. 4. JS, letter to CC, July 1, 1942; letter to Charles E. Bess, June 2, 1941; inscription to NDNS in presentation copy of *MM,* Jan. 18, 1944, JS Collection, Morehead State University, Morehead, KY. JS spells Miss Ives' name "Marion," commencing in "FFN," *JSSB#4,* pp. 74–75 (1935), the spelling adhered to here. Maxwell Perkins, letters to JS, March 14, June 24, July 11, Nov. 19, 1941.

Edgar Lee Masters, "To JS," *News and Views about Dutton Books and Authors,* pamphlet, New York, March/April 1940, noted in *JS:LW,* pp. 40, 278. Also see file labeled "Edgar Lee Masters" in JS Collection, University of Louisville. JS, letters to NDNS, Nov. 8, 10, 12, 17, 1939; Feb. 25, 1940, in which he mentioned his conversations with Masters. JS, "New-Ground Corn," orig. pub. in *American Prefaces,* vol. 5 (Feb. 1940), 66–72; repr. in *MOM* (1979), pp. 65–79, most recently in *BLSSJS,* pp. 159–171. Edgar Lee Masters, letter to JS, Nov. 25, 1941. JS, letters to NDNS, Feb. 3, 6, 1942; letters to AD, Aug. 26, 1942, and Sept. 7, 1943; "Poem for My Daughter," *Commonweal,* vol. 39 (Oct. 29, 1943), 30–31; repr. in *KML,* pp. 45–50. I#70; I#81. I#1 (orig. MS). I#17 (title for *TPT*). For a listing of pubs. of *TPT,* see *JSB,* pp. 24–25. I#6; *YMR,* p. 253. JS, "Preliminary Placement

Questionnaire," Apr. 22, 1944, in file labeled "Stuart, Jesse Hilton, Lt. jg.," JS Collection, University of Louisville.

⁶JS, letters to NDNS, March 31, April 9, 10, 14, 16, July 24, 1944. JS, *DJ*, Aug. 25, 1944. John Bird, letters to NDNS, Aug. 22, and to HER, Sept. 30, 1983. JS, *DJ*, Sept. 3, 9, 29, Oct. 1, 3, 4, 5, 9, Sept. 14, 1944 (last entry includes a copy of JAS.'s letter). JAS./ HER, Interview, Louisville, KY, July 19, 1982. JS, *DJ*, Nov. 23 and Dec. 7, 1944; Jan. 22, 1945. JS, *AD; DJ*, Oct. 16, Dec. 13, 30, 6, 1944. For JS's pubs. in the *Naval Aviation News*, see *JSB*, which lists thirteen of these on p. 157. JS, *DJ*, Nov. 17 and 21, 1944. "Thanksgiving Hunter," *Time to be Young*, ed. Whit Burnett (Philadelphia: Lippincott, 1945), pp. 318–323; orig. appeared in *Household*, vol. 43 (Nov. 1943), 1, 26–27, repr. most recently in *BLSSJS*, pp. 386–392. JS, *DJ*, Nov. 24 and 29, 1944.

JS, *TTRST*, pp. 256–257; *DJ*, Nov. 29–30, 1944.

JS, *DJ*, Dec. 7, 1944; Feb. 3, March 20–22, 29–30, 1945. *JSB*. JS, *DJ*, Oct. 15–16, Nov. 1, 1945; March 16, 25, April 12–13, 29, and Aug. 14, 1945. John Bird, letter to HER, Sept. 30, 1983. JS, *DJ*, March 12, 28, 1945; "Introduction," Byron Herbert Reece, *Ballad of the Bones and Other Poems* (New York: Dutton, 1945), pp. 11–12. JS, letter to Charles E. Bess, April 19, 1945; "Life in These United States," *Reader's Digest*, vol. XLVII (Sept. 1945), 64. JS, *DJ*, March 16–April 12, 1945 *passim;* June 15, 21, July 24, 1945. "Uncle Fonse Laughed," orig. pub. in *Esquire*, vol. 6 (Sept. 1936), 32–33, 182, 184, 186; repr. in Arnold Gingrich, ed., *The Bedside Esquire* (New York: McBride, 1940), pp. 275–287, and most recently in *BLSSJS*, pp. 42–54.

JS, *DJ*, July 30, 1945, notes the five novels as *Magic Moonshine*, an "almost finished story"; *Look Down from Heaven* "about the Melungeons" (not the title he would keep, *DOL*); *Are We No Longer Free[?]*, "a farm novel"; "a story about George Alexander" (*GSLR*); and "Betwixt Life and Death," a story "I have always wanted to . . . convert . . . into a novel." JS, *DJ*, Oct. 30 and Nov. 3, 1945. JS discusses his offers in *YMR*, pp. 263–265; *DJ*, Oct. 3–4, 1945.

JS, *DJ*, March 14, June 6, Nov. 23, 1945 (National Theatre productions attended); March 1–6, 1945 (furlough to Greenup). JS, "Alien Atolls," *Saturday Review of Literature*, vol. 28 (March 24, 1945), 11; "Sheep Are Great Sprout Killers," *Progressive Farmer*, vol. 60 (Feb. 1945), 18, 57; "Washington Is a Swell Place," *Southwest Review*, vol. 30, no. 3 (Spring 1945), 243–246; *DJ*, May 14–15, June 16, 1945.

JS, *DJ*, Sept. 22, 1945. W. R. Moses, letter to HER, June 30, 1979. JS, *DJ*, Oct. 21, 1945.

NDNS/HER, Conversation, W-Hollow, Greenup, KY, Nov. 4, 1978. JS, *DJ*, Nov. 15–Dec. 9, 1945 *passim;* Dec. 21–31, 1945 *passim.*

⁷JS, *DJ*, Jan. 5, 8, 10, 16, 22, Feb. 6, 10, 20, March 28, 1946. NDNS/HER, Nov. 4, 1978.

JS, "Lesson in a Liberal College Education," *Saturday Review of Literature*, vol. 29 (Feb. 16, 1946), 26–27, 55–57; *DJ*, March 2, 17, 20, 23, 27, 28, April 4–6, 8, 19, 25–30, May 1, 16, 18, 1946.

JS, *TPGH;* "Another April," pp. 13–21, orig. pub. in *Harper's*, vol. 185 (Aug. 1942), pp. 256–260; repr. most recently in *BLSSJS*, pp. 362–369. JS, inscription "To Deane . . ." in *MM*, JS Collection, Morehead State University. DD, letter to JS, Oct. 15, 1946. JS, "JS: Why He Selected 'Another April,' " in Whit Burnett, ed., *This Is My Best* (New York: Dial, 1942), p. 407.

JS, "My Book Made My Town Mad," *Author and Journalist*, vol. 36 (Dec. 1951), 11–12, 26–28; *DJ*, May 22, 1946. Ruel E. Foster, *JS*, pp. 115–159.

JS, *DJ*, June 4, 18, 19, 1946, June 29–July 20, 1946 *passim.* "How Sportsmanship Came to Carver College," *Esquire*, vol. 26 (Dec. 1946), 111, 321–326; repr. in *PIH*, pp. 127–137. "Old Alec," *Country Gentleman*, vol. 118 (May 1948), 31, 175–177; repr. as "Alec's Cabin" in *PIH*, pp. 228–236. I#1. JS, "The Muddy Road," *Household*, vol. 46 (Nov. 1946),

5, 19, 21–22. "Road No. One," *Pic*, vol. 19 (Aug. 1947), 68–69, 96, 98; repr. in *CIS*, pp. 133–146. *DJ*, Aug. 2, 8, 16–17, 1946.

JS, "The Slipover Sweater," *Woman's Home Companion*, vol. 76 (Jan. 1949), 25, 52, 54; repr. most recently in *BLSSJS*, pp. 148–158. *DJ*, Aug. 20, 22, 27, 1946. "Tackie," *Woman's Day*, vol. 11 (Feb. 1948), 44–45, 70–73. "When the End Comes," later retitled "Competition at Slush Creek," *Salute*, vol. 2 (Jan. 1947), 22–23; repr. in *CIS*, pp. 185–193. *DJ*, Sept. 16–17, 1946; letter to Henry Lee Shattuck, Oct. 24, 1945. Henry Lee Shattuck, letter to JS, Oct. 25, 1945. JS, *DJ*, Oct. 25, 1945. JS, *DJ*, Oct. 26–27, 1945. The story was "A Christmas Present for Uncle Bob," *Philippines Free Press* (Manila), vol. 57, no. 51 (Dec. 19, 1964), pp. 66–67, 81–86, repr. *CGS*, pp. 31–44, JS, *DJ*, Oct. 3, 12, 16, Nov. 6–18, 1946. John Bird, letter to HER, Sept. 30, 1983. JS, *DJ*, Nov. 22, 1946. "Heart of America," *Country Gentleman*, vol. 117 (May 1947), 18, 136; repr. as "Kentucky Is My Land" in *KML*, pp. 11–17; "No Hero," *Blue Book*, vol. 87 (Oct. 1948), 15–19; repr. in *CIS*, pp. 169–184, and in *JSR*, pp. 47–58. *DJ*, Dec. 4, 8, Sept. 9, 13, 1946.

JS, "Last Leave," *Atlantic Monthly*, vol. 175 (May 1945), 79; repr. as "The Last Leave Home," *KML*, p. 82. *DJ*, Dec. 16, 1946.

CHAPTER 14

¹JS, undated postcard to STILL, likely 1946 or 1947. Harry Harrison Kroll, letter to JS, June 1, 1943. JS, *TPT*.

JS, *DJ*, esp. July–Sept. 1947 *passim;* July 26, 1947 (Mr. Brickey). Letter to AD, April 25, 1948; letter to Charles E. Bess, July 9, 1947.

JS's short stories pub. in 1947 included "Competition at Slush Creek," "My Heart Told Me This Was the Place," "Destiny in Your Hands," "Fight No. 25," "Evidence Is High Proof," "April Again," "The Prettiest Girls Live in Plum Grove," "Thirty-two Votes Before Breakfast," "Road No. One," "Old Dick," "Sooner," and "Takes Two to Agree," listed alphabetically with complete bibliographical information in Woodbridge, *JSB*, pp. 51–87. His poems included "New Life," *Household*, vol. 47 (Feb. 1947), 19; and a major work, "Heart of America," *Country Gentleman*, vol. 117 (May 1947), 18, 136, reprinted as "Kentucky Is My Land" in the *Louisville Courier-Journal*, mag. sec. July 27, 1947, pp. 16–17, and in *KML*, pp. 11–17. JS, *DJ*, Dec. 19, 1947. "The Slipover Sweater," *Woman's Home Companion*, vol. 76 (Jan. 1949), 15, 52, 54; repr. most recently in *BLSSJS*, pp. 148–158. Joe Creason, "JS,—a Literary King Midas," *Louisville Courier-Journal*, mag. sec. Jan. 5, 1947, pp. 5–7. Margaret Shelbourne, "JS: Young Man of the Mountains," *Holland's Magazine*, vol. 66 (Dec. 1947), 8–9. Other pieces: "How I Became a Novelist," *Author and Journalist*, vol. 31 (Feb. 1947), 10–11, 18; "Mollie," *Louisville Courier-Journal*, mag. sec. Feb. 2, 1947, pp. 10–13; "Every Day Is Mother's Day," *Pic Magazine* (May 1947), pp. 8–9; "Fast Flying Virginian," *Railway Progress*, vol. 8 (May 1947), 24–29; "Kentucky Is My Land," *Louisville Courier-Journal*, mag. sec. July 27, 1947, pp. 16–17; "Corn Cuttin's Pretty Work," *Farm Journal*, vol. 71 (Oct. 1947), 2–23; and "I Can't Afford to Teach," *Pic Magazine* (Nov. 1947), pp. 38–39, 121–122.

JS, *DJ* (loose, longhand pages in back of notebook), Jan. 13, 1948 (according to internal evidence); Jan. 13–15, 1948; Feb.–March 1948 *passim*. JS, "The Use of Biography in *TTRST*" (lecture), Eastern Kentucky University, Richmond, KY, Dec. 9, 1966 (hereafter "The Use of Biography"). JS, *TTRST*.

JS, letter to AD, April 30, 1948. Albert Einstein, "On Education," *Out of My Later Years*, in HER, *How to Think and Write* (New York: Scott, Foresman, 1971), p. 175. JS, letters to NDNS, Nov. 10 and 12, 1948.

²JS, "The Use of Biography"; JS, letter to NDNS, Nov. 10, 1948; *TTRST*, condensed in *Ladies' Home Journal*, vol. 66 (May 1949), 46–47, 122, 124, 128, 131–134, 137, 139,

141–142, 144–145, 147, 149–150, 152–155, 157–158, 160–161, 163, 165–168, 170; *DJ*, March 2, 1952; outline of JS's second European trip, this time with NDNS, pp. 1–7, is in letter folder "To Deane from Jesse 1944–1949," JS Collection, University of Louisville. Harriette Arnow, *New York Times*, Sept. 25, 1949, p. 27. Worth Tuttle Hedden, "When JS Fought and Taught: The Poet-Novelist's Lively Memoir of Kentucky Hills Education," *New York Herald Tribune Weekly Book Review*, Sept. 25, 1949, sec 7, p. 24. J. H. Jackson, *San Francisco Chronicle*, Sept. 26, 1949, p. 14; Jack Conroy, *Chicago Sun*, Sept. 28, 1949. (Review), *Nation*, vol. 169 (Oct. 1, 1949), p. 333. Joy Elmer Morgan, *Journal of the National Education Association*, vol. 39 (Jan. 1950), 7, reprinted in Souvenir Program, JS Day, Greenup, KY, Oct. 15, 1955, in *EMcSB*. Foster, *JS*, p. 26.

JS, "The Use of Biography"; *HTH*. Whit Burnett, "Teen-Age Heart of Kentucky," *New York Herald Tribune Book Review*, vol. 26, pt. 2, May 14, 1950, p. 18.

JS, *CIS*. Charlotte Capers, *New York Times*, Nov. 19, 1950. E. P. Nichols, *Library Journal*, vol. 75 (Oct. 1, 1950), 1662. J. H. Jackson, *San Francisco Chronicle*, Dec. 7, 1950, p. 24. Kelsey Guilfoil, *Chicago Sunday Tribune*, Nov. 12, 1950, p. 3. Coleman Rosenberger, *New York Herald Tribune Book Review*, Nov. 19, 1950, p. 6. HER, "About the Story," *BLSSJS*, pp. 378–379. JS, letter to CW, Nov. 27, 1951.

[3]JS, *DJ*, Jan. 15, 1950. Joe Creason, "The Author Who Writes So True," *Louisville Courier-Journal*, mag. sec. Jan. 15, 1950, pp. 5–7. JS, "JS's Characters . . ."

JS, *DJ*, Feb. 18, 20, March 14–16, Aug. 15, 18, Sept. 10, Oct. 15, 31, 1950. T. M. Longstreth, *Christian Science Monitor*, Nov. 18, 1950, p. 7. JS, letter to AD, Nov. 21, 1950.

JS, *DJ*, memoranda after entry for Dec. 31, 1950.

[4]JS, *DJ*, May 3–14, 23–24, 1951; Poem 5, *MWBTP*, p. 27; *DJ*, June 2–3, 1951; July 16–Sept. 15, 1951, *passim;* "What America Means to Me," *The American Magazine*, vol. CLI, no. 5 (May 1951), 10–16, ed. note, p. 10. JS, letter to STILL, Nov. 1, 1951 (gratitude for nomination); JS, *DJ* memoranda following entry for Dec. 31, 1951.

JS's six short stories pub. in 1951 included "Death and Decision," "Teacher to Fit the Schedule," "The Moon Child from Wolfe Creek" (pt. of orig. *TTRST* MS which had been cut), "Mom's World—and Mine," "The Rainy Day on Big Lost Creek," and "The Devil and Television," and are listed alphabetically with other publication facts in Woodbridge, *JSB*, pp. 51–87 *passim*. The eight poems pub. the same year included "Rise Up, Old Pioneers" and "Clearing the Slopes" in the *New York Herald Tribune;* "Upon This High Hill" in *Ladies' Home Journal;* "May I Be Dead," "Jane and Sleep," and "Corn Song" in the *Saturday Evening Post;* "Marching" in the *Saturday Review of Literature;* and "My Land Is Fair for Any Eyes to See" (repr.) in J. K. Agnew et al., *Prose and Poetry Adventures* (textbook); all are listed with other pub. facts in *JSB*, pp. 89–123 *passim*. Essays and articles by JS in addition to "What American Means to Me" (listed above) included "Greenup: My Native Town," *Louisville Courier-Journal* mag. sec., Nov. 18, 1951, pp. 40–44; "My Book Made My Town Mad," *Author and Journalist*, vol. 36 (Dec. 1951), 11–12, 26–28; and "Education for a Free People," American Association of School Administrators, *Official Report 1951*, pp. 15–31, rev. and repr. as "Education and American Democracy," National Association of Secondary School Principals *Bulletin*, vol. 36 (April 1952), 418–434.

[5]JS, *DJ*, March 21 and April 7, 1952; "Author's Introduction," *JSR*, pp. 170–171. I#12. Also see HER, "About the Story," *BLSSJS*, p. 241.

JS, *DJ*, July 25–28, Sept. 21, 1952; *KML*. JS's stories for 1952: "With April in Their Eyes," "Tradelast," "Who Is Dolly?" "The Chase of the Skittish Heifer," "A Happy Reunion," "Christmas in the Valley," and "Back Track," listed alphabetically with other bibliographical information in *JSB*, pp. 51–87. His poems for 1952: "Love Song," "To Call Our Own," "Love Ballads of the Night," "Up Silver Stairsteps," "April," "October Love," "Mountain Funeral" (repr. also in *KML*), "Clay from the Heart of It," "The Builder and the Dream" (repr. also in *KML*), "Deserted Coal-Mine Camp" (repr. also in *KML*), and "The Undefeated," listed alphabetically in *JSB*, pp. 89–123. His essays for 1952: "How

I See America," *Current Events*, vol. 51 (March 17–21, 1952), 196–198; "Memorial Day Incident," *Country Gentleman*, vol. 122 (June 1952), 72, 97, 100; and "Community with a Future," *Russell Times*, Aug. 10, 1952, pp. 32–35, repr. Aug. 22, 1952, p. 6. The three theses: Beulah Mitchell, "A Study of the Life and Works of Jesse Stuart," East Texas State Teachers College, 1952, M.A. thesis, 154 pages; Mae D. Dixon, "Jesse Stuart and Education," Western Kentucky State College, 1952, M.A. thesis, 64 pages; and Halsey P. Taylor, "The Short Stories of Jesse Stuart," University of Southern California, 1952, M.A. thesis, 123 pages.

I. L. Salomon, *Saturday Review of Literature*, vol. 36 (Dec. 26, 1953), 21. Russell MacFall, *Chicago Sunday Tribune*, Jan. 11, 1953, p. 5. (Review), *San Francisco Chronicle*, Nov. 23, 1952, p. 31. (Review), *Kirkus*, vol. 20 (Aug. 15, 1952), 531. DD, letter to E. L. Blair, April 19, 1954, in *JS: LW*, pp. 149–150.

JS, *DJ*, April 15, July 20, Aug. 15, 19, Dec. 20, 1952; memoranda following Dec. 31, 1952.

JS, *DJ*, July 21, 1952. DD, letter to JS, Oct. 28, 1952.

JS, *DJ*, Aug. 24, 1952; memoranda following Dec. 31, 1952; July 20, 1952.

[6]JS, *DJ*, Jan. 17, May 10, June 2, 5, 23, 26, 1953; endnotes under "Recapitulation," 1953.

JS's short stories in 1953, including "From the Mountains of Pike," "The Greatest Short Story in the World," "Green Clouds Against the Wind," "Blue Morning Glories," "The Man Who Painted School Houses," and "Red Rats of Plum Fork," are listed alphabetically with other bibliographical facts in *JSB*, pp. 51–87. JS's poems pub. in 1953, "Heart-Summoned" (repr. *WJS*), "Cief Didway" (repr. from *AD*), "Prayer for My Father" (repr. in *KML*, *SJS*), are listed alphabetically with pub. facts in *JSB*, pp. 89–123 *passim*. JS's essays for 1953 included "My Father Was a Railroad Man," *Tracks*, vol. 83 (April 1953), 2–7; "Don't Stay Away Too Long," *Lincoln Memorial University Alumnus*, vol. 4 (Spring 1953), 14–15, 18; "Background and Results of Regional Writing," *Peabody Reflector*, vol. 26 (Jan. 1953), 3–6; "Earth Is My Father's Book," *Land*, vol. 11 (Jan. 1953), 245–250. JS, *The Good Spirit of Laurel Ridge* (New York: McGraw-Hill, 1953); *The Beatinest Boy* (New York: Whittlesey House, 1953).

JS, *DJ*, May 21–23, 1953; endnotes, 1953.

JS, "Meeting Mr. New England, America's Greatest Poet," *Educational Forum*, vol. 23 (1959), pp. 291–292; *DJ*, July 8–14, 1953. DD, letter to JS, Aug. 10, 1953. JS, letter to DD, May 16, 1955; letter to DD, July 29, 1953; *DJ*, July 14–22, 1953, *passim*.

[7] JS, "The Builder and the Dream," *KML*, pp. 83–95; *DJ*, Jan. 1–21, 1954, *passim*: Jan. 24, 26–28, Feb. 2–3, 1954.

JS, *DJ*, Feb. 8–12, Feb. 14–17, 1954. DD, letter to JS, March 5, 1954.

JS, *DJ*, March 18–19, May 11–12, 1954; Feb. 2, 17, 23, March 15, April 3, 1954. "Around This World," *Land*, vol. 12 (1953/1954), 403–407; "Soddy," *Chicago Magazine*, vol. 1 (March 1954), 52–57; "Character and American Youth," *Baylor Line*, vol. 16, no. 3 (May/June 1954), 5; *DJ*, May 26–31, 1954.

JS, "The Reaper and the Flowers," *Georgia Review*, vol. 8 (Summer 1954), 157–166, reprinted in *PIH*; "The Clearing," *Ladies' Home Journal*, vol. 71 (Aug. 1954), 46, 60; "This Farm For Sale," *Progressive Farmer*, vol. 69 (Nov. 1954), 19, 56–57, 114–116, reprinted in *JSR*, *BLSSJS*; "Come Gentle Spring," *Esquire*, vol. 42 (Dec. 1954), 208–210, reprinted in *CIS*, *CGS*; "Pockets Full of North Wind," in James McConkey, *Kentucky Writing*, Morehead, Morehead State College, 1954, pp. 43–55; *A Penny's Worth of Character* (New York: Whittlesey House, 1954); and *Hurra for Soldat Tussie*, trans. E. Thermaenius (Stockholm: Ljus, 1954). Allen Tate, *Sixty American Poets* (Washington, DC: Library of Congress, 1954), pp. 129–130.

JS, *DJ*, June 3–8, 1954, *passim;* July 2, 15–16, Aug. 18–Sept. 1, 1954, *passim*.

JS, *DJ*, Sept. 13–30, 1954, *passim*. Dick Perry, *ROJS*, p. 50. JS, letter to DD, Sept. 21,

1954. JS, *DJ*, Oct. 1–7, 8, 1954. John D. Minton/HER, interview, April 25, 1980. JS, *YMR*, pp. 7–8; *DJ*, Oct. 12, 15–16, 21, 1954; Oct. 9, 25, 29, 1954.

JS, *DJ*, Nov. 23–28, 1954, *passim; YMR*, pp. 22–23, 29. HER, "About the Story," *BLSSJS*, pp. 378–379. JS, *DJ*, Dec. 17–23, 1954, *passim; GO*, pp. 246–247.

CHAPTER 15

¹JS, *DJ*, Dec. 25–27, 29–30, 1954.

JS, "A Ribbon for Baldy," *Coronet*, vol. 40 (Sept. 1956), 140–152, repr. in *JSR*, pp. 178–182; *DJ*, Jan. 1–17, 1955, *passim;* "Angel in the Pasture," *Esquire*, vol. 51 (June 1959), 49–50, orig. pub. in earlier form in *YMR*, pp. 1–14. JS, "Love Is a Quadratic Equation," *Ball State University Forum*, vol. 9 (Summer 1968), 57–61.

JS, *DJ*, Jan. 1–31, 1955, *passim;* memoranda following Jan. 31, 1955. "Uncle Jeff Had a Way," *Southwest Review*, vol. 43 (Autumn 1958), 313–319; repr. in *Best Articles and Stories*, vol. 3 (May 1959), 4–8. *JSR*, pp. 32–44; *YMR*, p. 23.

JS, *DJ*, March 27, 1955; "When the Percoon Blooms, It's Spring," *Louisville Courier-Journal*, mag. sec., March 27, 1955, pp. 60–61; *DJ*, Feb. 2 and 4, 1955. JS, "As a Man Thinketh," *Esquire*, vol. 44 (Oct. 1955), 66, 151–153; repr. in *MLHV*. "Sweetbird for Sheriff," *Esquire*, vol. 45 (March 1956), 54, 132–134; repr. in *32V*. *DJ*, June 6 and 8, 1955. "Come Gentle Snow," *Colorado Quarterly*, vol. 5 (Spring 1957), 336; repr. in *SJS*, p. 136.

JS, *YMR*, pp. 58–62; *DJ*, March 7–8, April 1, 4, May 9–10, typed note at end of memoranda after Dec. 31, 1955. Lewis Gannett, "When JS's Heart Warned Him: 'Stop!' " *New York Herald Tribune Book Review*, vol. 33, Dec. 2, 1956, p. 1; V. P. Hass, *Chicago Sunday Tribune*, Dec. 9, 1956, p. 3; William Hogan, *San Francisco Chronicle*, Dec. 3, 1956, p. 29.

JS, *YMR*, pp. 137, 107, 135–136, 130–131, 150–151; letter to AD, June 10, 1955; "My Heart Attack and I," *Saturday Evening Post*, vol. 228 (Aug. 13, 1955), 25, 70, 72; *YMR*, pp. 143–145, 148.

JS, *DJ*, Aug. 1–13, 24, 1955.

²JS, *DJ*, Oct. 7–14, 1955, *passim*. Elinor Richey, "Great Day at Greenup," *Tracks: Chesapeake and Ohio Railway*, vol. 40, no. 11 (Nov. 1955), 3–4. Malcolm Conley, "2,000 Attend Ceremonies Honoring JS," *Ashland* (KY) *Daily Independent*, undated clipping in *EMcSB* (internal evidence suggests Oct. 16, 1955); "University Presidents are Featured on JS Day Program," *Ashland Daily Independent*, Oct. 16, 1955, pp. 1, 10, clipping in *EMcSB*. JS, *YMR*, pp. 254–257 *passim*.

JS, *YMR*, p. 257; *DJ*, Oct. 16, 1955. DD, letter to JS, Oct. 28, 1955. JS, letter to DD, Nov. 3, 1955. AD, letter to JS, Jan. 11, 1956. JS, letter to AD, Jan. 7, 1956.

³JS, *MGS; DJ*, Oct. 30, 1955; *TTTL*, p. 233. HER, review of *MGS, Los Angeles Herald-Examiner*, sec. G, July 28, 1968, n.p. JS, *MGS*, p. 50; *DJ*, Feb. 4, 1957; *MGS*, pp. 313–317; *DJ*, Feb. 14, March 12, April 9, Jan. 25, April 15, 1957. Paula Wells, letter to HER, March 25, 1980. JS, *DJ*, May 16, June 25, 1957. *Man*, esp. "Chronology of Events" [p. 6].

Through June 1957, JS's only story was "Flight to Freedom," *Classmate*, vol. 64 (May 26, 1957), 2–3, 14–15. His poems: "The Snow Lies Patched," "Spring Song," "The Two Houses," "Be in a Joyful Mood," "Come Gentle Snow," "The Undefeated," "Enchanted April," "Earth Was Their Banker," and "Songs That Sing Themselves," listed alphabetically with bibliographical facts in Woodbridge, *JSB*, pp. 89–123. His articles and essays: "Phone-strike Struck, School 'Hot-rodders' Impersonate Mercury," "Disputing Warriors," "JS Calls for more FL [Foreign Language] Study," "Teachers and Hen's Teeth . . . ," "When Nature Cleans House, It's Wonderful to be Alive," "Oh, JS's Aching Pocketbook—the Cost of Discipline Runs High," "An Uninvited Guest Shares a Glass of Blackberry Jelly," "The Line's Busy at W-Hollow . . . ," "The Master's Accolade . . . ," "Whippoorwill Love Song Brings Flood of Memories," "Lesson after School," "Wounded Sand Hornet Adds Vivid

Unscheduled Drama to Baccalaureate Address," "The Locust Hath Murdered Sleep, Down among Trees and Wiregrass," and "Pond Opens Up a New World for Second-grade Pupils," listed alphabetically with bibliographical facts in *JSB*, pp. 125–149. "Enchanted April" appeared in the *Colorado Quarterly*, vol. 5 (Spring 1957), 357, reprinted in *WJS*, p. 105. JS, letter to Mims, Dec. 23, 1957.

JS (vacation to the Northeast), *DJ* memoranda following Aug. 1, 1957; Aug. 14–25, 1957, *passim;* Aug. 26–28, Nov. 14, Oct. 3, 29, Sept. 11–12, 16, 1957; memoranda following Sept. 1, 1957. JS's short story "Flight to Freedom" is cited above in this note. E. R. Hagemann and James E. Marsh, "Contributions to *Esquire*, 1933–1941," *Bulletin of Bibliography*, vol. 22 (May/Aug. 1957), 71. JS's thirty-two *Louisville Courier-Journal* pieces for 1957 are listed in *JSB*, pp. 145–148 *passim.* His other essays that year were "Disputing Warriors," *American Forests*, vol. 63, no. 4 (April 1957), 68–71; "Morning of the Laundered Wind," *American Forests*, vol. 63, no. 7 (July 1957), 32, 67; "Revolution in Greenup County," *American Petroleum Institute Quarterly* (Autumn 1957), 20–25; "How to Handle Hoodlums," *Together*, vol. 1 (Oct. 15, 1957), 26; "Pioneers in Integration," *Kentucky School Journal*, vol. 36 (Nov. 1957), 9; "Guidance with a Heart," *Education Summary*, Nov. 5, 1957, pp. 4–5; and "America's Last Carbon Copy," *Saturday Review of Literature*, vol. 40 (Dec. 28, 1957), 5–7. His translations that year are listed in *JSB*, pp. 159, 162. JS, *DJ*, Nov. 8–9, 19–20, 23, 25, 30, Dec. 5, 1957.

⁴JS, "Jesse Has a Big Letter-Answering Job," *Louisville Courier-Journal*, mag. sec., March 30, 1958, pp. 44–46. Robert A. Thornbury, "Show Behind a Show: The Little White Lies Were Many," *Louisville Courier-Journal*, mag. sec., March 30, 1958, pp. 40–42. JS, *DJ*, Feb. 9–12, March 30, 1958; Feb. 19, March 25–27, 19–20, June 21–Aug. 1 (*passim*), Aug. 29, 1958. JS, letter to AD, June 11, 1958; letter to Mims, Sept. 11, 1958.

JS's short stories in 1958 included "The Cousins," "County Gather-All Day," "Two High C's," "Uncle Jeff Had a Way," "The Day the Greenoughs Triumphed," and "Here," listed alphabetically with bibliographical details in *JSB*, pp. 51–87.

JS's poems (1958): "Ides of March," "Empty Hours," "Sincere Song," "Heart Flies Home," "Unforgotten," "Shadows," "The Gone," "Raindrops," "Dawn," "Jack Porter," "Scottish Thistle," and "Small Wonder," listed alphabetically with pub. facts in *JSB*, pp. 89–123.

JS's essays (1958): "Can You Teach without Teachers?" "A Do-It-Yourself Refuge," "Association," "No More Depressions," "When Heart and Death Lie Down Together in a Lonely Land," "The Writer and His Puppets," "In Moments of Reflection," "Byron Herbert Reece: In Memoriam, I," and "Sophia Keeney, Sister of Integrity," listed alphabetically in *JSB*, with bibliographical information, pp. 125–142.

JS's articles including newspaper pieces (1958): "Retirement's Just a Word to Dr. and Mrs. Donovan," "Woman Who Wasn't There Still Baffles Two Couples," "Following 'Manifest Destiny,' the Stuarts Lose Their Race with Sun but Change Worlds," "Staff Receives Letter from JS" (Untitled piece in *Ashland Daily Independent*, Feb. 19, 1958, p. 11), "Greenup Ex-teacher, 92, Housekeeps in Old School," "Jesse Has a Big Letter-Answering Job," "Writing and Reading and JS," "Oregonians Are as Friendly as Their State Is Spacious," "When the Red Worms Crawl, They Write a Language for the Birds and the Fishermen . . . ," "Ott Willis Is a Hunter Who Doesn't Kill," "Writer Reports on Trip to Hazard . . . ," "Spirit of Vikings Is Still Potent Factor in the Lives of the North Dakota Folks," "Greenup Writer, Companions Marvel at Beauty of West," "Tour of Nevada Is Step into a Fabulous Period of America's History," "Breathitt at the Top—Why Not More Trophies for Scholastic Merit?" "Call of the Wild—Takes a Lot of Dunking to Snap a Moose . . . ," and "In Fond Memory of a Post Office," listed with further information in *JSB*, esp. pp. 143–149, 153.

JS, *DJ*, Jan. 8–22, 1958, *passim,* comments on the "Whitie" MS Helga Sandburg, *New York Herald Tribune Book Review*, vol. 35, Sept. 14, 1958, p. 6. H. B., *San Francisco Chronicle*, Dec. 28, 1958, p. 16. V. P. Hass, *Chicago Sunday Tribune*, Sept. 14, 1958, p. 11. Borden

Deal, *Saturday Review of Literature*, vol. 41 (Sept. 20, 1958), 26. "Jane Stuart Basketball Queen of 57–58," *The Tiger Gazette*, student pub. of Greenup High School, Jan. 1958, n.p., clipping in *EMcSB*. JS, *DJ*, Jan. 6–7, 1958; letter to Mims, Sept. 11, 1958; letter to DD, Nov. 14, 1958; *DJ*, Sept. 13–14, 1958. I#80 (inscription in *YMR*, signed "Jesse" and dated "Christmas / Dec. 22nd, 1956"); *DJ*, Dec. 20 and 30, 1958. JS, letter to DD, Dec. 24, 1958; "Byron Herbert Reece: In Memoriam, I," *The Georgia Review*, vol. XII, no. 4 (Winter 1958), 359–361.

⁵JS, letters to AD, Dec. 15, 1957, Jan. 16 and 25, 1959; letter to DD, Feb. 21, 1959. DD, letter to JS, April 12, 1959. JS, letter to DD, May 15, 1959. Allen Tate, letter to DD, May 15, 1950, in Fain and Young, pp. 350–351. DD, letter to JS, Dec. 7, 1958. JS, *DJ*, April 22, 1959. Flannery O'Connor, letter to Cecil Dawkins, May 21, 1959, and letter to Dr. T. R. Spivey, April 26, 1959, in *The Habit of Being*, letters of Flannery O'Connor, ed. Sally Fitzgerald (New York: Farrar, Straus, Giroux, 1959), pp. 333–334. *JS:LW*, pp. 185–186. I#54. DD, letter to JS, May 20, 1959.
JS, *DJ*, April 24–26, 1959. John Bird, "My Friend." JS, *DJ*, April 14, 1959.
JS, *DJ*, May 28–30, 1959; memoranda following May 31, 1959. *MWBTP* (1959 ed.); *RO; DJ*, June 12, 1959. Translations: See *JSB*, pp. 159–162 *passim*.
JS, *DJ*, June 17–July 3, 1959, *passim*; July 5, 1959. DD, letter to JS, July 14, 1959. JS, *DJ*, Aug. 27, July 3, Aug. 14, 1959; memoranda following Dec. 31, 1959.
JS, *DJ*, Dec. 8, 12, 13, 1959; letter to AD, Dec. 30, 1959.

⁶JS, *DJ*, Jan. 14, Feb. 11–12, March 15, 8–12, 14, 22–24, 1960. *JS:LW*, pp. 186–189. JS, *DJ*, March 16–21, 1960, *passim*; April 1, 4–6, 14, 21, 11–12, 26, 1960. DD, letter to JS, Sept. 23, 1959 (Mims' death, Sept. 15, 1959). JS, "What Vanderbilt," p. 20; letter to Ella Puryear Mims, Feb. 7, 1960.
JS, *DJ*, Jan. 3, 1960; Jan. 10, 1952; April 7–8, 25, 30, 1960.

CHAPTER 16

¹JS, "Challenge in Cairo," *NEA Journal*, vol. LI (May 1962), 46–47; letter to E. L. Blair, Oct. 24, 1960, in *JS:LW*, p. 232; *DJ*, May 30–31, June 4, 12, 1960; letter to Charles E. Bess, June 11, 1960. *JSB* (1960), 74 pp. JS, *DJ*, June 15, 20, 25, 27, 29, July 2, 6, 9, 13–18, 24, 1960.
JS, *DJ*, July 25–30, 1960; July 31–Aug. 20, 1960, *passim*. Prof. John C. Rolfe, "Virgil," *Encyclopedia Americana*, vol. 28 (1954), 111. JS, *DJ*, July 21–24, 1960, *passim*. For further details of JS in Italy, see his "JS's Italian Diary," in the *Huntington* (WV) *Herald Advertiser*, Sun. mag., July 29, 1962, pp. 1–3; Aug. 5, 1962, pp. 4–5; Aug. 12, 1962, pp. 4–5; Aug. 19, 1962, pp. 12–13; Aug. 26, 1962, pp. 4–5; Sept. 2, 1962, pp. 4–5.

²JS, *ED* (MS). Annie Laurie Williams, letter to Edward Kuhn, Jr., July 28, 1961, in folder with MS *ED*. Bruno R. Neumann, "Reader's Opinion," Nov. 3, 1961, in folder with MS *ED*. JS, *ED*, pp. 1–31 *passim*; *MW*, p. 90; arrival at AUC, *ED*, pp. 32–34; Morland House, *ED*, pp. 39–42, 53–55, 58, 66, 83–84, 78–79, 88.

³JS, *DJ*, Sept. 1–2, 1960; *ED*, pp. 109, 52, 80–81, 85, 64, 48, 112–113 (braying of donkeys); letter to AD, May 4, 1960; *DJ*, Sept. 21, 1960.
JS, *DJ*, Sept. 24, 1960. Carl Leiden, letter to HER, April 18, 1980; Leiden's "JS: A Kentucky Greek in Cairo," a longhand paper prepared for presentation at *JS and the Greenbo Sessions* (symposium), JS Lodge, Greenbo Lake State Resort Park, Greenup County, KY, May 22–25, 1980.
JS, "Challenge of Cairo . . . ," pp. 46–47; "My Fourteen Originals," *Scholastic Teacher*, vol. 2, no. 15 (May 20, 1965), 5–6; *DJ*, Feb. 6–26, 1961, *passim*.

JS, *DJ*, Nov. 28, 1960; letters to AD, Dec. 21 and 6, 1960. Helga Sandburg, "A Tender Salute to a Kentucky Father," *New York Herald Tribune Book Review*, vol. 37, Nov. 13, 1960, p. 3. Fanny Butcher, *Chicago Sunday Tribune*, Nov. 20, 1960, p. 4. DD, letter to JS, Jan. 14, 1955.

⁴JS, *DJ*, Oct. 5–7, Nov. 25, Oct. 12, 1960; *ED*, pp. 324–330 *passim;* letter to AD, Dec. 22, 1960; *ED*, pp. 132–134; *DJ*, Oct. 21, 1960; *ED*, pp. 350–358 *passim; DJ*, Feb. 13, 1961.

JS, *DJ*, Dec. 6–7, 1960 (flight of Shwiker Elwan); *ED*, p. 72. Cf. Carl Leiden, "JS: A Kentucky Greek in Cairo."

JS, timelessness of Egypt, *ED*, pp. 111–112, 96–100 *passim.*

JS, memories of Egypt, *DJ*, Nov. 4, 24–25, Dec. 29, 1960; Jan. 6, 25, 1961; Dec. 31, 1960; May 21, April 23, 30, 1961; March 3–May 29, 1961, *passim;* May 2, 8–9, 15, 22, 1961; notes following May 31, 1961; June 1, 8, 11–13, 1961.

⁵JS, *DJ*, June 13–18, 1961; June 18–21 (Munich and Bayreuth), 1961. JS, *Kentucky Melodie* (Bayreuth: Hestia Verlag, 1960), trans. Rudolf Roder; *Der gute Geist von Laurel Ridge* (Bayreuth: Hestia Verlag, 1957), trans. Rudolf Roder.

JS, *DJ*, June 21–25, 1961, *passim; Drangen i Dalen*, trans. Hanne Zahle (Copenhagen: Gyldendal, 1963); *Een syvende Pose*, trans. Hanne Zahle (Copenhagen: Gyldendal, 1963); *DJ*, June 22–July 12, 1961, *passim.*

⁶JS, *DJ*, July 17, Oct. 2–5, 1961; notes at the end of Oct. 1961. "Egypt Has Little Freedom, JS Tells Kiwanis," undated clipping in *EMcSB*, next to *Ashland Daily Independent* clipping "Famed Greenup Co. Author Goes to . . . Cairo," dated April 17, 1960. JS, *DJ*, Sept. 4, 1961; Sept. 10–Dec. 7, 1961, *passim.*

JS, *DJ*, Feb. 2–5, 1961, *passim*. Robert Hillyer, letter to E. L. Blair, March 3, 1961, in *JS:LW*, p. 76. JS, letters to DD, Feb. 26 and Sept. 15, 1961.

JS, *DJ*, Nov. 3–8, 1961. *JS:LW*, pp. 76–77. JS, "Hold to a Living Dream," *Saturday Review of Literature*, vol. 28 (June 16, 1945), 20; repr. in *KML*, p. 54. "I Cannot Write Tonight . . . ," *KML*, p. 71; repr. in *WJS*, p. 48. Poem 1, *MWBTP*, p. 3.

⁷JS, *DJ*, notes following Nov. 30, 1961; Nov. 7, 1961. *HA*. JS, *DJ*, Nov. 24, 1961; March 12, 1962; Oct. 30, 1961.

JS, *DJ*, comments on his lectures, June 10, Jan. 21, 1962; the Eastern Kentucky University trip, March 6–7, 1962; Tennessee lectures, April 10, 16–19, 1962; "Are We a Nation of Digits?" *Saturday Evening Post*, vol. 235, no. 28 (July 28, 1962), 8, 10.

JS, *DJ*, June 24, July 24, Sept. 2, 1962.

JS, *DJ*, June 29, Sept. 16–18 (flight to Iran), 1962; Sept. 18–31, 1962, *passim. Man* [p. 20]. JS, *MW*, p. 85.

JS, *DJ*, Sept. 30–Oct. 16, 1962, *passim* (Egypt); *al-Khayt al-Haqq "Qissat Kifah Mu'allim,"* trans. Fatimah Mahjub, rev. and with a pref. by Ahmad Zaki Muhammad (Cairo: Maktahat al-Nahdah alMisiyah, 1962); *MW*, p. 90.

"JS Leaving Lebanon on Tour for Information Service," clipping in *EMcSB*, near another dated Nov. 23, 1962. JS, *DOA*, pp. 43, 49, 125–144 *passim;* "Where Pindar Lived," *Caravel: A Magazine of Verse*, no. 14 (Fall 1965), 33, repr. in *WJS*, p. 247; *DJ*, Oct. 17–Nov. 16, 1962, *passim*, esp. Oct. 17, 21, 25, 27, Nov. 4, 9, 11 (Delphi), 1962.

"JSs Leaving Lebanon . . . ," clipping in *EMcSB*. JS, *DJ*, Nov. 16–Dec. 1, 1962, *passim* (Lebanon), esp. Nov. 22, 19, 23, 26 (Baalbek), 25 (autographing party), 1962; *Qati al-Ajus*, trans. Antoine Samya (Beirut: al-Mu-assasah al-Ahliyah lil-Taba'ah wa-al-Nashr, 1962). NDNS, letter to HER, Feb. 28, 1983.

JS, *DJ*, Dec. 2–14, 1962, *passim* (West Pakistan). "Mr. JS, American Poet . . . ," photocopy of clipping with photo of JS lecturing to an audience of students at Lady Maclagan Teachers Training College, Lahore and Rawalpindi, JS Collection, University of Louisville.

JS, *DJ*, Dec. 1–24, 1962, *passim* (East Pakistan). "The Simple Joys," *Country Beautiful*, vol. 3, no. 1 (Dec. 1963), 20–21; repr. in *LSALS*, pp. 81–85.

JS, *DJ*, Dec. 24, 1962–Jan. 13, 1963, *passim* (Philippines); the Asian Writers Conf., Dec. 26–28, 1962; "The Poet and Tomorrow," *Hawk & Whippoorwill*, vol. 2, no. 2 (Spring 1961), 10, repr. in *WJS*, p. 87. JS, *DJ*, Jan. 13–15, 1963 (Hong Kong); Jan. 15–23, 1963, *passim* (Formosa); "By Train to Taichung," *Student Review* (in both English and Chinese), vol. 12, no. 3 (n.d., either 1963 or 1964), pp. 32–35. JS, *DJ*, Jan. 24–Feb. 12, 1963, *passim* (Japan and Korea); Feb. 12–13, 1963 (Japan, Hawaii, journey home).

⁸Summarized pubs. are listed in *JSB*, pp. 3–194, *passim*. Hal Marc Arden, letter to Mrs. Ethel McBrayer, July 31, 1963, and clipping "Hechler to Speak with Heart Film," *Ashland Daily Independent*, Jan. 15, 1964, along with untitled clipping next to it, all three in *EMcSB*. JS, *DJ*, Sept. 9–14, 1963, *passim*. George Wolfford, " 'Heart of a Town' Shown in Courthouse at Greenup," clipping and photograph of JS, "star of the picture," with Mayor James R. Leslie, U. S. Congressman Ken Hechler, and M. Frederick Arkus, New York public relations counsel of the American Heart Association, in *EMcSB*. JS, letter to Mrs. Ward McBrayer, April 27, 1964, also in *EMcSB*. JS, *DJ*, memoranda under "Good Causes," following Dec. 31, 1964.

Man, 1960s chronology [p. 33]. JS, *DJ*, Nov. 7, 1966. JS's tenure as "author-in-residence" at Eastern Kentucky University commenced March 15, 1966: see *DJ*, March 15, 1966. *Man* [pp. 33–34]. JS, *MW*, p. 86. JS, *DJ*, memoranda following Dec. 31, 1964; Dec. 31, 1968; June 11, 1967; Feb. 18–26, 1965; memoranda following Dec. 31, 1969. *YMR*, p. 34. JS, *DJ*, July 16–28, 1967, *passim*; grandson born July 21, 1967, esp see *DJ*, July 22, 1967. JS's "Love in the Spring" appeared in *CGS*, pp. 55–69; and in Whit Burnett, ed., *This Is My Best in the Third Quarter of the Century* (Garden City, NY: Doubleday, 1970), pp. 575–578. For further details on Burnett's selection of this story, see HER, ed., "About the Story," *BLSSJS*, pp. 338–339. JS, *DJ*, memoranda after Dec. 31, 1969. *TTTL*, pp. 256–303. JS, *DJ*, memoranda after Dec. 31, 1968, and Dec. 31, 1969.

CHAPTER 17

¹"JS Receives 12th Honorary Degree," *Ashland Daily Independent*, undated clipping in *EMcSB*. JS, *DJ*, June 11, 1977, receipt of fifteenth honorary degree. G. Sam Piatt, "NDS retains hope for coma-stricken Jesse," *Ashland Sunday Independent*, vol. 87, no. 16 (Jan. 2, 1983), 1, 16, notes JS's 1978 honorary degree from Transylvania University.

JS, letter to John Bird, Sept. 19, 1973, and undated note attached to a copy of the review, William Boozer, "In Touch with the Folks," *The Commercial Appeal*, Memphis, TN, Apr. 18, 1974, sec. 6, p. 6. JS, *DJ*, Sept. 14, 1973.

JS (*nom de plum*), "Virtue Is Not a Private Matter," *Guideposts* (Nov. 1968), pp. 28–30. Leonard E. LeSourd, letter to JS, Dec. 16, 1968. JS, letter to Mary Virginia Robinson, Dec. 26, 1968. JS, letters to Leonard E. LeSourd, Jan. 10, 1969 [example of JS's ref. to "TRUE CONFESSIONS Guideposts" (sic)], Dec. 22, 1968, and Dec. 16, 1968. Leonard E. LeSourd, letter to JS, Feb. 4, 1969 (enclosing dozen copies Mar. issue of *Guideposts*). JS, letter to Leonard E. LeSourd, Feb. 28, 1969. See "Item of Regret," *Guideposts* (Mar. 1969), p. 13.

Summarized JS pubs. are listed in Woodbridge, *JSB*. JS, *LBR*. Martin Levin, "New and Novel," *New York Times Book Review*, April 15, 1973, p. 34. *Choice*, vol. 10 (Oct. 1, 1973), 1199. R. F. Cayton, *Library Journal*, vol. 98 (Feb. 1, 1973), 434. JS, *DJ*, Feb. 24–March 12, 1971, *passim*; letter to HER, April 22, 1971. See jacket copy, *LBR*, 1973.

JS, *DJ*, Jan. 11–16, 1971, *passim*; "It Can Happen to You, Too," *Greenup News*, vol. 119 (Feb. 19, 1976), 28–30.

JS, letter to HER, copy of "Itinerary Prepared for Mr. and Mrs. JS," Dec. 3, 1973; *DJ*, Oct. 13–Nov. 1, 1973, *passim*; "My Health Is Better in November" (Poem), *New York Quarterly*, no. 20 (1978), 44–47.

R. L. Brooks, *Library Journal*, vol. 100 (Sept. 1, 1975), 1554. Wade Hall, "Kentucky Poet Laureate: From Selfhood to Brotherhood," *Louisville Courier-Journal*, Nov. 9, 1975, p. D7. JS, *MW*, p. 86.

²JS, *TKW*, p. 27, describes his own handwriting. These JS pubs. are listed in *JSB* with full pub. details. JS, *DJ*, Oct. 14–31, 1976, *passim*, treats the Stuarts' journey to the Orient and Far East; his observation on Alaska is dated Oct. 15, 1976.

James Woodress, *American Fiction, 1900–1950: A Guide to Information Sources* (Detroit: Gale Research, 1974), esp. pp. 189–191. JS, *DJ*, March 2, 22, May 17, July 4, Aug. 1, 6, 1977 (Sugarlump). Farley's photo appeared in the *Ashland Daily Independent*, Aug. 8, 1977. JS, *HCLS;* also *TKW*, p. 70; *DJ*, April 2–4 (Abrams-Scala visit), 5–27 (heart attack), 1977, *passim*. JS's honorary degree from Ohio University would be formally granted June 11, 1977 (*DJ* of that date). JS, "Nine Bean Rows," *Saturday Evening Post*, vol. 249, no 4. (June 1977), 16, 28–29, 120.

JS, *DJ*, April 30 (post-cardiac depression), May 1–7, 1977; "Recapitulation" following Dec. 31, 1977. *JS:EOHW*. J. R. LeMaster, ed. with Introduction, *JS: Selected Criticism* (St. Petersburg, FL: Valkyrie Press, 1978); *JS:KCP*.

³See JS, "Forewords" for the *First Summer: The JS Creative Writing Workshop, 1969* (Murray State University, Murray, KY, 1970, pp iii-viii) through the *Seventh Summer . . . , 1977*, JS, *DJ*, July 10–29, 1977, *passim*. JS–Terry McBrayer photo is in the JS Collection, W-Hollow, Greenup, KY.

JS, *DJ*, July 31, Aug. 7–8, 1977 (70th birthday); *DJ*, Aug. 17, Sept. 5–12, 1977 (Florida trip); the Stuarts' second grandson, Erik Markstrom Norris Juergensmeyer, was bn. Nov. 5, 1970; Aug. 31, Sept. 10, 15 (*DOA*), Sept. 23, 1977 (*JS:EOHW*). William Boozer, "10 Scholars Have Praise for Stuart" (review of *JS:EOHW*), *Nashville Banner*, Feb. 25, 1978, n. p.

⁴JS, *DJ*, Aug. 31, Sept. 10, 15, 1977. JS, "Are Birthdays Measurements of Time?" *JSLN*, vol. 10, no 2 (May/Aug. 1977), p. 59. JS, *DJ*, Sept. 28, 1977; *TKW*, onset of coronary, pp. 1–16; Jean's wild drive to Aukland, pp. 17–22; intensive care scene, pp. 27–29; Shan's escape from the hospital, pp. 29–44; the return home, pp. 44–48; the ridge path, pp. 49–62; home and parents, pp. 62–79; walk to Three Mile, pp. 79–91; detraining of head children, pp. 92–110; Plum Grove, pp. 111*ff*; Shan's rejection by neighbor, pp. 112–113; quotations on death, p. 116; funeral, pp. 117–139; second meeting with parents, pp. 145–149; "Kingdom Within," pp. 137, 148; Shan's revival in hospital, p. 149; conf. with doctor, pp. 152–157; return to W-Hollow with Jean, pp. 158–168 *passim*.

Charles E. Bess, "JS of W-Hollow," *St. Louis Post-Dispatch*, May 11, 1980, p. 4J. Don Edwards, "Stuart Brightens Literary Annals of Kentucky," *Lexington Herald-Leader*, Feb. 7, 1982, p. G6. JS, *TKW:* Ohio R. Valley comparison to Macao, p. 59; the climb up steps of Temple of Lindos, p. 39; reflection on the elevator re McGraw-Hill Bldg. in NYC, p. 39; comparison of Ohio and Tiber rivers, p. 163.

I#7. See Ch. 2, note 39. J. R. LeMaster, "JS: an Interview," *Indiana English Journal*, vol. 8, no. 4 (Summer 1974), 6–25. JS, *DJ*, Nov. 18, Dec. 20–29, 1977, *passim*. The *Ashland Daily Independent* photo of JS with Boy Scouts, by G. Sam Piatt, appeared on Dec. 29, 1977, clipping enclosed by JS in letter to HER, Jan 18, 1978. I#72; for ref. to "Wolfe-Parkinson-White syndrome," see JS, *DJ*, Dec. 28, 1977.

JS, *DJ*, Aug. 24 and 29, 1977 (G. B. Johnson's visits); letter to HER, Jan 31, 1978.

JS, letters to HER, Jan. 31 and Feb. 17, 1978.

JS, *Hari no me wa toru sugu ni nobiru ito wo*, trans. by Fumi Onoyama (Tokyo: Kanazawa Hinosuke, 1978), 314 pp. I#31. G. Sam Piatt, "JS Faces Battle of His Life," vol. 82, no. 69, *Ashland Daily Independent*, June 4, 1978, pp. 1, 16. JS/HER, interview with Ken Cherry and NDNS, W-Hollow, Greenup, KY, June 30, 1978.

I#6. JS, *YMR*, pp. 163–164. "Articles of Incorporation of the JS Foundation, Inc.," Office of the Secretary of State, Frankfort, KY, issued June 7, 1979. I#5; see jacket copy of *BLSSJS*, 1982. Other directors of the JSF who have since been elected include, from Kentucky, Albert Christen, Louisville; Judy B. Dailey, Ashland; William F. Ekstrom and Herbert Garfinkel, Louisville; Richard Hannan, Frankfort; Sue McCullough, Ashland; Robert R. Martin, Richmond; Katherine Potts, Jeffersontown; John B. Stephenson, Lexington; James M. Stuart, Greenup; and, from Washington, DC, Harry M. Zachem. "Contract between JS and NDS and the JSF," Jan. 17, 1980, files of Chair, JSF. One exception to the literary property transfer is *TTRST*, the rights being retained by the Stuarts and Charles Scribner's Sons.

Stuart scholars taking part in the presentations also included Wade H. Hall, Bellarmine College, author of *The Truth Is Funny: A Study of JS's Humor* (1970); John Howard Spurlock, Western Kentucky University, author of *He Sings for Us: A Sociolinguistic Analysis of the Appalachian Subculture and of JS as a Major American Author* (1979); Poet-Professor Jim Wayne Miller, Western Kentucky University; William J. Marshall, Head of Special Collections, University of Kentucky; and Jerry A. Herndon, Professor of English and Curator of the JS Collection, Murray State University. For these and other faculty and participants, see *Jesse Stuart and the Greenbo Sessions: A Weekend in "Stuart Country"* (brochure-program), May 22–25, 1980, JSF [Louisville, KY]. Report prepared by Delinda Stephens Buie, Ass. Dir., *JS and the Greenbo Sessions*, JSF, files of the Chair. John T. Flanagan, letter to JS, May 26, 1980. Maud Adelaide ("Addie") Hochstrasser, letter to Mr. and Mrs. JS, June 9, 1980. William Boozer, "An Appreciation," p. 68.

Wade Hall, "Foreword," JS, *TOH* (1980). JS, *IIWSA. LSALS.* Robert Penn Warren, "Foreword," *HOWH* (1979). *MOM. JSB.* "JS Turns Over Part of Farm for Park," *Louisville Courier-Journal*, Dec. 9, 1979, p. B8. "JS Land in Greenup Co. Acquired by State," *Louisville Courier-Journal*, June 26, 1980, p. C3.

[5]CC, letter to JS, Oct. 16, 1979. Apparently Caldwell at eighty-three at this writing (1984) is the only remaining living American fictioneer of the forty-four listed in Woodress's *American Fiction, 1900–1950* (1974). JS, *DJ*, Sept. 15, 1973; May 8, 25, Oct. 3, 1977. I#35; Heaberlin died Sunday, June 8, 1980. JS, *DJ*, Jan. 9, 1947. JS, "Letter to AD" (poem), *Wisconsin Academy Review*, vol. 19, no. 2 (Aug. 1973), 5–7; repr. in part in *Hawk & Whippoorwill Recalled*, vol. 1, no. 1 (1973), 22–24, and in *AD Society Newsletter*, vol. 2, no. 1 (1978) [1–3].

EPILOGUE

[1]NNS and JS, letter to HER, Oct. 20, 1981. NDNS, letters to HER, Jan. 4, 14, 1982. HER, letter to Mr. and Mrs. JS, Jan 5, 1982. Robert Penn Warren, Introduction, *BLSSJS*, pp. vii–ix. *LHCW.* NDNS/HER, conversation, Ironton, OH, Aug. 17, 1982.

NDNS/HER, conversation, Ironton, OH, Aug. 17, 1982. NDNS, letter to HER, May 25, 1983. Andy Mead, "There's Hope in W-Hollow: Stricken Author's Wife Cherishes Her Memories," *Lexington Herald-Leader*, Jan. 20, 1983, pp. C2, C4. G. Sam Piatt, "NDS Retains Hope for Coma-Stricken Jesse," *Ashland Sunday Independent*, Jan. 2, 1983, pp. 1, 16; Piatt, letter to Frank G. Rankin, Feb. 14, 1983. NDNS, letters to HER, July 5 and 14, 1982. JAS./HER, interview, July 19, 1982, Louisville, KY.

NDNS/HER, conversation, Ashland, KY, Nov. 20, 1982; JS/HER, meeting, Ironton, OH, Nov. 20, 1982. JS, "If You Should Pass" (poem), *Adena*, vol. 4, no. 1 (Spring 1979), 4.

John Patterson, "JS Magic Still Alive," *Pittsburgh Press*, Jan. 12, 1983. William Boozer, "Cannon County Hills Need a JS," *Nashville Banner*, Jan. 15, 1983. Beaufort Cranford, "W-Hollow Revisited," *Detroit News*, Nov. 14, 1982, p. 2-H. Norbert Blei, "The World of Stuart's Kentucky," *Milwaukee Journal*, Nov. 14, 1982. Morton S. Corin, "Stories from the Kentucky Hills Transcend Their Humble Origins," *Miami Herald*, Feb. 13, 1983, n. p.;

Corin, letter to Mrs. JS, Feb. 22, 1983. Katherine Paterson, "JS's Stories of Old Kentucky Homes," *Washington Post Book World,* Oct. 24, 1982. NDNS, letter to HER, Dec. 9, 1982.

Frank G. Rankin, "JS's Home—'a landmark of Literature' " (letter), *Louisville Courier-Journal,* June 8, 1982. The historic marker was formally presented to Mrs. Stuart Sept. 25, 1982, by Dr. Morris L. Norfleet, Chair of the Jesse Stuart Foundation; see "JS's Home Named on National Historical Register," *The Morehead News,* (KY), Sept. 28, 1982.

NDNS, letter to HER, Dec. 9, 1982. G. Sam Piatt, "NDS Retains Hope for Coma-Stricken Jesse." Andy Mead, "Stricken Author's Wife Cherishes Her Memories." NDNS, letters to HER, Feb. 28 and March 18, 1983. NDNS/HER, conversation, W-Hollow, Greenup, KY, April 30, 1983. JS, "Hold April," orig. pub. in *Lyric,* vol. 36 (Spring 1956), back cover; repr. in *HA,* p. 87, and *WJS,* p. 110.

HER, Conversation, W-Hollow, Greenup, KY, Sept. 23, 1983. JS, Poem 1, *MWBTP,* p. 3; *YMR,* pp. 239–240.

JS/HER, Visit at Jo-Lin Health Care Center, Ironton, Ohio, Apr. 30, 1983. NDS/HER, Conversation, W-Hollow, Greenup, Ky., Sept. 23, 1983. JS, Poem #1, *MWBTP,* p. 3; *YMR,* pp. 239–240.

JS, "Give Me My Winter Land," *WJS,* p. 168. NDS/HER, Conversation, W-Hollow, Greenup, Ky., Feb. 19, 1984, 10:00 A.M. Jas./HER, Conversation, Raccoon Road, Greenup, Ky., Feb. 19, 1984, 3:00 P.M. Dr. Max Wheeler/HER, Telephone Conversation, Feb. 24, 1984, 10:35 A.M.

JS noted in *GO,* pp. 254–255, that his younger brothers' bodies were removed from his Grandfather Hilton's farm and reburied at Plum Grove shortly before his father's death. "Stuart Country," p. 11.

JS, *TKW,* p. 132; cf. JS, "This Is the Place," *MOM,* p. 330.

JS, *DJ,* Aug. 24, 1952. William Boozer, "Pilgrimage to Kentucky: JS: A Celebration," *Nashville Banner,* February 25, 1984, p. A-5. Robert T. Garrett, "Simple ceremony marks passing of author Jesse Stuart," Louisville, Ky., *Courier–Journal,* Feb. 21, 1984, pp. A1–A8.

JS, "February Winds" (poem), *WJS,* p. 163; *TKW,* p. 135. Shirley Williams, "Stuart's prose, poetry are 'imperishable monument,' " *Courier–Journal,* Feb. 19, 1984, p. B4. JS, *TKW,* p. 125; Poem # 618, *MWBTP,* 1959 ed., p. 318; "Log Shacks and Lonesome Waters," *HOWH,* p. 342.

JS, Poem #157, *MWBTP,* 1959 ed., p. 85; *YMR,* pp. 73, 86; "My Land Has a Voice," *Arizona Quarterly,* Vol. 22, No. 3 (Autumn 1965), pp. 197–211, *passim.* This essay won the *AQ* Award for best essay, noted in Vol. 11, No. 1 (Spring 1966) issue, p. 4.

Index